Bernard Shaw and the French

THE FLORIDA BERNARD SHAW SERIES

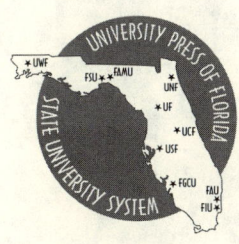

Florida A&M University, Tallahassee
Florida Atlantic University, Boca Raton
Florida Gulf Coast University, Ft. Myers
Florida International University, Miami
Florida State University, Tallahassee
University of Central Florida, Orlando
University of Florida, Gainesville
University of North Florida, Jacksonville
University of South Florida, Tampa
University of West Florida, Pensacola

Bernard Shaw and the French

Michel W. Pharand

University Press of Florida
Gainesville · Tallahassee · Tampa · Boca Raton
Pensacola · Orlando · Miami · Jacksonville · Ft. Myers

Copyright 2000 by the Board of Regents of the State of Florida
Printed in the United States of America on acid-free paper
All rights reserved

05 04 03 02 01 00   6 5 4 3 2 1

Frontispiece: Bernard Shaw in 1911. By permission of the
Agence Photographique Roger-Viollet, Paris.

Library of Congress Cataloging-in-Publication Data
Pharand, Michel W.
Bernard Shaw and the French / Michel W. Pharand
p. cm.—(The Florida Bernard Shaw series)
Includes bibliographical references (p.) and index.
ISBN 0-8130-1828-5 (cloth: alk. paper)
1. Shaw, Bernard, 1856-1950—Knowledge—France. 2. Shaw, Bernard, 1856-1950—Appreciation—France. 3. English drama—Appreciation—France. 4. English drama—French influences. 5. France—In literature. I. Title. II. Series.
PR5368.F7 P47 2001
822'.912—dc21   00-061519

The University Press of Florida is the scholarly publishing agency for the State University System of Florida, comprising Florida A&M University, Florida Atlantic University, Florida Gulf Coast University, Florida International University, Florida State University, University of Central Florida, University of Florida, University of North Florida, University of South Florida, and University of West Florida.

University Press of Florida
15 Northwest 15th Street
Gainesville, FL 32611-2079
http://www.upf.com

en souvenir de ma mère,
Aline Pharand

THE FLORIDA BERNARD SHAW SERIES
Edited by R. F. Dietrich

This series is devoted to works of and about Shaw, Shaw's literary production, and Shavian topics of interest. While supportive of traditional approaches, the series also aims to encourage scholars with new critical paradigms to engage Shaw's works.

Pygmalion's Wordplay: The Postmodern Shaw, by Jean Reynolds (1999)
Shaw's Theater, by Bernard F. Dukore (2000)
Bernard Shaw and the French, by Michel W. Pharand (2000)

In dealing with Englishmen you must make them believe that you are appealing to their brains when you are really appealing to their senses and feelings. With Frenchmen you must make them believe that you are appealing to their senses and feelings when you are really appealing to their brains.

—Bernard Shaw, quoted in R. F. Rattray,
Bernard Shaw: A Chronicle

Contents

List of Illustrations   xi
Foreword by R. F. Dietrich   xiii
Preface   xv
Introduction: Shaw as Francophobe and Francophile   1

Part I. Shaw et les Beaux-Arts
1. Shaw in the Picture-Galleries: "I am no critic of Art"   15
2. Shaw in the Concert Halls: "I purposely vulgarized musical criticism"   24

Part II. Shaw et le Théâtre
3. The Old Grooves: Shaw and the French Theater   49
4. The Siren on the Rock: An Exasperation with Sarah Bernhardt   70
5. The Ruthless Revealer: An Encomium to Eugène Brieux   84

Part III. Shaw Traduit et Critiqué
6. Shaw Frenchified: Augustin and Henriette Hamon Rewrite Shaw   101
7. Outrageous: Shaw and the French Press   129

Part IV. Shaw et Jeanne d'Arc
8. The Trials of Jeanne d'Arc: From Peasant-Warrior to Piteous Waif   149
9. Jeanne after Joan: Shaw's Joan and Two French Incarnations   172
10. The Disabled Skeptic: A Limited Esteem for Anatole France   182

Part V. Shaw et la Guerre
11. Shaw's Man of Destiny: The Decline and Fall of Napoleon Bonaparte   197
12. The Politics of Pacifism: At War with Romain Rolland   208

Part VI. Shaw et les Penseurs
13. The River-God and the Thinker: At Meudon with Auguste Rodin   225
14. Creative Evolution: The Rise of the Life Force   239

15. Optimistic Vitalism: Converging Toward God   253
16. Shaw's Protoexistentialism: In Hell with Jean-Paul Sartre   262
Conclusion: Irreconcilable Differences   274

Appendix A. Shaw on Stage: The Pitoëff Productions   281
Appendix B. Shaw in France: Travels Across the Channel   283
Appendix C. Shaw in Print: A Chronological Bibliography of Works by and about Bernard Shaw in French and on Shaw and French Culture and Literature   289
Notes   325
Works Cited   379
Index   397

Illustrations

Frontispiece. Bernard Shaw in 1911
1. Yvette Guilbert at about the time Shaw saw her perform   43
2. Sarah Bernhardt in Victorien Sardou's *Théodora* in 1884   73
3. Eugène Brieux in 1911 by Chéri-Rousseau, Paris   86
4. Poster announcing a series of lectures by Augustin Hamon at the Université de Paris, beginning on 16 February 1910, on *You Never Can Tell, The Devil's Disciple,* and *John Bull's Other Island*   120
5. The premiere of *Sainte Jeanne* at the Théâtre des Arts, Paris, 28 April 1925, with Ludmilla Pitoëff as Jeanne d'Arc in the triptych designed by her husband, Georges Pitoëff   160
6. Ludmilla Pitoëff in *Sainte Jeanne* at the Théâtre des Mathurins, Paris, December 1934   168
7. Anatole France in 1900   188
8. Romain Rolland around 1906   211
9. Bust of Bernard Shaw by Auguste Rodin, 1906   229
10. Henri Bergson around 1911   245

Foreword

On the one hand, Shaw has been enthusiastically declared "the Irish Voltaire," "the Irish Rousseau," and "the Irish Molière."

On the other hand, many Frenchmen have found Shaw to be inimical, if not downright offensive, to the French spirit. That the truth lies in between has been amply proven in Michel Pharand's *Bernard Shaw and the French,* which emphasizes the misunderstandings that were a part of Shaw's affinity for the French. As he explains the misunderstandings, Pharand details just how deep and broad Shaw's affinities with things French were. Shaw was often appreciative of French culture and behavior, even wondering if reading in the French hadn't contributed greatly to his taste for accuracy and the clear-cut, but he could just as easily be devastating in his criticism of them. And he could combine criticism and compliment at the same time: "The French would be a very tolerable nation if only they would let art alone," he wrote in 1894. "It is one thing for which they have no sort of capacity; and their perpetual affectation of it is in them what hypocrisy is in the English, an all-pervading falsehood which puts one out of patience with them in spite of their realities and efficiencies." This passage also illustrates how Shaw typically used the French as a stick to beat the English. Not the least of Shaw's efficiencies as a writer was his ability to offend the maximum number of people and nations in the fewest words. Shaw is thus much to blame for the misunderstandings that plagued his relations with the French, but Pharand shows that there's good reason to share the blame with others, for Shaw was ill served by those who sought to make him known to the French, most notably his translators, who are more accurately portrayed here as Shaw's *mis*translators. Pharand's account of this and nearly every other encounter of Shaw with the French is a welcome addition to the Florida Bernard Shaw Series.

We are especially happy to publish this book as it also stands as a memorial to Fred Crawford, editor of the journal *SHAW,* among other things, who, as Michel Pharand testifies in his preface, recommended the manuscript to us when the Shaw series was just being launched. I looked forward to many more such recommendations from Fred, for a better manuscript scout you could not want, but his untimely death has taken that, along with so many other valuable qualities and capabilities Fred offered, from us. Luckily, Fred's first and last recommendation to this Press is, particularly in the quality and thoroughness of its scholarship, a fitting memorial.

R. F. Dietrich
Series Editor

Preface

The influences of French culture and literature upon English and American writers have been well documented in essays and monographs, even full-length studies: Marie-Reine Garnier, *Henry James et la France* (1927); Mina Moore, *Bernard Shaw et la France* (1933); Georges-Paul Collet, *George Moore et la France* (1957); F. J. W. Harding, *Matthew Arnold the Critic and France* (1964); Jeanne Delbaere-Garant, *Henry James: The Vision of France* (1970); Betsy Erkkila, *Walt Whitman Among the French: Poet and Myth* (1980); Geert Lernout, *The French Joyce* (1990); Yves Hervouet, *The French Face of Joseph Conrad* (1990); and Edwin Sill Fussell, *The French Side of Henry James* (1990). Yet unlike Conrad, who borrowed from and imitated French writers on an impressive scale, or James, who made frequent use of the French language and culture in his works, Shaw has an engagement with France that is far less obvious. It is also pervasive enough to warrant exploration beyond Mina Moore's early, untranslated study.

The overall structure of this book is chronological insofar as Shaw's earliest contacts with French culture were as an art and drama critic. But the primary focus is on people: those for whom Shaw felt an ideological kinship as well as those who offended his literary sensibilities. For Shaw was a man of strong enthusiasms and dislikes, and when it came to the French, he expended vast energies both in defending and condemning them. His translators Augustin and Henriette Hamon, the actress Ludmilla Pitoëff and her husband, Georges, the director, Émile Zola, Eugène Brieux, Anatole France, Romain Rolland, Auguste Rodin, Henri Bergson, Voltaire, Camille Saint-Saëns, Victorien Sardou, Sarah Bernhardt, Yvette Guilbert, Jeanne d'Arc, Napoléon Bonaparte—the impact of these figures upon Shaw was considerable.

Since Shaw was born a Victorian and outlived existentialism, this study concludes with an examination of his Sartrean characteristics. Given Shaw's numerous French connections, however, an overview such as this one cannot be exhaustive. Shaw's affinities with Guy de Maupassant, Auguste Comte, Pierre Proudhon, and Maurice Maeterlinck—some mentioned here only in passing—might form the subject of a separate study. Still another essay could be written on Shaw's plays in French translation:

one could analyze his many emendations to the Hamon versions or compare those versions to the new translations of Shaw's *Théâtre complet*, a series begun in 1974 by the Paris publishers L'Arche, whose most recent volume was *Sainte Jeanne* (1992).[1] Therefore, I hope readers will approach *Bernard Shaw and the French* as Shaw approached humanity itself: as a work in progress to be improved upon by succeeding generations.

* * *

I have retained Shaw's idiosyncratic English spelling (dont, ninetynine, oneanother, and so forth), as well as his habit of not underlining titles of books, artworks, or musical compositions. I have transcribed Shaw's passable French as he wrote it, complete with errors. Unless otherwise noted, all translations are mine. To minimize textual clutter, I have left some expressions or short passages in French where sufficient English cognates make the meaning readily apparent.

Acknowledgments

Research for this book was carried out initially at the Pattee Library of the Pennsylvania State University at University Park, and later at the libraries of the University of Ottawa, the University of Guelph, the University of Texas at Austin, and the University of Georgia. Special thanks are due to the Department of Comparative Literature of the University of Georgia for its hospitality during my residence there as a visiting research scholar in 1998. I am also grateful to Kansai Gaidai University in Osaka, Japan, for a Research Fund Travel Grant, which allowed me to consult the Hamon Collection in the Archival and Special Collections of the McLaughlin Library at the University of Guelph, and to the Harry Ransom Humanities Research Center of the University of Texas at Austin for a Mellon Fellowship, which enabled me to examine its Shaw archives. I wish to thank Darlene Wiltsie of the McLaughlin Library and the congenial staff of the HRHRC Reading Room, in particular Pat Fox, for their unstinting helpfulness.

Many people have made considerable professional or personal contributions to this book. I am very grateful to Dan H. Laurence, the ultimate Shavian authority, for his most gracious assistance over the last two years, and I am particularly obliged to Stanley Weintraub—like Shaw an undaunted pragmatist—for over a decade of generous guidance and invaluable advice. And of course the ongoing support of my family has been essential: Donat Pharand, Sylvia Herrera, Bernard Pharand, Gisèle

Pharand, and Tom Schneider. Their contribution to the making of this book is greater than they realize.

I owe a large debt of gratitude to others who played an important role during the later stages of my project: Dezsö Benedek of the University of Georgia, for being the crucial impetus to the book's first major revision; Bernard Katz, head of the Archival and Special Collections at the McLaughlin Library of the University of Guelph, for his superb cooperation; Keith Wilson of the University of Ottawa, for his unflagging encouragement; Jeremy Crow of the Society of Authors, for his constant forbearance; and Eun Benedek, Martha Campbell, John Anson Warner, and Rodelle Weintraub for their friendship and good counsel. I am especially grateful to Colleen Franklin, who sustained my efforts with loving constancy and gave the final draft a thorough reading. All remaining errors and lapses are mine.

It was my privilege to have known and worked with the late Fred D. Crawford, whose untimely death occurred while I was revising this book. It was typical of Fred that, unbeknownst to me, he recommended my work in progress to the University Press of Florida for its Shaw series. This was in early January of 1998; one year later, only three weeks after he died, I learned that my manuscript had been accepted. Thanks to the example of Fred's outstanding scholarship, to his faith in my work, and to his sound advice, this book became a reality.

* * *

Portions of this book, in early stages of development, appeared in the following journals: 1. "The Siren on the Rock: Bernard Shaw vs. Sarah Bernhardt," *SHAW, the Annual of Bernard Shaw Studies* 18 (1998): 33–44. 2. "Bernard Shaw's Bonaparte: Life Force or Death Wish?" in *Shaw and Other Matters: A Festschrift for Stanley Weintraub* (1998): 41–52. 3. "Works by and About Bernard Shaw in French, and on Shaw and French Culture and Literature: A Chronological Bibliography," *Cahiers Victoriens et Édouardiens* 45 (April 1997): 83–114. 4. "Bernard Shaw, Proto-Existentialist: 'Don Juan in Hell' and Jean-Paul Sartre's *Huis clos*," *Journal of Inquiry and Research* 64 (August 1996): 59–70. 5. "The River-God and the Thinker: Auguste Rodin Reinvents Bernard Shaw," *Journal of Inquiry and Research* 63 (February 1996): 137–52. 6. "From Shavian Warrior to Gallic Waif: Bernard Shaw's *Saint Joan* on the French Stage," *Text and Presentation: Journal of the Comparative Drama Conference* 12 (1992): 75–81. 7. "Above the Battle? Bernard Shaw, Romain Rolland, and the Politics of Pacifism," *SHAW, the Annual of Bernard Shaw Studies* 11

(1991): 169–83. 8. "Shaw's Life Force and Bergson's *élan vital*: A Question of Influence," *Cahiers Victoriens et Édouardiens* 33 (April 1991): 87–101. 9. "Iconoclasts of Social Reform: Eugène Brieux and Bernard Shaw," *SHAW, the Annual of Bernard Shaw Studies* 8 (1988): 97–104. Complete bibliographical data will be found in appendix C.

Grateful acknowledgment is made to the following for their kind permission to reprint the revised versions of the above articles: Associated University Presses, London: 2; the Pennsylvania State University Press, University Park: 1, 7, 9; University of Florida, Gainesville: 6; Kansai Gaidai University, Osaka: 4, 5; Université Paul-Valéry, Montpellier: 3, 8.

I also wish to thank the following for their kind permission to reproduce copyrighted material in this volume: for photographs, the Archival and Special Collections of the McLaughlin Library, University of Guelph, and the Agence Photographique Roger-Viollet (Paris); for Bernard Shaw's extracts from various published works, unpublished letters, and various other unpublished sources, the Society of Authors, on behalf of the Bernard Shaw Estate. Significant efforts were made to trace the copyright holder(s) of all quoted materials. Should there be any omissions in this respect, the author and publisher apologize and shall be pleased to make the appropriate acknowledgments in future editions. We welcome any information as to whom to contact about any of the materials for which permission has not been obtained due to unknown rights holders.

Introduction

Shaw as Francophobe and Francophile

At a symposium at the Saint Martin's School of Art in London on 30 July 1946 to celebrate Bernard Shaw's ninetieth birthday, critic Denis Saurat stated: "I will step into the breach and tell you that Shaw should have been a Frenchman. That is the key to the whole of Shaw's character. . . . Shaw is a pacifist, an anti-nationalist, everything that the Irish are not. How is it that he decided not to be a Frenchman? Because his job in France has already been done by Voltaire."[1]

Shaw as the Irish Voltaire? Or an Irish Rousseau, as Jacques Barzun once showed?[2] Or was Shaw "le nouveau Molière," as he was dubbed at the turn of the century by his French translator Augustin Hamon? These labels do not seem to fit the man whose quintessence was more Ibsenist and Wagnerite than Molièresque, and whose attitude toward France was anything but cordial. Yet despite Shaw's carefully cultivated adversarial stance—an attitude that provoked and irritated the French—his life was filled with French interests, influences, friendships, and readings.

When asked (in the early 1930s) about his knowledge of French literature, Shaw listed Molière, Corneille, Beaumarchais, Voltaire, Dumas, Hugo, Zola, Maupassant, France, and Rostand, adding in a footnote: "Je garde Bossuet sur un rayon dans ma chambre" [I keep Bossuet on a shelf in my room].[3] Shaw read some works in translation, among them Émile Zola's *Thérèse Raquin* in 1886[4] and the historical novels of Alexandre Dumas *père*—"with great entertainment"—from which he claimed to have learned everything "from the conquest of the nobility by the monarchy under Richelieu to the French Revolution."[5] In one instance, because an English version was unavailable, Shaw read the most influential book in his life, Karl Marx's *Das Kapital*, in Gabriel Deville's French translation.[6]

According to his early diaries, Shaw also read many works in the original: Brantôme's *Discours sur les duels* (1887) on 17 March 1887;

Théodore de Banville's *Gringoire* on 28 March 1888; Prosper Olivier Lissagaray's *Histoire de la Commune de 1871* (1876) between 6 April and 3 July 1888; Eugène Labiche's play *La Cagnotte* on 23 January 1889; Balzac's prose drama *Vautrin* on 13 January 1889 and novel *La Peau de chagrin* (1830) on 13 February 1890; Zola's *La Bête humaine* (1890) on 16 and 17 April 1890; Hugo's *Les Misérables* between 5 March and 23 April 1893 ("Was quite affected by the end," he noted on 23 April); a detective novel by Fortuné Du Boisgobey on 19 February 1893; Jean Lucien Adolphe Jullien's *Richard Wagner, sa vie et ses oeuvres* (1886) on 20 December 1888 and his *Hector Berlioz: Sa vie et ses oeuvres* (1888) on 3 February 1890. Shaw purchased issues of *La Semaine Française* on 15 March and 2 April 1880, Molière's *L'Étourdi* on 28 February 1888, Zola's *Le Rêve* on 31 November 1891, and books by Rabelais and La Rochefoucauld on 1 May 1880.[7] He told H. G. Wells that he had read Rousseau's *Les Confessions* (1782) "in the original from end to end" when a breakdown of his car had held him up in Nancy for fifteen days; "There were heaven knows how many volumes."[8] Indeed, there were too many volumes: "I have been intending to read Balzac (I have all his books) ever since I read one of them sixty years ago," Shaw wrote in 1948, "but I have not time now and never shall have."[9] He was ninety-two.

* * *

It is important to note at the outset that Shaw championed those who were most like himself. One representative example is Émile Zola (1840–1902), the fervent social realist. From his diaries, we know that in 1886 Shaw read *Thérèse Raquin* (whose 1873 preface became an early manifesto of the naturalist movement), *La Bête humaine* in 1890, and bought *Le Rêve* in 1891. Zola continued to promote the naturalist cause between 1873 and 1880 as drama critic for various journals and delineated his principles in *Le Roman expérimental* (1880) and "Le Naturalisme au théâtre" (1881). In the latter essay, he denounced Victorien Sardou's characters as mechanical puppets and his plays as ingenious contrivances, just as Shaw did fourteen years later in "Sardoodledom" and other reviews.

In his 18 January 1888 lecture to the Blackheath Essay and Debating Society, titled "That Realism Is the Goal of Fiction," Shaw stated that Zola's naturalism "has come to be regarded as naturalism *par excellence*. It has even been called realism; but that is a blunder which need not detain us. Realism *in excelsis* transcends naturalism as far as Shelley transcends M. Zola. And I would contend that the lowest, merely fanciful fiction must advance towards Naturalism, whilst naturalistic fiction must advance towards Realism." Shaw was prescient in commenting that Zola's works, "freely sprinkled with deliberate and apparently gratuitous nastiness," were "expressly meant" to make a scandal.[10] That year, Henry Richard Vizetelly (1820–94), who had published inexpensive translations of Zola's works in England, was prosecuted for "obscene libel" for his English version of Zola's *La Terre* (1876). He pleaded guilty and paid a fine of £100, but the defense and the loss entailed by the suppression of the books cost him nearly £1,000.

The Vizetelly affair prompted Shaw to write a pseudonymous letter to the *Star* on 2 November, condemning the paper's "absurd" attempt "to defend what is called M. Zola's obscenity on the ground that Rabelais was obscene." The real issue, Shaw believed, was "whether a writer may or may not expose to society its own wickedness," claiming that the jury had found Vizetelly guilty on a false issue. Between the British pharisee's view that it was Zola's duty to hide the evil and pretend it does not exist, and Zola's view that was his duty to "drag it into the light and have it seen to," Shaw sided with Zola.[11] His frustration is palpable: the author of five unpublished novels was still five years away from exposing society's wickedness in his first play, *Widowers' Houses*.

The following year, in an unpublished manuscript of June 1889, Shaw again mentioned the Vizetelly case: "Are the novels . . . in which the most serious problems of life and conduct are glozed or shirked . . . more or less pernicious than the very coarsest book which their folly and insincerity have provoked M. Zola to write?" he asked. His answer was "Certainly not less," and he hoped that some publisher would issue a complete edition of Zola's works "in flat defiance of persecution. The very people who set this Vizetelly prosecution on foot ought to have been the last to believe that literature or society can be purified by a *police de moeurs*."[12]

In May 1895, the year after Vizetelly's death, Shaw discussed Zola in "The Problem Play: A Symposium," subtitled "Should Social Problems Be Freely Dealt with in the Drama?" Zola's case, Shaw wrote, was typical of the hold of social questions on the poetic imagination: "Zola's novels are the product of an imagination driven crazy by a colossal police intelligence, by modern hospitals and surgery, by modern war correspondence, and even by the railway system: for in one of his books the hero is Jack the Ripper and his sweetheart a locomotive engine."[13] This was taking realism as the goal of fiction about as far as it could go. In his 1909 preface to Eugène Brieux's plays, Shaw called the book in question, *La Bête humaine*, "a simple and touching story, like Prévost's Manon Lescaut. But into it Zola has violently thrust the greatest police sensation of the XIX century: the episode of Jack the Ripper." Why? Because Zola wanted to relate "that part of the truth that was tabooed. For the same reason, when he found a generation whose literary notions of Parisian cocotterie were founded on Marguerite Gauthier, he felt it a duty to shew them Nana,"[14] a reference to the prostitute and heroine of the infamous 1880 novel of that name.

One read Zola—as one attended a play by Brieux—to see social taboos in action. In 1900, Shaw recommended that William Archer read *La Fécondité* (1899), published that year by Vizetelly.[15] In "The Revolutionist's Handbook" from *Man and Superman,* Jack Tanner calls it "eloquent and powerful" and laments that in England "any attempt to deal with the relations of the sexes from any other than the voluptury or romantic point of view must be sternly put down."[16] Zola's work was also prized for its ability to effect social change: in the Brieux preface, Shaw credited *L'Assommoir* (1877) with having "effectively deterred many young men from drunkenness."[17]

"Zola was vulgar; Zola had no humor; Zola had no style," Shaw wrote to Hamon in 1910, three charges, ironically, brought against Shaw by French critics. "Yet he was head and shoulders above contemporaries of his who had refinement, wit, and style to a quite exquisite degree."[18] But if Zola had had a sense of humor, he would have "incurred the mistrust and hatred of the majority of Frenchmen, who, like the majority of men of all nations, are not merely incapable of fine art, but resent it furiously."[19] As will be seen, Shaw's own sense of humor went a long way in making the French mistrust his ideas and hate his plays.

* * *

Zola is one of a handful of exceptions to Shaw's stance on most French writers, some of whom he dismissed on the basis of undue notoriety or popularity alone. In 1887 he wrote that Théophile Gautier's *Mademoiselle de Maupin* (1835)—a novel that scandalized the public of its day— was "unreadably dull to little bookworms whose choice of literature is still subject to the parental censorship,"[20] calling it in 1905 "a reputedly improper book, but quite harmless, as no sane human being could possibly read it through."[21] In 1909, commenting on *Le Barbier de Séville* (1775) and *Le Mariage de Figaro* (1784), he stated that the French "have never read Beaumarchais, and therefore do not know how very little of him there is to read, and how, out of the two variations he wrote on his once famous theme, the second is only a petition in artistic and intellectual bankruptcy."[22] Yet when Shaw embraced the likes of Zola and Brieux, it was because he found them particularly suited to his antiromantic temperament.

But Shaw's French interests extended beyond literature and drama. In his diary on 20 January 1886, he noted reading *Qu'est-ce que la Propriété?* by socialist and anarchist Pierre Joseph Proudhon, probably in the first edition (Paris: J.-F. Brocard, 1840). One critic has shown how Shaw, despite forever quoting Proudhon's maxim "La Propriété c'est le vol" — Property is theft — was in fact quite frustrated with him.²³ Shaw was also familiar with social theorist Charles Fourier, author of the utopian *Le Nouveau Monde industriel et sociétaire* (1829), on the reorganization of society into cooperative communities governed by elaborate rules controlling the conduct of its inhabitants. In a book review of 1886, he alluded to Fourier's *phalanstères* (buildings occupied by a socialistic community called a phalanx) and *familistères* (buildings housing a group of people living together as one family).²⁴ A. M. Gibbs has studied the influence of philosopher Auguste Comte on Shaw's conception of a perfectible God, since the "new Deity" of positivism was a being whose nature is relative, modifiable, and perfectible, and of whom its worshipers form a part.²⁵

At times certain events in French history took on symbolic importance for Shaw. For example, he considered the French Revolution to be a touchstone of human cruelty. After reading Louis Madelin's *La Révolution* (1911), Shaw bemoaned in his diary on 1 January 1917 the helplessness of the French under the "infernal blackguards" of the Directoire, adding that "the same thing is occurring here and now through the war."²⁶ Nothing had changed three decades later, when Shaw wrote in 1946 that "insane cruelties of every description made the French Revolution stink in the nostrils of history just as the corruption by power of the German Government under Hitler did in our nostrils after 1933."²⁷ Commenting on the Dreyfus Affair in 1895, Shaw thought it was "French in the most un-English way, because it was not only theatrical, but theatrical at the expense of commonsense and public policy. . . . Our plan is to govern by humbug, and to let everybody into the secret. The French govern by melodrama, and give everybody a part in the piece." In France, someone like Dreyfus "instantly has all the national limelights flashed on him, whereas here he would be quietly extinguished in support of the theory that such conduct as his could not possibly occur in the British army."²⁸

Countless quotations from and allusions to French writers, thinkers, artists, statesmen, and historical events in his diaries, letters, plays, reviews, and essays are evidence of Shaw's ongoing interest in France. In conversation with Mina Moore, he once admitted: "Nous ne lisons jamais rien sans en retenir quelque chose; il se peut que j'aie reçu quelque chose de l'esprit français, le goût du précis, du nettement tranché" [One never reads anything without remembering something; it could be that I received something from the French esprit, a taste for accuracy, for the sharply clear-cut].[29] This admission of a temperamental affinity with the French is ironic, in light of Shaw's vexed relationship with France.

* * *

Shaw's readings in the original certainly helped him achieve a passable mastery of French, but he was not solely self-taught. Beginning in January 1881, three nights a week, he had tried assimilating French through music by singing in French to Richard Deck, an Alsatian *basso profundo* who was teaching him French (in exchange for English lessons). These "lessons" were probably an ineffectual way for Shaw to acquire grammatically or idiomatically correct French. According to Shaw, "Properly speaking [Deck] knew no language at all; for he had forgotten his native Alsatian dialect of German, and had adopted an unacademic French, which, though appallingly fluent, was seldom free from quaint Italian locutions and scraps of slang from all the countries in which he had sojourned."[30] In any event, these sessions with Deck (who died from fever in late 1882), combined with Shaw's own readings, provided a rudimentary knowledge of the language.

A few years later, Shaw began to learn French systematically. In 1884, Edith Beatty—wife of his friend Pakenham Beatty, an amateur pugilist— ex-music pupil of Charles Gounod, began teaching Shaw French. The experience resulted in a French playlet, *Un Petit Drame,* Shaw's earliest complete work for the stage. Composed on 7 October 1884 as an exercise for Beatty, it is a dialogue between L'oncle Arri (Uncle Harry) and Madame Malade (Mrs. Ill). Arri "rappelle Amleth, un peu usé" [reminds one of Hamlet, a little worn-out].[31] Arri Wilson is a medical doctor who arrives at Madame Malade's home highly distraught because he has recently been abandoned by his wife and daughter: they have left him nothing, not even the furniture. He is also quite inebriated: he trips on the carpet, falls into a chair, and sobs uncontrollably. His wife, he says, has unjustly maligned him: "Peut on croire qu'elle a osé dire que je suis ivrogne—moi!" [Can one believe that she dared say I was a drunkard—me!], and he quickly downs a brandy. Clearly his wife has left him because he is an alcoholic.[32] Although he refers to her as "ma seule consolation," he later wishes his friend "le père Shaw" would seduce her: "Plût-à-Dieu qu'il l'enlevasse" [Heaven grant that he should carry her off]. Arri ends the playlet with a diatribe on alcoholism, condemning drunken husbands and praising his own moderation: "C'est affreux de voir les jeunes hommes abimé par cette habitude fatale" [It is horrible to see young men ruined by this fatal habit], he exclaims, leaving in search of a hearse to take him home.

Shaw's farcical sketch is important for many reasons: as an early parody of popular French melodrama; as a miniature "badly made" play—complete with frenetic action, incoherent plot, and ambiguous denouement; and as a template for a number of Shaw's favorite themes and hallmarks. The latter include character archetypes, husband-wife rivalry, hilarious stage business, witty repartee, tirade on a social evil, ambiguous ending, and an overall irony and satire. These became staples of numerous Shavian domestic and social *petits drames*. Moreover, judging from this vaudevillian skit, Shaw's knowledge of French in his late twenties, even if he used a dictionary, was quite adequate. There are about sixty mistakes in the work's approximately one hundred lines, but most are minor: accents, hyphens, gender agreements, and literal translations from English.

Shaw continued to be plagued by such lacunae, and yet his French correspondence with Hamon and others indicates a competent understanding of *la langue de Molière*. It should be pointed out, however, that if Shaw's letters are not riddled with many serious mistakes, some credit is due to his wife, Charlotte, who was fluent in French and often revised her husband's letters. But in most cases, judging from his heavily corrected drafts, Shaw himself took pains to refine his French using a dictionary. Without examining the originals, however, it is impossible to know how much of Shaw's own French found its way into the final versions of his letters.[33]

If Shaw was not fluent, neither was he the hopeless linguist he often claimed. By his own admission, he managed well in a few languages. "I can read French as easily as English," he once boasted, "and under pressure of necessity I can turn to account some scraps of German and a little operatic Italian; but these I was never taught at school."[34] On another occasion he wrote: "I can read French easily, I can speak it after a barbarous fashion provided I am not asked to go more deeply into grammar than the present of the indicative; I can understand it when it is spoken as badly as I speak it, that is to say, by everybody except the French."[35]

Shaw's early readings and brief training in French took a practical turn around 1905, when he began struggling to improve upon Hamon's awkward (mis)translations of his plays. Shaw and Hamon had parallel situations: Shaw relied on Charlotte to correct his French correspondence, and

Hamon (who got all the credit) could not translate without the help of his wife, Henriette, who was apparently fluent in English. But when the couple began muddling his plays with inaccurate and misleading French equivalents, Shaw intervened. In long letters (some in French) filled with corrections, suggestions, and admonitions, the irate Irishman salvaged what he could of his frenchified Shavianisms. As will be shown, some emendations evidence Shaw's understanding of linguistic and cultural differences, and a surprising mastery of French idiom.

Shaw's training in French was eclectic, as was his relationship to French literature. His magpie borrowing is satirized in the famous Max Beerbohm cartoon of Shaw attempting to sell his tattered clothes to Danish critic Georg Brandes, characterized as a "marchand d'Idées" [merchant of Ideas]. When Brandes claims to have handled those goods before, Shaw replies: "Ah, but look at the patches."[36] Many of those philosophical and literary patches have been scrutinized; a partial list includes Nietzsche, Wagner, Mozart, Shelley, Bunyan, Butler, Blake, and Ibsen. But if some of the French patches have been acknowledged—Henri Bergson and Eugène Brieux, for example—many have gone unnoticed.

One reason is Shaw's relentless critique of the French. He railed against Paris and inveighed against the plays of Eugène Scribe and Victorien Sardou—while using their techniques, in satirical or parodic forms, in his early plays. He castigated Sarah Bernhardt for her histrionics and Hamon for his awful frenchifications. He was at odds with Romain Rolland over his pacifism and with Anatole France over his portrayal of Joan of Arc. He found little worth salvaging from the dull and derivative music of Camille Saint-Saëns. And with what was (in retrospect) a delightful Shavian irony, he ranted against Georges and Ludmilla Pitoëff's production of *Saint Joan* only to discover that they had unwittingly created his first and greatest triumph on the French stage.

Conversely, these criticisms were balanced by Shaw's sporadic, at times fanatic, devotion to those he considered kindred spirits. When Shaw came across an incarnation of the Life Force, he embraced it zealously. He eulogized Brieux and defended Hamon because they shared his socialist ideals, even though one was a second-rate dramatist and the other a mediocre translator. He hailed Bergson as a philosophical soul mate, claiming to better understand him than Bergson himself. He maintained that only Auguste Rodin had captured Shaw without his "GBS" persona, and cursed the French for not recognizing the sculptor's genius—and his own. And he admired and promoted the innovations of the French impressionist painters. In short, the Shavian debt to France spans his whole career:

from Scribe's *pièce à thèse* in Shaw's early plays, through Bergson's *élan vital* as a mirror of his personal theology in *Man and Superman,* to his tribute to France's patron saint in *Saint Joan*. One can even trace his affinities to French thinkers beyond his lifetime in Pierre Teilhard de Chardin, Jean Giraudoux, Jean Anouilh, and Jean-Paul Sartre.

* * *

Despite the scope and intensity of his interest in the French, Shaw remained only partly appreciated or recognized across the Channel, even among drama specialists and Anglophiles. As late as 1935, almost a decade after the astonishing success of *Sainte Jeanne,* François Closset was writing about "cet Irlandais que les Latins connaissent mal et dont périodiquement la presse anglo-saxonne nous souligne une manifestation politique, littéraire ou simplement . . . humoristique dont nous ne comprenons pas toujours bien le sens et la portée" [this Irishman whom the Latins know poorly and whose political, literary or simply humoristic expression the Anglo-Saxon press emphasize to us, but whose meaning and scope we do not always understand].[37]

Of course, part of the problem was Shaw's own playfulness in his works and in his attitude toward the French. Jean-Richard Bloch's views are those of the typical Parisian theater critic. Writing to Romain Rolland in 1913, he gave this assessment of the Irish dramatist: "Il use trop de paradoxe insultant, et comme il ne vise qu'à insulter le public anglais, ses paradoxes ne valent rien, passé l'eau. . . . [i]l n'atteint pas à la réalité, il reste dans une convention clownesque aussi éloignée de nous que la convention littéraire des dramaturges contemporains" [He overdoes the insulting paradox, and since he aims to insult only the English public, his paradoxes are worth nothing beyond the Channel. He does not reach reality, he remains in a clownesque convention as remote from us as the literary convention of contemporary playwrights].[38] Shaw's humor was too unorthodox and incomprehensible for the French to fully understand his message, and his attitude not earnest enough for them to take him seriously. As a result, his plays were produced in Paris only in small coterie theaters rather than in the more commercial *théâtres du boulevard*.

In addition, Shaw's disregard for French sensibilities contributed significantly to the reluctance of the French to accept him. For instance: "Paris is easily the most prejudiced, oldfashioned, obsolete-minded city in the west of Europe," he wrote in 1909 under the heading "Parisian Stupidity." The placard announcing the 18 February 1912 premiere of *La Profession de Mme Warren* was accompanied by some lines of a letter to

Hamon: "Paris is always the last city in the world to discover and accept an author or a composer of international reputation. London is twenty-five years behind the times and Paris is ten years behind London. Paris is a marvellous city, but Parisians have not yet discovered Paris. It is not surprising then that they have not yet discovered me."[39] Such flamboyant bellicosity certainly alienated those who might otherwise have been better disposed toward Shaw; with the French, he was his own worst publicist.

Flippancy, exhibitionism, invective, masquerading, obstinacy; "in few other cases," it has been observed, "did [Shaw] suffer the consequences of his unpredictable nature worse than in his relations with France and the French theatre."[40] The more Shaw infuriated the French with anti-Parisian diatribes in the press, the more he shocked theatergoers with heterodox ideas and strange paradoxes, the less the French wanted to hear what he was saying. Their bafflement was understandable even to the English: "Mr. Shaw is not very congenial to the *génie latin*," wrote the *London Times* in 1928, only three years after the *Sainte Jeanne* triumph. This is not surprising, it was observed, because "the French, after all, have seldom had much sympathy with the Puritan faith and philosophy which Mr. Shaw . . . has consummated in dramatic form."[41]

* * *

Although the Puritan gadfly did not leave the French alone, and they in turn lambasted him in the press, Shaw's French affinities are numerous yet sparsely documented. Aside from short studies on specific aspects, or essays synthesizing Shaw's career and reception in France,[42] there is only one book on Shaw's relations with the French: Mina Moore's useful but outdated *Bernard Shaw et la France* (1933). Three of the other four books on Shaw in French—Charles Cestre's *Bernard Shaw et son oeuvre* (1912), Hamon's *Le Molière du XXe siècle: Bernard Shaw* (1913), and Closset's *G. Bernard Shaw: Son oeuvre* (1935)—were written to spread the Shavian gospel and are not always very critical. Of these, only Hamon's panegyric was translated (1915). The only other extended study by a French scholar is Jean-Claude Amalric's *Bernard Shaw: Du réformateur victorien au prophète édouardien* (1977), which does justice to Shaw's infinite variety as orator, journalist, critic, novelist, playwright, socialist, and feminist. It remains the most comprehensive introduction to Shaw for French readers.

Aside from academic or scholarly interest in Shaw, the French seem to know him only slightly. As one of Shaw's French translators remarked in 1994: "Hormis *Pygmalion* . . . l'oeuvre de Bernard Shaw est aujourd'hui presque complètement inconnue du public français" [Aside from *Pyg-*

malion, Shaw's work is today almost completely unknown to the French public].⁴³ English speakers, on the other hand, although more familiar with his work, ignore the extent and impact of his engagement with France. This book attempts to place Shaw within his French sociocultural milieu by analyzing his French enthusiasms and concerns, and by examining his plays through Gallic eyes to see why they were often dismissed as outrageous or absurd (a view that, to some extent, persists to this day). If he was not the Irish Molière of Augustin Hamon's imagination, Shaw was sufficiently fascinated by France to make one reevaluate the epithet.

I

Shaw et les Beaux-Arts

Shaw in the Picture-Galleries

"I am no critic of Art"

"The French would be a very tolerable nation if only they would let art alone," wrote Shaw in 1894 in one of his music reviews. "It is one thing for which they have no sort of capacity; and their perpetual affectation of it is in them what hypocrisy is in the English, an all-pervading falsehood which puts one out of patience with them in spite of their realities and efficiencies."[1] Like other Shaw hyperboles, especially ones about the French, there is some truth to this one about "perpetual affectation." Yet it may be more applicable to French drama or music than to French art.

While writing musical critiques in the *Star* (1888–89), Shaw was publishing articles in the *World* in his capacity as official art critic, a post he held from February 1886 until January 1890, with occasional pieces for Annie Besant's socialist journal, *Our Corner*. His career as art critic has been thoroughly documented by Stanley Weintraub in *Bernard Shaw on the London Art Scene, 1885–1950* (1989); as this title indicates, Shaw wrote about art until he was ninety-three. Unlike the dramatic and musical criticism, however, his art criticism was "mostly unsigned, never reprinted, and largely unknown,"[2] many articles appearing under the heading "In the Picture-Galleries."

In his forays into the galleries, Shaw must have seen hundreds of French landscape, figurative, and genre painters, mentioning them in his reviews often only in passing, commenting kindly on one aspect of an artist's work, sometimes dismissing him with a few adjectives, as he did Louis Edouard Dubufe on 24 October 1888 with "skilful, pretty, and insincere, as usual."[3] Others whose paintings Shaw discussed have been eclipsed by greater talents. Their names, familiar to Shaw's age but nowadays only to art historians, evoke not a single canvas or period: Pierre Célestin Billet, Émile Adelard Breton, Jean Charles Cazin, Émile Auguste Carolus Duran,

Jean-Baptiste-Paul Lazerges, Madeleine Jeanne Lemaire, Jules Louis Marchand, Francisque Noailly, Aimé Perret, Jean Henri Zuber, and others.

At times a review was merely a speaker's platform, Shaw pausing just long enough to vent his frustrations. In his 2 June 1886 review of sixteen pictures by Jacques-Joseph Tissot (1836–1902), he criticized the spectators for turning into "moralising prigs in spite of laboriously acquired and proudly cherished *savoir faire* and *savoir vivre*." As for the art, even when Shaw liked it, there was usually a caveat. With Tissot, "Impressionism is carried with great skill just to the right point of representing everything as we see it in Nature when our eyes are wide open. Thus the verisimilitude of the newspapers and play-bills is perfect, though they cannot be read even with a magnifying-glass. M. Tissot shows us our decorative taste exactly as the books of our upholsterers and house-furnishers prove it to exist."[4] He chided the British on 13 April 1887 in a review of an exhibition of the Société d'Aquarellistes Français, a group whose watercolors were "quite enough to make them think rather poorly of our boasted English school, and yet not enough to shake our insular conceit for a moment." Paul Albert Besnard's (1849–1934) "outrageously unobservant impressionism might sober even the New English Art Club or the British Artists."[5]

At other times, Shaw was genuinely pleased—with the usual reservations. Although he had written that the Napoleon of his *Man of Destiny* had nothing in common with the Napoleons of military genre painter Jean-Louis-Ernest Meissonier (1815–91), Shaw had only kind words for his work. On 10 February 1886, he mentioned the famous *La Rixe* [The Brawl] and praised (ambiguously perhaps) the *Flute-player,* with "the sheen of his white satin coat undimmed, and his immaculate finger-nails still perfect in their pearly finish. Comment would be superfluous." On 3 November, he thought *Voyageur* "the chief attraction" at an exhibition; on 23 March 1887, he praised a watercolor study for the smoker in the *Sign Painter* for its "quiet mastery of expression and breadth of handling." On 2 May 1888, he praised Meissonier's technical skill with the enormous watercolor *1807:* the uneven ground and long grass upon which ride the cuirassiers were "as consummate as the minute elaboration of the sword-hilts," and the "Napoleon with the face of an ecclesiastic is a novelty." Everything about the work was "dignified and impressive, without being in the least heavy or unhandsome," although the idea of the spectacle of heavy cavalry "is growing old-fashioned."[6]

Shaw's assessments of the more talented or famous artists show respect, even admiration, for their work. In 1885, he called Barbizon painter Jean

François Millet (1814–75) "the great Millet." In 1886, a vast panorama by Joseph-Benjamin Constant (1845–1902) exhibited "all the luxurious light and color that we expect" from him. Shaw was delighted with sixty-four watercolor drawings by Gustave Moreau (1826–98), illustrating *Les Fables* of Jean de La Fontaine. "He is not a consummate draughtsman," he wrote on 3 November 1886, "or an exceptionally dexterous manipulator of the brush . . . but he has the insight of a poet, and the true painter's faculty of mixing his colours with imagination. . . . The illustrations have humour; but they are not comic." Shaw even praised Jean-Baptiste-Camille Corot (1796–1875), master of idealized romantic landscapes, whose twenty-two works he found "inexhaustibly beautiful" in 1889.[7]

What sometimes excited Shaw was a work's verisimilitude. In 1890, he characterized realist painter Gustave Courbet (1819–77) as "a strong man if you please, though his range of color was limited." In his 9 November 1912 article "Rodin" in the *Nation,* Shaw compared his bust by Rodin to the one Rodin had made of Pierre Puvis de Chavannes (1824–98), who had protested to Rodin that his was not a proper likeness. Shaw disagreed. Rodin had shown Puvis "as distinct from his collars and his public manners. Puvis, though an artist of great merit, could not see himself." Frequent references to Rosa Bonheur (1822–99), the leading French animal painter of her time, indicate that Shaw esteemed her work. In 1924, he referred to "Bonheur painting in male blouse and trousers, and George Sand living a man's life," claiming that Joan of Arc might have been canonized much sooner had she "not been one of those 'unwomanly women'."[8]

Shaw even became quite defensive when poet and art critic Laurence Binyon wrote in the *Saturday Review* (7 December 1907) that "few but fanatics share Mr. Bernard Shaw's contempt" for the art of Eugène Delacroix (1798–1863). In the 14 December issue, he reminded Binyon how, in the 1880s, he had on occasion troubled the British Museum library attendants by asking for the *Faust* and *Hamlet* lithographs to find out if they could still fascinate anyone as they had fascinated him. "Has any living man done more for Delacroix without being paid for it?"[9] Years earlier, Shaw had written that "Berlioz's vividly imaginative treatment of the picturesque element" in Goethe's *Faust* could only be compared to Delacroix's "indescribable lithographs."[10]

Sometimes an art review was an opportunity for Shaw to take a stand against censorship, as when he attended an exhibition at Waterloo House of illustrations by Jules Arsène Garnier (1847–89) for new editions of the *Gargantua* (1534) and *Pantagruel* (1532) of François Rabelais. Garnier's illustrations were seized by the police following the successful prosecution of the exhibitors by the National Vigilance Society on the grounds of obscenity. On 22 October 1890, Shaw objected to the "absurdity" of displaying a dozen out of the 160 pictures, "on the score of indecency," in a separate room to which admission was possible only by providing a name and an address. Shaw praised Garnier's "humorous sense of colour" and "fantastic realism" but concluded that he "did not succeed in perfectly reconciling the artistic with the literary motive," although "Rabelais-fanciers who are not picture fanciers will find the collection worth pottering through."[11]

* * *

In addition to making cursory or general comments, Shaw had his favorite artists and movements. He championed the literary naturalists, especially Zola; defended the Pre-Raphaelites (Dante Gabriel Rossetti, Holman Hunt, Edward Burne-Jones) past their heyday; and took up the cause of the French Impressionists in his art reviews. In 1892—using political terminology well suited to the context—Shaw recalled that when he was an art reviewer, "certain reforms in painting which I desired were advocated by the Impressionist party, and resisted by the Academic party. Until those reforms had been effectually wrought I fought for the Impressionists—backed up men who could not draw a nose differently from an elbow against [Frederick] Leighton and [Adolphe William] Bouguereau—did everything I could to make the public conscious of the ugly unreality of studio-lit landscape and the inanity of second-hand classicism," Monet having made Bouguereau's backgrounds "ridiculous."[12] Members of the "Academic party," like their contemporaries writing for the stage, were stuck in "the old grooves."

Shaw was especially fond of Claude Monet (1840–1926), who gave the Impressionist movement its name when, in 1874, a Parisian journalist used it as a derisive epithet for Monet's *Impression: Soleil levant*. So many artists found the term apt in describing their work, it was officially adopted for the third Impressionist exhibition in 1877. Shaw remarked (on 30 November 1887) that Monet, "rebelling against the sacrifice of vivid colour to truth of tone, impressionises in violent aniline hues, which justify themselves to the eye at a certain distance."[13] It was only a matter of perspective; progress for Shaw meant change, and one had to adapt to that change by adjusting one's perspective, by stepping back. Shaw stressed this idea the following year, on 18 January 1888, in a lecture to the Blackheath Essay and Debating Society titled "That Realism Is the Goal of

Fiction," in which he compared the methodology of the naturalist and Impressionist movements. He spoke of writers (like Zola) "who have some conscience, some sense, some independence," and who go "to Nature to study their materials afresh." The Impressionists are doing it today, Shaw said, and finding that "their particular form of Naturalism is as old as the century.... The naturalism of the Impressionists... seems new only because they have suddenly become conscious of the fact that atmosphere is a visible and paintable phenomenon; and we, accustomed from childhood to see pictorial scenes represented as occurring in a vacuum, are put out by the shock to our habits."[14] The solution, as Jean-Baptiste Lamarck had shown, was to acquire new habits.

One (so-called) art critic in particular who irritated Shaw was Max Nordau (1849–1923), a Hungarian physician who moved from Budapest to Paris in 1886, the year Shaw began writing for the *World*. When Nordau attacked as decadent the modern art movements in a work titled *Degeneration*, Shaw countered with "A Degenerate's View of Nordau," a lengthy review-essay in *Liberty* (New York) on 27 July 1895. Shaw asserted that as an art critic, he had "vigorously" supported the Impressionist movement because, "being the outcome of heightened attention and quickened consciousness on the part of its disciples, it was evidently destined to improve pictures greatly by substituting a natural, observant, real style for a conventional, taken-for-granted, ideal one." Yet there were also many "absurdities" produced in imitation of Whistler and others, "at the time when people could not see the difference between any daub in which there were shadows painted in vivid aniline hues and a landscape by Monet. Not that they thought the daub as good as the Monet: They thought the Monet as ridiculous as the daub; but they were afraid to say so, because they had discovered that people who were good judges did not think Monet ridiculous."[15] Shaw would later search in vain for "a natural, observant, real style" in French drama as theater critic for the *Saturday Review*.

On 24 April 1889, Shaw recommended twenty pictures by Monet exhibited in one room at the Goupil Gallery. Again, he cautioned that they were not "what the British gallery-goer is accustomed to." However, "a glance at the super 'Mediterranean: Vent de Mistral' would convince any one that Monet, his apparently extravagant violets and poppy reds notwithstanding, is one of the most vividly faithful landscapists living." But Shaw's praise, as usual, was qualified: "In the 'Thaw: Argenteuil,' cold and sloppy, and the 'Moulin d'Orgemont,' bathed in hot sleepy sunlight given quite newly and truly in a *gray* tone, his independence of the more startling resources of his palette is proved. In the two pictures described as 'Prairie and Figures' his inferiority to Mr. Sargent in dealing with figures is very marked."[16]

Monet's antithesis, Adolphe William Bouguereau (1825–1905), painted historical, mythological, and religious subjects and, according to Weintraub, was "best known for his ability to paint white on white." In *Our Corner* (March 1886), Shaw commented on several works by Bouguereau, "the illusion of whose smooth and solid flesh-painting will endure the closest inspection," mentioning only *La Patrie* by name. On 21 July 1886, Bouguereau's *Spring* was ambiguously described as "the inevitable masterpiece of ivory nakedness . . . more interesting and not less beautiful than its many forerunners."[17] In a 1910 speech, Shaw commented on Bouguereau's "extreme interest in beautiful women. He tried to make their flesh look like ivory. . . . Bouguereau wants his pretty women with skin like a visiting-card."[18] Bouguereau reached "an illusionistic perfection and a mawkish eroticism much admired in his day, but his flesh tones now seem to be lifeless waxworks, and his fashionable subjects an accumulation of platitudes."[19] Shaw writes as if Bouguereau had died long ago, but he was only sixty-one, with two more decades to live.

Shaw also admired postimpressionists Henri Matisse (1869–1954) and Paul Cézanne (1839–1906). In the *Nation* on 15 February 1913, Shaw mentioned Matisse's "trained professional hand,"[20] and he believed that both men were possessed "of a distinguished mastery of their art in its latest academic form [and] . . . finding themselves intolerably hampered by so much ready-made reach-me-down thoughtstuff . . . deliberately returned to primitive conditions so as to come in at the strait gate and begin at the beginning with all the knowledge of the men who begin at the end."[21]

*   *   *

A second aspect of Shaw's engagement with French art is the extent to which it influenced his work. As we will see, Shaw's sources for a few of his French dramatic characters came from art: a fifteenth-century helmeted female head seen at Orléans in 1913 fits almost exactly Shaw's description of Joan of Arc; a painting by historical artist François Flameng seems to describe the young, long-haired Napoleon of *The Man of Destiny*; and Shaw admitted that Rodin's *Burgesses of Calais* inspired *The Six of Calais*. But there were other French influences at work, some of them more or less conscious.

Shaw was familiar with the work of Jean Léon Gérôme (1824–1904), the popular neoclassical realist painter who took his themes from antiquity. In 1886, Shaw described "a small group of pious Mussulmans . . . in very unequal preservation, one half of the surface being dry and cracked and the other apparently fresh—perhaps repainted," and the following year noted the "technical power" of Gérôme's *Master of the Harem*. Critics have seen important Gérôme echoes in Shaw, Weintraub pointing out that Shaw was familiar with a number of Gérôme's Roman scenes—the widely reproduced *Ave Caesar, Morituri Te Salutant* (1859), *The Gladiators* (1874), and *The Christian Martyrs' Last Prayer* (1883)—"which enriched *Androcles and the Lion* (1913)."[22] Another work may have influenced the so-called rug scene in act 2 of *Caesar and Cleopatra*, where Cleopatra is delivered to Caesar wrapped in a carpet; it has been suggested that the famous *Cléopâtre apportée à César dans un tapis* (1866),[23] exhibited at the Royal Academy in 1871 (five years before Shaw's arrival in London), may have been one of Shaw's sources for that scene.[24]

A more direct influence on *Caesar and Cleopatra* was no doubt *Repos en Égypte* (1879) by Luc-Olivier Merson (1846–1920), first exhibited in the salon of 1879. A sketch of the painting appeared in *Scribner's Monthly* (December 1880), where it was (mis)titled "The Flight into Egypt."[25] Shaw explained to Hesketh Pearson in 1918 that the Sphinx scene in his play "was suggested by a French painter of the Flight Into Egypt. I never can remember the painter's name, but the engraving, which I saw in a shop window when I was a boy, of the Virgin and child asleep in the lap of a colossal Sphinx staring over a desert, so intensely still that the smoke of Joseph's fire close by went straight up like a stick, remained in the rummage basket of my memory for thirty years before I took it out and exploited it on the stage."[26] As Martin Meisel points out, Shaw used the painting as an intertextual echo, since Caesar "explicitly equates himself with his successor, the unborn Christ."[27]

Repos en Égypte also influenced Shaw's staging of the play in France. Writing to director Georges Pitoëff on 23 January 1929 about the failure of *César et Cléopâtre,* Augustin Hamon explained that Shaw had written to him that the Sphinx scene was inspired by Merson's *héliogravure*: "L'avantage de cette présentation est que, losque le rideau se lèverait Cléopâtre apparaîtrait pour le public entre les pattes du Sphinx, alors que César étant sur le côté ne la verrait pas" [The advantage of this presentation is that, when the curtain rises, Cleopatra would appear to the public between the legs of the Sphinx, whereas Caesar, being at the side, would not see her]. Hamon even included a small drawing and emphasized that Shaw considered the monologue a key scene that would decide the fate of the entire play.[28]

Shaw borrowed clothes rather than setting from French artists for *Saint Joan*. Weintraub suggests that since Joan appears at the trial in a "page's black suit," the garb was possibly suggested by a painting of Jules Eugène Lenepveu (1819–98), *Le Départ de Vaucouleurs,* a work that became part of his Pantheon mural in Paris. Shaw was also familiar with illustrator Louis-Maurice Boutet de Monvel (1851–1913), and we know from his diary that on 20 December 1888 he looked at some of Monvel's drawings. One book in particular, *Jeanne d'Arc* (1907), contains "a too-prettified Joan . . . clothed in page's garb for her trial."[29] Another character dressed from art is the twenty-six-year-old Dauphin, the future Charles VII, described by Shaw as *"a poor creature physically; and the current fashion of shaving closely and hiding carefully every scrap of hair under the headcovering . . . makes the worst of his appearance. He has little narrow eyes, near together, a long and pendulous nose that droops over his thick short upper lip, and the expression of a young dog accustomed to be kicked."*[30] Weintraub comments: "That the Dauphin seems to have been imagined from the Jean Fouquet portrait on wood of Charles VII now in the Louvre is unquestionable,"[31] not only due to the accuracy of Shaw's description, but because in the play's epilogue, Charles is in bed *"looking at the pictures in Fouquet's Boccaccio."*[32]

There are also times when Shaw used paintings to establish character and help define personality. Paul Delaroche's *Hémicycle* (1837–41) finds its way into Roebuck Ramsden's study in the opening scene of *Man and Superman* as *"an impression of Dupont's engraving of Delaroche's Beaux Arts hemicycle, representing the great men of all ages."*[33] The original, in a semicircular frieze of the Palais des Beaux-Arts amphitheater, depicts seventy-five colossal figures of the great artists of the world, "a complement to Ramsden's own miniature collection of Victorian celebrities. Ramsden's study is, then, in effect a 'Hemicycle' in miniature," writes Weintraub. Delaroche's theme would have appealed to the pompous, conservative Ramsden.[34]

*   *   *

Shaw's comments on French art, coupled with his occasional use of pictorial suggestion in a few of his plays, exhibit a less adversarial attitude than one would expect from his vituperative theater criticism. Then again, "I am no critic of Art," Shaw insisted in 1889, while he was writing in the *World*. "I hate the whole confounded cultus, which is only a huge sponge to sop up the energies of men who are divinely discontented."[35] His over six decades of art appreciation are evidence that Shaw had energy to spare, and that he was not all that discontented with the French, at least where art was concerned.

2

Shaw in the Concert Halls

"I purposely vulgarized musical criticism"

A Night at the Opera: "Gallic glitter and grandiosity"

Reviewing Arthur Hervey's *Masters of French Music* on 28 February 1894, Shaw wrote: "I will not say that Mr Hervey expresses my own feelings about French music; for no book could be abusive enough for that and at the same time be entirely fit for publication. But then I should write a very bad book on the subject."[1] These are strong words for someone without training in music theory or composition—hence the "bad book" qualification. Yet if he was no musicologist, Shaw knew a great deal about music, having grown up with a father who played the trombone and a mother who developed her fine mezzo-soprano voice under charismatic teacher George John Vandeleur Lee, who took young Shaw to the opera and to his own Amateur Musical Society concerts. At fifteen, his family having broken up, Shaw "learnt the alphabet of musical notation from a primer, and the keyboard from a diagram," and "soon acquired the terrible power of stumbling through pianoforte arrangements and vocal scores," including those of Bizet, Berlioz, Meyerbeer, and Gounod.[2] Later on, every evening for thirty years until his wife's death in 1943, Shaw would sit at the Bechstein and play and sing for Charlotte in what he once called "an uninteresting baritone voice of no exceptional range."[3]

Shaw complemented his informal training with readings in musical technique, history, and biography, recalling in 1935 that he had "studied academic textbooks" and "read pseudo-scientific treatises," resulting (he claimed) "in my knowing much more about music than any of the great composers, an easy achievement for any critic, however barren."[4] "Did nothing but read Gevaert on Instrumentation at the [British] Museum," he wrote in his diary on 4 September 1885,[5] alluding to the *Traité général d'instrumentation* (1863, rev. 1885) by Belgian musicologist François Auguste Gevaert, whose *Histoire et théorie de la musique de l'antiquité* (2 vols. 1875, 1881) Shaw mentioned two years later.[6] The next year he read Jean Lucien Adolphe Jullien's *Richard Wagner, sa vie et ses oeuvres* (1886); in 1893 he went through the two volumes of Georges Noufflard's *Richard Wagner d'après lui-même* (Paris, 1893), reviewing it favorably the following year. Although Noufflard, "being racially out of sympathy" with Wagner, "never entirely comprehends him," he is also "remarkably free from the stock vulgarities of French operatic culture: for instance, he washes his hands of Meyerbeer most fastidiously; and he puts Gluck, the hero of French musical classicism, most accurately in his true place."[7]

Dan H. Laurence has assembled Shaw's entire musical criticism, which includes unsigned notices in the *Hornet* (1876–77), reviews in the *Star* (1888–89) as "Corno di Bassetto" and in the *World* (1890–94) as "G.B.S.," *The Perfect Wagnerite* (1898), and many occasional (and previously uncollected) pieces—the last published nine days after his death—amounting to over 2,700 pages. Shaw's energy was prodigious; during one six-day period (14 to 19 May 1894) he heard seven operas: on Monday, Puccini's *Manon Lescaut*; Wednesday, Gluck's *Orfeo ed Euridice* and Mascagni's *Cavalleria Rusticana*; Thursday, Gounod's *Philémon et Baucis* and Leoncavallo's *Pagliacci*; Friday, Bizet's *Carmen*; and Saturday, Verdi's *Falstaff*. Of course this is merely a selection of his weekly activities. Shaw usually had many other personal and social engagements.

In his music reviews, Shaw expressed himself with vehemence, explaining in 1935: "I purposely vulgarized musical criticism, which was then refined and academic to the point of being unreadable and often nonsensical."[8] He had his prejudices, not all of them French: the religious oratorios of Mendelssohn were offensive; Brahms was intellectually pretentious.[9] But the French composers he mentions most often—Berlioz, Bizet, Gounod, Massenet, Meyerbeer, Offenbach, Saint-Saëns—are more derided than praised. Georges Liébert, who translated a large selection of Shaw's music reviews, asserts that as far as French music is concerned, Shaw, "malgré sa francophobie ostentatoire, est loin de la dédaigner. Saint-Saëns excepté" [despite his ostentatious Francophobia, is far from despising it. Saint-Saëns excepted].[10] Yet if Shaw enjoyed some French music, Saint-Saëns was definitely not the sole exception.

Certainly Shaw had his favorite singers (soprano Emma Calvé, baritone Victor Maurel), musicians, composers, and works. But seduced as he was by Bach, Handel, and especially Mozart, by Wagner's verbal allegories and the originality of Richard Strauss and Edward Elgar, Shaw was not entranced by any French composer, aside from some works by Meyerbeer and Berlioz. But were his critiques of French music and musicians as "abusive" as he claimed they could be, or as abusive as were his reviews of French plays and playwrights? Upon entering Covent Garden in 1891, Shaw was astonished to find that the music (Gounod and Wagner) "was being conducted with immense spirit by a French gentleman who did not understand one bar of it, but who 'worked up' the finish with a truly Gallic glitter and grandiosity."[11] Was this all there was to French music?

* * *

Shaw's music critiques exhibit what one recent commentator called "passionate subjectivity."[12] Shaw on "La Marseillaise": "incurable vulgarity . . . mechanical tramp and ignobly self-assertive accent"; on inept musical direction: "[in Paris,] the opera is generally mutilated, and ill-done by people who dont understand opera"; on the Paris Opéra: "that detestable blight of bravado and flunkey-like attitudinizing."[13] Shaw complained in 1917 that for a century, "that disgusting overgrowth, the Grand Opera of Paris, has been compelling quite charming composers to . . . turn out dainty operettas and ballets in Handelian-Wagnerian armor." Properly done, Meyerbeer's *Dinorah,* the third act of *Les Huguenots,* and Gounod's *Mireille* "are not gigantic obsolescent bores" but "charming and dramatic in their romantic little way."[14]

As he did in his critiques of French drama, Shaw singled out Paris—repeating himself often—as the locus of a culture outdated and overblown: "a pedant-ridden failure in everything that it pretends to lead"; "in music, as in most other things, Paris is still in the year 1850"; "Paris remains . . . incapable of high art"; "a metropolitanism that is fifty years behind the time"; "I long ago gave up Paris as impossible from the artistic point of view"; "going to Paris means going back fifty years in civilization"; London "is as far ahead of Paris in musical judgment as in most other things."[15] Passionate subjectivity indeed! Although Shaw faulted the age he lived in, where composers make tenors bleat, baritones shatter with their vibrato, and sopranos sound like "a locomotive whistle without its steadiness,"[16] his music reviews exhibit a dissatisfaction with almost all manner of French music.

Some works were dispatched in a title, as was Ambroise Thomas's "Hamlet: A Foolish Opera," or in a line: "The two pieces by Saint-Saëns were clever trash."[17] Others were used to illustrate silly extravagance:

alluding to Ferdinand Hérold, Shaw noted "the endless repetitions, sequences, and *rosalias,* the *crescendos,* doubles and redoubles, of the operatic instrumental style, the absurdity of which culminated in that immortal composition, the overture to Zampa."[18] The romantic opera *Lakmé* (1883) by Léo Délibes was produced, Shaw claimed, not in recognition of its merit, but to display the lead singer's talent, she and her French colleagues singing "with a shattering *tremolo* and a nasal tone to which French audiences are better accustomed than English ones."[19] Even compliments were dubious: in *Les Pêcheurs de perles,* "Bizet is only himself— his immature self—in the love music."[20]

Shaw appreciated some works merely for their literary background. On 25 November 1891, he reviewed Alfred Bruneau's *Le Rêve* (1890), a light opera based on the dramatic poem that Louis Gallet had made from the 1888 novel of the same title by Bruneau's friend Émile Zola: "Like all Frenchmen, Bruneau vindicates his originality by a few *hardiesses* . . . the whole affair is frightfully sentimental."[21] On 30 November, he wrote that it was "full of delicate and noble themes in what I may call the celestial style of Gounod, and woven together in the fashion of Wagner."[22] But his curiosity was piqued, and the next day Shaw bought Zola's novel. In 1894, he referred to Bruneau as "really a tone-poet in his way."[23]

At times one does not know if Shaw is being witty or if he is in earnest. He warned against the "wicked" music of Offenbach's *Les Brigands* (1869): "Every accent in it is a snap of the fingers in the face of moral responsibility: every ripple and sparkle on its surface twits me for my teetotalism."[24] Claude Debussy was reduced to the subject of witty anecdote. In a 1913 causerie written to be read to a society of musicians in France, Shaw recounted meeting "a Parisian who had heard of Debussy, and even had a theory that he must have been employed in an organ factory, because of his love of the scale of whole tones." In 1914, he mentioned that Debussy's scale of whole tones was "long familiar to organ builders, but strange to the musical public." And in an undated essay, Shaw ascribed the first attempt at "new music . . . to the accident of a musical Frenchman named Debussy living next door to an organ factory, or perhaps being employed in one." He explained that in an organ factory, the tuning proceeds by whole tones, "so that anyone within earshot soon becomes accustomed to a scale which you can play on your piano as C, D, E, F sharp, A flat, B flat, C. . . . Debussy wrote music in the whole tone scale, melody, harmony and all; and immediately there was a genuine new music."[25]

Generally, then, Shaw's comments reveal frustration and disappointment with French music and musicians. Exasperated by interpretations or compositions that fell below his exacting standards, Shaw countered with as much wit as he could muster after attending what were often lengthy or lackluster performances. But he ceased to be playful with those for whose music he truly had no use, such as Camille Saint-Saëns.

Camille Saint-Saëns (1835–1921)

Shaw heard Saint-Saëns at the organ and piano in Saint James's Hall in 1885, making only a few remarks about the C minor piano concerto and a septet for strings, piano, and trumpet.[26] But after seeing *Ascanio* on his first trip to Paris in 1890, he reported that the opera did not have "an original phrase in it from beginning to end. The tragic scenes are secondhand Verdi; the love scenes are secondhand Gounod; the 'historic' scenes are secondhand Meyerbeer." He found both libretto and music "a string of commonplaces," and on the whole it was a dull "potboiler," "an elaborate and expensive tomfoolery." Three years later, he recalled his "prodigious boredom."[27]

Shaw found nothing to commend in Saint-Saëns. In 1892, he was "disheartened" to hear his "heavy and barren" variations for two pianos on a theme by Beethoven.[28] *Le Rouet d'Omphale*, conducted by the composer, was "trivial," Shaw wrote in 1893, noting that after playing his G minor concerto, Saint-Saëns was recalled for a solo but did not understand, "and the audience had at last to give over the attempt."[29] Four months later, Shaw reported that Slivinski, in trying to treat that concerto seriously, made it "very dull, whereas in the hands of the composer it is at least gay," its only highlight borrowed from the prelude to Bach's organ fugue in A minor.[30] The following week, Shaw heard the violin concerto in B minor, "with its trivially pretty scraps of serenade music sandwiched between pages from the great masters."[31] Eight months later, finding the symphony for orchestra with pianoforte and organ "a model of elegant instrumentation," Shaw complained that it degenerated at the finale. "All that barren *coda* stuff, its whipping of rhythms, and its ridiculous scraps of *fugato*, should be ruthlessly excised: it has no real theme, and only spoils the rest."[32]

Shaw remarked in 1909 that for years *Samson et Dalila* (1877) was forbidden in England because the Lord Chamberlain objected to them as "scriptural characters."[33] But his review of the opera on 4 October 1893 began: "Who wants to hear Samson and Delilah? I respectfully suggest, Nobody." He left after the second act. Granted, sluggish conducting was partly to blame; but Shaw was annoyed at the stage antics, and after describing how Saint-Saëns might treat a historical opera titled *Ulster*—"with a grand climax of all the national airs of Ireland worked in double counterpoint with suitable extracts from the Church music of the rivals' creeds, played simultaneously on several military bands and a pair of organs"—he concluded, "This is the sort of thing a French composer dreams of as the summit of operatic achievement."[34]

Shaw found Saint-Saëns simply too trivial to be taken as seriously as most people did. In his review of Hervey's *Masters of French Music* four months later, he remarked that from the sixty-five pages about Saint-Saëns—giving the pleasantest impression of his cleverness, technical ingenuity, fine orchestration, keyboard skills, and "wide knowledge of modern music"—one would never guess that by removing his borrowings from Meyerbeer, Gounod, and Bach, one would have nothing left except "graceful knicknacks—barcarolles, serenades, ballets, and the like."[35] For Shaw, being derivative was perhaps a composer's greatest sin against music.

Giacomo Meyerbeer (1791–1864)

Shaw had more respect for Giacomo Meyerbeer, a Berliner who took up permanent residence in Paris in 1834 and whose operas *Les Huguenots* (1836), *Le Prophète* (1849), and *L'Africaine* (1865) had librettos by Eugène Scribe. According to Shaw, Meyerbeer "deliberately cultivated *bizarrerie* in order to impress the French with the idea that he was 'superior and powerful' (and succeeded)," Paris regarding him "as a sort of musical Michael Angelo."[36] Shaw, too, esteemed "his striking individuality, his inexaustible variety," called him "the impressive, the original, the historical, the much imitated inimitable," and considered the duet in the fourth act of *Les Huguenots* as "the most exciting situation in lyric drama."[37] "From my earliest recorded sign of an interest in music," Shaw wrote in 1935, "when as a small child I encored my mother's singing of the page's song from the first act of Les Huguenots . . . music has been an indispensable part of my life."[38]

This is how Shaw summed up Meyerbeer's characteristics as a composer: "the singularity which is not always individuality, the inventiveness which is not always fecundity, the love of the curious and piquant, the fastidious industry and cleverness, the intense and jealous individualism with its resultant treatment of the executants as mere instruments and not as artistic comrades and cooperators, the retreating from any effect that cannot be exactly and mechanically planned by himself as from an impossibility, the love of the fantastic, legendary, non-human element in folk music, ... and the almost selfishly concentrated feeling, the fire, the distinction, the passion that flash out occasionally through much artifice and much trifling."[39]

The problem was that Meyerbeer, a victim of his place in musical history, was more sinned against than sinning. In 1894, Shaw reminded his readers that "Wagner accused Meyerbeer of following the great masters as a starling follows the plough, picking up the titbits which their force unearthed, and serving them up to Paris unmixed with noble matter."[40] Meyerbeer, who had "a very remarkable and original dramatic talent," was "maimed" by having come after Mozart and before Wagner, and "could only cobble up his fine dramatic phrases into childish couplets, quatrains and quadrilles by such means as an able prose writer might employ to turn a straightforward love letter into a bad valentine."[41] After seeing *Le Prophète* with bilingual libretto in hand, Shaw called it "the oddest medley of drinking songs, tinder-box *trios,* sleigh rides, and skating quadrilles imaginable."[42] But this may not have been entirely Meyerbeer's fault, for "Paris encouraged Meyerbeer in posing as the successor of Mozart and Beethoven, as it encourages Saint-Saëns and Massenet in posing as the successors of Meyerbeer"; "No doubt Saint-Saëns had to copy Meyerbeer, just as poor Meyerbeer had to copy himself from the day when he made a speciality of religious fanaticism in Les Huguenots."[43]

A second problem was the way in which Meyerbeer's work was performed. For instance, the opening scene of the fifth act of *Les Huguenots* was "excised and the *finale* recklessly mutilated," the remaining acts "extensively and tastelessly curtailed." This was recorded in "The Merits of Meyerbeer" (1877), where Shaw's praise is unqualified: "We are acquainted with no work of similar length which is more highly finished in all its parts; which contains such a profusion of original and varied melody without being eked out by conventional manufacture; which displays greater fertility in orchestral device; and which at the same time bears so exclusive a stamp of one individuality."[44] Shaw saw the opera again at Drury Lane on 20 July 1887 and in 1891 at Covent Garden, in a performance that was "the result of music butchery perpetrated half a century ago in order to bring the performance within reasonable limits of time. In accordance with the taste of that Rossinian period, the whistlable tunes were retained, and the dramatic music sacrificed." Shaw suggested further cuts to be made as well as the restoration of excised scenes.[45] He knew the opera well, having examined the score in the British Museum in April 1880 and recently on 28 May 1890.[46] After seeing it again in 1894, he railed against "the mutilated state of the work as performed at Covent Garden," with "intolerably slovenly" choral singing and a third act "too silly for description."[47]

What Meyerbeer possessed, and what even bowdlerized performances could not suppress, was energy. In "The Religion of the Pianoforte" (1894), Shaw urged that youths, instead of reading descriptions of duels, escapes, and "raptures of passion," should experience "the stirring of the blood, the bristling of the fibres, the transcendent, fearless fury which makes romance so delightful" by pitching "your Three Musketeers into the wastepaper basket" and getting a vocal score of *Les Huguenots*. "Then to the piano, and pound away. In the music you will find the body and reality of that feeling which the mere novelist could only describe to you."[48]

However, Meyerbeer was no musical Michelangelo. In *The Perfect Wagnerite* (1898), Shaw assessed him as "a profounder genius" than Mozart, but "all this effect of originality and profundity was produced by a quite limited talent for turning striking phrases, exploiting certain curious and rather catching rhythms and modulations, and devizing suggestive or eccentric instrumentation." He produced "neither a thorough music-drama nor a charming opera" yet "had some genuine dramatic energy, and even passion."[49]

Jules Massenet (1842–1912)

Also possessing energy and passion, Jules Massenet lacked true musical greatness. According to Shaw, his prelude to *Hérodiade* was mere "French routine music."[50] In 1885, Shaw reviewed an English *Manon* (1884), advising those who found the libretto bewildering "to read the novel, which is prodigiously superior to the opera." The libretto must have been very badly translated, Shaw refusing to quote from it for fear of creating "uproarious mirth." He recommended the scarce 1838 and scarcer 1797 French editions of the book, while "the much vaunted *édition de luxe* of 1875, with the preface by Alexandre Dumas *fils*, and the etchings by Leopold Flameng, will repay careful avoidance."

Des Grieux, Shaw wrote, "wins all the sympathy that the readers of the novel feel, in spite of their moral sense, for the amiable hero whose honor rooted in dishonor stood, and whose faith unfaithful kept him falsely true." Soprano Marie Roze, "not a first-rate singer" in previous roles, triumphed as Manon: "The intelligence and determination that have enabled her to achieve it are still masked by the infantine simplicity, the plaintive eyes, and the innocent beauty that used to blunt the critical pen and sweeten the critical ink. But the artlessness that was once only too genuine now conceals carefully premeditated acting, based on an exhaustive study of the original description of the character." Shaw commended Roze for "giving up her old fashion of desperately assaulting vocal difficulties in the hope of vanquishing them by force or by good luck," thus saving her voice from deteriorating.

But in *Manon* and elsewhere, Massenet was "one of the loudest of modern composers" who "pours forth all his energy in a screeching, grinding, rasping *fortissimo* of extraordinary exuberance and vigor. He is perhaps better at a stage tumult than any living composer." The music was "pretty, spirited, easy to follow, varied with considerable fancy and ingenuity, never dull, and only occasionally trivial or vulgar," but Shaw complained of the "excessively strident" instrumentation and "immoderate fury" of the climaxes. At any rate, had Meyerbeer and Gounod "not made a path for M. Massenet, it is impossible to say whither he might have wandered, or how far he could have pushed his way."[51] Two months later, Shaw noted Massenet's "very obstreperous" orchestral style, pointing out that his librettists had "kept the Sunday side" of des Grieux but "suppressed the episodes in which his failings would lead him into actual disgrace."[52]

After seeing *Werther* (1892), Shaw remarked on 20 June 1894 upon "a certain frank naturalness which never deserts Massenet . . . as long as he steers clear of the traditions of Parisian grand opera. On his own ground he has an engaging force and charm of expression." Shaw lavished accolades on tenor Jean de Reszke, whom he heard often, for his Werther (though "Werther is hardly to be counted a great part").[53] One week later, he praised the excellent staging and realistic scenery of *La Navarraise* at Covent Garden, with its cannonades and "almost smokeless explosives," and called Emma Calvé "a living volcano, wild with anxiety, to be presently mad with joy, ecstatic with love, desperate with disappointment, and so on in ever culminating transitions through mortification, despair, fury, terror, and finally . . . silly maniacal laughter." Massenet, "bashfully concealed in the wing," refused to come on stage at the curtain despite yells from the audience. The triumph did not stop Shaw from calling the opera "a prescription" whose events were "credible and touching, and the assumptions, explanations, and pretexts on which they are brought about so simple and convenient that nobody minds their being impossible."[54]

Georges Bizet (1835–1875)

When soloists mangled a composition, Shaw was merciless. He liked Georges Bizet's *Carmen* (1875) and thought Emma Calvé (1858–1942) "a soprano of innate dramatic force,"[55] but her Carmen so enfuriated him that he berated her for years, beginning on 30 May 1894: "I *hate* performers who debase great works of art: I long for their annihilation. . . . But I am necessarily no less extreme in my admiration of artists who realize the full value of great works for me, or who transfigure ordinary ones. Calvé is such an artist," one who possesses "a beauty of . . . that sort of action which is the thought or conception of the artist made visible." Shaw was shocked "beyond measure" by a Carmen that was merely a "a superstitious, pleasure-loving good-for-nothing . . . with no power but the power of seduction, which she exercises without sense or decency," honesty or courage. The dying Carmen was transformed "into a reeling, staggering, flopping, disorganized thing." Despite the applause, it was evident to Shaw that the audience was uncomfortable.[56]

Six weeks later, Shaw alluded to Calvé "scoring cheap triumphs with trashy one-act melodramas,"[57] and in 1895 wrote that she had "wrecked an innocently pretty opera by suddenly springing upon the delicate romance of Bizet's and Prosper Mérimée's fancy the worthless, fierce, sensual, reckless, rapscallionly Carmen of real life."[58] "Calvé, an artist of genius," he wrote eight months later, "divested Carmen of the last rag of romance and respectability: it is not possible to describe in decent language what a rapscallion she made of her." If "the comedy of her audacities was irresistible"—and Shaw gave examples of their "genuine artistic force"—Calvé allowed Carmen "no courage, . . . no heart, no worth, no positive vice . . . and she made her die with such frightful art that . . . you felt that there was nothing lying there but a lump of carrion." Calvé's performance may have been "great acting in all its qualities, interpretation, invention, selection, creation, and fine execution, with the true tragicomic force behind it," but the achievement was "too cheap to counterbalance the degradation of her beauty and the throwing away of her skill on a study from vulgar life which was, after all, quite foreign to the work on which she imposed it." Like others before her, Calvé had "substituted the Zola Carmen for the Mérimée Carmen."[59] In 1891, Shaw had written that Mérimée's Carmen, "with all her subtle charm, was only a gentleman's dream."[60]

Georges Liébert explained recently Shaw's extreme dissatisfaction with *Carmen* by suggesting that if his comments "sentent l'injustice, c'est parce que Bizet prend l'amour trop au sérieux" [reveal a certain unfairness, it is because Bizet takes love too seriously]. According to Liébert, it is a case of Shaw exhibiting his "indignation puritaine."[61] That may be so, but it may simply be that Shaw felt that a crude and abrasive Carmen did not do justice to the poetry of her literary source.

Charles Gounod (1818–1893)

"Gounod had devoutly declared that Don Giovanni has been to him all his life a revelation of perfection," wrote Shaw in 1891, "a miracle, a work without fault. I smile indulgently at Gounod . . . but I am afraid my fundamental attitude towards Mozart is the same as his."[62] This is perhaps the most generous comment Shaw ever made about Charles Gounod, whom he sometimes used "as a whipping boy to register his admiration for Mozart," according to Richard Corballis.[63] Then again, four years earlier Shaw had alluded to "the maudlin Mozart idolatry of M. Gounod, whom I of course do not consider a great musician."[64]

Shaw continued to whip Gounod even in his own work, slipping him with Mozart into the "Don Juan in Hell" interlude of *Man and Superman* by having a *"very Mephistophelian"* Devil enter to the sound of Mozart's music, which *"gets grotesquely adulterated with Gounod's,"* and soon after singing *"in a nasal operatic baritone, tremulous from an eternity of misuse in the French manner."*[65] Corballis believes that for Gounod's adulterating music, "Shaw presumably had in mind the fortissimo woodwind chords which accompany the first entrance of Méphistophélès in *Faust*," and for the "nasal" French manner, interpreters like Jean-Baptiste Faure,[66] principal baritone at the Paris Opéra, whom Shaw termed "a vocalist of the French school, and a bad one," and his Méphistophélès "respectable, not to say occasionally a trifle dull."[67]

Shaw did not think highly of *Faust* (1859), which he described in 1885 as "Faust with all Goethe's thought left out."[68] Four months later, he called Faust "a refined but weak sentimentalist" and Méphistophélès "a mountebank who grimaces in the glow of a red limelight, . . . the most childish and ridiculous travesty of a serious conception that the public has ever disgraced itself by taking in earnest."[69] Five years later, in 1890, he complained, "I have heard Gounod's Faust not less than ninety times within the last ten or fifteen years; and I have had enough of it."[70] Three years after that, he suspected that if the music "were less seraphically soothing, it would have long ago produced an inflammatory disease—Faustitis—in my profession. Even as it is, I am far from sure that my eyesight has not been damaged by protracted contemplation of the scarlet coat and red limelight of Mephistopheles."[71]

Shaw recognized in 1890 that some of the fault lay with the critics, who, had they not set the fashion of writing up Méphistophélès "as an acting part of all but unfathomable profundity, we should not now be plagued with the puerile inanities of baritones with impossible eyebrows, who spend the evening in a red limelight and an ecstasy of sardonic smiling."[72] Shaw, who in childhood had wished for "un visage Méphistophélique" in the Gounod manner, thought that only Victor Maurel managed (in part) a dignified portrayal. At an 1891 Covent Garden performance, Shaw commended his Méphistophélès as a character with "no sentimental trace of the fallen son of the morning" or "any of the stage puerilities of the pantomime demon." Maurel, with "ashen face and beard" and "loveless tigerish voice," was "that grim Gothic fancy of an obscene beast of prey with the form and intellect of a man." Yet Shaw also found him deficient in humor and, in the serenade and duel scene, "cumbrous and heavy," taking the scene "as tragically as Faust himself, instead of being the one person present to whom it is pure sport."[73] Six weeks later, Shaw praised Belgian Heldentenor Ernest Van Dyck, whose bad cold did not prevent him from being "by far the best Faust" he had ever seen. "Little as there is in the part as treated by Gounod, it is surprising to find how far that little can be made to go by an artist of genuine power and abundant vitality."[74]

Faust was not the only Gounod work Shaw did not like. Others annoyed him, mostly for the cloying sentimentality that often turned them into frivolous, pointless, frequently endless exercises: the music of *Le Cinq Mars* was "valueless";[75] the great length of *Roméo et Juliette,* despite its exquisite music, made it "tedious" and "monotonous";[76] the "Ave Maria" on Bach's C minor prelude showed Gounod's "old tendency to save himself the trouble of composing by simply setting everything to the ascending chromatic scale," whose "heavenly felicities" were by this time "palling" on Shaw; and *Philémon et Baucis* was enjoyable only as "pure play from beginning to end."[77]

Although Shaw recorded in his diary on 27 August 1885 that he played through Gounod's *Messe Solennelle,* and on 20 October 1887 that he played and sang it with his mother,[78] he found Gounod's other long religious works problematic. About the oratorio *Mors et Vita* on 29 August 1885, performed that week at the Birmingham Festival, Shaw wrote: "Religious music of this sort is only remarkable as *naïve* blasphemy, wonderfully elaborated, and convinced of its own piety."[79] In his 7 November review, he thought it "on the whole, a bore," although "the grace of his enchanting music, by making us forget its subject matter, banishes our sense of its absurdity. But he has treated the Christian religion with the same utter frivolity as he formerly treated Goethe's Faust; and criticism must now [sic] allow itself to be bribed to ignore that fact by the sensuous beauty of his music." And Shaw did find it "impeccably beautiful from beginning to end . . . all is clear, smooth, articulate, harmonious, and in exquisite taste. Many of the strains are quite angelic. . . . On the other hand, the sequences and repetitions are almost beyond all patience." Shaw concluded that the Supreme Judge, given his dignity and refinement, had been "apparently conceived by M. Gounod on the lines of that noble gentleman, Athos, in Les Trois Mousquetaires."[80]

The following month, writing about the London premiere of *Mors et Vita* on 4 November, Shaw referred to Gounod as "the romantically pious Frenchman whose adoration of the Virgin Mother is chivalrous, whose obedience to the Pope is filial, and whose homage to his God is that of a devoted royalist to his king. It follows that he is a deep thinker. But his exquisite taste, his fastidious workmanship, and an earnestness that never fails him even in his most childish enterprises, make him the most enchanting of modern musicians within the limits of his domain of emotion and picturesque superstition." Shaw concluded that Gounod's "piety is inane, and so, at bottom, his music is tedious. . . . Feeling that the consummate musician is a puerile thinker, we are compelled to deny that he is a great composer whilst admitting the loveliness of his music."[81]

Gounod's previous oratorio *Rédemption* (1882), performed six months later at the Crystal Palace with three thousand singers and four hundred musicians, was "extremely tedious . . . because its beauties are repeated *ad nauseam*." In Gounod's hands, the Redeemer—like the Supreme Judge six months earlier—became "a smooth-spoken gentleman! There is a plague of smoothness over the whole work. . . . M. Gounod is to Handel as a Parisian duel is to Armageddon."[82] When *Rédemption* was performed at the Albert Hall seven years later, Shaw was again put out, this time by the composer's self-plagiarism; in the death on the cross scene, Shaw discovered the same eight bars (transposed from D to B) Gounod had used two decades earlier in *Faust* to accompany the death of Valentin, thus turning him into "a saint and a martyr." Shaw also found the oratorio wearisome, noting that those who did not "would not mind going through five miles of pictures by Fra Angelico,"[83] an allusion to what he had written two years previously, after reading (in French) the recently published (1890) biography by Marie Anne de Bovet: "For Gounod's music I have never found any better words than heavenly and angelic, in the simplest, childish sense," and so was delighted to learn that when Gounod was studying in Vienna, he had written in the margin of one of his scores, "O heiliger Fra Angelico: wo ist die Musik deiner Engeln!"[84]

It is no surprise to find Shaw writing in April 1894 of the two oratorios that "their sweetness made them cloy after half an hour or so, full-length performances being all but insufferable"; and in July, that "we have found by our experiments with Mors et Vita and The Redemption that a whole concert of Gounod is insufferable."[85] Very shortly after Gounod's death, Shaw attended a Crystal Palace concert that included the "Marche Religieuse" and the overture to *Mireille;* Shaw remarked upon the "beautiful smoothness of its lines and the transparent richness and breadth of its orchestral coloration." Two weeks later, however, he complained about the printed slip that had been circulated at the Crystal Palace asking the audience to stand during the march: "I took no part in it. . . . I object to confer on a trumpery *pièce d'occasion* the distinction which is the traditional English appanage of Handel's Hallelujah Chorus."[86] As with the work of Saint-Saëns, Gounod's music was greatly inferior to its reputation.

Jacques Offenbach (1819–1880)

In 1909, Shaw classed Jacques Offenbach as one of the "art confectioners . . . who hasten to make pretty entertainments out of scraps and crumbs from the masterpieces," as did Offenbach by turning Beethoven's seventh symphony into "J'aime les militaires." Such people bring to their work "love of beauty, desire to give pleasure, tenderness, humor, everything except the high republican conscience, the identification of the artist's purpose with the purpose of the universe, which alone makes an artist great."[87]

Offenbach was no genius, but he was lively and amusing. Shaw was especially fond of *La Grande Duchesse de Géroldstein* (1867), a satire on war and militarism, which he praised in 1890 as "an original and complete work of art."[88] In July 1893, he noted its "witty book and effervescent score," recalling the days when it was considered "something frightfully wicked, . . . and young persons were withheld from the interpolated *can-can* in the second act as from a spectacle that must deprave them for ever."[89] Four months later, after hearing a ponderous interpretation at the Criterion Theatre, Shaw lamented the absence of "the true Offenbachianisms—the restless movement, the witty abandonment, the swift, light, wicked touch, the inimitable *élan.*" "Even the big drum, which always marked Offenbach out as a musical blackguard in spite of his cleverness, thumps away without any of the old enjoyment." Yet it was a tribute to its "grace, gaiety, and intelligence" that it held its own when performed "without any of the piquancies of style which he and his librettists had in contemplation."[90]

In 1896, Shaw called the opera's score and its libretto "classics compared to anything we seem to be able to turn out nowadays. Still, if La Grande Duchesse had been entrusted to a mere comic song tune compiler and a brace of facetious bar loafers, it would have been none the more up to date now in dramatic weight and musical richness."[91] Offenbach is perhaps the one French composer praised solely on the grounds that he was amusing and entertaining.

André Messager (1853–1929)

An organ pupil of Saint-Saëns, André Messager eventually became musical director at Covent Garden from 1901 to 1907 and at the Paris Opéra from 1908 to 1914, long after Shaw had reviewed his music. Shaw was particularly taken with the D'Oyly Carte production of the comic opera *La Basoche* (1890), which he reviewed at length on 11 November 1891. He praised "the dainty combination of farce and fairy tale in an historical framework," Messager having avoided the hackneyed operatic turns "in a fresh, clever, cultivated, and ingenious way." The work had "neither tomfoolery nor sentimentality: the atmosphere is that of high comedy." Shaw concluded that with *La Basoche* one reaches "that happy region which lies between the pity and terror of tragic opera and the licentious stupidity and insincerity of *opéra bouffe*." Nonetheless, it remained "the work of a French author and a French composer. Such drawbacks, however, cannot be helped as long as we abandon high musical comedy to the French." He ended his review with a warning that "if we do not take kindly to The Basoche, we may make up our minds to ninetynine chances in the hundred of having to fall back on something worse in its place."[92]

On 16 November, Shaw saw Messager's *Fauvette* (which ran for only six performances) but failed to review it, "suggesting his disappointment," as Weintraub notes.[93] Commenting upon the music season some weeks later, Shaw qualified *Fauvette* as "elaborate and polished in style, without being pretentiously and emptily heavy, and amusing without being slangy or vulgar."[94] He found in 1894 that the love story of Messager's new work *Mirette* was too simple, that the music was "commonplace," and that the opera went "in pointlessness and tediousness, to the extreme limits compatible with production at the Savoy Theatre."[95]

Hector Berlioz (1803–1869)

That Shaw took a special interest in Hector Berlioz, the great representative of French musical romanticism, is evident from his thorough study of his life and works. Shaw's diaries tell us that in 1880 he read Berlioz's *Voyage Musical en Allemagne et en Italie* (1844) and *Mémoires* (1870), both in French; that he requested the *Traité d'instrumentation et d'orchestration* (1843) at the British Museum in October 1888, and on 10 December "looked over several of Berlioz's scores" there;[96] and that he was reading Jean Lucien Adolphe Jullien's *Hector Berlioz: Sa vie et ses oeuvres* (1888) in February 1890. Shaw may also have known, at least by reputation, the abundant musical criticism that Berlioz published in *Le Journal des débats* from 1835 to 1864; Shaw wrote in 1890 that Berlioz was "almost as good a critic as I."[97] Jacques Barzun believes that "Shaw on his own made himself into one of the best-informed and most perceptive critics of the music of Berlioz."[98]

Shaw believed that Berlioz "actually towers above Gounod as a French composer,"[99] mild praise in light of Shaw's opinion of Gounod. Unfortunately, few orchestras lived up to the demands of Berlioz's monumental works, and Shaw complained in 1885 that the "massive Symphonie Funèbre et Triomphale" at Saint James's Hall and the "gigantic Te Deum" in the Crystal Palace failed in producing their "prodigious effects" because the orchestras were simply too small.[100] In 1893, reviewing an Albert Hall performance of *La Damnation de Faust* (1846), Shaw observed that it managed "to comb that wild composer's hair, stuff him into a frock-coat and tall hat, stick a hymn book in his hand," and replace the "brimstonish orgy in Auerbach's cellar" with an evening at the YMCA. The "dull and suburban" performance suggested to Shaw a new title: "Berlioz's Damnation."[101]

Shaw was very annoyed by the British treatment of the *Symphonie Fantastique* (1830), one of Berlioz's most powerful and poetic works. In "Berlioz's Episode" (5 December 1885), he was irked to find that Berlioz's program, which the composer had requested should be distributed among the audience, was replaced by a distorted English summary. Shaw provided an excerpt from Berlioz in translation (presumably his own) and the equivalent passage from the W. A. Barrett version (written in 1882). Berlioz: "A young musician of morbid sensibility and ardent imagination poisons himself with opium in a fit of despair caused by love." Barrett: "... a young musician, whose soul is consumed by that infinite yearning, that soul sickness, which has been called the 'vague passion,' and which forms the subject of so much modern rhythm, miscalled poetry." Shaw also quoted in French Berlioz's fifteen-word description of the musician finding his beloved at the ball, and Barrett's "too expansive" sixty-four-word translation. Berlioz would be unable to refrain from laughing at "vague passion" as a translation of his *"vagues de passion,"* wrote Shaw, pointing out that "the march to the scaffold" became "March to the Gallows," "in spite of the tremendous crash with which the guillotine axe cuts short the *idée fixe* [the beloved] at the end of it." Shaw even took out his watch and clocked the first movement—112 minims per minute instead of Berlioz's stipulated 132—and found it two-thirds of the proper speed: "The music lost the character, *agitato e appassionato,* that Berlioz insisted on."[102] He reviewed another performance three weeks later and timed the movement again, finding the orchestra "jogging along under easy sail at the rate of sixteen minims less than Berlioz's explicit *tempo*." Shaw specified this time that when Berlioz speaks of *"ce vague des passions,"* "he is quoting Chateaubriand, who somewhere wrote that the further nations advance in civilization, the more intense becomes '*cet état du vague des passions.*' [Théophile] Gautier has given in the earlier chapters of Mademoiselle de Maupin a capital description of the unaccountable disquietude referred to."[103]

Jacques Barzun has written of the many psychological affinities between Berlioz and Shaw: "Both were natively shy men who schooled themselves to showmanship, that is, self-exhibition"; as critics, both appreciated Mozart when he was neglected, and nothing could violate the integrity of their judgments, even if it meant praising the work of an opponent; as artists, Berlioz taught orchestras and conductors how to perform his works and Shaw taught actors and directors how to put on his plays; as writers, their prose is "lucid . . . rapid, dazzling. . . . The thought modulates briskly; it links remote ideas unexpectedly"; and Shaw's lifelong belief that "music was drama—character and conflict in sound" is answered in every bar of Berlioz's music.[104]

The impact of Berlioz on Shaw was not only personal but literary, as one can see from Shaw's recently published "A Reminiscence of Hector Berlioz," dated 29 February 1880,[105] a story that incorporates many of his British Museum readings. Barzun, who edited the story, believes that it "contains the essence of Shaw's musical creed, not borrowed from Berlioz, but helped into being by the teachings derived from reading him."[106] The story records the infatuation of Berlioz for the narrator, a young Englishwoman, who sets down in 1827 remembered events of late 1824 and early 1825; the postscript informs us that she is "now" (in 1879) eighty years old.

The story opens as the narrator unexpectedly comes upon Berlioz speaking to himself: "Accursed be this miserable world, the paradise of pedants: the hell of genius." The tale of failed courtship is also one of artistic struggle, and its importance lies in its portrayal, in the guise of a tormented young Berlioz, of Shaw's own frustrations and aspirations. According to Barzun, the following lines from Berlioz's love letter to the narrator "amount to a Shavian self-portrait and thereby confirm Shaw's identification of himself at that time with the young genius he found in the *Memoirs*": "Do not think me arrogant—intoxicated with self regard. Consider the ridicule I risk, and the burning faith I must have in my inward gift to brave it. Besides, how else can I recover your esteem, except by pleading that I am not one of those common men to whom alone a burst of heartfelt fury is never pardoned." Near the end of the story, after having been rebuffed definitively, Berlioz reminds his beloved: "I will one day be acknowledged a great man."[107] Twenty-four-year-old Shaw wrote "A Reminiscence of Hector Berlioz" while trying to find his voice as a novelist, unaware that his "inward gift" would be for the drama.

*   *   *

If there was more to French music than "Gallic glitter and grandiosity," there was sometimes not much more. But Maurice Valency reminds us that music for Shaw "had not primarily a musical significance. He was deeply moved by the beauty of sound and was certainly aware of musical design; but design, for him, suggested idea: without idea, music ceased to have utility and fell within the category of art for art's sake."[108] This may help explain Shaw's attitude toward Gounod, for example, as well as his overall antipathy to all music he considered frivolous or meaningless. Shaw himself recognized the quandary: "The poet tries to make words serve his purpose by arranging them musically," he wrote in 1894, "but is hampered by the certainty of becoming absurd if he does not make his musically arranged words mean something to the intellect as well as to the feeling."[109] While many French composers failed to achieve this synthesis, one French artist, Yvette Guilbert, succeeded.

Yvette Guilbert: "A fine intensity of mordant expression"

Whereas Sarah Bernhardt was the doyenne of classical and contemporary French drama, the famous chanteuse Yvette Guilbert (1867–1944) ruled the stage at the cabaret and *café-concert*. Her fame had crossed the Channel long before she did, but her bawdy repertoire of songs and skits about the seamy side of life was not always palatable to the British middle class. Her first ten-day engagement in London was greeted with mixed enthusiasm. "Some critics objected to her use of drawling recitative; complained of monotony; found her songs deficient in melody." Although Shaw had similar objections to Bernhardt, he enjoyed Guilbert well enough to publish a long, enthusiastic appreciation of her. It has even been claimed that Shaw was "the first to recognize that a new planet had just swum into the ken of the English vaudeville public."[110]

Despite Guilbert's reputation and popularity, Shaw admitted that before he and William Archer attended a reception in her honor at the Savoy Hotel on 7 May 1894, "I had never heard of her."[111] But when twenty-seven-year-old Yvette made her London debut at the Empire Theatre two days later—singing "La Promise," "À La Villette," "Sur la scène," and "La Femme à Narcisse"—Shaw was seduced. In his review of her performance in the *World* on 16 May 1894, Shaw wrote that not only was she "no mere music hall star," but she embodied what he called a "female Efficient Person," a woman "fit for active service of the roughest kinds" who horrifies certain "chivalrous gentlemen . . . who will not suffer the winds of heaven to breathe on a woman's face too harshly lest they should disable her in her mission of sewing on buttons."

Calling her "one of the best singers and pantomimists in Europe," Shaw remarked that Guilbert sang "with a fine intensity of mordant expression that would not be possible without profound conviction beneath it," praising "the perfect integrity of her self-respect"—which sounds like a description of Shaw's own work. "In spite of her superb diction, I did not understand half her lines myself," he wrote, but thought her "a highly accomplished artist. She makes all her effects in the simplest way, and with perfect judgment." Shaw was most impressed by Guilbert's "perfectly well-controlled declamation; . . . a fine ear and a delicate rhythmic faculty. Her command of every form of expression is very remarkable, her tones ranging from the purest and sweetest pathos to the cockiest Parisian cynicism." If "Madame Bernhardt" was the height of mannered artificiality, the art of "Mlle Guilbert" was "classic self-possession and delicacy without any loss of gaiety."[112]

Aside from her versatility and energy, it was Guilbert's unabashed realism that attracted Shaw. He described in detail one of her poignant treatments of sordid miseries, an "almost frightful" song, *La Pierreuse,* which ends with the guillotining of a thief: "You positively see his head flying off; above all, you feel with a shudder how the creature's impulses of terror and grief are overcome by the bestial excitement of seeing the great State

1. Yvette Guilbert at about the time Shaw saw her perform. By permission of the Agence Photographique Roger-Viollet, Paris.

show of killing a man in the most sensational way." The French government, Shaw surmised, "would certainly abolish public executions . . . if only they would go and hear Mlle Guilbert sing *La Pierreuse*."[113]

Over the years Guilbert kept in touch with Shaw in a relationship so cordial that a possible collaboration was discussed. Writing from Lausanne on 19 March 1907, a dozen years after her London debut, Guilbert gently (but firmly) reminded Shaw that she was still interested in acting for him: "I hope also you did not forget that you—I do not want to say—promised me but made me hope that you would write one day a play for me . . . . thanks to *my* persuasion Mr. Reding manager of the Parc Theatre there [in Brussels] to whom I spoke of your works had decided to produce your Candida. The performance was very excellent, the play splendidly translated. I should like very much to play *in Paris* Man and Superman in French. Will you kindly authorize me to do it, I would play Ann."[114] Augustin Hamon recorded that in 1906, Reding had indeed first heard of *Candida* from Guilbert and her husband, Dr. Max Schiller.[115]

Shaw never wrote a play for her and she never played Ann Whitefield, but he kept up with her career. The following year, 1908, he wrote to Hamon that Guilbert was singing at the Palace Theatre, "no doubt getting an enormous salary"; "I am told she is enormously successful, all of which looks as if it would be more and more difficult for her to break loose from the variety stage."[116] As he had done fourteen years earlier, Shaw recognized Guilbert's potential for more dramatic roles: "The fact is," he had written in the *World,* "Mlle Guilbert's performance was for the most part much more serious at its base than an average Italian opera *scena.*"[117]

Two decades later, on 9 June 1928, Guilbert lunched at Shaw's home and, that day, remembered fondly in her diary Shaw's "long, enthusiastic criticism" in the *World*. She also recalled the last time they met, again at the Shaws', in June 1914, at a luncheon attended by Auguste Rodin. "His [Shaw's] bellicose intelligence, which misses no contemporary happening and attacks every stupidity, fills me with delight!" Guilbert was charmed but, like many of the French, puzzled: "Even with intelligent people he likes to emphasize the exaggeration of his sallies, his paradoxes. Perhaps after all to him there are no intelligent people? Or perhaps (and who knows if this is not the real truth?) it is an excessive shyness that makes him spur his brain so hard to attain that audacious ease, that iconoclastic boldness, of his among his friends." She comes closer to understanding him when she writes, "Bernard Shaw, of you I preserve a gay memory . . . having divined beneath your high-handed effronteries, your jarred sensitiveness, all your human heartburning at seeing humanity still so stupid and so pitiful!"[118]

In 1957, eighty-year-old Archibald Henderson recalled another luncheon at the Shaws', with Guilbert, Max Beerbohm, and Rodin (on his way to Oxford to accept an honorary degree). He remembered Yvette as "homely of face and she had no figure, but her charm was so great no audience cared, even though she was ugly."[119] In 1898, Bliss and Sands published an English edition of Henri de Toulouse-Lautrec's lithographs of Guilbert—they are rather unflattering—titled *L'Album: Yvette Guilbert*. Since Lautrec had done those drawings in 1894, the year of Guilbert's English debut, it may have been partly due to Shaw's panegyric that she achieved English recognition. If the new French planet swimming into the ken of the English vaudeville public was not as alluring as the Divine Sarah, she was bold, clever, witty, and mocking—something of a female Shaw.

II

Shaw et le Théâtre

3

The Old Grooves

Shaw and the French Theater

Speaking Automatons: Shaw on French Actors and Acting

Historically, stage performers have been reviled as wanton pariahs or adulated as godlike superstars—often both at the same time. Dramatist and critic Octave Mirbeau, in "Le Comédien" (*Le Figaro*, 26 October 1882) and "Cabotinisme" [sham acting] (*La France*, March 1885), complained of the prestige accorded to leading actors by an infatuated public, calling the members of the Comédie-Française a privileged "band of ignoramuses." Three years later, in "Mummer Worship" (*Universal Review*, September 1888), George Moore complained that "the public has almost ceased to discriminate between bad and good acting," and that "the actor is applauded not for what he does, but for what he is."[1] Shaw had less trouble with a cult of personality than with stage deportment and considered French actors in particular mere speaking automatons.

Their rigid acting style was in part the result of the teaching of François Delsarte (1811–1871), a professor of vocal training and diction whose elaborate laws of speech and gesture had a widespread influence in France (and in the United States until about 1920). Delsarte's aim was "to codify external manifestations of speech and gesture with mathematical precision,"[2] and his emphasis on gesture is especially important when one considers how the reputations of some actors—such as Sarah Bernhardt—thrived on histrionics. Writes Delsarte: "The artist should have three objects: To *move*, to *interest*, to *persuade*. He interests by *language;* he moves by *thought;* he moves, interests and persuades by *gesture.* . . . Gesture corresponds to the soul, to the heart; language to the life, to the thought, to

the mind. The life and the mind being subordinate to the heart, to the soul, gesture is the chief organic agent."[3]

Shaw experienced these principles firsthand on 31 July 1886 at a lecture on Delsarte given by an American couple, and in September he wrote about it at length in *Our Corner*. Although he deplored Mr. Russell's "acting the lecture as if it were a dramatic monologue, and even accompanying it with imitative gestures," Shaw was impressed by his enunciation and concluded that Delsarte was someone whose work "had an important bearing on moral, as popularly distinguished from physical, welfare."[4] Yet he continued to denounce the physical manifestations of Delsartism— exaggerated gestures, bombastic speeches—year after year in his theater reviews. And Delsarte alone was not responsible for French theatricality; it was the order of things. "To act in the nineteenth century," write John Stokes and his coauthors, "involved participation in a conventionalized bravura display; its distance from 'real life' was an accepted part of the code, even though the emotions aroused in the spectators were assessed in terms of their closeness to reality. There were handbooks of poses. . . . Performers and spectators colluded in the arrangement of signs."[5] Shaw was up against a pervasive, entrenched performance style, but he did not collude; Bernhardt and her kind always exasperated him.

In 1883, W. H. Pollock translated Denis Diderot's *Paradoxe sur le comédien* (1773–78), an important work in which Diderot, hostile to the artificiality of classical French acting, advocated realistic portrayals of life. Shaw discussed the book with William Archer on 18 October 1887, and on 4 September 1888 read the proofs of Archer's own book on the *Paradoxe,* "annotating it with my own theory of the matter."[6] Five months later, on 1 February 1889, in a pseudonymous article in the *Star* titled "Royalty Theatre . . . French v. English Histrionics," Shaw concluded: "The French actor is no actor at all, but only that horrible speaking automaton, an elocutionist, and . . . his proceedings on the stage represent not life, but that empty simulacrum called a style. In genuine Art, *le style, c'est l'homme*. On the French stage, *l'homme, c'est le style*." The ordinary French actor, he concluded, was "galvanised" by pedantic formalities.[7]

That is exactly the way the French actor was trained: the mission of the French Conservatoire's drama school, founded in 1786, was (as its name implied) to preserve the authenticity of the work of Molière and his contemporaries. Even Frédérick Lemaître (1800–76), one of the leading actors of his age, decried the Conservatoire's "routine désespérante" [sickening routine], which consisted in transmitting to future generations "le geste, l'inflexion de la voix, le regard, classés, numérotés, stéréotypés; sans

distinction de nature, de tempérament ou d'instinct; études qui, ne servant qu'à jeter la jeunesse dans la gaine de la tradition, ne sont bonnes qu'à faire et à perpétuer des pantins à ressort, tirés uniformément par une ficelle toujours la même, dignes émules de chiens dressés, d'oiseaux savants et de perroquets bavards" [gesture, vocal inflection, glance, classified, numbered, stereotyped; without allowances for different natures, temperaments or instincts; studies that only serve to imprison youths in hidebound tradition, useful only to produce and perpetuate jumping-jacks pulled all alike by the same string, worthy rivals of trained dogs, performing birds and chattering parrots].[8]

It should be noted, however, that Lemaître had failed his entrance examination and was admitted into the Conservatoire only as a nonparticipant "auditeur," presumably because of his pronounced Norman accent.[9] But the "hidebound tradition" he described persisted until Shaw's day, and in "The Stage as a Profession," a letter to the *Morning Post* of 29 November 1897, Shaw echoes Lemaître's disgust with the French actor's rigid training and artificial style. In the Conservatoire, he wrote, "in addition to the oldfashioned calisthenics and elocution, actors are to be taught that there is one 'right' way (all others 'wrong')" of sitting, kneeling, shaking hands, and "howling an alexandrine." The advantage, however, was that French teachers could turn a housemaid into the Queen in *Ruy Blas* "without commiting a single solecism; whereas an English manager must look for a lady of sufficient natural and socially acquired qualifications" to please a London audience. This "French machine made acting" makes for a bad actor precisely "because he has been taught to act," while an English actor is bad "because he is not a trained artist."[10]

Fifteen years later, in the preface to *Overruled* (1912), Shaw resumed his comparison, this time focusing on psychological differences: "French actors are often scandalized by what they consider the indecency of the English stage, and French actresses who desire a greater license in appealing to the sexual instincts than the French stage allows them, learn English and establish themselves on the English stage." This sounds extravagant, until Shaw explains that "French prudery does not attach itself to the same points of behavior as British prudery, and has a different code of the mentionable and unmentionable, and for many other reasons, the French tolerate plays which are never performed in England until they have been spoiled by a process of bowdlerization; yet French taste is more fastidious than ours as to the exhibition and treatment on the stage of the physical incidents of sex." On the French stage, a kiss is a "purposely unconvincing convention," but in England, "realism is carried to the point at which nobody except the two performers can perceive that the caress is not genuine. And here the English stage is certainly right," for any incident "will be offensive, no matter whether it be a prayer or a kiss, unless it is presented with a convincing appearance of sincerity."[11]

One should point out that things had begun to change fifty years before Shaw's drama reviews. According to F. W. J. Hemmings, the old style of acting—clarity of diction, nobility of gesture, dignity of demeanor—began to look outmoded, especially after the death in 1826 of that master of declamation, François Joseph Talma. The following year, when a troupe of British actors (including Charles Kemble, Edmund Kean, and Harriet Smithson, who married Berlioz in 1833) were invited to the Odéon to play the major Shakespearean tragedies, the French were astounded by an acting style unlike anything they had ever seen. Soon afterward, many French actors began to introduce "a modest dose of realism into the somewhat wooden style of acting." Instead of declaiming speeches downstage near the footlights, standing near the prompter's box, they adopted a British acting style known as "jouer à l'anglaise," to the disgruntlement of conservative critics like Francïsque Sarcey, who felt uneasy about seeing actors sitting down, speaking to one another, and being generally remote from the audience.[12]

* * *

But the "modest dose of realism" did not prevent French actors from their usual histrionics, and where Shaw demanded subtlety, he found only rhetoric, pedantry, and artificiality. Jean Sully Mounet (1841–1916)—known as Mounet-Sully—famous for his tragic roles, "plasters his cheeks with white and his lips with vermillion, and positively howls his lines ... with a meaningless and discordant violence," Shaw recorded in 1895. Six years earlier, he claimed to have been "driven out" of the Théâtre de la Monnaie in Brussels after only one act of Mounet declaiming Oedipus (his most famous role).[13] And in 1899, he wrote to Ellen Terry from France that Charlotte "insisted on my going to hear that bellowing donkey, Mounet Sully, as Othello. . . . Poor Moony Silly grinned like a fairy queen ... & howled like a newsboy."[14] Shaw recalled that the sailors in Edmond Rostand's *La Princesse lointaine* bawled "their phrases like street cries, in the manner of M. Mounet Sully and the Comédie Française."[15] Sarah Bernhardt's opinion of her costar—and lover for two years—was naturally different: "Mounet Sully avait une voix admirable, donnant tous les sons. C'est à sa voix mélodieuse, forte et vibrante, qu'il devait la plus grande part de sa réputation" [Mounet Sully had an admirable voice, giving all the sounds. It is to his melodious, strong and vibrant voice that he owed the greater part of his reputation].[16]

If Mounet embodied male histrionics—the "divine" Sarah was his female counterpart—Benoît Constant Coquelin (1841–1909), famed interpreter of Molière and Rostand, was the epitome of refinement. In 1889, Shaw called Coquelin the greatest of French players, in 1895, "the greatest comedian known to us," and in an 1889 lecture, spoke about "the citadel of Coquelin's self-respect."[17] Shaw's views on Coquelin can be read as a corrective to what he considered the deficiencies of French acting: "So far from being a mere mask with no individuality, . . . [Coquelin] is one of the few points in the human mass at which individuality is concentrated, fixed, gripped in one exceptionally gifted man, who is, consequently, what we call a personality, a man preeminently himself, impossible to disguise, the very last man who could under any circumstances be an actor. Yet this is just what makes him the stage player *par excellence*. We go to see him because we know he will always be Coquelin, because every new part he plays will be some new side of Coquelin or some new light on a familiar side of him, because his best part will be that which shews all sides of him and realizes him wholly to us and to himself."[18]

Shaw had seen Coquelin as Mascarille in Molière's *L'Étourdi* in 1888, and in Alexandre Bisson and Fabrice Carré's *Les Surprises du divorce,* in which he clowned it by "bounding into the air and throwing forward his arms and legs as if to frighten off some dangerous animal."[19] When Shaw finally met him in London in 1908 (eight months before his death) at a garden party—"I went into [the most distinguished circles] for the express purpose of meeting him"—he was most impressed by the actor's cordiality and manners. He also found his imitation of an Englishman speaking French "excessively funny; but I was the only person who enjoyed it, because I was the only person present who knew the difference between our English dipthongs and French vowels."[20] In addition, Coquelin's integrity, versatility, and humor were complemented by stamina: writing in 1929, Shaw remarked how "Coquelin, without turning a hair, [could] get through a night's work that would have worn most of our actors to rags or driven them to stimulants to pull them through." In "The Stage as a Profession," Shaw had given a description of the ideal performer: "The actor should be a first-rate athlete," with "a skilled command of his nerves and muscles, . . . complete control of the muscles of his face. . . . an expert's ear for phonetics."[21] Coquelin was probably the only French actor to approach this ideal.

Given this admiration, Shaw was probably familiar with Coquelin's famous book, *L'Art et le comédien* (1880, translated 1881), which stressed that verisimilitude destroys all illusion and effect on the stage. Shaw may have read "L'art du comédien" (1886, published in *Harper's New Monthly Magazine* in May 1887), which described an actor's dual personality as "first self" (character, player, role) and "second self" (individuality, ego, instrument).[22] The first should control the second, wrote Coquelin, something that Henry Irving failed to do; Coquelin called him "a kind of methodical Mounet-Sully."[23] Irving responded in June with "An Actor's Notes" (*Nineteenth Century*), in which he insisted that denying one's individuality on stage is neither possible nor desirable. In November, in "A Reply to Mr. Henry Irving" (*Harper's Weekly*), Coquelin ascribed their differences to national traits: the English favor inspiration and originality (they are general), the French adhere to tradition (they are specific); Shakespeare creates individuals, Molière creates types. William Archer entered the debate in 1888 with *Masks or Faces?* which "guardedly supported Coquelin."[24] Shaw was certainly not alone in trying to come to terms with national acting styles.

What Coquelin was to Mounet, Gabrielle Réjane (1857–1920) was to Bernhardt. Réjane's acting, Shaw wrote in 1895, "has the quick sensibility which is the really moving quality in fine comic acting, and it is perfecly honest and self-respecting in its impudence." Even in mediocre plays such as Maurice Donnay's *La Douloureuse,* it was impossible to dislike her: "Her cleverness, goodfellowship, and queer personal charm put that out of the question."[25] But Coquelin and Réjane are exceptions. What the French did on stage was generally badly done, and London should be so informed.

Stage Sardoodledom: French Failures in *Our Theatres*

According to Maurice Valency, the drama in the 1880s was not a vital art: "Its prevailing attitudes were materialistic, its moral standards, bourgeois. Its subject matter was principally domestic relations, and its interest was focused predominantly on problems of sex, money, marriage, legitimacy, and adultery."[26] This was the stuff—and often the nonsense—of the so-called *pièces bien faites,* "well-made" or finely constructed plays, and of the *pièces à thèses,* "thesis" or lesson-teaching plays. Both types were in effect sentimental and sensational entertainments that passed for dramas of ideas. By means of a socially meaningful subject and a relatively complex plot, most of them treated what Valency calls "the consequences of individual aberrations from the standards of good society."[27] And while

Francïsque Sarcey, drama critic for *Le Temps* (1867–99), was championing Eugène Scribe's well-made plays and Victorien Sardou's thesis plays, Shaw was denouncing them in the *Saturday Review*. In his opinion, the "individual aberrations" were the plays themselves.

That the popular bourgeois drama at the close of the century offered mostly escapism, idealism, and romanticism is clear from Shaw's weekly essays written between January 1895 and May 1898, which he collected in 1932 in three volumes under the title *Our Theatres in the Nineties*. For Shaw, most French plays were "constructed things with no true life in them, yet sometimes more amusing than real plays, just as a clockwork mouse is more amusing than a real mouse, though it will kill the cat who swallows in good faith."[28] Yet Sardou and his cohorts were turning out clockwork mice at an alarming rate, and few Parisian boulevard audiences were choking on them. When an exasperated Shaw titled one review "Sardoodledom," the barb stuck and became synonymous with any predictable, mechanical stage confection.

Shaw had an agenda. In his October 1906 preface to *Dramatic Opinions and Essays,* titled "The Author's Apology," he characterized his *Saturday Review* essays as "a siege laid to the theatre of the XIX century" in which he had brought "authors, actors, managers, and all, to the one test: were they coming my way or staying in the old grooves?" Begging the reader not to mistake his pronouncements for final estimates of the worth of dramatic artists and authors, Shaw admitted that his essays did contain "something like a body of doctrine." The "Apology" is important also for Shaw's famous statement on the sacrosanct nature and purpose of the theater as "a factory of thought, a prompter of conscience, an elucidator of social conduct, an armory against despair and dullness, and a temple of the Ascent of Man." Hence his view of actors and actresses as "hierophants of a cult as eternal and sacred as any professional religion in the world."[29] Most French plays and players failed to meet these exacting standards.

Shaw's "doctrine" on the French drama in particular can therefore be gleaned from his remarks on dozens of French plays, many of them in English adaptations. While some were dismissed in a paragraph, many inspired long digressions: diatribes against the theatrical world, disquisitions on the art of acting, or comparative appraisals of performers. And if the adaptation was often more to blame for a play's failure to please Shaw—"French farces were regularly subject to 'refinement' in the process of adaptation to English taste," writes Valency[30]—he found fault with almost every work: Raimond Deslandes's *Antoinette Rigaud* had "impossible pretexts"; Rostand's *La Princesse lointaine* lacked "the force which comes from wisdom and originality"; Alexandre Bisson and Fabrice Carré's *Monsieur le directeur* was "persistent Philistinism"; François Coppée's *Pour la couronne* was a "vortex of academic nonsense"; Maurice Donnay's *La Douloureuse* was "false sociology"; Georges Feydeau and Maurice Hennequin's *Le Système Ribadier* was a "piece of farcical clockwork"; Alfred de Musset's *Lorenzaccio* bewildered him with "false starts, dropped motives, no-thoroughfares"; Prosper Mérimée's *Carmen* was "tedious, inept, absurd, ... positively asinine."[31] French playwrights were definitely staying in the old grooves.

Shaw could sometimes excuse a play's shortcomings if the acting was outstanding. Alexandre Dumas *fils*'s *La Femme de Claude* was saved by the electrifying presence of Eleonora Duse—whom Shaw adored—in a "highly intellectual" interpretation; Réjane was outstanding in Henri Meilhac's *Ma Cousine*; and when he saw Aurélien Lugné-Poë's production of Maurice Maeterlinck's *Pelléas et Mélisande* at the Théâtre de l'Oeuvre on 26 March 1895, Shaw was overwhelmed by the "vigilant artistic conscience in the diction, the stage action, and the stage picture, producing a true poetic atmosphere," with the "remarkable subtlety and conviction of expression" of the acting, and with "M. Maeterlinck's fragile word-music," all of which was contrasted to the "costly and highly organized routine" of the Comédie-Française.[32] In general, aside from a few brilliant performances and the socialist dramas of Eugène Brieux, Shaw found French acting and playwriting formulaic, unimaginative, and mediocre.

Before discussing Shaw's relationship to five French playwrights, it would be useful to examine briefly his reservations about one prominent French literary critic, Augustin Filon (1841–1916), whose survey of English drama, *Le Théâtre anglais: Hier, aujourd'hui, demain* (1897), translated as *The English Stage,* Shaw reviewed on 5 June 1897 in a long essay titled "Quickwit on Blockhead." If our blockhead was "unable to see any merit in Ibsen," he was at least objective (an argument Shaw himself used to justify writing *Saint Joan*): "Thanks to his nationality, his vision of our theatre is quite unclouded by our own stupidity." Yet Filon was "too French" to comprehend the distinction between the theater as "a self-contained artistic contrivance" (Filon's view) and as "a response to our need for a sensible expression of our ideals and illusions and approvals and resentments. As such it is bound to affect our ideas, and finally our conduct." Shaw also pointed to the emptiness of Filon's "neatly turned phrases" on Sarcey and Jules Lemaître: "M. Filon does not know what a French critic is like because he is a French critic himself." And Filon's praise of Irving—"Sir Henry has rarely been more thickly buttered"—led Shaw to remark that Irving possessed a "constitutional imperviousness to literature." Understandably, Shaw was particularly offended by "the most astonishing remark" that "'dramatic criticism and musical criticism, owing to the natural gifts they require, are two absolutely different callings'." Shaw rebuffed this thesis by saying that "your typical XIX century Frenchman" is "always cleverer than your stupid Englishman, and always fifty years behind him."[33] Not only were the French incapable of good playwriting and fine acting, but when it came to understanding the English, some French critics were blockheads, apparently.

Clockwork Mice: Augier, Scribe, Sardou, Dumas *fils*, Feydeau

Shaw once claimed that his plays simply wrote themselves, that he had little control over the creative process: "I am not governed by principles," he wrote in 1912; "I am inspired, how or why I cannot explain, because I do not know; but inspiration it must be; for it comes to me without any reference to my own ends or interest." He called the result "sane hallucination."[34] Far from being the result of inspiration, Shaw's plays were written, at least in the beginning, in order to show mediocre playwrights just how it ought to be done. Yet, as we will see, Shaw may have been "inspired" by some of the very French playwrights he disparaged. Let us take five of the most popular ones and examine the reasons for Shaw's dissatisfaction with them, as well as the extent of his creative borrowing.

Eugène Scribe (1791–1861)

It has been said that "without Scribe . . . there would have been no Ibsen, no Shaw, no Pirandello, no Brecht."[35] Augustin-Eugène Scribe began as a writer of one-act *comédies-vaudevilles:* farcical entertainments with song and dance aimed primarily at the gallery. But in the 1820s he refined these into "serious" dramas; light sketches of manners became long comedies of manners, prototypes of the *pièce bien faite,* the well-made play. For the next forty years, "often with a team of assistants and buying ideas when his own supply was low,"[36] Scribe became the ruling figure of the French stage. It is estimated that he (and his workshop of lackeys) manufactured a total of 374 works for the theater.[37] He grew enormously rich (by imposing a new system of royalties) and very famous: by 1836 he had been elected to the Académie Française—which had refused Molière.

Valency describes Scribe's dramas as "realistic" insofar as they are concerned with "the desire for power, money, a rich marriage—in short, the desire to succeed at all costs."³⁸ Good always triumphs and evil is punished, but the outcome is often in doubt because the antagonists are almost evenly matched; suspense runs high. His plays, writes John Russell Taylor, inculcate "the spacing and preparation of effects so that an audience should be kept expectant from beginning to end. That, and that only, is what Scribe meant by a well-made play."³⁹ Otherwise, Scribe's world was "without moral seriousness," writes Valency, "the prevailing mood of which was a sense of irony, which was perhaps a sublimation of despair," a world "held together by logic alone. It could therefore not fail to be other than superficial, and was not presented with any pretense of profundity."⁴⁰

In short, Scribe's plays rely for their effect on complexity of form. According to Tom F. Driver, the characteristics of Scribe's *pièce bien faite* are the following: (1) The plot is based on a secret known to the audience and withheld from major characters until the climactic scene, at which point an unsympathetic character is unmasked and the hero restored to good fortune. (2) The plot describes the culmination of a long story begun before the start of the play ("late point of attack") and made known to the audience via "exposition." (3) Action and suspense rise in intensity via entrances, exits, letters, revelations, and so on. (4) The hero, in conflict with an adversary, experiences good and bad turns in fortune. (5) The lowest point in the hero's fortune is soon followed by the highest in an "obligatory" scene (the *scène à faire*, so termed by Sarcey) via the disclosure of secrets. This scene must also contain some sort of moral judgment. (6) The plot is frequently knotted by a misunderstanding (*quiproquo*) in which a word or situation is understood in opposite ways. (7) The denouement is logical and clear, without unresolved or puzzling elements for the audience. (8) The overall action pattern of the play is reproduced in each act, the principle according to which each minor climax and scene is constructed.⁴¹ This last point was essential: "Each scene had its initial situation, its progression, complication, climax, peripeteia, and conclusion, so that it formed an autonomous whole within the total arrangement."⁴² The inexorable (yet contrived) logic of *Le Verre d'eau* (1840) is typical: a glass of water spilled on Queen Anne's dress brings about the disgrace of the Duchess of Marlborough, the collapse of the Whigs, the rise to power of Bolingbroke, and a reversal of English foreign policy. The ultimate effect: "a *reductio ad absurdum* of human greatness."⁴³

Ironically, one finds many Scribean characteristics in the works of the man who once asked: "Who was Scribe that he should dictate to me or anyone else how a play should be written?"⁴⁴ Shaw was protesting too much. Since the elaborate Scribean blueprint "acquired in its day the authority of a science" and became *le système du théâtre*,⁴⁵ and since plays by Scribe and others using this recipe were translated and adapted en masse for the English stage, Shaw could not help but fall under Scribe's influence. More important, during his apprenticeship at Bergen (1851–56), Shaw's idol Henrik Ibsen had directed about seventy well-made plays, twenty-one by Scribe.⁴⁶ Since Ibsen made frequent use of Scribean intrigue in his early work, keeping the form (while adding symbolism and sociology) in his more mature work, Eric Bentley thinks it quite possible "for a writer in 1890 to denounce Scribe and Sardou and simultaneously to steal their bag of tricks—from Ibsen."⁴⁷ Shaw opened the French bag fully aware of its provenance. In the 1891 edition of *The Quintessence of Ibsenism,* he commented that *The League of Youth* (1869) was "clever enough in its mechanical construction to entitle the French to claim that Ibsen owes something of his technical education as a playwright in the school of Scribe." In the 1913 edition, he wrote that *A Doll's House* (1879) "might be turned into a very ordinary French drama by the excision of a few lines, and the substitution of a sentimental happy ending for the famous last scene."⁴⁸ If Scribe did not "dictate," he was ubiquitous.

There is no doubt that some of Shaw's early work is Scribean in structure and, to a degree, in theme. Bentley notes that *Man and Superman* "bears every sign of careful workmanship—all of it School of Scribe": the pursued hero, the clandestine marriage, the self-sacrifice of the lovelorn hero, the villain who impedes for a while a happy ending, farcical coincidence, and a subplot (about the Malone family) resting upon a secret withheld, then skillfully released. In this "utterly Scribean 'closed' structure," the shrewd female pursues the male fool, illustrating that "in our trivial, tawdry, clever, Scribean world, intellect is futile and ever at the mercy of instinct."⁴⁹ There are probably many similar parallels.

One Scribe play that seems to have had an impact on Shaw is *La Bataille des dames* (1851). Bentley discusses its influence on *Arms and the Man*—which Valency called "a textbook example of the well-made play"—claiming that Shaw may have "lifted" parts of it and adapted "the main situation": "even when Shaw's story diverges from Scribe, it remains Scribean."⁵⁰ Bentley maintains that "the passion and preoccupation of Scribe was the idea of climax," while in Shaw "there was almost as great a predilection for anticlimax," citing the disenchantment of Raina and Sergius as an example.⁵¹ Stanton even called *Arms and the Man* "an ingenious reworking" of *La Bataille des dames*.⁵² He has also discussed at length the similarities between *La Bataille des dames* and *The Devil's Dis-*

ciple, Captain Brassbound's Conversion, Man and Superman, and especially *Candida* (1895), whose structure he considers "thoroughly well-made." Stanton shows how Shaw reverses Scribe's triangle—one man, two rival women—by centering Candida between two rival men. There are other parallels as well: "Léonie learns the virtue of poise and self-control, just as the poet learns that he can stand alone. Both characters 'grow up'. Henri serves in a sense as a catalyst, as does Candida. The protagonists are Henri and Candida, the antagonists Léonie and Marchbanks; the countess and Morell are victims of the conflict."[53] These and other similarities, however, have less to do with adapting Sribe than with a typical Shavian reversal of commonly accepted dramaturgy. One suspects that "without Scribe," Shaw would have done very well indeed.

Émile Augier (1820–1889)

Shaw had tried his hand at playwriting in 1878 with two acts of something he called *The Household of Joseph;* it was not until 1884 that William Archer, then an established drama and art critic, convinced him to collaborate on a play he titled *Rhinegold.* Shaw would work out the dialogue while Archer supplied the scenario; the theme was tainted money. But the idea was hardly original; Shaw and Archer were borrowing from *La Ceinture dorée* (1855), a comedy by social dramatist Émile Augier, whose plays were rooted in conventional bourgeois morality. Shaw began writing on 18 August and by 12 September had completed the first act; a month later, the second act was done. But in mid-November, after twenty-three lines of the third act, he stopped. According to Michael Holroyd, Shaw was having trouble "matching this contrived Parisian structure to an analysis of contemporary slum landlordism."[54] It was not until 1892 that *Rhinegold* was reincarnated as *Widowers' Houses,* in which Archer was astounded to see "my sentimental heroine . . . transmuted into a termagant who boxed the ears of her maid-servant. Still, however, it is possible to discern in the play fragments of my idea, and to trace its relationship to *Ceinture Dorée.*"[55]

In *La Ceinture dorée,* an honest young man is in love with a girl whose father has acquired his fortune by dubious means. The marriage is thus a social impossibility—until the ruin of her father removes the obstacle. When the young man discovers that his bride's dowry comes from a tainted source, Shaw, "throwing the monkey wrench . . . of character" into "this perfectly functioning machine of the well-made play" (in Bentley's words),[56] makes his people act according to the laws of psychology, not according to the expectations of an audience—as the well-made play decreed they should. Hence Augier's hero could not consider marrying a woman with a tainted dowry, while Shaw's hero asks his fiancée to give up the dowry for his sake. The dilemma is solved in Augier by the outbreak of war—the deus ex machina—that ruins the father; in Shaw, with the hero "accepting the nature of capitalism"—that is, by the logic of situation. Despite these differences, Bentley considers *Widowers' Houses* to be "an adaptation of an adaptation of a well-made play," and Valency believes that with the play Shaw "meant to follow the latest French fashion."[57]

In 1897, over a decade after the aborted *Rhinegold* collaboration, Shaw reviewed Augier's "tissue of arrant respectability worshipping folly," *Le Mariage d'Olympe* (1855): "Augier was a true bourgeois: when he observed a human impulse that ran counter to the habits of his class, it never occurred to him that it opened a question as to their universal propriety. To him those habits were 'morality'; and what was counter to them was 'nostalgie de la boue.' Accordingly, the play is already a ridiculous inversion of moral order."[58] Augier's play was meant as a corrective to the apparent sanction of illicit love in Dumas *fils*'s *La Dame aux camélias* (1852). In both plays, a young man wants to marry a seemingly redeemed courtesan, but the premiere of *Le Mariage d'Olympe* was hissed: "All Paris was by now sick of the courtesan on the stage." So was Shaw, who concluded that Augier's play "plainly shews that it is better for a woman to be a liar and a rapscallion than a mere lady."[59]

Victorien Sardou (1831–1908)

Sardou was essentially a moralist. His one aim was "to attract an audience and strengthen its attachment to respectable virtues."[60] From about 1860, with a highly professional Paris theater and many good actors, he established himself as the master of the *pièce bien faite* and became a major force in French theater. But his fame was ephemeral; although he was elected to the Académie Française in 1878, fifty years later "his laurels were already withered beyond recognition."[61]

In his heyday, Sardou intoxicated audiences with "fantastic mixtures of incompatible genres (tragical-comical, historical-melodramatic) tricked out with lavish *mise en scène*."[62] Whatever the genre, Shaw's *Saturday Review* critiques bristled at all of them: *Dora* (1877) was "a sham," *Delia Harding* "the worst play I ever saw." In his famous 1 June 1895 essay, "Sardoodledom," he found the "stale mechanical tragedy" of *Fédora* (1882) "an entertainment too Bedlamite" to believe, and the antiquated claptrap of *Gismonda* (1894) "surpassingly dreary." He began his 13 July 1895 review of *Madame Sans-Gêne:* "I have never seen a French play of which I understood less"; when he saw it again in 1897, he thought that "Sardou's Napoleon is rather better than Madame Tussaud's, and that is all that can be said for it." *Divorçons* (1880), in an adaptation by Herman Merivale titled *The Queen's Proctor* (1896), put him in the "worst possible temper with the whole perfomance." In an 1890 review in the *Star* of *La Tosca* (1887), he exclaimed, "The French well-made play was never respectable even in its prime; but now, in its dotage and *delirium tremens*, it is a disgrace to the theatre," dismissing the play as "an old-fashioned, shiftless, clumsily constructed, emptyheaded turnip ghost of a cheap shocker."[63] Sardou's confections were abysmal.

With one exception. Although *Divorçons*—known as *Let's Get a Divorce!*—had displeased him, he admitted being "unable to maintain this unfavorable attitude" and ended by praising its "witty liveliness."[64] Martin Meisel sees the play as a precedent for the "auction scene" in *Candida*,[65] and he explains how some of its elements found their way into *Getting Married* (1907–8). The parallels are "not only in the overall fusion of Farce with a genuine discussion of marriage and divorce but in particulars and details." For instance, in both plays, books upset the equilibrium: Cyprienne des Prunelles is passionately interested in such works as *Divorce!* and *About Divorce;* in Shaw, the groom is reading Belford Bax's *Men's Wrongs,* and the bride a pamphlet titled "Do You Know What You Are Going to Do? By a Woman Who Has Done It." In both plays, the divorcing couples are reconciled "partly through the wife's recognition that the substitute husband would be, as husband, just as prosaic and perhaps less comfortable."[66]

Holroyd goes even farther and finds that *Getting Married* "is in places little short of an ingenious adaptation" of *Divorçons:* "It is as if a conventional well-made play were being performed backstage, and we witness the performers discussing its event-plot during the intervals."[67] He also points out that the play progresses by means of duologues and trios. Shaw had singled out this conversational aspect in his 1895 review of *Madame Sans-Gêne:* "Of course I admire the ingenuity with which Sardou carries out his principle of combining the maximum of expenditure and idle chatter with the minimum of drama," but it was "beginning to pall" on him.[68] It certainly palled on the critics of *Getting Married;* many complained about its interminable talking.

Shaw's last word on *Divorçons* came in 1910, when he used it in his preface to *The Shewing-Up of Blanco Posnet* as an example of how, "if a play is irresistibly amusing, it gets licensed no matter what its moral aspect may be." Shaw recalled that Sardou's play "was certainly the very naughtiest that any English manager in his senses would have ventured to produce," and it passed the licenser except for a reference to impotence as grounds for divorce, "which no English actress would have ventured on in any case."[69]

Sardou's laurels may have withered, but St. John Ervine, Shaw's future biographer (*Bernard Shaw,* 1956), marked the centenary of Sardou's birth in 1931 with a panegyric article in which he took issue with Shaw's derisive treatment of the French playwright. "It is not wise to be contemptuous of a good craftsman, which Sardou was, for when we begin to despise skill we obtain sloppiness, and Mr. Shaw would have done better, at times, if instead of jeering at the Frenchman's work, he had tried to acquire his technique." Ervine censured Shaw for denouncing Sardou "for his ridiculous 'situations'. . . . People did not behave like that, said Mr. Shaw, or if they did, they ought not to. That raises a pretty problem. What is an author to do? Portray people as he sees them, or as he would like them to be? Was Sardou right when he filled his plays with men and women who behaved melodramatically, or ought he to have divested them of their humanity and have made them behave 'reasonably'?" After quoting from Shaw's critique of *Fédora,* Ervine concluded: "The most banal melodramatist would know better than to write such intolerable tosh as that." He then cited *Diplomacy*'s three revivals: "A play which is immeritable and merely mechanical cannot possibly excite the enthusiasm of three separate decades."[70]

Alexandre Dumas, *fils* (1824–1895)

In his 12 June 1897 review of Sydney Grundy's adaptation of *Le Mariage sous Louis XV* (1841) by Dumas *père* (1802–1870), Shaw had written: "Dumas was not, like his son, a man of problems. He had no need of them, being full of stories about charming imaginary people, whose affairs he manipulated with such delicacy, geniality, and humor, that nothing that they could do ever raised any moral questions. What in the son's work is murder, adultery, and the rest of the seven deadly sins, is in the father's simply natural history."[71]

Like Sardou, Dumas *fils* was a moralist: marriage and family were sacred; motherhood was a woman's highest duty; adultery was unforgivable. It was his ambition to transform the *pièce bien faite* into a *pièce à thèse,* to write meaningful plays with clever plots. His motto: "Le réel dans le fond, le possible dans le fait, l'ingénieux dans le moyen" [The real in the substance, the possible in the fact, the ingenious in the means].[72] With these goals in mind, Dumas took up the social problems of his day and dramatized them using Scribean logic; he even wrote some plays beginning with the denouement! A Dumas play contained "a quasi-tragic action based upon a social problem, climaxed by a sermon." A *raisonneur*—Dumas's mouthpiece and often a protagonist—kept the author "constantly in view of the public with an incessant patter of comment and admonition."[73] Shaw himself used this technique and was familiar with it in Dumas; in a 5 January 1895 review, he discussed a character "charged with the duty of accompanying the play by an explanatory lecture in the manner of Dumas *fils*."[74]

Dumas's dramatic aims were similar to Shaw's, and the preface to *Le Fils naturel* (1858) sounds uncannily like a Shavian call to arms: "Par la comédie, par la tragédie, par le drame, par la bouffonnerie . . . inaugurons donc le théâtre *utile,* au risque d'entendre crier les apôtres de *l'art pour l'art,* trois mots absolument vides de sens" [Through comedy, through tragedy, through the drama, through buffoonery . . . let us inaugurate the *useful* theater, at the risk of hearing the protests of the apostles of *art-for-art's-sake,* words absolutely devoid of meaning].[75]

But these lofty aims, if Shaw knew of them, had no effect on his critiques. When on 8 June 1895 he reviewed *La Femme de Claude* (1873), he found Duse as Claude's wife, Césarine, "so fascinating that it is positively difficult to attend to the play instead of attending wholly to her." Thus he did not discuss the play at all, but the following week (on 15 June) referred to Claude's wife as "a mere predatory creature." On 9 November, he reviewed an adaptation of *L'Ami des femmes* (1864) titled *The Squire of Dames,* finding the original "a bad play with good material in it. The material is what we now call Ibsenite: the technique is that of Scribe. In it, accordingly, we have serious characters philosophically discussing themselves and oneanother quite undramatically in long speeches," and so on. Again, Shaw did this too. But his review was mostly about the failure of R. C. Carton's adaptation: the translation was faulty—"Ça passera" became "That will pass" instead of "Ah, you will get over that"—and the acting made Dumas's characters insignificant or foolish. Only Chantrin survived the adaptation, "so that the part is as dangerous in English as in French: that is, it remains the part of a bore who actually is a bore, and not an unconscious humorist."[76]

Dumas had assumed the role of social critic and reformer twenty years prior to Shaw by writing prefaces that Valency characterised as "long discourses on a variety of subjects associated with, but not limited by the plays to which they are prefixed, . . . describing the genesis and the history of his play, the difficulties attending its production, and the nature of the critical reception, . . . discussing the moral and social problems raised in the play in question, touching upon related questions of a social and political nature, arguing, demonstrating, admonishing, posing questions and resolving them."[77] All of this is remarkably Shavian, and the "plays and prefaces become tribunals, as they became later for Shaw, but unhappily those of Dumas *fils* are much less often enlivened by objectivity or wit."[78]

Martin Ellehauge noted the "essential identity of thought" between the 1867 preface to *La Dame aux camélias* (1849, adapted from the 1847 novel; first performed in 1852) and *Mrs Warren's Profession*.[79] Dumas points to society as the criminal: Your son loves a young woman who, instead of selling herself, remained honest and chose to toil for pittance to support herself and her mother on bread and potatoes, a little meat and some water. Would you make her your daughter-in-law? "Non. Qu'est-ce qu'elle gagne donc à rester honnête?" [No. Then what does she gain from remaining honest?].[80] Shaw too points the finger at a social system that made Mrs. Warren's life of vice necessary. Although he refers often to *La Dame* in his drama criticism and book reviews, and given the play's impact on English drama, it is surprising that Shaw wrote no sustained appreciation of it. Meisel notes that he wrote *Mrs Warren* in the latter half of 1893, and that in London on 24 May, Eleonora Duse had starred in *La Dame*.[81] In a review of 8 June 1895, Shaw does mention Duse's performance as Marguerite Gautier, and on 15 June he singled out her "unspeakably touching . . . exquisitely sympathetic" portrayal. However, any "identity of thought" probably came from the zeitgeist, not from Dumas.[82]

Shaw was familiar with other Dumas plays he did not write about. He recorded in his diary on 12 June 1886 that he had seen *Denise*,[83] a play first performed at the Comédie-Française in 1885 and produced at the Lyceum by Henry Irving. When Shaw wrote to actress Elizabeth Robins in 1891, he suggested that "in order to bring *Denise* up to date, you should get me to play Thouvenin & to rewrite the part from my own point of view. But this is the only departure from the original that ought to be tolerated."[84] Given Shaw's self-proclaimed role as rationalist and reformer, the identification with Thouvenin came easily; he is the play's talkative *raisonneur*.[85]

Shaw also knew about Dumas's views on women—none of them Shavian. He alludes three times (1897, 1928, 1929) to the letter from Dumas to a young woman of means and position who wished to go on the stage in which he assured her that it was out of the question for a person in her social position to do so. In an 1895 theater review, Shaw mentions "the Tue-la of Dumas *fils*," an allusion to "L'Homme-Femme: réponse à

M. Henri D'Ideville" (1872), a notorious essay that underwent numerous editions that year.[86] Dumas the arch-moralist thought adulterous women odious. In his 11 September 1886 book review of *Vendetta!* by Marie Corelli, Shaw had quoted the essay's most infamous passage in the original: "Ce n'est pas la femme, ce n'est même pas une femme; elle n'est pas dans la conception divine, elle est purement animale; c'est la guenon du pays de Nod, c'est la femelle de Caïn; tue-la" [She is not Woman, she is not even a woman; she is not in the divine conception, she is purely animal; she is the she-ape from the Land of Nod, she is Cain's female; kill her].[87] In a 23 July 1888 review of another Corelli novel, Shaw referred to the "creed" of her second novel and its foundation in Dumas: "It carried his 'Tue-la' doctrine to the extent of exhibiting a husband deliberately murdering his unfaithful wife under circumstances of diabolical cruelty as a matter of duty."[88]

Brian Tyson notes that Shaw quotes only the last lines of a 177-page essay—the final words of advice from a father to his son after nine conditional clauses that "modify the savagery of the thought."[89] But Shaw was obviously disturbed by Dumas's outrageous bias. He would certainly have been shocked at this passage from the 17,000-word preface (1869) to *L'Ami des femmes* (1864), in which Dumas answers his question "What then is Woman?" as follows: "La Femme est un être circonscrit, passif, instrumentaire, disponible.... C'est la seule oeuvre inachevée que Dieu ait permis à l'Homme de reprendre et de finir.... Elle n'a rien inventé, rien découvert pour sa plus-value collective" [Woman is a limited being, passive, instrumental, available.... She is the only uncompleted work that God has permitted man to take in hand and finish.... She has invented nothing, discovered nothing, to increase her collective value].[90]

Georges Feydeau (1862–1921)

Like Shaw's, many of the thirty-nine plays by Georges Feydeau are filled with discussions about ideas and attitudes that are at odds with conventional morality. But unlike Shaw, Feydeau seldom suggests that these attitudes or institutions should be changed. Feydeau's manic plays, filled with extravagant buffoonery, sent audiences into waves of laughter; the now-forgotten *Champignol malgré lui* (1892) ran for 1,000 performances, and *L'Hôtel du Libre-Échange* (1894) was resurrected on Broadway in 1957 as *Hotel Paradiso*. When Shaw reviewed *A Night Out*, the English version of *L'Hôtel du Libre-Échange*, on 9 May 1896, he found it "not in the main badly acted," despite the "unecessary noisiness" of some scenes as well as some "shockingly ugly" moments in others. On 31 October 1896, he found *Le Système Ribadier* (1892), adapted as *His Little Dodge*, "outrageously funny" at first. "But our disenchantment was all the more irritating. The moment it became apparent that all these interesting and promising people were only puppets in a piece of farcical clockwork, the old disappointment, the old worry, the old rather peevish impatience with the remaining turns of the mechanism set in."[91] That mechanism was airtight, and the events in a Feydeau play, writes one French critic, "are linked together with the precision of a well-oiled machine." His plays "have the consecutiveness, the force, and the violence of tragedies. They have the same ineluctable fatality. In tragedy, one is stifled with horror. In Feydeau, one is suffocated with laughter."[92]

Like his more "serious" compatriots, Feydeau had an impact on Shaw. One critic cites *Getting Married* as an example of Feydeauvian farce, where "Shaw uses farce's immunity from judgment to forestall the outright condemnation of unusual proposals and thus permit a a genuine dialogue to take place." He also claims that the difficulties that Cecil anticipates if he marries Edith are realized in Feydeau's *Hortense a dit: "Je m'en fous!"*[93] Yet compared with other dramatists, Feydeau remains a minor influence, Shaw being less interested in creating "ineluctable fatality" than in making people laugh at themselves.

* * *

Shaw always considered himself an iconoclast and innovator, yet even as he composed his *Saturday Review* essays, a growing distaste for the type of entertainment provided by exponents of the well-made play had been in the air for some time—at least in France. As early as 1838, Balzac had written, "Scribe is finished. New talents must be sought,"[94] a sentiment echoed in Zola's *Le Roman expérimental* and "Le Naturalisme au théâtre," and by his disciple, director André Antoine, in *Le Théâtre Libre* (1890). "With the notable exception of Brieux," writes Valency, the seriousness of "the heirs of the Scribean tradition"—Augier, Dumas, Sardou—as social critics was open to question. What is interesting is that "outside of France they were taken with complete seriousness,"[95] hence the importance of Shaw's diatribes.

If Shaw's ideological affinities were with writers of the "realistic" school—Proudhon, Taine, Comte, Brieux, Maupassant, Zola—his early drama reflects the preoccupations, even the style, of the *pièce bien faite* and the *pièce à thèse*. There are even instances of a debt to the hated clockwork mice: Shaw may have built some of his works, as Stanton phrases it, "out of materials from the house of Scribe," but he "combined them differently, so as to ridicule with an ironic twist both the audience's acceptance of conventional thrills and suspense and the Victorian attitudes that enabled them to accept these conventions."[96] He did this, as Stanton demonstrates, in *Candida,* and there are other instances. Valency claims that *Mrs Warren's Profession* is a *pièce à thèse* in the manner of Dumas, and that the technique of *Widowers' Houses* is Scribean; that the chemistry of love in *You Never Can Tell* had been anticipated by Dumas in *L'Étrangère* (1876); and that Shaw introduced *Saint Joan* as a *pièce à thèse,* with the example of Ireland in mind.[97] Meisel points to some uncanny parallels between the English adaptation by Pierrepont Edwards and Lester Wallack of *Le Roman d'un jeune homme pauvre* (1858) by Octave Feuillet (1821–90) that he considers an "anticipation" of *Heartbreak House:* "Captain Laroque is an ex-privateer in a stage of impressive and eccentric senility. Like Captain Shotover, he is the head of an aristocratic country house dominated by women . . . and is in closest sympathy with the Ellie-like young girl."[98]

Meisel believes that the tone of *The Shewing-Up of Blanco Posnet* (1909) is close to an English adaptation of *L'Auberge des Adrets* (1823) by Benjamin Antier (1787–1870), starring the clever rogue Robert Macaire. G. H. Lewes described the Macaire type as a peculiar union of "a certain ideal grace and *bonhomie* with the most degraded ruffianism and hardness,"[99] and Shaw was very familiar with Macaire. He had seen Henry Irving's version ("a more horribly evil-looking beast of prey than his Macaire never crossed the stage") and had twice read *Macaire; A Melodramatic Farce* (1885), the popular adaptation by Robert Louis Stevenson and William Ernest Henley: the old version ("quite unreadable") and the new one ("wittily and whimsically turned"). He also saw the new version and in his 8 June 1895 review emphasized how the adaptation had beaten the original author at his own craft: "outwritten him, outwitted him, outstaged him." He drew attention, among other things, to Macaire's new dialogue, "an epigrammatic philosophy expressed in lines which a distinguished actor need not be ashamed to speak."[100]

According to Meisel, the indomitable, flamboyant Macaire "looks and acts like Shaw's Mendoza, but thinks and philosophizes like John Tanner and Andrew Undershaft."[101] As with Feuillet's play, the parallels here are striking. Stevenson and Henley's Macaire: "What is crime? discovery. Virtue? opportunity. Politics? a pretext. Affection? an affectation. Morality? an affair of latitude. Punishment? this side the frontier. Reward? the other. Property? plunder." The Devil in *Man and Superman:* "What is his religion? An excuse for hating me. What is his law? An excuse for hanging you. What is his morality? Gentility! an excuse for consuming without producing. What is his art? An excuse for gloating over pictures of slaughter. What are his politics? Either the worship of a despot because a despot can kill, or parliamentary cock-fighting."[102]

* * *

Shaw was not alone in being influenced by the popular French dramas of his day: Oscar Wilde modeled *Lady Windermere's Fan* (1892) on Scribe's adultery play *Une Chaîne* (1841); Arthur Wing Pinero's *The Second Mrs. Tanquery* (1893) resembles Augier's *Le Mariage d'Olympe* (1855), to cite only two prominent examples.[103] Even Shaw had to acknowledge the popularity of French clockwork mice. In the section "The Pedantry of Paris" from his 1909 essay on Eugène Brieux, he defined the well-made play of Scribe and his school as "a nuisance which was not a failure" and admitted that for a playwright of manufactured comedies to rise out of obscurity, "you must be a Scribe or a Sardou, doing essentially the same thing, it is true, but doing it wittily and ingeniously, at moments almost poetically."[104]

Yet Shaw's distaste for these manufactured dramas was as intense as his desire to eradicate them, and he remained a self-proclaimed mechanoclast until he died. In 1924, discussing with Archibald Henderson what he called the "transfiguration" of British drama in the early twentieth century, Shaw referred to it as an era in which new playwrights were trying to write real plays, "not 'constructing' cats' cradles and clockwork mice like the machine-made *nouveautés Parisiennes* of the eighteen sixties."[105] In a 1938 letter to Augustin Hamon, this is how Shaw recalled his career as dramatic reviewer: "In London I bombarded the West End theatres with criticisms which now fill three volumes. . . . . Feuilletons of 2000 words a week for years were needed to establish a convention . . . that Sardou was obsolete and ridiculous."[106] In late 1947, the nonagenarian reminded the readers of the *Strand* that he had been part of the transfiguration in drama, alluding to "Scribe's mechanically constructed 'well-made' pieces (I helped to kill them)."[107] Even if Shaw did not succeed in killing them off, eventually most of them broke down.

4

The Siren on the Rock

An Exasperation with Sarah Bernhardt

On a morning at the end of May, 1879, "La Divine Sarah" and the fifty-odd members of the Comédie-Française landed at Folkestone and were greeted by thousands of cheering admirers. Among them were Johnston Forbes Robertson, who handed her a gardenia, and Oscar Wilde, who scattered an armful of lilies at her feet. In eighteen performances during the next two months, Bernhardt would conquer London in *Phèdre*, *L'Étrangère*, *Le Sphinx*, *Zaïre*, *Andromaque*, *Ruy Blas*, and *Hernani*. Meanwhile, Shaw was living at home with his mother and writing *Immaturity*, a first novel begun in early March. Sarah Henriette Rosine Bernhardt (1844–1923) was thirty-four and at the height of her fame on her first visit to England, but twenty-two-year-old Shaw was fourteen years from the premiere of his first play and eight years from his first critique of a Bernhardt performance. While Shaw gave up novels and poured his energy into a stream of letters, speeches, reviews, pamphlets, and plays, Sarah continued to portray on stage the decadent femmes fatales that created her legend: Théodora, Phèdre, Cléopâtre, Tosca, Médée, and Marguerite Gautier, to name a few. "She lived to mesmerize," we are told, "to dazzle, to lure the public into the mysteries of sensuality and poetic illusion. He [Shaw] was the rock of truth; she the siren on the rock."[1]

Bernhardt began as a classical actress trained for the archconservative Comédie-Française; her most famous role was Racine's Phèdre, later a sensation in London. But by the time Shaw saw the siren in her element, she had romanticized those great classical roles and was adept in the so-called late romantic style of acting, "where it was enough that a performer simply intoxicate with a display of emotional force."[2] She certainly intoxicated twenty-three-year-old D. H. Lawrence in 1908; after seeing her play Marguerite Gautier in *La Dame aux camélias* in Nottingham, he described the sixty-three-year-old Bernhardt as "the incarnation of wild emotion . . . the primeval passions of woman. . . . I could love such a woman myself, love her to madness; all for the pure wild passion of it."[3] Such was her charisma that playwrights wrote dramas for her, as did Wilde with *Salomé*—in which she never appeared, thanks to the intervention of the Lord Chamberlain—and Victorien Sardou with *Fédora* and *La Tosca*. Her repertoire became an idiosyncratic mixture of commissioned works, popular plays, and classics such as *Phèdre,* whose second act—where Phèdre confesses her incestuous love to Hippolyte—was often played separately.

But it was Sardou more than any dramatist who helped make Sarah Bernhardt the most famous actress of the Comédie-Française. In a paper read on 5 February 1889, titled "Acting, by One Who Does Not Believe in It," Shaw gave an amusing account of their highly profitable collaboration: "He [Sardou] deliberately took that part of Madame Bernhardt's nature which she shares with any tigress, and he exploited that to the utmost farthingsworth. Finding that it paid, he did it again."[4] And often in the very same way: most of Sardou's heroines were women "torn between uncontrollable impulses of power-hungry aggression and passive subservience" who fell in love with men they either sacrificed or destroyed.[5] Even though many French critics saw that Sardou's melodramas and those of his fellow playwrights were often of little merit—calling these Bernhardt vehicles "mediocre" or "feeble"—she managed to remain, writes Robert Horville, "a specialist in theatrical deaths" who "died each time in a different way, to the great admiration of the audience."[6] In the words of one of Bernhardt's contemporaries, "With Sarah Bernhardt, grief and death have an air of intoxicating exaltation."[7]

However, after a few years of Théodora and Tosca, the critics complained that Bernhardt had become vulgarized. Yet why, Shaw asked, did they not immediately protest against *Théodora* "as a vile degradation of the actress, of the stage, of the drama, and of the playgoing public?"[8] One reason was sheer spectacle: *Théodora* had a mise-en-scène of extraordinary splendor, eight tableaux that included immense arcades, oriental drapes, and decorations of enamel, silver, and gold, with Sarah in a "flower-patterned tunic set with precious stones, her blue satin cloak emblazoned with peacocks in sapphires, emeralds and rubies, her head covered by a bejewelled helmet."[9] Another was popular demand: the stereotype of the nineteenth-century *femme féroce* was at the height of its vogue in the 1880s, and Bernhardt "found it advantageous to make a specialty of the role."[10] From her opening performance at the Gaiety Theatre on 2 June 1879, she took London by storm. Francïsque Sarcey wrote back to Paris: "Nothing can give any idea of the craze Sarah is exciting. It's a mania."[11]

Long after the storm had passed, A. B. Walkley recalled: "It was the Gaiety French season of 1897 that turned Sarah Bernhardt into Sarah Barnum,"[12] and that is what she remained for Shaw. Her emotionalism was an extreme example of everything he despised in bad acting, especially bad French acting. In his pseudonymous essay in the *Star* of 1 February 1889, "Royalty Theatre . . . French v. English Histrionics," he took issue with what Walkley had called "that Gallic system of histrionics which holds illusion and naturalness subservient to perfect elocution and consummate finish of style." As we have seen, Shaw argued that French actors were merely elocutionists "galvanized" by stage formalities.[13] These formalities, however, were a complex technique known as *détailler*, involving "precise inflection, throwing certain phrases into relief without losing sight of an underlying rhythm."[14] Bernhardt had studied with the famous Edmond Got (1822–1901), a master of this type of acting. Jules Lemaître recalled Bernhardt's imperial diction in *Théodora* as "la plus artificielle peut-être qu'on ait jamais hasardée au théâtre" [perhaps the most artificial ever attempted in the theater].[15]

The histrionics and "wild emotion" that had moved young Lawrence went against all of Shaw's dramaturgical goals: self-control, natural delivery, portrayals of real life. One French critic explained Bernhardt's appeal this way: "Though intoxicated, she remains lucid in her intoxication. She is frenzied, but yet within the bounds of logic, style and clarity."[16] Yet for Shaw, her intoxication always overshadowed those three Gallic traits. "Disliking French drama of most periods," writes one critic, "Shaw was predisposed to dislike French acting of almost every kind."[17]

As Doña Sol in *Hernani* in 1879, Bernhardt would suddenly switch from despair and hatred to resignation and content in an entirely believable manner. Such shifts in mood, combined with an ostinato delivery and spasmodic bodily movements, became the foundation of her success,[18] as well as Shaw's perennial Bernhardt hobbyhorse. The critic, Shaw wrote in 1897, "is the policeman of dramatic art; and it is his express business to denounce its delinquencies."[19] As we will see, if his denunciations had no effect on Bernhardt's acting or on her immense popularity in France and in England, her flamboyant acting and speaking styles were responsible for some of Shaw's most colorful passages of theater criticism.

* * *

2. Sarah Bernhardt in Victorien Sardou's *Théodora* in 1884. By permission of the Agence Photographique Roger-Viollet, Paris.

Shaw first mentioned Bernhardt in print in a passing reference in *Our Corner* (August 1885) to her role in Sardou's *Théodora*.[20] The following year, in his 13 October art review in the *World* of a Hanover Gallery opening, he called attention to "the Bastien Lepage portrait of Sarah Bernhardt, with its vaunted cut-steel frame,"[21] a work of 1879, the year of her first visit to London. Nine months later, Shaw recorded in his diary for 18 July 1887, "First night Sarah Bernhardt's engagement at the Lyceum. Sardou's *Theodora*."[22] The next day, his first critique of a Bernhardt performance appeared under "From Our London Correspondent," an unsigned review in the *Manchester Guardian:* "The great actress met all the demands made on her by M. Sardou's play with consummate ease and mastery," he wrote, "the enthusiasm of the audience growing steadily from her reception to the fall of the curtain."[23]

Shaw's early praise was short-lived. This was the beginning of a long and eloquent antipathy, during which he saw Bernhardt perform in at least thirteen plays. In order of composition, they were Victor Hugo, *Hernani* (1830); Alfred de Musset, *Lorenzaccio* (1834); Alexandre Dumas *fils, La Dame aux camélias* (1852); Henri Meilhac and Ludovic Halévy, *Frou Frou* (1869); Jules Barbier, *Jeanne d'Arc* (1873); Victorien Sardou, *Fédora* (1882); Sardou, *Théodora* (1884); Sardou, *La Tosca* (1887); Hermann Sudermann, *Heimat* (1893); Maurice Maeterlinck, *Pelléas et Mélisande* (1893); Sardou, *Gismonda* (1894); Edmond Rostand, *La Princesse lointaine* (1895); and Rostand, *L'Aiglon* (1900).

In all of these plays, Bernhardt displayed her virtuoso acting, which consisted mostly of "the continual repetition of movements, gestures and expressions from a variety of stage positions,"[24] emphasizing what Reynaldo Hahn called "feline suppleness" and Jules Lemaître "the windings of a snake."[25] In reality, Bernhardt's slenderness verged on emaciation: "arms of a skeleton," she said of herself.[26] In her 1908 memoirs, Ellen Terry recalled Bernhardt as "hollow-eyed, thin, almost consumptive-looking."[27] Bernhardt's sinewy, statuesque poses were described by Théodore de Banville as a model for "a Greek statue, wishing to symbolise Poetry"; Rostand went so far as to dub her "the queen of posture." Bernhardt's posturing, combined with an abruptness of gesture that one contemporary critic called "a kind of feverishness and hyperaesthesia," continued to fuel Shaw's fiery remarks in play after play.[28] It should be emphasized that this stylized acting was entirely in keeping with the stage pictorialism of the day, where actresses posed when immobile or "glided" when walking. "Statues achieved a sublime fixity of attitude that acting could only try to imitate. But at the same time the statuesque style threatened to imprison the living potential of the performer."[29]

By the time Shaw saw Bernhardt again on 11 July 1892 in *Frou Frou*, she was forty-eight, "well past her prime," he believed, "and relied on paint and cleverness."[30] To his exasperation, she also relied on that combination of exaggerated elocution and formulaic acting that made her performances as predictable as the "well-made" plays themselves. At least once, Shaw found her incomprehensible and arrogant; he reported in 1894 that in the Albert Hall, Bernhardt was audible but unintelligible—mostly because of her French accent—and that after polite applause, "she conveyed to us very plainly by the manner of her withdrawal that she considered us a parcel of imbeciles."[31] Her unintelligibility seems odd in light of the usual clarity and perfection of her diction, one French critic recalling "the marvellous articulation which saved the listener any effort of attention."[32] But by forcing her voice, Bernhardt "produced an unharmonious tone which made her words practically incomprehensible,"[33] which she may have done in the Albert Hall, notorious for its poor acoustics. And as Lemaître observed, Bernhardt's words sometimes rushed out in such cascades that "on n'entend plus que leur bruit sans en concevoir le sens" [one hears but their noise without understanding their sense].[34]

But no matter how much she irked Shaw, Bernhardt, more than any male or female performer of any nationality, remained a touchstone in his advice to actresses and in his discussions about acting (and overacting). In the *Saturday Review* of 30 March 1895, he complained that in Ibsen's *Rosmersholm*, Marthe Mellot played Rebecca West "in the manner of Sarah Bernhardt, the least appropriate of all manners for the part," exploiting "the explosive, hysterical, wasteful passion which makes nothing but a scene," with "a tearing finish in the Bernhardt style."[35] To Janet Achurch on 23 April 1895, Shaw praised Bernhardt's ability to move an audience, as when an actress must speak her part "with a pathetic intensity that makes you forget that the actual words do not mean anything pathetic at all, affecting the public as Sarah Bernhardt affects people who do not know a word of French, or Duse people who do not know a word of Italian." And about Achurch's performance in *The Wild Duck*, he wrote on 20 May 1897, "It is clear that you are not going to act any more: it is all Sara [sic] Bernhardt now—no brains, no pains, none of the distinction and freshness of thoughtful, self controlled work, nothing but letting yourself go and giving it to 'em hot and strong." And on 4 July 1897, he even told Ellen Terry—Bernhardt's friend and admirer—that Bernhardt had "reduced her business to the most mechanical routine possible" and was nothing more than "a worn out hack tragedienne."[36]

Bernhardt's melodramatic mannerisms were only part of what Shaw could not stomach. As a singer, amateur organist, and professional music critic, he was especially offended by her legendary "golden voice," an unfortunate (and vague) phrase coined by Victor Hugo at the banquet celebrating the hundredth performance of his play *Ruy Blas*. In actuality, although Bernhardt's voice was melodious, it could become strident and declamatory. More than one French critic complained about her "hammered diction," the result of her habit of laying stress on certain words or syllables, "of introducing strongly accented words by any means whatever."[37] Yvette Guilbert, her admirer and parodist, recalled: "Mon coeur se refusait au truquage de sa voix, de sa prononciation saccadée qui cliquetait parfois comme des castagnettes, mais éteignait la vérité, au profit des fioritures" [My heart refused to be taken in by the tricks of her voice, by her jerky pronunciation that sometimes clicked like castanets, but that sacrificed truth for the sake of elaboration].[38] Bernhardt's voice was also rather thin, forcing her "to play in a minor key, which grated when it needed to go into the upper register."[39] None of this affected the young Sigmund Freud, who saw Bernhardt in Paris in 1885 in *Théodora* and reported, "After the first words of her lovely, vibrant voice I felt I had known her for years."[40] Shaw himself had referred to Bernhardt in 1889 as an "internationally musical speaker of the highest class" but remarked the following year that as Jules Barbier's Joan of Arc, with music by Charles Gounod, she "intones her lines and poses like a saint" and "sends the lines out in a plaintive stream of melody throughout which only a fine ear can catch the false ring. You would almost swear that they meant something and that she was in earnest."[41] Like Guilbert, Shaw was not taken in.

Although others, like de Banville (quoting Lamartine), thought Bernhardt spoke verse "as the nightingale sings, as the wind sighs, as the stream murmurs," and critics compared her voice to flute, cello, violin, sea, and sun, many agreed with Shaw and reported that it often sounded "strangled ... raucous, and ... ineffectual," "too violent and jerky," and "strident."[42] "Able only with difficulty to make use of differences of range," writes one critic, "she skilfully exploited flexibility and variations of tone. By this means she was able to give her phrasing smoothness and a flowing quality. . . . Apt at bringing out the lyricism of the verse, her delivery could easily become monotonous, falling into a tedious chanting."[43]

Shaw was especially haunted by this "tedious chanting." Following a performance of Sardou's *Gismonda,* his 1 June 1895 *Saturday Review* critique ("Sardoodledom") attacked "that 'voix céleste' stop" that she keeps always pulled out "like a sentimental New England villager with an American organ," in a performance that was "vulgar and commercial, . . . hackneyed and old-fashioned."[44] Writing to Florence Farr on 6 June 1902, he complained that Bernhardt's "abominable 'golden voice,' which has always made me sick, is cantilation, or, to use the customary word, intoning."[45] In 1897, he had written that Ada Rehan's voice, compared with Bernhardt's, was "as all the sounds of the woodland to the chinking of twenty-franc pieces."[46] Shaw was only satisfied when he could *not* hear Bernhardt; after seeing the silent film *Elisabeth, Reine d'Angleterre* (1912), he wrote to Ellen Terry in 1915 that it was "very fine, and much better without that voix d'or that always set my teeth on edge than with it."[47]

One wonders, therefore, how Bernhardt's acting—unmusical, predictable, hyperdramatic—could entrance her audiences, both French and foreign, for so long. In his article of 15 June 1895 titled "Duse and Bernhardt"—which Bernard Dukore calls "by common consent . . . the best criticism of acting in the English language"[48]—Shaw contrasts Bernhardt to the equally famous Italian star Eleonora Duse (1859–1924) in their roles as Magda in Hermann Sudermann's *Heimat.* While Shaw could pardon Bernhardt's overpainted face because of its unashamed and artful execution ("Her lips are like a newly painted pillar box"), he deplored "the childishly egotistical character of her acting, which is not the art of making you think more highly or feel more deeply, but the art of making you admire her, pity her, champion her, weep with her, laugh at her jokes . . . and applaud her wildly when the curtain falls," of "cajoling you, harrowing you, exciting you—on the whole, fooling you. . . . She does not enter into the leading character: she substitutes herself for it." This was far from Shaw's idea of the thinking actor, but the crowds loved her—even though, as Shaw mocked, Bernhardt's "stock of attitudes and facial effects could be catalogued as easily as her stock of dramatic ideas: the counting would hardly go beyond the fingers of both hands."[49] And Shaw was right; her bewitching personality enveloped a role to the extent that, as Gabriel Boissy observed of her *Andromaque,* she ended up "playing herself all the time."[50] And yet, writes Horville, "she studied her rôles with great care and it was her gift to be able to know how to adapt her own powerful personality to the psychological demands of those rôles."[51]

Médée or Cléopâtre, Phèdre or Andromaque, Théodora or Tosca—they were all incarnations of the Divine Sarah.

What appalled Shaw most of all was in effect the secret of Bernhardt's success: her appeal to the emotions. Her performances were nothing if not explosions of feeling; "Our tears flow freely and sincere," she claimed in a 1921 interview, "and often the last sob still weighs on us when the play is over."[52] Shaw had written in 1896 that compared with Duse, Bernhardt was nothing but "a hackneyed provincial melodramatic actress."[53] Little wonder some believe that it was Shaw more than any other critic "who led future generations to think of Sarah as a moneygrubbing queen of melodrama and Duse as an otherworldly priestess of high art."[54]

Shaw's descriptions are very much pen portraits of the "queen of melodrama" in full Dionysian mode. In his 22 June 1895 review of *La Princesse lointaine* by Rostand, he described her tearing through her lines: "At the utmost pitch and power of her voice, she shews no further sense of what she is saying, and is unable to recover herself when, in the final speech, the feeling changes" and she "finally rushes off the stage in a forced frenzy." He suggested that her "ranting" be "replaced by a genuine study and interpretation of the passages which are sacrificed to it," concluding with his usual stab at her voice: the critic "who finds melody in one sustained note would find exquisite curves in a packing case."[55] On this last point, one French critic remarked of *La Princesse lointaine* that "she doubtless thought that it would be impossible to over-use the drawling singsong."[56] Two years later, in his 26 June 1897 review of Musset's *Lorenzaccio*, Shaw summed up Bernhardt's stage antics as a combination of "golden voice," "celebrated smile," "businesslike and competent" acting, and "tearing a passion to tatters," a routine "which is refurbished every year with fresh scenery, fresh dialogue, and a fresh author, whilst remaining itself invariable."[57] How different is the anonymous French review of the same play in Paris the previous year: "Without over-exaggeration of purple passages, without excess and without cries, she moves us to the very depths of our souls."[58] That same performance led Anatole France to praise Bernhardt's "sureness of gesture, the tragic beauty of her pose and glance, the increased power in the timbre of her voice, and the suppleness and breadth of her diction"[59]—everything that Shaw deplored.

But Shaw was not completely immune to Bernhardt's charisma. One odd instance, considering how he felt about her histrionics and stiff acting, was the suggestion to his French translator Hamon in 1906 that Bernhardt "ought to play" Mrs. Warren![60] Shaw also admired Bernhardt as a businesswoman; as one who took an interest in all aspects of the theater, he acknowledged her shrewdness in writing to Ellen Terry in 1903 that Bernhardt's "plan of always keeping her stage full of the prettiest women she can find is a very worldly-wise one."[61] And he told actress Gertrude Kingston in 1917: "No single success can keep up a theater unless it be that of a man who can play the big Hamlet Macbeth repertory which has no female equivalent. It has been tried again and again; and the only apparent solid result is Sarah, who always built herself in with the prettiest women and strongest men she could lay her hands on."[62]

Yet Shaw was adversarial even at Bernhardt's death. In his short, mixed tribute for the *Manchester Sunday Chronicle* of 1 April 1923, ambiguously titled "Handicaps of a Queen of Tragedy," Shaw admitted that he had been touched "by her Pelléas as she never touched me in any other part." On the other hand, "She was not an author's actress. The only character she gave to the stage was her own.... She never got into the skin of her parts: she simply exploited them, preferring her own skin, sometimes with good reason." He went on to recall the first time he saw her, forty years earlier in *Hernani*. (Although he left no record of his views on that performance, he had written in his 26 June 1897 review of *Lorenzaccio* about "the fascination which, as Dona Sol, she once gave to Hernani.")[63] He mentioned "an unforgettable moment in the last act" that, he emphasized, had reappeared in every play as "a mechanical rant." Shaw even got a last word on her voice, writing that the "famous voix d'or was produced by intoning like an effeminate Oxford curate." While admitting that "she improved with age, becoming much jollier and more sensible," he finished with a left-handed compliment: "Only a clever, resolute, self-centred woman could have imposed 'the Divine Sarah' on Europe and America."[64]

* * *

Shaw may have been somewhat disingenuous in his memorial epitaph because he was apparently "coerced" into writing it.[65] In any event, he was mistaken in stating that if Bernhardt "had any other part in the great dramatic development that took place in her time, it did not reach us here."[66] Florence Farr, who acted in Gilbert Murray's versions of Greek tragedies, "certainly studied her delivery closely."[67] Stokes points out that thanks to Arthur Symons and others at the turn of the century who made French acting into something of a cult, Bernhardt became "even in her decline, an unexpected influence upon English Modernism."[68] Such was the English admiration for the French theatrical scene that Henry Irving urged the foundation of a school for British actors on the model of the

École Royale Dramatique, an idea that bore fruit only in 1905 (the year of his death) with the establishment of the Royal Academy of Dramatic Art.[69]

More important, Meisel believes that *Saint Joan*, as a play written for a woman star, "is a direct continuation of the line of the most 'legitimate' women-plays of the nineteenth century, historical, tragic, and rhetorical, elevated in diction and sentiment,"[70] all of which describes the plays that Bernhardt's productions made famous. She may even have been part of the impetus behind *Saint Joan;* in her journal (on 19 May 1923) Lady Gregory noted: "G.B.S. says he chose Joan of Arc because of Bernhardt and others having played so many parts turning on sexual attraction he wanted to give Joan as a heroine absolutely without that side."[71] One wonders what Bernhardt would have done with *Sainte Jeanne,* had she lived to displace the meek, waiflike (and hugely popular) Ludmilla Pitoëff from the stage. Most likely she would have played Jeanne as she once described the saint: "un être frêle conduit par une âme divine. Un ange invisible soutient son bras porteur du lourd étendard" [a frail being led by a divine soul. An invisible angel supports her arm carrying the heavy standard].[72] It was exactly the opposite for Shaw. And since Bernhardt's tears, according to one critic, "were almost as famous as her voice,"[73] she might have outdone even Ludmilla, who, as will be seen, played Joan with an overabundance of tears.

Paradoxically, Bernhardt did contribute to French "dramatic development" thanks in part to her experiences in English theaters. While Shaw was ranting against her, she was giving interviews in English newpapers: "I have suppressed the *claque*. It never saved a piece yet, and it is an unfair attempt to lead the opinion of the audience. I have, also, suppressed the *surtaxe* on tickets—the extra prices charged for booking seats in advance—and I have done away with the *ouvreuses,* those too-officious women attendants to whom foreigners object so strongly. In a word, I have formed the Théâtre Renaissance on the best English models."[74] Even though her comments were meant to endear her to English readers (and audiences), the fact remains that Bernhardt streamlined her own theater in accordance with theaters across the Channel.

In his low opinion of Bernhardt's acting, Shaw was in good company; some French critics deplored in their national stage heroine the very affectations and mannerisms that made Shaw bristle. In 1877, Gabriel Boissy lamented that in *Andromaque*, "instead of Racine, she searches for theatrical effects." "She overdid all the stage effects," wrote René Doumic in 1896; "she replaced the utterance, the gesture, the postures by an incensed mimic."[75] Even more strident was novelist and playwright Romain

Rolland, who considered the romantic dramas of Dumas *fils,* Sardou, and Rostand a threat to his idea of a "théâtre populaire," and Bernhardt as the one performer who exerted a definitive influence on the success of his fellow dramatists. Like Shaw, Rolland objected to Bernhardt's gaudiness and mechanical acting, in one instance outdoing Shaw's use of epithets in describing her. Writing in 1903, he singled her out as the one who best characterized "ce néo-romantisme byzantinisé,—où américanisé,—raidi, figé, sans jeunesse, sans vigeur, surchargé d'ornements, de bijoux vrais ou faux, morne sous son fracas, blafard dans son éclat" [stiff, rigid, without youth, without vigor, weighed down with ornaments, with jewels real or fake, bleak beneath its bluster, pallid in its glitter].[76]

It is interesting that Shaw's and Rolland's descriptions of Bernhardt's shortcomings are at odds with what she herself wrote in a chapter titled "Le Naturel" in her book, *L'Art du théâtre*. She expected the artist to exhibit "les sentiments qui doivent l'agiter, comme les manifestent dans la réalité la moyenne de ses contemporains" [the feelings that are supposed to stir him, as they are expressed in real life by average men amongst his contemporaries]. After what Shaw had seen of (and written about) Bernhardt's acting, he would have been astonished to read this: "Être naturel . . . c'est exclure tout ce qui est rigide et permanent, pour se plier aux innombrables vicissitudes de l'existence. . . . Rien n'est plus malséant que de jouer d'après une formule toujours répétée" [To be natural is to exclude all that is stiff and permanent, in order to adapt oneself to the innumerable vicissitudes of existence. Nothing is more distasteful than to act according to a formula that is constantly repeated].[77] Ironically, this very formula propelled Bernhardt and her playwrights to stardom.

In keeping with these views on naturalism in acting—and despite her "romantic" temperament and stage characterizations—is Bernhardt's idea of the theater as a didactic medium for an intellectual audience. While excoriating her acting style, Shaw would have found it difficult to disagree with her idea of the theater as "un enseignement vivace et concluant" [a perennial and effective form of instruction] and "le porte-voix le plus direct des idées nouvelles philosophiques, sociales, religieuses et morales" [the most direct megaphone of new philosophical, social, religious and moral ideas]. Like Shaw, Bernhardt thought of the theater as an institution that invites the public "à penser, à comprendre et à tirer de ce qui se passe sur la scène autre chose qu'un vulgaire plaisir visuel" [to think, to understand, and to extract from what happens on the stage something other than a commonplace visual pleasure].[78] Her views echo very closely Shaw's famous definition of the theater (mentioned earlier) as "a factory of thought, a prompter of conscience, an elucidator of social conduct."[79] Despite the emotionalism and spectacle of her performances, it seems that Bernhardt and Shaw were thinking along similar theoretical lines.

In light of her interest in realistic acting and didactic drama, it is not surprising that of all her famous peers—Sardou, Augier, Rostand, Dumas *fils*—the playwright that Bernhardt held in highest esteem was the one that Shaw too thought the greatest of all living French dramatists: Eugène Brieux (1858–1932), the ardent socialist to whom Shaw wrote a long panegyric and some of whose plays Charlotte Shaw translated into English.[80] Bernhardt praised his work as "courageux, probe et lumineux" [bold, upright and lucid]. "Les tares de l'hypocrisie sociale y sont mises a nu. . . . Et rien de ces thèses philosophiques, morales ou sociales ne nuit à l'action prenante de l'intrigue" [The blemishes of social hypocrisy are laid bare. And nothing of his philosophical, moral or social doctrines interferes with the engrossing action of the plot].[81] Yet Bernhardt never appeared in a work by Brieux, most likely because his dramas were designed to illustrate controversial topical issues, such as venereal disease, birth control, the dowry system, prostitution, and divorce. They were not showcases for a prima donna who could portray famous historical or mythical tragic figures in plays that featured, in the words of one critic, "blackmail, treason, torture, suicide, murder and *lots* of adultery."[82]

Such plays turned Bernhardt into the richest, most important French actress of her time, the first modern female superstar. She became an internationally recognized tragedienne of Sophocles and Racine, as well as the heroine (or hero) of the most popular dramas and melodramas of the day. Her contribution to French culture was honored with the medal of the Légion d'Honneur in 1913 and a requiem mass in Westminster Cathedral.

One critic has asked: "Where would Sarah be if we had only the testimony of Bernard Shaw?"[83] Fortunately, her place in theater history was ensured by many other famous English and Irish writers. When she spoke, her most fervent English admirer, Maurice Baring, heard "the voice of the masters of the *bel canto*," "so soft, so melting, so perfectly in tune and in time, with so sure a rhythm, and so perfectly clean-cut that one never lost a syllable." A. B. Walkley was "spellbound" by Phèdre's "low, wailing melody." James Agate, her devoted worshiper, believed that "those who remember her acting at its best will marvel at the panegyrist's ineffectual poverty." W. B. Yeats, a devotee of verse drama, saw in Bernhardt "an endorsement of the ideal of rhythmic delivery and minimal movement that . . . he had been reaching towards with the production of his own plays." And he of the armful of lilies, the Bernhardt fanatic Oscar Wilde, praised "the superb elocution of the French—so clean, so cadenced, and so musical."[84]

And if Shaw's was not the only dissenting Anglo-Saxon voice—Matthew Arnold described her as "a fugitive vision of delicate features under a shower of hair and a cloud of lace," pointing out in August 1879, three months after her London debut, her want of "high intellectual power"[85]—Shaw's was certainly the loudest and most sustained. Yet Bernhardt enjoyed the same controversial renown as Shaw's: both were caricatured as well as apotheosized by the press; both possessed an often exaggerated sense of their amazing capabilities; both took an active part in the staging, casting, and production of their plays; and both were adept at self-promotion and garnered enormous profits from the theater.[86] "Was she really a great actress," Sir John Gielgud queries, "or merely a great star personality with a genius for publicity and showmanship?"[87] We need only replace "actress" with "playwright" to form the question that has been asked of Shaw more than of any dramatist in history.

But the similarities end there. Sarah Bernhardt was too French for Shaw, a man "more dedicated to Anglo-Saxon matter than to Gallic manner,"[88] to making a point rather than creating an effect. Although she became an international cult figure, the spellbinding siren never lured the Irishman "into the mysteries of sensuality and poetic illusion." Bernhardt's plaintive song failed utterly to enchant the "policeman of dramatic art."[89]

5

The Ruthless Revealer

An Encomium to Eugène Brieux

On 2 February 1927, a document was issued in Paris titled "International Protest Against the Unauthorized & Mutilated Edition of 'Ulysses' in the U.S.A." It was signed by 167 luminaries, including T. S. Eliot, Virginia Woolf, W. B. Yeats, Benedetto Croce, Italo Svevo, Luigi Pirandello, André Gide, Paul Valéry, Thomas Mann, and "Eugène Brieux, de l'Académie Française." One notable name was missing.

Shaw approved of Joyce's accurate portrayal of Dublin mores but did not like the language (nor the price) of *Ulysses,* and his refusal to sign is no surprise. What is odd is to find Eugène Brieux (1858–1932) among the avant-gardists of modernism, odder still to know that Shaw bothered with him at all. That Shaw admired Molière, Wagner, Ibsen, and Strindberg is understandable; that he wrote an encomium to a man whose epitaph was "Il a fait de son mieux" [He did his best] can only be explained by his unrelenting promotion of those who shared his ideas even if, like Hamon, they were not first-class minds.[1] Both Shaw and Brieux were socialists, and Brieux's quest to better society by holding up to it the mirror of its shortcomings struck an intellectual nerve in Shaw. Brieux turned out approximately fifty plays and short stage pieces between 1880 and 1929, while Shaw wrote about thirty major plays between 1884 and 1939.[2] Ironically, recognition came early for the lesser talent: Brieux was elected to the Académie Française in 1909, the year of Shaw's encomium; Shaw was awarded the Nobel Prize in 1925.

Shaw's awakening to Brieux must partly be credited to Charlotte, who was quite moved when she read *Maternité* (1903) during the winter of 1906. Eight years later, she recalled feeling that "an event had occurred, and a new possession come into my life."[3] So taken was she by the play that she spent the next few months translating it. The censor refused to license her version, so she and other members of the Stage Society put on *Maternity* clandestinely on 8 April 1906. In his 17 April review in the *World* of *Maternity* and *Captain Brassbound's Conversion* (at the Court Theatre), titled "Brieux and Bernard Shaw," H. Hamilton Fyfe observed that "tradition demands a definite plot; and M. Brieux has not had the courage to defy the demand. The result is that he hangs his discussion upon a tedious little story about the seduction of a silly girl . . . who does not interest us in the very least. . . . It is in his attitude towards 'the plot' that Mr. Shaw proves himself so much more a master of the discussion-play method than is M. Brieux."[4]

Nonetheless, Brieux's popularity in England was on the rise. The previous year, the Stage Society had performed *Les Trois Filles de M. Dupont* (1897) [*The Three Daughters of Monsieur Dupont*, translated by St. John Hankin], and John Pollock had translated *Les Avariés* (1901) as *Damaged Goods*. When Charlotte wrote to Brieux for permission to publish these two plays and *Maternity* as one book, he enthusiastically agreed. Unfortunately, the project was rejected by many publishers, and *Three Plays by Brieux* appeared only in 1911, after he had been elected to the Académie Française. Four months later, a doctor wrote to Charlotte requesting several thousand copies of *Damaged Goods* in pamphlet form to be distributed "among the youth of our Connecticut colleges, especially Yale University,"[5] and ten thousand copies were published. In December 1913, Charlotte's translation of *La Femme seule* (*Woman on Her Own*) was produced by the Actresses' Franchise League, and *Damaged Goods* was given a private production at the Little Theatre. The censor could no longer turn the other way; *Damaged Goods* was given its first London performance on 16 February 1914.[6] With the help of Charlotte and, as we will see, her husband, the most popular dramatist in France had made his mark on England.

* * *

When Charlotte became interested in Brieux, Shaw too read him and from then on alluded to him often, always with admiration: "Dramatic Censorship" (1907), an article written at the time of Charlotte's first translation, discusses *Les Avariés* and venereal disease; the preface to *Getting Married* (1909) mentions *Les Avariés, Les Trois Filles de M. Dupont, Maternité,* and *Les Hannetons;* the preface to *The Shewing-Up of Blanco Posnet* (1909) mentions *Maternité* and *Les Avariés* in relation to censorship; "What I Owe to German Culture" (1911, in German) mentions *Les Trois Filles de M. Dupont, Maternité,* and *Les Hannetons* as attacks on moral-

3. Eugène Brieux in 1911 by Chéri-Rousseau, Paris. Frontispiece of *Three Plays by Brieux. With a Preface by Bernard Shaw. The English Versions by Mrs Bernard Shaw, St. John Hankin and John Pollock* (London: A. C. Fifield, 1911).

ists and immoralists; the preface to *Overruled* (1914) mentions *La Foi* and *Le Bourgeois aux champs;* the preface to *Heartbreak House* (1919) mentions *Les Avariés;* an address, "Censorship as a Police Duty" (1928), discusses *Les Avariés* and venereal disease; and *Everybody's Political What's What?* (1944) mentions *Les Avariés* and censorship.

For Shaw (and like him), Brieux was a voice challenging authority by staging taboo issues. Shaw paid homage to him with "Brieux: A Preface," a fifteen-thousand-word essay written late in 1909 and published in *Three Plays by Brieux,* Shaw's longest essay on any French writer. Yet instead of an analysis of Brieux's works, the essay is a short history of modern European drama, with Brieux and his plays acting as the impetus for long disquisitions on conventionality, censorship, taboos of the stage, venereal disease, and other issues dear to Shaw. It is also a paean to Brieux himself with, on occasion, the usual (and by now expected) jibes against Brieux's homeland: "In fine art, France is a nation of born pedants. . . . Paris is easily the most prejudiced, oldfashioned, obsolete-minded city in the west of Europe. . . . there is nothing she hates more than a Frenchman of genius. . . . They [Parisiens] never know [a great Frenchman] until the English tell them."[7] These outrageous pronouncements—as well as others elsewhere, such as "Europe has today a Sophocles in the person of Eugène Brieux"[8]— were intended less to insult than to arouse the French into taking Brieux seriously.

While he wanted his preface to shock Paris, Shaw wanted Brieux to be completely satisfied with it. Shortly after completing it, he sent it to Hamon (on 24 January 1910) requesting him to translate it and forward it to Brieux. "Will you also ask him to deal with it quite freely," Shaw specified, "in the way of modifying or altering or omitting anything that may be for any reason disagreeable or inconvenient to him." He told Hamon to assure Brieux that no public allusion would be made to the preface being submitted to Brieux for his approval; "he will not be in any way responsible for my views."[9] Two months later, he urged Hamon to assure Brieux "that he need not have the slightest delicacy about doing exactly what he likes with that preface of mine. There must be some things in it which are not quite right as matters of fact; and there may possibly be some expressions of opinion which may jar on him. At all events, beg him to treat me as a friend to the extent of making as free with my preface as he would with one of his own."[10] For Shaw to allow anyone such latitude with his work shows how deeply he admired and respected Brieux, who seems to have had similar feelings for Shaw. On 14 April 1910, the day after he and André Antoine attended a performance of *Candida,* Brieux wrote to Shaw about "l'incompréhension de la critique," lamenting that he could not understand how they could have remained "insensible aux beautés de votre oeuvre."[11]

Ironically—and thankfully—only part of Shaw's vituperations crossed the Channel. In a letter of 10 June 1911 to his German translator, Siegfried Trebitsch, Shaw regretted that Hamon had "allowed himself to be seduced by the editor of L'Illustration into giving him two or three columns extracted from the preface; and after that none of the magazines would touch it." The excerpt, "De Molière à Brieux," had been published on 7 May 1910, but Shaw felt that his preface "would have made a considerable sensation in Paris if it had been published there in full."[12]

The sensation created by the excerpt was considerable enough. It was attacked as yet another example of Shaw's misunderstanding of French literature, although Brieux was also targeted. Writing in *Le Journal des débats* on 13 May, Henry Bidou concluded that Brieux "a peint des travers, qui deviennent dramatiques en précipitant à faux des malheureux dans l'engrenage social. Et le plus curieux dans ce tissu d'erreurs élémentaires, c'est que M. Shaw aime visiblement M. Brieux pour les qualités qu'il lui prête d'abord, mais aussi pour son rôle d'instructeur et ses qualités de prédicant, qui en sont justement l'opposé" [has portrayed failings that become dramatic by erroneously hurling down wretches into the social gear-wheels. And the most curious thing in this tissue of elementary blunders is that Mr. Shaw obviously likes Mr. Brieux, first of all for the qualities that he attributes to him, but also for his role as schoolmaster and his qualities as preacher, which are precisely the opposite].

That same day, an anonymous reviewer in *L'Action française* was incensed: "On y voit à cru l'ignorance et l'outrecuidance absurde d'un auteur qui prétend, d'ailleurs, nous donner des leçons et nous apprendre ce qu'est le lamentable primaire dont l'Académie va faire jeudi prochain un immortel. Voici l'exorde de cette incomparable bouffonnerie" [Here we can observe in the raw the ignorance and absurd presumptuousness of an author who claims, moreover, to give us lessons and to teach all about this pitiful simplist whom the Académie will make 'an immortal' next Thursday. Behold the exordium of this incomparable buffoonery]. The following day, in *La Dernière Heure,* Maurice de Waleffe was no less amazed at how the "London panegyrist" dared equate Brieux with Molière. Although he applauded (perhaps sarcastically) "l'intronisation de ce très honorable ouvrier de lettres" [the enthroning of this very honorable workman of letters], he chided both men for turning stage into pulpit, where Brieux's characters debate their author's opinions on everything from maternal breast-feeding to reform of the magistrature. "Le théâtre, ô cher M. Bernard Shaw! consiste à faire vivre devant nous des hommes et des femmes, non pas transformés en pasteurs protestants ou en colonels de l'Armée du Salut" [is about making men and women come to life before us, not in transforming them into Protestant ministers or Salvation Army colonels].[13]

* * *

Shaw's was only one of many voices being raised for or against Brieux. He may have inspired H. L. Mencken, who, two years after Shaw's preface, published one of his own. Perhaps imitating Shaw's title, Mencken called his volume *Two Plays by Brieux*. But if Shaw's preface is more about theater history than about Brieux, Mencken's is a useful chronology of the Brieux canon in French and English production. Finding Shaw's praise of Brieux "somewhat extravagant," Mencken admits that "all the acknowledged giants of the French drama since Molière have been giants of dramaturgy rather than giants of truth." However, "in many of the latter plays, the mark is overshot, the untypical is mistaken for the typical, the argument finds its answer in its unsound premises. I need cite only 'Suzette,' 'Ménage d'Artistes,' 'La [sic] Berceau' and 'Les Avariés.' In each of them Brieux states a case which, in part at least, misrepresents the thing he attacks."[14] Another American, Hugh Allison Smith, thought that "Brieux is not primarily a thinker, much less a scientific one. Only a critic as uniquely original as Shaw could call him both."[15] Arnold Bennett, well versed in French literature and culture, warned about what he called "the Brieux craze" that would follow the publication of Shaw's selection. He also shared some of Mencken's reservations: "I have seen most of Brieux's plays," he wrote in 1910; they "always begin so brilliantly, and they always end so feebly, in such a wishwash of sentimentalism." Moreover, "Brieux is too violent a reformer ever to be a serious dramatist. Violent reformers are unprincipled, and the reformer in Brieux forces the dramatist in him to prostitution." Yet Bennett accords Shaw faint praise: "He is deficient in a feeling for beauty; he is deficient in emotion. But that is not the worst of him. Mr. Shaw is deficient in these supreme qualities. But Mr. Shaw is an honest playwright."[16]

What fascinated Shaw about the mediocre Brieux was that he was a French "policeman of dramatic art." "His fisticuffs are not aimed heavenward," wrote Shaw; "they fall on human noses for the good of human souls." Shaw liked in Brieux those qualities that he himself possessed: "For it is the business of Brieux to pick out the significant incidents from the chaos of daily happenings, and arrange them so that their relation to one another becomes significant, thus changing us from bewildered spectators of a monstrous confusion to men intelligently conscious of the world and its destinies. This is the highest function that man can perform: the greatest work he can set his hand to."[17] Shaw was concerned more with the lessons of Brieux's plays than with the plays themselves.

If their ideologies were similar, their plays were structurally antithetical. An amusing section in Shaw's preface is his tongue-in-cheek formula for the creation of a well-made play, "How to Write a Popular Play."[18] This is ironic, given the kind of plays Brieux was writing. In the preface to the 1921 edition of his complete works, Brieux summed up his life's work as a desire to reform society by changing its laws by means of the thesis-play. "J'ai donc passé ma vie à écrire ce qu'on appelle des pièces à thèse. J'ai toujours envisagé le théâtre non comme un but, mais comme un moyen. J'ai voulu par lui, non seulement provoquer des réflexions, modifier des habitudes et des actes, mais encore . . . déterminer des arrêtés administratifs qui m'apparaissaient désirables" [I have therefore spent my life writing what are called thesis-plays. I have always regarded the theater not as an end in itself, but as a means to an end. I wished by means of the stage not only to provoke thought, alter habits and actions, but also . . . to establish administrative bylaws which to me seemed desirable].[19] To provoke thought, alter habits and actions was unmistakably Shavian, especially since Shaw was interested in many of the same issues that fascinated Brieux, such as marriage, women's rights, prostitution, poverty, religion, and venereal disease.

* * *

Shaw's long preface, in which seven Brieux plays are mentioned briefly or given short plot summaries, closes with a discussion of *Damaged Goods*, Brieux's only play dealing with venereal disease. "No play ever written was more needed than Les Avariés," writes Shaw. He goes on to praise sexuality as the crux of all creativity: "Sex is a necessary and healthy instinct; and its nurture and education is one of the most important uses of all art; and, for the present at all events, the chief use of the theatre." Like poverty, or wealth gone sick, sexuality gone sick undermines the social fabric; hence the importance for both Shaw and Brieux of philanthropy and marriage. By the end of the preface, Shaw's hyperbole no longer shocks: "If half the scientific evidence be true, a marriage contracted by a person actively affected in either way is perhaps the worst crime that can be committed with legal impunity in a civilized community."[20] Shaw's

1933 postscript to the preface mentions the progress made in eradicating venereal disease and promoting birth control by Marie Stopes in England and Margaret Sanger in the United States.[21]

The topic was dear to Shaw, and on 28 February 1914, in an Oxford lecture titled "On the Nature of Drama," he compared *Les Avariés* (which had had its London premiere less than two weeks earlier) to, of all plays, *Oedipus Rex*. The lecture is quoted at length by Charlotte Shaw in her foreword to *Damaged Goods. A Play by Brieux* (1917). According to Shaw, Brieux had dealt with his issue even more forcefully than Sophocles forcing the horror of parricide and incest "on the public unflinchingly and ruthlessly." Brieux "surpasses Sophocles" in driving "a man quite comfortable in his conscience and happy in his circumstances . . . to an overwhelming conviction of guilt and disaster." Loches, the respected member of parliament of *Les Avariés* who is reduced "to utter moral nakedness and bankruptcy," is a more effective Oedipus, according to Shaw, because "our prejudices, our convictions, our virtuous indignations have been exactly those of the man on the stage, and . . . we too have been left naked. Sophocles cannot do that to us, because we are not Edipuses." Granted, Shaw was using Brieux to illustrate Sophoclean technique, but his claims that *Les Avariés* could be turned into Greek drama by replacing the second act by declamatory narrative—and that Brieux must be ranked "with the greatest of tragic poets and theatrical craftsmen"—are overblown, to say the least.[22] When John Pollock published a revised translation of *Les Avariés* in 1943, he too quoted in his preface the passages cited by Charlotte.[23]

Syphilis is only one of the targets in Brieux's catalogue of social degeneration: *Ménage d'artistes* (1890) denies the artist the right to sacrifice his family to his work; *L'Engrenage* (1894) depicts the evils of universal suffrage; *Les Bienfaiteurs* (1896) satirizes fashionable charity; *Les Trois Filles de M. Dupont* (1897) shows the evils of the dowry system; *Résultat des courses* (1898) attacks gambling; *Le Berceau* (1898) discusses divorce; *La Robe rouge* (1900) exposes the corruption of the judicial system; *Les Remplaçantes* (1901) shows the horrors of wet-nursing; *Maternité* (1903) shows the necessity of birth control; *La Déserteuse* (1904) is about divorce; *L'Armature* (1905) deals with avarice; *Les Hannetons* (1906) shows that free love can be more enslaving than marriage; *Simone* (1908) denies the right of a man to kill his wife for adultery; *Suzette* (1909) promotes the rights of mother and child; *La Foi* (1909) shows the desirability of religious faith; and *La Femme seule* (1912) denounces the injustices done to working women.

This brings us to one major difference between Brieux and Shaw: Shaw's female protagonists tend to behave heroically, or at least stoically, in the face of struggle, while Brieux's are frequently victims of domestic or social injustice. When the eponymous young peasant girl of *Blanchette* (1892), after receiving a fine education, is sent away by her father to Paris for having made costly modernizations to his shop, she attempts suicide and, in despair, becomes a prostitute. The three sisters of *Les Trois Filles de M. Dupont* are similarly victimized: when Angèle becomes pregnant, she is turned into the street by her father; Julie is merely her husband's plaything; and Caroline is unhappily chaste in religious penury. Exclaims Angèle: "On nous méprise tant ... on n'a pas d'amis, pas de pitié, pas de justice.... On est volée, exploitée." [We are so despised ... we have no friends, no pity, no justice.... We are robbed, exploited].[24] On the other hand, Shaw is not interested in helpless females. Candida, Vivie, Barbara, Ann, and Joan triumph; in Joan's case, from beyond the grave. Even Shaw's own "fallen woman," Mrs. Warren, is a far cry from Brieux's hapless creatures of circumstance; the aggressive entrepreneur secures money, property, independence.

Brieux's married women fare no better. In *Maternité*, undowried Lucie marries a man who turns out to be an alcoholic who rapes her. She sums up the situation tersely at the abortion trial, telling the judge that the only thing men have to offer is "l'amour pour amorce et la loi pour complice" [love as bait and the law as accomplice].[25] Like Angèle, Lucie is a victim of social inequity. What is worse—and this is typical of Brieux's catholic outlook—is that an unhappy wife cannot escape once the union is consecrated. In *Les Trois Filles de M. Dupont,* Julie finds in Lignol the companionship her husband, Antonin, cannot provide. However, since the parents will not hear of divorce, she continues seeing Lignol in secret, remaining trapped in sad domesticity. Generally, there is a somber tone to Brieux's plays, and their characters seem doomed even before they begin their sometimes interminable speeches pleading for compassion.

What saves Shaw's people from becoming mouthpieces for reform or merely downtrodden failures is their will, their Life Force. His women are more resourceful than Brieux's, and more conniving. Julia in *The Philanderer* (1905) poses as an emancipated "Unwomanly Woman" to trap Charteris into marriage, as much for status and security as for sex. With *Getting Married* (1908), Shaw distinguishes between marriage and sexuality, and one has little to do with the other. Brieux's morality may appear "liberal," but nothing in his work approaches Lesbia's views on motherhood. Whereas Shaw's work advocates impregnation followed by state support of the child, Brieux advocates in *Suzette* (1909) the sanctity of children and family, and marriage as the preservation of the race. Shaw does Brieux one better by striving for the perfectibility of the race, not only its survival by propagation.

Given the ills that plague society, especially its women, can the children of the future inherit a harmonious world? Anxious not to disturb the family structure, Brieux makes little Julien in *Le Berceau* (1898) a symbol of his parents's mystic union, and in *Suzette* states that the family must remain together if there are children. But to the Shaw of the "Treatise on Parents and Children" (1910), his preface to *Misalliance,* a child is merely "an experiment. A fresh attempt . . . to make humanity divine."[26] The Life Force is eugenic, not social. While Shaw's characters are willing to live passionately, even dangerously, for the eventual improvement of humankind, Brieux's people bend to a safer ethic so as to preserve a tolerable social status quo. In *Maternité,* for example, on the assumption that his audience approves of a high birth rate for religious and nationalistic reasons, Brieux proposes to reform the laws concerning women's rights. The alternatives are not pleasant; Anette dies of an illegal abortion, and Lucie aborts herself, although the latter case is mitigated by the suggestion that the child would likely have been defective due to the father's intemperance. Moreover, many of Brieux's characters are from the lower middle classes. A furious Lucie sums up the situation as an aphorism for her obtuse husband: "Pas de maternité sans mariage, et pas de mariage sans dot" [No children without marriage, and no marriage without a dowry].[27] Most of Shaw's characters are from the well-to-do bourgeoisie, and children rarely make an appearance unless they are of a marriageable age.

There are some interesting parallels between Brieux's *Les Bienfaiteurs,* produced in English by the Stage Society in 1904, and *Major Barbara,* a variation on the same theme, completed and produced within the year. Both plays deal with the issue of philanthropy, and some characters mirror one another. Féchain, like Snobby Price, is an undeserving pauper and fraud who is helped by self-made millionaire Valentin Salviat, an Undershaft figure, whose charity only encourages Féchain's profligacy. The conflict is between institutional and private charity, and both are ineffectual. Whereas Shaw would have the unemployed repudiate their situation by individual will, Brieux looks to the state to provide employment as a birthright for all citizens. Again, the focus for Brieux is national, for Shaw personal. Brieux indicts the evils of the environment upon the victim; Shaw demonstrates how the individual can triumph over that environment. For instance, Salviat's motto, "D'abord moi" — "Me first" — sounds more selfish than Undershaft's "Unashamed," but the idea is the same. However, Salviat makes his money in a few lucky speculations and thus cannot be, like Shaw's philanthropist, a symbol of human potential actualized through strength of will. "I was a dangerous man until I had my will," says Undershaft; "now I am a useful, beneficent, kindly person."[28] Whereas Undershaft puts the poor to work and provides them with comfortable living arrangements, Salviat's workers are manipulated by their boss Pluvinage to become mere units of production. What is important for Brieux is work for its own sake, the Christian ethic: "Le travail, qui est sacré, ne doit jamais céder" [Work, which is sacred, must never give way].[29]

This brings us to another topic important to both playwrights: religion. As men of great faith—"religious" for Brieux, "secular" for Shaw—they held that one must believe in something, even an illusion. This is the lesson of *La Foi,* literally "Faith" but translated as *False Gods,* which one critic claims may have influenced an episode in Shaw's most famous "religious" drama: "the Archbishop's cynical speech about miracles in *Saint Joan* echoes the philosophy of the High Priest in Brieux's play, *La Foi,* written eleven years previously. Here Shaw skilfully appropriated what suited his purpose, heightening its effect by a characteristic touch of caustic humour."[30]

If one parallels certain passages, the similarities are striking. Brieux's High Priest: "La religion est un appui. Elle soulage et console" [Religion is a buttress. It soothes and consoles]; Shaw's Archbishop: "A miracle, my friend, is an event which creates faith. That is the purpose and nature of miracles." The High Priest: "Il n'est pas, pour eux, de bonheur sans religion. . . . Si tu lui enlèves sa religion, quelle morale soutiendra sa vertu? . . . Lui enlever la crainte des dieux, c'est déchainer ses plus viles instincts" [There is no happiness for them without religion. . . . If you take away their religion, what morality will keep them virtuous? . . . Removing their fear of the gods would let loose their vilest instincts]; the Archbishop: "Frauds deceive. An event which creates faith does not deceive: therefore it is not a fraud, but a miracle." "Miracles are not frauds because they are often—I do not say always—very simple and innocent contrivances by which the priest fortifies the faith of his flock."[31]

Yet, as with the topic of women, Brieux and Shaw approach "faith" from almost opposite perspectives. In *La Foi,* the young priest Satni (an anagram for "saint") is portrayed as a cold, rationalistic skeptic, one of the few characters in Brieux who embodies intellect. Although he knows that the masses worship false gods, Satni takes pity on them and, pulling the lever that bows the head of the statue of Isis, performs a "miracle." When the faithful throw down their crutches and begin to dance—Brieux was inspired by a visit to Lourdes—and Satni is moved to tell them the truth, the crowd massacres him in a frenzy.

François Mauriac once remarked that Brieux was commonly referred to as a "chrétien sans la Foi,"[32] a faithless Christian. One is tempted to call Shaw a "païen croyant," a pagan believer. Yet Brieux's faith is grounded in a reliance on faith alone; what counts is social equilibrium, maintained even at the cost of illusory gods. Shaw's faith is geared not to dreaming but to doing and becoming. Brieux's version of Shaw's Life Force is universal harmony. "En un sens," he writes, "le dieu de chaque homme sera son prochain. C'est là la religion de l'avenir" [In one sense, each man's god will be his neighbor. That is the religion of the future].[33] The difference is that for Brieux, one's personal god is "thy neighbor"; for Shaw, it is oneself.

One could complement the above parallels with others. Martin Ellehauge believed that *La Française* (1907) and *Fanny's First Play* (1910–11) "both contain a controversial portrayal of French national characteristics from mainly the same point of view."[34] Maurice Valency drew attention to similarities between *Blanchette* (1892) and *Pygmalion* (1912). Blanchette is highly educated but as the daughter of a village innkeeper is unable to secure the academic position for which she is qualified. According to Valency, both plays touch upon the problem of "finding a place in the social structure for exceptional individuals of lower-class origin emancipated by the widening trends of popular instruction, and educated beyond the capacity of society to absorb their services."[35] In any case, since Brieux and Shaw were attracted to the same issues and took similar stances on the controversial topics of their day, these and other similarities are not surprising.

*   *   *

Four years after his long preface, Shaw wrote a second defense of Brieux, "The Play and Its Author," a two-thousand-word essay on *La Femme seule* (1912), translated by Charlotte as *Woman on Her Own* and produced by the Actresses Franchise League at the Coronet Theatre, London, from 8 to 13 December 1913. Shaw's essay was the souvenir program for the last performance. Bennett thought Brieux "deficient in a feeling for beauty," and Shaw agreed: "No playwright was ever less of a confectioner and beautymonger," he wrote, and like this one, other comments apply to Shaw himself: "Brieux is great, as all great writers are great, in virtue of his judgment of the absolute weight and relative importance of things, and of his concern for the welfare of the world and the enhancement of life." "According to his custom, he shews you powerfully and accurately where you are, and leaves it for you to consider whether you like it, and, if not, how you are going to get out of it."[36]

Shaw maintained that in *La Femme seule,* Brieux had dealt with the topic of prostitution "much more disturbingly" than he had in *Mrs Warren's Profession,* because "whereas I was content to shew how society brings about and supports prostitution by paying poor girls better and treating them better as prostitutes than in the sweated trades which are the sole alternative available to them, Brieux shews how educated, refined and highspirited women are not allowed even this alternative, because their attempts to support themselves bring them into competition with men in the labor market, and the men thereupon deliberately drive them out of the market and force them into marriage or prostitution without any alternative at all." Shaw concluded that "employers will not employ a woman as long as they can find a man, unless the woman offers to take less than the man or to give more. The men, in forbidding her to do this, are therefore forbidding her to work at all . . . the women are driven back to domesticity: to the occupation of wife and mother and housekeeper and nursemaid. Now as there are more women in the country than men, the supply of wives exceeds the demand; and the superfluous women must go to the streets or to the workhouse." *La Femme seule* does not spare the male trade unionist. "Brieux shews you the working man as selfish, foulmouthed, illbehaved and violent, objecting far more to the woman's capacity, orderliness, and industry, than to her weaknesses; jealous of her attempts to do without him; and afraid of being dominated by her in industry, where he cannot resort to his fists, as he often does in his home."[37]

* * *

After reading *Suzette,* Bennett recorded in his diary on 31 October 1909: "Very workmanlike and good first act. The other two acts no good at all. It is simply astounding that a man so imperfectly endowed as Brieux can make such a deuce of a reputation among intelligent people."[38] Literary historian René Lalou wrote in 1923 that Brieux's plays consisted of "absence de nuances psychologiques, constructions mécaniques, émotion facile, abus des tirades de conférencier, prosaïsme de l'inspiration et du style" [absence of psychological nuances, mechanical constructions, facile emotion, overuse of lecture-like tirades, mundaneness of inspiration and style].[39] According to drama critic Jacques Copeau, Brieux was merely "un philosophe primaire, un moraliste sans portée" [a simplistic philosopher, an inconsequential moralist].[40] Nevertheless, *Les Avariés* went on tour in the United States, was novelized by Upton Sinclair in 1912, and in Europe was "taken up as a moral tract, far out-distancing the effect of Ibsen's vastly superior *Ghosts*."[41]

All this would have astonished Bennett, but he has been proven right in the long run. "Nothing can keep Brieux's plays alive," he wrote in 1910; "they are bound to go precisely where the plays of Dumas *fils* have gone, because they are false to life."[42] Even Shaw allowed himself the occasional (but private) irritation with his French idol. When Siegfried Trebitsch proposed to publish *The Doctor's Dilemma* (in German) without the last act, Shaw wrote to him on 18 April 1908 that it was "the maddest" of all suggestions: "Am I Brieux, to cut out a vital limb of my play because a few newspaper men complain of it?"[43] The allusion was topical: four days earlier, Brieux had defended his rewriting of the third act of his latest play, *Simone,* to which a dress-rehearsal audience (of invited critics, most likely) had objected.[44]

But this is a rare critique in Shaw's unflagging promotion of the Frenchman's "deuce of a reputation." When the two met on 16 June 1921 to address the Institut Français in Paris, an invited guest, John W. Klein, thought Brieux's remarks platitudinous. After listening to him read at length from *La Française,* Klein wondered how Shaw could follow such a "puerile piece of banal patriotic propaganda" with "a paean of praise" exalting Brieux above all modern dramatists.[45] Klein missed the point; Brieux was Shaw's continental ally—his only French one, really, aside from Hamon—and shared his socialist ideas, which was enough for Shaw. "The truth is that what determines a writer's greatness," he had written to Hamon, "is . . . solely his power of perceiving the relative importance of things." Like Zola, Marx, Proudhon, and Hamon himself, Shaw concluded, "Brieux knows what is important and what is not."[46] This is why for all his detractors, Brieux remained, in Shaw's words, "a ruthless revealer of hidden truth and a mighty destroyer of idols,"[47] which is an apt description of Shaw himself.

III

Shaw Traduit et Critiqué

6

Shaw Frenchified
Augustin and Henriette Hamon Rewrite Shaw

Beguiling the Anarchist: A Reluctant Translator

In the mid-1890s, while Shaw was writing on Fabianism, Wagner, Ibsen, and turning out plays as well as music and art criticism, in France a social psychologist named Augustin Frédéric Adolphe Hamon (1862–1945) was busy illustrating the socially determined nature of human behavior. Author of a few works on general topics—*Étude sur les eaux potables et le plomb* (1884), *Survivances animiques et polythéiques en Bretagne* (1891), *La France sociale et politique* (1891)—Hamon began drawing upon the philosophies of anarchist, Communist, and Socialist movements, publishing his findings in *La Psychologie du militaire professionel (étude de psychologie sociale)* (1894, and an 1895 edition "augmentée d'une défense"); *La Psychologie de l'anarchiste-socialiste* (1895); *Déterminisme et responsabilité* (1898, translated in 1899 as *The Universal Illusion of Free Will and Criminal Responsability*), and *Une Enquête sur la guerre et le militarisme* (1899).

In 1893, Hamon had begun a series of "Studies in Social Psychology" whose first volume, *La Psychologie du militaire professionnel,* outlined his antimilitarism. Using published accounts of military antisocial behavior, he demonstrated how a profession—in this case life in the army—could socialize an individual to behave criminally or to abuse power. Some editors considered Hamon's research less than objective and scientific, while others dismissed the book as antimilitary polemics. But after being turned down by half a dozen publishers, it was eventually published and became a scandalous best-seller.[1]

It was at about this time that Shaw became interested in Hamon's ideas, over a decade before the eccentric Breton was to become Shaw's official—and at first very reluctant—French translator. Hamon approached Shaw by sending him in July 1893 his essay "La France sociale et politique." Shaw replied briefly that he would study the work and had been "vivement interessé au premier coup d'oeil" [keenly interested at first glance].[2] Encouraged, Hamon sent Shaw his *Psychologie du militaire professionnel* in early November, and on the twenty-sixth, Shaw recorded in his diary that he had spent the evening "beginning a new play—a romantic one."[3] This was to become his own antimilitaristic statement, *Arms and the Man,* which premiered on 21 April 1894. Although Archibald Henderson maintains that there is "no reason to believe that Shaw was under any indebtedness to this book,"[4] Hamon's treatise may have provided the impetus (perhaps the theme) for Shaw's play. Certainly it would have been difficult for Shaw to write on antimilitarism without Hamon's tract in mind.

Shaw's first meeting with Hamon was the indirect result of a French national calamity. While Hamon was writing his *Psychologie de l'anarchiste-socialiste* (1895), president Sadi Carnot was assassinated on 24 June 1894 by anarchist Santo Caserio. The timing could not have been worse; Hamon's activities and writings on behalf of anarchist causes had recently brought him under police surveillance,[5] and when laws were passed after Carnot's murder outlawing anarchist propaganda, Hamon was forced to flee to London. There he finished his book and, at a Fabian congress in November 1894, meet the man who, ten years hence, would change the course of his professional life forever.[6]

When Hamon returned to France the following year and his work was rejected by mainstream social science editors and publishers, he began his own journal, *L'Humanité nouvelle,* an eclectic social science, political, and literary periodical that published avant-garde pieces by controversial figures such as Leo Tolstoy, Edward Carpenter, Havelock Ellis, and Peter Kropotkin. When Hamon asked Shaw to contribute an article, Shaw replied that he had no time to write one and suggested instead a translation of "The Illusions of Socialism," "pour enrager vos abonnés socialistes" [to outrage your socialist subscribers]. Excerpts from the essay had been published in 1896 in the Viennese paper *Die Zeit,* but as Shaw specified, "pour éblouir l'Europe il faut une traduction Française toute complète" [to dazzle Europe a complete French translation is necessary].[7] It appeared in *L'Humanité nouvelle* in August 1900 in a translation by Henriette-Marie-Hortense Rynenbroeck, a Belgian who married Hamon in 1901. This was

Shaw's second appearance in French journals. The previous year, "The Transition to Social Democracy"—first published in *Our Corner* in 1888—had appeared as "Le Chemin à parcourir" in two issues of *La Revue socialiste* in a translation by Jules Magny, a French journalist living in London who had joined the Fabians in 1890 and was writing a series of articles about them.[8]

L' Humanité nouvelle proved to be an unstable venture. In early 1901, when Hamon refused to censor some antimilitaristic and antigovernment articles (as well as some erotic poetry), his publishers closed down the operation. Eighteen months later, thanks in part to Shaw's continued financial support, *L'Humanité nouvelle* resumed publication, only to fold for good with the December 1903 issue. Fortunately for Hamon, who was by no means self-sufficient, Shaw forgave him all his debts on the grounds that the money had "all gone into the pockets of the lawyer," Shaw wrote in January 1904. It was obvious that Hamon would never "make a living as a social psychologist, writer or journal editor holding politically marginalized anarchist beliefs."[9] After seven years of devotion to anarchist causes, Augustin Hamon had no career and no income.

* * *

Then the unexpected occurred: Shaw proposed to the financially desperate anarchist that he and his wife translate all of Shaw's works into French. "Few odder things have ever happened in the history of the theatre," wrote Henderson, "than Shaw's pouncing on Hamon, who was no more concerned with the theatre than with polar exploration, and much less interested in it, and forcing him to take up the rôle of a French Bernard Shaw."[10] The idea came to Shaw early in 1904, when Hamon sent him a young Frenchman, Ali Ben Muraour, then studying in London, hoping that Shaw would allow him to translate *Man and Superman*. Shaw turned him away. He "is far too young for a piece of work that would tax the capacity of Sardou,"[11] he wrote to Hamon, suggesting instead that Hamon and his wife begin translating his plays.

The stupefied Hamon immediately refused, protesting vehemently that he knew nothing of drama, was not a man of the theater, had written only scientific studies in hygiene, sociology, and psychology, and did not possess an adequate mastery of English.[12] This last statement was no exaggeration; his friend Robert de Smet—the Belgian poet, critic, and translator—once remarked that Hamon "ignorait la langue anglaise au point de ne pouvoir demander son chemin dans les rues" [was ignorant of the English language to the point of being unable to ask his way in the streets].[13]

In addition to these linguistic deterrents, Hamon was regarded with suspicion by literary circles because of his anarchist tendencies. He claimed, somewhat boastfully, that he was "trop un iconoclaste, un démolisseur" [too much of an iconoclast, a wrecker].[14] His new role as the translator of comedies by one of the most controversial playwrights in England could not endear him to theater critics in France. Of course all of these ironies appealed to Shaw, who had found in Hamon all the requisite Shavian trademarks: he was a socialist, a "naturalist" in his approach to human behavior, and an iconoclast. "That Hamon was . . . a walking revolutionary with exemplary collectivist principles," writes Michael Holroyd, "obviously pleased him."[15]

But if, from a literary standpoint, Shaw had chosen the wrong man, Hamon took his new vocation very seriously. "Le traducteur devient interprète de l'auteur," he wrote to Shaw in November 1905, "altérant en somme le texte pour conserver l'esprit. C'est une vraie collaboration. . . . Ce serait vraiment ridicule que nous ne puissions pas vous RENDRE en Français et vous faire COMPRENDRE au public" [The translator becomes the author's interpreter, essentially altering the text to retain the spirit. It is a true collaboration . . . It would be truly ridiculous if we could not CONVEY you in French and make you UNDERSTOOD by the public].[16] It is ironic that Hamon unwittingly hits upon what was to be the major complaint of reviewers and critics for years to come: Shaw's text had been so altered that his wit was unrecognizable.

Yet with such determination and noble intentions—and a self-confidence that Shaw may have identified with—there seemed no reason not to entrust Hamon with full control of his works. "You must write my plays as I would have written them had I been a Frenchman. The idea of asking you to undertake the work came to me from reading an account of a Socialist Congress by you. You used dialogue with some dramatic instinct; and I have no doubt you will, after some practice, create a style which shall be both Shavian and French, both English and Hamonique. But do not be too much afraid of neologisms & turns of expression borrowed from English. Languages enrich each other in that way. Classicism, pedantry, is the besetting sin of the Frenchman. Do not hesitate to épater les académiques."[17]

Early in their partnership, Shaw was giving Hamon the freedom to transpose his plays not only into a new idiom but into a new "Hamonique" ideology. He had taken exactly this stance a few years earlier with Trebitsch: "As a work of art, your translations seem to me better than the originals in several ways, and to have a certain charm of style and character that cannot be purchased for money or contrived by corrections & the like."[18]

In 1922, when Shaw had turned a play by Trebitsch into *Jitta's Atonement* and Hamon was trying to adapt *Pygmalion* for a French audience, Shaw advised him to be flexible: "A literal translation would not have told Trebitsch's story or presented his characters to an English audience. I have told the story and presented the characters; but there is hardly a speech in my version which corresponds word for word with the original text. If I could write French as I write English I would make a version of Pygmalion that would astonish you." The following month, he wrote to Hamon that if he were asked to find a French equivalent for Higgins—a name with "a certain comic flavour about it"—"I should give Hamon as pretty near to it; and I am not at all sure that the touch of blague [practical joke] in using your own name would do any harm." Unable to resist his 'inclusion' into a Shaw play, Hamon went along; Henry Higgins became Henry [*sic*] Hamon.[19]

But if even Shaw's help did not save the translations from almost unanimous condemnation, he always maintained that his translators were up to the job. He explained to Hamon that Henriette's "intimate knowledge of English" and Hamon's understanding of "the modern social organism" and of "human nature" qualified the couple to tackle his plays.[20] These credentials were not enough for the critics, and Shaw constantly justified his apparently aberrant choice, even though he had orchestrated the collaboration from the outset. As he told Henry Arthur Jones in 1908 about all his translators: "Sometimes the men came of their own accord as devoted disciples. Sometimes I picked a man who had never dreamt of the job and hypnotised and subsidised him into it,"[21] which was the case with Hamon.

Shaw could have added that he had turned away a number of disciples before and after young Muraour. Comte Auguste Gilbert de Voisins, son of famed ballerina Maria Taglione, was the first to approach Shaw for translation rights, according to Dan H. Laurence. On 6 October 1898, he wrote from Paris to remind Shaw that they had met in England that summer and to say that he had translated the first act of *Arms and the Man*. Since the *Revue Blanche* was interested in a complete translation, he asked Shaw for permission to finish his own, promising to try and convey in French as much of Shaw's humour as possible. Shaw declined to authorize the project.[22] When one Rémy Salvator wrote from Marseille in early

1902, wishing to translate *Widowers' Houses* and have it produced at the Théâtre Antoine or the Théâtre Gémier, Shaw replied that he could only deal with a manager or publisher.[23] In February 1903, when Georges Saint-Clair wrote to ask about adapting *Arms and the Man* for the Théâtre de la Bodinière in Paris, with sole rights for the French translation and adaptation, Shaw replied that he would make no arrangements before knowing the results of the German and Austrian performances.[24]

In 1905, when Hamon encouraged Stéphane Epstein-Etienne, whose translations of Arthur Schnitzler and Hugo von Hofmannsthal had been played in Paris, to translate *Arms and the Man,* Shaw wrote to Hamon that he would have nothing to do with it: "I want no introductions to Paris theatres and will accept none."[25] A week later, when he learned that the interloper had already translated the play, Shaw wrote to him at length (and tersely) about the perils of illegal copyright violations: "The fact that M. Hamon did not expressly warn you that the play belonged to the author and not to himself will not be held to justify you in assuming the contrary without evidence." He specified that "an authorization to translate is not transferable or assignable. The translator's personality, his professional skill, his reputation are essential parts of the arrangement."[26]

Shaw may have been wise to remain steadfast in reserving his work for the Hamons. When one misguided soul, Henri de Gérardel, transformed some of *Caesar and Cleopatra* into rhyming alexandrines, the result was an unintentionally comical solemnity. For example, Caesar's address to the Sphinx—"Salut, Divinité, qui représente un âge. / C'est bien toi, je te vois; je connais ton visage"—would resonate as: "O hail Divinity, who represents an age. / It is you that I see; and I know your visage."[27]

Fortunately or not, Shaw got the personality (stubborn), skill (polemical), and reputation (anarchistic) he wanted, confessing to Arnold Bennett in 1910 that Hamon "had about as much notion of becoming a translator of plays as of becoming a banker or a bishop; . . . I beguiled him into it."[28] Thus Augustin and Henriette Hamon were duly appointed Shaw's authorized French translators, a position all three defended tenaciously. Augustin, the unsuccessful social scientist and political essayist, in his forties and at a professional and financial crossroads, left Paris with his wife and three young children to begin his new career. His self-imposed exile took him to his native Brittany, where, thanks to Shaw's loan of thirty thousand francs, he and his wife moved into a house at Port Blanc en Penvénan (Côte-du-Nord) called Ty an Diaoul, "The House of the Devil." From their secluded outpost, over the next forty years, the Hamons translated virtually all of Shaw's works and penned countless lectures, articles, reviews, essays, and letters promoting and defending their benefactor. Given the magnitude of their task and its often hellish consequences, the house that Shaw financed was aptly named.

The Halt Leading the Blind: A Perilous Collaboration

Shaw's plays were finally published and acted in the one European country that had waited the longest to recognize them. Yet this was exactly the problem: the French still did not recognize them. Audiences were introduced to works that had been until then unknown or misunderstood, but the French versions were seldom faithful to the original. "Translating a drama," writes Ortrun Zuber, "means facing most of the difficulties encountered in translating any other literary genre, considering semantic as well as cultural, historical and socio-political aspects, and also the form-content dichotomy. Not only the meaning of a word or sentence must be translated, but also the connotations, rhythm, tone and rhetorical level, imagery and symbols of association."[29] This is a challenge even for professionals; it was a nightmare for amateurs like the Hamons.

Shaw's choice seemed absurd to everyone. Urged by Jacques Rouché, proprietor of the Théâtre des Arts (where *Mrs Warren's Profession* was about to be produced), and by artist Hermann-Paul, who designed the scenery and costumes, Fabian journalist Robert Dell wrote to Shaw from Paris on 11 January 1912 to inform him that all three of them believed Hamon's translations were "extremely bad and calculated seriously to injure you in France." Hermann-Paul in particular objected to the Montmartre argot spoken by Mrs. Warren, which made her "an obvious *propriétaire de bordel* whose profession would be easily visible to everyone at the first glance." Rouché "begs me to tell you that both [André] Antoine, the director of the Odéon, and Max Maurey, the director of the Grand-Guignol, have declared that they will never present a play of yours translated by M. Hamon.... It is a pity that you did not get hold of a man like [Henry-D.] Davray, whose translations of Wells are so good that they read like books written originally in French, and are correct into the bargain."[30] Ironically, the following year, when novelist and critic Remy de Gourmont wrote to Hamon to thank him for *Pièces déplaisantes* (which included *Mrs Warren's Profession*), he praised the translation! The plays, Gourmont thought, "n'ont pas l'air d'être traduites, d'ailleurs, tant le style français parait naturel" [do not seem to be translated, actually, so natural seems

the French style].[31] In 1950, Shaw recalled Gourmont's accolades but ascribed them to a liking for what he termed Hamon's "ultra-revolutionary politics."[32]

Gourmont is an unusual exception to the widespread condemnation of the Hamon versions. Like the Pitoëff production of *Sainte Jeanne,* they did not render Shaw's meaning or wit. Hamon was too literal: "Bring me a couple of chairs" became "Apportez-moi une couple de chaises." *You Never Can Tell* was *On ne peut jamais dire* [One can never say], despite happier potential choices such as *On ne sait jamais* [One never knows] and *On ne peut jamais prévoir* [One can never foresee]. Larousse in hand, Shaw tried to polish Hamon's efforts, telling him that the expression "useless, dangerous, and ought to be abolished" was impossible to render in French because it was "the wording of the resolution by which the Long Parliament abolished the House of Lords."[33] He also stressed that exact repetition was often essential, as in *The Man of Destiny:* the Lieutenant says he gave the letters to the thief "to shew his confidence in him," a phrase used later on when the Strange Lady—the thief in question—tells Napoleon, "You see I shew my confidence in you." Shaw warned Hamon that unless he used "the same words in both places the play will fail."[34]

Hamon was bound to fail, considering the obstacles posed by Shaw's mastery of English. He used slang, aphorisms, idioms, allusions; his characters spoke satirically or ironically, using words with multiple meanings; key words and phrases were repeated in different places verbatim or with a significant variation. After a career as a critic of art, music, and drama, Shaw's style was supple, voluble, lucid—and his vocabulary was enormous. It was easy for the Hamons to misunderstand and misrepresent his ideas and intentions: "stone dead" became "morte comme une pierre"; "pulled the house about our ears" became "tiré les oreilles à toute la maison" instead of "nous a entraîné dans la ruine" [dragged us into ruin]; "he sits down in dudgeon" became "il s'assied dans le donjon" [dungeon!]; "chuckleheaded" went untranslated.[35]

If the shortcomings of Shaw's translated works were ascribed almost exclusively to the Hamons, the collaboration itself contributed to mangling the plays. Early in their partnership, in January 1904, Hamon had proposed the following methodology: "*Première* traduction étant faite par nous deux, je vous l'envoie—pièce par pièce—. Vous revisez, corrigez, annotez et me renvoyer. Alors nous récrivons la pièce en tenant compte de vos corrections etc. Nous vous expédions cette deuxième traduction. Vous rerevisez. Vous réexpédiez. Nous re-récrivons la pièce et faisons imprimer" [*First* translation having been made by both of us, I send it to

you—piece by piece—. You revise, correct, annotate and send it back to me. Then we rewrite the play taking into account your corrections etc. We dispatch this second translation to you. You re-revise. You re-dispatch. We re-rewrite the play and have it printed.]³⁶

By July 1906, the Hamons had further refined (and complicated) the process: "Ma femme traduit toute la pièce. Je la lis seul d'un trait, toute entière. Je la reprends seul, corrigeant sur la copie à la main.- Repos.- Copie à la machine en corrigeant. La copie est alors lue et corrigée par ma femme et vous est envoyée ensuite. Votre copie est retournée: lecture par ma femme et moi.- Correction sur le Mss par moi.- Repos.- Copie à la machine qui est ensuite lue et corrigée par ma femme et moi. . . . C'est le seul procédé qui permet d'avoir une bonne traduction, à la fois précise, exacte, *vivante* [My wife translates the whole play. I read the entire play at a sitting. I examine it alone, correcting by hand on the copy.- Rest.- Typing while correcting. The copy is then read and corrected by my wife and is then sent to you. Your copy is returned: reading by my wife and me.- Correction on the MS by me.- Rest.- Typing followed by corrections by my wife and me. . . . It is the only procedure that allows for a good translation, at once precise, accurate, and *alive*].³⁷

Yet the French plays that emerged from these multiple revisions were less precise and accurate than ambiguous and confusing. And if Augustin was chief Shavian propagandist, he was merely reviser and typist of the plays, while Henriette was chief translator. Given her apparent fluency in English, this makes the flawed translations something of a mystery. Furthermore, the convoluted method just described probably muddled Shaw's work. Even if all three managed to keep to the intended scenario, Shaw's literary, political, and business affairs made vigilance sporadic. And although his French was more than adequate, he was not fluent and could not detect many of the Hamons' lacunae, even with a dictionary. In the end, his revision of the "stodgy" and "naïve" translations, writes Dan H. Laurence, was "a classic example of the halt leading the blind."³⁸ As Mina Moore observed, "L'esprit qui est le souffle créateur du texte anglais ne passe pas dans le texte français: il y tombe à plat" [The wit that is the English text's creative breath does not pass into the French text: it falls flat].³⁹

No wonder the translations (and Hamon) were perpetually criticized as impediments to Shaw's acceptance in France. And when a better translator intervened, it created tension between Hamon and everyone else, and Shaw had to act as peacemaker. In 1912, for instance, the stage director of the Théâtre des Arts, Vicomte Robert d'Humières (1868–1915)—a dramatist himself and translator of Conrad and Kipling—published an essay in which he concluded that Shaw was attached to his translator "comme le pendu à sa corde. Et c'est bien un suicide—au seuil de notre admiration" [like a hanged man to his rope. And it is indeed a suicide—on the brink of our admiration].[40] The remark stemmed from his frustrations with Hamon, whose work he had tried to improve a few years earlier. On 1 May 1908, Shaw had written to Hamon that d'Humières had sent him a list of twenty-two corrections to Hamon's version of *Candida* (which ran from 7 May at the Théâtre des Arts for only twenty-eight performances). To placate Hamon—always fiercely protective of his Shavian mission—Shaw had called the corrections "decided improvements" and urged him to cooperate with d'Humières:

> He has got one enormous advantage over you. In making the translation, you were working from an English original; and you produced a version under the direct influence of that original. The Marquis, unobsessed by this original, starts perfectly fresh on your French version and instantly sees how it can be made more French and more clear. You have occasionally made an obscure translation because, as the meaning was not quite clearly into your head by the original, you could not become conscious of the obscurity in the translation. The Marquis, starting completely in the dark, detects your obscurity at once and clears it up. The truth is, we are lucky to have so intelligent a critic; and you had better encourage him to tear the whole thing to pieces as much as he likes. . . . The Marquis is very much afraid of you, because he thinks you are very touchy, and I have told him that you are the responsible party and must have your own way—also that you are as obstinate as twenty thousand devils. But in the theatre it is no use being touchy.[41]

Hamon was indeed very touchy and must have been annoyed by this intrusion because two weeks later, Shaw again took up the sensitive topic of d'Humières, this time discussing what he called Hamon's "moral case":

> You can be conscientious as you like about your own conduct; but you must allow D'Humières to act according to his own conscience, and not according to yours. His conscience is just as valid as yours. And he is quite entitled to despise you if he feels inclined that way. Why shouldnt he? To begin with, he is a Vicomte with very good manners; and you are a bourgeois with no manners at all—nothing but moral categories. Free your soul from moral categories and get

rid of all this fictitious anger and resentment (mere instinctive anger and resentment, *without moral pretensions,* is quite a different thing and may be forgiven to anybody), and your Vicomte will respect you at once. But as long as you keep trumping up a moral case against him, and making it an excuse for malice towards him, you will be in a state of hopeless inferiority.... When the theatrical world is no longer strange to you, and you have learnt the practical applications of your instinct for the theatre, you will look back with a blush at the barbarity of your recent proceedings.[42]

Eighteen years later—and no doubt having read of Shaw's admirable "suicide" in *Le Mercure de France*—Hamon mentioned d'Humières in the 1926 preface to the translation of *Le Disciple du diable*. He noted that d'Humières had been so dissatisfied with "le comique brutal et accentué" [blunt and pronounced] of Burgess that he had translated Burgess's lines—despite Hamon's objections—into "un ton comique accentué. L'effet fut déplorable."[43] Mentioning *Candida*'s short run, Hamon implied that d'Humières's translation was largely responsible for the play's poor reception.

The fact is that Hamon took his task as Shaw's official translator as seriously as he took Shaw's plays—even the comedies. Shaw had to admit to Bennett that Hamon "has no sense of humor," relating how poor Augustin had been baffled, at the 7 February 1907 premiere of *Candida* at the Théâtre du Parc in Brussels, when he was congratulated on the laughter his translation had produced: "It was such a revelation to him that he straightway plunged into the opposite extreme and now regards me as an author of harlequinades."[44] Hamon had been amazed by the audience's reaction. "Je ne croyais pas," he told de Smet, "que cette pièce fût drôle. Elle traite de questions si sérieuses" [I did not think this play was funny. It deals with such serious questions]. He was also horrified at the idea that he had betrayed his mentor. "Mon Dieu, on rit!" he exclaimed. "Tout est perdu! Ma maladresse a ruiné Shaw" [My God, they're laughing! All is lost! My clumsiness has ruined Shaw]. He had been so absorbed by the sociology and psychology of the play, "que je n'en avais perçu l'intense comique!" [that I had not discerned its intense comic aspect!].[45]

The Brussels *Candida* was thus an important psychological turning point for Hamon, and years later he continued to relate the premiere's impact: "Et ces rires m'étonnèrent, me choquèrent au point que, mezzo voce, je criais leur bêtise à ces spectateurs qui voyaient à rire là où étaient des idées si justes, si grandes, si profondes et parfois si amères. Les spectateurs avaient raison et le sot c'était moi, qui n'avais pas vu le comique intense et puissant de Candida. . . . L'accueil que la critique fit à notre traduction me convainquit que la langue dramatique n'était ni en dehors, ni au-dessus de nos moyens" [And this laughter astonished me, shocked me to the extent that under my breath I cursed these spectators who saw fit to laugh where the ideas were so just, so great, so profound and at times so bitter. But the spectators were right whereas I, who had not recognized the intense and powerful comedy of Candida, was the fool. . . . The critical reception to our translation convinced me that the language of the theater was neither beyond nor above our abilities].[46] In light of this last comment, one understands Hamon's vehement resentment of d'Humières's improvements the following year.

It should be emphasized that credit for Shaw's first French-language production goes to Hamon, who had lectured on criminology in 1897 at the Université Nouvelle de Bruxelles (founded in 1894 by dissident professors of the orthodox Université Libre). Hamon also knew the manager of the Théâtre du Parc, Victor Reding, a broad-minded man who took an interest in new foreign plays, and had begun negotiating with him in the summer of 1906 for a performance of Candida. Following the 7 February 1907 premiere, Hamon lectured on Shaw at the Université Nouvelle on 9 and 14 February, and at the Foyer Intellectuel de Bruxelles on 21 February. His 14 February talk, "Shaw et son théâtre," appeared in September in *La Revue socialiste* and was Hamon's first published commentary on Shaw.

As Oskar Wellens illustrates in his account of the Brussels *Candida*, Hamon's lecture drew upon Shaw's comments in letters to him, for instance, about Candida staying with her husband out of love, not duty. (Three years earlier, Maurice Muret had asserted precisely the opposite in "De Nora à Candida.") Wellens notes that Hamon's socialist bias raised the issue of whether Shaw was primarily a dramatist or an ideologist, a question perennially debated among French critics.[47] Aside from *Le Vingtième Siècle* (which dismissed the lecture as subversive propaganda and the play as incoherent) and *Le Matin de Bruxelles* (which denounced the play as devoid of action), critical responses to the Brussels *Candida* were very favorable; even the translation was praised as "excellent" and "elegant."[48]

* * *

The Brussels accolades for the translation were unusual. "My wife translates the whole play," Hamon had told Shaw, and he emphasized in print that "la langue anglaise est quasi aussi familière que sa langue maternelle" [the English language is almost as familiar to her as her native tongue].⁴⁹ Yet despite her crucial, even dominant, role, Henriette remained a silent partner, while poor Augustin was bombarded by Shaw's queries and corrections in letters that reveal a concern for absolute accuracy, down to the most minute details.

Their exchanges during the translation of *Mrs Warren's Profession*, for example, show how even expletives and speech formalities were problematic for Hamon. Shaw wrote on 25 March 1905 to explain that "Oh my eye!" cannot be rendered as "O mon oeil!" nor can "Oh Lord" be translated as "O Seigneur." It was a question of culture: "In France everybody says 'Mon Dieu' on the most trifling provocation: in England a man says 'My God' only when his wife is struck by lightning or his house swallowed up by an earthquake." But Hamon stuck to his French guns and on 6 April replied that "O mon oeil" was a widely used expression, and that some people say "Ah Seigneur! just as others say Sapristi! Nom d'un chien! Dieu! Nom de Dieu! etc." Ten months later, on 18 January 1906, Shaw wrote that he found Hamon's dialogue in *Mrs Warren* "effective & *speakable*" (Shaw's emphasis), yet he implored Hamon to form his own style: "Don't try to make it like anybody else's dialogue, or give it literary elegance. Get it right according to your own feeling & stick to that, no matter what anyone says."

Four days later, Shaw sent Hamon act 3 and told him that the change from the formal *vous* to the informal *tu* was of great dramatic value in French. "It seems to me that Frank would 'tutoyer' his father all through, whilst his father would call him 'Monsieur' & 'vous' whenever he tries to be pompous. And I should think Frank would 'tutoyer' Vivie also whenever they are alone together, though Vivie would call him 'vous' whenever she wishes to snub him. Would not Mrs Warren occasionally 'tutoyer' Crofts or Praed?"⁵⁰ Hamon followed Shaw's advice (for once), but in his review of the play, Jean Schlumberger pointed out that Hamon had made Shaw's characters unrealistically pass from the formal *vous* to the informal *tu*: "Je sais que Frank est déluré et que la grosse dame est facile, mais jamais on ne me fera croire qu'il ose la tutoyer après une heure de promenade" [I know that Frank is sharp and that the big woman is easy, but nobody will convince me that he dares 'tutoyer' her after an hour's stroll]. Frank's *tutoiement* falsifies his relations with Vivie, Schlumberger emphasized, "de la façon la plus choquante" [in the most offensive manner].⁵¹

Year after year, Shaw riddled Hamon's typescripts with his near-microscopic writing, crossing out words and replacing them by Shavian *mots justes*, explaining—often in minilectures—the meaning of idioms, puns, proverbs, slang, legal terms, colloquialisms, quotations, allusions, English customs, and biblical passages, the latter always problematic because they were imbedded in Shaw's dialogue and went unrecognized by Hamon. Shaw would give one or more alternatives for Hamon to choose from, or cross out and dismiss something as "untranslatable." For instance, "grim" and "grimly" became, from play to play, "sévère," "d'un ton sombre," "avec une expression de férocité," "aigrement." None of these would do. In *Too True to be Good,* Hamon was baffled by "tell me another," "put a sock into it," and "off the deep end"; and while Meek "dismounts and races his [motorcycle] engine with a hideous clatter," Hamon's Meek "court ensuite à toutes jambes avec elle" [runs beside his motorcycle as fast as his legs can carry him].[52] Yet Shaw urged Hamon to use slang when appropriate, imploring him often to avoid what he called "academic" or "literary" language, choosing to omit a word rather than see it transmuted into a long circumlocution, as when "handicapped" was rendered "ce qui le met dans un certain état d'infériorité" [that which puts him in a certain state of inferiority].[53] The Hamons had two besetting sins: literalness and prolixity.

The care taken by Shaw in revising the Hamons' work is astonishing. Take, for instance, one of the "Maxims for Revolutionists" in *Man and Superman:* "Make your cross your crutch; but when you see another man do it, beware of him," which Hamon had rendered as "De votre croix, faites votre béquille; mais si vous voyez un autre homme faire de même, gardez-vous de lui," but had put a question mark beside it in the margin of the typescript. Shaw explained:

> To make your cross your crutch is an English proverb. It refers to the cross of Christ. Christ "took up his cross": that is, he accepted sorrow & death as his duty and bore it without complaining. In England when a man suffers some misfortune—loss of money, or his wife taking to drink, or anything you like—and he resigns himself to bear it without complaining, he is said "to take up his cross." Now the patient endurance of suffering is supposed to strengthen and ennoble one's character. The sorrow you bear becomes a support to you. This is called "making your cross your crutch." Or if a man loses his eyesight and one of his legs, and makes a good deal of money by begging through the pity his estropiage [crippled state] inspires, he may equally be said to be "making his cross his crutch." My maxim is only a variation of the one on the previous page, "Gardez vous de l'homme qui ne vous rend pas votre coup." These pious people are dangerous.[54]

Shaw's annotations are often fascinating for what they tell us about his own views. Another maxim, "The right to live is abused whenever it is not constantly challenged," was translated oddly as "Le Droit de vivre est violé quand il n'est pas tout à fait mis au rancart" [The Right to live is violated when it is not entirely scrapped]. Substituting *abusé* for *violé*, Shaw explained: "To abuse a right is quite a different thing to violating it. It means to make an excessive and unjust use of it. For instance, the Tsar abuses his power in Russia. The capitalist abuses his power. The priest abuses his power. The man who beats his wife abuses his power. If he forces intercourse on her when she is ill, he abuses his marital rights. The meaning is 'You must allow that every man has a right to live; but he will abuse this right by living at your expense unless you continually demand that he shall justify his right to live — by producing his own subsistence, for example'."[55]

In another vein altogether, here is Shaw illustrating (literally) how sartorial and class differences mirror one another. The expression that baffled Hamon is from "The Revolutionist's Handbook": "'Moleskins & belchers' means the costumes that laborers used to wear in the old days when they dressed differently from the middle classes. A belcher was not a 'foulard' [scarf], but a coarse red cotton handkerchief tied round the neck instead of a collar. Moleskin was like corduroy: a material that no gentleman ever wore. The French equivalent should be used. 'In moleskins & belchers' should be, for French purposes, 'in blouses & caps'. The contrast is between [drawing of "artisan 1848" with "BLUE BLOUSE" written on jacket] and [drawing of "artisan 1909" with arrow pointing from "a chic tweed" to jacket]. 'Draps elegants' [fashionable cloths] is absurd. It should be 'chic tweeds' or whatever French tailors call tweeds."[56] Shaw's two caricatures are clearly of French, not English, artisans.

In *Candida*, when Hamon wrote that Burgess (incrédule) exclaims: "Sacrebleu! . . . C'est une image de 'Igh Church'," Shaw enlightened him:

> This term Haute Eglise — High Church — is difficult to translate. The State Church in England is divided into parties — High Church, Broad Church, and Low Church. The High Churchmen regard the Church as Catholic, but Anglican Catholic instead of Roman Catholic, and use candles, pictures, vestments, incense &c. The Low Churchmen are Protestants, and abhor the Pope. They will not tolerate candles, and consider vestments and incense almost as wicked as confession or prayers to the Virgin or saints. Burgess is Low Church; and when he sees the picture of the Virgin, he suspects Morell of worshipping it. Almost all the Socialist clergymen of the

Established (State) Church are High Churchmen. Broad Churchmen hold the views of Ernest Renan, but remain in the Church because it is respectable. "A high church picture" should therefore be translated "un tableau catholique"—or better still "un tableau papist," since Burgess wishes to denigrer the picture.[57]

Despite Shaw's many (and often better) alternatives, Hamon did not always incorporate his suggestions. In the page proofs of *Le Disciple du diable,* Shaw had crossed out "la cour martiale" and replaced it with the correct expression, "pour passer au conseil de guerre," noting that "Cour martiale is surely not right. A court martial is a military tribunal." But the published version reads "la cour martiale."[58] Often Shaw had his French audience in mind, as in the case of *Sainte Jeanne*. One month before the Paris opening, he changed Warwick's line to Joan (near the end of the play) from "We sincerely regret our little mistake"—correctly rendered by Hamon as "Nous regrettons sincèrement notre petite erreur"—to the stronger "Vous savez combien je regrette cette gaffe deplorable à Rouen." But the obstinate Hamon's published version read "cette gaffe de Rouen."[59]

One interesting example of Shaw's altering his text to suit French readers and spectators occurs at the end of the second act of *La Profession de Madame Warren,* where his additional stage directions during the long interchange between Mrs. Warren and Vivie are clearly intended to soften Mrs. Warren's character and thereby increase empathy for her. After Vivie asks her mother if it is not "part of what you call character in a woman that she should greatly dislike such a way of making money," Shaw adds that Mrs. Warren's answer should be "(en mère indulgente) [like a lenient mother] beaucoup plus lent, plus doux, plus maternelle." When Vivie asks her if such work is lucrative, her mother should answer "(en femme d'affaires)" [like a businesswoman], but between "It's far better than any other employment open to her" and the next sentences, Shaw adds: "(Ici le ton d'affaires se changent en ton de la sensibilité sincere et même un peu solennelle"). This precedes "I always thought that oughtnt to be. It cant be right, Vivie, that there shouldnt be better opportunities for women." Finally, in the middle of Mrs. Warren's forceful diatribe against socially imposed "starvation and slavery"—which in the original is marked "[*indignantly*]"—Shaw precedes "The only way for a woman to provide for herself decently is for her to be good to some man that can afford to be good to her" with a mollifying instruction: "Tendresse maternelle, comme si elle enseigne à sa petite fille la prière" [maternal tenderness, as if she were teaching her little girl a prayer].[60]

*   *   *

Despite Shaw's ongoing problems with Hamon, it is easy to understand the basis of Shaw's allegiance to his mediocre translator in light of his near-worship of the mediocre Eugène Brieux: ideology. The underlying philosophy of Hamon's commitment to anarchism-communism, write Ian Lubek and Erika Apfelbaum, involved an "institution-blame approach" that sought to reform society by expanding "the traditional range of criminal acts to include consideration of 'political and professional crimes'," such as cheating and corruption by businessmen, politicians, and bureaucrats.[61] No wonder Shaw was drawn to Hamon. As he told de Smet in Malvern around 1930, "Monsieur Augustin Hamon *partage toutes mes idées politiques. Il ne saurait donc me trahir*" [Hamon *shares all of my political ideas. Thus he could never betray me*].[62]

Thus the more Hamon was reviled, the more Shaw defended him. When in 1908 a note in *The Athenaeum* signed "C.G." mentioned Hamon's poor translations as an impediment to Shaw's Parisian productions, Shaw replied at length in the 4 April 1908 issue (with a letter dated 26 March) that following the Brussels premiere of *Candida*, "the translation was spoken of in the highest terms," noting that the object of such attacks as C.G.'s was to "humbug" him "into allowing one of the numerous gentlemen who assure me that they have influence with managers, and that they know how to adapt my plays to the requirements of 'the boulevard', to fasten themselves as collaborators on the harvest of fees my plays are expected to sow in France." C.G. replied in the 11 April issue that he had attended Hamon's lecture, "Bernard Shaw; or, the New Molière," as well as the Brussels *Candida*, and after reading the play in French, had concluded: "I once more felt that M. Hamon has an incomplete knowledge of our language."[63]

Two months later, Shaw was not amused to discover that another Frenchman was translating his plays: "The existence of your version is a violation of the rights of my authorized translators," he cautioned one Dr. Ch. Barbaud. "You really might as well write to me to say that you had stolen M Hamon's watch, Mme Hamon's parasol, and my hat."[64] Nothing dissuaded him from defending the Hamons. On 13 April 1924, two weeks before the Paris *Sainte Jeanne*—two decades after initiating the Hamon partnership—Shaw wrote in the *New York Times:* "If a Frenchman says to me that the translations of Hamon are infamous, I can evidently not contradict him.... But when, as generally happens, the gentleman who denounces Hamon shows the most disastrous and complete incomprehension of my works and sometimes undisguised hostility toward them, I begin to ask myself whether Hamon has not made enemies for himself by attempting to be too faithful to me instead of turning my works into Parisian articles, like the others think they could do so adroitly. . . . The better his translation is, the worse it seems."[65] Yet "infamous" the translations remained, and Shaw's protests did not change the reality that his plays had become, despite his emendations, simply too Hamonique.[66]

Shaw as the Irish Molière: A Dubious Apotheosis

Hamonique or not, Shaw's appointed frenchificator continued to translate prefaces and plays, write paeans to Shaw in newspapers and journals, and lecture on his drama in Paris and Brussels. But Shaw had reason to worry about the kind of Shavian image Hamon was presenting to French audiences. Only one month before the Brussels lectures of February 1907, Shaw had warned him about distorting his views: "Life appears a mere chaos of accidents, & your attempt to make an 'Annual Register' of it necessarily as devoid of dramatic interest as a Post Office Directory. . . . If you tell the world that the essential idea in my works is Determinism, I solemnly swear that I will go over to Brussels & murder you."[67] Perhaps he should have. With unimpeachable logic and dogmatic argumentation, Hamon concluded his 1911 lecture on "The Technique of Bernard Shaw's Plays" by solemnly declaring:

> The Life Force determines more or less directly all individual, and, consequently, all collective phenomena, since the collectivity is composed of individuals. Hence, it results that this philosophy of life is determinist. Also, by reason of the philosophy which inspired its construction, the drama of our author is determinist, as we have already noted. We must make the best of events—we can do nothing against them. We cannot withstand destiny; what must be, will be. This is the message in a greater or lesser degree of *Mrs Warren's Profession, Arms and the Man, Man of Destiny, Caesar and Cleopatra, Candida, The Devil's Disciple,* and, above all, *Man and Superman.* Man is not free; he is determined inevitably; and whether he wishes it or not, he submits to the Life Force.[68]

So much for Shaw's cautionary measures. By 1908 the Hamons had translated most of the pleasant and unpleasant plays, which were published in one volume in 1913 as *Pièces plaisantes et déplaisantes.* Hamon and his wife even settled in England and spent "almost three years near

Ayot St. Lawrence during World War I, and saw a great deal of the Shaws."[69] Having successfully done so in Europe, Hamon had planned to finance his English sojourn by lecturing, a scheme that Shaw considered "stark raving lunacy.... The English dont care twopence about Molière; and they don't want to hear you lecture in a foreign language on me when they can hear me lecture in their own language on myself."[70] Disregarding Shaw's advice, in London Hamon gave ten lectures on Shaw titled *La Comédie* at the Institut Français du Royaume-Uni (Marble Arch) from October to December 1914, repeating them at Birkbeck College from 6 May to 8 July 1916.[71] The Shavian gospel was spreading *malgré* Shaw.

* * *

More than all of Hamon's lectures and essays, one work, published the same year as *Pièces plaisantes et déplaisantes,* marks the apex of his Shaviolatry: *Le Molière du XXe siècle: Bernard Shaw.* The book collected the first six of ten lectures on "Le Théâtre de Bernard Shaw" given in February 1909 at the Sorbonne (and again in March at l'Université Nouvelle de Bruxelles) and was translated as *The Twentieth Century Molière: Bernard Shaw* in 1915. This was the second book on Shaw in French—Charles Cestre had published his 1909 University of Bordeaux lectures the previous year as *Bernard Shaw et son oeuvre*—and it provoked widespread irritation within the literary community both in France and in England. "I once scandalized the French bellettrists by remarking that Brieux is the greatest playwright since Molière," boasted Shaw.[72] Now it was Hamon's turn; the French were astounded to discover that one of their own had inflated the already controversial Irishman to Molièresque proportions.

Hamon had already published at least twenty articles on Shaw in French periodicals—some of them lengthy excerpts from his lectures—and was well known to French literati as Shaw's apologist. But as Henderson points out, *Le Molière du XXe siècle* was an "evangelistic" book that was "not taken quite seriously in the world of literature, the drama or the stage."[73] Hamon admitted that he knew nothing about dramaturgy before meeting Shaw, and it is no surprise that his comparisons between Shaw and Molière were "negligible," in Henderson's opinion, "since similarities common to all dramatists were stressed to establish *liaisons* which were really neither distinctive nor significant for the two great artists under discussion."[74] This was reiterated by many French critics, whose comments may have inspired Hamon to add to the English translation of his book a "Synoptic Table of the Resemblances Between

> **RÉPUBLIQUE FRANÇAISE**
> **UNIVERSITÉ DE PARIS – FACULTÉ DES LETTRES**
>
> # COURS LIBRE
> autorisé pour l'année scolaire 1909-1910
>
> # LITTÉRATURE ANGLAISE
>
> Le lundi et le mercredi à 2 heures
> (Amphithéâtre Quinet)
>
> M. Augustin HAMON commentera trois pièces du théâtre de BERNARD SHAW : *On ne peut jamais dire*, – *Le Disciple du Diable*, – *La Seconde Ile de John Bull*, au point de vue de la technique dramatique, des caractères, des mœurs et des idées.
>
> **OUVERTURE DU COURS LE MERCREDI 16 FÉVRIER 1910**
>
> Vu : Le Président du Conseil de l'Université,   Le Doyen de la Faculté des Lettres,
> **L. LIARD.**   **A. CROISET.**
>
> Paris. — Imprimerie CHAIX (Succursale B.), 11, boulevard Saint-Michel. — 350-10.

4. Poster announcing a series of lectures by Augustin Hamon at the Université de Paris, beginning on 16 February 1910, on *You Never Can Tell, The Devil's Disciple*, and *John Bull's Other Island*. By permission of the Hamon Collection, Archival and Special Collections, University of Guelph Library, Guelph, Canada.

the Dramatic Works of Molière and of Bernard Shaw." Yet this too seems ineffectual. Under such headings as situations, plots, incidents, denouement, realism, depiction of characters, comedy, style, family, religion, ethics, and meliorism, Hamon lists many similarities, only to conclude (predictably) that both playwrights wage war upon established institutions, the bourgeoisie, the professions, and hypocrisy.[75]

Mina Moore, to whom Hamon provided information for her *Bernard Shaw et la France,* summarized his book in her study while remaining impartial about his conclusions. Only once did she take exception with him, disagreeing with his idea that one must blame the institution of marriage, and that parental authority is always and everywhere nefarious: "Rien ne porte à croire que Molière, transporté au XXe siècle, eût défendu les remèdes conseillés par Shaw" [Nothing leads one to believe that Molière, transported to the 20th century, would have defended the remedies advised by Shaw]. She concluded that Shaw demands a more intense intellectual effort and does not provoke outright laughter, as does Molière.[76]

Other French critics were not so restrained. A. Barbeau was aghast at Hamon's worshipful attitude — "Que d'épithètes louangeuses! quelle constance dans l'admiration! quel ton dithyrambique!" [What laudatory epithets! what steadfastness in admiration! what a dithyrambic tone!] — and at his poor French: "des négligences, des incorrections, des néologismes inutiles, et aussi des affectations" [carelessness, inaccuracies, useless neologisms, and affectations as well]. Shaw must find it amusing, wrote Léon Blum, to see "ériger en dogmes ses bluffs et ses plaisanteries" [his bluffs and jokes erected into dogma]. The anonymous critic of the *Dundee Advertiser* described Hamon's book as a eulogy expressed in "a painfully affected French, where archaic forms abound and inaccuracies are not rare." When the *New Witness* reviewed the English translation, it found the book's depiction of Shaw "radically false."[77]

Not only were Hamon's tone and style awkward, but the Molière/Shaw parallel was deemed unconvincing or absurd. Ernest Rhys thought Molière's comedy "rich, hearty, constructive and recreative," while Shaw's left one "without any sense of vision of the humane deliverance to follow." The *Pall Mall Gazette* called the book's title a "foolish and facile label." Maurice Boissard remarked that Molière's characters were universal but that Shaw's "sont Anglais, uniquement Anglais, rien qu'Anglais." Jethro Bithell thought they were insensitive: "Il y a du tragique dans la folie de Molière. Dans celle de Shaw il n'y en a point de trace.... Nous aimons le *Misanthrope* de Molière. Quel personnage de Shaw nous inspirerait une telle sympathie?" [There is a tragic element in Molière's madness. There is no trace of it in Shaw's.... We love Molière's *Misanthrope*. Which character in Shaw inspires in us that kind of sympathy?]. André Maurois thought the comparison made no sense: "Le ton de Molière me semble plus fort, plus direct, plus soutenu. Les scènes de Molière sont mieux charpentées que celles de Shaw" [To me, Molière's tone seems stronger, more direct, more sustained. Molière's scenes are better constructed than Shaw's].[78]

Henry Bidou's long review adumbrates arguments against a Molièresque Shaw made by many of his colleagues. First, Molière was no "réformateur des institutions." Second, the vices under fire in *Mrs Warren* and *The Philanderer* "ne sont pas des défauts éternels et permanents de l'humanité; ce sont des vices de classe, des défauts inhérents à l'ordre social où nous vivons" [are not eternal and permanent deficiencies of humanity; they are class vices, faults inherent to the social order in which we live]. Third, Molière depicts "la méchante nature des hommes" [the wicked nature of men] and Shaw "la mauvaise construction de la société" [the evil construction of society]. Fourth, "aucun personnage de Molière ne se corrige" [none of Molière's characters are reformed]—Harpagon is a miser to the end—whereas Shaw imagines a reformed society where the bourgeois would not exploit others, nor women sell themselves. Fifth, Shaw (unlike Molière) remains on stage in the midst of his characters, an "affirmation excessive de la personne" that Bidou finds "le caractère le plus gênant du théâtre de Shaw" [an excessive affirmation of the individual that is the most discomforting aspect of Shaw's theater]. And sixth, Molière lets his characters behave naturally, objectively; Shaw's are but "des marionnettes entre ses mains" [puppets in his hands].[79]

The recurring note of frustration in the way critics debunked the Molière analogy might be explained by the following excerpt from a Hamon article, which illustrates how relentlessly he and his wife hammered away at the parallel: "Le théâtre de Bernard Shaw est de même technique que le théâtre de Molière, Bernard Shaw est le Molière contemporain. Nous ne savons pas quand tous accepteront de lui décerner ce nom. Peut-être sera-ce bientôt, peut-être faudra-t-il cinq, dix ou vingt ans encore. Mais ce que nous savons avec certitude, c'est qu'à un moment donné, en France, ce sera un lieu commun de considérer Bernard Shaw comme le Molière du xxe siècle" [Bernard Shaw's theater and Molière's share the same technique; Bernard Shaw is the contemporary Molière. We do not know when everyone will accept to award him this name. Perhaps it will be soon, perhaps it will take another five, ten or twenty years. But what we know with certainty is that at some point, in France, it will be a commonplace to consider Bernard Shaw the Molière of the twentieth century].[80]

Such heavy-handed proselytizing only deafened the critics to the Hamon creed. Ironically, even Shaw Molièrized Hamon's panegyric, changing "personnage farcesque" and "comique farcesque" to "Molièresque," and turning "comique farcesque en un comique sérieux" into "comique Shavien en un comique pseudo-psychologique moderne." Shaw also replaced Molière, "le premier des auteurs de farces," with "grand écrivain et profond philosophe sans jamais cesser d'employer la méthode du cirque et de la comédia dell'arte Italienne." Hamon's published text omitted "moderne" and added "les procédés de la farce médiévale et des clowneries de la foire [fairground]."[81]

* * *

Yet Hamon did not fail completely. Many were amused or outraged by his belabored comparisons, but some found Molière a plausible Shavian parallel. Émile Cammaerts thought it was "absurd to pretend that Shaw's outlook on life is similar to that of Molière," but contrasted the playwrights as follows: "Molière uses the weapon of reason, which is to oppose current ideas and fashions to older and firmer traditions based on experience—what we are accustomed to call common sense or popular wisdom. Shaw uses the weapon of paradox, which is to contend that if such and such an idea is sound, another idea, which ought to horrify the defenders of the first one, is just as sound in the light of their arguments. The first weapon may be likened to a shield and is most effective in the defence, the second may be likened to a sword and is most effective in the attack."[82]

Another critic considers Shaw's basic comic formula to be precisely the reverse of Molière's. At the center of a relatively rational world, Molière places a fool—Tartuffe, Alceste, Harpagon—who threatens to upset it and who is ousted at the end of the play, when order is restored. In a stupid and irrational world, Shaw places a superior character who tries to change it by inviting it to face and pursue reality. "The world usually prefers its own illusions."[83] On the other hand, Jacques Barzun claims that Shaw wrote his plays "in the classical tradition; he is the modern Molière and Aristophanes, where also you will find the point of the piece exhibited in long, self-aware declarations and arguments. Think of the *Misanthrope*: Alceste and Philinte, Alceste and Célimène carry on virtually scholastic debates about life in society, hypocrisy and truthfulness."[84] This would have delighted Hamon, especially since Shaw had agreed with him that "Tanner is the nearest thing in my gallery to the misanthrope."[85]

That Shaw admired Molière and was familiar with his plays is clear from numerous allusions and quotations to them in letters, prefaces, essays, and reviews. Writing to one of his biographers in 1916, Shaw admitted: "My clown and ringmaster technique of discussion . . . is plain Molière."[86] He spoke "officially" on Molière before the Royal Society of Literature in London on 18 January 1922, at a luncheon marking the latter's tercentenary, following a lecture on Molière by Maurice Donnay (whose *La Douloureuse* he had once called "false sociology"). According to Henderson, Shaw commented that the British Academy could do no better "than take in hand the task of bringing into existence a standard edition of Molière, so that the only rivalry between the French and British nations would be as to which could give the best representations of the greatest dramatist who ever lived."[87] Two months later, Shaw wrote to Hamon that he had been too busy to write on Molière for *Le Peuple*, "and all petitions for Molière articles had to remain ungranted, and even unanswered." He told Hamon that he had based his Royal Society speech on an article by Paul Bourget, "in which he said that Molière was great because he incarnated the French nation.... I said that the great French statesmen—Clemençeau, Briand, Millerand, Poincaré—had all enchanted us with the most remarkable qualities; but that the one thing we had never noticed in them was even the very slightest resemblance to Molière."[88] For Shaw here, Molière was merely a politically expedient means of achieving Anglo-French harmony—tongue-in-cheek, of course.

Henderson accurately compares the two dramatists: "Molière was not a social reformer; he accepted French society as he found it. He made a fetish of conservatism and the golden mean, and in the name of common sense declared that 'the correction of social absurdity must at all times be the subject matter of true comedy.' Shaw makes a fetish of radicalism and image-breaking, and in the name of uncommon sense declares that the unmasking of convention, the destruction of illusions, and the basic reorganization of society are the prerogatives, nay the duties, of the true comedic dramatist." Henderson concluded that the central character in Molière became with Shaw

> a code of conduct, a philosophy of life, incorporated in an individual.... Shaw does not, like Molière, satirize the generalized human specimens fit for study by the psychologist, the pathologist, the psychiatrist: the miser, the misanthrope, the hypocrite, the coxcomb, the pedant, the quack, the parvenu, the bore, the coquette. Shaw portrays class types, *hommes-idées,* as the French express it, representative of different strata of our so-called civilized life: the Cockney, the chauffeur, the mechanic, the Salvation Army officer, the munition maker, the professional soldier, the brigand, the gentleman, the lady, the cowboy, the labor leader, the politician, the statesman, the king, the dictator, the prelate, the genius, the saint.[89]

Around 1948, at Henderson's request, Shaw commented upon the Molière analogy. Writing in the third person, he stated that "Molière does not criticise his doctors: he guys them. He represents them as humbugs... makes them ridiculous by making one of them stammer." In *Tartuffe,* the "satire on clericalism achieves nothing more than a warning that a priest may be a scoundrel, which no intelligent Catholic has ever doubted. The tradition of satire which vilifies what it criticises lasted well up to Shaw's time.... Shaw reverses the procedure." In *Candida,* (Shaw went on,) Morrell is "'a first rate clergyman' without a single mean trait"; in the "unpleasant" plays, "the slum landlord is not a Harpagon but a clean living man and a fond father; the vivisector is not cruel outside his laboratory; the jealous termagant is pitiable rather than odious; . . . even the clergyman in *Mrs. Warren's Profession* . . . is no worse than a misplaced fool." "Shaw is not really interested in villains and guys. They are to him pathological specimens; and he holds that disease is not dramatic."[90]

* * *

If Hamon's Molière analogy was tenuous, his hold over Shaw was solidly defended, and negative reviews or articles condemning his idol often provoked an irate response. In his review of Cestre's *Bernard Shaw et son oeuvre,* literary critic Émile Faguet called Shaw Francophobe, insincere, violent, and preachy (among other things). Hamon replied with a seven-page letter to Faguet in *Pan,* countering that Shaw has "revêtu le vêtement du bouffon afin de mieux faire avaler la pilule amère de ses critiques sociales" [donned the buffoon's garb to help us swallow the bitter pill of his social critiques]; and that his farces are "le miel dont l'auteur enrobe l'amertume de sa leçon morale" [the honey with which the author coats the bitterness of his moral lesson].[91] This argument was marshaled whenever Shaw was accused of being clownish, acerbic, or didactic.

The earnest and hardworking Hamon was also a temperamental, obstinate fellow who could fire off letters filled with righteous indignation. When he wrote to Jules Delacre of the Théâtre du Marais in Brussels on 26 March 1924 demanding the return of *La Première Pièce de Fanny* and *Comment il mentit au mari* (sent six months earlier), he alluded to Robert de Smet's 4 March letter in the Paris theatrical daily *Comoedia*—"Les 'adaptateurs' défigurent-ils leurs auteurs étrangers?" [Do 'adaptors' disfigure their foreign authors?]—which had characterized Hamon's translations as "de véritables *trahisons*" (absolute *betrayals,* de Smet's emphasis). On 2 June, Hamon wrote to complain of Delacre's silence. Delacre finally responded on 7 July to answer what he called Hamon's "lettre très désagréable" filled with "vif mécontentement" [sharp dissatisfaction]: "*J'ignorais absolument* . . . qu'il y eût une polémique Shaw-Hamon. . . . J'ai fait des réserves sur *tous les traducteurs en général*" [*I absolutely ignored* that there had been a Shaw-Hamon polemics. . . . I had reservations on *all translators in general*]. Delacre could not imagine that Hamon thought his work so impeccable that "l'ombre seule d'une critique de détail vous paraisse insupportable" [the shadow of a single critique of some detail would seem unbearable to you]. This did not appease Hamon, who replied on 12 July that it was clear from de Smet's letter that Delacre found his translations "*irreprésentables*" [*unperformable*], but blamed de

Smet, who did not hide his "désire de nuire [injure] aux Hamon." He told Delacre that he never pretended his translations were impeccable. "Mais nous regimbons contre la condamnation en blôc de nos traductions, contre les affirmations sans preuves que nous avons trahi l'auteur" [But we adamantly reject the wholesale condemnation of our translations and the groundless assertions that we have betrayed the author].[92]

Worse than bald accusations of faulty translating were specific examples of it. In a long letter to director Georges Pitoëff of 23 January 1929 about the failure of his *César et Cléopâtre,* Hamon explained that he was dissatisfied and annoyed by the corrections. The ignorant child-woman Cleopatra could not have said "musclés" but could have used "rond et fort" to describe an arm; the majordomo's "rose leaves" was changed from Hamon's "feuilles de roses" to "pétales de rose," which Hamon said was the scientific word, not the popular word, which an uncultured domestic would use. He took a petulant tone verging on sarcasm: "Voyez-vous, chers amis, vous seriez bien, bien gentils de laisser notre texte tel qu'il est, sans le retoucher. Croyez bien qu'il est *étudié* avec soin, travaillé, et que l'emploi d'un mot plutôt qu'un autre est raisonné. Il est de notre texte, comme de vos décors. Vous les travaillez et retravaillez, n'est-ce pas. Eh bien, nous aussi. Et de même que vous n'admettriez pas que nous modifiions vos décors, souffrez que nous n'acceptions pas que vous modifiiez notre texte" [You see, dear friends, you would be very, very kind to leave our text as it is, without altering it. Rest assured that it is *studied* with care, worked over, and that the use of one word instead of another is reasoned. Our text is like your sets. You work them over again and again, don't you. Well, so do we. And just as you do not allow us to alter your sets, allow us not to accept that you alter our text].[93]

When it came to his translations, Hamon became almost paranoid over the thought of losing his Shavian dominion. On 4 January 1931, a Mlle. J. R. Roux wrote from Lyon that she had sought permission from Shaw to translate *The Perfect Wagnerite* and that Shaw had directed her to Hamon. On 19 February, Hamon replied tersely that he had already translated the book, adding with finality that Shaw's complete works "doit paraître" in the Hamons' translation.[94] Yet he was eager to spread the Shavian gospel when others asked for help with their research. To François Closset, who wrote in December 1931, Hamon recommended a "dissection" of the plays and prefaces from a sociological perspective, explaining that Shaw's "appréciation élogieuse de l'oeuvre des Soviets est la conséquence fatale, inéluctable de son socialisme" [eulogistic assessment of the work of the Soviets is a fatal, inescapable consequence of his socialism].[95] Although he told Closset that his work would be *"très originale* et *nouvelle"* [Hamon's emphases], Hamon himself had given a sociological analysis of Shaw's first twelve plays in his (unpublished) lectures at the Sorbonne from 1909 to 1912. Writing from Liverpool the following month, Mina Moore deluged Hamon with questions: Why did Shaw defend Mussolini? Did Shaw go to France often? How is his French? Does he have prejudices against the French? Are there any critical works on Shaw? She mentioned that the French do not take to Shaw because he is not at all a psychologist, having "remplacé les ressorts normaux des actions humaines par des 'forces' qui font agir et parler les hommes comme des marionettes" [replaced the normal springs of human actions by "forces" that make men act and speak like puppets].

Hamon replied to this onslought on 10 February with three typed pages of single-spaced commentary. The purpose of a Soviet dictatorship is to abolish classes, and so *The Apple Cart* supports it. Shaw praised the good done by Mussolini but averred that "le pire criminel n'est pas toute sa vie mauvais" [the worst criminal is not evil his whole life]. Hamon discussed the differences between catholicism and soviet atheism, lamenting how "les Eglises ont défiguré l'enseignement communiste, de liberté de pensée, etc, qui en ressort" [Churches have distorted communist teaching, the freedom of thought, etc, that stems from it]. On Shaw in France: "Le succès de Shaw en France a été inhibé parce que les maîtres capitalistes ont trop bien compris la puissance de sa critique. . . . Ils pourrissent la littérature et l'art dramatiques français par la glorification d'oeuvres sans valeur, médiocres, banales. . . . Il est impossible d'écrire des *caractères* comme ceux de ses pièces, sans être . . . très grand psychologue" [The success of Shaw in France has been inhibited because the capitalist masters have but too well understood the power of his criticism. . . . They rot French literature and dramatic art by the glorification of worthless, mediocre, banal, works. . . . It is impossible to write *characters* like those in his plays without being . . . a great psychologist]. Three years later, on 29 January 1934, Moore sent Hamon and his wife a copy of *Bernard Shaw et la France*.[96]

A few years after assisting Moore, Hamon suggested to Adrien Sobra, a student at Dijon, the topic "Shaw et les femmes" for his "Mémoire de diplôme d'études supérieures." In 1933, Sobra sent him the completed study, which he emphasized was "entièrement originale, car je n'ai pu me procurer aucun ouvrage de critique sur l'auteur" [completely original, since I was unable to obtain any critical work on the author]. The following month, ten days after his graduation, Sobra wrote to Hamon that no author had given him "des plaisirs intellectuels aussi intenses."⁹⁷ Excerpts of "Les Femmes dans le théâtre de G. Bernard Shaw" appeared serially in 1936 in four issues of the *Revue de l'enseignement des langues vivantes*.

* * *

What began as mild coercion became uneasy collaboration and culminated in idolatrous devotion. "Vous vouliez un traducteur," wrote Hamon to Shaw in the "Épitre Dédicatoire" to *Le Molière du XXe siècle*, "qui fît mentir le proverbe '*Traduttore, traditore*', qui pût rendre toute l'âme révolutionnaire de votre oeuvre" [You wanted a translator who would give the lie to the proverb "*Traduttore, traditore*," who would convey the revolutionary spirit of your work].⁹⁸ Hamon believed that he had been a godsend, even though he and his wife had frequently muddled Shaw's textual and ideological intentions. However, they brought Shaw's plays and ideas into the French limelight, and if readers or audiences were reluctant to accept or unable to understand them, the Hamons were only partly to blame; if their frenchifications were the result of their own ineptitude or ignorance, Shaw zealously promoted and defended them.

Even after Hamon's death in 1945, Shaw refused to let anyone touch his plays. In 1946, Jean-Marie Rojé asked to translate *Arms and the Man*, but Shaw replied that all his plays had long been translated.⁹⁹ In 1948, when Pierre Montillier asked for *Saint Joan*, Shaw wrote that no new translation could be authorized.¹⁰⁰ In 1949, when Maurice Grinberg asked for "*In Good King Charles's Golden Days*," suggesting Louis Jouvet as Charles, Shaw replied: "My authorized French translator is Madame Henriette Hamon. . . . I do not know whether she has yet translated King Charles nor whether she is prepared to do so. It is not a one-part play: L.J. alone could not pull it through."¹⁰¹

It has been suggested recently that Shaw encouraged such mediocre talents as the Hamons and Trebitsch because of "his obsessive need to control. Had he hired talented translators, his plays might have slipped out of his hands, taking on—as with all good translations—artistic lives of their own."¹⁰² Whatever the reasons, the Irish Molière got the translators he deserved—although not the translations the French, or Shaw himself, required.

7

Outrageous

Shaw and the French Press

La Critique and Monsieur Shaw: Mutually Baffling

By the time Augustin Filon published *Le Théâtre anglais* in 1897, Shaw had written and produced eight plays. Yet Filon mentions him in passing and only as a drama critic. In the chapter "Mr. Archer and Ibsen," he notes that one must add to the name Arthur B. Walkley "that of Mr. George Bernard Shaw, whose articles in the *Saturday Review* have attracted much notice during the year 1895, and have constituted a veritable campaign in Ibsen's honour."[1]

This is the only reference to Shaw in a survey by an important French literary critic of the day. Despite *Mrs Warren's Profession, Arms and the Man, Candida, The Devil's Disciple,* and *Man and Superman,* Shaw would remain almost completely unknown in France as a playwright until the Hamons began translating and publicizing him in 1904—and it took until 1907 for some of their translations to be published. Aside from Maurice Muret's article, "De Nora à Candida" (1904), French critics paid little attention to Shaw until the Brussels premiere of *Candida* in February 1907. Even as late as 1911, Jacques-Émile Blanche, a portrait painter who often worked in London, wrote to Shaw: "I had never heard of your works being translated into french [*sic*]. . . . A friend of mine just told me your books were most difficult to secure in Paris . . . & that the translation was as poor as could be."[2]

Ironically, it was Shaw's American biographer, Archibald Henderson, who first awakened French interest in Shaw. To discover why Shaw was popular in Germany and Austria—where his plays had scored early triumphs—but almost completely unknown in France, Henderson wrote letters of inquiry to five distinguished literary men, including Jules Lemaître, dramatic reviewer for *Le Journal des débats* and *La Revue des deux mondes* and one of the finest critics of his day, and playwright Jules Claretie, who in 1885 had become director of the Théâtre Français. Lemaître and Claretie "replied that they had never discussed Shaw in their *Chroniques théâtrales*," he reported. Émile Faguet knew nothing about him. Belgian dramatist Maurice Maeterlinck confessed that he had never heard of Shaw: "Je l'avoue avec une profonde confusion" [I admit it with a deep embarrassment]. Even Filon admitted that "owing to some contradictory aspects of the man, I have not yet been able to form a clear and definite estimate of his meaning and worth."[3]

The situation changed in late 1905 when, at Henderson's insistence, Filon wrote "M. Bernard Shaw et son théâtre" for *La Revue des deux mondes*, a twenty-eight-page essay that marked the beginning of a French awareness of the Irish dramatist. Filon characterized Shaw as an Ibsen who had slid into the skin of Beaumarchais and in so doing had lost "les trois quarts de sa puissance dramatique et la moitié de sa philosophie" [three quarters of his dramatic power and half his philosophy]. The piece is rather unflattering overall, and Filon closed by stating it was high time that Shaw, purporting to be both reformer and iconoclast, "build us something." "Indulgents et amusés, nous avons souri aux fantaisies de l'iconoclaste, qui, d'ailleurs, n'a cassé jusqu'à présent que des réductions en plâtre, à bon marché, des statues de nos dieux immortels: nous attendons le réformateur" [Indulgent and entertained, we have smiled upon the fantasies of the iconoclast who, moreover, has so far broken only plaster miniatures, cheap ones, of the statues of our immortal gods: we await the reformer].[4]

Henderson took matters in hand again in July the following year and published "La Carrière de Bernard Shaw" in Hamon's journal, *L'Humanité nouvelle*. This was followed at year's end by Jean Blum's twenty-one-page article in *La Revue germanique*, which examined (and praised) Shaw's socialist convictions. The avalanche of articles, essays, reviews, and critiques from France had begun.

* * *

Any mention of Shaw in the French press was always controversial, provoking everything from amazement and bafflement to qualified praise, from resentment and disgust to indignation and condemnation. On the one hand, eminent critic and novelist Remy de Gourmont wrote in 1913: "C'est pourtant le seul génie dramatique de la présente heure européenne et c'est le seul théâtre qui traduise une vie un peu élevée et une vie profondément originale" [Yet he is the only dramatic genius of present-day Europe and his is the only theater that expresses a somewhat elevated and a profoundly original life].[5] In 1912, Paul Grosfils placed Shaw far above "La galerie des femmes hystériques et détraquées [deranged] de M. A.-W. Pinero, la dramaturgie puérile de M. J.-M. Barrie, Sherlock Holmes et les fantoches [puppets] de M. A. Conan Doyle, les lourdes [unwieldy] moralités de M. Hall Caine." And in 1927, Marcel Brion praised Shaw's perspicacity and candor, his "observation exacte et ironique de la vie."[6]

On the other hand, even positive assessments had caveats about Shaw's peculiar humor, English biases, and disturbing paradoxes. Charles Cestre, to give only one example, was indignant with Shaw's satirical treatment of heroism and patriotism in *Arms and the Man*. Granted, the play is a comedy; "Mais a-t-on le droit de faire intervenir le rire et le ridicule en si grave matière?" he asked [But do we have the right to bring laughter and ridicule into so serious a topic?][7] Generally, most critics tried to label Shaw as misogynist or megalomaniac, clown or charlatan, and many found his work deeply unsettling.

Charles Hermeline (1908) found that his plays "fourmille d'invraisemblances" [teem with improbabilities]; Maurice Dekobra (1910) thought them fine reading but thought Shaw a "dramaturge manqué" [failed dramatist]; for Émile Faguet (1912), he was "très francophobe, ou plutôt *misogallo*" [Faguet's emphasis], "un clown qui s'habille en prédicateur" [a clown who dresses up as a preacher]; Maurice Muret (1912) called Shaw a journalist and a polemicist, and deplored the "pessimisme desséchant" [desiccating pessimism] of his theater. Lucien Dubech was particularly irked: in 1922, he labeled Shaw's ideas "un tissu d'incohérences" [a fabric of incoherences]; in 1932, "mornes platitudes" [dreary platitudes]; in 1933, he thought Shaw "un très regrettable fumiste" [a very unfortunate fraud], "un fabricant de farces lourdes et banales" [a manufacturer of awkward and banal farces].[8] French critics simply did not know what to make of him.

A cursory sampling of the countless essays on Shaw and his plays will illustrate why the French found him so baffling and irksome. Some believed he was an ineffectual theorist, and Denis Saurat (1925) writes for many when he faults Shaw for bookishness: "Cet homme ne semble jamais avoir vécu, ni eu d'expérience réelle. Il a habité un monde à part construit d'idées socialistes bien calmes et de souvenirs de lectures mélangés à des statistiques que lui fournit son ami Sydney Webb" [This man seems never to have lived, nor had any real experience. He has lived in a world apart built out of very unruffled socialist ideas and of memories of readings mixed with statistics provided by his friend Sydney Webb]. Like many, G. Locria (1912) thought Shaw's creations mere bloodless talking heads. He characterized them as "fantoches sans vie réelle, sans émotion aucune, personnages falots qui n'agissent qu'à peine, et encore de façon futile, incohérente, inexplicable, bavards qui s'adressent toujours à notre esprit, jamais à notre coeur, qui veulent nous faire penser, jamais sentir" [lifeless puppets, queer characters who barely act, and then again in a futile, incoherent, inexplicable manner, chatterboxes who always speak to our mind, never to our heart, who want to make us think, never feel].

Even more than Shaw's characters, what grated on French sensibilities was the way in which Shaw himself seemed to flog reader or spectator with intellectual acrobatics. This is how Jacques Nayral (1912) summed up Shaw's dramatic method: "Développer à outrance une proposition en apparence paradoxale, heurter de front, violemment, nos habitudes de juger, bafouer, sans ambages, notre morale coutumière, puis, par des examples irréfutables, des déductions irrésistibles, des observations cruelles, mais sûres, des rapprochements imprévus, mais foncièrement exacts, nous entraîner, hors d'haleine, jusqu'au point où il veut nous mener, et nous obliger à conclure avec lui, et malgré nous, que son paradoxe est vérité, que nos jugements sont préjugés et que notre morale est hypocrisie, tel est le procédé cher à M. Bernard Shaw" [To develop to excess an apparently paradoxical proposal, to violently run head-on into our habits of judging, to jeer unequivocally against our customary morals, and, by means of irrefutable examples, irresistible deductions, cruel but absolutely certain observations, unexpected but fundamentally exact parallels, to drag us along, breathless, to where he wants to lead us, and to force us to conclude with him, and despite ourselves, that his paradox is truth, that our judgments are presumptuous and that our morals are hypocrisy, such is the process dear to M. Bernard Shaw].

Nayral also pointed out, as did others, that the virulence of Shaw's attacks was disproportionate to their targets: "La morale courante est raillée et bafouée sans pitié, avec des rires. . . . Il semble qu'il prenne la société comme on prendrait je ne sais quel corps hideux mais somptueusement vêtu, et que, le déshabillant pièce à pièce, il s'amuse à en faire apparaître successivement toutes les difformités, tous les ulcères" [Current morals are jeered and scoffed at without pity, with laughter. . . . It seems he [Shaw] takes society as one would take who knows what hideous but gorgeously dressed body and, stripping it piece by piece, enjoys himself by producing one after another all of its deformities, all of its ulcers]. Abel

Hermant (1913) went farther: "Il est d'une cruauté presque sadique" [He is of an almost sadistic cruelty].

One major stumbling block to a French understanding of Shaw was culture. Émile Faguet (1912) faulted Shaw on seven points: lack of sincerity, weak endings, mouthpiece characters, clownishness, preachiness, paradoxes, Englishness. This last flaw was especially vexing to the French. Like Maurice Boissard (1913), who thought Shaw's characters "Anglais, uniquement Anglais, rien qu'Anglais," Faguet thought Shaw's theater "presque exclusivement anglais. . . . M. Bernard Shaw . . . est *anglais, presque rien qu'anglais*. Ce sont des travers tout anglais, qu'il houspille ou qu'il flagelle" [almost exclusively English. . . . M. Bernard Shaw . . . is *English, almost nothing but English*. Those are English faults that he berates or scourges] (Faguet's emphasis).

In short, the French found Shaw problematic simply because his sensibility was not French. Some became outrightly anti-English, such as Gaffié (1913), who called Shaw's works "immorales au dernier chef. Il leur a donné cette marque de fabrique tout à fait spéciale, qui fait le fond du caractère anglais et qui s'appelle l'hypocrisie" [immoral in the utmost. He has given them this very special trademark, which is at the core of the English character and is called hypocrisy]. Others like Octave Uzanne (1913) blamed everything on language: "Toute l'essence de son comique original ne peut être versée, décantée, sans y perdre, hors de la vieille pinte de wisky où elle se développe, pour se conserver intacte dans une de nos bouteilles de bourgogne ou de bordeaux" [The whole essence of his inventive comedy cannot be poured or decanted, without losing something, out of the old pint of whisky where it develops, in order to remain intact in one of our bottles of bourgogne or bordeaux]. And not a few, such as Louis Gillet (1919), were nonplussed by the apparent absence of sexual passion in Shaw's characters: after a long analysis of *Candida*, he concluded that the main characteristic of Shaw's theater was "le dédain de l'amour" [the scorn of love].[9]

* * *

Regarded with suspicion and attacked often and vehemently, Shaw could not resist contributing to the general disgruntlement of French critics. Of all the controversial statements he made regularly in the French press, the following five exchanges between Shaw and poet-dramatist Henry Bernstein (1876–1953) in 1925 are typical of Shaw's deliberately provocative stance in the Paris newspapers. One of his articles in *Le Temps* (10 August) so infuriated Bernstein that he countered with a long two-part reply,

"G.B.S. et Paris," in *Le Temps* (7 and 14 September). Shaw retaliated with "Lettre ouverte à Henry Bernstein" in *Le Temps* (16 November), which was published alongside Bernstein's reply, "Lettre confidentielle à Bernard Shaw." Naturally, Shaw had the last word: "Mon pseudo-antisémitisme ou post-scriptum à la controverse Bernstein-Shaw" appeared in *La Volonté* (23 December).[10] The controversy was lively and deserves a brief summary, as it is one of the few recorded "dialogues" between Shaw and a prominent French playwright, as well as one of Shaw's most virulent onslaughts upon the French.

Pierre Brisson's headnote to Shaw's "Réflexions," the article that sparked the exchange, warned readers that Shaw's accusations were not of a "courtoisie exquise," but that coming from such an eminent mind, "tous les paradoxes méritent d'être accueillis" [all paradoxes deserve to be welcomed]. Shaw began by summarizing a negative critique of *Candida* by Catulle Mendès, sarcastically calling it a model of what the oldest English critics could have written about him. He even admitted that Hamon becoming his translator was a situation as bizarre as if Labiche had proposed to John Stuart Mill that he translate his plays simply because Mill appreciated Comte. As for Parisians, they were "parmi ceux qui ont le moins de savoir-vivre au monde" [among the most ill-mannered people in the world]. He discussed the "intense provincialism" of Paris, a city that was intellectually "un chaos labouré d'obus, couvert de ruines de la pensée et du goût du dix-neuvième siècle" [a chaos plowed with shells, covered in the ruins of nineteenth-century thought and taste], and yet thanks to *Sainte Jeanne* (he gloated) he was "nearly canonised by Paris before my death."

Bernstein's two-part rebuttal was a mixture of bafflement and ire: "L'insolence du ton ne nous a pas caché l'indigence extrême de la pensée" [The insolence of tone has not hidden the extreme indigence of thought]. He quoted at length from Frank Harris's essay in *La Nouvelle Revue française* (1 July 1925) and was astounded to find that Shaw was a "Molière-Bazarof." He also found Shaw's self-portrait in the same issue just as shocking; chastity is an instinct—very funny, but is it humorous? Shaw was in high spirits at his mother's cremation: "'Il a ri, et il avait emmené du monde pour le voir rire'" [He laughed, and he had brought people to see him laugh]. *Sainte Jeanne* was anachronistic and paradoxical; to call it "poetic" is childish. Shaw, Bernstein concluded, was nothing but another Alexandre Dumas *fils,* with his prefaces and manifestos: "Shaw, comme Dumas, chérit la tirade qu'il sait adroitement briser, le morceau de bravoure, un certain balancement narquois. . . . . ils ne cessent de plaider.

... Leurs pièces à thèse, ils y voient des satires, mais, pour fouetter l'homme, il faut d'abord de la chair et du sang, et ils ne savent pas.... Sous la boursouflure de l'un, sous l'outrance drolatique de l'autre, paraîtrait aisément un dogmatisme prétentieux et, ma foi, naïf" [Like Dumas, Shaw cherishes the tirade which he knows how to break off skillfully, the bravura piece, a certain cunning balancing.... They cannot stop arguing.... They think their thesis plays are satires, but to flog a man, one must first have flesh and blood, and they do not know.... Beneath the turgidity of one, beneath the comic audacity of the other, one can easily make out a pretentious and naive dogmatism].

Eight weeks later came Shaw's unexpected "open letter." It was natural, wrote Shaw, for Bernstein to admire and adore him because "cela a toujours été la faiblesse généreuse du Juif de pousser son idéalisme jusqu'à l'idolâtrie absolue" [it has always been the Jew's generous weakness to push his idealism to absolute idolatry]. For you, the Parisian is "un être héroïque ... splendide, fier, sensible, éperdument dévoué à une femme qui le trahit ou à la femme de quelqu'un d'autre qui refuse de trahir son mari, un idéaliste toujours dans une situation noblement tragique, et par conséquent toujours à la fin de l'avant-dernier acte" [a heroic being ... splendid, proud, sensible, madly devoted to a wife who betrays him, or to someone else's wife who refuses to betray her husband; always an idealist in a noble and tragic situation, and consequently always at the close of the penultimate act]. The Théâtre-Français? A "vieil hospice d'octogénaires" [old hospice for octogenarians]. A Frenchman? "Le mouton que tout le monde tond, l'âne écrasé sous tous les fardeaux de l'Europe" [The sheep everyone fleeces, the donkey crushed beneath the burdens of Europe]. "Et le Juif parle toujours de la gloire, de la patrie, parce qu'il veut faire égorger tout Paris, toute la France, tout le monde pour devenir milliardaire" [And the Jew is always talking about glory and homeland because he wants to slaughter all of Paris, all of France, and everyone to become a millionaire].

Bernstein replied indignantly that Shaw had revealed an "inflexible contempt": "Vous dénoncez mon sémitisme aux nationalistes et mon nationalisme aux autres" [You denounce my semitism to the nationalists and my nationalism to others], but this has been done before, and with more style, "dear multimillionaire and antisemite socialist!" Five weeks later, Shaw published a hyperbolic "post-scriptum," in which he claimed that there was no anti-Semitism in England, although there were of course the same prejudices against Jews as against Scots, Irish, French, and all foreigners. England is "saturated from infancy" by the Old Testament; "elle est Sioniste," he stated, despite the overzealous, converted Catholic

G. K. Chesterton and the anti-Semitic Hilaire Belloc.[11] Although Shaw stressed his strong Jewish sympathies and friendships, he emphasized that he repudiated "pro-Judaism as emphatically as I do anti-Semitism," noting that Bernstein's imperialistic flag-waving was laughable, as were his attempts to be "more French than the French."

The polemic died down, and, amazingly, a few years later the two men reconciled. Shaw reported to Hamon in 1927 that "l'affaire Bernstein est raccommodée" [patched up]. Bernstein was entertained in London at the Anglo-French Luncheon Club, and Shaw, unable to attend, sent Bernstein a note "assuring him that my absence had nothing to do with our polémique" and begging him to count on Shaw as a friend during his visit. "The result was that Henri," Shaw told Hamon, "with perfect savoir faire, called on me immediately on rising from the lunch, and made himself very agreeable. He is not only an exceptional man, but an exceptional Jew," with a "talent for combining an unquestionable authority with the most genial and disarming frankness. He made a great success of our meeting by his tact."[12]

* * *

The "affaire Bernstein" is only one example of Shaw's epistolary epics to translators, actors, directors, and critics that attest to a bellicose attitude toward almost anyone involved in staging his plays in France. Like Hamon, Shaw brooked no opposition. When actor-manager Firmin Gémier produced *Le Héros et le soldat* at the Comédie-Montaigne on 30 March 1921, it was almost unanimously praised for its gaiety, humor, and merciless truth. Shaw was still not satisfied: "I give Gémier no credit whatever for succeeding as Bluntschli," he wrote to Hamon. "The part is actor-proof: no amateur has ever failed in it. After the war, the play is also actor-proof; . . . I beg you to let G. know that his coupure [cut] has produced the worst possible impression on me. Unless you contrive to spread a perfect terror in the theatres of meddling with my plays, cutting them, and adapting them to the supposed tastes and susceptibilities of the Parisian playgoer, you will have failure after failure."[13]

The following year, when Aurélien-Marie Lugné-Poë (1869–1940), actor-manager of the Théâtre de l'Oeuvre, hired mediocre actors for his production of *Le Dilemme du docteur,* Shaw instructed Hamon, "Do not let him have any other play of mine," and two years later he refused to consider Lugné-Poë for *Sainte Jeanne:* "I do not believe Lugné understands how to treat my work: his failure with The Doctor's Dilemma shattered my faith in him as a possible Shaw producer."[14] Fifteen years earlier, when Shaw was approached by a Monsieur Boulestin, one of Lugné-Poë's associates, with a request that the latter produce *Mrs Warren's Profession*, he angrily turned it down because Boulestin had written that such a "pornographic" play was sure to succeed with Lugné-Poë's wife, Suzanne Després, in the title role. Shaw wrote to Lugné-Poë that this was horribly disrespectful to Després as a woman and as an artist, adding: "D'ailleurs, je ne suis pas pornographist" [Besides, I am no pornographer]. Nonetheless, Shaw told him to read Hamon's translation to Suzanne, whom he had seen on stage three or four times and in whose talent and personality he had found "une qualité très touchante" [a very touching quality]. The next year (1907), Lugné-Poë refused Shaw's terms and negotiations broke down.[15]

Shaw was particularly put upon by Georges Pitoëff, the actor-director responsible for his *Sainte Jeanne* triumph. Two months before the 17 January 1928 premiere of *Heartbreak House*—awkwardly translated as *La Maison des coeurs-brisés,* the house of the broken hearts—at the Théâtre des Mathurins, Shaw warned Pitoëff not to cut a single word. Cutting lines here and there would lead to cutting the entire play and substituting "un chef d'oeuvre de Scribe ou Augier." Shaw cautioned that "le jeu shawien est précisément le contraire du jeu du boulevard. Tout effort de concilier le boulevard doit fatalement manquer son but et mettre assez d'eau dans le breuvage pour le rendre incapable d'enivrer" [the Shavian game is precisely the opposite of the boulevard's. Any effort to gain the esteem of the boulevard must fatally miss the mark and put enough water in the drink to make it unable to intoxicate].[16]

Ten months later, when *César et Cléopâtre* failed (with Georges and Ludmilla in the title roles), Shaw was concerned more with Hamon's state of mind than with the Pitoëffs' performances. "Le Père Hamon is ready to hang himself," he wrote to them on 13 January 1929. "Why do you not console this worthy man instead of letting him write me frantic letters, ten pages long, accusing me of being corrupted by my fabulous wealth, and of being a party to the conspiracy against you?" Because Georges had worked so hard in producing the play and acting a big part at the same time, at the *répétition générale*—the final dress rehearsal attended by critics—he was "half asleep, and the critics soon are wholly asleep. Thus the producer betrays the actor and both of them betray the author." Shaw also hated the scenery, advising Georges to "sell it, pawn it, burn it, and let it never be seen again on your stage."[17] As he explained to Hamon a few days later, Georges had "overrated his talent and his authority with the Paris public; and he must take the consequences. Nothing on earth could make Caesar fail in the hands of a great actor, nor make it succeed in the hands of a small one."[18]

Shaw was harder on Pitoëff in January 1930, when he learned (via Hamon) that Georges was planning to produce *La Charrette de pommes* and to play Magnus. "Do you want to ruin me? I cannot afford another failure like that of Caesar: it would be the end of me as a dramatic author in France.... The part of the King needs a first rate actor.... It is also necessary that he should be a French actor, not a foreigner. Now you, dear Georges, though you do not know it, are an execrable actor, monotonous to a maddening degree, and a foreigner into the bargain."[19] Georges was a Russian of Armenian origin and spoke with a thick Georgian accent, and Joseph Kessel had been appalled to see Caesar distorted by "un Slave dégingandé [ungainly] et un peu hystérique."[20] Shaw excoriated Georges for his "crashing, smashing, ridiculous failure [as Caesar], ruinous to you, ruinous to Hamon, ruinous to my reputation in France. It established you forever as a perfectly damnable actor, absolutely the worst in the world." Neither was Shaw happy with Georges's staging:

> You murder them [my plays] always by some barbarous extravagance which destroys their credibility.... By sticking up a senseless ship's mast in the middle of the room [in *Heartbreak House*] you proclaimed that the captain was in his dotage, and upset all my stage business, besides distracting the attention of the audience from the play: the very thing no producer should ever do. In Caesar, instead of the massive solidity of Egypt you perpetrated extravagances which made the buildings look like houses of cards with figures from a nightmare. [In *Saint Joan*] the structure looked flimsy, the atmosphere was one of weak pathetic piety instead of overbearing strength.[21]

The following year, despite Shaw's injunctions against a production of *La Charrette de pommes,* Georges went ahead with it and cast himself as Magnus. Shaw was in Paris and saw the play on 24 April, writing to Trebitsch four days later that the production had been "ugly, silly, and incompetent,"[22] as he knew it would be. Shaw's high anxiety with the Pitoëffs and the Hamons was typical of the irritation he felt with many of those involved in his French productions. Year after year, he remained frustrated by what he—and most French critics—considered the ineffective and incompetent treatment his plays were receiving in France.

La Critique on Shaw's Plays: Colliding Cultures

Shaw had praised Bernstein for his "genial and disarming frankness," but there is nothing genial and disarming in the frankness of the reviews of Shaw's plays in performance. Despite the usual suspects—acting, staging, translation, ideology, cultural differences—each play presented specific difficulties that made it unpalatable, often repulsive, to French audiences. A brief overview of critical opinions on *Candida, Mrs Warren's Profession, You Never Can Tell,* and *Pygmalion* will illustrate the obstacles French audiences encountered in trying to understand and appreciate Shaw. Like the general comments on Shaw just examined, we will see that some of these critiques were gallocentric.

On the occasion of *Candida*'s 1908 Paris premiere at the Théâtre des Arts, the London correspondent for the *Daily Telegraph* cautioned that "there is nothing more solemn than a Parisian who does not see a joke. . . . But the worst peril of all was the Parisian humour, which is cruelly sensible, and picks out an ounce of naïveté in a ton of philosophy, and will laugh down a whole scene in the name of common sense for one ingenious slip of the author's. . . . Candida sitting down to talk it all over and choose between the two men went down as farce," and the poet's exit was "the greatest joke of all."

But French critics did worse than misinterpret Shaw's comedic intentions; they were put off by the sexlessness of a play in which they expected adultery. Fernand Nozière concluded that Shaw's idea of marriage was the "union du prétentieux égoïsme avec la vaniteuse abnégation" [union of pretentious egotism with conceited self-denial]. The absence of sexual desire is shocking for the French spectator, wrote Léon Blum, who finds it difficult to understand that in a woman's choice between two men, "l'attrait physique, la préférence physique n'intervienne pas." In Candida's decision, "pas un instant le facteur sexuel n'entre apparemment en jeu. Cette particularité est bien anglaise" [not for a moment does the sexual factor come into play, apparently. This is a very English characteristic]. When Candida did show mild passion, J. Ernest-Charles was perturbed by her "familiarités grossières et précipitées" [coarse and hasty intimacies]: alone with Marchbanks, Candida allowed him to press his head against her knees, where she kissed it. These actions, thought Ernest-Charles, revealed "des moeurs frustes et une vulgarité blessante" [crude manners and an offensive vulgarity].

Was there something inherent in the English psyche that made Candida behave so inappropriately? In *Comoedia*, Robert d'Humières explained that English morality is upheld by "l'absence du tempérament sensuel. Ces hommes et ces femmes ... n'ont ni le cerveau, ni les reins exigeants" [the absence of a sensual temperament. Neither the mind nor the loins of these men and women is very exacting]. D'Humières quoted from one of his previous articles: "'L'amour représente pour l'Anglais une distraction à laquelle on peut donner le change par le travail ou le sport; chez les types supérieurs, la passion revêt un caractère d'idéalisme respectueux; chez les autres, c'est un assouvissement brutal et rapide'" [Love represents for the Englishman a diversion from which one can get sidetracked by work or sports; in superior fellows, passion takes on the characteristics of respectful idealism; in others, it is a swift and brutish satiation]. As for Candida's desires: "Pour une salle française, l'épouse, afin de ne pas déconcerter les habitudes d'esprit, sera généralement adultère" [For a French audience, the wife, in order not to disconcert the usual mind-set, will generally be adulterous]. It is clear from these comments by d'Humières and others that some national biases made it very difficult for Shaw's plays, *Candida* in particular, to be readily embraced by French audiences at the turn of the century.

At the suggestion of d'Humières—perhaps to mollify the audience—actress and singer Georgette Leblanc-Maeterlinck, wife of playwright Maurice Maeterlinck and the principal actress in his plays, read a paper before one of *Candida*'s performances. In this fascinating lecture (published in *Le Figaro*), she compared English and French mores in an attempt to defend Shaw's treatment of the passions. Had Morell strangled Marchbanks and killed Candida, she wrote, "on trouverait cela injuste, mais naturel; barbare mais normal" [we would find this unjust, but natural; barbaric but normal], emphasizing that it was the characters' "effort de sagesse qui les rend absolument illogiques" [effort of wisdom that renders them absolutely illogical]. Yet Candida is a woman of enlightened instincts; when she speaks to her husband about the poet's love for her, it is "la vision d'une perfection morale absolue." Leblanc-Maeterlinck warned the audience that the scene in which Marchbanks declares his love for Candida is highly unusual: "Il faut penser que l'éducation anglaise diffère de notre éducation française et que la froideur physique qu'on prête, à tort ou à raison, aux Anglo-Saxonnes, leur permet plus d'abandon" [One must understand that English education differs from our French education and that the physical coldness that we attribute, rightly or wrongly, to Anglo-Saxon women, allows them to be more unconstrained].

Her lecture took the tone of a paean to womanhood when she defended

Candida's choice of Morell over Marchbanks: "Candida n'aime pas le jeune poète, elle aime son mari, et je pense que ce serait encore amoindrir la haute volonté de l'auteur que de croire que son héroïne obéit à un devoir en restant avec le pasteur. Non! Elle obéit à une loi plus profonde et plus naturelle, elle obéit à la seule loi sur laquelle nous ayons le devoir d'appuyer nos forces et notre bonheur: elle obéit à son choix" [Candida does not love the young poet, she loves her husband, and I think that it would be to diminish the author's higher will to believe that his heroine yields to duty in remaining with the minister. No! She yields to a deeper and more natural law, she yields to the only law upon which we have the duty to found our strength and our happiness: she yields to her choice].[23]

If *La Profession de Madame Warren* was less baffling, its topic was thought passé, having been better dealt with by Guy de Maupassant, as Anglophile critic Henry-D. Davray pointed out, in *Yvette*. "Mais toutes ces diatribes contre la Société, contre l'hypocrisie sociale, nous les avons entendues, déjà, maintes fois. . . . Nous les avons déjà vus, tous ces personnages contradictoires; nous les avons vus et entendus, en mieux!" [But all these diatribes against Society, against social hypocrisy, we have already heard them many times. . . . We have already seen all of these contradictory characters; we have seen and heard them, and better]. Jacques Nayral also thought that Shaw's play recalled *Yvette,* with a difference: where Maupassant "n'a vu qu'une petite fille un peu frivole, sentimentale, qui veut être aimée quand même et qui se résigne, Bernard Shaw a généralisé, il a fait le procès de l'organisation sociale tout entière" [saw merely one rather frivolous, sentimental little girl who wants nonetheless to be loved and who resigns herself, Bernard Shaw has generalized, he has put the entire social structure on trial].[24]

Lucien Dubech thought Shaw's thesis unworthy of dramatization altogether, finding ridiculous the premise that in today's society, "les femmes ne peuvent vivre qu'en se vendant aux hommes" [women can live only by selling themselves to men]. And in an analogy much quoted by others, Gustave Lanson called the play "une bouteille de vitriol jetée à la figure de la prude Angleterre, et toute la société moderne en reçoit des éclaboussures" [a bottle of vitriol thrown at the face of prudish England, and the whole of modern society is splattered].[25] In general, most French critics thought the sound and fury of *Madame Warren* less shocking than its author did.

They found *On ne peut jamais dire* more disturbing, but for cultural rather than dramatic reasons. Here was a play that went counter to the cherished French values of order, reason, logic, clarity, balance, and pro portion. "Notre caractère, nos moeurs sont, en effet, trop éloignés des moeurs anglaises" [Our character, our mores are, in effect, too far removed from English ones], wrote Albert Blavinhac. Paul Souday believed that there was something in the play that was "spécifiquement britannique qui nous échappe un peu" [which eludes us a little bit]. Edmond Sée found it "énigmatique," a patchwork of Scribe, Labiche, Meilhac, Dumas *fils*, Regnard, and Molière. Guy Métives qualified Shaw's language as "des exercises de clown philosophique et dramatique." "Nos cervelles françaises," he clarified, "façonnées à l'école de l'équilibre, de la raison, du juste milieu—mon Dieu, oui!—et surtout de la belle clarté, ne peuvent aimer que par contraste ce genre de productions" [Our French brains, molded in the school of balance, reason, the happy medium—my God, yes!—and especially beautiful clarity, can love this kind of production only by contrast].

Robert de Flers wrote that a play combining German ideology with "la raideur saccadée et un peu clownesque de l'humour britannique" [the stiff and somewhat clownish jerkiness of British humor] should never have been performed in front of "un public latin épris [enamored of] d'ordre et de clarté." And Abel Hermant's vituperative (anti-English) review explained that racial and cultural differences were insurmountable: "Les Anglais ont un caractère si tranché, si personnel, qu'ils ne ressemblent point ni à nous-mêmes, ni aux autres peuples" [The English have such a distinct and personal nature that they do not resemble either ourselves or other peoples]. Moreover, "la plupart d'entre eux ne sont pas cultivés avec excès, ni spécialement intellectuels" [most of them are not exceedingly cultivated, nor especially intellectual].[26]

As they had in *Candida,* French audiences looked for romance in *Pygmalion*. After attending the opening performance at the Théâtre des Arts on 28 September 1923—with Paulette Pax as Eliza and Michel Simon as Doolittle—Pierre Veber affirmed: "Un auteur français aurait au troisième acte marié Pygmalion et sa créature" [A French author would have married off Pygmalion and his creature in the third act]. An exasperated Shaw wrote to Hamon: "Paris can now boast of being the only city in the world where it has failed. . . . But if theatrical people persist in regarding the play as a love affair between Higgins and Eliza, they deserve all they get in the way of failure."[27]

The French remained disturbed by this aspect of the play for years. Reviewing the 1955 production by Claude-André Puget (with Jean Marais as Higgins and Jeanne Moreau as Eliza), Gabriel Marcel recognized that "dans une certaine optique française conventionnelle, Eliza ne peut être qu'amoureuse de Higgins, même sans s'en douter, et il faudra bien qu'à la fin celui-ci, non seulement s'en aperçoive, mais réponde à cet amour" [within a certain conventional French perspective, Eliza can only be in love with Higgins, even without knowing it, and in the end he will not only have to realize it, but also respond to that love]. The play succeeded for precisely the same reasons that *Sainte Jeanne* triumphed: just as Ludmilla Pitoëff's Joan had seduced French audiences, so did Jeanne Morcau's Eliza. "Elle est irrésistible dans les scènes bouffonnes, émouvante dans les passages de sensibilité, diverse, complète, admirable" [She is irresistible in the farcical scenes, touching in the passages of sensibility, ever-changing, complete, admirable], wrote Georges Ravon. And Pierre Marcabru ascribed the play's acclaim to a shift in focus from the "insupportable" Higgins—"Sa brutalité cassante, sa goujaterie feinte, sa sécheresse de coeur étaient pour l'auteur de rares vertus" [His imperious brutality, his sham caddishness, his unfeelingness of heart were for the author rare virtues]—to "la douce Eliza."

The lovemaking in *Pygmalion* was not French enough, yet the production itself was almost too French. Morvan Lebesque wrote that Marais had "'parisianisé' à l'excès cette comédie anglaise qui prend avec lui des allures de Boulevard" ["parisianized" in the extreme this English comedy to which he gives Boulevard aspects], and Véra Volmane complained that "tout le côté satirique cède le pas à un comique de boulevard" [the whole satiric side gives way to boulevard comedy]. One J. L. thought that Marais had turned it into "une habituelle et banale comédie de Boulevard de chez nous . . . et l'humour cède constamment le pas à la farce" [our kind of regular, commonplace Boulevard comedy . . . and the humor constantly gives way to farce]. On the other hand, Lebesque had always thought that the play "demeurait presqu'injouable dans la traduction Hamon farcie de niaiseries argotiques et bizarrement francisée" [remained almost unplayable in the Hamon translation crammed with slangy nonsense and queerly frenchified], but that "M. Puget a nettoyé tout cela" [Mr. Puget has cleaned up all that].[28] And although Béatrix Dussane praised Puget's linguistic equivalents, missing were "le brin d'humour irlandais, un trait ça et là, de caricature arbitraire, irréductible, et par là même poétique" [that bit of Irish humor, a stroke here and there of arbitrary, indomitable, even poetic caricature].[29]

Ten years later, *Pygmalion* underwent another linguistic metamorphosis to perform a unique role in French-Canadian drama. Shaw had written to Hamon on 13 June 1922 that any attempt "to disguise Pygmalion as a French play about French people . . . would be as ridiculous as an attempt to make an English play of *Le Misanthrope* or *Le Bourgeois Gentilhomme*."[30] Yet one Montreal director succeeded in disguising it as a Canadian play about Quebecois people. The event occurred at a crucial moment when "joual" had become the centerpiece of Quebec theater. Joual, a mostly urban working-class language designating a particular way of life and social class, with its own vocabulary, accent, and diction, was utilized by many dramatists "as the sign of oppression and of neglect."[31] This phenomenon was the result of something that began in the 1930s, when language replaced religion as the major nationalist issue and became the primary vehicle of modern, secular Quebec nationalism. Thus when Éloi de Grandmont adapted *Pygmalion* for the stage in 1968, he used Quebec joual rather than Parisian argot.

"Why such a decision was made," writes a Canadian critic, "and approved by the Théâtre du Nouveau Monde, already becoming at the time a major theatrical institution of Quebec, is still a point of interest, however, for one cannot fail to notice that it is a dramatization of the problem of language and class. Popular language is opposed to a more educated way of speaking, and this opposition is coupled with two others concerning 'good' and 'bad' taste or manners, as well as the tension between a male and a female character." Shaw's *Pygmalion* was in effect "a *new* translation, written to *replace* a more traditional French translation, with *joual* taking over *Parisian argot* as the target language. The recognition of Quebec's popular use of French language, as a *legitimate* language of translation, was the newest idea put forward by Grandmont's work."[32] Linguistically "disguised," Shaw's play contributed to push the boundaries of French-Canadian theater by innovatively portraying class differences in the province of Quebec.

* * *

Jean-Claude Amalric observed that Shaw in France is "well-known superficially and widely misunderstood as far as his ideas and attitudes are concerned. The witty, paradoxical jester, famous for his repartees and humorous anecdotes, still prevents a part of the public from taking his message seriously or from understanding his aims."[33] For example, a performance of *Mrs Warren's Profession* scheduled for 22 March 1955 at the Salle Luxembourg in Paris was banned by the selection committee of the Comédie-Française. Shaw had been enjoying a revival—with *Pygmalion* at the Bouffes-Parisiens and *Le Héros et le soldat* at the Théâtre Gramont—but *Mrs Warren's Profession* was judged unsuitable because it was, reports Henderson, "'amoral' (not immoral), 'bad', and (shades of Voltaire!) 'boring'."[34]

Shaw's work continued to elicit mixed responses in France after his death, many of them positive. When Edmond Rostand's son, renowned biologist Jean Rostand, prefaced a 1959 edition of *Retour à Mathusalem* with a summary of Shaw's creative evolutionism, he began with a rather astonishing statement. Shaw's position, he wrote, "loin d'être une position désuète et condamnée par le savoir, rejoint certaines préoccupations et inquiétudes de la philosophie biologique contemporaine" [far from being out-of-date and reproved by scholarship, foreshadows certain preoccupations and concerns of contemporary biological philosophy]. Rostand mentions the French scientists who share Shaw's Lamarckism—Albert Vandel, Lucien Cuénot, Paul Chauchard, Henri Bergson, Teilhard de Chardin, and Édouard de Hartmann—and gives a brief overview of their theories. He concludes that their ideas "eussent certainement retenu l'attention de Shaw et lui eussent paru beaucoup moins absurdes et odieuses que le darwinisme" [would certainly have held Shaw's attention and appeared to him less absurd and odious than Darwinism].[35]

Another instance of a positive French reevaluation of Shaw is Jean Cocteau's translation of Jerome Kilty's *Dear Liar* (1960), a two-person play based on letters of Shaw and Mrs. Patrick Campbell written between 1899 and 1939. The acting was superb (Pierre Brasseur and Maria Casarès were enthusiastically acclaimed), and *Cher menteur* was hailed as a "beauté tremblante." One critic thought Cocteau's translation "éblouissante" [dazzling].[36] Why did this play appeal to poet-dramatist Cocteau? "A vrai dire," he wrote, "voilà une pièce abstraite et réaliste. Elle brave l'espace et le temps. On en arrive à oublier que les protagonistes furent célèbres et la marche de l'intrigue amoureuse l'emporte même sur l'intérêt historique de l'entreprise" [To tell you the truth, this is an abstract and realist play. It defies space and time. One comes to forget that the protagonists were famous, and the course of the love story prevails over the historic interest of the enterprise].[37]

Productions of Shaw's own works have fared equally well. There was Pierre Vaneck's *Pygmalion*; Georges Neveux's 1964 adaptation of *Saint Joan* (with Danièle Delorme as Joan); Jean Desailly's 1972 *Candida* (in a translation by Marie Dubost); Guy Rétoré's 1975 *Androcles and the Lion*; Georges Perros's *Heartbreak House*; Jean Marais's *Pygmalion, Caesar and Cleopatra*, and *The Devil's Disciple*; and Jean Mercure's *Heartbreak House*, to name the most important. And just as *Cher menteur* was enhanced by Cocteau's translation, Raymond Gérôme's 1965 production of *Don Juan in Hell* "was well received, in an adaptation by André Maurois which enhanced the brilliance of Shaw's dialogue."[38]

Ironically, Shaw's attitude toward the Comédie-Française remained ambivalent, even as a nonagenarian. Yvette Guilbert's husband, Dr. Max Schiller, sent Shaw a letter (25 July 1950) by P. A. Touchard, *administrateur général* of the Comédie-Française: the idea of mounting *Sainte Jeanne* "me séduit beaucoup" [seduces me very much], he wrote, cautioning that the final decision rested with the Comité de Lecture. Three months before his death, Shaw replied by advising ninety-year-old Schiller not to spend too much time persuading Touchard: "If you succeed it will probably be on such conditions that I shall refuse to authorise it." Shaw was thankful that Hamon "did not cut out all the Shaw and all the true Joan, and substitute Scribe and Sardou, which is, I suspect, what Mons. Touchard wants.... The sole advantage of the Français for me is that the company is trained in declamation by the Molière tradition; and if I, as Hamon contended, am *le Molière de nos jours,* their style would serve me fairly well."[39] Twelve years later, it did: on 18 December 1962, Hamon's translation of *La Grande Catherine,* adapted by Georges Neveux, was performed at the Comédie-Française.

And Shaw is still being discovered by the French: only in 1970 was *Major Barbara* (1905) performed in France. This is not surprising. So imbued were the French with long-standing prejudices and misconceptions about Shaw that it was not until *Sainte Jeanne* in 1925 that he won critical acclaim in Paris. As we will see presently, this belated success was highly ironic. Had it been staged according to Shaw's intentions, *Saint Joan* might have generated even greater antagonistic press than did his other plays. It took an entirely un-Shavian production for the French to concede that this madcap, would-be Molière was a playwright after all.

IV

Shaw et Jeanne d'Arc

8

The Trials of Jeanne d'Arc

From Peasant-Warrior to Piteous Waif

Pauvre Pucelle: Shaw Reinvents Jeanne d'Arc

On 17 July 1429, an illiterate tax collector's daughter turned soldier presided over the coronation of the dauphin Charles VII in the cathedral at Reims. On 30 May 1431, she was burned for heresy, witchcraft, and sorcery on the Place du Vieux-Marché in Rouen. She was nineteen years old. The verdict was annulled in 1456, and she was rehabilitated. In 1803, Napoleon restored her annual feast day of May 8, and in 1869, Félix Dupanloup, archbishop of Orléans, appealed to Rome to have her beatified. After four decades of research, she was designated "venerable" in 1904, beatified in 1909, and canonized by Pope Benedict XV on 16 May 1920. It took half a millennium for Joan of Lorraine to go from peasant-sorceress to patriot-saint.

Joan's literary history was turbulent.[1] The French at first found her a source of inspiration and patriotism, but the British villainized her. In Shakespeare's *Henry VI, Part One*, she was a witch and prostitute, an agent of diabolical powers. Voltaire's ribald mock-epic *La Pucelle d'Orléans* (completed 1730, published 1762)—parodying the devout patriot of Jean Chapelain's *Poëme héroïque: La Pucelle ou la France délivrée* (1656)—was a scathing attack on church and state centering on the preservation of Joan's virginity. The romantics reinstated her: Robert Southey's *Joan of Arc* (1793) and Friedrich von Schiller's *Die Jungfrau von Orleans* (1801) made her a freedom fighter, while Jules Michelet's *Histoire de France* (1865) turned her into a scapegoat and martyr, a portrait, says Valency, which "served to characterize her for all subsequent ages."[2] Others romanticized her: in Mark Twain's *Personal Recollections of Joan of Arc* (1896), she was a "sweetly pathetic child saint, surrounded by ugly monsters."[3] Anatole France, in his *Vie de Jeanne d'Arc* (1908), interpreted her visions as hysterical hallucinations and her mission as a priestly stratagem. Andrew Lang's *The Maid of France* (1908) showed that Joan's supernatural qualities could not be tested by reason or science. And in Charles Péguy's *Le Mystère de la charité de Jeanne d'Arc* (1921), she embodied universal peace and freedom. Shaw took some pains to underscore that most of these accounts owed more to artistic imagination than to historical fact.

With Joan's official recognition by the Church in Shaw's time, there occurred a resurgence of popular acclaim for the patron saint of France, especially from dramatists. There were countless French and English versions of her trial and martyrdom, most of them sentimental or melodramatic: Joseph Boubée's *Jeanne d'Arc à Poitiers* (1909), Jules Baudot's *Jeanne d'Arc* (1909) and *La Vocation de Jeanne d'Arc* (1912), Émile Moreau's *Le Procès de Jeanne d'Arc* (1909), Joseph Fabre's *La Délivrance d'Orléans* (1913), Charles Péguy's *Jeanne d'Arc* (1897), *Jeanne et Hauviette* (1904), *Le Mystère de la charité de Jeanne d'Arc* (1910), and *La Tapisserie de Sainte Geneviève et de Jeanne d'Arc* (1912), Percy Mackaye's *Jeanne d'Arc* (1906), Will Hutchins's *Jeanne d'Arc at Vaucouleurs* (1910), Julia Chadwick's *Joan of Arc: Three Scenes from her Life* (1912), Edward Garnett's *The Trial of Jeanne d'Arc* (1913), and Harold Brighouse's *The Maid of France* (1917). Putting an end to this series of mostly undistinguished Joans came Shaw's *Saint Joan,* written and performed in 1923, and published in 1924.[4]

* * *

Given Joan's religious and dramatic legitimization, it is not surprising to find a Shavian variation on such a popular theme. And as we have seen, Martin Meisel considers *Saint Joan,* a vehicle for star performer Sybil Thorndike, one of the many "women-plays" of Shaw's time.[5] What is puzzling is that *Saint Joan* took so long in coming, although it had been incubating in Shaw's mind for over a decade. From Orléans, in what he called "Joan of Arc country," Shaw had written to Mrs. Patrick Campbell in 1913:

> I shall do a Joan play some day, beginning with the sweeping up of the cinders and orange peel *after* her martyrdom, and going on with Joan's arrival in heaven. I should have God about to damn the En-

glish for their share in her betrayal and Joan producing an end of burnt stick in arrest of Judgment. "What's that? Is it one of the faggots?" says God. "No," says Joan "it's what is left of the two sticks a common soldier tied together and gave me as I went to the stake; for they wouldnt even give me a crucifix; and you cannot damn the common people of England, represented by that soldier[,] because a poor cowardly riff raff of barons and bishops were too futile to resist the devil." That soldier is the only redeeming figure in the whole business. English literature must be saved (by an Irishman, as usual) from the disgrace of having nothing to show concerning Joan except the piffling libel in Henry VI, which reminds me that one of my scenes will be Voltaire and Shakespeare running down bye streets in heaven to avoid meeting Joan.[6]

Thus the tragicomic, farcical epilogue, foreshadowing Joan's canonization five centuries later, probably was conceived first. As we see here, Shaw's dissatisfaction with other treatments of Jeanne d'Arc gave him all the more reason to redeem her. What was needed was a Shavian saint.

After the treatment Shaw's other plays had received in the French press, what was also needed was French support. Shaw knew of the recent attack on *Saint Joan* by A.-Louis Thomas, the New York correspondent for *Comoedia*, who had seen the New York premiere in December 1923. In his 13 January 1924 review—headed "Une Clownerie déplacée" [a misplaced clowning about]—Thomas had written of Shaw's "mégalomanie offensante," accusing him of turning the saint into "une petite sotte, sans profondeur, sans beauté, sans mystère" [a little fool, without depth, beauty or mystery]. "C'est cette Jeanne, bonne Lorraine, que quinze cent mille Français sont allés retrouver au Paradis des Braves, depuis 1914. M. Bernard Shaw essayera vainement de la diminuer par ses explications prosaïques, qui montrent seulement les limites de son talent" [It is this Jeanne, good Lorraine, that one million five hundred thousand Frenchmen have joined in the Paradise of the Brave, since 1914. M. Bernard Shaw will try in vain to diminish her by his prosaic explanations, which only serve to demonstrate the limits of his talent].[7]

Thomas's comments, and others by him in a second article (22 February) denigrating Hamon's translation as "un mortier crayeux" [chalky mortar],[8] may have spurred Shaw to write to the French ex-premier and minister of foreign affairs, René Viviani, on 13 March, inviting him to attend the opening of *Saint Joan* at the New Theatre. Shaw mentioned Thomas's second essay and tried to justify his own approach to the French

saint: "J'ai écrit cette pièce comme un acte de justice et de piété envers Jeanne outrageusement traitée par Shakespeare, S[c]hiller, Voltaire, Anatole France, de même que Barbier et autres dramaturges de seconde zone. Il est bon que la vérité soit dite en anglais, puisque les Anglais sont les 'vilains' de la pièce, si, toutefois, il y en a dans une affaire tout à fait claire. Un auteur français pourrait être suspect de patriotique partialité" [I wrote this play as an act of justice and of reverence toward Joan outrageously dealt with by Shakespeare, Schiller, Voltaire, Anatole France, as well as by Barbier and other second-rate playwrights. It is good that the truth be told in English, since the English are the "villains" of the play, if, however, there are any in an entirely clear matter. A French author could be suspected of patriotic partiality]. Shaw singled out Voltaire as having conceived a Joan who was an affront to French patriotism, emphasizing that "je n'ai pas suivi les traces de Voltaire" [I have not followed in Voltaire's footsteps].[9] There would be nothing in *Saint Joan* that could embarrass a representative of an ardently nationalistic France. Shaw may have read Voltaire's 8,300 lines of rhymed decasyllabics, but as historian Johan Huizinga remarks, "it is rather silly to call the *Pucelle* blasphemous"; "this lighthearted burlesque does not deserve automatic condemnation."[10]

Three days later, in a long letter published in *Comoedia* (although it was written on 7 March), Shaw was less diplomatic: "Voltaire made of her a heroine of licentious and scandalous extravagance,"[11] implying that his own version would not offend. The letter was addressed to Gabriel Boissy but meant as a counterblast to Thomas's attack. Since Thomas, according to Miron Grindea, was a "fanatical Roman Catholic,"[12] Shaw argued that he recognized that Joan was widely celebrated in France as a saint, but suggested that "the real woman in her is still as unpopular in her own country" as she was with the French Church and Inquisition. Shaw explained that the French are incapable of appreciating her either as saint, nationalist, or masterful woman. "I will have to overcome all these prejudices and weaknesses when I show France her national heroine without fear or favor, as she was." "I have not belittled Joan," he cautioned, "as would have been the case if I had turned her story into a melodrama about a wicked Bishop and a virtuous virgin." Then came the (by now usual) invective: Paris suffers "from a special kind of Eighteenth Century provincialism"; the French theater "addresses itself less and less to an intelligent public"; France "is almost at the bottom of the form" in appreciating Shaw's plays, something which has "become a proof of civilization." "If Paris perishes in ignorance of my works, then the loss will be for Paris and not for me."[13] Shaw was not endearing himself to the French public.

François Mauriac answered him in *La Nouvelle Revue française:* "M. Bernard Shaw nous donne l'illusion qu'il est le seul dans son bon sens et que le reste du monde extravague" [Shaw gives us the illusion that he alone makes sense and that everyone else is delirious], adding that "l'Irlandais demeure bien en arrière de notre Péguy" [the Irishman remains far behind our Péguy].[14]

"I am violently and arrogantly Protestant by family tradition," declared Shaw in 1906,[15] a remark that helps explain Jeanne d'Arc's impact upon his thinking. Shaw identified closely with his saint, an iconoclast who used wit and common sense to baffle her detractors. "Joan was the first great Protestant, and France has never shown herself friendly to Protestantism," Shaw wrote in his *Comoedia* letter.[16] Yet was she really a Protestant? Huizinga maintains that there is no justification for Shaw's toying with the word "Protestantism" because the term "makes sense only with regard to persons who, after having tested the whole medieval Catholic concept of the Church, deliberately rejected it. . . . True Protestantism can only lie on the yonder side of the whole system of Scholastic theology; Joan's ignorant faith falls completely on this side of it—or outside it. Her spirit has nothing in common with those of Huss or Wycliffe. . . . Protestantism presupposed humanism, intellectual development, a modern spirit; in her faith Joan of Arc was in the full sense of the word a primitive."[17] All of this is true, although Shaw's usage of the word is far simpler than Huizinga implies. If "the supremacy of private judgment for the individual [is] the quintessence of Protestantism," as Shaw puts it in the preface to *Saint Joan,* Joan was certainly a Protestant; he was even more explicit in a BBC radio talk on the five hundredth anniversary of the burning of Joan on 30 May 1931: "She was a Protestant: that is to say, she said that God came first with her."[18] For Shaw, the violently arrogant Protestant, that was enough.

* * *

A psychologically unromantic Joan corresponds to Shaw's idea of her as an unsentimental, almost asexual being. On his 1913 trip to France, he had seen at Orléans a fifteenth-century helmeted female head, of which he wrote in 1924: "I am convinced that it is Joan because it is not an ideal head, and yet it is [so] amazingly unlike any ordinary person that I ask 'If it is not Joan, who *is* it?'"[19] According to tradition, when Jeanne entered Orléans in triumph, a sculptor used her as the model for a head of Saint Maurice. In his shorthand manuscript, Shaw had described his Joan as having "an uncommon face, eyes very wide apart and bulging as they often do in very imaginative people, a long well-shaped nose with wide nostrils, a short upper lip, resolute full-lipped mouth, and a handsome fighting chin."[20] This portrait, aside from the sculpture's half-closed eyelids, accurately describes the helmeted head.

Joan's language, like her features, was also "uncommon": she spoke bluntly, as would have any peasant. Shaw based her speech on his own "north country talk" because Joan was also from the north, with "just a touch of rough country dialect" to distinguish her from the court people.[21] Shaw's verisimilitude pleased nobody. A. B. Walkley thought Joan's "rusticity of speech" was "a superfluity. Joan spoke the speech of Lorraine; you cannot represent that in an English play by making her speak the speech of an English peasant."[22] James Agate asked: "May I beseech Mr Shaw to allow her to drop the dialect? Whatever the quality of Lorraine peasant-speech, it cannot have been Lancashire."[23] Mina Moore wrote that by not rendering Shaw's dialect into French, the Hamons "ont supprimé un effet très déplaisant et que l'auteur n'avait nullement besoin de produire" [have suppressed a very unpleasant effect, one that the author did not in the least have to produce]. However, she found it difficult to believe that, no matter how modest her origins, Joan would have used the "expressions vulgaires" and "grossièreté triviale" [crude uncouthness] that Shaw attributes to her, citing the innocuous (at least to our ears) "muck," "fatheads," and "noodle."[24]

But Joan needed to be crude to remind the world that, unlike her literary antecedents, she was not an ethereal girl inspiring prayer; she was a passionate woman inspiring men into battle, "always the adventurous impetuous masterful girl soldier," as Shaw called her.[25] Joan's language reflected a forcefulness that the French were used to; Jeanne d'Arc had been a symbol of military prowess during the First World War when, in books and on posters, she fought alongside French soldiers. Shaw too claimed to have been inspired by the spirit of his warrior-maiden: "As I wrote she guided my hand," he reported, "and the words came tumbling out at such a speed that my pen rushed across the paper and I could barely write fast enough to put them down."[26] Although *Saint Joan* is a long work that entailed much research, it was begun on 29 April 1923 and recorded as completed on August 24. Shaw was sixty-seven, his Life Force still burning.

*   *   *

To reinstate Joan as a plausible heroine, Shaw was determined to remain faithful to French history. He chose as his primary source an abridged translation of the official Latin text of Joan's trial in 1431 and rehabilitation in 1456: the English version of Jules-Etienne-Joseph Quicherat's *Procès de condamnation et de réhabilitation de Jeanne d'Arc, dite La Pucelle,* in five volumes (Paris: J. Renouard, 1841–49), translated by T. Douglas Murray as *Jeanne d'Arc, Maid of Orleans, Deliverer of France; Being the Story of Her Life, Her Achievements, and Her Death, as Attested on Oath and Set Forth in the Original Documents* (London: Heinemann, 1902).[27] Even though Joan's words came to Shaw in an English translation of a French translation of the Latin original, Shaw let her speak for herself in his play as she had done at her trial. Aside from Murray, "I took particular care not to read a word of anything else until the play was finished," he wrote in 1924. "Then I amused myself by looking through Anatole, Lang, and Mark Twain."[28]

What he found was not amusing. Lang's Joan was a mere "border-ballad beauty," Twain's a "Victorian schoolmarm in armor." France was "disabled by his Anti-Feminism: he could not credit Joan with mental superiority to the Statesmen and Churchmen and Captains of her time." Voltaire's burlesque was "an uproarious joke," Schiller's play "romantic flapdoodle."[29] Plays or biographies, fictions or histories—all lacked verisimilitude. With Quicherat at his side, Shaw set about rehabilitating Joan as patriot-saint of French history and, in the process, turning her into a Shavian saint of the Life Force.

Brian Tyson has traced thoroughly Shaw's debt to Murray's translation of Quicherat, and his meticulous comparison of Murray to the shorthand manuscript of *Saint Joan* shows how faithful Shaw was to the French records; much of Joan's wit and many of her shocking statements are not Shaw's but Jeanne's. Joan says she was called "Jenny" just as Jeanne said they called her "Jeannette"; to Pierre Cauchon's crucial demand that Joan submit to the Church, she replies, "I will obey the Church . . . provided it does not command anything impossible," which is identical to Jeanne's answer: "I will refer to the Church Militant, provided they do not command anything impossible"; Joan's famous reply to Cauchon—who asks if she dares pretend to be in a state of grace—is this: "If I am not, may God bring me to it: if I am, may God keep me in it!" Jeanne's reply in Murray is this: "If I am not, may God place me there; if I am, may God so keep me." When taunted with a naked archangel Michael, Joan asks, "Do you think God cannot afford to clothe him?" just as Jeanne had replied: "Do you think God has not wherewithal to clothe him?"; Joan's reference to the English as "goddams" comes from Jeanne, who called them "godons"; and even Joan's "Miracle of the Eggs" has a factual parallel.[30] There are many other cases where Joan owes more to Jeanne than one suspects. Tyson concludes that Shaw read Murray "alert for fine lines and central issues; for the best and apparently most Shavian lines in the Trial scene are all to be found in Murray's translation of Quicherat."[31] Unlike his predecessors, Shaw was not rewriting history; he was merely rewording it.

Of course he was immediately accused of distorting history by providing Joan with a naturalistic explanation for her voices as messages of God working through her imagination. Yet here too there was a precedent: according to Huizinga, at the 1431 deliberations, Jehan Beaupère, master of theology, "was inclined to consider the phenomena 'to be not supernatural, but traceable, in part, to physical causes, and in part to imagination and human invention'."[32] This is crucial. Of all the charges against Joan, her main offense was her declaration that she was responsible to God rather than to the Church, a stance which for Shaw was the crux of her Protestantism. On the issue of imagination, it seems at least one member of Jeanne's tribunal thought like Shaw.

But Shaw did more than recast Murray. As well as being the mark of the Shavian hero, imagination is the key to Shaw's historical method. In 1893, he wrote that any book that claims to be "an extraordinarily erudite criticism of contemporary institutions . . . is really a work of pure imagination, in which a great mass of facts is so arranged as to reflect vividly the historical and philosophical generalizations of the author, the said generalizations being nothing more than an eminently thinkable arrangement of his own way of looking at things, having no objective validity at all."[33]

He was even more explicit the following year: "Historical facts are not a bit more sacred than any other class of facts. In making a play out of them you must adapt them to the stage, and that alters them at once, more or less. . . . Things do not happen in the form of stories or dramas; and since they must be told in some such form, all reports, even by eyewitnesses, all histories, all stories, all dramatic representations, are only attempts to arrange the facts in a thinkable, intelligible, interesting form—that is, when they are not more or less intentional efforts to hide the truth, as they very often are."[34] This explains in part how *Saint Joan* turns out to be, as Maurice Valency called it, "a brilliant interpretation of a period the author knew next to nothing about, and was thus able to explain with perfect clarity."[35] It would be more accurate to say with M. A. Cohen that "Shaw obviously believed that he had been true to the historical *essentials* despite the (inevitable) license with particulars."[36]

However, on the issue of the fairness of Jeanne's trial, Shaw may have been led astray unwittingly precisely by adhering to his source. After reading Murray, he was convinced that Joan had been tried, as he put it to the Reverend Joseph Leonard, "mercifully and fairly, all things considered." "They tried her quite mercifully," he said in his 1931 BBC radio talk. "They did not try to trap her." And he wrote in 1936, "That procedure was strictly legal, strictly reasonable, strictly pious."[37] The accusations were founded on fact: Joan was a heretic because she put God before the Church, a witch because she heard voices and saw visions, and unnatural in her desire to fight battles and to dress as a male soldier. The Rouen judges were not unjust or lawless; they simply mistook a saint for a witch. Huizinga points out that Joan's trial was a cause célèbre, and that any compassion shown to her was only "feigned gentleness" to make her condemnation seem unimpeachable. "Shaw was perhaps unaware that the words used on transferring a condemned person from the ecclesiastical court to the secular arm, 'with the request to deal with her tenderly,' were nothing more than a customary formula that no one expected to lead to anything but the bonfire."[38] This seriously undermines Shaw's (hyperbolic) claim that "Joan got a far fairer trial from the Church and the Inquisition than any prisoner of her type and in her situation gets nowadays in any official court."[39]

Facts and records aside, Joan's symbolic value was more important than history proper. Although Shaw based his play on what he believed were definitive accounts of her trial and recantation, he was concerned with what Jeanne d'Arc represented: Protestant, Nationalist, Militant Woman, Life Force. The play, writes Cohen, is "first and foremost a fable, and greater fidelity to the facts about Cauchon would have produced an essentially un-Shavian fable."[40] The same applies to the facts about Jeanne, and it is a measure of Shaw's genius that he did not let history override poetic license. If Joan speaks like Jeanne, she thinks like Shaw.

Conquering Paris: Georges and Ludmilla Pitoëff Reincarnate Joan

Seven plays by Shaw had been produced in Paris prior to *Sainte Jeanne*, none of them successfully. Hamon's flawed translations and polemical articles in the French press had probably alienated audiences, and Shaw's disparaging remarks about the French did not help. In addition, the 1923 world premiere of *Saint Joan* in New York had generated many articles in Parisian newspapers—such as the one by Thomas—portraying Shaw as unable to enter into the miraculous spirit of the Middle Ages or incapable of grasping Joan's religious qualities.[41] It appeared that *Sainte Jeanne* was doomed to be yet another French failure.

Due to a unique combination of factors, however, *Sainte Jeanne* turned into Shaw's greatest dramatic triumph in France. In particular the credit goes to two Russian émigrés, Georges Pitoëff (1886–1939) and his wife, Ludmilla (1895–1951), who, by reversing Shaw's well-planned characterization of Joan, created his first and most enduring Parisian success. Even the most famous English Joan was convinced: "Had I seen Ludmilla in *Saint Joan* before playing her myself," Sybil Thorndike told Shaw, "I would never have dared play her. Ludmilla is Joan herself."[42] Ironically, Ludmilla was the very Joan that Shaw despised: tearful, frail, vulnerable, sentimental, melodramatic, and saintly. The French loved her.

The road to Paris had not been easy for the Pitoëffs. From his early experiences before the war in Petrograd—where he had staged *Candida* in Russian—through five years in Geneva, where he met Ludmilla, Georges struggled against destitution. "Pitoëff has produced more plays for less money than any manager who ever lived," wrote John Palmer three months after the premiere of *Sainte Jeanne*, "and he has produced them without giving any impression of meanness or of conceptions thwarted by a lack of capital."[43] Palmer recalled seeing *Androcles and the Lion* played to an audience of twenty. Eventually, Jacques Copeau of the Vieux Colombier, Lugné-Poë of L'Oeuvre, and Firmin Gémier of L'Odéon visited Geneva and heard about or saw Georges's creations and Ludmilla's performances at the Plain-Palais. When the French critics discovered them, the couple moved to Paris in 1922, where they went on to perform works by Ibsen, Tolstoy, Pirandello, Cocteau, and others.[44]

In 1907, when Lugné-Poë was arguing over Shaw's terms for a production of *Mrs Warren's Profession* at the Théâtre de l'Oeuvre, Shaw sent him a long letter: "I am not a poor & obscure man of genius needing the aid of a defricheur [pioneer]: I am a shark eager to devour French artists & French theatres. . . . I have the constancy of a shark as well as its voracity." He concluded, "I shall conquer Paris in due time."[45] With the help of the Pitoëffs, he did—but not quite as he had planned.

* * *

Thorndike was right; Ludmilla was Joan herself—but a frail, vulnerable Joan, the very opposite of a strong suffragette. The stern-willed warrior was completely absent in the Pitoëff production, something Shaw observed firsthand when the Pitoëff company came to London before the Paris opening. André Maurois also saw the play, and when he praised Ludmilla's performance, Shaw exclaimed, "Your Mme Pitoëff is charming, touching, but she would never have driven a single Englishman out of France."[46]

Ludmilla's transfiguration was masterminded by her husband; Georges had staged *Sainte Jeanne* as a mystic drama that evoked precisely the holy atmosphere Shaw wanted to avoid. His intentions were clear: "Je veux qu'on sente une seule chose: que Jeanne est une sainte. Ce que je m'attacherai à rendre sensible, avant tout, par-dessus tout, c'est le sentiment religieux qui émane de l'héroïne avec une incomparable puissance d'ingénuité, parce qu'elle est toute foi en sa mission, absolument possédée de l'idée qu'elle est l'envoyée de Dieu. Alors, en dépit de l'intérêt historique ou philosophique de tel ou tel épisode, c'est le personnage de Jeanne-Ludmilla qui, dans son esprit, domine toute la pièce" [I want people to feel only one thing: that Joan is a saint. What I will strive to embody, first and foremost, is the religious feeling which emanates from the heroine with an incomparable power of ingenuousness, because she is all faith in her mission, absolutely possessed of the idea that she is God's messenger. Thus, despite the historical or philosophical interest of this or that episode, it is the character of Jeanne-Ludmilla who, in her spirit, dominates the whole play].[47]

Georges was in full control of all aspects of the production. "Le metteur en scène impose donc sa vision et coordone tous les autres intermédiaires," he wrote. "C'est la personnalité du metteur en scène qui fera ressortir le sens général de l'oeuvre" [The producer imposes his vision and coordinates all the other intermediaries. It is the producer's personality which will make the general meaning of the work stand out]. To enhance his wife's miraculous aura, he created a set consisting of a huge triptych, "un cadre gothique immuable" [an unchanging gothic frame], he called it, which evoked cathedral windows depicting the legends of the saints[48] and enveloped Jeanne-Ludmilla from the coronation at Reims to the trial at Rouen. "Backed by an open sky for exterior scenes or curtains for the interiors (black in the judgement hall, red and gold for the epilogue in the King's bedchamber), or flanked by railings for Reims cathedral, this motif allowed for dramatic variety whilst preserving the all-important thematic continuity."[49] Tyson calls the set "an exciting one, conceived under the influence of the Cubists,"[50] but Jean Hort was disappointed with its lack of perspective and found the heavy, outmoded scenery reminiscent of "un dadaïsme datant de 1925." This background, "au lieu d'habiller la pièce, en déformait les résonances par son archaïsme primaire et son charactère inachevé" [instead of dressing up the play, deformed its resonances by its primitive archaism and unfinished character].[51]

5. The premiere of *Sainte Jeanne* at the Théâtre des Arts, Paris, 28 April 1925, with Ludmilla Pitoëff as Jeanne d'Arc in the triptych designed by her husband, Georges Pitoëff. By permission of the Hamon Collection, Archival and Special Collections, University of Guelph Library, Guelph, Canada.

Whatever its beauties or defects, Georges's gothic triptych was overshadowed by Ludmilla. It is ironic that Shaw's description of her resembles his description of the head of Saint Maurice, which had "an uncommon face, eyes very wide apart and bulging." Shaw described Ludmilla as "an extraordinarily fascinating creature" with "big eyes," a woman "so exquisitely and *originally* made that she seems to be acting all over."[52] The poster of Ludmilla by Kees Van Dongen for the 1926 production of *Sainte Jeanne* at the Théâtre des Célestins in Paris shows her striking physiognomy, especially the large, bulging eyes. Such was her stage presence that "she invariably transformed all her roles into something unreal and dreamlike."[53]

Ludmilla was serious about her metamorphosis into Saint Joan. To get as close as possible to the saint, she had often visited Rouen to examine the historical documents and to see Jeanne's prison. Henri-René Lenormand relates how she began to identify with Joan: "Le rôle commençait à l'habiter; derrière le rôle, le personnage, et derrière le personnage, la grande âme de la Sainte l'enveloppait, la cernait, l'attaquait de toutes parts. Elle subissait avec ferveur cette imprégnation. . . . Elle changeait, dans le rythme et l'orientation de sa vie intérieure. . . . Une Jeanne vivait en elle"

[The role began to inhabit her; behind the role, the character, and behind the character, the great soul of the Saint enveloped her, encircled her, attacked her from all sides. She suffered this impregnation with fervor. . . . She changed, in the rhythm and orientation of her interior life. . . . Joan inhabited her].[54] As Hort puts it, she played Joan with "un visage illuminé par la foi radieuse" [a face illuminated by radiant faith].[55] Ludmilla's self-imbued saintliness reached its apex when she underwent a religious crisis and, tormented by her own impurity, undertook religious pilgrimages.[56]

To the religious atmosphere and the radiant Ludmilla, one must add a reworked dialogue as a third factor contributing to Shaw's unwitting Parisian success, for the Pitoëffs not only betrayed the spirit of Shaw's intentions but also the spirit of his text. This was understandable; their initial enthusiasm for the English version turned to dismay when they read the Hamons' translation. And since the couple had always stubbornly refused to alter their work—they were adamant about not changing a word—the Pitoëffs approached the young dramatist Lenormand. For several weeks, he and Ludmilla secretly revised the Hamon version with the help of Shaw's original. Almost nothing was altered except Joan's lines, but the task must have been daunting. Lenormand called Hamon's text "l'épaisse matière verbale dont les Hamon avaient barbouillé l'original," an "étrange pâte à reluire" [the thick verbal matter with which the Hamons had smeared the original, a strange polishing paste].[57] Anything was an improvement.

But in trying to save *Saint Joan,* the Pitoëffs had antagonized almost everyone. When André Antoine's review of the play alluded to the retouched translation without mentioning the culprit—he wrote about "un des jeunes maîtres du théâtre actuel" [one of the young masters of the current drama][58]—Augustin Hamon countered in mid-July with in an open letter that this was a slander punishable under British law! Antoine replied in *L'Information* that he was simply not authorized to name the playwright. Shaw then sent Lenormand angry and ironic letters—thanking him for ensuring Shaw's glory—and Lenormand did not reply because he could neither admit nor deny his meddling without placing the Pitoëffs in an embarrassing position.[59] Out of this muddle of wounded vanities, only Ludmilla emerged triumphant. Shaw lost the battle to retain his saint's integrity, but *Sainte Jeanne* won Shaw's war on Paris.

*   *   *

The French were accustomed to pious, poetic dramas; over one hundred Joan plays had appeared in France since 1890.[60] Four months before

Sainte Jeanne, Parisian audiences at the Théâtre de la Renaissance had witnessed the failure of François Porché's *La Vierge au grand coeur* (1925), a romantically earnest work in which Jeanne "declaims endlessly with a false poetic lyricism" and saints and angels participate in Jeanne's apotheosis on stage. In stressing her divine inspiration rather than her victimization by earthly powers, Porché omitted the entire trial scene! Writes Daniel C. Gerould, "Shaw's abandonment of the customary lyric manner and rhetorical piety could not but be welcome to the French for whom the subject had seemed thoroughly exhausted."[61]

Georges had (in Shaw's eyes) botched the mise-en-scène, but he shrewdly took precautions with the French press. At the *répétition générale*—a final dress rehearsal crucial to a play's reputation, since the daily newspaper reviews appeared before the next evening's *première représentation,* opening night—he sat his friends amidst influential critics: Georges Duhamel beside André Antoine, the Vildracs beside Paul Ginisty, and so on for critics Henri Bidou, Edmond Sée, Gaston de Pawlowski, Étienne Rey, Pierre Audiat, Pierre Veber, Régis Gignoux, Lucien Descave, and others. In this way, they "would overhear only favourable comments and, separated from their critical brethren, be unable to conspire against the piece!"[62]

These precautions, along with the gothic sets, a pious Jeanne, and a revitalized translation, had the desired effect: at the Théâtre des Arts on 28 April 1925, *Sainte Jeanne* became Shaw's first French success and ran to over one hundred packed performances. The Pitoëff production is "still considered one of the great French theatrical events of the century."[63] Critics agreed that the play was full of reverence for Joan, who remained historical, heroic, and surprisingly undefiled by a dramatist whose previous treatment of Napoleon (in *The Man of Destiny*) had been less than respectful. "Ce n'est pas une guerrière bardée d'acier," wrote *L'Illustration,* "c'est une vierge frêle, presque une enfant, mais d'un tel rayonnement intérieur, d'une telle flamme mystique, qu'elle en est comme transfigurée. Et pourtant, au faîte même de la sublimité, elle demeure pathétiquement humaine" [She is not a warrior blazing with armor, she is a frail virgin, almost a child, but of such an interior radiance, such a mystical flame, that she appears transfigured. And yet, even at the height of sublimity, she remains pathetically human].[64]

Pierre Veber, drama critic for the *Petit Journal,* was beside himself, calling the play "une chose splendide, unique, féroce, terrible et savoureuse, d'une facture prodigieuse, d'une virtuosité ironique invraisemblable" [a splendid thing, unique, fierce, terrific and delectable, of prodigious workmanship, of incredible ironic virtuosity].[65] Paul Blanchart wrote that Shaw had "brossé un tableau d'une étonnante justesse, qui parfois déconcerte, mais, bien vite, séduit et qui emporte le spectateur dans une vie hallucinante" [painted a picture of an astonishing accuracy, which at times disconcerts but very quickly seduces and carries the spectator into a hallucinating life].[66] Roger Martin du Gard wrote to Pitoëff on 15 May that his mise-en-scène was "d'une ingéniosité très spirituelle" [of a very spiritual ingenuity], and that he had found Ludmilla "*incomparable* dans la scène de l'interrogatoire" [*incomparable* in the interrogation scene].[67] And André Rivoire, who had found the French *Pygmalion* execrable in 1923, congratulated the Hamons on their brilliant translation of *Saint Joan*, unaware that this time it was not entirely theirs.[68]

"I am too old to educate Paris," Shaw had lamented in his *Comoedia* letter.[69] Yet *Saint Joan* educated the Parisian critics in a number of ways. They were impressed with the way Shaw had emphasized "Joan's nobility and purity by reserving all his satire for the other characters whom he debased and ridiculed," a contrast that "was considered his masterstroke." "Juxtaposing the saint and the almost farcical world of Shavian satire seemed an amazing technical feat whereby Shaw avoided sullying Joan as the French had feared and instead glorified her as never before by exercising his ironic wit on her opponents." They also found *Sainte Jeanne* amusing as well as edifying, and thought "familiar" and "lively" Shaw's anachronistic technique of making historical figures think and speak like their contemporaries.[70]

Most of all, they were delighted with Joan. Thorndike's "British" interpretation, imbued with energy and willpower, seemed vulgar to the French. They preferred Ludmilla's "Gallic" emotionalism, especially during the trial scene, where the audience wept as a frail, childlike Joan confronted the unrelenting tribunal. With the court behind Ludmilla—who sat facing the audience—"her judges seemed of a different world than Joan's spiritual universe of voices and inner light." Since "the French had been so awed by the Saint that they were unable to make her sufficiently human," Shaw's "simple peasant, almost a child, directed by divine light," seemed a radical departure from other versions. That Joan alone heard the voices and that no miracles were performed on stage (for once) increased the audience's belief in the supernatural forces at work.[71]

Inevitably, there were critiques. Those writing from a Catholic viewpoint were offended by Shaw's presentation of Joan as Protestant and by his rehabilitation of Cauchon. The depiction of Charles VII and his court was judged excessively farcical: "By debasing the characters who surrounded Joan to the level of burlesque figures . . . Shaw put his saintly heroine in the company of buffoons."[72] The epilogue also jarred French sensibilities. Palmer claims that it "would never have been criticised as unnecessary if its critics had seen the Pitoëff production. The scene is grotesque, but grotesque in the spirit of the mediaeval miracle play."[73] Yet most French critics thought it was superfluous: "Its bizarre form, combining fantasy and humor, . . . was unwelcome, and the half-burlesque, half-fantastic treatment seemed forced and unnatural."[74] Clownish and noble characters, parodic and dignified scenes, irony and drama—this alternatingly comic and serious play puzzled the French, and they found Shaw's mixture of genres disconcerting yet amusing. "Because of the skillful combination of these diverse elements, *Saint Joan* never ceased to interest and to entertain," writes Gerould, and Shaw's placing Joan "uncontaminated into a burlesque setting was regarded as a technical *tour de force* of great difficulty."[75] After all of his previous failures, it seemed that with *Sainte Jeanne,* Shaw could do no wrong.

After seeing the Pitoëff production at the Globe Theatre in London in 1930, Desmond MacCarthy believed the French production had improved on the original! He wrote that those who had been troubled about historical accuracy or intellectual anachronisms "will have learnt from seeing *Sainte Jeanne* how unimportant these points were." He found in Thorndike's Joan "more of Lady Astor about her than of a peasant who saw visions," and that Ludmilla's Joan forced "politicians, bishops and generals to do what she wanted . . . thanks to the magic of pure goodness rather than energy of character. . . . She was perhaps too much of a piteous little waif in her misery, and too much of a darling in armour at other moments to suggest completely the strange power of a saint." Shaw's jokes seemed "less prominent in translation," which made the play dramatically effective. MacCarthy found Shaw's unpoetical recantation scene—"when he calls upon the Muse of Words to do more for him than to define and state, she does not answer"—much improved in French. Joan's lyrical passage about "young lambs crying through the healthy frost" was unconvincing: "No mediaeval shepherdess would think the frost healthy. Well, in *Sainte Jeanne* these false notes, this poor diction, were partially veiled from English ears."[76]

MacCarthy was in good company at the Globe, for Shaw was there. At a reception in honor of the playwright and the Compagnie Pitoëff at the Savoy on June 20, Shaw met the entire Pitoëff cast. Some he found more romantic than robust. To Louis Salou (La Hire), he said, "Vous étiez un beau chevalier! Enfin, vous avez plu à ma femme, mais pas à moi!" [You were a handsome knight! In short, my wife liked you, but not me!]. La Hire, Shaw explained, was "un ancien berger" [an old shepherd] who must "bound like a lion" because he envies Dunois and wants to replace him. "Il ne faut pas chercher à comprendre," he told the French actors. "Chez l'acteur, l'instinct doit suffire.... Pour jouer mes pièces, il faudrait des acteurs qui n'y comprennent rien comme ceux du Théâtre Français" [One must not try to understand. In an actor, instinct must suffice.... To act my plays, one would need actors who don't understand them, like those of the Théâtre Français].[77]

But it was Ludmilla's emotionalism that especially displeased Shaw. One critic described Jeanne in the 11 June 1930 *Daily Herald*: "She is shaken with terror, she grimaces, the tears roll down her face."[78] It appears that Shaw was not exaggerating when he told her: "Vous aimez pleurer. ... Jeanne d'Arc ... est aussi une guerrière tandis que vous ne jouez que la sainte.... Vous êtes déjà dans le ciel au premier acte" [You love to weep. ... Jeanne d'Arc ... is also a warrior but you play only the saint.... You are already in heaven at the first act].[79] Aniouta Pitoëff, Ludmilla's daughter, describes her mother's unstoppable tearfulness: "On se demandait comment elle pouvait pleurer tant de larmes et recommencer le lendemain. Dans les coulisses, après le tableau du procès, on la voyait sortir de scène, le visage décomposé.... Titubante, transfigurée, elle se guidait à travers ses larmes" [We wondered how she was able to cry so many tears and start over again the following day. In the wings, after the trial scene, we used to see her coming off stage, her face distorted.... Staggering, transfigured, she guided herself through her tears].[80] And yet those tears brought Ludmilla one step closer to the historical Jeanne d'Arc, judging from a contemporary account by De Boulainvilliers, who reported in June 1429: "*abundantia lacrimarum manat,*" "she sheds tears freely."[81] But Ludmilla was not at all Shaw's Joan. With Thorndike translating, she tried to mollify Shaw by arguing that any great role could be interpreted in a number of different ways. "No, there's only one right way," Shaw retorted, "and that's the way that the author wrote it."[82]

Jean Hort suggested that Shaw was merely "furieux de jalousie" because Ludmilla had succeeded in arousing passions that the author had never intended.[83] This may be true, and Shaw told her bluntly "that she had given a wonderful representation of a scullery maid being sentenced to a fortnight's imprisonment for stealing a pint of milk for her illegitimate child."[84] He wrote in the *Era* in 1934 that Ludmilla had "revived the snivelling womanly heroine of the old sentimental melodramas with appalling intensity. But the effect she made in Paris was not repeated in

London, and will never, I hope, overcome that made by Miss Thorndike in London."[85]

Yet some English critics thought Joan's innocence and faith were obscured by Thorndike's energy and coarseness,[86] and Huizinga agreed: "I was put off by an excess of dramatic art—a rapturous note in her voice and gesture, a touch of high tragedy that served as a disturbing rather than a contributing factor."[87] Not only was Ludmilla too tearful and pitiful, she was too attractive. Shaw went so far as to tell her: "You put too much sex in the part. Look at the English Joan"—pointing to Sybil Thorndike—"she hasn't got an inch of sex."[88] (Thorndike's rejoinder, if there was one, went unrecorded.) Shaw's comment may sound off the mark, but it is consistent with what he had told Lady Gregory only three weeks after beginning the play. In her journal for 19 May, she recorded that because Sarah Bernhardt and others had "played so many parts turning on sexual attraction [Shaw] wanted to give Joan as a heroine absolutely without that side."[89] That Ludmilla infused sex appeal into Shaw's saint is itself something of a miracle.

Ironically, it may be that Georges Pitoëff's idiosyncratic production was more memorable than the one starring Thorndike. Palmer's comparison of the two productions provides an insight into that phenomenon:

> [*Saint Joan* was only] adequately conveyed to the English public in London. . . . You got from it neither more nor less than from a reading of the book. One scene followed another, intelligently acted, perfectly clear and logical, but the total effect was that of a series of charades which put together gave us the title *St. Joan*. . . . The author's ideas were in all essential respects carried out. But never for one moment did we have the feeling, which only the great producers give, that the play was a world unto itself, that it had its own peculiar atmosphere, a unity and character which belonged to that particular play. . . . There was never one instant of that complete illusion when the play itself has an existence and a quality that leave a permanent impression on the imagination.

But *Sainte Jeanne* at the Théâtre des Arts refuses to be forgotten precisely because of the "element of saintship and of the miraculous in which the London exposition of *St. Joan* was so fatally deficient." The three arches of Georges's triptych reaching heavenward convey "continuously but without undue insistence a religious background. . . . The imagination is prepared for a miracle."[90]

When Thorndike and Pitoëff did perform Joan's most famous miracle—her discovery of the dauphin upon her arrival at the court—their radically different interpretations crystallize the gap between Shaw's conception and the French interpretation. "I have a vague recollection of Miss Thorndike," writes Palmer, "striding into the scene, full of vitality and *nous,* picking him out with a bustling and instinctive competence that refused to be baffled. There was no suggestion of a miracle—nothing to explain the conversion of the unbelievers or to justify the immediate leadership which it enabled the heavenly maid to assume." In Pitoëff's version, "The maid enters, a tiny figure, shrinking a moment from the hall blazing with light and from the alien laughter. For a breathless instant she pauses like a child, sensitive to mockery, bewildered. Then suddenly uplifted by her inspiration and purpose she braves them all, and, led by the intuition with which she is suddenly illumined, goes straight to her goal. We do not see the dauphin ourselves. She suddenly dives into the midst of them and brings him forth."[91]

Perhaps the most ironic aspect of Shaw's first French triumph was that it was not at all an "intellectual" one. Shaw's attempt to explain the opposition to Joan as an alliance of the feudal Church and state was less significant or important to Parisian audiences than the portrayal of Sainte Jeanne d'Arc. Shaw's preface had not yet been translated at the time of the Paris premiere, but that may not have made any difference; two years later, Pierre Brisson showed that the preface's ideas assumed little importance in appreciating the performance.[92]

* * *

"I love the real Joan," Shaw had written in his *Comoedia* letter, "but the conventional Joan of the stage makes me sick."[93] Three months before he died, Shaw referred to "Joan in tears all the time and half burnt already on her first entry, like all the other French Joans."[94] Yet this saintly, tearful, conventional Joan was hailed by the French as a brilliant portrait of their national patriot-saint. Huizinga had complained that "by using familiarity and humor to fumigate his work of the romantic [Shaw] also banishes the heroic," and wondered whether Shaw "has not thrown out the baby of tragedy with the bath of romanticism."[95] This may have been true of the English production, but the Pitoëffs infused enough pathos into the play to seduce French audiences. Of the seventeen comedies by Shaw produced in Paris during his lifetime, *Sainte Jeanne* was by far the most enthusiastically received.

6. Ludmilla Pitoëff in *Sainte Jeanne* at the Théâtre des Mathurins, Paris, December 1934. By permission of the Agence Photographique Roger-Viollet, Paris.

The play's sensation went beyond the premiere. The Pitoëffs revived *Sainte Jeanne* in Paris numerous times between 1925 and 1934, and it remained the most dependable play in their repertory. It was even staged alongside other contemporary French plays on Joan of Arc: in 1929 and 1931 with René Arnaud's *Le Vray procès de Jehanne d'Arc,* and in Orléans in 1936 with the Domrémy scene from Charles Péguy's *Jeanne d'Arc.* But even after his Paris triumph, Shaw continued to worry about his saint: "The old conventional Joan with the sad eyes . . . and reeking with pious pathos, will kill my play dead," he wrote to Hamon in 1928.[96] It is almost as if Shaw refused to believe that the French were delighted with something other than what he had intended. Ironically, Ludmilla performed the role with even more "pious pathos" as the years went by. In reviewing the 1934 production, one critic remarked: "Pendant ces dix années, l'âme de Jeanne s'est imposée à elle, prenant possession de tout son être, en sorte que maintenant nous n'avons même plus sous les yeux une actrice incomparable, mais Jeanne en personne qui prie, agît et agonise devant nous" [During these ten years, Jeanne's soul has asserted itself upon her, taken possession of her entire being, so that now we behold not an incomparable actress, but Jeanne in person who prays, acts and agonises before us].[97]

Benjamin Crémieux declared in 1938 about *Sainte Jeanne* that "ce fut beaucoup plus le triomphe de Jeanne d'Arc que de Bernard Shaw" [it was much more the triumph of Joan of Arc than of Bernard Shaw].[98] It was also the triumph of Ludmilla: "Bernstein was exactly right," wrote Shaw to Hamon in 1937, "when he said that her success was due to the fact that her every word and gesture was a flat contradiction of the Shavian text."[99] Yet one must not give all the credit to the Pitoëffs; Shaw too had a hand in his French conquest. He may even have created a completely new genre for the French theater. In his review of 1 June 1925, Lucien Dubech called *Sainte Jeanne* a "vaudeville philosophique," and from then on the expression was used to describe Shaw's plays.[100] And in his survey of the drama, *Destin du théâtre* (1930), Jean-Richard Bloch mentioned *Saint Joan* as a model for a new historical drama.[101] Shaw's irony, humor, and fantasy cleared the French stage of decades of solemn history plays full of high rhetoric and false piety. Shaw, the voracious shark, had devoured them all—thanks to Ludmilla-Joan.

Surviving Vichy: Jeanne During the Occupation

The symbol of the saintly *pucelle* brutally put to death was exploited during the entire period of the Occupation. It represented France victorious against its enemy, and its enemy was Germany. The Resistance adopted the Croix de Lorraine as the emblem of Free France, and "parallels were frequently drawn between De Gaulle and Joan."[102] When Charles Péguy's *Le Mystère de la charité de Jeanne d'Arc* (1910) was staged by the Théâtre des Arts in June 1940, its message was unmistakable: "C'étaient des barbares, des armées barbares, des armées innombrables, des armées païennes. Cent fois plus barbares, cent fois pires, infiniment plus barbares, infiniment pires que les Anglais mêmes" [They were barbarians, barbarian armies, innumerable armies, pagan armies. A hundred times more barbarous, a hundred times worse, infinitely more barbarous, infinitely worse than the English themselves]. In 1941, Paul Claudel, author of *Jeanne d'Arc au bûcher* (1937), called Jeanne d'Arc "la grande réunisseuse de notre pays" [the great reunifier of our country].[103]

But Jeanne was more than a forger of political unity; she was a warrior-mystic in the Shavian sense. Shaw's play contributed to this resurgence of interest in the saint, if only because *Sainte Jeanne* was the first Joan play to be staged in occupied Paris, on 24 December 1940. "Double malice," wrote theater critic Béatrix Dussane, "devaient penser les censeurs de l'armée occupante, puisque'il s'agissait d'une héroïne française dressée contre les Anglais et célébrée par le plus irréductible des Irlandais" [Double malice, the censors of the occupying army must have thought, since what was involved was a French heroine standing up against the English and celebrated by the most indomitable of Irishmen].[104] In truth it was the success of *Sainte Jeanne* that encouraged another company to mount Péguy's play in July 1941. Then came Claudel's that same month, and finally Claude Vermorel's *Jeanne avec nous* (completed in 1938) on 19 January 1942, whose final performance in August marked the end of Joan on the Parisian stage for the rest of the Occupation, with the exception of a reprise of Claudel's play on 9 May 1943. Dussane claims that Vermorel's play finally opened German eyes; it was taken off at the height of its popularity.[105]

Ironically, then, Shaw was the impetus for the presentation of French Joan plays in the country where he had been the most maligned. For *Sainte Jeanne*, Raymond Rouleau's company, with Jany Holt as Jeanne, used the Hamon translation for their Théâtre de l'Avenue production, which ran until the end of January 1941. That reviews were comparatively few, writes Gabriel Jacobs, indicates that the performances "were neither deliberately didactic, nor deliberately contentious, nor deliberately ambiguous." The majority of them concentrated on the literary and dramatic merits of the play, and only the theater critic of *L'Illustration* commented on 14 January on "its enormous latent value as propaganda beyond that of its conspicuous anti-British ethos." He found Shaw's Joan "miraculeuse dans la mesure où elle a galvanisé pour un idéal un pays aveugli par la défaite" [miraculous insofar as she has galvanized for an ideal a country blinded by defeat].[106] During the Occupation, that was some miracle.

Jacobs believes that "Jeanne's 'rien ne comptant, en dehors de Dieu, que la France libre et Française' (p. 216) [aside from God, nothing counts except France free and French], may have sounded too much like a call to arms not to have caught the attention of the censor." Of other passages, such as Jeanne's "Notre ennemi est à nos portes et nous sommes là sans rien faire" [Our enemy is at our doors and we do nothing] (on p. 73), he asks: "Could the audiences of the winter of 1940 have been insensitive to such patent implications, heavy with overtones of pre-war hesitation, infighting, self-indulgence and low military morale, in the face of order, discipline and blitzkrieg tactics? It would seem that Jeanne's symbolic role was as yet too ill-defined in the national consciousness, or the critics unsure of how far it was appropriate to press the point home."[107]

That the censors did not close down *Sainte Jeanne* is puzzling; that the French chose to stage it at all is baffling. Paris walls sprouted placards representing the British as the betrayers of France; one showed Joan burning at the stake and a silhouette of Napoleon brooding at Saint Helena, beneath which was written: "Our two great national martyrs, Joan of Arc and Napoleon, are England's victims."[108] In addition, Shaw's attitude during the early days of the war was "characteristically exasperating," writes Hobson. He took "a perverse pleasure in annoying those who most firmly believed in Britain's capacity to resist the Nazis." Yet in typical Shavian paradox, "more than any other British writer he stimulated the hopes of those French men and women who had the spirit of resistance in them."[109] Perhaps, writes Jacobs, "its strong anti-English flavour (and the fact that Shaw was Irish was emphasised in a number of reviews of the play) had considerable appeal at the end of 1940, when Albion was still exceptionally perfidious for a part of the French bourgeois theatre-going public."[110] One critic, writing in *Les Nouveaux temps* on 6 January 1941, went so far as to recommend *Sainte Jeanne* as a cure for Anglophilia![111]

The apotheosis of Joan of Arc on the French stage during the war occurred at the "Fête de Jeanne d'Arc" of 10 May 1942, a gala matinee organized by the Théâtre National Populaire at the Palais de Chaillot. Excerpts were performed from François Porché's *La Vierge au grand coeur* (1925), Saint-Georges de Bouhélier's *Jeanne d'Arc la pucelle de France* (1934), Vermorel's *Jeanne avec nous* (1938) and the plays of Claudel, Péguy, and Shaw, among others.[112] A few months after the celebration, André Gide recorded in his diary that he was rereading *Saint Joan* "avec un très vif contentement" [keen satisfaction]; the play seemed to him "une merveille d'intelligence, de pertinence et d'ingéniosité" [a marvel of intelligence, aptness and cleverness].[113] Despite his dissatisfaction with the Pitoëffs, Shaw survived his first French triumph and Joan survived the Occupation.

9

Jeanne after Joan

Shaw's Joan and Two French Incarnations

Jean Giraudoux and *Ondine*

One of Shaw's favorite masks was the sermonizer pontificating in the theater, which he referred to as "the week-day church." A good play, he maintained, was "essentially identical with a church service as a combination of artistic ritual, profession of faith, and sermon."[1] One playwright with similar ideas was Jean Giraudoux (1882–1944). "Le spectacle est la seule forme d'éducation morale et artistique d'une nation," he wrote. "Il est . . . le seul moyen par lequel le public le plus humble et le moins lettré peut être mis en contact personnel avec les plus hauts conflits, et se créer une religion laïque, une liturgie et ses saints, des sentiments et des passions" [Entertainment is a nation's only form of moral and artistic education. It is . . . the only means by which the most lowly and uneducated public can come into personal contact with the highest conflicts, and create for itself a lay religion, a liturgy and its saints, feelings and passions].[2] Giraudoux also called the art of the theater, whose language he considered liturgical in its solemnity and exuberance, a "prophecy or divination."[3]

In the same way that pulpitlike speeches were a Shavian hallmark, Giraudoux's characteristic trait was the tirade—long set speeches whose words stress symbolic rather than representational value.[4] "Sans style rien ne vit," he wrote, "et rien ne survit: tout est dans le style" [Without style nothing lives, and nothing survives: everything is in the style].[5] He went so far as to maintain that the audience itself expressed "cette vénération pour le style et le vocabulaire, [pour] ce qu'un peuple possède de plus précieux, son langage" [this veneration for style and vocabulary, [for] a people's most precious possession, its language].[6] But Giraudoux's style was problematic, and Tristan Bernard considered him "an author of great talent who spoiled the pleasure of his finest ideas by expressing them in a form intentionally complicated and sybilline."[7] Accusations of verbosity were also directed at Shaw, who once defined the drama of Ibsen and his followers—of whom he was one—as "a forensic technique of recrimination, disillusion, and penetration through ideals to the truth, with a free use of all the rhetorical and lyrical arts of the orator, the preacher, the pleader, and the rhapsodist."[8]

Both Shaw and Giraudoux saw the drama as didactic and the theater as a forum for the heightened, almost spiritual, awareness of its audience. They conveyed this awareness through well-known historical, biblical, mythical, or archetypal figures and situations: Shaw with Pygmalion, Androcles, Caesar, Napoleon, Don Juan, and Joan of Arc; Giraudoux with Amphitryon, Electra, Siegfried, Judith, the Trojan War, and the female water-spirit, the undine. Both men wrote a play on the theme of the inability of a mundane world to accept the mystical, with heroines that are neither altogether human nor meant for the human world.

It has been said that "Ondine, like Joan, represents a threat of anarchy to a system which can survive anything except the penetration of the exceptional."[9] Joan is up against a religious system, Ondine against a social one. Both are rigidly stratified worlds with their own codes of behavior and penalties for breaking them. The girls are exceptional creatures: as "supernatural" beings set against the "natural" social order, they are passionate and idealistic, often unintelligible to others, doomed to disappointment, and condemned to death. They embody individuality and the self-sacrifice that follows its rejection. Neither saint nor spirit can survive the world; the maid and the mermaid must be destroyed to maintain religious, political, and social equilibrium.

Contemporaneous to the historical Jeanne d'Arc, Ondine's story began as an anonymous fourteenth-century poem revived in a story by Friedrich de La Motte-Fouqué, *Undine* (1811), of which Giraudoux's *Ondine* (1939) is an adaptation. In Giraudoux's version, knight-errant Hans seeks shelter in the hut of Auguste and Eugénie, whose fifteen-year-old adopted daughter, the sea nymph Ondine, falls madly in love with him. Forsaking the natural for the supernatural, he abandons his fiancée, Bertha, for the elusive Ondine, bringing her back to the palace as his wife. But the untamed Ondine—the ideal of beauty, simplicity, and love—fails to adapt to the artificial, hypocritical constraints of the court; Hans too is incapable of assimilating her magical, mystical, nature. What is more, Ondine was conceived in violent lust and thus embodies a powerful sexuality. Such absolute passion overwhelms Hans; he retreats to Bertha's domesticity, preferring the security of a submissive wife over the evanescent bliss of a free spirit. Bertha convinces him to have Ondine arrested and tried for witchcraft, and, despite his passionate efforts to save her, Ondine is condemned to beheading. Though the king of the Undines sentences the knight to death for adultery, Hans dies naturally, of disillusionment, torn between the mundane and the miraculous.

That Joan and Ondine are temperamentally unsuited for the real world is nowhere more evident than in their trial scenes, during which, according to one critic, both women "exhibit the same natural candor, and in both plays stolid bureaucrats are ridiculed."[10] The two are accused of witchcraft and tried by Church and state: Joan before an ecclesiastical and secular tribunal, Ondine before "les juges d'évêché et d'empire, qui jugent des cas surnaturels," [the judges of the bishopric and empire, who judge supernatural cases].[11] Both women acknowledge their otherworldly nature: Joan confesses to hearing voices, Ondine admits to being a sea nymph. Their "crime" is that they are not like other people. Like Ondine, whose untamed nature cannot adapt to the constraints of the court, Joan craves open spaces; what she fears most is to be shut out from the sky, fields, flowers, and "the blessed blessed church bells that send my angel voices floating to me on the wind."[12] Neither woman can survive without freedom.

Condemned to death, neither Joan nor Ondine "dies," which underscores the playwrights' optimism. Joan's heart will not burn, and, in the words of the executioner, "She is up and alive everywhere,"[13] returning in the epilogue to end the play with the famous question, "How long, O Lord, how long?" In the same way that Joan's spirit is transfigured into a heavenly realm, Ondine is transmuted into a watery world. As the play closes, she exclaims to the dying Hans: "Comme c'est dommage! Comme je l'aurais aimé!" [What a shame! How I would have loved him!]. Although Joan's and Ondine's last words might be interpreted as admissions of defeat, they are also admonitions to the world at large that something is very wrong with it. The two women have failed to make love triumph in the world. Gross reality has ousted the ideal.

When the real world finally recognizes the validity of their vision, it is too late. The Inquisitor realizes Joan's greatness only in the epilogue as he kneels before her and, on behalf of the judges, praises her for having "vindicated the vision and the freedom of the living soul."[14] Ondine's tribunal also realizes its mistake, concluding at the end of the trial, "elle n'apporta ici que bonté et amour" [she brought here only goodness and love], sparing her—as Joan was spared—"la torture et le supplice public" [torture and public torment], but sentencing her to a more merciful beheading.[15]

One critic sums up the basic principle of Giraudoux's thought as: "life is a fatal course toward compromise and debasement."[16] Giraudoux does tend to side with humanity over destiny, just as Shaw prefers realism over idealism. Valency has suggested that *Ondine* and *Pygmalion* can be read as domestic dramas about the inability of a young woman of the lower classes to conform to the demands of polite circles.[17] In each case, the illiterate women are out of their element; they undergo a metamorphosis but are eventually discovered as impostors.

Another motif common to Shaw and Giraudoux is that of the individual faced with a choice, and in most instances the person involved is a young woman. The choices of Alcmène in *Amphitryon 38* (1929), Isabelle in *Intermezzo* (1933), and Agnès in *L'Apollon de Bellac* (1942) are analogous to those of Candida and Eliza. In each case, a young woman must choose between a pedestrian existence and union with a godlike or more "spiritual" being. Alcmène rejects Jupiter and remains with her husband, Amphitryon; Isabelle rejects the ghost and marries the superintendent; Agnès rejects Apollo and marries the president. Similarly, Candida sends Marchbanks into the night and remains with Morrell; Eliza, although her last line seems to foreshadow the beginning of a domestic relationship with Higgins—"What you are to do without me I cannot imagine"—according to Higgins, she will marry Freddy.[18] All these women choose humanity over mystery, the commonplace over the adventurous.

It has been claimed that Shaw and Giraudoux "must have been considerably aware of one another," and that "Destiny for Giraudoux is the Life Force for Shaw."[19] The first is doubtful, the second debatable, but the two playwrights did express their shared affinities with similar characters and situations, Joan and Ondine being striking examples. Both men were fascinated by these medieval beings and with them demonstrated how the world is often incapable of coming to terms with the miraculous.

Jean Anouilh and *L'Alouette*

In 1958, André Frank commented that the success of *Saint Joan* had contributed to the resurgence of Joan of Arc as a subject for the theater: "On peut même se demander si, sans elle, sans la liberté d'allure à laquelle elle nous a habitués, nous aurions connu *Jeanne parmi nous, L'Alouette,* d'autres encore" [We can even ask ourselves if, without her, without the freedom of her ways to which she has accustomed us, we would have known *Jeanne parmi nous, L'Alouette,* still others].[20] Can Shaw's *Saint Joan* have been the impetus to one of the most controversial plays by the leading French playwright of the twentieth century? At the age of sixteen, Jean Anouilh (1910–87) was already "haunting Parisian theatres and reading Shaw, Claudel and Pirandello."[21] He wrote his first play at nineteen, had his first stage success at twenty-two, and went on to write about fifty plays in as many years.

There are a number of resemblances between those plays and Shaw's. Anouilh's plays "deal with the confrontation of a hero or heroine obsessed with an ideal of purity and sincerity—integrity is perhaps the best word . . . with the conventions, the compromises, the pretences and the falsehoods on which society is based."[22] Like Shaw, Anouilh was a man of the theater and made use of the same Shavian devices: mistaken identities, stock characters, harangues, witty remarks. Shaw divided his works into *Plays Pleasant, Plays Unpleasant,* and *Three Plays for Puritans;* Anouilh categorized his own as *Pièces noires, Pièces roses, Pièces grinçantes, Pièces brillantes, Pièces farceuses,* and *Pièces costumées:* gloomy, light, grating, sparkling, clownish, and fancy-dress plays. Some of Anouilh's stage archetypes are also Shaw's: *Antigone* (1942) is a Jeanne d'Arc figure; *L'Alouette* (1952) is a version of Joan's trial; *Ornifle, ou le courant d'air* (1955) is a Don Juan play; and *La Foire d'empoigne* (1958) is about Napoleon Bonaparte.[23]

Yet Shaw and Anouilh were temperamental opposites: Anouilh was unassuming and reclusive; Shaw was gregarious, often overwhelming. Anouilh was a cynic and a pessimist, while Shaw had a basically optimistic, playful temperament (behind the G.B.S. mask). On the other hand, Anouilh described himself as a "comic misanthrope,"[24] an epithet not a few French critics might have applied to Shaw.

* * *

Antigone firmly established Anouilh's reputation when it was produced during the Occupation. The play became a rallying point for a country that saw in Antigone's uncompromising defiance of Créon its own oppression during the Vichy regime. Like Philippe Pétain, Créon became a modern-day "collaborateur," sympathetic but not to be trusted, a man whose relationship to Antigone is akin to that of Shaw's Cauchon to Joan. Valency points out that the situation in *Androcles and the Lion* is similar to that of Anouilh's play: Antigone, in her insistence on dying "for nothing," exemplifies "something of the existential posture which Lavinia innocently assumes."[25] Ten years later, Anouilh returned to the theme of the young woman at odds with Church and state in *L'Alouette,* and eleven years after Lavinia came *Saint Joan.*

As a teenager, Anouilh read Shaw, but as an adult he became more familiar with Shaw's works and reputation. This is clear from his recollection in his memoirs of Georges Pitoëff's production of *The Apple Cart.* Anouilh recalls Shaw's fury at how Pitoëff had furnished the king's quarters with "[tables and chairs] en tubulure et formica, dénichées on ne sait où. Bernard Shaw, convié au spectacle lors d'un passage à Paris, faillit s'étrangler d'indignation et malgré les supplications des traducteurs, refusa d'aller dans les coulisses rencontrer Pitoëff—à qui il devait pourtant le succès de l'admirable *Sainte Jeanne*" [tubular and formica tables and chairs tracked down who knows where. Bernard Shaw, invited to the performance while in Paris, almost strangled himself with indignation, and despite the translators' pleas, refused to go in the wings to meet Pitoëff— to whom he nevertheless owed the success of the wonderful *Sainte Jeanne*]. Anouilh goes on to relate how "tout Paris avait frémi de sa fibre patriotique blessée parce que Pitoëff avait osé jouer Charles VII (où il était étonnant) dans la *Sainte Jeanne* de Shaw. Un roi de France avec l'accent russe—où allions-nous?" [all of Paris had shuddered to have its patriotic feelings hurt because Pitoëff had dared play Charles VII (as whom he was astonishing) in Shaw's *Sainte Jeanne*. A king of France with a Russian accent— what next?][26]

Anouilh was thus very familiar with "l'admirable *Sainte Jeanne,*" produced in Paris at the Théâtre des Arts in 1925–26 and published in *La Petite Illustration* in 1928. Although one critic has remarked, "Il paraît certain qu'Anouilh l'a lue mais il s'en est entièrement détaché" [It appears certain that Anouilh read it, but he has entirely detached himself from it],[27] Eric Bentley thinks otherwise, as we will see. Anouilh may have seen *Sainte Jeanne* during the Occupation, in December 1940 at the Théâtre de l'Avenue. Since *Antigone* was written soon afterward, one cannot rule out the possibility that Shaw may have been a catalyst for Anouilh's defiant heroine.

L'Alouette premiered in Paris at the Théâtre Montparnasse Gaston Baty on 14 October 1953 and had a long run. But like *Sainte Jeanne,* it was greeted with a mixture of praise and denunciation, and not a few parallels were made to Shaw's play. Wrote one critic: "Même après Bernard Shaw, M. Jean Anouilh a réussi à renouveler, à raviver, à ranimer le sujet" [has succeeded in renewing, reviving, reanimating the subject]. *La Revue des deux mondes* for 1 November 1953 stated that this kind of "théâtre historique et psychologique" resembled Shaw's.[28]

But unlike Shaw, who had scrutinized the historical records pertaining to Jeanne d'Arc trial, Anouilh claimed to have written *L'Alouette* "sans plan, sans date, sans documents sur mes souvenirs de petit garçon, sans rien qu'une inexplicable joie" [without a plan, without a date, without documents on my boyhood memories, with nothing but an inexplicable joy].[29] More imagination than research went into Anouilh's version. As one critic wrote: "Il n'y a pas lieu de rechercher à quelles sources Anouilh s'est documenté. Il n'a jamais été et ne sera jamais un chevalier de la documentation" [There is no use researching which sources Anouilh used as documentation. He has never been and will never be a champion of documentation].[30] This may explain why Anouilh diverges radically from history in his characterization: here is a Jeanne who does not think miracles are essential, who pardons Cauchon (portrayed as a benign counselor) instead of blaming him for her death—"Évêque je meurs par vous" [Bishop I die by your hand]—and who is Baudricourt's object of passionate desire.[31]

Joan may be a mere peasant girl, but to show that saintliness is within reach of everyone, Anouilh made her commonplace and crude. The critics were not amused. "Jean Anouilh met tout son talent," wrote Jacques Lemarchand, "tout son art, dont il n'a jamais été si maître, au service de la vulgarité qu'il camoufle en poésie" [Jean Anouilh puts all his talent, all his art, which he has never so well mastered, in the service of vulgarity that he camouflages as poetry]. Morvan Lebesque thought that Anouilh had told Joan's story as if Joan of Arc were "la fille du bistro du coin."[32] As we have seen, similar attacks were made on Shaw's Joan: T. S. Eliot called her in 1924 "perhaps the greatest sacrilege of all Joans," and in 1926, "one of the most superstitious of the effigies which have been erected to that remarkable woman."[33] It is not surprising that Anouilh, like Voltaire and Shaw, was accused of debasing and trivializing the French saint, despite the fact that Anouilh ended his play not with Jeanne's death but with her coronation. As one critic remarked, Anouilh wanted his audience "to remember Joan as the inspiring force, the symbol of man's fight for freedom and independence, rather than the humiliated martyr."[34]

To show that Jeanne had more faith in human beings than in God, Anouilh downplayed her spiritual qualities to such an extent that Brooks Atkinson described *L'Alouette* as overly cerebral and thus inferior to *Saint Joan:* "Anouilh's reasoned speculation has little of Shaw's intellectual passion. For Shaw was a political philosopher bent on condemning the errors and malice of institutions. Monsieur Anouilh's drama is more like an intellectual reverie."[35] This may have been an effect created by Anouilh's use of anachronism and by his characters speaking as self-conscious actors, forcing the viewer to concentrate intellectually rather than emotionally.[36] The mystical element is definitely missing from Anouilh's play. The "intellectual reverie" stems in part from the flashbacks to Jeanne's youth, and from a courtroom that must evoke a battlefield, a village, or a prison cell. These devices make for a "modern" play but a fragmented and episodic one. The theatricality makes Jeanne's rise and fall inevitable, gives them an ambiguous aura of predestination, almost of fatalism.[37] This is seen in Warwick's opening words — "Plus vite elle sera jugée et brûlée, mieux cela sera" [The sooner she is judged and burned, the better it will be] — as well as in Cauchon's remark that "nous ne pouvons que jouer nos rôles, chacun le sien, bon ou mauvais, tel qu'il est écrit, et à son tour" [we can only act our roles, each his own, good or bad, just as it is written, and each in turn].[38] Anouilh himself had warned the audience in a program note: *L'Alouette* "n'apporte rien à l'explication du mystère de Jeanne" [does nothing to explain Jeanne's mystery].[39]

According to Eric Bentley, *L'Alouette*'s lack of mystery may be explained in part by a lack of historical and religious perspective. He even maintains that Anouilh followed Shaw's version of the facts as if it were history, and that "in this the least imaginative of his works he also displays so little interest in the truth — the truth about Catholicism, for example," that as a thinker he possesses "the narrow-mindedness we traditionally associate with the religious, only in his case it's the fact that his mind contains *no* religion that makes him narrow."[40] Exactly the opposite may be said of Shaw, for whom religion and history were paramount, and who portrayed the saint in more realistic — if not more flattering — terms than did Anouilh. Whereas Shaw's characters explain history, as in the dialogue between Warwick and Cauchon about Protestantism and nationalism, Anouilh, according to Howarth, "offers a wholly arbitrary, subjective explanation of his characters' behaviour." Thus we can accept *Saint Joan* as a reconstruction of historical events in a way impossible with *L'Alouette*. "Anouilh's Joan is no more than the particular illustration of an *a priori* generalisation, whereas Shaw makes us believe in the existence as individuals of Joan and the other characters, and in her tragedy as the actual outcome of the experiences leading up to it."[41] A similar view is held by Harold Kasimov, who finds that Anouilh's Jeanne is an accurate portrayal of a Christian mystic, more archetypal than historical, with the result that "Anouilh does not concentrate on the authenticity of Joan's miracles and revelations to the same degree as Shaw."[42]

Part of the problem is that Shaw's play is chronological, while Anouilh rearranges the events as "flashbacks" within a framework that Howarth explains as "retrospective comment from the vantage-point of the future glory of the canonised saint," with scenes "re-enacted by protagonists conscious of playing allotted parts, so that the spectator inevitably feels that everything is pre-ordained: characters' roles, tragic ending, future apotheosis." Shaw's people are "forced to act in a certain way by the pressures of history; whereas Anouilh's characterisation tends to make us see all his characters almost exclusively in terms of their conduct towards Joan herself."[43] *L'Alouette* moves through Joan's trial, her defense, recantation, denial, and execution; but it ends with a scene that Shaw left out, the high point of Joan's career: the coronation of the dauphin at Reims as King Charles VII. Anouilh gives his saint a traditional "happy ending."

Paul Hernadi's eloquent comparison of the two plays focuses on what he calls Anouilh's "retrospecting consciousness": "The very structure of Anouilh's play is designed to evoke not an actual sequence of past events but their imagined presence in *memory*—be it the playwright's memory and the spectator's or the memory of each and every stage figure." Whereas Shaw has Joan say what he thinks she would have said, in *L'Alouette,* "Joan's voice and Joan's Voices are emphatically identified as the voice of the actress playing the part."[44]

Bentley has suggested that Anouilh adhered closely to the events of *Saint Joan.* He goes one step farther: "Anouilh, when he was adapting Shaw's play, noticed that Joan flirts with Robert de Baudricourt in Scene I. So Anouilh had to go all the way and have her making passes at the guy. A Frenchman doesn't believe in a sexless Saint Joan: Voltaire said she'd *have* to be a saint to remain a virgin in the French Army!"[45] Anouilh never actually "adapted" *Saint Joan,* but there is evidence that *L'Alouette* is to a degree a retelling of some of the events in Shaw's play, Jean Bastaire pointing out Anouilh's "pillant sans vergogne" [shamelessly borrowing wholesale] from *Saint Joan* for his situations and characters.[46] For if we believe Anouilh's claim that he had no plan or documents, it is more difficult to explain away some scenes and passages that parallel Shaw's uncannily. When asked if sainte Marguerite and sainte Catherine are nude, Jeanne asks, "Croyez-vous que Notre-Seigneur n'ait pas les moyens de payer des robes à ses saintes?" [Do you believe that Our Lord lacks the means to buy dresses for his saints?]. When asked if she is in a state of grace, Jeanne replies, "Si je n'y suis, Dieu veuille m'y mettre; si j'y suis, Dieu veuille m'y tenir" [If I am not, may God put me in it; if I am, may God keep me in it]. Even her last question, "O Rouen, Rouen, tu seras donc ma dernière demeure? O Jésus!" [O Rouen, Rouen, you will thus be my last home? O

Jesus!],⁴⁷ echoes Joan's last words: "O God that madest this beautiful earth, when will it be ready to receive Thy saints? How long, O Lord, how long?" Closer comparison may reveal that Anouilh's debt to Shaw was considerable. If so, Shaw's Joan underwent the most convoluted metamorphosis in the history of drama: *L'Alouette* becomes a French play based on an Irish play based on an English version of a French translation of a Latin text!⁴⁸

The ironic coda to Anouilh's relationship with Shaw's saint occurred in 1959, five years after *L'Alouette,* with the release of Otto Preminger's film version of *Saint Joan,* starring Jean Seberg. Although it was a critical and commercial failure (despite a screenplay by Graham Greene, who apparently followed the outlines of Shaw's play), it was thanks to Anouilh that French audiences saw the film. One might even say that he "translated" Shaw's play (or at least Greene's version), because when *Saint Joan* was shown in France, the subtitles were by Jean Anouilh.⁴⁹

10

The Disabled Skeptic

A Limited Esteem for Anatole France

It was during the second half of a monthlong visit to Rome, from about 2 May to 1 June, 1904, that Shaw first met the most popular writer in France. It was not an auspicious encounter. Miron Grindea recounts that Shaw and Anatole France were in the Sistine Chapel, and that Shaw approached him and adressed him in French: "Bonjour, Monsieur, moi aussi je suis un génie" [Good day, Sir, I too am a genius]. To which France retorted: "Tiens! Je suis enchanté non seulement d'avoir rencontré un génie, mais d'apprendre en même temps que j'en suis un" [Indeed! I am delighted not only to have met a genius, but also to learn that I am one].¹ Hesketh Pearson's version is more telling. France, examining the ceiling's frescoes at close quarters while perched on a scaffold, began "firing off all the conventional phrases—Angelo's wrist of steel and heart of fire and so on." He descended and, turning to Shaw, asked who he was. "'Like yourself, a man of genius,' answered Shaw. Staggered by this (to a Frenchman) almost incredible exhibition of bad taste, Anatole could only shrug his shoulders and reply, 'Quand on est courtisane on a le droit de s'appeler marchande de plaisir'."² Delicately translated: "When one is a courtesan one has the right to call oneself a pleasure-merchant."

If Shaw was the most famous literary figure of his day in England, Jacques-Anatole-François Thibault (1844–1924) held the same position across the Channel. The skeptical France was considered by many (for a time) the ideal French man of letters—he received the Nobel Prize for literature in 1921—and like Shaw was very prolific, writing numerous essays, plays, novels, criticism, and journalism. Also like Shaw, he was often cynical about human institutions³ and possessed many Shavian traits: lucidity and grace of language, shrewdness of observation, detachment from human problems without losing contact with them, irony interrelated with pity but tempered by charity, and a strong pacifism.[4] France embraced socialism and, later in life, communism, and like Shaw was known for his wit and irony, and for a passion for social justice.[5] One of France's biographers compared the two men this way: "One was a master technician in words and so was the other; both were pre-eminent among their countrymen in the domain of letters; both were preoccupied with the stupidities of life; both pilloried the pretensions of propriety, the cruelties of its dominion, and the vanities of men. Both were Socialists, bent on the regeneration of a hopeless world.... Both had their doubts and contradictions, but they were often dissolved in the mighty vision of a better world."[6]

That world never came. Instead, the Great War reinforced the pessimism of *L'Ile des Pingouins* (1908), a bleak vision of a materialistic, hyperindustrialized society of the future that ends with an atomic blast. Shaw knew the book, and in a letter to the editor of the *Nation and Athenaeum* (London) of 26 March 1921, he compared the Lord Chamberlain — the licensor of plays who had caused him such trouble — to one of its characters: "He was exactly like Maubec, the aristocrat in Anatole France's 'Ile des Pingouins', whose reply to a democratic remonstrance ended with the formula, 'Recevez mon pied dans vos sept cents derrières'."[7] The analogy must have delighted Shaw because he repeated it a decade later in an American interview: "He was exactly like the prince in Anatole France's 'Ile des Pingouins,' who wrote to a democratic Association 'Receive my foot in your six hundred *derriers*'."[8]

Shaw's esteem for France must have been sufficiently well known because publisher John Lane approached Shaw in 1908 with a request for a preface to a uniform edition of France's works. Shaw replied that a preface by himself or any other Englishman (A. B. Walkley, Edmund Gosse) would be "nothing but an impertinence. A solemn impertinence would be insufferable; and a vivacious impertinence would be like flat ginger ale compared with Anatole's champagne." Shaw suggested instead a preface by France himself, "an entirely frank statement of his impressions of the English and of his attitude towards them." He proposed that Lane tell France that "the substitution of a sort of literary chairman's speech for it would be an insufferable banality." He closed with a reminder that France's 1904 preface to Émile Combes's *Une Campagne laïque* (1902–3) "first sold up an enormous edition of the pamphlet and was then reprinted without the pamphlet," and he assured Lane that something similar, with "enough Anatolian pepper and salt in it," would be financially profitable.[9]

Shaw could have read the thirty-one-page preface by France to the 463-page compilation (hardly a pamphlet) of anticlerical speeches by Combes when it was published in Georges Clemenceau's newspaper *L'Aurore* a week before Combes's book.[10] The preface would have interested Shaw. It is a short history of the parting of Church and state in which the Dreyfus Affair—France had joined the crusade when Zola published "J'accuse!" in *L'Aurore* on 13 January 1898—is used to castigate anti-Semitic Jesuits. But "l'affaire de 1897" is also the impetus to condemn "monks"—France's blanket term for all religious groups—for meddling in affairs of state: "Les moines étaient pleins de courage. Ils avaient l'Affaire, la bienheureuse Affaire, suscitée, pensaient-ils, par Dieu lui-même pour ramener la France à la foi catholique" [The monks were full of courage. They had l'Affaire, the blessèd Affaire, conjured up, they believed, by God himself to bring France back to the Catholic faith].[11] The highly polemical preface is essentially anticlerical propaganda and contains more than "enough Anatolian pepper and salt."

At the time that Shaw was reading France—there were translations by Frederick Chapman, Lafcadio Hearn, and Lewis May—his fame "was now almost as great in England as in France."[12] When France paid an official visit to London in 1913, he was treated like a visiting dignitary. Among those present at the 10 December banquet in his honor at the Savoy Hotel were Walter Crane, Marie Corelli, James G. Frazer, John Galsworthy, Jerome K. Jerome, W. W. Jacobs, Edward Marsh, H. W. Massingham, Alfred Sutro, H. G. Wells, and Israel Zangwill.[13] The following evening, when France addressed the Fabian Society at the Suffolk Street galleries of the Royal Society of British Artists, Shaw chaired the meeting. France began his speech, in French, with the customary "Mesdames et Messieurs," and then turned to Shaw and added with a bow and a smile, "et le Molière d'Angleterre!"[14] Shaw too spoke, and when he finished France sprang up, threw his arms around Shaw, and kissed him repeatedly on both cheeks.[15] Upon this occasion, "the Irishman and the Frenchman," writes Jacob Axelrad with an excess of fervor, "had reached the milepost of Socialism in different ways, in accordance with their different natures. To the Fabian, it was a cerebral loyalty to manifest logic; to the Frenchman, it was a spiritual, emotional, aesthetic response to his quest for certainty. For one it was as scalpel to a surgeon; to the other as healing balm for a piteous wound."[16]

The analogy is clever but misleading. France could be as cutting as Shaw (as in the Combes preface), and he remained for Shaw a touchstone of political integrity. When Gilbert Murray invited Shaw in 1914 to be a signatory to an open letter, "To our Colleagues in Russia," Shaw replied that he would sign only if the document "expressly and emphatically damns the Tsardom uphill, down dale, and all the way to hell.... I shall be as explicit as Anatole France's peasant who, having prayed in vain for rain to the child in the arms of the statue of the Virgin, burnt a candle to her instead, with the explanatory remark, 'It is not to you, you son of a whore, that I offer this candle, but to your sainted mother'."[17] When he included the anecdote in a proposed volume on religion to be published as part of his *Collected Works*, Shaw elaborated upon the story and substituted "wanton" for "whore": "Anatole France tells the story of a peasant who, praying before a statue of the Virgin and Child, addressed the latter in these terms: 'It is not to thee, son of a wanton, that I offer my prayer, but to thy sainted mother.' On a previous occasion he had made his petition to the Infant Christ without success; and when it was not granted he abused the obdurate deity just as Russian peasants, when they have prayed in vain for good weather to their Ikons, take them into the fields and beat them."[18]

Shaw was using France's anecdote in a discussion of idolatry and iconoclasm. "We want intelligent obedience instead of idolatrous obedience," he wrote, "as that is our only guarantee against the abuse of power for the private ends of whom we must trust with it." France's story illustrated for Shaw "the danger that arises from the fact that idolators always expect too much from their idols, and in the fury of their disappointment often outdo the iconoclasts when an insurrection is provoked by famine or defeat." In politics, it takes the form of the pendulum swing in general elections:

> Our Party leaders are idolized. The inevitable consequence is that impossibilities are expected of them. They are held accountable for the harvests, for the fluctuations of trade, for the fortunes of war, for every private mishap and every public calamity, whilst at the same time they get no credit for beneficial measures that are beyond the comprehension of their idolators. Consequently they are thrown down and smashed, and the Opposition set up on their pedestals and worshipped until the pendulum swings again, when they are set up again and given another turn. At last the governing classes become entirely cynical as to democracy and set themselves deliberately to perfect themselves in the art of exploiting idolatry.[19]

Aside from politics and their socialist ties, Shaw admired France's sardonic, comedic side. In the *London Mercury* of May 1921, Shaw published "Tolstoy: Tragedian or Comedian?" in which he showed how familiar he was with France's works:

> Since Dickens one can think of no great writer who has produced the same salad of comedy and tragedy except Anatole France. He remains incorrigible: even in his most earnest attempts to observe the modesties of nature and the proprieties of art in his autobiographical Le Petit Pierre he breaks down and launches into chapters of wild harlequinade (think of the servant Radegond and the Chaplinesque invention of Simon of Nantua and the *papegai*) and then returns ashamed and sobered to the true story of his life, knowing that he has lost every right to appear before the Judgment Seat with Le Petit Pierre in his hand as the truth, the whole truth, and nothing but the truth, so help him Rousseau. On his comic side Anatole France is Dickens's French double, disguised by culture. In one of his earliest stories, Jocaste, the heroine's father is a more perfect Dickens comic personage than Dickens himself ever succeeded in putting on paper.[20]

Shaw alludes to the first of two novelettes published together in 1879 as *Jocaste et le chat maigre*. M. Fellaire de Sizac, Hélène Haviland's father in *Jocaste*, is considered by critics a sort of French Micawber, always optimistic despite life's mishaps.[21] Like his praise of Brieux, Shaw's esteem for France was based upon similar affinities, in this case a sense of humor. There even occurred an incongruous pairing of their works when the two men shared a double bill in 1915: the first offering of the New Stage Society of New York, under the direction of Harley Granville Barker, combined *Androcles and the Lion* and France's *La Comédie de celui qui épousa une femme muette* (1913)—translated as *The Man Who Married a Dumb Wife*—at Wallack's Theater, from 27 January to March.

A last and most interesting example of Shaw's admiration for France is found in an account by the noted Berlin critic Alfred Kerr. In 1913, Kerr reported that Shaw told him he would have preferred to have France translate his works instead of Augustin Hamon! "But whoever has something to produce himself doesn't translate," Shaw wrote in the *Neue Rundschau*. He wrote to Siegfried Trebitsch that it had been indiscreet of Kerr to repeat what Shaw had told him; "Fortunately Hamon does not read German."[22] Although Shaw always defended his choice of Hamon in print, these private misgivings indicate that he may have regretted that choice. And he must have been sufficiently familiar with (and pleased by) France's works in French to consider him capable of translating his works.

* * *

Shaw's reverence for Anatole France underwent a radical change after he wrote *Saint Joan* and read France's massive two-volume biography, *Vie de Jeanne d'Arc* (1908), which he found extremely biased. Like Shaw, France had examined closely Quicherat's *Procès de condamnation et de réhabilitation de Jeanne d'Arc*. But he also consulted dozens of French sources unavailable to Shaw; these are listed in his meticulously documented eighty-three-page preface. However, if his research was thorough, there is some doubt as to its integrity. In writing her own biography, *Saint Joan of Arc* (1936), Vita Sackville-West examined France's book and was very disappointed: "References as to sources of information unbelievably inaccurate: mistrust them all."[23] Shaw too may have mistrusted them, referring in 1948 to "Anatole France's book (as far as it is really his)."[24] Yet Sackville-West placed the author of *Saint Joan* in the same camp as France in referring to "such brilliant and untrustworthy artists as Mr. Bernard Shaw and M. Anatole France."[25]

Scholarship aside, Shaw was displeased by France's portrayal of Jeanne d'Arc as a Church puppet without military skills. Writing in 1924, he complained that France "was completely disabled as to Joan herself by a simple disbelief in the existence of *ability* (in the manly sense) in women."[26] And in the preface to *Saint Joan,* although he refers to France as a "man of genius," Shaw deplored that France had denied Joan "any serious military or political ability." He stated that it had been advanced that France was "a Parisian of the art world, into whose scheme of things the able, hardheaded, hardhanded female, though she dominates provincial France and business Paris, does not enter; . . . But this explanation does not convince me. I cannot believe that Anatole France does not know what everybody knows. I wish everybody knew all that he knows. One feels antipathies at work in his book. He is not anti-Joan; but he is anti-clerical, anti-mystic, and fundamentally unable to believe that there ever was any such person as the real Joan."[27]

Shaw also criticized France's biography in *Le Temps* on 10 August 1925: "Feu mon ami Anatole France a passé des années à lire l'histoire du quinzième siècle et à écrire une oeuvre qui est un chef d'oeuvre de commérages historiques sur tous ceux qu'a jamais rencontrés la Pucelle, . . . en ce qui concerne la Pucelle, une gaffe si prodigieuse que seul un Français réellement grand pouvait la commettre" [My late friend Anatole France spent years reading histories of the fifteenth century and in writing a work that is a masterpiece of historical gossiping on everyone the Maid

7. Anatole France in 1900. By permission of the Agence Photographique Roger-Viollet, Paris.

ever met, . . . as far as the Maid goes, a gaffe so prodigious that only a truly great Frenchman could have committed it].[28]

How did this gaffe come about and in what way was France "completely disabled"? William Searle has examined thoroughly what he terms the "philosophical Naturalism" of the *Vie de Jeanne d'Arc*—a book that took twenty-five years to write—and how the conspiracy against Alfred Dreyfus had much to do with France's antiheroic approach: "To France that young Jewish officer had fallen victim to precisely the sort of mindless religious intolerance which he here attributes to the Maid." Hence the book "became imbued with an anti-religious bias which had formed no part of its original conception, and which tended to confirm France's view that history cannot be otherwise than subjective."[29] Even Jeanne's miracles, France believed, could they be scientifically verified, would remain subject to debate! And when one thinks that France, in his zeal to explain away Jeanne's visions, appended to his book a seven-page letter from a Sorbonne neuropathologist to the effect that Jeanne's "hallucinations hystériques" may have been the result of a "hémi-anesthésie" (hemianesthesia) of the right side,[30] Shaw's "anti-mystic" tag seems euphemistic. In all fairness, it must be noted that Shaw, in the preface, also gives Joan's visions a "scientific" underpinning of sorts: "Joan was what Francis Galton and other modern investigators of human faculty call a visualizer," Shaw's point being that "the street is full of normally sane people who have hallucinations of all sorts which they believe to be part of the normal permanent equipment of all human beings."[31]

"Because France did not share Shaw's belief in inspiration," writes Searle, "he denied emphatically that Joan's voices could have offered her any constructive advice." Her voices fostered in her the conviction that she had the backing of God, which in turn made her "dangerously unrealistic and fatuously overconfident."[32] France went so far as to conjure up an unknown priest of Lorraine who inculcated in Jeanne the delusion that she was divinely appointed! This exploitation also denied her the "military or political ability" that made her heroic. Jeanne believed that if men fought in a state of grace, they would be victorious: "C'était là toute sa science militaire, hors toutefois qu'elle ne craignait pas le danger" [That was her entire military science, albeit that she did not fear danger]. Interestingly enough, France's seemingly odd ideas on medieval warfare (few battles, lackluster fighting), as well as his conclusion that "ces guerres perpétuelles étaient peu meurtrières" [these perpetual wars were not that deadly],[33] are supported by the historian Huizinga, who writes that "in the uncomplicated situation of her day military talent was still largely a matter of penetrating common sense."[34] Shaw's Joan certainly embodies that quality.

France and Shaw also differ radically as to Jeanne d'Arc's role as patriotic symbol. Where Shaw, following the anticlerical Michelet, considered her a precursor of French nationalism, France maintained that Jeanne could have had no idea about a "patrie telle qu'on la conçoit aujourd'hui; . . . elle ne se figurait rien de semblable à ce que nous appelons la nation; c'est une chose toute moderne." "Le mot de patrie n'existait pas au temps de la Pucelle. On disait le royaume de France. Personne, pas même les légistes, n'en savaient au juste les limites, qui changeaient sans cesse" [homeland such as we conceive of it today; . . . she imagined nothing similar to what we call a nation; it is a thoroughly modern thing. The word homeland did not exist in the Pucelle's time. One said the kingdom of France. Nobody, not even jurists, knew exactly what were its limits, which changed constantly].[35] Once again, Shaw also knew this to be true, writing in his preface that "the idea we call Nationalism" was "foreign to the medieval conception of Christian society."[36]

Despite these and other differences, Shaw and France are in complete agreement on one essential point: the sincerity of Jeanne's judges and the fairness of the trial. Like Shaw, France wished to be fair to the intentions of the Rouen tribunal. He concluded that its members "pensaient, la plupart, procéder vraiment en matière de foi.... Plusieurs sans doute imaginaient, par leur sentence, maintenir, contre les fauteurs du schisme et de l'hérésie, l'orthodoxie catholique et l'unité d'obédience; ils voulaient bien juger" [believed, most of them, that they were proceeding truthfully in matters of faith.... Many of them no doubt imagined that, by their sentence, they were maintaining Catholic orthodoxy and the unity of obedience against the inciters of schism and heresy; they wanted to judge well].[37] This echoes the *Saint Joan* preface, where Shaw maintains that Joan was not "done to death by a superstitious rabble of medieval priests"; "the tribunal was not only honest and legal, but exceptionally merciful," and "the decision was strictly according to law."[38] Shaw stressed the point again in 1936, writing that the procedure of the Rouen trial, "which had been held up to public execration for centuries as an abominable conspiracy by a corrupt and treacherous bishop and a villainous inquisitor to murder an innocent girl," was "strictly legal, strictly reasonable, strictly pious."[39]

But Shaw does not seem to have considered that aspect of France's biography worth mentioning, continuing to berate the *Vie de Jeanne d'Arc* in extreme old age, calling it in 1946 a "pile of literary rubbish." The nonagenarian neither forgot nor forgave: "A.F. had XIX century limitations. He could not believe that a woman could have military ability and political leadership. To him women's place was not even in the home: it was in the bed. His book is a compilation of unmemorable and finally unreadable twaddle about nobodies: hack work by his assistants mostly."[40] Two years later, he wrote: "Anatole France I used to relish (I read French as easily as English, though I am a very poor linguist); but I cannot forgive his silly little gaffe about Joan of Arc."[41]

John Middleton Murry echoed Shaw's frustrations in an article titled "The Two Joans," published in the *Adelphi* in May 1924. His extended comparison leaves no doubt as to his dissatisfaction with France's biography, "a suave and careful repository of facts compared to Bernard Shaw's revivification of the thing that was.... The *Vie de Jeanne d'Arc* is a work of history: *Saint Joan* is a creation." Therefore, "Shaw's *Saint Joan* is better than Anatole France's, and more subtle, and more true." According to Murry, France turned Joan into "a charming, naïve innocent peasant girl who dreams dreams, a pathetic and deluded visionary who distorts the secret promptings of her heart into the voices of God and his angels: in a word, she is mad." But for Shaw, "she is not mad: she is one of those who have had a glimpse of what is beyond this mortal world. . . . Shaw's Joan disturbs and inspires men by what she is, Anatole France's Joan moves them by what in their folly they imagine her to be."[42]

In fairness to Shaw, it should be mentioned that his assessment of France was generally high, especially when weighed against that of others. A poll conducted after his death, whose results were published in 1929 as "Anatole France: A Post-Mortem Five Years Later" in *Le Tambour,* found him to be a fine writer but no great original. There was something archaic about him: he was "primarily a 'period' writer" (Waldo Frank); amusing but not profound (H. L. Mencken); "his brand of cultivated scepticism is out-of-date, alas!" (Bertrand Russell); "an embodiment of the French intelligence after it had assimilated Voltaire, Stendhal, Flaubert and Renan" but with "a facile side" (Edmund Wilson); "merely a dilettante" (Paul Morand). In answering the question "How do you rate Anatole France? For what reasons?" Shaw returned again to *L'Ile des Pingouins* and to Jeanne d'Arc: "His books seem to me likely to survive as Sterne's have survived in England; but just at this moment his XIXth century anti-clericalism 'dates', as we say, very badly. His failure with Jeanne d'Arc eclipses his success with la Reine Pédauque. People want to find a way out of Penguin Island: they are out of patience with the Voltairean pessimism of his conclusion of its history. But when this phase passes, and his works are read disinterestedly as entertaining literature his vogue will revive; and he will take his appropriate place among the classics."[43]

* * *

Shaw and France may be "classics," but they were not always paired flatteringly by their contemporaries. Even Hamon concluded a 1912 article, "Bernard Shaw romancier," with this analogy: "Ces romans de Bernard Shaw rappellent un peu Anatole France, mais avec moins de délicatesse dans la critique. Tandis que les personnages d'Anatole France font sourire, ceux de Bernard Shaw font franchement rire" [These novels of Bernard Shaw remind us a little of Anatole France, but with less scrupulousness in the criticism. While Anatole France's characters make us smile, those of Bernard Shaw make us laugh outright].[44]

What Hamon saw as Shaw's lack of refinement was targeted following the Paris premiere of *Candida* in 1908 by the anonymous reviewer for the

English Mail, who remarked that Shaw "is to be compared to no modern French writer. The rather gross inspiration of Zola is as alien to him as is the delicate 'finesse' of Anatole France."[45] Two days later, J. Ernest-Charles, in his critique of the play, went farther. He found that the fictional creations of both men were nothing more than mouthpieces for ideologies lacking in substance: "Nous devons surtout le comparer à Anatole France. . . . Mais il est nihiliste comme Anatole France, à la manière d'Anatole France. Le théâtre et le roman ne lui sont que des moyens pour exposer, avec une fantaisie agréable, sa philosophie de l'univers contemporain. La philosophie, même réformatrice, est essentiellement sceptique. Il ne croit à aucune doctrine, pas plus qu'à aucun des héros qu'il crée. Il abandonne chaque idée à l'instant même qu'il la soutient. Et ses personnages sont incohérants parce que en eux se succèdent toutes les négations caustiques de Bernard Shaw" [We must compare him above all to Anatole France. . . . But he is a nihilist like Anatole France, in the manner of Anatole France. The theater and the novel are but his means of exposing, with a pleasing fancy, his philosophy of the contemporary universe. Philosophy, even one of reform, is essentially skeptic. He believes in no doctrine, no more than in any of the heroes he creates. He abandons each idea in the very act of upholding it. And his characters are incoherent because in them we find the succession of Bernard Shaw's caustic negations]. Ernest-Charles thought that Bergeret and so many other characters were nothing more than "Anatole France et ses doctrines," implying a similar relationship between Shaw and his characters.[46]

Generally speaking, it was Shaw who was found wanting. In 1925, an anonymous Lyon reviewer of *Pygmalion* found Shaw un-Gallic in the extreme: "Au regards de l'anarchiste Shaw, notre bon maître Anatole France fait figure de timide bourgeois. Gardez-vous d'ailleurs d'aller demander à celui-là les subtiles émotions que nous prodiguait celui-ci. L'Irlandais Shaw ne se soucie nullement de la mesure, du sens des proportions, voire du bon goût latin" [In the eyes of the anarchist Shaw, our good master Anatole France takes on the appearance of a timid bourgeois. Moreover, be sure not to expect from the former the subtle emotions lavished upon us by the latter. The Irishman Shaw does not concern himself whatsoever with moderation or a sense of proportion, let alone Latin good taste]. Other critics drew parallels—at times ironic ones—between the literary affinities of France and Shaw. Henri d'Hennezel, in "Bernard Schaw" [*sic*], called him "l'ironiste, nourri de [Ernest] Renan et d'Anatole France" [the ironist nursed on Renan and Anatole France]. Firmin Roz in 1908 asserted that "si M. Anatole France avait voulu s'inspirer de

Schopenhauer, d'Ibsen et de Nietzsche plus que de Voltaire et de Renan, être ou paraître ainsi plus profond et laisser sa fantaisie tremper les ailes dans la métaphysique, il pourrait assez bien nous donner l'idée de M. Bernard Shaw" [had M. Anatole France wanted to inspire himself from Schopenhauer, Ibsen and Nietzsche more than from Voltaire and Renan, in order to be or appear to be more profound and to let his fancy dip its wings in metaphysics, he could pretty well give us an idea of M. Bernard Shaw]. Fernand Gregh, reviewing *You Never Can Tell* in 1913, was even more ambiguous: "Faites collaborer l'esprit de M. France et un clown échappé du répertoire shakespearien, et vous avez tout Bernard Shaw" [Have Mr. France's wit collaborate with a clown escaped from the Shakespearian repertoire, and you have Bernard Shaw whole].[47]

Shaw and France were judged harshly by their peers, and some modern views have also been inimical. This is how Richard Aldington, scholar and translator of French literature, compared them in a 1931 review of *Frank Harris on Bernard Shaw: An Unauthorised Biography*: "His exaggerated and brilliantly self-fostered reputation rests on far flimsier foundations than that of Anatole France, and will crumble with even more astonishing swiftness."[48] An almost identical analogy was made by John Steinbeck: "He [Shaw] and Anatole France will be buried together and will be forgotten together."[49]

Aldington was only half-right. France's reputation crumbled,[50] but neither man is forgotten; they are enshrined with Joan of Arc in a stained-glass window in the Ethical Church, Bayswater Road, London. Blanche Patch, Shaw's longtime secretary, wrote that Shaw "appears with Anatole France on the other side and St. Joan between them."[51] In reality, Shaw stands close behind France, and with his left hand helps him hold an open book, to which France points with one hand. Joan is to their left (the viewer's right), her arms raised heavenward. Ironically, this Bayswater Joan bears a marked resemblance to Sybil Thorndike in her role as Saint Joan: similar hairstyle, thin lips, square jaw, and far-off gaze.[52] It would have amused Shaw to see himself so close to France, with Jeanne d'Arc—their sole disagreement—hovering nearby. The "religious" symmetry is fitting; Shaw (the atheist) and France (the archskeptic) first met in a Roman basilica and are "buried together" in a London church.[53]

V

Shaw et la Guerre

11

Shaw's Man of Destiny

The Decline and Fall of Napoleon Bonaparte

Many early stage treatments of Napoleon Bonaparte portrayed him as the oversimplified hero of popular mythology, or, in the words of one critic, as "an illustrative example, chosen for powerful emotional effect, of the precariousness of human happiness in the face of a hostile destiny."[1] But with characteristic mischief, Bernard Shaw debunked this icon in a one-act play, *The Man of Destiny* (1895),[2] a not-so-trivial playlet in which the twenty-seven-year-old general is outmaneuvered and outwitted by a woman. Shaw's Bonaparte is in effect the antithesis of the hero of those "romanticist" playwrights who preferred their history diluted with equal parts of myth and fantasy. He is also the first of two Shavian demystifications of French military leaders; Shaw's version of Joan of Arc's trial came three decades later.

Shaw did not think highly of his playlet. He dismissed it as "ridiculous," "a mere stage brutality," "a silly little play," a "baby comedietta," a "bravura piece to display the virtuosity of the two principal performers," "a display of my knowledge of stage tricks," and "a harlequinade."[3] In a review published one month after the play's three performances, William Archer agreed: it was nothing but "a piece of mechanical and meaningless claptrap."[4] Critic Maurice Muret found Shaw's "harlequinade" deeply offensive: "Il a écrit contre Napoléon un pamphlet (sous forme de drame) aussi injurieux qu'ennuyeux" [He has written against Napoleon a pamphlet (in the form of drama) as insulting as it is tedious].[5] Whatever its flaws, *The Man of Destiny* is a gem of characterization in miniature, perhaps "one of the great *jeux d'esprits* of dramatic literature."[6] Not only is it Shaw's most developed—albeit whimsical—characterization of the French hero; it is also his very first stage portrayal of any famous historical figure. More important, Shaw's Bonaparte is an early seriocomic embodiment of the Life Force, an incarnation that bears a striking resemblance to Shaw himself.

Yet the play is only one of Shaw's attempts to come to terms with a historical figure who seemed to embody the Life Force. Over time, Shaw found himself in an increasingly painful dilemma. As he matured, he saw Bonaparte as something of a monster, and if Bonaparte embodied the Life Force, then the Life Force was also monstrous. In the end, Shaw could not confront the full implications of his discovery, for to have done so would have required an extensive and disorganizing personal redefinition. His solution, as we will see, was to revert to a bellicose defense of the French hero. Therefore, if we examine briefly what Shaw's Bonaparte owes to biography and art, compare him to one famous contemporary French stage Napoleon, and analyze how Shaw's estimate of the historical Bonaparte varied with the times, we will better understand why the very idea of a Napoleon remained essential to Shaw's thinking, and why this Great Man continued to fascinate him to the end of his life.

Aside from the lighthearted trivialization of his play and despite its subtitle, "A Fictitious Paragraph of History," Shaw was more than a little intrigued by Bonaparte the man. He doubtless knew Arthur Lévy's *Napoléon intime* (1893), translated the next year as *The Private Life of Napoleon*. He was familiar with the history behind his "fictitious paragraph": the empress Josephine once admitted in a letter that if she were to marry the general, Vicomte Paul François de Barras would have her husband named as commander of the army in Italy.[7] However, since there is no evidence that Napoleon obtained the promotion by any means other than military competence, the episode in *The Man of Destiny* remains pure invention.

Although Shaw claimed to have written his play "out of the vacuitude of the densest historical and geographical ignorance,"[8] there is evidence to the contrary. On 27 August 1895, three days after completing the first version of the play, he wrote to T. Fisher Unwin requesting issues of *Century Magazine* (New York) in which William Milligan Sloane's *Life of Napoleon Bonaparte* was being run serially (from November 1894 to October 1896). Shaw was still reading Sloane as late as 30 December,[9] and Charles Berst has shown how Sloane's *Life* was important in shaping Napoleon's character in *The Man of Destiny*, demonstrating that Shaw "adapted materials from the biography to strengthen and refine the play's historical references, characters, dramatic values, and theme." By close scrutiny of the "extensively, almost chaotically revised" facsimile manuscript, Berst demonstrates how Shaw incorporated some of Sloane's ideas on Napoleon's personality, the Napoleon-Josephine-Barras love triangle, and in particular the "theater-of-life" metaphor, wherein Napoleon (in Sloane's words) was a "leading actor" who played out "a human tragicomedy."[10] That Shaw consulted available documents is not surprising; he typically used historical materials to suit his purpose, as with the translated transcripts of the trial of Jeanne d'Arc for *Saint Joan*.

Shaw not only examined published sources for his psychological portrait of Bonaparte but to some extent based his physical portrait on artistic ones, carefully dissociating him from the common French heroic representations. One stage direction cautions that his general is not the Napoleon of Paul Delaroche or Jean-Louis Meissonier, whose well-known paintings were the usual mid-nineteenth-century apotheoses of a successful conqueror "which later ages expect of him."[11] Shaw was recalling Meissonier's *Napoleon in 1814* (1863) and *Campaign of France* (1864), and Delaroche's *Napoleon at Fontainebleau* (1845), *Napoleon Crossing the Alps* (1848), and *Napoleon at Saint Helena* (1852), all exhibited in London in Shaw's day.[12] These dignified and military scenes are far removed from our first glimpse in *The Man of Destiny* of a young man seated at a table hard at work while finishing a meal, his map under a clutter of dishes and glasses, his long hair trailing into the risotto. It has been suggested that Shaw's tableau may have been partially inspired by an untitled painting by the historical artist François Flameng, depicting a youthful, long-haired Napoleon working at a table piled with books and papers. Shaw's diary for 31 March 1894 notes the opening of "François Flameng's Napoleon pictures at the Goupil Gallery."[13] Having missed the opening, he may have returned to the Goupil later and remembered the painting.[14]

Despite the playlet's debt to historical and artistic sources, Shaw's man of destiny thrives not on verisimilitude but on domestic discord: the general is fighting in the boudoir rather than on the battlefield, trying to avert at all costs a personal, not a military, defeat. The discovery of a billet-doux from Josephine to his *Directeur* Barras—with whom she has some influence in advancing her husband's career—would force him to fight a duel for his wife's honor. Bonaparte realizes that "by taking care not to know,"[15] as he puts it, he could avoid being ridiculed as a cuckold, alienated by his future benefactor, and embroiled in a public scandal that could ruin his career. A few years ago, a performance of the play was followed by a symposium in which it was observed that *The Man of Destiny* is precisely about being realistic, about Napoleon's "various intersections" with the truth.¹⁶ Shaw's young Napoleon is involved in a battle of wits for personal and political survival, as well as in a fight to preserve his dignity in the face of scandal; his posturing and theatricality, combined with a vicious streak and nervous energy, often make him behave like a man on the edge. He refers to himself as a "vile vulgar Corsican adventurer," and when he is informed that there is no red ink, he facetiously tells the innkeeper, "Kill something and bring me its blood."¹⁷ The wit does not altogether mitigate his heartlessness, which emerges later in his willingness to sacrifice the foolish Lieutenant to safeguard his public image. Shaw's Bonaparte may be ruthless, but we will see that this is often the only way that embodiments of the Life Force can carry out its design for the improvement of the human race.

But can this madcap avatar really be in earnest? Is this young Bonaparte, as was so often the case with Shaw, too much the posturing actor for his pronouncements to be taken seriously? Shaw has chosen to involve him in what has been called "a long mutual seduction, a play of sexual titillation,"¹⁸ in which posturing and theatrics prevail. It may be precisely the paradoxical nature of this cruel-yet-comic figure that Shaw wishes to underline by the Great Man's Shavian histrionics and hyperbole. According to Berst, some of the key elements in *The Man of Destiny* include role-playing, pretense, deception, bluffing, trickery, masking and unmasking, and a life-as-theater theme that is the play's "one continuous dominating issue."¹⁹ For example, Napoleon "deliberately poses for an oration" on fear, which he calls the only "universal passion" and "the mainspring of war," even denying that there is any such thing as a real hero when the Strange Lady calls him one. "I win battles for humanity: for my country, not for myself," he says. "Self-sacrifice is the foundation of all true nobility of character," he proclaims. Clearly Bonaparte embodies for Shaw the essence of creative evolution: "You teach us what we all might be," the Strange Lady tells him, "if we had the will and courage."²⁰ Unfortunately, young Bonaparte is also caught in the grip of the Life Force itself by the extravagant Josephine, a woman who has lied to him about her age and income and who is incapable of fidelity to people or principles. Yet he cannot help loving her.

The irony is that despite his ambition, talent for warfare, flair for public posturing, and a certain ruthless temperament, Shaw's Bonaparte remains a slave to his passions. He must be taken seriously precisely because he is human and not the godlike icon of historical romance. He has been called "one of Shaw's masterful realists, unhampered by idealism or altruism, by conscience or morality."²¹ For Bonaparte, heroism is a matter of survival, by trickery if necessary. To avoid dishonor, he must rid himself of the bundle of dispatches as if they had never existed, and at the very end of the play, the incriminating billet-doux is destroyed: "Caesar's wife is above suspicion. Burn it."²²

In doing what is most expedient, Bonaparte resembles Shaw. Maurice Valency goes so far as to observe that in the young general "it is far easier to recognize Shaw at the age of thirty-nine than Napoleon at twenty-six."²³ The underlying premise of Bonaparte's final, grandiloquent diatribe against the English is creative evolution, Shaw's credo of human perfectibility. In this light, *The Man of Destiny* concerns two issues of some interest to Shaw: religion and nationality. One could say that Napoleon is outwitted by heredity itself, because the Strange Lady's grandfather was English—which accounts for her "conscience," "devotion," "self-sacrifice," and "goodness"—and her grandmother Irish, which accounts for her "brains."²⁴ The English, whom Bonaparte criticizes at length as a race chained to its rigid principles and moral convictions, seem a lost cause. One might almost believe that Shaw's admiration for Napoleon owes something to his own exasperation with the English. "It seems hardly possible," Shaw wrote three years later, "that the British army at the battle of Waterloo did not include at least one Englishman intelligent enough to hope, for the sake of his country and humanity, that Napoleon might defeat the allied sovereigns."²⁵ As we will see, this is one of Shaw's milder statements.

Shaw created a Bonaparte in his own image, and the stage directions complete the self-portrait: an "original observer" with "prodigious powers of work, and a clear realistic knowledge of human nature in public affairs," a man "imaginative without illusions, and creative without religion, loyalty, patriotism or any of the common ideals."²⁶ What is this if not the Life Force in action? The essential feature of Shaw's Napoleonic ideal is that only someone capable of changing the destiny of nations is of any value to Shaw, who, in his own struggling way, considered himself capable of doing so. Jack Tanner's "Revolutionist's Handbook," for example, goes so far as to claim that real change is impossible "until there is an England in which every man is a Cromwell, a France in which every man is a Napoleon, a Rome in which every man is a Caesar, a Germany in which every man is a Luther plus a Goethe."²⁷ Although this is Tanner, Shaw too was convinced that an individual will to power is necessary for world progress. He may have overstated his case to Gilbert Murray in 1915, but he leaves no doubt as to how far thought can reach: "Not like Napoleon, who said 'I make circumstances' or like me, who, going one better than Nap, say '*I* am a circumstance'."[28]

* * *

In contrast to Shaw's *Man of Destiny,* one should examine the stage Napoleon of the playwright whom Shaw considered, as we have seen, the nadir of French drama: Victorien Sardou, whose *Madame Sans-Gêne* (1893) was yet another example of incompetent playwriting. Shaw had begun his Napoleon play on 10 May 1895 and was still working on it when he saw the French version of Sardou's play on 8 July. If he "adopted or paralleled" some of Sardou's plot or prop devices in later stages of his draft, *The Man of Destiny* is not so much an "answer" to Sardou as a touchstone for his theater reviews.[29] "I have never seen a French play of which I understood less," he wrote, calling it "a huge mock historic melodrama which never for a moment produces the faintest conviction," a work in which Sardou had combined "the maximum of expenditure and idle chatter with the minimum of drama."[30] When he reviewed the 10 April 1897 performance of the English version, he was no less scathing: Ellen Terry had sailed "the Lyceum ship into the shallows of Sardoodledom," and Sardou's Napoleon was reduced to "nothing but the jealous husband of a thousand fashionable dramas, talking Buonapartiana."[31] The roles were unchallenging, the settings garish, and the literal translation an odd mixture of ready-made locutions and artificial eloquence. But Shaw defended Terry from critics who accused her of portraying a vulgar character on the grounds that Madame Sans-Gêne is a washerwoman, and that coarseness and slang befit a laundress-turned-duchess.

Madame Sans-Gêne is forgettable, but Shaw's defense of Terry's Sans-Gêne shows that he recognized even in a Sardou character certain worthy (that is, Shavian) traits: iconoclasm, a determined will, a passion for survival. Shaw was even approached to write an English version of Sardou's play as an opera but refused for lack of time, "time meaning will," he noted. Yet he told Terry that if they had asked him to do it for her, he "would have obliterated them from the surface of the globe."[32] That opera would have been an ironic triumph; by adapting a Sardou melodrama, Shaw would have taught the French how to write a good play.

What is interesting is that these "Napoleon plays" focus on two different characters: Shaw's is mostly Napoleon, Sardou's mostly Catherine, Madame Sans-Gêne. In her use of idiom and slang amidst the court aristocrats, Catherine recalls the faltering Eliza Doolittle. But unlike Shaw's flower girl, who merely plays a princess, hiding her lowly origins and cockney accent, Catherine has married into the nobility and has no qualms about her old profession or uncouth language. Because she is now legitimately part of the aristocracy, she can boast: "Blanchisseuse, oui, princesse. Et j' m'en cache pas, vous voyez! Y a pas d' sot métier, y a que de sottes gens! Qu' si j' parle l' jargon du peuple, c'est que j'en suis, du peuple, et en belle compagnie, j'peux l'dire" [Laundress, yes, princess. And as you can see, I don't hide it! There's no stupid occupations, there's only stupid people! 'Cause if I speak the people's lingo, it's 'cause I'm part o' the people, and in good company, I'll say].[33] Sardou's Napoleon may be a mere stereotypical jealous husband, but there is something endearing about feisty young Catherine, who used to air "dirty linen" in public—and who metaphorically still does.

These differences do not eclipse resemblances that may or may not be due to Shaw's having seen *Madame Sans-Gêne* while writing *The Man of Destiny*. Arthur Ganz points out that in both plays, "Napoleon flirts with and loses his temper with a clever woman trying to protect a secret of his wife's, and in both he intrigues for and intercepts a letter concerning her fidelity."[34] But the resemblance ends there. Like other successful historical comedies, *Madame Sans-Gêne* is an example of historical events "reduced to the level of domestic trivia."[35] On the other hand, Valency finds *The Man of Destiny*, as a parodic interpretation of romantic comedy, "openly subversive of the established tradition."[36] In the end, Sardou's play is little more than a flourish of period costumes and settings, whereas Shaw, as J. L. Wisenthal puts it, wanted "to present something of Napoleon's spirit and will, the human qualities that raise a Man of Destiny above the ordinary jealous husband."[37] It remains to be seen how long Shaw would continue to uphold that "spirit and will" in the turbulent years that followed.

Shaw's stage coda to the Napoleon theme occurred immediately after the Great War. It took the form of the "saturnine and self-centred" general in military uniform in part 4 of *Back to Methuselah* (1918–20), where Napoleon is reincarnated as Cain Adamson Charles Napoleon, emperor of Turania: "I am the Man of Destiny."[38] Although his encounter with the Veiled Woman is reminiscent of the younger Napoleon's with the Strange Lady two decades earlier, there is a note of anguish and anger in Shaw's attitude toward the Napoleon figure now. One senses here a disillusionment stemming from Shaw's struggle to master his own postwar bitterness. The result is a pronouncement on the folly of warfare and an account of the now-dubious role of the Great Man in history. Shaw's new, futuristic Bonaparte is an archrealist who proclaims, "I do not believe in metaphysical forces."[39] Shaw may have endowed his creation with some of his own beliefs (or lack thereof). One critic quotes Shaw as affirming that the historical Napoleon was an atheist, but cites evidence to the contrary: the emperor's last will and testament, in which he writes, "Je meurs dans la religion apostolique et romaine" [I die in the apostolic and Roman religion], and a letter of Napoleon to his surgeon, which begins: "Je suis loin d'être athée" [I am far from being an atheist].[40] But this Turanian "atheist" embodies the Life Force to such a degree that there seems to be even more of Shaw in him than in the younger general of *The Man of Destiny:* "The truth is that my talent possesses me. It is genius. . . . I am great when I exercise it. At other moments I am nobody."[41]

But this talent for organizing the slaughter of warfare "to give mankind this terrible joy which they call glory" does not make him happy. There is more Cain than Adam in his Life Force: "I have the virtues of a laborer: industry and indifference to personal comfort. But I must rule, because I am so superior to other men that it is intolerable to me to be misruled by them. Yet only as a slayer can I become a ruler." "I matter supremely: my soldiers do not matter at all," he says, realizing that he is invincible only at the cost of "the demoralization, the depopulation, the ruin of the victors no less than of the vanquished." This is a Bonaparte conscious that ultimately there are no winners in war, and his megalomania is tinged with lucidity. There is something of Shaw's own pellucid thinking here: nine-tenths "common humanity," but "the other tenth is a faculty for seeing things as they are that no other man possesses. . . . I mean that I have the only imagination worth having: the power of imagining things as they are, even when I cannot see them." In light of these amazing gifts, how does Napoleon come to terms with the fact that warfare causes bloodshed and death? The Veiled Lady, revealed early on as the Oracle, shows him the way out of that quandary: "To die before the tide of glory turns."[42] To this end, she shoots at him at close range—but misses. It appears that Napoleons are necessary evils after all.

* * *

Shaw's views on Napoleon became cautionary in the aftermath of World War I, an event that diminished his admiration for the man of destiny. In "Common Sense About the War," Napoleon takes on the appearance of a megalomaniac. Shaw found that one can maintain the Militarist hold over the imaginations of the people only by feeding them with continual glory. You must go from success to success: the moment you fail you are lost. . . . Napoleon conquered and conquered and conquered; and yet, when he had won more battles than the maddest Prussian can ever hope for, he had to go on fighting just as if he had never won anything at all. After exhausting the possible he had to attempt the impossible and go to Moscow. He failed. . . . His success had made him the enemy of every country except France: his failure made him the enemy of the human race. . . . Nothing can finally redeem Militarism. When even genius itself takes that path its end is still destruction.[43]

In 1921, as a witty response—but also as a critical rebuttal—to H. G. Wells's comments on Napoleon in *The Outline of History*, Shaw sent him the Napoleon scene from *Back to Methuselah*. Napoleon's egotism and pettiness were encroaching upon his heroism; in wartime, Cain was beginning to overtake Adam. This is evidenced by Shaw's unsent letter to Wells, for which he had substituted the Napoleon scene. A quarter of a century after *The Man of Destiny*, although Shaw still considered the general an incredible tactician with an amazing memory, the historical Bonaparte emerges more flawed than great: "If he hadn't been a soldier he would have been a nobody. He tried writing and everything else that he could try in his youth, and failed at them all. He was useless even as a subaltern: only for the revolution he would have been kicked out of the army as a disgrace to it. But from the moment when he got a military command he never looked back until he was defeated, and then he was nothing. All the other things he did could have been better done by other men. Peace was fatal to him. . . . He spoke as an artist when he described a field strewn with corpses as a beautiful sight."[44]

"Peace was fatal to him." At times it is difficult to tell if the passage is praise or censure, but the ambiguity is typical of Shaw's attitude toward Bonaparte in later years, during which he continued to be preoccupied by the Napoleon figure. He used him to great effect in a toast to Albert Einstein in 1930, where he received "laughter and applause" from his Savoy Hotel audience when he stated: "I could say many flattering things about Napoleon. But the one thing which I should not be able to say about him would be perhaps the most important thing, and that was, that it would perhaps have been better for the human race if he had never been born."[45] The following year, Shaw used "Napoleon" on the stage one last time in *Too True to be Good* (1931): the Lawrence of Arabia figure who runs the army from the ranks and who rides about the desert on a motorcycle is Private Napoleon Alexander Trotsky Meek.

In 1935, in his preface to *The Millionairess,* Shaw ridiculed Bonaparte outright as "a very ordinary snob in his eighteenth-century social outlook," citing his assumption of the imperial diadem, his remanufacturing of a titular aristocracy, and "his silly insistence on imperial etiquette" at Saint Helena as evidence that "for all his genius, he was and always had been behind the times." As the disastrous march to Moscow had proved, he was "fundamentally a commonplace human fool." But once again, this is the paradox of greatness: that a "shabby-genteel Corsican subaltern" could eventually place upon his head the crown of Charlemagne. In Shaw's opinion, Napoleon's apotheosis was the result of the idolatry of a nation that had been taught "to measure greatness by pageantry and the wholesale slaughter called military glory."[46] The French got the hero they deserved.

Another volley came in 1944 in *Everybody's Political What's What?* — Shaw's attempt to make sense of the second great upheaval of the century. With the rise of fascism, he had already been making controversial statements. As early as 1927, he had written that "Mussolini . . . has done for Italy what Napoleon did for France."[47] But by 1944, Napoleon had fallen from grace utterly; he had been "a scourge and a tyrant," "a snob, a cad, an assassin, and a scoundrel," even a precursor to Adolf Hitler: "Our contemporaries die for their upstart Führer as Frenchmen used to die for their upstart Emperor." Such dictators demonstrate that "barbarism, surviving in a disguise of chivalrous heroism, has ended in an idolatry of famous warriors." Hence the necessity of recognizing that military heroism thrives less on nobility of character than on "popular pugnacity, idolatry, and glory worship," the "impregnable bulwarks" of all conquerors.[48] In the aftermath of two world wars, Shaw's Bonaparte had degenerated from Life Force to Death Wish.

Two years later, he was berating Napoleon again, this time in an essay published on 19 May 1946, "Idolatry of the Glory Merchant Is Sheer Illusion," a review of *Military Leadership* by Field Marshal Viscount Montgomery of Alamein. Although his comments were tamer, Shaw continued to harp on "idolatry and glory worship." The "excessively professionalised" Napoleon, he wrote, "was driven to his fatal attack on Russia not so much by ambition to conquer the world as by the fact that it was only as a great glory merchant that he had been deified in France, and that only by continued French victories could he maintain that idolatry."

Montgomery declared that "the idolatry of glory merchant is mostly sheer illusion." "Napoleon rose . . . not by lust for domination but by sheer gravitation. Command came to him because France had to be governed; and he was the only man capable of the job. To such men power is not a luxury, but a responsible and very hard-working duty."[49]

Shaw's ambiguous attitude shows that his postwar condemnation of the glory-seeking "upstart" did not erase Napoleon's importance as idea and symbol. Whatever his flaws, Bonaparte was a man, "not an anthropomorphic god," as Shaw pointed out.[50] He was also a man with a mission, capable of nothing else but accomplishing that mission, even at the expense of human lives. This is precisely the way the Life Force wields its power through a superbeing: progress requires sacrifices. "France had to be governed."

Two years after his book review, ninety-two-year-old Shaw defended Napoleon against those he believed had treated him as the mythical hero of a glorious military romance. His letter to the *New Statesman and Nation* of 9 October 1948, "The Acquired Habits of Napoleon," shows that Shaw still considered Napoleon an avatar of the Life Force. He maintained that historian A. J. P. Taylor's essay on Napoleon was "farther off the mark than H. G. Wells's *gaffe* on the same subject in his *Outline of History.*" He ascribed Napoleon's "extraordinary natural aptitude for the tactics dictated in his technical schoolbooks" to his "overwhelming habit of mind," decrying as "schoolboy romance" Taylor's claim that Napoleon supposed he "could master the world by will alone" (in Taylor's words). Shaw concluded that "Napoleon's professionalism is the key to his whole career."[51]

This brings us full circle to the Bonaparte of *The Man of Destiny:* an original observer with prodigious powers of work, a realistic knowledge of human nature, and an imagination without illusions. If we add to these qualities a professionalism, natural aptitude, and habit of mind, we have listed the traits of an embodiment of the Life Force, of Shaw himself. His esteem for the Great Man of history was tempered by contemporary political reality, but Shaw's continued interest in the Napoleon figure is evidence that this "vile vulgar Corsican adventurer," for all his shortcomings, formed an integral part of Shaw's ideology.

12

The Politics of Pacifism

At War with Romain Rolland

Along with Émile Zola and Anatole France, one French contemporary to rival Shaw's literary output is Romain Rolland (1866–1944): five novels, ten biographies, fifteen plays, about twenty-four volumes of musical essays and sociopolitical criticism, over thirty volumes of correspondence, and an important volume of drama theory.[1] Furthermore, aside from Augustin Hamon and the critics who recorded Shaw's progress on the French stage, Rolland was one of few Frenchmen to follow Shaw's career from across the Channel.

At the outset, Rolland had his reservations. In 1912, he thought *Mrs Warren's Profession* "amusant, mais conventionnel—même quand cela veut être au rebours des conventions" [entertaining, but conventional—even when it flies in the face of conventions].[2] This was probably his introduction to Shaw, and in a letter of 6 December 1913 to Jean-Richard Bloch, he admitted being rather unfamiliar with Shaw, and that any judgment on his work must be considered provisional: "Il a vu des choses neuves et profondes, surtout dans l'âme féminine. Il a troué les voiles de la moderne hypocrisie, sociale, morale et littéraire. Pour mon goût, son oeuvre est viciée par le bluff et le dandysme—comme celle de plus d'un Anglais, en lutte avec les mensonges de sa race (voir Byron). Je trouve plus de probité dans l'effort de Wells, qui a moins de génie, et qui pourtant va loin, à force de sérieux" [He has seen new and profound things, especially in the feminine soul. He has pierced the veils of modern hypocrisy, social, moral and literary. For my taste, his work is tainted by bluff and dandyism—like that of more than one Englishman, struggling with the lies of his race (see Byron). I find more integrity in the effort of a Wells, who has less genius, and who nevertheless goes far, by dint of seriousness].[3] Like many Frenchmen, Rolland felt that Shaw's flippant, cynical persona got in the way. Rolland was no ironist, and it was perhaps difficult for him to appreciate Shaw's witty polemics. As we will see, his comments on *Mrs Warren's Profession* are mild compared with his scathing condemnation of *Sainte Jeanne*.

In addition, the basic difference in temperament between the playful Shaw and the more serious Rolland is evident in Rolland's appreciation of Shaw's "courageuse défense" in the *Manchester Guardian* (22 July 1916) of Sir Roger Casement, soon to be executed for high treason for planning to incite the Sinn Fein rebellion. In the speech that Shaw wrote for him to read at his trial, Casement was portrayed not as an English traitor but as an Irish patriot. Shaw's speech was read to the jury, but Casement was found guilty and hanged. Unfortunately, wrote Rolland, "le ton habituel de plaisanterie paradoxale qui est sa marque est, pour la majorité de ses lecteurs, un prétexte à ne pas le prendre au sérieux" [the usual tone of his paradoxical jokes that is his hallmark is, for the majority of his readers, a pretext for not taking him seriously].[4] Once more, what Rolland interpreted as a lack of earnestness went counter to his own uncompromising stance, a stance that would eventually alienate many of his closest friends when he needed them most.

However, something about Shaw fascinated Rolland, for at the end of 1916 he listed six plays as his "lectures de ces derniers temps" [latest readings]: *Candida, Le Héros et le soldat, L'Homme du destin, L'Homme aimé des femmes, Non Olet,* and *On ne peut jamais dire*—far more works by a single author than his other readings.[5] Yet he was disappointed, writing to his mother that he was reading Shaw "sans enthousiasme, et même avec quelque étonnement [some amazement] de la médiocrité du talent, parfois."[6] Nonetheless, Rolland's reservations about Shaw the dramatist did not prevent him from enlisting his help as a fellow pacifist.

* * *

Although Rolland was as spiritually *engagé* as Shaw was during the Great War, he preferred to remain neutral. From self-imposed exile in Switzerland, he wrote articles urging intellectuals to act on the dictates of conscience rather than on the false idealization of militaristic patriotism. Rolland felt that they had been swept up by the war effort and forsaken their duty as guardians of culture. These sixteen open letters, essays, appeals, and manifestos were published in 1915 under the title *Au-dessus de la mêlée*, a title that Shaw disparaged as elitist and escapist. The tract is usually translated as *Above the Battle* (or *Above the Conflict*), but the expression is ambiguous: a *mêlée* is a scuffle, fray, or free-for-all; to be *au-*

dessus de la mêlée or *à l'écart de la mêlée* means to stay on the sidelines or to remain aloof.[7]

If Shaw thought jingoism abhorrent and admired Rolland's political commitment, he did not subscribe to what he interpreted as the Frenchman's philosophical aloofness. "For I entirely refused Romain Rolland's invitation to *planer au dessus de la mêlée*," he recalled, "and survey the war from the empyrean of a morality which none of the combatants could possibly practise even if, like myself, they recognized that morality as their natural own, and regarded war with implacable horror and disgust."[8] For Shaw the pragmatist, Rolland's position was untenable. In the essay "Pro Aris," for instance, Rolland does sound rather lofty: "L'esprit est la lumière. Le devoir est de l'élever au-dessus des tempêtes et d'écarter les nuages qui cherchent à l'obscurcir. Le devoir est de construire, et plus large et plus haute, dominant l'injustice et les haines des nations, l'enceinte de la ville où doivent s'assembler les âmes fraternelles et libres du monde entier" [The spirit is light. It is our duty to lift it above tempests and thrust aside the clouds which seek to obscure it. It is our duty to build, higher and stronger, dominating the injustice and hatred of nations, the enclosure of the city wherein the fraternal and free souls of the entire world must assemble].[9] Rolland's rhetoric suits his abstract idealism; that Shaw balked at its utopianism is not surprising.

Shaw was not alone in misconstruing and condemning Rolland's manifesto. To the French, Rolland's neutrality and his pleas for Franco-German cooperation and reconciliation made him an intellectual traitor, even a collaborator. Many parents forbade their children to read his work. "In months, the darling of the French literary left and the cultivated public became a pariah.... After 1914 his works were misrepresented and slandered.... For the remainder of his life, opponents would attack Romain Rolland ad hominem by invoking the slogan 'above the battle'."[10] In his letters discussing both world wars, Shaw himself did so at least half a dozen times.

The construction metaphor of "Pro Aris" was appropriate. The article was a protest against the German bombing of Reims cathedral, a devastating event that Auguste Rodin, in a letter to Rolland, compared to the fall of Constantinople, the burning of the library of Alexandria, and the destruction of the Temple of Jerusalem.[11] When Rolland sent a draft of "Pro Aris" to his English publisher Heinemann, he published it without Rolland's permission in a deluxe edition on slick paper, in a badly edited version. The new document, wrote Rolland, had a "violence déclamatoire excessive." This was an especially misleading tone in view of Rolland's

8. Romain Rolland around 1906. By permission of the Agence Photographique Roger-Viollet, Paris.

opinion of his protest as "un brouillon de lettre hâtivement envoyé dans un moment de passion" [a mere draft of a letter sent hastily in a moment of passion].[12]

Still, almost all of the thousand or so to whom he sent "Pro Aris" signed it. Of the 279 English intellectuals—of whom 110 were authors, including Arnold Bennett, John Galsworthy, Edmund Gosse, Rudyard Kipling, George Moore, Gilbert Murray, Arthur Wing Pinero, H. G. Wells, and W. B. Yeats—Shaw was one of the few who refused to sign. He wrote to Heinemann that Rolland ought to know better than to repeat "halfpenny newspaper rubbish": "I am one of the two or three people in Europe who really care about Rheims; but if I were a military officer defending Rheims I should have to put an observation post on the cathedral roof; and if I were his opponent I should have to fire on it, in both cases on pain of being court-martialled and perhaps shot. If this war goes long enough there will not be a cathedral left in Europe; and serve Europe right too! The way to save the cathedrals is to stop fighting, and not to use them as stones to throw at the Germans. I won't sign."[13]

Rolland replied to the disgruntled Shaw on 18 November 1916 to reassure him that Shaw was perfectly justified in abstaining, something Rolland himself would have done had he seen his protest printed in such large type and grandiose format. He said that although he admired Shaw the writer, "je crains que vous n'eussiez été bien mauvais général. Les batailles ne se mesurent pas au nombre de morts qu'on fait et de pouces de terrain qu'on gagne" [I am afraid you would have made quite a bad general. Battles are not measured by the number of dead we make and of inches of ground we win].[14]

Shaw responded to Rolland indirectly in a letter to Mrs. Mary Bedford on 8 December 1916 to explain that fear of censorship had prevented him from speaking out freely, urging her to tell Rolland: "Not only are his [Rolland's] views sympathetic to me; but he is, like myself, an old musical critic, apparently nursed on music as I was; so that I have a key to his writings that our unmusical literary men lack." He went on to explain some of his own struggles with controversial documents: he could not let his *Common Sense About the War* be translated into French (in any case, Hamon refused); neither did Hamon translate a long interview made by Shaw for France, but instead made a précis which failed to get published at the right moment. "I have been violently attacked in the French papers, but without any knowledge of what I think." He ended by stating that if he "could only get a hearing in any French paper, I should astonish M. Davray and the rest of my French critics very considerably."[15] Like Rolland, Shaw had been maligned by the press, and although he sympathized with Rolland's plight, he steadfastly refused to participate in "Pro Aris."

But the refusal did not deter Rolland from requesting Shaw's support a second time a few years later. In the hope of restoring tolerance among the intellectual elite, and as an antidote to the destructive militarism around him, Rolland proposed in 1918 the formation of an "Internationale de l'esprit" [International of the Mind],[16] whose apolitical, pacifist members would help curb the prevalent cultural nationalism, ethnocentrism, and xenophobia. His elitism was tempered by the suggestion that all endeavors should be immediately accessible to the masses via reports, a newspaper, and a multilingual journal. "Fière Déclaration d'intellectuels" appeared in Paris in the French socialist newpaper *L'Humanité* on 26 June 1919, two days before the signing of the Treaty of Versailles. It was cosigned by some of the world's leading thinkers, among them Albert Einstein, Hermann Hesse, Benedetto Croce, Bertrand Russell, Israel Zangwill, Stefan Zweig, Maxim Gorky, Alfred Stieglitz, Upton Sinclair, Rabindranath Tagore, Alain, Henri Barbusse, Georges Duhamel, and Augustin Hamon.[17]

The declaration was an ambiguous document. It began with a call to the "Workers of the Mind" to regroup into a fraternal union but soon turned into a harsh indictment of intellectuals for their betrayal of noble ideals in the service of warfare. Rolland urged them to follow the Mind, to sweep aside nationalism in the name of "le Peuple—unique, universel, . . . le Peuple de tous les hommes, tous également nos frères" [the Nation—unique, universal, . . . the Nation of all men, all equally our brothers]. But the unrelenting accusations only served to weaken the closing plea for "l'Esprit libre, un et multiple, éternel" [the free Mind, one and manifold, eternal], and some intellectuals were very critical of this *Déclaration d'indépendance de l'esprit* [Declaration of independence of the mind], as it was titled in final draft.

As Rolland soon recognized, there were two main objections to his manifesto: first, some thinkers were afraid to make an openly international profession of faith; second, they were reluctant to condemn the misbehavior of fellow intellectuals during the war.[18] Others had personal reasons. Marie Curie refused to sign, and Anatole France did not respond at all. According to Rolland, the elderly skeptic "se calfeutrait . . . dans un prudent silence capitonné" [shut himself up smugly . . . in a discreet, padded silence], while Curie could not forget the sinking of the *Lusitania*.[19] Some who signed did so hesitatingly. Benedetto Croce and Heinrich Mann had reservations; Max Eastman published Rolland's manifesto in the New York City periodical the *Liberator* but appended his own Marxist critique.

Bertrand Russell's support included reservations about the penultimate paragraph, which he found accusatory. He wrote to Rolland in French that many intellectuals regretted what they had done during the war, that he had "no wish to impose upon them the task of saying publicly: Peccavi." On May 4, he sent Rolland a long alternate paragraph, which stated that "les intellectuels devraient contribuer à la réédification du monde en ruines" [intellectuals should contribute to the rebuilding of a world in ruins], and which urged moral and intellectual unity. Rolland disagreed. He felt that one should "ne pas se hâter de passer l'éponge sur les trahisons d'hier, car on livre ainsi la place aux trahisons de demain" [not rush to wipe away the treasons of yesterday, for in so doing we give way to the treasons of tomorrow]. He expressed his disillusionment to

Russell on June 4, lamenting that it was impossible to unite a few free intellectuals around even a harmless, watered-down text. "Ma Déclaration a reçu de différents côtés tant de demandes de modifications ou d'atténuations, qu'en les réalisant, il n'en resterait plus rien que le titre" [My Declaration has received so many demands for modifications or toning down from different sides, that if I made them, nothing would be left but the title].[20] When one considers the sheer number of proposed changes to the document, this is no exaggeration.

Not surprisingly, the most critical reaction of all—and certainly the most fully documented by Rolland—came from Shaw. Rolland wrote to him on 25 April 1919, urging him to support "ce défi . . . à l'asservissement volontaire de presque toute l'élite européenne" [this challenge . . . to the voluntary enslavement of nearly the whole European elite]. His was a plea on behalf of "une jeunesse intellectuelle qui attend, désorientée, angoissée, que les aînés la rallient et lui rendent confiance dans le pouvoir de l'Esprit libérateur" [an intellectual youth which waits, disoriented, anguished, for its elders to rally it and render it confident in the power of the liberating Mind]. Instead of swords, he wrote, idealist intellectuals employed their pens.[21]

Shaw did Russell one better. With his reply to Rolland in French dated 7 May 1919, he returned the extensively revised declaration with a cautionary note: "Il faut une confession plutôt qu'un reproche: sans cela, nous aurons l'air d'être Pharisien, même snob. Pour l'éviter, j'ai osé raccommoder un peu votre brouillon. Qu'en pensez-vous? Naturellement, vous saurez rédiger mon baragouin: je suis vil linguiste" [We must have a confession rather than a reproach: without that, we will appear to be Pharisees, even snobs. To avoid this, I have dared to mend your draft a little. What do you think of it? Naturally, you will know how to compose my gibberish: I am a vile linguist].[22] The self-deprecation was perhaps intended to assuage Rolland's reaction to Shaw's considerable "mending": he had completely rewritten about one third of the document.

The tone of the original declaration was at times vituperative: "Les penseurs, les artistes, ont . . . travaillé à détruire la compréhension mutuelle entre les hommes. Et, ce faisant, ils ont enlaidi, avili, abaissé la Pensée, dont ils étaient les représentants" [Thinkers and artists have . . . worked to destroy mutual understanding among mankind. And, in so doing, they have disfigured, demeaned, debased, and degraded Thought, of which they were the representatives].[23] Shaw left this passage untouched but manipulated the preceding paragraph to make it seem that the conditions of war had obliged the intellectuals to act as they did, as opposed to Rolland's placing the blame entirely on the intellectuals themselves. "La guerre a jeté le désarroi dans nos rangs" [The war has cast confusion in our ranks], wrote Rolland. "La plupart des intellectuels ont mis leur science, leur art, leur raison, au service des gouvernements" [Most intellectuals have put their science, their art, their reason, at the disposal of governments]. In Shaw's version, this became "Elle [war] nous a obligés à mettre notre science, notre art, notre raison, au service de nos gouvernements" [It has forced us to put our science, our art, our reason, at the disposal of our governments].

Shaw went on to replace Rolland's realization of "la faiblesse des âmes individuelles et la force élémentaire des grands courants collectifs" [the weakness of individual souls and the elemental force of great collective currents] with the somewhat brutal advice that in time of war, "il faut sacrifier et même prostituer à la défense nationale non seulement la vie, mais l'âme, l'esprit, la conscience, et manier le mensonge aussi peu scrupuleusement que la baïonnette et la bombe. Nous avons beau chercher à planer au-dessus de la mêlée. Inutile: à la guerre, le premier devoir est au foyer, au voisin, la tâche suprême d'en détourner la mort" [one must sacrifice and even prostitute not only life, but soul, spirit, and conscience for the sake of national defense, as well as handle lies as unscrupulously as one would a bayonet and a bomb. It is no use trying to soar above the battle: in wartime, one's first duty is to the home, the neighbor, and the supreme task is to keep them away from death].

No wonder the gentle Rolland considered this passage shocking and deeply offensive, antithetical as it was to his goal of quashing what he would later refer to as "nationalismes sanglants" and "religions de patriotisme jaloux" [bloody nationalisms and religions of jealous patriotism],[24] as well as to his persistently reiterated insistence on pan-nationalism: "Non, l'amour de ma patrie ne veut pas que je haïsse et que je tue les âmes pieuses et fidèles qui aiment les autres patries. Il veut que je les honore et que je cherche à m'unir à elles pour notre bien commun" [No, love of my country does not demand that I hate and kill those pious and faithful souls who love other countries. It wants me to honor them and seek to unite myself to them for our common good].[25]

After placing the blame on war itself and, in typical Shavian rhetoric, propounding survival at whatever intellectual or moral costs, Shaw apologized for the actions of the intellectuals. He replaced "Debout! Dégageons l'Esprit de ces compromissions, de ces alliances humiliantes, de ces servitudes cachées! [Rise up! Release the Intellect from its compromises, from its humiliating alliances, from its hidden servitude!] with an even more forceful passage:

> Tout cela n'est peut-être pas plus horrible pour nous, penseurs et artistes, que ne l'est le meurtre, l'incendie, surtout la famine voulue, pour nos frères poilus. Mais c'est infiniment plus difficile d'en arrêter l'opération. A l'armée, on donne l'ordre: 'Bas le feu partout!' et le feu cesse. Qui sait donner pareil ordre à la pensée fausse, à l'empoisonnement de l'esprit? Pourtant, il faut faire l'essai. La menace qui nous a forcés de piller les trésors et profaner les temples de l'esprit n'existe plus. La paix nous rend la liberté. Hâtons-nous donc de nous dégager de ces alliances, de ces servitudes dénaturées, imposées par la guerre.
>
> [All that is perhaps no more horrible for us, thinkers and artists, than murder, fire, and deliberate famine are for our fellow soldiers. But it is infinitely more difficult to stop its operation. One gives the army the order to "Cease fire!" and it does. Who can give such an order to false thought, to the poisoning of the mind? And yet, one must try. The menace which has forced us to plunder the treasures and desecrate the temples of the mind no longer exists. Peace restores freedom to us. Let us therefore hasten to extricate ourselves from these alliances, from these unnatural constraints, imposed by war.]

"Tout cela," of course, refers in part to Rolland's scathing accusation that intellectuals had "enlaidi, avili, abaissé, dégradé la Pensée." In comparing intellectuals to soldiers, Shaw reiterated his thesis that war calls for drastic measures by thinkers as well as fighters, with the essential difference that soldiers can be ordered and controlled, whereas thought has a volition all its own.

Despite Shaw's gentler concluding remarks urging immediate extrication from the shackles of war, Rolland remained offended by what must have seemed to him a callous attitude. In his reply of 28 May, he admitted that Shaw was correct in warning against self-righteousness, but objected vehemently to Shaw's propounding of sacrifice and self-prostitution in the service of the state: "Jamais je n'admettrai que le premier devoir de l'homme de pensée soit la défense nationale; il est, pour moi, la défense de la pensée. Je ne mets pas la nation, la patrie, le foyer, avant tout. Avant tout, je mets la conscience libre. . . . Que l'esprit reste sauf!" [Never will I concede that the thinking man's first duty is to defend his country; it is, in my opinion, to defend the intellect. I do not place country, homeland, family, before everything. Before everything, I place the free conscience. . . . May the mind remain unharmed!]. He ended with a plea for "une Internationale de la pensée, une Conscience mondiale!" [an International of the mind, a worldwide Conscience!].[26]

Shaw answered on June 27, criticizing Rolland's notion of the omnipotence of Thought or Intellect, reminding him that the man of intellect did not exist. "Moi, je ne suis pas la Pensée. Je suis Bernard Shaw. Vous êtes Romain Rolland. Nous mangeons, et huit heures après, nous oublions notre philosophie, et sentons seulement la faim. . . . Nul homme n'a été au-dessus de la mêlée. Une telle prétention répugnerait le monde et briserait notre influence. Pardonnez-moi ma brusquerie: en écrivant l'anglais, j'ai assez de tact; mais dans une langue étrangère, on écrit comme on peut" [I am not Thought. I am Bernard Shaw, and you are Romain Rolland. We eat, and eight hours later, we forget our philosophy, and feel only hunger. . . . No man was ever above the battle. Such a claim would disgust people and ruin our influence. Pardon my bluntness: in writing English, I have some tact; but in a foreign language, one writes as one can].[27]

Rolland replied on 29 June that it was not necessary to forget one's ideas when one is hungry; even then men were dying for their ideas. "Je ne suis pas au-dessus des mêlées,—de toutes les mêlées. J'ai été, je suis, je serai toujours 'au-dessus de la mêlée' des nations et des patries. Mais je suis dans le combat contre les nations, contre les patries, contre les castes, contre toutes les barrières qui séparent les hommes" [I am not above battles,—all battles. I have been, I am, I will always be "above the battle" of nations and homelands. But I am in combat against nations, against homelands, against castes, against all barriers separating human beings].[28] This important distinction helps clarify Rolland's adherence to an international *mêlée* of intellects struggling for world harmony, as well as his denunciation of one nationalistic *mêlée* fighting another in a struggle for military glory. The difference is one of theory and practice; while striving to create a world community of pacifist nations, Rolland had to confront the more pragmatic—and human—emotions of patriotism and individualism. He was disappointed. Ironically, despite the recommendations and objections of Shaw and others, the published declaration was virtually identical to Rolland's first draft of 16 March 1919! Only a single sentence was altered: the original read, "Nous prenons l'engagement de ne servir jamais que la Vérité" [We are engaged to serve only Truth]; the final version read, "Nous honorons la seule Vérité."

When Rolland looked back upon his debate with Shaw almost two decades later—in his 1935 introduction to *Par la révolution, la paix*—the controversy seemed to have been one of form rather than content. He came to the conclusion that the form was not only more suited to Shaw's nature but also probably "la plus efficace à flétrir le servile égarement de la pensée enrégimentée pendant la guerre" [the most effective for condemning the servile aberration of enlisted thinking during the war].[29] More important, the passionate debate with Shaw over the declaration had provided Rolland with the impetus to define the ideology behind the unfortunate expression *au-dessus de la mêlée*. Echoing his letter to Shaw, Rolland wrote that he was above the bloody battles of a nationalism "se baignant dans des torrents de sang,—sang infécond, sang maudit, qui ne fait qu'appeler le sang vengeur" [bathed in torrents of blood,—barren blood, cursed blood, which only summons up vengeful blood]; but he emphasized that he was very much "*dans la mêlée,* délibérément, ou, d'un terme plus digne, dans le combat organisé contre toutes les forces oppressives du passé, ..." [*in the fray,* deliberately, or, to use a more dignified term, in the struggle organized against all the oppressive forces of the past].[30] Yet despite Shaw's pragmatic advice, Rolland's credo had been repeated, contradicted, and ultimately ignored.

* * *

Shaw's political differences with Rolland did not prevent him from endorsing the latter's satiric antiwar play, *Liluli,* which Rolland had sent him soon after its completion in November 1918. Shaw read the play in French and responded almost one year later, on 7 October 1919. The controversy over the declaration was just over three months old, and Shaw's overabundant enthusiasm may have been a conciliatory gesture: "*Liluli* est kolossal, grossartig, wunderschön, magnificent. Je l'ai goûté énormément; sans bornes, avec extase. Ma femme partage mon admiration" [*Liluli* is colossal, grand, very beautiful, magnificent. I enjoyed it enormously; boundlessly, with ecstacy. My wife shares my admiration]. Shaw went on to say that he had suggested to H. W. Massingham, editor of the *Nation,* to obtain the rights to produce the play in serial form, and to have it translated by Laurence Housman, "plume délicate, esprit sympathique."[31] Thanks to Shaw, *Liluli* was performed in England.

Liluli is one of Rolland's rare forays into the ironic mode, and—despite Shaw's praise—not altogether a successful one. In keeping with the frenzy of war which it mocks, it is fraught with fast-paced confusion. We meet the conniving, blond enchantress Liluli, or Illusion; Truth, the dark, lively gypsy; the barbarous Llôp'ih, mute Opinion; the majestic, ineffectual, white-bearded Master-God; Polonius, the pompous, bemedalled Academician; armed Peace; indifferent Love; three termagant sisters: Equality, Liberty, Fraternity—and so on. Polichinello, the play's Everyman, rejects Liluli's enticements, for she has already lulled the innocent eighteen-year-old Altaïr into the arms of army recruiters. Polichinello also refuses the headstrong seductions of Truth, admitting that "un mignon petit mensonge est bien plus doux à peloter" [a pretty little lie is nicer to fondle].[32] Master-God sells little idols and fetishes, and always sides with the powerful. The two crowds—one French, the other Germanic—join in a cacophonous, gluttonous orgy, while the Diplomats maintain that diplomacy is a chess game: "Pour gagner, la règle veut que l'on perde des pions. Les pions sont là (*Ils montrent les peuples*)" [To win, the rule says that one must lose pawns. The pawns are there (*Pointing to the people*)]. When half-naked Truth is bound and gagged on a throne, the leering crowd cheers, "Long live Truth!" Bloodthirsty Liluli encourages best friends Altaïr and Antarès to kill one another, exclaiming: "À qui perd gagne! Qui me veut gagner, qu'il se perde! [Whoever loses, wins! Whoever would win me, let him lose himself!]. Naked, cadaverous Opinion presides over the final conflagration, during which the Intellectuals, having spoken eloquently, look on and mop their foreheads: "Souffrez, mourez, manants! C'est pour mon chant" [Suffer, die, yokels! It's for the sake of my song].[33] The play culminates in everything collapsing on Polichinello's head.

This summary leaves unmentioned the dozens of other groups that weave through the allegory: children, fat men, thin men, pageants, "fettered brains," workers, peasants, merchants, et cetera. Like a dissonant fugue, the harried, topsy-turvy madness builds upon puns, rhymes, and an endless conglomeration of characters until the entire hullabaloo explodes onto poor Polichinello.

Ironically, the outright didacticism of *Liluli* runs counter to Rolland's theory of drama propounded fifteen years earlier in *Le Théâtre du peuple: Essai d'esthétique d'un théâtre nouveau*, in which he vehemently condemns all moralizing and didacticism: "Le théâtre populaire doit éviter deux excès opposés, qui lui sont coutumiers: la pédagogie morale, qui, des oeuvres vivantes, extrait de froides leçons, . . . et le dilettantisme indifférent, qui veut se faire uniquement, à tout prix, l'amuseur du peuple" [The popular theater must avoid two customary opposing excesses: moral pedagogy, which extracts cold lessons from living works, . . . and indifferent dilettantism, which only wants to be, at all costs, the people's entertainer].[34] As a savage attack on militarism and a highly entertaining spoof, *Liluli* does not conform to Rolland's theoretical precepts, although it complements his declaration as a diatribe against the vanities of war. In praising *Liluli,* Shaw may have wanted to bridge their differences over the declaration, and a satirical attack on human foibles in dramatic form may have appealed to Shaw more than the chiding of a formal manifesto.

* * *

Very different from Shaw's praise of *Liluli* is Rolland's critique of *Saint Joan.* His comments are hidden in the epilogue to the second volume of his *Péguy,* a work he completed in 1944, the year of his death. Although he admits that *Saint Joan* is "une assez bonne pièce, qui a de l'esprit et de l'émotion, qui est intelligente, vive et humaine" [a fairly good play, which has wit and emotion, is intelligent, lively and human], after Péguy's staunchly Catholic interpretation, Shaw's version fails dismally. It is "superficielle, dénuée de toute vraie spiritualité, surtout absolument étrangère à l'esprit du catholicisme" [superficial, devoid of all real spirituality, most of all absolutely foreign to the spirit of Catholicism]. Even the trial scene, bolstered as it is by historical documents, is "déplorablement sommaire, futile, un paresseux dessin d'élève brillant et léger, qui a feuilleté à peine les textes, y a piqué ça et là quelques répliques authentiques de Jeanne, sur un fond de dialogue de théâtre, fait pour des spectateurs frivoles et pressés" [deplorably brief, futile, a lazy drawing by a brilliant and thoughtless student who has barely skimmed through the texts, picking here and there a few of Jeanne's authentic lines, on a background of stage dialogue made for shallow and hurried spectators].[35]

Even more serious is that Shaw is not a "believer" in the strict religious sense, and any attempt at portraying a passionately religious being can only be artificial and ineffective. *Saint Joan* is therefore based on "le vide esthétique et moral d'un cosmopolitisme d'art 'intellectuel', qui ne croit pas à la réalité intérieure de ce qu'il raconte.... Il [Shaw] n'a aucune idée du monde intérieur qui remplit l'âme de Jeanne" [the aesthetic and moral void of a cosmopolitanism of "intellectual" art which does not believe in the interior reality of what it tells.... He has no idea of the interior world which fills Jeanne's soul].[36] Harsh as these "fighting words" from Rolland the pacifist appear, they do coincide with those of other French critics, as we have seen.

* * *

Rolland's noble efforts to gather the intellectual community under a single ideological banner proved ineffectual. When in late 1919 and early 1920, along with Georges Duhamel and Henri Barbusse, he attempted to prepare for the first in a series of International Congresses of Intellectuals, nothing came of it.[37] In the words of one critic, "Despite disclaimers, Romain Rolland tended to attribute to the intellectual priestly qualities and divine functions." He wrote to "inspire his readers to goals he deemed transcendent and eternal."[38] This sounds remarkably like Shaw, except that his approach was often more pragmatic. The fact remains that despite his admiration for Shaw's independent and idiosyncratic temperament, Rolland, the solitary, indignant moralist, was ultimately disappointed that Shaw did not take a more militant stand in troubled times. What he was aiming for can best be summarized as "un organisme intellectuel mondial, qui fût en quelque sorte le cerveau de la société à venir" [a worldwide intellectual organism, which would be, as it were, the mind of the society to come].[39] With the difference that this organism is communal and Shaw's is individual, Rolland's aspiration is very Shavian.

Requests for Shaw to participate in the war effort with other intellectuals continued into the Second World War. Henri Barbusse, campaigning with Rolland, invited him to join the organizing committee of an antiwar coalition called the Congress Against War, under the aegis of the Committee of International Co-operation (CIC) created in 1921 by the League of Nations to foster internationalism in art, science, and literature. The congress had some twenty members, including Rolland, Barbusse, Einstein, Dreiser, Dos Passos, Upton Sinclair, Gorky, Wells, Russell, and Gilbert Murray, who served as chairman from 1928 onward.[40]

Shaw wrote to Barbusse on 4 May 1932 that he would allow his name to be used only with great reluctance: "All that happens is that our names lose all their value by futile repetition." He stipulated that the CIC should organize the congress, especially since it had long been "impotent and almost useless because nobody takes any notice of it." He also chided Barbusse for convening his congresses as if the CIC did not exist, noting the futility of "reading moral lectures at Geneva." To Murray, he wrote that "Barbusse, Romain Rolland & Co . . . repudiated my suggestion as 'bourgeois'." It is no wonder, he informed Hamon, that people took "no more notice of a Barbusse-Romain Rolland manifesto than of the clock of Notre Dame striking twelve."[41] Indeed, the CIC itself fell upon hard times: the franc's devaluation reduced its effectiveness, and, according to Shaw, "intellectually it sank into profound catalepsy."[42] Its only merit for Shaw seems to have been as impetus for a new play, *Geneva* (1936), which satirizes the committee's efforts to achieve world peace, but, as he wrote Murray, "in such a way as to make this the first step to its publicity and popularity."[43]

In the end, Rolland's romantic panhumanism and idealistic internationalism proved incompatible with Shaw's pragmatic turn of mind. Yet despite significant ideological differences, Shaw's estimate of Rolland remained high, writing in 1930 that his opinion of the Frenchman would require "a book as long as Romain Rolland's opinion of Beethoven."[44] Only in 1940 did Shaw allow himself to make light of Rolland's infamous slogan: "I can only *planer au dessus de la melée* like Romain Rolland when the siren does not remind me that I am crawling *au dessous des bombiers.*"[45] Shaw knew that in wartime bombs fall on sidelines as well as battlefields, something about which Rolland, the apologist for nonviolence, needed to be reminded.

VI

Shaw et les Penseurs

13

The River-God and the Thinker

At Meudon with Auguste Rodin

Rodin Reinvents Shaw: From Mephistopheles to Moses

Countless artists have captured a likeness of the physical Shaw. He was caricatured by Max Beerbohm and David Low, painted by Augustus John and Feliks Topolski, sculpted by Jacob Epstein and Sigmund Strobl, photographed by Alvin Langdon Coburn and Yousuf Karsh, even enshrined in stained-glass windows.[1] "I have sat to so many well-known sculptors and painters," Shaw claimed, "that H. G. Wells complains that he cannot move about Europe without knocking against some image of me."[2] But of all these images, Shaw's favorite likeness was done by Auguste Rodin (1840–1917), the most famous French sculptor of his era.

A Rodin portrait bust of Shaw was Charlotte's idea. When Rodin was in London to open the International Society Exhibition in 1906, she invited him to Adelphi Terrace in the afternoon of Friday 1 March. According to Shaw, Rodin had told Charlotte, "I know nothing of Monsieur Shaw's reputation, but what is there I will give you."[3] However, "never having heard of me," wrote Shaw, Rodin "made every possible excuse to avoid a job that had no interest for him."[4] Shaw too seemed reluctant to undertake the sittings. When Rodin left that evening, Shaw wrote to Siegfried Trebitsch: "My wife insists on dragging me to Paris for twelve days at Easter so that Rodin may make a bust of me!!!!!"[5]

Charlotte first ascertained Rodin's terms from his secretary, the poet Rainer Maria Rilke: 25,000 francs (£1,000) for a marble, 20,000 francs (£800) for a bronze. She then wrote to Rodin, informing him that she wished to assure a worthy memorial of her husband, who was "comme vous, travailleur acharné et vous êtes le seul artiste auquel il consente à poser" [like you an inveterate worker and you are the only artist he agrees to pose for].[6] According to Shaw, she explained to Rodin that her husband had declared "that he would go down to posterity as a fool if, being within reach of Rodin, he selected any lesser genius." She deposited £1,000 in Rodin's bank on the understanding that it was a contribution to the general expenses of his art and that he was under no obligation to do the bust or finish it once he began. Wrote Shaw, "Rodin could not resist such treatment."[7]

Shaw had been scheduled to sit for Rodin at the Dépôt des Marbres, near the Grand Hôtel de la Gare du Quai d'Orsay, where he and Charlotte were staying. But the sculptor had been ill with influenza, and although he was feeling better, wanted to avoid going into Paris. Shaw agreed to sit for him at his home in Meudon, twenty-five minutes by train from the city. From 16 April to 8 May, Rodin completed plaster, bronze, and marble busts of the world's most famous living writer. "These *séances* at Meudon became one of the features of Paris's spring season."[8]

Rilke described the sittings in an account published in 1930. Rodin began by taking Shaw's head measurements with large iron calipers. "After he had scooped out the arches of the eyes very quickly, so that something like a nose began to form, and had made a cut that established the position of the mouth, the way children do with a snowman, he began . . . to form first four profiles, then eight, then sixteen; and after every three minutes or so the sitter had to turn." During the third sitting, "he placed Shaw in a nice little child's chair (which gives the ironic and, incidentally, not uncongenial satirist a great deal of pleasure) and cut the head off the bust with a wire." Soon the bust was "making tremendous progress thanks to the determination and energy that Shaw displays as a model. He stands there like something that has the will to stand."[9]

Shaw's own version offers a glimpse of Rodin as technician and creator. His 1912 essay is a portrait of the artist as miracle worker: "He plodded along exactly as if he were a river-god doing a job of wall-building in a garden for three or four francs a day. . . . If the bust's nose was too long, he sliced a bit out of it, and jammed the tip of it up to close the gap, with no more emotion or affectation than a glazier putting in a window pane. If the ear was in the wrong place, he cut it off and slapped it into its right place, excusing these ruthless mutilations to my wife (who half expected to see the already terribly animated clay bleed) by remarking that it was shorter than making a new ear."[10]

In 1932, Shaw reported in a French journal that Rodin would fill his mouth with water and spray the clay in order to keep it soft and workable. "Absorbé par son travail, il . . . en aspergeait abondamment mes vêtements. A la fin de la séance, . . . j'avais généralement l'air de m'être promené sous la pluie pendant une bonne heure" [Absorbed by his work, he . . . would splash my clothes a great deal. By the end of the sitting, . . . I usually looked like I had been strolling in the rain for an hour"].[11] Rodin was merely doing his job. "He knew what is important and what is not, and what can be taught and what cannot," Shaw had written, praising "the divinest workman of his day" for his "incorruptible veracity" and "a profounder and more accurate vision than anyone else's."[12] A few days into the sittings, Shaw wrote to Sydney Cockerell that Rodin "cares about nothing but getting the thing accurate and making it live."[13]

Shaw admired more than Rodin's technical skill. The following lyrical passage describes the discovery of another exemplar of the Life Force in action:

> Yet a succession of miracles took place as he worked. In the first fifteen minutes, in merely giving a suggestion of human shape to the lump of clay, he produced so spirited a thumbnail bust of me that I wanted to take it away and relieve him from further labor. . . . But that phase vanished like a summer cloud as the bust evolved. I say evolved advisedly; for it passed through every stage in the evolution of art before my eyes in the course of a month. After that first fifteen minutes it sobered down into a careful representation of my features in their exact living dimensions. Then this representation mysteriously went back to the cradle of Christian art, at which point I again wanted to say: "For Heaven's sake, stop and give me that: it is a Byzantine masterpiece." Then it began to look as if Bernini had meddled with it. Then, to my horror, it smoothed out into a plausible, rather elegant piece of eighteenth-century work, almost as if Houdon had touched up a head by Canova or Thorwaldsen, or as if Leighton had tried his hand at eclecticism in bust-making. At this point Troubetskoi would have broken it with a hammer, or given it up with a wail of despair. Rodin contemplated it with an air of callous patience, and went on with his job, more like a river-god turned plasterer than ever. Then another century passed in a single night; and the bust became a Rodin bust, and was the living head of which I carried the model on my shoulders. It was a process for the embry-

ologist to study, not the aesthete. Rodin's hand worked, not as a sculptor's hand works, but as the Life Force works.[14]

Nothing like this, Shaw wrote to Jacob Epstein, had ever happened to him in other sittings. Creative evolution was alive and well and living at Meudon.

But since Shaw had as many faces as reputations, which face was this one? Charlotte later wrote to Rodin that the bronze portrait bore such a striking resemblance to her husband that sometimes it frightened her.[15] Rodin's ignorance of Shaw's fame as acerbic critic and iconoclast was an advantage. Charlotte had told him that artists and photographers had tried to depict her husband "as the Mephistopheles they imagined him to be; they were drawing his reputation without bothering to look at the man."[16] Incidentally, the devilish appearance and persona that Shaw cultivated were of French origin: as a child, Shaw had often been to see Gounod's *Faust*. "Ce qui me plaisait surtout," he had reported in his 1932 interview, "c'était la figure de Méphistophélès. J'étais littéralement possédé du désir d'avoir un visage méphistophélique.... Par un étrange hasard, mon voeu s'est réalisé et j'ai, aujourd'hui, un visage méphistophélique" [What I liked most of all was the figure of Mephistopheles. I was literally possessed by the desire to have a mephistophelian face.... As luck would have it, my wish came true and I have, today, a mephistophelian face].[17]

Shaw's reputation had eluded Rodin, but not his physiognomy. "Shaw's satanic locks, forked beard and sardonic smile prompted Rodin to say: 'Do you know, you look like—like the devil!' And Shaw ... answered ... 'But I *am* the devil'." "On the contrary," Rodin wrote to Charlotte five weeks after completing the bust, "M. Shaw has a great sensitivity which is, oddly enough, sometimes mistaken for pride. There is something in his character that is difficult to define, as in the *Gioconda*'s smile."[18] Shaw was very amused when Rodin later wrote to him that some who had seen the bust thought it made Shaw look like "'a young Moses'!!! Justice at last—from a Frenchman, of course."[19] Indeed, from a certain angle Shaw's hair does seem parted into two small "horns" similar to those on Michelangelo's famous statue of the sitting Moses.

The marble bust arrived at Adelphi Terrace in October. Charlotte got her memorial, quite a realistic one according to Shaw: "Look at my bust, and you will not find it a bit like that brilliant fiction known as G. B. S. or Bernard Shaw. But it is most frightfully like me."[20] "Before Rodin's bust," writes Holroyd, "[Shaw] wanted to feel cleansed of the revulsion that

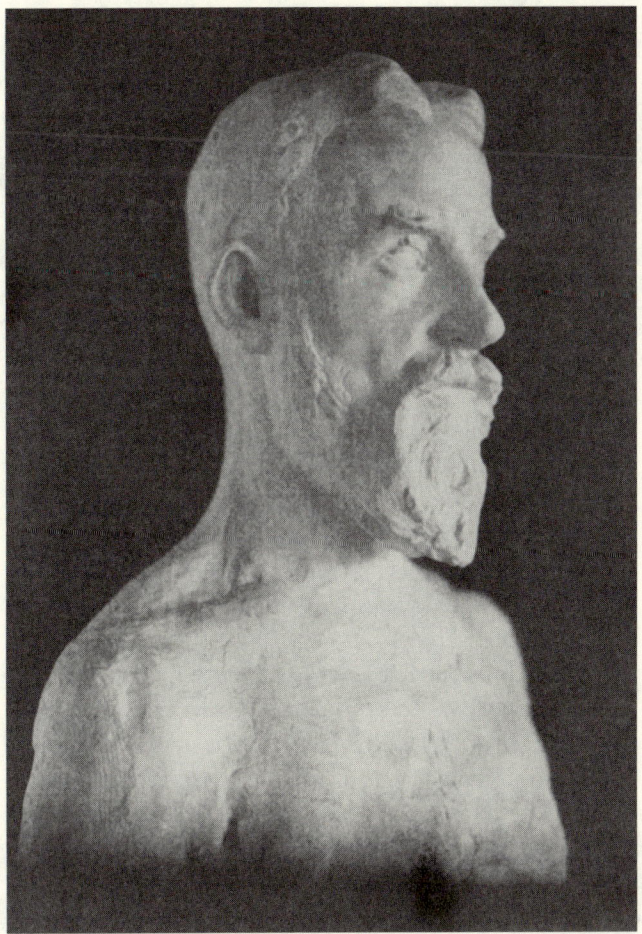

9. Bust of Bernard Shaw by Auguste Rodin, 1906. Frontispiece of *Selected Passages from the Works of Bernard Shaw. Chosen by Charlotte F. Shaw* (London: Constable, 1912).

periodically rose up in him over his own notoriety. He wanted it to extinguish G.B.S."[21] Perhaps he succeeded. Shaw wrote to Frank Harris in 1919 in the guise of Harris writing on Shaw: "'G.B.S.' he says 'is . . . a legend created by myself: a pose, a reputation. The real Shaw is not a bit like him.' Now this is exactly what all his acquaintances say of the Rodin bust, that it is not a bit like him. But Shaw maintains that it is the only portrait that tells the truth about him."[22]

* * *

But not the whole truth. Something vital was missing: humor. A letter Shaw wrote to Trebitsch shortly before the sittings (13 April 1906) closes with a delightful caricature of Rodin's bust as Shaw imagined it might look: arched eyebrows, upturned mustaches, immensely oversized ears.[23] The farcical self-portrait is a sample of the mischief that the "river-god" failed to capture. A friend of Rodin's, Anthony Ludovici, remarked upon the "unfamiliar meekness, gravity and absence of Shavian 'roguishness'" of the bust.[24] How could Rodin have left out such an intrinsic aspect of Shaw's character?

To blame was not so much his ignorance of Shaw's works or reputation but, if we believe Shaw, Rodin's own lack of humor. "I am obviously a brain worker, not a manual laborer," Shaw wrote. "All this Rodin conveyed perfectly. . . . I made myself known to Rodin as an intellectual and not as a savage, nor a pugilist, nor a gladiator. He gave that in the bust unmistakeably. But I am a comedian as well as a philosopher; and Rodin had no sense of humor. . . . Accordingly, the bust has no sense of humor; and Shaw without a sense of humor is not quite Shaw, except perhaps to himself. Here the barrier of language was unsurmountable. I am hopeless as a linguist and cannot joke in French."[25]

Rodin was gracious: "Monsieur Shaw ne parle pas bien; mais il s'exprime avec une telle violence qu'il s'impose" [Mr. Shaw does not speak well; but he expresses himself with such violence that he makes an impression].[26] But this "impression" failed to inspire Rodin into infusing blarney into the bust. Six years later, when the "Moses" photograph mentioned earlier became the frontispiece to an anthology of Shaw passages selected by Charlotte, Shaw recommended the book as "an excellent volume omitting all his humor."[27]

Rodin would have disagreed. "The cold reason," he asserted, "which he [Shaw] could, were it unhampered, apply to the problems of this life, is modified, reduced to vapor by his delicate temperamental sensitiveness, and by his keen Irish sense of humor. It is, in fact, to his Irish blood that Bernard Shaw, as we know him, is due. With the cold Anglo-Saxon current, only, in his veins, he would have proved the 'bore' *par excellence* who tries to divert us while reforming society, to win our applause by mere idol-breaking."[28] Despite his awareness of Shaw's "keen Irish sense of humor," Rodin did not translate it into the bust.

According to Shaw, "it was clear that he [Rodin] never regarded a portrait bust as finished as long as the sitter was alive."[29] Shaw said later that he found the notion of an unfinished bust quite natural because Rodin wished to represent "eternally changing man."[30] Shaw even described the marble bust as if it had a life all its own: "It does not look solid: it looks luminous; and this curious glowing and flowing keeps people's fingers off it; for you feel as if you could not catch hold of it."[31] He also deplored Augustin Hamon's failure to capture the marble's elusive quality. The French version of "Rodin" appeared in *Le Gil blas* on 24 November 1912; Shaw wrote to Rodin on 5 December: "Hamon a mal traduit mon effort de décrire le marbre. Mais peu importe; le facon dont la lumière coule sur le marbre est indescriptible. Seulement cette idée de Hamon de se servir du mot 'emaner' est une idée de littérateur et je me hate de me disculper. Pardonnez lui" [Hamon has badly translated my effort to describe the marble. But it doesn't matter; the way in which the light flows on the marble is indescribable. Only Hamon's idea of using the word "emanate" is a literary hack's idea and I hasten to exonerate myself. Forgive him].[32]

Rodin's bust is thus an appropriate symbol of the ever-evolving Life Force of which Shaw felt he was a part. Shaw maintained that Rodin had surpassed most efforts by other artists: Paul Troubetskoy's bust was "Mephistopheles, not suburban, but aristocratic"; Augustus John's three portraits, in their depiction of Shaw's public assurance, were "more than lifesize"; De Smet's portrait was of "a quiet delicate elderly gentleman"; the statuette by Lady Kennet of the Dene was merely "friendly and literal"; and John Collier's portrait was "prosaic." Shaw called Epstein's bust "some aboriginal ancestor," and when she saw its photograph, Charlotte warned her husband, "If that thing enters this house I leave it."[33] She stayed.

Rodin was the only one to capture Shaw's quintessence—minus the humor. As a token of his esteem, Shaw had presented him with a valuable Kelmscott Chaucer, which he inscribed with some (happily) rare verses:

> I have seen two masters at work: Morris who made this book,
> The other Rodin the Great, who fashioned my head in clay:
> I give the book to Rodin, scrawling my name in a nook
> Of the shrine their works shall hallow when mine are dust by the way.[34]

Shaw had declared that any man who allowed his bust to be made by anyone but Rodin would go down to posterity as "a fool" and "an ignoramus," as "a stupendous nincompoop."[35] In a reply to the editor of *Le Comoedia illustré* to a request for a recent portrait, he expressed amazement that anyone, let alone a Frenchman, would want any portrait other than Rodin's: "Toute le monde en Europe, excepté un Français, comprenait qu'un homme qui a posé pour Rodin ne saurait condescendre à poser pour un simple mortel peintre" [Everyone in Europe, except a Frenchman, would understand that a man who has sat for Rodin could not condescend to sit for a mere mortal painter].[36] He declared that a thousand years hence, he was sure of a place in every biographical dictionary as "Shaw, Bernard: subject of a bust by Rodin: otherwise unknown."[37]

* * *

Shaw's admiration for Rodin reached its apex when he became the living incarnation of Rodin's most famous sculpture. On 21 April, the young American photographer Alvin Langdon Coburn accompanied the Shaws to Paris for the unveiling of Rodin's *Le Penseur* outside the Panthéon. The next morning, much to Coburn's surprise, Shaw suggested that after his (Shaw's) bath, Coburn should photograph him, nude, in the pose of Rodin's statue. Coburn had photographed Shaw two summers earlier, and in a preface to the catalogue for an exhibition of Coburn's work, Shaw had compared his photograph of Chesterton to Rodin's statue of Balzac.[38] Coburn remarked: "I had photographed him in almost every conceivable way, [Shaw] said, so now I might as well complete the series as 'The Thinker'—his true role in life."[39] Shaw's idea of himself as a man devoted to the life of the mind corresponds to Rodin's own conception of *The Thinker,* whom he called a man "lost in contemplation. His fertile thoughts slowly unfold in his imagination. He is not a dreamer; he is a creator."[40]

These affinities did not prevent the Shavian Thinker from arousing controversy when it was exhibited as *Le Penseur (Bernard Shaw)* at the London Salon of Photography. Here was arguably the most famous author of the day sitting completely naked on the edge of his bath! In fact some reporters found it difficult to believe that this was Bernard Shaw at all, and critics suggested that Coburn had faked his photograph by superimposing Shaw's head on another torso. Although it was never published in Shaw's lifetime, this Thinker-Shaw remains a tribute to Rodin as well as a fitting symbol of Shaw's "true role in life" as a proponent of the Life Force.[41]

Shaw Reinterprets Rodin: From *Les Bourgeois de Calais* to *The Six of Calais*

On 25 January 1885, Rodin signed a contract for a monument commissioned by the city of Calais to commemorate the burghers whose self-sacrifice had saved the town in 1347, during the Hundred Years' War. Jean Froissart relates how King Edward III of England offered to lift the eleven-month siege on the starving city if "sixe of the chief burgesses of the towne come out bare heeded, bare foted, and bare legged, and in their shertes, with haulters about their neckes, with the keyes to the towne and castell in their handes, and lette theym sixe yelde themselfe purely to my wyll."[42] Led by Eustache de Saint-Pierre, they came forward in tatters and surrendered to the king, who would have made an example of them had not his consort, the pregnant Queen Philippa, interceded on their behalf. Thanks to her, the six men were set free.[43]

Rodin's interpretation of this famous event was entirely original: he wished to portray the moment when the hostages leave Calais and descend toward the English camp in a cube rather than in the common triumphal pyramidal form of attitudes struck for posterity. He believed that works conceived in the spirit of the pyramid were, in his words, "cold, conventional, and lack movement,"[44] and he was criticized for creating the antithesis of works traditionally elevated upon pillars and pedestals. Even the members of the Calais committee insisted that Rodin alter not only the group's composition as a whole but also what they called the "dejected" attitude of his figures, which constituted, in their opinion, "an offence to our religion."[45] Critics complained that the statue portrayed humiliation and capitulation, that it would be better to show the moment when Eustache volunteers dressed as the rich bourgeois he was. The local newspaper, *Le Patriote*, deplored the fact that the six men were portrayed as "exhausted by famine, deprivation, and the fatigue of a long siege," and that the monument emanated "sorrow, despair, and endless depression" rather than "feelings of greatness and devotion," and a "noble and graceful pose."[46]

What Rodin wished to arouse was patriotism inspired by an identification with heroes subject to an unjust fate. "I did not hesitate to make them as thin and as weak as possible," he wrote in 1914. "The more frightful my representation of them, the more people should praise me for knowing how to show the truth of history.... They are still questioning themselves to know if they have the strength to accomplish the supreme sacrifice— their soul pushes them onward, but their feet refuse to walk." For Rodin, their pathos was inseparable from their grandeur. The subject imposed, he wrote, "a heroic conception" of "human patriotism, abnegation, and virtue," and he believed that a statue at ground level would enable the public "to enter more easily into the drama of suffering and sacrifice."[47]

There certainly was "drama" at the work's first public appearance in plaster in 1889 at a joint retrospective of 145 Manet paintings and 36 Rodin sculptures. *Les Bourgeois de Calais* was the most heatedly discussed work on display. Although one critic thought that the figures reminded him of "clowns in our lowest form of entertainment," the critical consensus was that Rodin had struck a blow for modernity. Another critic called the monument "a watershed in the history of sculpture."[48] Its inauguration a decade later, on 2 and 3 June 1895, was even more dramatic: torchlit parade, gymnastics competition, music festival, ball, fireworks, and banquet, with thirty thousand people in attendance. Yet Rodin's victory was undercut by the council, which disregarded his wish for a ground-level placing. Instead, they elevated the statue on a plinth, fenced it in by a wrought iron grille, and, to Rodin's dismay, flanked it by an outdoor toilet! The greatest official triumph of Rodin's career was also a personal and artistic disappointment.

* * *

Eventually Rodin's burghers crossed the English Channel. When the British government purchased a new casting of *Les Bourgeois de Calais* in 1911, Shaw was as concerned with the statue's placement as Rodin had been. He wrote at length to Rodin on 24 May 1913 about the folly of a raised pedestal: "Faites un beau piédestal si vous voulez: cela sera magnifique. Mais mettez au dessus un chef d'oeuvre du Salon.... A vingt cinq metres de hauteur les mauvaises statues sont beaux et les bons sont perdus" [Make a beautiful pedestal if you wish: that will be splendid. But top it off with a Salon masterpiece.... At a height of twenty-five meters the bad statues are beautiful and the good ones are lost]. In short, only mediocrity—conventional and conservative art—requires a pedestal. Shaw pleaded: "Pas de pilier, pas de piédestal: laissez nous regarder Eustache de St Pièrre en face.... Le piédestal de ces Bourgeois doit etre rien que la terre solide et éternelle" [No pillar, no pedestal: let us look at Eustache de Saint-Pierre face to face. The pedestal of these Bourgeois must be nothing but the solid and eternal earth].[49]

One week later, in an anonymous article in the *New Statesman* (31 May), Shaw asked the British public to find a prominent place for Rodin's burghers: "The usual plan of dumping a statue in the handiest open space or at the nearest crossroads (a method of disposal formerly reserved for the bodies of suicides) will not suit this extraordinary work, which is not in the conventional monumental form, as it consists of four [sic] standing figures placed with an art so well concealed that it is impossible to call them anything as artificial as a group. There is only one place in London worthy of them, and that is Westminster Hall." Shaw was acting as a diplomat of sorts, since Raymond Poincaré, recently elected president of the Republic, was planning a trip to England. "Monsieur Poincaré's visit affords us just the right opportunity to pay a magnificent compliment to the French nation by offering it to their greatest living genius. We have not been too happy hitherto in giving distinction to Presidential visits ... and Monsieur Poincaré's threatens to be no exception to the rule unless Rodin's masterpiece saves the situation for us."[50] With Shaw's help, it did: Rodin came to London that year to install his sculpture near the Houses of Parliament.

* * *

Like Jeanne of Orleans, the burghers of Calais had come to symbolize French courage and self-sacrifice in the face of tyranny. Like Joan's trial and execution at Rouen, the Calais episode had a prominence in the new history textbooks, especially since the first celebration of Bastille Day as a national holiday on 14 July 1880. In the same way that the idea for *Saint Joan* (1923) had come to Shaw during a trip to the Lorraine region, inspiration for *The Six of Calais* (1934) came while Shaw traveled through France. He reported in the *Daily Chronicle* on 5 March 1917 that he had kept mentally busy "on an evening stretch of the journey" between Calais and Boulogne "by inventing a play on the Rodin theme of the Burgesses of Calais."[51] But Rodin's sculpture rather than history was Shaw's immediate inspiration, for it was not until 1934 that he consulted Froissart's *Chronicles* and wrote *The Six of Calais,* subtitled "A Mediaeval War Story in One Act, by Jean Froissart, Auguste Rodin and Bernard Shaw." How different are Shaw's clowns from Rodin's heroes, who convey, according to one critic, "compliance, defiance, interrogation, supplication, and resignation."[52] Shaw's play is a satiric slap in the face of French history, a debunking of the Calais episode as irreverent as Rodin's monument is noble.

Written in only four days, from 13 to 16 May 1934, and first performed on 17 July, *The Six of Calais* hardly seems to warrant mention. Shaw dismissed it as having "no moral whatever," claiming that it was "an acting piece and nothing else." He complained that he "had to improve considerably on the story as told by that absurd old snob Froissart.... He made a very poor job of it in my opinion." The play left the critics "prostrated with shock, damn their eyes!"[53] What shocked them was the outrageous behavior of Edward III; they were scandalized to behold, in Shaw's words, "a medieval soldier monarch publicly raging and cursing, crying and laughing, asserting his authority with thrasonic ferocity and the next moment blubbering like a child in his wife's lap or snarling like a savage dog at a dauntless and defiant tradesman: in short behaving himself like an unrestrained human being in a very trying situation instead of like a modern constitutional monarch on parade keeping up an elaborate fiction of living in a political vacuum and moving only when his ministers pull the strings."[54] In the England of George V, monarchs did not do such things.

The play opens with thirty-five-year old Edward at his wit's end, his army bankrupt, diseased, and mutinous: "I will have every man, woman, and child torn to pieces with red hot pincers for it." He has not threatened a single knight of Calais since it is their duty to oppose him, but he curses the "purseproud" burgesses, "these swine, these bloodsuckers," six of whom he has sentenced to public hanging. His wife's entrance turns his wailing to whining, and he becomes a doting expectant father: "Madam: are you well wrapped up? Is it wise to come into the cold air here?" Thirty-three-year-old Philippa has borne him eleven children and claims he is "the greatest baby of them all." In her presence the king can only utter uxoriously, "Yes, yes, yes, my love."

When the burghers enter, the queen in turn becomes the doting mother: "Old men in their shirts in this weather!! They will catch cold." But Edward sends her away, and all kneel save the recalcitrant Piers de Rosty, nicknamed Peter "Hardmouth."[55] "On your knees, hound," says the king, using the canine imagery that, along with sartorial metaphors, pervades the play. "I am a good dog, but not of your kennel, Neddy," Peter retorts, challenging the king to single combat; "we shall see which is the better dog of the two," he barks at the astounded monarch. The meeker Eustache de Saint-Pierre intervenes, confounds the king with rhetoric in the manner of Jesus before Pilate, and implores mercy. But the "anointed king," as Edward twice calls himself, sends the "traitors" away, except for the unrepenting Peter. The queen returns, promising the burghers hot wine and warm clothes, but when Edward is unrelenting she begins to cry. Like Eustache, she equates divine and kingly power—"it is as if you were God himself"—and her pleas finally make him break down in tears: "I am never allowed to do anything I want. I might as well be a dog as a king." He gives up: "Banquet them: feast them: give them my crown, my kingdom," he says dejectedly.

She wins the battle but not the war. In a last tête-à-tête between Edward and Peter, the roles are reversed again. At first the queen pleads for mercy: "But he is blue with cold. I fear he is dying." Yet at Peter's insolence to her husband—"Henpecked! Kiss mammy!"—Philippa is furious, and now it is Edward's turn to say that Peter "is to be pitied, shivering there in his shirt." The mood turns absurd when the king, realizing that Peter is "a dog of Champagne" like himself, begins to growl with the burgher chin to chin, in imitation dogfight. When Philippa threatens to have Peter chained and muzzled, the king, in a salacious parody of her earlier demands, says: "I have asked you for many favors, and had them granted me too, as the world, please God, will soon have proof." To confuse things further, Peter now sides with the queen: "If I had sworn to hang the six of us as he swore, no shrew should scold me out of it, . . . Do your worst, dame: I like your spunk better than his snivel." Philippa is in a rage, and Peter is dragged away braying like a donkey. "That is how they build men in Champagne. By the Holy Rood I care not if a bit of him gets into our baby," says the king, somewhat blasphemously. He snatches his wife in his arms, and as the soldiers and courtiers laugh uproariously, Philippa cries "for shame! for shame!" and Edward stops her with a kiss. The stage note reads, "Peter brays melodiously in the distance," and Shaw's little "war story" comes to a riotous close.

Perhaps one clue to the play's significance is the phrase "war story." *The Six of Calais* is Rodin's monument in reverse: dignity and high seriousness give place to bickering and pettiness. By transposing a famous incident from international warfare to the arena of domestic politics, Shaw illustrates three truths: kings are human, humans are vainglorious, and war is absurd. That the critics derided the first point and ignored the third is evidence of the second. Even Shaw realized he was too subtle for his own good: "Every year or so I hurl at [journalist critics] a long play full of insidious propaganda, with a moral in every line. They never discover what I am driving at. . . . A play of mine in which I am not driving at anything more than a playwright's direct business is as inconceivable by them as a medieval king."[56] The play is highly propagandistic: it interweaves international and domestic politics using the metaphors mentioned earlier—dogs and clothes—to demonstrate that in their struggle for power—in the home or on the battlefield—human beings are intrinsically bellicose. By pitting the cruelty of canine savagery (warfare) against the importance of keeping warm (nurturing), and by confounding the audience in having his characters constantly change "sides" in that dispute, Shaw demonstrates that in time of war, confusion reigns and everyone is victimized, or at least made absurdly ridiculous.

How is harmony reestablished? Behind the larger historical perspective of the stalemate between the king's exasperated army and the town's starving citizens, there are human emotions at play: a man's pride versus a woman's compassion; or, at another level, a king's power versus a townsman's will to survive. Only when these polarities are reversed, with Edward as womanly man and Philippa as manly woman, or with Edward as growling dog and Peter as unbending scapegoat, is equilibrium established. The two rulers are also counterbalanced by the two burghers: resigned and subservient Eustache against stubborn and insolent Peter. But beneath the trappings of political office, Edward is a mere husband and only, like Peter, "a dog of Champagne." Kinship overrules kingship, and both men can communicate, albeit primitively and hilariously, at some level other than as hostile monarch and rebellious prisoner. There are no villains or heroes; human beings are not that simple.

At first, then, Rodin's monument to self-sacrifice seems to have nothing in common with Shaw's slapstick satire. Yet both men seized upon the Calais episode as a symbol of human frailty: Rodin shows us the pathetic, Shaw the comic, side of human beings under duress. *The Six of Calais* may be a harmless little "war story" with "no moral whatever"; but like the sculpture, it is a reminder that the Life Force does not always triumph. Rodin's burghers are portrayed in pathos and suffering, and Shaw's "anointed" Edward discovers that he is not God. It is a measure of Edward's humanity that he spares the burghers; he is Champenois husband first, king second. Shaw's "war story" turns out to be a "peace story" whose moral might well be the old saw, "Love conquers all" — even, in this case, the conqueror.

14

Creative Evolution

The Rise of the Life Force

"I want to write a big book of devotion for modern people," Shaw wrote to Frederick H. Evans in 1895, "bringing all the truths latent in the old religious dogmas into contact with real life—a gospel of Shawianity, in fact."[1] Shaw never wrote that book, but one can argue that his collected dramatic and prose works form a "book of devotion" in that they share a single-minded spiritual or religious concern: the universe has mind and purpose behind it, and all progress stems not from randomness but from consciousness.

Shaw's personal religion might be summed up as follows: the Life Force (individual will) works through creative evolution (eugenic procreation) to produce the Superman (pure intellect) who strives toward God (divine perfection). The Life Force is an impersonal, amoral power that progressively and experimentally transforms us into a superior species of "artist-philosophers" through the union of the subconscious will with the female. In Shaw's view, our flaws and failings are as essential to our development as are our social accomplishments and intellectual triumphs. Furthermore, it is clear from Charles A. Berst's synthesis of the workings of Shaw's personal religion that in some ways we are all vitalists in the making: "The Holy Spirit is Life in its evolutionary action, an action represented by the Hero. Most completely, philosophical poets are Heroes because through their art they perceive and articulate the Holy Spirit: insofar as they accordingly create, reveal, and redeem they are God in action, the Word made flesh."[2]

As early as 1878, in the unfinished *Passion Play*, the spiritual nature of Shaw's new theology was exemplified in his portrayal of Jesus himself as the archetypal vitalist, a believer in "a grand, ineffable, benevolent Power . . . all composed of Love," whereas the atheist Judas was depicted as a rationalist and skeptic who shuns "the snare of self delusion."[3] In the preface to *Androcles and the Lion* (1912), Jesus becomes in effect the very first evolutionist and "a first-rate biologist" because "he declared that the reality behind the popular belief in God was a creative spirit in ourselves called by him the Heavenly Father and by us Evolution, Élan Vital, Life Force and other names."[4] Creative evolutionism is rooted in a faith in spiritual progress, wherein (as Shaw wrote in 1921) "the driving force behind Evolution is a will-to-live, and to live, as Christ said long before, more abundantly."[5]

Some of Shaw's "other names" or incarnations of his "creative spirit" include Shelley's Prometheus, Goethe's Faust, Ibsen's Julian, Wagner's Siegfried, Nietzsche's Zarathustra, even Bunyan's Pilgrim, all of them archetypes struggling toward higher consciousness. The all-embracing nature of Shaw's concept is stunning. As late as 1945, he found analogies to the Life Force in Phlogiston, Functional Adaptation, Natural Selection, Design in the Universe, Bergson's Élan Vital, Kant's Categorical Imperative, and Shakespeare's "divinity that shapes our ends."[6] One critic sees in the Life Force a synthesis of Lamarck's "force vitale," Schopenhauer's "Wille zum Leben," Nietzsche's "Wille zur Macht," and Bergson's "Élan de vie."[7] Shaw's Life Force is nothing if not versatile and universal.

But Shaw's Life Force is more than a synthesis of famous principles. The important difference between these manifestations and the Shavian idea is that Shaw's superbeings are only incidental participants in a perpetual and unfinished process. Jack Tanner, Louis Dubedat, Andrew Undershaft, Joan of Arc, Napoleon Bonaparte, and Julius Caesar have this in common: their methods may be questionable, but they are positive forces in an ongoing evolutionary progress. The Life Force, Shaw wrote in 1944, struggles "towards its goal of godhead by incarnating itself in creatures with knowledge and power enough to control nature and circumstances."[8] The ultimate end—an omnipotent, omniscient, and benevolent God—is unobtainable, a necessary attribute of absolute perfection.[9]

According to Jonathan Rose, there was "a curious, monotonous Edwardian obsession with that simple word [life].... It could mean the surrogate religion of vitalism, the worship of the life process as a spiritual force. It could specifically mean the creation of new life, an erotic impulse breaking out of Victorian constraints and sometimes worshipped as a religion in itself. Life could also be a mysterious spiritual quality that endowed human beings with identity, consciousness, a moral sense, and free will—a vital spark very like the Christian concept of the soul."[10] Shaw used the expression Life Force—at times to the point of obsession—in all three senses: vitalist religion, erotic impulse, and intellectual consciousness.

Jean-Baptiste Lamarck and the *force singulière*

Although Shaw was familiar with the new evolutionary theories being developed by his British contemporaries—Samuel Butler, Francis Galton, and Lester Ward, for instance[11]—the true origins of his eugenic vitalism are found in what he called in 1891 "the Lamarckian theory of functional adaptation."[12] Shaw was refering to the influential eighteenth-century naturalist Jean-Baptiste Lamarck (1744–1829), who coined the word "biology" in 1802, and whose *Philosophie zoologique* (1809) maintains that necessity is literally the mother of invention. Evolution, he claimed, occurs through the inheritance of characteristics acquired in response to environmental demands. There is little in Lamarck that Shaw or his peers could have accepted as scientific fact, but Shaw found that the Frenchman's concept mirrored the underlying principle of his Life Force idea: "that living organisms change because they want to."[13]

Lamarck believed that circumstances cause certain wants that can be satisfied only when certain habits are developed, a process accomplished through force of will perfecting the desired organs. He described this will as a "force singulière, qui prend sa source dans la cause excitatrice des mouvements organiques, et qui . . . fait exister la vie" [remarkable force, which takes root in the inciting cause of organic movements, and which . . . brings forth life].[14] Whereas Darwin, in *The Origin of Species by Means of Natural Selection* (1859), attempted to show *how* giraffes acquired longer necks in his "survival of the fittest" theory, Lamarck fifty years earlier had explained the phenomenon as sheer effort of will, an idea that Shaw found appealing, even plausible. As he told H. G. Wells in 1901, "A man who cannot see that the fundamental way for a camelopard to lengthen his neck is to want it longer, and want it hard enough, . . . ought really to be locked up!"[15]

Compared to Lamarck's "open-eyed intelligent wanting and trying," Shaw wrote, "the Darwinian process may be described as a chapter of accidents," concluding that the "hideous fatalism" of natural selection was nothing less than "a blasphemy,"[16] "the most horrible of all religions . . . which teaches us to regard ourselves as the irresponsible and helpless prey of circumstances, appetites, and senseless accidents."[17] But in retrospect, Shaw's use of Lamarckism as an alternative to Darwinism is unfortunate, especially since the assumptions underlying Lamarck's theory—that characteristics acquired by a parent can be inherited by its offspring—has been proven false.[18] Yet what mattered for Shaw was the principle that evolutionary change originates from within as a response to circumstances. This is a key element in his thinking, and he would refer to this idea of evolution through inherited characteristics as "Lamarckian," in contradistinction to the "Darwinian" process of natural selection. Rather than die of hunger, Lamarck's giraffes grew longer necks as they strained to reach the acacia leaves upon the higher branches, thereby willing the necessary length of neck into existence and passing this acquired characteristic to their offspring. According to Shaw, this evolution from the instinctual to the temporarily conscious would eventually become permanently unconscious.

Since these ideas form the crux of the theory of the Life Force, it is worth quoting in full the important passage from the preface to *Back to Methuselah* in which Shaw delineates what he calls "the Lamarckian evolutionary process":

> You are alive; and you want to be more alive. You want an extension of consciousness and of power. You want, consequently, additional organs or additional uses of your existing organs: that is, additional habits. You get them because you want them badly enough to keep trying for them until they come. Nobody knows how: nobody knows why: all we know is that the thing actually takes place. We relapse miserably from effort to effort until the old organ is modified or the new one created, when suddenly the impossible becomes possible and the habit is formed. The moment we form it we want to get rid of the consciousness of it so as to economize our consciousness for fresh conquests of life; for all consciousness means preoccupation and obstruction.[19]

Shaw called this evolutionary process a "metabiology" in 1911 and a "psychobiology" in 1948, and would insist that the Life Force "is as obvious a reality to me as magnetism or gravitation."[20] However, A. M. Gibbs speaks for the majority when he writes that "Shaw's account of Creative Evolution is decidedly weakened by the fact that he nailed his flag so firmly to the mast of Lamarckian and neo-Lamarckian theory."[21] Others have been less diplomatic. As early as 1905, the distinguished biologist William Bateson wrote that "not one scrap of tangible evidence was ever produced pointing to the existence of the Life Force."[22] Even H. G. Wells (along with Julian Huxley and G. P. Wells) sarcastically dismissed the Shavian Life Force idea: "It is Lamarckian in caricature . . . the essence of the Life Force is purpose. Quite apart from the difficulty of ascribing even rudimentary purpose and foreknowledge to a tapeworm or a potato or collective aspiration to the tapeworm race or the potatoes of the world, there remains the impossibility of transmitting the results of this purposeful striving to posterity. If, as we have given ample reason for believing, acquired characteristics cannot be inherited, Mr. Shaw's Life Force does not exist."[23] And recently: "Shaw's promotion of Creative Evolution," writes Tom Shippey, "was always wrong, always shallow, and often rather cheap." Moreover, "Shaw's arguments in Preface and play alike are false, ill-informed, unfair, shallow, scientifically disproved."[24]

Just how far-reaching and pragmatic Shaw believed Lamarck's theory was can be seen from his application of it to the politics of his day: "If the Western Powers had selected their allies in the Lamarckian manner," Shaw claimed in 1921, "intelligently, purposely, and vitally, . . . there would have been a durable League of Nations and no war."[25] Achieving world peace, like the giraffe obtaining a longer neck, was a matter of wanting it badly enough.

Henri Bergson and the *élan vital*

Shaw's intellectual affinities with Lamarck resemble those with the philosopher Henri Bergson (1859–1941), who rejects, in his *L'Évolution créatrice* (1907), the idea of Darwinian evolution in favor of human progress resulting from effort, a process implying "conscience et volonté" [consciousness and will]. The resulting variation is a new species which, writes Bergson, "naîtrait de l'effort même de l'être vivant pour s'adapter aux conditions où il doit vivre" [would spring from the very effort of the living being to adapt itself to the conditions in which it must live]. He concludes that neo-Lamarckism is therefore, "de toutes les formes actuelles de l'évolutionnisme, la seule qui soit capable d'admettre un principe interne et psychologique de développement, encore qu'il n'y fasse pas nécessairement appel" [of all the current forms of evolutionism, the only one capable of admitting an internal and psychological principle of development, although it is not bound to do so].[26] Bergson calls this important psychological component "un des points les plus solides" [one of the most solid points] of neo-Lamarckism.

Where Bergson diverges from Lamarck—and hence from Shaw—is in the notion of heredity. In 1935 he attempted to show that his own ideas in *L'Évolution créatrice* do not exactly coincide with those of Lamarck, whom he called nonetheless "le vrai père de la doctrine de l'évolution"

[the real father of the evolutionary doctrine]. Bergson went on to stress that "l'évolution créatrice implique, avant tout, que les habitudes acquises ne se transmettent pas héréditairement, que les variations ne sont pas dues à des efforts individuels, que ces variations surgissent au contraire tout d'un coup, chez tous les représentant d'une espèce, ou du moins chez beaucoup d'entre eux" [creative evolution implies, above all, that acquired habits are not transmitted hereditarily, that the variations are not due to individual efforts, that, on the contrary, these variations emerge all of a sudden, in all the representatives of a species, or at least in many of them].[27] Bergson's idea of social progress is sporadic and communal, in contradistinction to Shaw's perfectability, which is hereditary and individual. Despite these reservations, Bergson endorses the fundamental Lamarckian principle of effort and will as the genesis of evolutionary progress, refining that idea by maintaining that change toward complexity is related to "un effort autrement profond que l'effort individuel, autrement indépendant des circonstances" [an effort of far greater depth than individual effort, far more independent of circumstances].[28] This is much more abstract than Shaw's personal and pragmatic triumph over circumstances by effort of will.

This common interest in Lamarck indicates that Bergson and Shaw had been developing their ideologies independently but along parallel lines, both men reaching their creative apex simultaneously: they were forty-eight years of age when their most important works were published, *Man and Superman* in 1903 and *L'Évolution créatrice* in 1907. Shaw won the Nobel Prize in 1925, Bergson in 1927. Oddly enough, the two men do not seem to have known about one another until 1911, when Bergson's major work was translated into English and he began lecturing in Great Britain. This is odd since, according to one critic, Bergson's fame "eclipsed that of any other philosopher," and he "was established as the pre-eminently fashionable philosopher of his day."[29] Yet Shaw makes no mention of reading Bergson in translation, nor of an awareness of his lectures in English at Oxford, Birmingham, Leeds, London, and Edinburgh, about a dozen appearances between 1911 and 1913.[30]

By this time, Bergson had published four of six major works: *Essai sur les données immédiates de la conscience* (1889), *Matière et mémoire* (1896), *Le Rire* (1900), and *L'Évolution créatrice* (1907); the others are *Durée et simultanéité* (1922) and *Les Deux sources de la morale et de la religion* (1932). It is also odd that Shaw does not comment on Bergson's famous analysis of humor, *Le Rire* [Laughter], subtitled "Essai sur la signification du comique," which first appeared as two articles in *La Revue*

10. Henri Bergson around 1911. By permission of the Agence Photographique Roger-Viollet, Paris.

de Paris. Augustin Hamon examined Shaw's humor in light of *Le Rire* in 1913 in *Le Molière du XXe siècle:* "Bergson a conclu que le comique est produit par la mise en lumière du raide, du tout fait, du mécanique dans la vie.... 'Pour transformer le drame de la vie en comédie, il faut montrer que la liberté est apparente, qu'elle recouvre un jeu de ficelles'. On peut dire que le théâtre entier de Shaw est une illustration de cette pensée Bergsonnienne. Il montre l'apparence de cette liberté par la sincérité, la franchise avec laquelle s'expriment ses personnages qui s'ôtent leurs masques les uns les autres, à la grande confusion de chacun d'eux" [Bergson con-

cludes that the comical is produced by a display of the rigid, of the mechanical element in life. "To transform the drama of life into comedy, one must show that freedom is only apparent, that it conceals the puppet strings." It may be said that the whole of Shaw's drama illustrates this Bergsonian idea. It illustrates the illusory nature of this freedom by the sincerity and frankness with which his characters express themselves, stripping off one another's masks to their mutual confusion].[31]

More recently, Charles Berst has suggested that "Bergson wrote with Molière as his model, and consequently found the comic laugh to be directed at the errant individual who mechanically pursued his unsocial ways into eccentricity and estrangement from the norm: laughter in this context supports the social consensus. Shaw most typically does exactly the opposite. He supports the individual in his lack of sociability, occasionally enjoying his falls, as in Tanner's *faux pas,* but in the long run extolling as marks of genius the insights and courage of the nonconformist." However, Berst notes that many Shaw characters exhibit Bergsonian man-as-machine humor: Ptolemy, Eliza, Sergius, Tanner, Vivie, Bluntschli, and Higgins possess the mechanical traits of robots, dolls, and machines; Mangan, Stogumber, Undershaft, and the Inquisitor incarnate "profound aspects of Bergsonian humor" as "characters in whom the individual has become an automaton through surrendering his soul to an abstraction."[32]

But if Bergson was not mentioned, one cannot conclude that he was not read. His immense popularity would have been difficult to ignore, especially after his most significant works had been translated: *Time and Free Will* in 1910, and *Matter and Memory, Laughter,* and *Creative Evolution,* all in 1911. Despite a relentless schedule, Shaw kept abreast of world intellectual developments and certainly could have come across some of the many reviews, articles, and critical essays on Bergson published in countless English newspapers and journals, the earliest one in May 1890.[33] Moreover, Shaw was in France at the height of Bergson's popularity, spending three weeks in Paris in 1906 posing for Rodin, and later touring the country by car: two weeks in 1907, four weeks in 1910, and three months in 1911.[34] This last visit included ten days with Augustin Hamon, who had firsthand knowledge of the latest developments in Continental philosophy.

Shaw's knowledge of Bergson aside, the ideas behind creative evolution and the Life Force had been germinating in him long before Bergson put his label on them. Shaw admitted to appropriating from him the expressions *évolution créatrice* [creative evolution] and *élan vital* [vital impetus or momentum, life-drive], terms that became the keystones of Shaw's personal religion. But the Shavian doctrine had been clearly formulated and played out years before *L'Évolution créatrice,* between 1901 and 1903, with *Man and Superman.* "When I wrote Man and Superman," he told H. G. Wells in 1921, "I had never heard of Bergson."[35] This play was "the first attempt," he wrote in 1919, "to dramatize [a creed of creative evolution] in English. My Life Force is Bergson's *élan vitale* [sic]."[36] Shaw's acknowledgement of Bergson was more likely a tribute to a similarity in thinking rather than a recognition of intellectual debt, since *L'Évolution créatrice* was not published until 1907, and its English translation by Arthur Mitchell only in 1911.

"Bergsonism" was already part of European discourse when Shaw first mentioned "the philosophy of Bergson" in 1912 in a footnote added to the second edition of *The Quintessence of Ibsenism.* The next year, in a causerie written to be read to a society of musicians in France, Shaw chided the French for ignoring Bergson's genius: "I should explain that Mr Bergson is a French philosopher well known in England. When he has been as long dead as Descartes or Leibnitz, his reputation will reach Paris."[37] Shaw was fond of censuring Paris for not recognizing his genius; Bergson now joined Rodin and Shaw as great thinkers unjustly ignored in France.

* * *

It should come as no surprise that some of Bergson's ideas have strong Shavian overtones: for example, the validity of mystical intuition leading to creative action—as in *Saint Joan*— or a belief in the continuity of pure memory beyond bodily decomposition—as in *Back to Methuselah.* But the most striking similarity between Bergsonian and Shavian metaphysics is the idea of an inner force moving toward perfection. Bergson conceives his *élan* as "une poussée intérieure qui porterait la vie, par des formes de plus en plus complexes, à des destinées de plus en plus hautes" [an inner thrust which would carry life, through more and more complex forms, to higher and higher destinies].[38] Colin Wilson has suggested that Bergson's theory is cruder than Shaw's because Bergson "over-emphasises the inability of reason to grasp the flowing contours of life," failing to stress the importance of the intellect (as Shaw does) in his focus on the development of intuition and instinct.[39] Bergson's *élan* is quite impersonal: "Tout se passe comme si un être indécis et flou," he writes, "qu'on pourra appeler, comme on voudra, homme ou surhomme, avait cherché en route une partie de lui-même" [Everything happens as if an indecisive and vague being, whom we might call, as we wish, man or superman, had searched en route a part of himself].⁴⁰ Yet this is precisely how Shaw's Life Force works: as an instinctual, albeit conscious, inner power struggling to perfect itself, transforming man into superman. What Wilson fails to take into account in Shaw is that consciousness, in time, refines itself *into* "habit" in its drive toward the superbeing.

When we examine Bergson's best-known definition, we see that its characteristics are very Shavian. At the beginning of the section titled "Signification de l'évolution" is his summary definition of his concept: "*L'élan de vie* dont nous parlons consiste, en somme, dans une exigence de création. Il ne peut créer absolument, parce qu'il rencontre devant lui la matière, c'est-à-dire le mouvement inverse du sien. Mais il se saisit de cette matière, qui est la nécessité même, et il tend à y introduire la plus grande somme possible d'indétermination et de liberté" [In short, the *impetus of life* we speak of consists of a necessity for creation. It cannot create absolutely, because it is confronted with matter, that is to say an inverse movement of its own. But it seizes upon this matter, which is necessity itself, and strives to introduce into it the largest possible amount of indetermination and liberty].⁴¹ Here are the two central traits of the Life Force: necessity struggling toward creation, and the idea of discontinuous progress, where human imperfections are necessary to progress. For Shaw as much as for Bergson, human nature gropes its way toward perfection, and as one of Bergson's biographers puts it, "the evolution of man is strewn with moments of regression, dead ends, false steps, hesitations, and stagnation. Viewed as a whole, it is progress all the same," and "in ourselves we touch and feel the stream of life which is coextensive with the divine consciousness."⁴² Human beings are merely gods-in-the-making unable to avoid setbacks while working toward perfection.

While Bergson and Shaw grappled with their respective philosophies separately but in tandem, the issue of common phraseology arose only long after both men had made their mark upon the intellectual scene. The matter of "debt" was finally settled by Shaw himself late in 1912, when he had completed a laborious revision of the French translation of *Man and Superman*. When Hamon suggested translating "Life Force" as "La Force de Vie" [The Force of Life], Shaw told him that it would be pointless to attempt to ignore Bergson's term, since the philosopher "is the recognized French exponent of the Life Force; and it is no use trying to change the term to which he has given currency." Shaw went on to dismiss "La Force de Vie" as unintelligible on stage as well as ungrammatical. "Therefore you must use L'Élan Vital. It is extraordinarily fortunate for us that

Bergson has provided us with such an admirably appropriate term. It is quite probable that if I had heard the expression Élan Vital when I was writing Man and Superman, I would have called the Life Force, the Life Impulse."[43] Shaw adapted existing ideologies to suit his own intellectual purposes, and Bergson was yet another convenient touchstone. Although it is clear from his suggestions to Hamon that Shaw was unaware of the French neologism until he had completed *Man and Superman,* as early as December 1904, Shaw had anticipated Bergson's famous expression when he wrote about "the life to come" and "the mightiness of that belief and the vital Force of All Forces that is behind it."[44]

Following Bergson's popular recognition in England in 1911, Shaw would continue to pay tribute to his kindred spirit across the Channel. He would often juxtapose his own term with Bergson's, referring in 1912 to "the Shavian Life Force, the Bergsonian Élan Vital," and in 1921 to God as "an *Élan Vital* or Life Force,"[45] thereby demonstrating the universality of his concept and legitimizing it for a skeptical public. Shaw would go even farther in 1918 when he discussed the third act of *Man and Superman* in relation to Bergson's *L'Évolution créatrice:* "These are totally independent of one another: Bergson and I would have written as we did, word for word, each if the other had never been born. And yet one is a dramatization of the other. Our very catchwords, Life Force and Élan Vital, are translations of one another. The Irishman and the Frenchman find their thoughts in focus at the same point."[46]

Shaw was delighted by the coincidence of great minds thinking alike; Bergson was not. Bertrand Russell relates how, at a London luncheon in the philosopher's honor, Shaw began to expound upon Bergson's thought. At first, reports Russell, the Frenchman "mildly interjected, 'Ah, no-o! it is not qvite zat!' But Shaw was quite unabashed, and replied, 'Oh, my dear fellow, I understand your philosophy much better than you do.' Bergson clenched his fists and nearly exploded with rage; but, with a great effort, he controlled himself, and Shaw's expository monologue continued."[47] Shaw's claim to a profound understanding of Bergson's ideas may have led Russell to the somewhat overstated conclusion that "*Back to Methuselah* is pure Bergsonism."[48] But one must not dismiss Bergson's impact on Shaw, as Mina Moore did, merely as "l'extrême simplicité de quelques brins de philosophie que Shaw lui emprunte pour les ériger en système religieux" [the extreme simplicity of a few bits of philosophy which Shaw borrows from him only to elevate them into a religious system].[49]

※　　※　　※

It has been said that Bergson, "just four years after publication of *Man and Superman*, transformed the Life Force into the *Élan Vital*."[50] But if Bergson did not adapt Shaw's epithet, one cannot discount the possibility that Bergson read Shaw during the writing of *L'Évolution créatrice*, which Bergson admitted in 1907 he had written over a period of eleven years.[51] This would mean that he was working out his theories as early as 1896, five years before Shaw began *Man and Superman*. Furthermore, thanks to his English mother, Bergson had been familiar with the English language from childhood,[52] and he claimed, again in 1907, that he returned to England between eight and ten days each year to visit his relatives.[53] Despite the personal nature of his visits, Bergson may also have been keeping abreast of current British artistic and literary developments. As an enthusiastic supporter of Herbert Spencer and good friend of William James, whose philosophy he found compatible with his own, he would have been hard-pressed not to have come across Shaw's name and reputation, if not his work.

The nearest Bergson comes to admitting an awareness of the Shavian intellectual circle is a reference to his familiarity with a movement called the New Theology: "Le mouvement de la Nouvelle Théologie de Campbell," he told an interviewer in 1907, "que je ne connais que superficiellement, et son succès, c'est là un fait des plus significatifs" [The New Theology movement of Campbell, which I know only superficially, and its success, is a most significant fact].[54] Although the New Theology League was formed in January 1907, its radical tenets had been preached for years by the Reverend Reginald John Campbell (1867–1956), from 1903 to 1915 minister of the City Temple in London. Campbell believed that "the recorded events of the 'historical' Jesus were merely legendary and often had little to do with the spirit of the divine Christ; and that the importance of contemporary Christianity lay in Christ's immanence, his presence in men and in history."[55] On 12 January 1907, he made this idea public to a lay audience in a *Daily Mail* interview, in which he used the phrase "the new theology." Later that year, while *L'Évolution créatrice* appeared in France, Campbell published his highly controversial book, *The New Theology*. That Bergson recognized the importance of this secular religion, which was being debated in England while he was formulating his own doctrine, shows that he was not unaware of contemporary British intellectual movements.

What is even more interesting is that the Reverend Campbell was in fact a longtime Fabian who finally had to resign from the Executive Committee because of his inability to attend meetings, a fact alluded to by Shaw in a 1908 reference to "Campbell's absolutely blank attendance sheet."[56] Campbell invited Shaw to lecture at the City Temple in 1906 ("The Religion of the British Empire"), 1909 ("The Ideal of Citizenship"), and 1913 ("Christianity and Equality"), as well as four times to its Literary Society. He even included Shaw's "Citizenship" speech in the appendix to the 1909 edition of *The New Theology*. Shaw himself had given a lecture titled "The New Theology" at Kensington Town Hall in 1907, stating that the aim of the New Theology was

> to conceive of the force behind the universe as working up through imperfection and mistake to a perfect, organized being, having the power of fulfilling its highest purposes. In a sense there is no God as yet achieved, but there is that force at work making God, struggling through us to become an actual organized existence, enjoying what to many of us is the greatest conceivable ecstasy, the ecstasy of a brain, an intelligence, actually conscious of the whole, and with the executive force capable of guiding it to a perfectly benevolent and harmonious end.[57]

This is in essence the doctrine of creative evolution, the tenets of which had been preached and published in England by Campbell, Shaw, and others while Bergson was working out his theories. Given Bergson's knowledge of the New Theology movement, it is unlikely that he was oblivious to Shaw while writing *L'Évolution créatrice*.

Bergson may have aware of the radical ideas propounded by exponents of the New Theology, but it seems unlikely that he "transformed" or incorporated Shaw's concepts into his version of evolutionism. As with Lamarck, Bergson recognized William James as a thinker with whom he shared certain ideas but to whom he owed no intellectual "debt." In an effort to clarify one French critic's assertion that he had written his *Essai sur les données immédiates de la conscience* under the influence of James's *Principles of Psychology*, Bergson wrote in 1905 that the *Principles* appeared in 1891, whereas the *Essai* was written between 1883 and 1887, and published in 1889. Rather than a combination of what he called a "French philosophy" and an "American psychology," Bergson ascribed their similar thinking to "un mouvement d'idées qui se produit un peu partout depuis quelques années, et qui tient à des causes bien autrement générales et profondes" [a movement of ideas which has occurred everywhere for some years, and whose causes are altogether more general and profound].[58]

Shaw acknowledged that his and Bergson's ideas were part of that movement when he boasted in 1924: "I am as indispensable as Bergson for a complete modern culture."[59] They began as Lamarckians but soon formulated separate philosophies, and while some of Shaw's ideas may have informed Bergson's theories, Shaw certainly owes him a debt beyond the use of his terminology. Both men evolved almost identical premises—Life Force and *élan vital*—but their intellectual cross-pollination was more complex and ambiguous than it appeared.

15

Optimistic Vitalism

Converging Toward God

Voltaire and *The Adventures of the Black Girl in Her Search for God*

While driving in South Africa in 1932, Shaw mistook the accelerator for the brake and plunged his car off the road and over a bank. His wife, Charlotte, was badly bruised, but the accident proved a "fortunate fall." It was during her monthlong convalescence that Shaw wrote his only fable, *The Adventures of the Black Girl in Her Search for God* (1933), a comic parable on his perennial theme: the quest for godhead. Having been given a Bible by a missionary, the black girl decides to find out for herself the nature of the Supreme Being. Taking the modified biblical exhortation "Seek and ye shall find me" literally, she strides off into the jungle in search of God, with the Bible as guidebook. What follows is a combination of *Alice in Wonderland* and *Candide,* an irreverent tale of a girl whose trek through the African forest leads to a series of encounters with a number of ancient and contemporary sages.

Although Augustin Hamon spent half a century drumming into the French what he considered the obvious similarities between his Irish sage and Molière, others have noticed a resemblance between Shaw and François Marie Arouet, *dit* Voltaire (1694–1778). If Denis Saurat believed that Shaw's job in France had already been done by Voltaire, Jacques Barzun maintains that Voltaire, as the leading intellectual playwright of his age, "displaces Rousseau as Shaw's counterpart in the eighteenth century."[1] Both Shaw and Voltaire were polemical playwrights as famous for their wit and personality as for their enormous literary output, and both were very interested in music, art, politics, and history. André Maurois believes that Shaw's "poésie intellectuelle" and "fran-

chise dure de la pensée" [intellectual poetry and harsh candor of thought] are reminiscent of Voltaire rather than of Molière: "Il a la même intelligence encyclopédique, le même mélange de la légèreté du ton et de la gravité du fond, la même vivacité du style et de la personne, la même vieillesse alerte et moqueuse. Peut-être Shaw a-t-il plus d'honnêteté intellectuelle que Voltaire; ses idées sur l'histoire sont moins déformées par le fanatisme de l'anti-fanatisme; son attitude envers le christianisme est moins injuste" [He has the same encyclopedic intelligence, the same mixture of lightness of tone and of seriousness of content, the same vivacity of style and of person, the same alert and mocking old age. Perhaps Shaw is more intellectually honest than Voltaire; his ideas on history are less distorted by the fanatism of anti-fanatism; his attitude toward Christianity is less unjust].[2]

Leaving aside the justness of Shaw's views on Christianity, it is true that both he and Voltaire were highly critical of organized religion. Voltaire (the deist) believed in a Supreme Being; Shaw (the evolutionist) examined the ongoing development of the divine spark within human beings. Shaw preached a "God within" in perpetual progress; Voltaire's "God without" (so to speak) was a force aloof from humanity and perhaps unmoved by earthly turmoil. According to Voltaire, God may merely allow evil to exist; according to Shaw, evil cannot help coming into existence as a result of the necessary blunders of a Life Force struggling toward higher consciousness. Both men are "believers" in an amoral divine force that must be recognized but not necessarily idolized or worshipped. Whereas Voltaire maintained that "if God did not exist, it would be necessary to invent him," Shaw did invent him and called him the Life Force.

"Everybody now sees that Voltaire did a great service to religion," wrote Shaw in 1889, "by winning the right to criticise and question the authority of the Church as if it were no more sacred than any other human institution. Yet he did this service by shocking the world with lampoons upon the most sacred subjects—lampoons which were chaste in comparison to the rhapsodies in many books of devotion, but which, to the prejudices of his contemporaries, were beyond measure indecorous and scandalous. These lampoons did not, as shallow people feared, destroy religion and corrupt the world: nobody reads them now; but they secured the right of discussion which many great thinkers immediately availed themselves of to let light into dark places and fresh air into unwholesome sanctuaries."[3] Shocking the world with lampoons to let light into dark places sounds Shavian enough, but Shaw did not like some of Voltaire's lampoons. As we have seen, he had strong objections to *La Pucelle d'Orléans,* and he also believed that "Mahomet, like Joan, needs to be rescued from Voltaire, whose play about him [*Mahomet,* 1741] is really an outrage."[4] Yet the fact remains that in many of their writings, Voltaire and Shaw had a common goal: to fight against those who persist in believing Voltaire's most famous (and most ironic) adage, "Tout est pour le mieux dans le meilleur des mondes possibles" [Everything is for the best in the best of all possible worlds].

In matters of religion, Shaw considered Voltaire the epitome of the enlightened man. In "English Voltaireanism," from the 1906 preface to *John Bull's Other Island,* Shaw notes "the ignorance of the ordinary Englishman" who "thinks of Voltaire as a French 'infidel,' instead of as the champion of the laity against the official theocracy of the State Church. The Nonconformist leaders of our Free Churches are all Voltaireans. The warcry of the Passive Resisters is Voltaire's warcry, 'Écrasez l'infâme.'"[5] In describing Voltaire's religious stance and "heroic energy," Shaw's language and ideas foreshadow *Saint Joan*'s Antigone-Creon conflict: "Voltaire convinced the Genevan ministers that he was the philosophic champion of their Protestant, Individualistic, Democratic Deism against the State Church of Roman Catholic France." And by calling Voltaire "the legitimate successor of Martin Luther and John Knox," Shaw makes him the heir of a Protestant tradition of which Shaw believed Joan of Arc was the originator and first martyr.[6]

* * *

Clearly Shaw knew and, for the most part, admired Voltaire. In 1928, in a letter to Mabel Shaw—no relation, but the prototype for his female missionary in *The Black Girl*[7]—he said it would have been a great "religious misfortune" to have missed Voltaire, "who at least loved justice and did mercy and walked humbly with his God, and believed that no further theology was required of him. Also he certainly loved mercy and, as far as his temperament would let him, tried to do justly. That is why he is still so readable." Shaw makes Voltaire's strategy sound exactly like his own dramatic technique: "Besides, as the wickednesses which he exposed and which he called on to the world's conscience to renounce were too frightful to be contemplated without some sort of anaesthetic, he used his sense of fun to make people come to scoff, knowing that that was the only chance of getting them to remain to pray."[8] Except for the praying, this is Shaw's method.

In addition to *La Pucelle* and *Mahomet,* Shaw knew *L'Homme aux Quarante Écus* (1767), which is read by the empress in the last act of *Great*

Catherine (1919), and about which Shaw once remarked: "I have always wanted to have Voltaire's Homme aux Quarante Ecus—the tract in which he smashed up old Mirabeau's Single Tax panacea (*l'impôt unique*)— translated & reprinted as a Fabian tract."[9] But most of all Shaw was familiar with *Candide, ou l'Optimisme* (1759). Voltaire's Candide is a bit of a simpleton, a "victim of circumstance" who has been taught by Pangloss—in the manner of Gottfried Wilhelm Leibniz in his *Théodicée* (1710)—to believe that manifest evil is hidden good. Shaw's black girl, on the other hand, for all her naïveté, has no qualms about fighting back. Steeped only in the Bible, she has none of Candide's illusions about cosmic harmony and does not hesitate to use her knobkerrie to fight off her antagonists. Like *Candide* and Romain Rolland's play *Liluli* (1918), Shaw's *Black Girl* is a quest story in which numerous archetypal or allegorical beings provide a naïve protagonist with a variety of ideas. Rolland's Polichinelle encounters Illusion, Truth, Opinion, Peace, Love, and other personifications. Voltaire's Candide escapes the Inquisition, meets wealthy Jesuits, is bullied in Buenos Aires, robbed in Eldorado, swindled in Paris, and besieged by the conflicting ideologies of Martin the Manichean, Pangloss the Optimist, and Cacambo the Pessimist. In the same vein, Shaw's black girl confronts Ivan Pavlov (thinly disguised as "Science"), Jesus (the "Conjurer"), Saint Peter, Saint John, Mohammed, the Wandering Jew, a red-haired Irish socialist (Shaw), and a wizened old gentleman (Voltaire) who advises her that the best place to seek God is in a garden. The events in the *Black Girl* and *Liluli* tumble at breakneck speed, leaving the protagonists exhausted and befuddled.

Interestingly enough, the notion of a transcendent power or deity is absent from *Candide*. But not from Shaw; along with the saints, prophets, and wise men, he provides his black girl with a Supreme Being, a deity whose composite portrait is strikingly similar to the Master-God of *Liluli*. Rolland's Maître-Dieu is a majestic, white-bearded old man of many faces. Disguised as a street Arab, he hawks cheap, all-purpose, discount gods in the form of amulets and fetishes: "De peur d'en manquer, en ces temps il est prudent d'avoir toujours un bon Dieu dans sa poche" [Not to run out of them, these days it is wise always to have a God in one's pocket]. And, as a military officer complete with epaulettes and gold braid, he incites the crowd to violence and murder: "Il est bien vrai que dans mes livres, il est écrit: *"Ne tue pas! Aime ton prochain!"* Mais l'ennemi n'est ton prochain. Et n'est pas tuer, se défendre" [It is quite true that in my books it is written: *"Thou shalt not kill! Love thy neighbor!"* But the enemy is not your neighbor. And self-defence is not killing].[10]

Shaw's God also has a double persona: he is two different beings altogether. The aristocratic old man with the imposing white beard and "ruthlessly severe expression" is the God of Abraham who demands that the black girl bring him her favorite child and slay it in sacrifice: "For I love the smell of newly spilled blood." Without animal offerings to propitiate him, he will smite her family with "the most horrible plagues." The kindly, bearded old man with an expression of "self-satisfied cunning" is the God of Job who delights in argument. "Dont worship me. Reproach me. Find fault with me," he tells the black girl. But he is at a loss to answer her questions about why he did not make the world all good instead of a mixture of good and evil: "Asking conundrums is not arguing. It is not playing the game," he replies.[11] Rolland and Shaw parody the same divine attributes of omnipotence and omniscience. Both portray the Supreme Being as warmonger and idealist: ruthless and bloodthirsty on the one hand, a purveyor of false panaceas or unsatisfactory answers on the other.

Only when the black girl arrives at the "very amateurish garden" being cultivated by a man whose "face was all intelligence" does she at last attain peace of mind. "I have found, after a good deal of consideration," the Voltaire figure tells her, "that the best place to seek God is in a garden. You can dig for Him here."[12] What follows is most likely Shaw's last use of a historical figure—others include Christ, Caesar, Jeanne d'Arc, and Napoleon—to incarnate the Life Force and serve as his mouthpiece. In the manner of Blanco Posnet, the Voltaire figure expounds upon creative evolutionism: "For we shall never be able to bear His full presence until we have fulfilled all His purposes and become gods ourselves. But as His purposes are infinite, and we are most briefly finite, we shall never, thank God, be able to catch up with His purposes. So much the better for us. If our work were done we should be of no further use: that would be the end of us. . . . Therefore come in and help to cultivate this garden to His glory. The rest you had better leave to Him."[13]

This is Shaw's answer to the problem of how to handle greatness. According to his Voltaire, "We hate it; we crucify it; we poison it with hemlock; we chain it to the stake and burn it alive,"[14] as in the case of Christ, Socrates, and Jeanne d'Arc. Conversely, we think so highly of ourselves that, like Semele wanting to be loved by a god in all his godhood, we explode from our hubris. "Do not be a fool like Semele," Shaw's Voltaire warns the black girl. "God is at your elbow, and He has been there all the time; but in His divine mercy He has not revealed Himself to you lest too full a knowledge of Him should drive you mad. Make a little garden for yourself: dig and plant and weed and prune; and be content if He jogs your elbow when you are gardening unskillfully, and blesses you when you are gardening well."[15] For Shaw, Voltaire's Edenic garden is a place of work and contemplation, similar in fact to the "heaven" to which the Don Juan of *Man and Superman* escapes. Unlike heaven, however, Voltaire's garden is a personal, pragmatic solution rather than an ideal toward which human beings strive.

And so it comes to pass that the black girl finally lays down her knobkerrie and begins to tend to her garden. She and the French philosopher are soon joined by a red-haired Irishman, who expounds upon the idea of God as an unfulfilled purpose: "He's not properly made and finished yet. Theres somethin in us thats dhrivin at Him, and somethin out of us thats dhrivin at Him," with that something making "plenty of mistakes in thryin to get there." Not only does Shaw put himself in his Voltaire's garden; at the philosopher's suggestion, he agrees to marry the black girl! But not without a struggle; only after an aborted escape and piteous protests does the Irishman succumb to the Life Force. Like Ann Whitefield holding Jack Tanner, "the black girl held him in a grip of iron (softly padded, however)," and her procreative function is soon realized.[16]

* * *

"The story is absolutely blasphemous," Shaw later admitted, "as it goes beyond all the churches and all the gods.... The truth is... I have finished with all these deities, who seem to me more or less grotesque signboards announcing that the Holy Ghost is lodged within, though It is there only as It is everywhere."[17] In *The Black Girl,* what lies beyond all churches and gods is Voltaire's garden of self-reliance and contentment. One cultivates it in an "amateurish" fashion to the best of one's ability and with sufficient effort. One can "dig for Him" yet not find him because the merit is in the searching, not the attainment. As Shaw's Voltaire says, one is never able to "catch up with His purposes." Besides, as he had cautioned the black girl, "Many people who have found God have not liked Him and have spent the rest of their lives running away from Him."[18]

Shortly after finishing *The Black Girl,* Shaw referred to it as "a Voltairian pamphlet," writing a dozen years later that "the Bible perished in the hand of my Black Girl when she tried all the gods in it and found more rest for her soul with Voltaire than with any of them."[19] Voltaire's garden was a refuge from the religions that failed to satisfy the black girl's curiosity. For her, even for Voltaire and Shaw, "the best of possible worlds"—a world of perfect creeds or religions—was an unattainable illusion, albeit a necessary one.

John A. Bertolini has shown that Shaw identified closely with Voltaire, pointing out that in *Great Catherine,* Catherine "can be taken as a figure of Shaw himself." When Princess Dashkoff implores her to give her brain a rest—"That is why you get headaches. Monsieur Voltaire also has headaches. His brain is just like yours"—Bertolini notes that "Shaw's susceptibility to crippling migraine headaches is well known. And the comparison to Voltaire obviously applies to Shaw, as he was considered by many the Voltaire of his times." He goes on to observe that when Catherine reads from her own Voltaire pamphlet to Edstaston (bound hand and foot), she finds it thoroughly amusing, a moment that "figures Shaw's own exuberant delight in his own comic powers."[20] In addition, Shaw had specified to John Farleigh, the illustrator of *The Black Girl,* that his philosopher should be drawn in the manner of Jean-Antoine Houdon, the renowned sculptor of more than one hundred busts of Voltaire. And when Shaw bequeathed his own bust (by Sigmund Strobl) to the Shakespeare Memorial National Theatre, he specified that it should be placed "in the foyer as the bust of Voltaire by Houdon is placed in the foyer of the Théâtre Français."[21] It seems that the Irish socialist of Shaw's Voltairian pamphlet wished to be remembered not so much as a new Molière but as the Voltaire of England.

Pierre Teilhard de Chardin and *la convergence*

We have seen how Shaw's melioristic theory of evolution was anticipated by Lamarck, reinforced by Bergson, and restated in *The Black Girl.* It also has a curious parallel in the writings of Shaw's near-contemporary, the Jesuit theologian-scientist Pierre Teilhard de Chardin (1881–1955), whose ideal world (like Shaw's) refined aggression, greed, and (in Teilhard) sexuality, out of existence.[22] Teilhard was in quest of a perennial religion-philosophy, a kind of cosmic pantheism, where the terminus of progress was godhead. This is in essence Shaw's creative evolutionism.

Because he was a priest, geologist, and paleoanthropologist, Teilhard's attempt at a reconciliation of science and religion into an evolutionary optimism seems natural enough. But like Bergson, whose works were put on the Index of Prohibited Books in 1914, Teilhard was eventually forbidden by his Jesuit superiors to lecture, teach, and publish. Thus most of his works appeared posthumously: *Le Phénomène humain* (1955, written 1938), *L'Apparition de l'homme* (1956), *Le Milieu divin* (1957), *L'Avenir de l'homme* (1959).

It has been said that *Le Phénomène humain* can be considered a scientific-religious realization of "The Gospel of the Brothers Barnabas" in *Back to Methuselah*. "For both thinkers," writes Daniel J. Leary, "the Thesis (Life or Life-Force) is progressively liberated from the Antithesis (Matter) leading to the mediate synthesis (Man-Thought) and the ultimate synthesis (Superman-Survival)."[23] In some respects, Shaw's Life Force has a parallel in Teilhard's "radial energy," a force that draws elements together into higher states of consciousness in an ecstatic merging of energies. It comes as no surprise that Teilhard's spiritual force is love itself, an all-encompassing flow of energy struggling toward "a single, new, conscious entity, one which will no longer be dependent upon a physical body. . . . a point of convergence, the Omega Point, where men become truly one in God," an idea similar to Shaw's "vortex of pure thought" that makes us divine.[24] Teilhard elsewhere describes the Omega Point as "a harmonised collectivity of consciousness equivalent to a sort of superconsciousness," and, in an essay titled "The God of Evolution," he writes that the end result of the development of mind is that "we have beings that have suddenly become *conscious of becoming every day a little more conscious* as a result of 'co-reflection,'" co-reflection being the consciousness of consciousness.[25]

Nothing could be closer in spirit or wording to the credo of Shaw's Juan of "Don Juan in Hell," who every day struggles toward "wider, deeper, intenser self-consciousness."[26] Teilhard's reflective consciousness and Shaw's intenser consciousness are means of attaining godhead. According to Teilhard, the Parousia—the second coming of Christ—will occur when human beings attain individuation, when "cosmogenesis" and "Christogenesis," creation and creator, converge.[27] Both men agree on life's final destination; only the means of attaining it differ: Shaw's Life Force pushes us toward godhead, Teilhard's divine Love pulls us into it.

Where Shaw and Teilhard diverge is in their conception of love. Jonathan Rose has argued convincingly that erotic love is the bait used by the Life Force to work its ends, and that Shaw was one of many Edwardians attempting to transmute Christianity into a "sanctified eroticism."[28] There is no doubt that Woman is vital to Shaw's secular religion. According to Shaw, Goethe's Eternal Feminine drawing us forward and upward was "the first modern manifesto of the mysterious force in creative evolution."[29] But the passion that draws Tanner to Ann and Juan to Ana, although it partakes of the divine spark of the Life Force, is very physical. It is a far cry from Teilhard's metaphysical idea of love, which he describes in rhapsodic terms: "Love alone is capable of uniting living beings in such a way as to complete and fulfill them, for it alone takes them and joins them by what is deepest in themselves."[30]

Although Shaw and Teilhard held fast to their respective concepts, neither achieved significant recognition for their theories in their lifetime. Shaw was not taken seriously because he insisted that his Life Force was as real as magnetism or gravitation, and Teilhard's teleology undermined the very foundations of Christianity. Warren Sylvester Smith believes that for the non-Christian Shaw, "humanity occupies no privileged position in the universe. If it cannot fulfill the purposes of the Life Force, some other creature in some other time-span or on some other planet must be evolved to do it. For the Christian, Teilhard, man is the especial child of God, and his failure would be a cosmic tragedy of Titanic scope."[31] In *Back to Methuselah*, higher consciousness can be reached only through human longevity—"as far as thought can reach"—a concept probably too anthropocentric for any Jesuit theologian. But as a follower of Bergson, Teilhard might have agreed on the power of what Franklyn Barnabas called "the tremendous miracle-working force of Will nerved to creation by a conviction of Necessity."[32] "To Shaw, to Teilhard, to Bergson, to Lamarck," writes Leary, "it was always man who created the environment, never the reverse. This difference between design outside the organism and design within it is one amounting to a philosophic revolution."[33] Not a revolution, really, but rather an awakening.

16

Shaw's Protoexistentialism

In Hell with Jean-Paul Sartre

The descent into the underworld is one of the most popular of all literary tropes, from medieval dream-visions to contemporary cinema. Hell is the setting for two one-act plays: the "Don Juan in Hell" section of Shaw's *Man and Superman* (performed 1905) and Jean-Paul Sartre's *Huis clos* (performed 1944), or *No Exit*, as it is usually mistranslated.[1] These short, polemical works discuss personal ethics and are as central to the thought of Shaw and Sartre as was the *Commedia*, the most famous journey into hell, to Dante's. Like his trilogy, these plays are semi-allegorical: Don Juan Tenorio—the seventeenth-century Spanish nobleman who shares "a resemblance, even an identity,"[2] with John Tanner, his twentieth-century incarnation—is also a Shavian mouthpiece; the three souls in *Huis clos* illustrate Sartre's views on responsibility, authenticity, and commitment, issues that are central to Shaw's philosophy.

Unlike the pilgrim Dante, who is merely passing through his *Inferno*, Shaw's Don Juan and Sartre's three bourgeois are in hell permanently. The plays also differ from one another in symbolic intention: Shaw's Juan is an example to emulate; Sartre's people are moral failures. Juan hopes to redeem humanity in his struggle toward godhead, and represents what we are capable of achieving when we embody the Life Force; Sartre's characters exemplify the self-destructive hubris of weak-willed selfishness. For Shaw, self-deification is a step toward the salvation of the race: in the end, Juan leaves hell for heaven. In Sartre's world, Joseph Garcin, Inès Serrano, and Estelle Rigault are so consumed by their egotistic passions that they are unable to leave hell even when its door is forced open. Shaw's linear path to progress and Sartre's cyclical road to perpetual strife are effectively symbolized in the last lines of each play: In Shaw, by the optimistic cry, "I believe in the Life to Come. A father! a father for the Superman!"[3] In Sartre, by the fatalistic entreaty, "Eh bien, continuons" [Well, let's go on].[4]

Regardless of damnation or escape, both plays posit responsibility as the only hope for progress. "Liberty means responsibility. That is why most men dread it," writes Jack Tanner in his "Maxims for Revolutionists."[5] This is only one instance of what one might call Shaw's existentialist temperament, and many critics have been drawn to that dimension of his work. He has been called an "existentialist before his time";[6] Maurice Valency compared Brassbound to Sartre's hero in *Les Mains sales*;[7] some believe that in composing *Heartbreak House,* Shaw "was in fact writing an Existential play," "an unconscious or unwitting forecast or prototype of Existential thought as posited by Sartre in *No Exit*";[8] Colin Wilson maintains that "in the profoundest sense of the word, he [Shaw] is an existentialist thinker" and "the key figure of existentialist thought";[9] one critic, writing recently about *Saint Joan,* claims that "Shaw sounds like—indeed in fact is—a practicing existentialist whom Camus would have recognized on the spot."[10] Perhaps Bernard Dukore offers a more balanced view when he refers to Shaw as "a protoexistentialist" and to "Don Juan in Hell" as an "existential parable" "whose protagonist is a prototypical existentialist hero."[11] Let us find out if some of these startling claims apply to "Don Juan in Hell," and determine whether or not Shavianism is an existentialism.

* * *

"Don Juan in Hell" forms the third act of *Man and Superman,* but Shaw thought of it as "a totally extraneous act."[12] "I wrote the third act of 'Man and Superman' and the whole of 'Back to Methuselah' without the least prospect of their being performed in my lifetime," he admitted in the *Era* of 10 January 1934.[13] Since it was first performed only on 4 June 1907, two years after the play's premiere on 21 May 1905, "Don Juan in Hell" can be read as an autonomous work with its own premises and conclusions. One might call it the "Philosophy" of the play's subtitle, "A Comedy (and a Philosophy)," a parenthetical and polemical commentary on *Man and Superman* in the way that *Huis clos,* according to one critic, illustrates the ideas developed by Sartre in the chapter of *Being and Nothingness* titled "Concrete Relations with Others."[14]

To elucidate the plays, it will be useful to examine the "lay sermon" read by Shaw at the Kensington Town Hall in London, "The New Theology," discussed earlier, and the famous lecture given by Sartre at the Club Maintenant in Paris titled "L'Existentialisme est un humanisme." Shaw spoke on 16 May 1907, two weeks before the premiere of "Don Juan in Hell," but *Man and Superman* was complete by 1902. Sartre spoke on 29 October 1945, a year after the premiere of *Huis clos* on 27 May 1944. In both cases, one can say that theory followed practice.

In these speeches, we find that Shaw's Life Force mirrors Sartre's "engagement" or commitment; each is a means for mind and will, and for the human race, to achieve progress. As developed in the sermon and *conférence,* this idea originates for Shaw with Jean-Baptiste Lamarck, as discussed earlier, and for Sartre with René Descartes. To Shaw, consciousness is the triumph of "purpose and will," exemplified by Lamarck as a giraffe straining its neck to feed on the top branches of tall trees.[15] To Sartre, it is *cogito ergo sum:* "Il ne peut y avoir de vérité autre," he writes, "au point de départ, que celle-ci: je pense donc je suis, c'est la vérité absolue de la conscience s'atteignant à elle-même"[At the outset, there can be no truth other than this one: I think therefore I am, the absolute truth of consciousness achieving itself].[16] Will and reason; these are the forces that propel the race toward higher goals, be they treetops or ideas.

Ironically, Shaw reverses Descartes's formula when he has Don Juan take it one step farther: "I had come to believe that I was a purely rational creature: a thinker! I said, with the foolish philosopher, 'I think; therefore I am.' It was Woman who taught me to say 'I am; therefore I think.' And also 'I would think more; therefore I must be more'."[17] Dukore's comment on this passage is worth noting: "Existent and sentient, Shavian man, like existential man, defines himself."[18] Another critic writing about this passage maintains that "Shaw would have agreed with modern existential thinkers that man is ultimately a subjective entity at the mercy of the life energies rather than a thinking being."[19] The purpose of the Life Force may be intellectual or cerebral, but its action is instinctual, as we will see with Doña Ana later on. Life Force and commitment aim for the greater good of the race: "If there is purpose and will in a microbe," writes Shaw, "there must be purpose and will through the whole universe."[20] In the same vein, Sartre links consciousness of the self to that of all beings in what he terms an *intersubjectivité* by which "l'homme décide ce qu'il est et ce que sont les autres" [man decides what he is and what others are].[21] For both playwrights, an individual's quest for higher consciousness is the first stage in improving humanity.

The difference between these two concepts of a will-to-progress is what Shaw calls the "ecstasy of a brain,"[22] a cosmic force working through individuals—Juan, for example—while Sartre's energy is innate insofar as individuals already possess the will to assert their authentic selves. Although the plays approach that concept from opposing perspectives—"Don Juan in Hell" is an affirmation of human potential, *Huis clos* an object lesson in its abuse—both plays are predicated upon the same principle: freedom of choice, the responsibility for determining our own salvation or damnation. According to Sartre, we create our own hell through inertia or by hiding behind excuses. This is very Shavian; for Shaw's Devil, earthly existence is a series of excuses for human self-destructiveness—religion, law, gentility, art, politics—where even duty and patriotism turn the most humane into "the most destructive of all the destroyers." Conversely, hell is the realm of what Juan calls the "seven deadly virtues": honor, duty, justice, and so on,[23] where the Devil—wrote Shaw in the program to the play's first production—"organizes his kingdom frankly on a basis of idle pleasure seeking, and worships love, beauty, sentiment, youth, romance, etc., etc., etc."[24] This realm of self-gratification is, in existential terms, a place of inauthenticity. "Here you call your appearance beauty," says Juan, "your emotions love, your sentiments heroism, your aspirations virtue, just as you did on earth." In heaven, "You face things as they are."[25]

Shaw's hell is for those who thrive on the escapism of "idle pleasure seeking." Paradoxically, Sartre's people are trapped in the hell of authenticity, where one can no longer hide behind excuses to justify one's degenerate behavior. "Nous sommes seuls, sans excuses," writes Sartre. "C'est ce que j'exprimerai en disant que l'homme est condamné à être libre" [We are alone, without excuses. It is what I will express by saying that man is condemned to be free]. He concludes, "Tout homme qui se réfugie derrière l'excuse de ses passions, tout homme qui invente un déterminisme est un homme de mauvaise foi" [He who takes refuge behind the excuses of his passions, he who invents a determinism is a man of bad faith].[26] Since he refuses to hide "behind the excuses of his passions"—since he is "without excuses," to use Sartre's expression—Juan is able to leave hell.

What, then, constitutes inauthentic behavior? Very simply: duplicity in one's relations with others. "It is not killing or dying that degrades us," Juan tells the Devil, "but base living, and accepting the wages and profits of degradation."[27] It is almost as if he were speaking about the souls of *Huis clos*, who had become experts at "base living": Garcin the adulterer, Inès the lesbian, and Estelle the infanticide are guilty of having accepted on earth "the wages and profits of degradation." Now in hell they attempt to justify with excuses and half-truths the acts that damned them: Garcin made his wife serve him and his mistress breakfast in bed, and eventually his wife died of grief. Inès stole her cousin's wife from him, and later he was crushed to death by a streetcar;[28] and Estelle drowned her baby while its father begged her to stop, after which he shot his head off. In light of these aberrant acts and their tragic consequences, there is more than a little truth to Juan's witticism that "the sex relation is not a personal or friendly relation at all."[29]

This brings us to Juan's ideas on relationships with "other people," in particular with women. The archetypal seducer calls marriage "a mantrap baited with simulated accomplishments and delusive idealizations." Moreover, since he has always believed that the sex urge "overrides and sweeps away all personal considerations," and since his interest in women was "a perfectly simple impulse of my manhood towards her womanhood," "there was nothing for it but lifelong servitude or flight."[30] But if Juan chose flight, this does not make him a "coward" in the existential sense of the word. Admittedly, he spent a lifetime philandering and avoiding earthly commitment to a single woman; but he was avoiding the futility and wasted energy of romantic love. As Shaw himself explains it, "Don Juan was consumed with a passion for divine contemplation and creative activity, this being the secret of the failure of love to interest him permanently."[31] Instead of giving in to his sexual instincts—the "impulse" of his "manhood," as Shaw phrases it—Juan's freedom of choice will result in a commitment to a higher consciousness in heaven. Garcin, Inès, and Estelle remain trapped in recriminations, replaying in hell their earthly "base living" and "degradation."

In other words, the lack of Life Force or of commitment generates cowardice. Sartre believes that we are free agents who must create our own lives: "l'homme . . . n'est donc . . . rien d'autre que sa vie" [man . . . is therefore . . . nothing other than his life],[32] he writes, which echoes what Inès tells Garcin, "Tu n'es rien d'autre que ta vie" [You are nothing else but your life].[33] He conceives earthly hell as the abuse of one's free will: "Les uns qui cacheront, par l'esprit de sérieux ou par des excuses déterministes, leur liberté totale, je les appellerai lâches" [Those who will hide their total freedom from themselves, by a seriousness or by deterministic excuses, I will call cowards].[34] This is what Sartre's people did on earth: the journalist Garcin was a pacifist and wartime deserter; civil servant Inès not only rejected the socially acceptable heterosexual behavior of her day but reversed another's psychosexual orientation; and the greedy Estelle married for money instead of love. All of them are cowards.

It is interesting that Sartre sees cowardice as the germ of inauthenticity in precisely the same way that Shaw's Juan does. When the Devil has finished his lengthy diatribe on Man's obsession with Death, Juan dismisses Man as "only a coward," and he concludes that "all his civilization is founded on his cowardice, on his abject tameness, which he calls his respectability." Respectability for Shaw represents the inauthentic facade behind which cowards hide their deepest fears. As Tanner reminds Ramsden, "The more things a man is ashamed of, the more respectable he is."[35] Sartre's people, therefore, are damned because they shunned commitment (the antithesis of cowardice), whereas Shaw's characters are saved because they embrace it: Ana by her instinctual desire to engender the Superman, and Juan by his psychosexual urge to father him.

* * *

The punishments in Dante's *Inferno* increase in severity in proportion to the number of people on earth affected by the crime: Judas Iscariot, the most heinous betrayer, is chewed upon by Satan. In what one might call "existential hell," the torment stems from within: for the French trio, it is the gradual and painful unveiling of truth; for Juan, it is the boredom of sensual gratification, which he now finds unfulfilling. Shaw's "utter void" of dull virtue, where one worships love and beauty and romance, is as stifling to Juan as Sartre's windowless, mirrorless drawing room is for his three souls. "But a lifetime of happiness!" exclaims Jack Tanner, Juan's earthly alter ego, "No man alive could bear it: it would be hell on earth."[36] And so it is in hell itself, where there is no striving after something "higher," thus no purpose or meaning to Juan's existence. For Sartre's bourgeois, hell is the addiction to other people. As Garcin often reminds his cohorts, they are "nus comme des vers" [naked as worms].[37] They can neither sleep nor blink nor cry beneath hell's eternally lit lamps, symbols of oppressive, ever-present truth. Inès tells Estelle, "Tu te retrouveras au fond de mes yeux telle que tu te désires" [You will find yourself deep in my eyes just as you wish yourself to be]. In this narcissistic world, where our self-image depends on how others perceive us, "L'enfer, c'est les Autres" [Hell is Others], as Garcin puts it, or as it is more commonly translated, "Hell is other people."[38] Furthermore, hell is other people because, as Inès puts it early in the play, "le bourreau, c'est chacun de nous pour les deux autres" [the torturer is each of us for the other two].[39]

The problem is that "Others" are essential to our survival in the world, because life is a perpetual tribunal during which the judgments of others deify or damn us in our own eyes. In Sartre's hell, these "Others" damn one another in a vicious circle of insatiable desire: Garcin the sensualist desires Inès the lesbian, who desires Estelle the nymphomaniac, who desires Garcin, and so on. Says Garcin, "Nous nous courrons après comme des chevaux de bois, sans jamais nous rejoindre" [We run after one other like wooden horses, without ever catching up with one another].[40] This carousel of unconsummated lust echoes the perpetual dissatisfaction of the earthly erotic triangles in which he and his fellow bourgeois were trapped: Garcin / his wife / his mistress; Inès / her cousin / his wife; Estelle / her husband / her lover. In typical Dantean symbolic retribution, Sartre dooms his people to repeat for eternity the inauthenticity of their earthly existence. They are trapped precisely in Shaw's definition of hell, what he calls "a society in a state of damnation . . . given wholly to the pursuit of immediate individual pleasure."[41] Only because Don Juan is no longer concerned with "immediate individual pleasure" can he make the existential choice to leave hell. Sartre's people are so mired in self-justification and egotism that they cannot leave even when the door finally opens and allows them that possibility.

And here is the ultimate irony: escape from both infernal realms is and was at all times possible. "Quel que soit le cercle d'enfer dans lequel nous vivons," writes Sartre, "je pense que nous sommes libres de le briser" [Whatever circle of hell we inhabit, I think that we are free to break it].[42] This is the very same kind of personal freedom that Shaw postulates; when Juan asks the Commander the way to the frontier of hell and heaven, the Statue replies: "Oh, the frontier is only the difference between two ways of looking at things. Any road will take you across it if you really want to get there."[43] This offhand but astounding revelation sums up the single most important "existential" principle in Shaw's play: freedom of choice. Juan "really wants" to get to heaven, but Garcin, Inès, and Estelle lack the will to escape their drawing room hell.

Ruby Cohn has remarked that "Shaw's hell is built with witty lies, Sartre's hell with cruel bad faith."[44] Comedy or tragedy, the end of torment lies in a choice between action or escapism, commitment or bad faith. The difference is that Juan makes an existential choice to leave what he calls "this Palace of Lies,"[45] while Sartre's people cannot break the circle of mutual dependency. Even when Garcin manages to force open the door, neither he nor the others are able to pass beyond it. "La voie est libre," Inès tells them, "qui nous retient?" [The way is clear, who is keeping us back?].[46] The question is not so much "who" as "what": without Juan's higher purpose, the French trio cannot pass through hell's open door.

* * *

If hell is a kind of moral and physical paralysis or entrapment, salvation is its opposite: praxis or action, what Shaw calls "Life Force" and Sartre "engagement," the means by which mind and will give existence purpose and meaning. Shaw and Sartre were orators and activists with unwavering sociopolitical programs. Neutrality was as abhorrent to them as it was for Dante, who reserved the vestibule of his poem for those angels who were neither for God nor for Satan. "The philosopher is Nature's pilot," says Juan; "to be in hell is to drift: to be in heaven is to steer."[47] A similar passage, from the "Epistle Dedicatory" to *Man and Superman*, is often quoted as the quintessence of Shavianism: "This is the true joy in life, the being used for a purpose recognized by yourself as a mighty one; ... the being a force of Nature instead of a feverish selfish little clod of ailments and grievances complaining that the world will not devote itself to making you happy."[48] In his lay sermon, Shaw reiterates this idea in speaking of "a will, a life-force ... a great purpose ... engaged in a continual struggle to produce something higher and higher."[49] Of all Shaw's stage creations, Juan is one of the most adamant exponents of that view: "I tell you that as long as I can conceive something better than myself I cannot be easy unless I am striving to bring it into existence or clearing the way for it. That is the law of my life. That is the working within me of Life's incessant aspiration to higher organization, wider, deeper, intenser self-consciousness, and clearer self-understanding."[50]

Juan and many of Shaw's other characters are engaged in this struggle toward a "higher" plane, and Sartre too believes in playing an active role in human affairs. "Ce qui compte, c'est l'engagement total" [What counts is total commitment],[51] a concept summed up in this famous passage: "Qu'est-ce que signifie ici que l'existence précède l'essence? Cela signifie que l'homme existe d'abord, se rencontre, surgit dans le monde, et qu'il se définit après" [What is meant here by existence preceding essence? It means that man exists at the outset, emerges into the world, and defines himself afterward].[52] Whereas Shaw's notion of progress is rooted in the idea of a higher, more intense consciousness setting our will in motion, Sartre's idea of progress begins with the stasis of *nausée*, or nausea (existence, or *en-soi*), and moves to the praxis of *néant*, or nothingness (essence, or *pour-soi*). In this sense, Colin Wilson's remark about Sartre also applies to Shaw: "All his work is *an act of protest at the limitation of human consciousness*."[53] This praxis-as-process is very Shavian in its optimism for the future of humanity: "Le futur n'est pas, il se *possibilise*" [The Future is not, it *possibilizes* itself].

One might also contrast here the Tanner/Ann synthesis leading to an as-yet unborn Superman to Sartre's genesis of the emergence of the self: "Le Futur est le point idéal où la compression subite et infinie de la facticité (Passé), du Pour-soi (Présent) et de son possible (Avenir) ferait surgir le *Soi* comme existence en soi du Pour-soi" [The Future is the ideal point where the sudden and infinite compression of facticity (Past), of Pour-soi (Present) and of its possible (Future) would make the *Self* emerge as existence in itself of the Pour-soi].[54] The Life Force is working toward Juan's "intenser self-consciousness" to create the Superman in the same way that "engagement" will culminate in the birth of Sartre's new "Self." Both of these goals take the form of a projected fusion of the human and the divine.

For instance, Juan's life is a force in perpetual improvement working toward perfection, "the ideal individual," as he tells the Devil, "being omnipotent, infallible, and withal completely, unilludedly self-conscious: in short, a god."[55] Shaw's lay sermon is clear: "The object of this whole evolutionary process is to realize God."[56] This is also the very terminus of Sartre's "engagement": "Être homme, c'est tendre à être Dieu" [To be man is to tend toward being God], which parallels what Shaw calls a "force at work making God."[57]

Whatever the terminology—"being God" or "making God"—Shaw's god-in-man is very similar to what Sartre terms a man-god: "Ainsi peut-on dire que ce qui rend le mieux concevable le projet fondamental de la réalité humaine, c'est que l'homme est l'être qui projette d'être Dieu.... l'en-soi-pour-soi, la conscience devenue substance, la substance devenue cause de soi, L'homme-Dieu" [Thus one can say that what makes the fundamental project of human reality most conceivable, is that man is the being who plans to be God.... the en-soi-pour-soi, consciousness become substance, substance become cause of the self, The man-God]."[58] In the same way that Shaw's "intenser self-consciousness" mirrors Sartre's "consciousness become substance," Shaw's projected superman seems a distant cousin, almost a forebear, of Sartre's projected man-god. "We are not very successful attempts at God so far," claimed Shaw in a speech of 29 May 1911 titled "The Religion of the Future," "but I believe that if we can drive into the heads of men the full knowledge that there never will be a God unless we make one—that we are instruments through which that ideal is trying to make itself a reality—we can work towards that ideal until we get to be supermen, and then super-supermen, and then a world of organisms who have achieved and realized God."[59] Striking remarks coming from two avowed atheists.

* * *

Ideologically, then, Shaw was an unwitting precursor of the philosophy that emerged in his lifetime known as "existentialism." Maurice Valency believes that "for Shaw, as for the later existentialists, there was no distinction between becoming and being. The individual was what he made of himself; things were what they became; and there was no a priori determinant to limit the direction of their development." Valency considers Blanco Posnet an innocent prefiguration of such a doctrine.[60] Wilson writes that "the true existentialist philosopher is the 'artist-philosopher' of whom Shaw spoke in Man and Superman."[61] This is Don Juan, who sings the praises of what he calls "the philosophic man: he who seeks in contemplation to discover the inner will of the world, in invention to discover the means of fulfilling that will, and in action to do that will by the so-discovered means."[62] Juan's doctrine of action or "praxis" is the essence of Sartrean thought.

In the final analysis, for change to occur, the optimism of Shaw's Life Force and of Sartre's "engagement" must move from individual to universal progress into greater spheres of mutual responsibility. What is "religious" about these two "atheists" is their devotion to a goal beyond earthly concerns. At the end of his "New Theology" sermon, Shaw entreats his audience to "stand up and say, 'I am God and here is God, not as yet completed, but still advancing towards completion, just in so much as I am working for the purpose of the universe, working for the good of the whole of society and the whole world, instead of merely looking after my personal ends.' . . . In that way I think we may turn towards the future with greater hope."[63] Like Shaw, Sartre sees civilization as progressing toward a higher, divine consciousness: "Même si Dieu existait, ça ne changerait rien; voilà notre point de vue. Non pas que nous croyions que Dieu existe, mais nous pensons que le problème n'est pas celui de son existence; il faut que l'homme se retrouve lui-même et se persuade de l'existence de Dieu. En ce sens, l'existentialisme est un optimisme, une doctrine d'action" [Even if God existed, it would change nothing; that is our point of view. Not that we believe that God exists, but we think that the problem is not that of his existence; man must find himself again and persuade himself of God's existence. In this sense, existentialism is an optimism, a doctrine of action].[64] This "greater hope" and "optimisme" are the praxis of Shaw's Life Force and of Sartre's commitment.

Interestingly, Shaw pushes the doctrine of action one step farther than Sartre. J. L. Wisenthal writes that "the Hell scene takes the principle of free choice to its utmost limit—beyond death."[65] I quoted at the outset

Doña Ana's last words—"A father! a father for the Superman!"—uttered just before "she vanishes into the void"; "my work is not yet done," she says."[66] Shaw clarifies her whereabouts and the nature of her "work" in his program note of 4 June 1907: "Love is neither her [Ana's] pleasure nor her study: it is her business. So she, in the end, neither goes with Don Juan to heaven nor with the devil and her father to the palace of pleasure, but declares that her work is not yet finished. For though by her death she is done with the bearing of men to mortal fathers, she may yet, as Woman Immortal, bear the Superman to the Eternal Father."[67]

It is important to note that Juan is only one half of Shaw's "existential" project. To use Shaw's terminology, Juan is the intellectual artist-philosopher, Ana the instinctive mother-procreator, and only their union will bring about progress. Wisenthal notes that in the hell scene, "the emphasis is on the need for more intellect," where Juan points out that "without intellect to give it direction, the progress that [instinctive willing] can make is limited. This is in precise counterpoint to the Comedy, where intellect is of value, but can make no progress without the instinctive force of Ann to give it power."[68] Whatever the emphasis, the human condition will not improve unless Juan and Ana join forces to create the Superman.

The importance of Ana's role must be emphasized in light of Juan's rejection of romantic love and of the tyranny of the sexual impulse. As one critic puts it, "Woman may pervert the soul of man and become the main obstacle in the way of an artist-philosopher's orderly realization of the self, but she is also the primordial creative energy."[69] Hell is a place of sensual gratification *for its own sake,* but if Ana joins Juan in heaven, their lovemaking will have a higher purpose: to be instruments of the Life Force, not slaves to their egotistic urges, as are Garcin, Inès, and Estelle. In the words of Jean-Claude Amalric, the advent of the Superman is "a great existential purpose,"[70] and at the end of the interlude in hell, that purpose remains to be achieved.

* * *

"Yet Shaw is not existentialist," asserts a critic in 1997. "The plots of his plays usually revolve around the sort of extreme situations preferred by existentialists, and his protagonists often do compromise their private values as existentialist heroes do. However, existentialists find that the fact of death makes the reality of life 'absurd,' leaving individuals lonely and impotent in the face of an implacably hostile or indifferent universe. Unable to accept the concept of a mindless and meaningless universe, Shaw assumes that it has order, reason, coherency, and a mysterious primal urge he calls the Life Force that guides evolution ever upward."[71]

With the above insightful caveat in mind, one could nonetheless explore Shaw's existential affinities beyond "Don Juan in Hell." Dukore has examined eight works—including "Don Juan in Hell"—from an existential perspective of alienation, despair, bad faith, and the absurd: *John Bull's Other Island, Heartbreak House, Too True to be Good, Major Barbara, Saint Joan,* "Tragedy of an Elderly Gentleman," and *The Doctor's Dilemma*. His gallery of existential heroes and heroines includes Don Juan; Mrs. Warren, who evolves into "existential woman" by "renouncing a life of bad faith"; Barbara Undershaft, "a classic case of existential development: an awareness of the loss of God, anguish, and finally affirmation through existential choice"; Saint Joan, who, after a period of "existential solitude," "chooses her fate"; and virtually everyone living in Heartbreak House, "an existential hell" whose people "fail to make the existential choices necessary to their survival."[72] Another critic, W. Stephen Gilbert, considers *The Devil's Disciple* "a kind of existential comedy" and reads Shaw's portrait of Dick Dudgeon as "an attempt at an existential hero."[73]

It appears that there is in "Don Juan in Hell" and other works a certain temper that aligns Shaw with existentialist thinking. As we have seen, Shaw and Sartre focus on key human values: truth, realism, action, will, free choice, responsibility, and authenticity. Shaw was ahead of his time in struggling with so-called existential issues, many of which continue to make people as uncomfortable as they must have made the spectators and readers of Shaw's day.

Conclusion

Irreconcilable Differences

Eric Bentley assessed Shaw's achievement in *Saint Joan* as the maintenance of an exact balance between Joan and her judges, between "individual and society, intuition and philosophy, conscience and convention, vitality and system." Such an opposition, he concluded, is "Shavian theatre in a nutshell."[1] This argument helps explain Shaw's annoyance with certain aspects of the French temperament, which he believed was constrained by social convention and conservative thinking. Not that Shaw himself was unsystematic or disorganized; his ideology was clearly defined, informed everything he wrote, and had its own idiosyncratic principles. But what prevented it from stifling under the constraints of its own form was Shaw's trial-and-error clause allowing for mistakes and failures. The Life Force is a divine spark within fallible vessels; without dialectic or paradox, there can be no creative evolution.

Shaw's idea of an evolving Life Force applies to his philosophical as well as his dramaturgical principles: "When the critics were full of the 'construction' of plays," Shaw wrote in 1890, "I steadfastly maintained that a work of art is a growth, and not a construction. When the Scribes and the Sardous turned out neat and showy cradles, the critics said 'How exquisitely constructed!' I said 'Where's the baby?' Of course, there never was any baby; . . . the French theatre, in which men and woman play the parts of puppets, is unendurable."[2] Evolution and progress require freedom of thought and movement, which Shaw did not find in the "neat and showy" French dramas of his day.

If Shaw's thinking was dialectical, paradoxical, and evolving, French thought, as he saw it, was sentimental, predictable, and stagnant. True, his barbs were aimed at anyone, French or English, "staying in the old grooves." But since most had Gallic targets, one must distinguish between Shaw's antipathy toward the French and his interest in select French individuals who were, in his estimation, superior beings. Certainly they were iconoclasts: Jeanne the mystic, Voltaire the atheist, Napoléon the dictator, Bergson the (élan) vitalist, Brieux the socialist, Zola the naturalist, Hamon the anarchist, Rodin the modernist, Rolland the pacifist. They were also exceptions. What the French majority applauded—Scribe's plays, Bernhardt's acting, Pitoëff's productions—was anathema to Shaw, who thought Gounod's music was sentimental, well-made plays lacked substance, Comédie-Française acting was formulaic, Ludmilla's Joan was febrile. One might call these aspects "romantic," whereas Shaw's French enthusiasms were, for the most part, "realistic."

This dichotomy is not as well balanced as it seems, and there is as much irony in it as in Shaw himself, especially if one agrees with Enid Starkie: "The power of seeing things as they are, without flinching and without expressed judgment, but with understanding and compassion, is one of the most fundamental characteristics of French literature."[3] The paradox is that the lucid vision that Starkie considers typically French is also typically Shavian. If the "old grooves" were static, Shaw's iconoclasts embodied that quintessential Shavian trait: vitality. Shaw maintained that it was his business "to incarnate the Zeitgeist, whereby I experience its impulse and universality."[4] When he discovered similar avatars, he promoted them passionately. The following was written about Bergson but applies to all those with whom Shaw felt an affinity: "People who, separately and often without being aware of the others' existence, design the shape of a recognizable entity in the history of culture meet, as it were, in an impersonal spiritual space which seems to have been waiting for a specific content, and the content comes from unconnected concerns and disparate sources."[5] In Shaw's case, many of those concerns and sources were French.

* * *

Aside from a few outstanding French figures, nothing allayed Shaw's antipathy toward the French. Conversely, neither did Shaw succeed in eradicating their mistrust of himself and his work. Even a year after his death, Archibald Henderson asked: "Will France accept Shaw? Will the future register the triumph of the Gaelic genius over a decadent classicism, or its repulse by Gallic conservatism, chauvinism, and insularity?"[6] Although that summer an exhibition titled "G.B.S. et la France" was held in London at the Institut Français, it came too late: during his lifetime, Shaw's "Gaelic genius" was an enigma for the French. Certainly "Gallic conservatism, chauvinism, and insularity" were obstacles: as John Palmer suggested in his essay on *Sainte Jeanne,* the French theater is "perhaps the most insular and the most faithful to traditions peculiarly national and academic."⁷ Critic Léon Blum admitted, "Nous nous tenons, en matière d'art et de pensée, pour le centre certain du monde" [In matters of art and thought, we hold ourselves to be the undoubted center of the world].⁸ It is no wonder that Shaw's paradoxes, unresolved dilemmas, and mistranslated intellectualizing did not move French audiences.

Yet as we have seen, a number of other factors made Shaw unpalatable to the French, one of them being the cultural gap between two ideologies. Like the journalist who remarked that Shaw was "not very congenial to the *génie latin*," biographer St. John Ervine asserted that Shaw's Irish Protestant turn of mind could not have been farther from a French Catholic one. He reasoned that "the coldness of G.B.S.'s women and the lack of passion in their lovers disconcerts the Latin mind," citing Vivie Warren and Ann Whitefield as examples; he could have added Candida and Eliza. Although there is some truth to this, Ervine (writing in 1956) lapses into cultural stereotyping: "The Frenchman has never allowed his intellect to interfere with his impulses and passions; and he has difficulty that is almost insuperable in understanding the Shavian man who does. It is notorious that Frenchwomen find Englishmen unsatisfying lovers. The French distaste for G.B.S.'s work, therefore, is more likely to be a matter of temperament than of translation. His insistence that intellectual passion transcends any physical passion alienates him from their liking or understanding; and their insistence that physical passion is more important than any other, since it stimulates the mind and elates the spirit, is merely disgusting to G.B.S."⁹ Simplistic as some of his remarks are, Ervine underscores one basic factor that prevented Shaw from seducing France: antithetical temperaments.

In any event—and this was a second factor Ervine pointed out—it may not be the rational element itself, but rather the intellect interfering with the passions, that baffled Parisian audiences. To paraphrase the subtitle of *Man and Superman*, they preferred "comedy" unhindered by "philosophy." When there was too much philosophizing, Shaw was attacked as an undramatic thinking machine. One A. Barbeau, writing in 1914, asked: "Et qui ressemble moins à notre comédie classique que ces pamphlets dialogués où, à travers une action ordinairement aussi inconhérente qu'invraisemblable, les personnages . . . semblent n'avoir d'autre raison d'être que d'illustrer par leurs actes ou par leurs paroles quelques unes des thèses philosophiques ou sociales, qui sont chères à l'auteur?" [And what could be farther removed from our classical comedy than these pamphlet-dialogues where, by means of an action usually as incoherent as it is implausible, the characters . . . seem to have no raison d'être other than to illustrate by their deeds or words a few of the philosophical or social theses dear to the author?].[10] The truth is that Shaw never pretended—or intended—anything else: the stage was his pulpit.

Xavier Heydet's review of *Bernard Shaw et la France* in *Elsaessisches Literatur-Blatt* (1 March and 1 April 1934) provides a good assessment of the French point of view: "Les idées de Shaw ne seraient qu'un chaos d'opinions mal mûries, receuillies un peu partout et offertes au monde dans leur état embryonaire. Ce théâtre est trop exclusivement anglais dans sa façon de flageller les travers humains" [Shaw's ideas are but a chaos of badly matured opinions, gathered here and there and offered to people in their embryonic state. This theater is too exclusively English in the way it flagellates human defects]. The French were irked by "sa mentalité protestante de moraliste et de propagandiste incompréhensible à l'esprit catholique français; . . . le peu d'importance attribué aux passions sexuelles, lacune que le Français considère comme antidramatique. . . . Shaw part de la thèse que le mariage est une prison d'où la femme ne peut s'échapper de peur de mourir de faim. En soutenant cette idée il ne se concilie pas l'approbation de la masse de la nation française dont la famille est la force centrale et essentielle" [his Protestant moralist and propagandist mentality incomprehensible to the French Catholic spirit; . . . the slight importance attributed to the sexual passions, a lacuna that the French consider antidramatic. . . . Shaw starts off with the thesis that marriage is a prison from which a woman cannot escape without dying of hunger. In supporting this idea he does not win the approbation of the bulk of the French nation of which the family is the central and essential force].[11]

The following year, Anglophile André Maurois (who was very familiar with Shaw's work), like Barbeau, pointed to Shaw's distance from French "comédie classique" as a factor preventing him from succeeding in France: "Le comique, pour atteindre en France au rang de littérature, y doit être coulé dans un moule classique. Les meilleures scènes de Courteline ou de Becque sont bâties d'après des modèles de Molière" [Comedy, to attain in France the rank of literature, must be poured in a classical mold. The best scenes by Courteline or Becque are modeled on Molière]. This is ironic, given Hamon's insistence that Shaw's plays are Molièresque in structure and substance. Maurois goes farther, maintaining that there is something in the French psyche that rejects a melding of the comic and tragic: "Enfin nous admettons assez mal le mélange des genres," he writes. "Qu'une métaphysique soit exposée dans une pièce bouffonne, cela nous surprend.

C'est sans doute pour cette raison que Bernard Shaw, grand écrivain, sérieux par ses intentions, mais délibérément paradoxal, n'a jamais obtenu en France le même succès que dans les pays anglo-saxons" [In short, we find it rather difficult to accept the mixing of genres. That a metaphysics should be expounded in a farcical play, this surprises us. It is doubtless for this reason that Bernard Shaw, great writer, serious in his intentions, but deliberately paradoxical, has never achieved in France the same success as in Anglo-Saxon countries].[12]

That Shaw was aware of this particular criticism (and its cultural roots) is clear from his annotations to Hamon's "Épître dédicatoire" to *Le Molière du XXe siècle*:

> Do not force the note about my plays being comic. You may leave that to the enemy. Your struggle will be to resist the notion that I am a mere farceur, and to convince people that I am serious. Besides, my plays are not really genre plays: they are human, natural plays. And yet they are quite in the English tradition of the old Christian "mysteries," which has persisted through Shakespear and Dickens, and which mixes the most solemn things with the most ludicrous. In the old mystery of Cain, & Abel, when God calls Cain solemnly to account, asking him where is his brother &c &c, Cain replies 'Demandez de mon cul,' 'Vous pouvez baiser mon derrière avec votre frères' &c &c &c, just as he talks to his farm servants in the comic scenes. Frenchmen have always been disgusted with this mixture of comic & serious, which seems to them a barbarous confusion of artistic genres, only possible to a grossly ignorant author—see Voltaire's later criticisms of Shakespear.[13]

This mixture of genres continues to be problematic: Amalric reports that according to one prominent director, French actors, especially older ones, "were trained to play Racine *or* Feydeau or Molière, but not a mixture of the two genres."[14]

Even historian of English literature Louis Cazamian, who praised *Candida* as a masterpiece and defended Shaw against charges of "gratuitous and systematic paradox," upheld the usual commonplaces. Most of Shaw's characters, he wrote in 1927, "are but the mouthpieces of the author. Many of his plays degenerate into endless dialogue.... Profound dramatic life is most often lacking in his work." Shaw's satirical study of English society was "the demonstration of a series of theses, which, according to a simple and almost mechanical device, reversed the usual order of certain terms."[15] And in 1994, Georges Liébert asserted that Shaw's characters "sont trop souvent que des marionnettes et ne parlent que d'une seule voix: la sienne" [are too often only puppets and speak with only one voice: his].[16] It appears the charges brought against Shaw in his lifetime have not yet been dropped.

Archibald Henderson, who first urged French critics to recognize Shaw's genius, ascribed Shaw's problems in France to five causes. First, since the prefaces were often untranslated when the plays were staged, Shaw's ironies and paradoxes bewildered drama critics. Second, theatergoers were shocked by Shaw's surfeit of words and debate. Third, Shaw's idea of passion—woman the pursuer and man the prey—was "antipathetic and antagonistic to a Catholic country such as France." Shaw replaced liaisons and adultery by an "assertive Puritanism" devoid of sentimentality and romanticism, an austerity, concludes Henderson, that stifles "in the normal Frenchman any overwhelming desire to know better this bloodless paragon, devoid of all human passions."[17] Fourth, the "normal Frenchman, rationalistic, lucid, philosophic," distrusts a worldview composed of ideas taken from Schopenhauer and Nietzsche to Bergson and Butler. Finally, the French public "reacts with violence against what it considers to be Shaw's cheap masquerade as a barker for the Shavian circus."[18]

These stumbling blocks, as well as others discussed in this book, point to an overriding concern with what was perceived as Shaw's lack of classical decorum or restraint. French audiences and readers were disconcerted at unorthodox ideas cloaked in levity, paradoxical or ironic situations, cerebral discussions, assertive women, and an eclectic philosophy. Add to this a discomfiture resulting from Shaw's aggressive, deliberately clownish self-promotion, and the French could only conclude that "G. B. S.," as Henderson phrased it, stood for "Genre Britannique Saltimbanque"—Genus British Showman.[19]

Certainly the "bloodless paragon" knew of the cultural differences hindering his acceptance in France. "In dealing with Englishmen," Shaw wrote, "you must make them believe that you are appealing to their brains when you are really appealing to their senses and feelings. With Frenchmen you must make them believe that you are appealing to their senses and feelings when you are really appealing to their brains."[20] But with the exception of *Sainte Jeanne,* Shaw's plays seldom affected French "feelings." "Il n'a pas réchauffé ni fait délirer les coeurs," wrote Robert d'Humières in 1912. "Ce satyre est un buveur d'eau" [He has neither warmed hearts nor made them rave. This satyr drinks water].[21] Yet it was never his intention to stir his audiences to emotional frenzy. Six months before his death at ninety-four, Shaw reiterated his most important dramaturgical principle: "The quality of a play is the quality of its ideas."[22] If those ideas suffered a linguistic and cultural seachange as they crossed the Channel, Jeanne's conquest of Paris—late as it was—alerted the French to the existence of a less misunderstood, but still controversial, "nouveau Molière."

Appendix A.

Shaw on Stage: The Pitoëff Productions

In Geneva:[1]

Grand Théâtre	*Candida*	13 November 1916
Salle Communale de Plainpalais	*Le Soldat de chocolat*	5 December 1918
Théâtre Pitoëff	*Le Disciple du diable*	19 November 1919
Théâtre Pitoëff	*Androclès et le lion*	26 December 1921

In Paris:

Comédie des Champs-Élysées	*Androclès et le lion*	3 March 1922
Comédie des Champs-Élysées	*Candida*	10 November 1922
Comédie des Champs-Élysées	*Androclès et le lion*	18 May 1923
Théâtre des Arts	*Sainte Jeanne*	28 April 1925
Théâtre des Arts	*Sainte Jeanne*	20 March 1926
Théâtre des Arts	*Sainte Jeanne*	9 May 1926
Théâtre des Arts	*Sainte Jeanne*	11 November 1926
Théâtre des Arts	*Sainte Jeanne*	18 April 1927
Théâtre des Mathurins	*La Maison des coeurs brisés*	17 January 1928
Théâtre des Arts	*César et Cléopâtre*	18 December 1928
Théâtre des Arts	*Sainte Jeanne*	31 December 1928
Théâtre des Arts	*César et Cléopâtre*	3 May 1929
Théâtre des Arts	*Sainte Jeanne*	12 May 1929
Théâtre des Arts	*Sainte Jeanne*	10 May 1930
Théâtre des Arts	*La Charrette de pommes*	14 April 1931
Théâtre Tristan-Bernard	*Sainte Jeanne*	10 November 1931
Théâtre des Mathurins	*Sainte Jeanne*	1 December 1934
Théâtre des Mathurins	*Le Héros et le soldat*	23 November 1935
Théâtre des Mathurins	*L'Argent n'a pas d'odeur*	16 September 1938

In Orléans:

Salle des Fêtes du Campo Santo	*Sainte Jeanne*	9 May 1936

Appendix B.

Shaw in France: Travels Across the Channel

Shaw's first trip to Paris, a weeklong visit with Sidney Webb in April 1890, was something of a disappointment. Nothing seemed to please him, judging from his report (as "Corno di Bassetto") in the *Star* of 11 April 1890, titled "Paris: A Pedant-Ridden Failure." Edmond Haraucourt's play *La Passion*—with Bernhardt as both Virgin Mary and Mary Magdalen—was met with yells of disapproval from the audience; Saint-Saëns's opera *Ascanio* was mechanical and unoriginal; Jules Barbier's *Jeanne d'Arc,* with music by Gounod and Bernhardt as Joan, was boring; and Molière's *Le Bourgeois Gentilhomme* at the Comédie-Française was merely "gag and horseplay." Monsieur Jourdain, Shaw wrote, "is himself bourgeois Paris incarnate," complete with "flunkeyism," "helpless incapacity for art," and "petty rationalism." Shaw concluded that "Paris is what it has always been: a pedant-ridden failure in everything that it pretends to lead."[1]

This initial visit by Shaw was only the first of many forays across the Channel, some of them lasting several months, most of them less frustrating. Despite his professed displeasure with most things French, Shaw probably went to France more frequently than to any other European country. Usually traveling incognito, he and Charlotte motored often enough through France that eventually they visited most of its important sites and cities. "Considering the state of the roads and the discomfort of the cars in the early decades of the twentieth century," writes Jean-Claude Amalric, "one is astounded by the length of Shaw's itineraries, both in terms of mileage and of motoring days."[2] Shaw was his own best chronicler; we know so much about his itineraries because he sent several reports to the Royal Automobile Club, "careful, accurate descriptions of the routes to follow, of the difficulties of the road, or of available accommodation."[3]

Throughout the years, Shaw's trips to France increased in frequency and duration. Yet these vacations, pleasant and relaxing as they could be, were hectic and often exhausting. Shaw was not very fond of traveling, and his dietary regimen—no meat, fish, fowl, or alcohol—must have made going through France especially difficult. Nonetheless, Shaw's first visit to Paris did not put him off completely, although it took six years before he returned to the "pedant-ridden failure," in November 1896, for only three days. He attended Lugné-Poë's production of Ibsen's *Peer Gynt*—Shaw had met him in London in March the previous year—but was unable to see Coquelin's production of Eugène Brieux's *Les Bienfaiteurs*.

The Shaws' first extensive tour of France began on 7 April 1901, when they went from Marseilles to Paris via Bordeaux (Marseilles, Arles, Saint Rémy, Avignon, Nîmes, Toulouse, Bordeaux, Tours, Chartres, and Paris). Five years later, Shaw was in Paris for three weeks (15 April to 8 May 1906), most of them spent with Auguste Rodin at Meudon. Although Shaw had planned a trip to Brittany to visit Augustin and Henriette Hamon—with whom he had been collaborating since 1904—the Rodin sittings delayed his visit to the Côte du Nord until 1911.

The Shaws were in Paris on May Day in 1906, and they went to the Place de la République to witness a demonstration of workers for a limitation of working hours. Police and soldiers quelled the riot and arrested a number of protesters. Shaw wrote to the *Labour Leader* the next day that it would "be well to organise some means of protecting the public against the police and military. The Government here wishes to win the general election by suppressing a revolution. Unluckily there is no revolution to suppress. The Government therefore sends the police and the dragoons to shove and charge the lazy and law abiding Parisians until they are goaded into revolt. No use: the people simply WON'T revolt. But several respectable persons have been shoved and galloped over and even sabred."[4] Neither Shaw nor his wife were hurt, but there had been enough real danger to make this Paris visit memorable. He wrote to Harley Granville Barker on 7 May that Charlotte "clung to lamp posts to see over people's heads, and got so furious when she saw a real crowd charged by real soldiers that she wanted to throw stones. By dignified strategy . . . we left the field without wounds."[5]

The following year, in 1907, the Shaws traveled from 30 March to 11 April, starting at Le Havre and visiting Yvetot, Caudebec, Rouen, Beauvais, Laon, Reims, and Amiens. Shaw found Rouen very interesting because of the Jeanne d'Arc connection, and he greatly admired Reims cathedral, returning for a second visit in 1912. In 1910, from 30 March to 2 May, the Shaws traveled again to Rouen, also visiting the Pyrénées from the Atlantic to the Mediterranean coast, the Languedoc, and the Limousin: Boulogne, Neufchâtel, Rouen, Le Mans, Poitiers, Périgueux, Bayonne, Biarritz, St.-Jean-de-Luz, Tarbes, St.-Girons, Perpignan, Bourg-Madame, Quillan, Tarascon, Toulouse, Carcassonne, Albi, Cahors, Tulle, Limoges, Blois, Chartres, Evreux, Beauvais, Amiens, and Boulogne.

In 1911 the Shaws embarked upon another marathon journey, a three-month voyage that lasted from 19 June to 4 October: Boulogne, Amiens, Doullens, Coucy, Soissons, Reims (three days), Châlon, Nancy, Gérardmer, Ballon d'Alsace, Belfort, Pontarlier, Annecy, top of Mont Cenis, Grenoble (five days), La Grande Chartreuse, Chambéry, Albertville, Beaufort, Haute Combe, Chamonix, Thonon, Evian, les Diablerets, Courmayeur, Albertville, Chambéry, Belley, Bourg, Bourges, Aignan, Tours, Saumur, Angers, Rennes, St.-Briac, Port-Blanc (where they spent ten days with the Hamons), St.-Brieuc, St.-Lunaire, Granville, Caen, Bayeux, Rouen, and Boulogne.

The Shaws motored through France and Germany from 27 July to 8 September 1912: Boulogne, Hesdin, Doullens, St.-Quentin, Hirson, Sedan, Nancy (twelve days awaiting the repair of the car, which had broken down in Germany), Freiburg, Gérardmer, Neufchâteau, Bar-le-Duc, Reims, Soissons, Ham, Péronne, Bapaume, Arras, Lille, Dunkerque, Calais, and Boulogne.

From 6 September to 17 October 1913, they traveled to Rouen, Orléans, Moulins, Mont-Dore, Le Puy, Valence (ten days), Vals les Bains, Mende, Albi, Toulouse, Lourdes, Pau, Biarritz (ten days), Bordeaux, La Rochelle, Nantes, Le Mans, Rouen, and Boulogne. It was from Orléans that Shaw wrote to Mrs. Patrick Campbell that he would one day write a play about Jeanne d'Arc—which he did, a decade later.

* * *

In 1917, Shaw returned to France not as a tourist but as a reporter. Commander in chief Sir Douglas Haig had invited him to visit the front and to write about it. Shaw set off, this time without Charlotte, to spend eight days (28 January to 5 February) traveling through Boulogne, Trancourt, Rollencourt, Arras, St.-Eloi, Ypres, Bailleul, Etaples, Montreuil, St.-Omer, Amiens, the Somme front, Aire, and Boulogne again. He related what he had seen of war-torn France in three issues of the *Daily Chronicle* (5, 7 and 8 March 1917), reprinting the essays in 1930 as "Bombardment," "The Technique of War," and "Consolations and Responsibilities"—under the odd heading "Joy Riding at the Front"—in *What I Really Wrote About the War*, volume 21 of his *Collected Works*.

The tone of "Bombardment" is ironic, and perhaps Shaw's quips and almost surrealistic analogies helped him deal with the devastation he encountered. He found the French army completely unkempt, "the Frenchman brusque, contemptuous of the graces, doing everything with a jerk and a snap, as if there were nothing in the world to be considered except getting it done. I judged, as it now seems rightly, that the Frenchman would be a very formidable fighter." Yet Shaw himself must have cut a strange figure, dressed in khaki, having discarded his cap "and, like Don Quixote, donned the helmet of Mambrino."

According to Amalric, Shaw was received as a distinguished visitor at the headquarters at Boulogne, and he insisted on visiting Ypres. Whatever turmoil he felt at the gruesome scenes before him was camouflaged in print by cavalier or witty descriptions. "A man lying by the roadside was not a tramp taking a siesta, but a gentleman who had lost his head. . . . Well, in time of peace he might have lost it much more painfully and mischievously. There are worse ways of ending one's walk in life." Arras cathedral was "a copy of a copy, looked better as a ruin than when it was intact." At the Somme front, Shaw noted the irony of the signposts. "'To Maurepas'; and there was no Maurepas. 'To Contalmaison'; and there was no Contalmaison. 'To Pozières'; and there was no Pozières. . . . As to the ground, you cannot find enough flat earth in a square mile to play marbles on. The moon seen through a telescope, or a slice of Gruyère cheese, is a tennis lawn by comparison."

Thus ended the "joy ride," an interlude that apparently left our reporter in good spirits. Shaw concluded by stating that amidst "the booming and whizzing" of gunfire, "I enjoyed myself enormously and continuously."[6] But as Amalric notes, this lighthearted tone may have been necessary: "The censorship imposed on war correspondents prevented him from expressing his ideas on that war and on the places he visited, at least at that time."[7]

* * *

A decade passed after Shaw's tour of the front before he and Charlotte returned to France. They spent from 15 July to 3 September 1928 on the Riviera, taking the boat train to Agay (five days), Cap d'Antibes, and making excursions to Vence, Cannes, Thorens, Monte-Carlo, Menton, Sospel, Var, Goyes de Coron, Fréjus, Beauvallon, St.-Raphaël, Monaco, and Nice. From Cap d'Antibes on 31 July, Shaw wrote to his old friend Frank Harris, declining his invitation to lunch with him at Nice. Shaw reminded him that Charlotte had once burnt Harris's notorious memoirs, *My Life and Loves* (1923–27), and that she refused to entertain "Frank Casanova" on any terms.[8]

From 23 April to 6 May 1931, the Shaws were in Paris again, where they saw Georges Pitoëff's production of *La Charrette de pommes*. Shaw had hoped to remain incognito but was recognized by one of the actors and consented to salute the audience. He congratulated the cast, in particular Georges, who had played King Magnus "as democratically as I hoped. I am grateful to you for doing so, for it was not the case in England, in Poland and in Germany."[9] He was being diplomatic; as we have seen, he found the entire production "ugly, silly, and incompetent."

This was Shaw's final glimpse of Paris.[10] It had been four decades since his first visit, when the unknown music critic was appalled at what he saw on the French stage. Now he was too famous to remain anonymous in the city he had so often berated. Ironically, Bernard Shaw spent his last visit to France watching one of his own plays performed in French in a Paris theater.

Appendix C.

Shaw in Print

A Chronological Bibliography of Works by and about Bernard Shaw in French and on Shaw and French Culture and Literature

The following bibliography includes everything from short newspaper reviews of Shaw's plays in performance to longer articles in periodicals and journals, as well as Shaw's own writings (articles, excerpts from plays and prefaces, letters to the press), most of them translated by Augustin and Henriette Hamon. All entries are listed as they appear in the published sources listed below, with as much information as was available. Since first compiling this bibliography in 1989, I have emended existing entries and added numerous others. It should be considered preliminary, to be augmented as new material becomes available. I would be grateful for any corrections or additions readers might provide.

I have consulted (among others) the following biographical, bibliographical, and archival sources, listed alphabetically: Jean-Claude Amalric, *Bernard Shaw: Du réformateur victorien au prophète édouardien* (Paris: Didier, 1977), 467–566; Amalric, "Shaw in France in Recent Years," *Shaw Review* 20.1 (January 1977): 43–46; *Catalogue général des lives imprimés de la Bibliothèque Nationale*, vol. 171 (Paris: Imprimerie Nationale, 1947); W. Eugene Davis, general editor, *G. B. Shaw: An Annotated Bibliography of Writings About Him,* 3 vols. (DeKalb: Northern Illinois University Press, 1986–87); Daniel C. Gerould, "*Saint Joan* in Paris," *Shaw Review* 7.1 (January 1964): 11–23; Augustin Hamon, "Bernard Shaw en France et dans les Pays de langue Française," *La Pensée Bretonne* (1 June 1913); Augustin and Henriette Hamon, "Au Lecteur. En guise de préface" [to *Le Disciple du diable: Mélodrame en trois actes*] (Paris: Calmann-Lévy, 1926), 1–36; Archibald Henderson, *G. B. Shaw: Man of the Century* (New York: Appleton, 1956), 492–505; Madeleine Horn-Monval, *Répertoire bibliographique des traductions et adaptations françaises du théâtre étranger du XVe siècle à nos jours,* vol. 5 (Paris: Centre National de la Recherche Scientifique, 1963), 173–80; Jacqueline Jomaron, *Georges Pitoëff, metteur en scène* (Lausanne: L'Age d'Homme, 1979), 158–82; Dan H. Laurence, editor, *Bernard Shaw: A Bibliography,* 2 vols. (Oxford: Clarendon, 1983); Mina Moore, *Bernard Shaw et la France* (Paris: Champion, 1933), 204–10; John R. Pfeiffer, "Shaw and Other Playwrights: A Bibliography of Secondary Writings," in *SHAW, the Annual of Bernard Shaw Studies,* vol. 13, *Shaw and Other Playwrights,* edited by John A. Bertolini (University Park: Pennsylvania State University Press, 1993), 159–75; Oskar Wellens, "*Candida* in French (1907)," *Shavian* 7.7 (spring 1995): 6–11 (reviews of the Brussels premiere); the manuscript of *SHAW, the Annual of Bernard Shaw Studies,* vol. 20, *Bibliographical Shaw,* edited by Dan H. Laurence and Fred D. Crawford, assisted by MaryAnn K. Crawford (University Park: Pennsylvania State University Press, 2000), 200–203; and the Bernard Shaw Papers in the British Library, London.

Included here are over one hundred items, not listed in the above sources, from the Hamon Collection in the Archival and Special Collections of the McLaughlin Library, University of Guelph, Guelph, Canada. Although some of these letters, essays, articles, and reviews are by the Hamons, many are by French literary historians and theater critics, some by Shaw in translation. Augustin Hamon collected virtually everything relating to Shaw and meticulously filed thousands of items: from three-line newspaper notices to full-length reviews and articles, as well as theater programs, posters, and photographs of the French productions of Shaw's plays, including twenty-one of the Pitoëff *Sainte Jeanne.* The Hamon Collection comprises sixty-two rolls of microfilm of more than 150,000 documents.[1]

*   *   *

1880

Shaw, Bernard. "A Reminiscence of Hector Berlioz." 1880. [reprinted in Dan H. Laurence and Margot Peters, eds., *SHAW, the Annual of Bernard Shaw Studies,* vol. 16, *Unpublished Shaw* (University Park: Pennsylvania State University Press, 1996), 71–87]

1886

Shaw, Bernard. No title. *World* 622 (2 June 1886): 15. [unsigned note on Jacques-Joseph Tissot; reprinted in Stanley Weintraub, ed., *Bernard Shaw on the London Art Scene, 1885–1950* (University Park and London: Pennsylvania State University Press, 1989), 117–18]

———. "Proudhon—Ch. IV. Propositions I–V. pp. 126–153." 1886. [report and commentary on Pierre Proudhon's *Qu'est-ce que la Propriété?* (1840), reprinted in Dan H. Laurence and Margot Peters, eds., *SHAW, the Annual of Bernard Shaw Studies,* vol. 16, *Unpublished Shaw,* (University Park: Pennsylvania State University Press, 1996), 133–37]

1887

Shaw, Bernard. "Molière's Things." *Pall Mall Gazette* (1 December 1887). [unsigned note on *Tartuffe*; reprinted in Bernard F. Dukore, ed., *Bernard Shaw: The Drama Observed,* vol. 1 (University Park: Pennsylvania State University Press, 1993), 81]

1888

Shaw, Bernard. "The Man Who Might Have Averted the French Revolution." *Pall Mall Gazette* (16 August 1888). [review of Léon Say, *Turgot* (1888); reprinted in Brian Tyson, ed., *Bernard Shaw's Book Reviews* (University Park and London: Pennsylvania State University Press, 1991), 431–33]

1889

Shaw, Bernard. "Le Chemin à parcourir." *La Revue socialiste* 10 (August–September 1889): 216–25; 284–98. [translation by Jules Magny of "The Transition to Social Democracy," *Our Corner* 12 (November 1888): 257–75; corrected by Shaw]

1894

Shaw, Bernard. "Yvette Guilbert." *World* (16 May 1894). [reprinted in Yvette Guilbert and Harold Simpson, *Yvette Guilbert: Struggles and Victories* (London: Mills and Boon, 1910), 238–44; in Dan H. Laurence, ed., *Shaw's Music: The Complete Musical Criticism* (New York: Dodd, Mead, 1981), vol. 3, 207–14; and in Stanley Weintraub, ed., *The Portable Bernard Shaw* (Harmondsworth, England: Penguin, 1983), 65–69]

1897

Davray, Henry-D. No title. *Le Mercure de France* (18 June 1897).

1900

Shaw, Bernard. "Les Illusions du socialisme." Translated by Henriette Rynenbroeck [Hamon]. *L'Humanité nouvelle* (August 1900). [originally in *Die Zeit* (Vienna) (24 and 31 October 1896)]

1903

Walkley, Arthur Bingham. "Le Théâtre de G. B. Shaw." *Le Temps* (18 July 1903): 2–3.

1904

Muret, Maurice. "De Nora à Candida." *Le Journal des débats* (21 June 1904).

1905

Filon, Augustin. "M. Bernard Shaw et son théâtre." *La Revue des deux mondes* 30 (15 November 1905): 405–33.

Walkley, Arthur Bingham. No title. *Le Temps* (28 August 1905): 1–2.

1906

Blum, Jean. "George Bernard Shaw." *La Revue germanique* 10 (November–December 1906): 634–55.

Fyfe, H. Hamilton. "Brieux and Bernard Shaw." [reprinted in Fyfe 1975]

Henderson, Archibald. "La Carrière de Bernard Shaw." *L'Humanité nouvelle* (July 1906).

1907

Anonymous. "Le Théâtre de Bernard Shaw." *Le Petit bleu* (7 February 1907). [on *Candida*]

Anonymous. No title. *Le Matin de Bruxelles* [Brussels] (8 February 1907). [on *Candida*]

Anonymous. No title. *Le Peuple* [Brussels] (8 February 1907). [on *Candida*]

Anonymous. No title. *La Dernière Heure* [Belgium] (9 February 1907). [on *Candida*]

Anonymous. No title. *Le Petit bleu* (9 February 1907). [on *Candida*]

Anonymous. No title. *Le Vingtième Siècle* [Belgium] (9 February 1907). [on *Candida*]

Cammaerts, Émile. No title. *L'Éventail* [Brussels] (10 February 1907). [on *Candida*]

"Fémina." "Bernard Shaw." *Le Figaro* (3 October 1907).

George, Walter Lionel, and Raymond Lauzerte. "Les Idées et le théâtre de G. Bernard Shaw." *Pages libres* 363 (14 December 1907): 601–17.

Hamon, Augustin, and Henriette Hamon. "Bernard Shaw et son théâtre." *La Revue socialiste* 46 (September 1907): 125–43, 220–30.

H. M. No title. *Le Peuple* [Brussels] (9 February 1907). [on *Candida*]

Michaud, Régis. "Bernard Shaw." *La Revue de Paris* (17 September 1907) and *Le Penseur* (December 1907).

Sepher, Olivier. No title. *Le Soir* [Brussels] (7 February 1907). [on *Candida*]

———. No title. *Comoedia* (16 December 1907).

Shaw, Bernard. *La Profession de Madame Warren*. Translated by Augustin and Henriette Hamon. *Comoedia* (23 December 1907–16 January 1908). [19 issues, complete]

Unsigned. No title. *Le Soir* [Brussels] (9 February 1907). [on *Candida*]

V. No title. *L'Indépendence Belge* (10 February 1907). [on *Candida*]

1908

Anonymous. "*Candida*." *Comoedia* (9 May 1908): 3.

Anonymous. "French Version of 'Candida'." *Daily Telegraph* [London] (9 May 1908).

Anonymous. "Dramatic Notes." *English Mail* [Frankfurt-am-Main] (14 May 1908). [on *Candida*]

Anonymous. "Les Femmes de M. Shaw." *XIXème Siècle* (31 May 1908).

Bidou, Henry. "*Candida*." *Le Journal des débats* (11 May 1908).

Blum, Jean. No title. *La Phalange* (15 July 1908).

Blum, Léon. "La Vie théâtrale." *La Grande Revue* (10 June 1908): 571–77.
Bordeaux, Henry. "La Vie au théâtre." *La Revue hebdomadaire* (6 July 1908): 104–12. [on *Candida*; reprinted in Bordeaux 1910]
Brisson, Adolphe. "*Candida.*" *Le Temps* (11 May 1908).
C. G. "Mr. Bernard Shaw in French." *Athenaeum* 4198 (11 April 1908) [response to Shaw's "Mr. Bernard Shaw in French," *Athenaeum* 4197 (4 April 1908): 418]
Chassé, Charles. "Bernard Shaw." *La Revue* (1 November 1908).
d'Humières, Robert. "'Candida,' Bernard Shaw et leurs critiques." *Comoedia* (10 May 1908).
E. L. B. "Un Dramaturge Féministe Anglais: George-Bernard Shaw. Conférence par M. Palante." *Le Réveil* (21 February 1908).
Ernest-Charles, J. "Bernard Shaw et *Candida* (au Théâtre des Arts)." *L'Opinion* (16 May 1908).
Florence, Jean. "La Personnalité littéraire de M. George Bernard Shaw." *La Phalange* (15 July 1908). [on Shaw and Beaumarchais]
Hamon, Augustin. "A French View of Bernard Shaw—un nouveau Molière." *Nineteenth Century and After* 64 (July 1908): 48–63.
Henderson, Archibald. "La Carrière de Bernard Shaw." *La Société nouvelle* 4 (May 1908): 186–205.
Hermeline, Charles. "Le Théâtre révolutionnaire en Angleterre: Bernard Shaw." *L'Univers* (20 November 1908).
Hirsch, Charles-Henry. No title. *Sports* (9 May 1908). [on *Candida*]
Leblanc-Maeterlinck, Georgette. "Une Conférence." *Le Figaro* (30 May 1908). [on *Candida*]
Nozière, Fernand. "Le Théâtre." *Le Gil Blas* (10 May 1908). [on *Candida*]
Pascal, Félicien. "Pour comprendre Bernard Shaw." *Gazette de France* (19 May 1908): n.p.
Rageot, Gaston. "A French Estimate of G. B. Shaw." *Bookman* 28 (July 1908): 474–77.
Roz, Firmin. "Bernard Shaw." *Revue bleue* (6 June 1908): 723–26.
———. No title. *La Phalange* (15 July 1908).
Shaw, Bernard. "Mr. Bernard Shaw in French." *Athenaeum* 4197 (4 April 1908): 418. [letter of 26 March responding to C. G., "Notes from Paris," *Athenaeum* (21 March 1908)]
———. *Candida*. Translated by Augustin and Henriette Hamon. Paris: A. Munier, 1908. [limited edition of 100 copies]
———. *Le Héros et le soldat*. Translated by Augustin and Henriette Hamon. Paris: A. Munier, 1908. [limited edition of 100 copies; serialized (act 1 only) in *Les Cahiers d'aujourd'hui* 6 (August 1913): 281–305]
———. *L'Homme aimé des femmes*. Translated by Augustin and Henriette Hamon. Paris: A. Munier, 1908. [limited edition of 100 copies]
———. *L'Homme aimé des femmes*. Translated by Augustin and Henriette

Hamon. *La Grande Revue* 47 (25 February 1908): 637–56; 48 (10 March 1908): 82–96); (10 April 1908): 516–44. [complete]

———. *L'Homme du destin.* Translated by Augustin and Henriette Hamon. Paris: A. Munier, 1908. [limited edition of 100 copies]

———. *Non olet* [later known as *L'Argent n'a pas d'odeur*]. Translated by Augustin and Henriette Hamon. Paris: A. Munier, 1908. [limited edition of 100 copies]

———. *On ne peut jamais dire.* Translated by Augustin and Henriette Hamon. Paris: A. Munier, 1908. [limited edition of 100 copies]

———. *La Profession de Madame Warren.* Translated by Augustin and Henriette Hamon. Paris: A. Munier, 1908. [limited edition of 100 copies]

Tarde, Alfred de. "Le Théâtre anglais à Paris: *Candide,* de Bernard Shaw. La question du nu au théâtre." *La Vie contemporaine* (June 1908): 220–22.

Van Vorst, Marie. "Rodin and Bernard Shaw." *Putnam's Monthly* (October 1907–March 1908): 534–35.

Walkley, Arthur Bingham. "*Getting Married.*" *Le Temps* (31 August 1908): 1–2.

1909

Barnes, Kenneth R. No title. *La Poétique* (1 November 1909).

Blum, Jean. No title. *Le Divan* (March 1909).

Filon, Augustin. "M. Bernard Shaw peint par M. G.K. Chesterton." *Le Journal des débats* (20 October 1909).

Florence, Jean. "De la méthode de M. Bernard Shaw." *Le Divan* (March 1909): 69–76.

Hamon, Augustin. "Bernard Shaw et la Censure." *La Grande Revue* (25 July 1909): 374–85.

———. "Introduction du Traducteur: Bernard Shaw et le Socialisme" [to *Le Manuel de poche du parfait révolutionnaire par John Tanner*] *La Grande Revue* (25 October 1909): 629–38. [excerpt of February Sorbonne lecture at 631–37]

———. "Bernard Shaw (Quelques notes sur l'homme)." *Pan Revue libre* 2.12 (December 1909): 206–14.

———. "Le Théâtre de Bernard Shaw." *Revue bleue* (11 December 1909): 752–55, 790–94.

———. "Sur quelques pièces de Bernard Shaw." *La Phalange* 42 (20 December 1909): 152–19.

Régnier, Henri de. "Une Pièce de Bernard Shaw." *Le Journal des débats* (9 August 1909). [on *Arms and the Man*]

Shaw, Bernard. "Ce que boivent et mangent les savants en Angleterre." *La Revue* (15 February 1909): 411–13. [translation of "What to Eat, Drink, and Avoid." *Review of Reviews* 37 (February 1908): 145–46]

———. *Le Manuel de poche du parfait révolutionnaire par John Tanner.* Translated by Augustin and Henriette Hamon. *La Grande Revue* 57 (25 October–25 November 1909): 629–55. [complete; later titled "Bréviaire du Révolutionnaire"]

1910
Anonymous. [on "De Molière à Brieux" in *L'Illustration*]. *L'Action française* (13 May 1910).
Bidou, Henry. "Quand on parle des étrangers." *Le Journal des débats* (13 May 1910). [on Shaw and Eugène Brieux]
Bordeaux, Henry. *La Vie au théâtre*. Paris: Plon-Nourrit, 1910. [Shaw discussed at 199–208 and 329–30]
Chase, Lewis Nathaniel. *Bernard Shaw in France*. Bordeaux: Imprimerie nouvelle F. Pech, 1910. [15 pp.]
———. "Shaw in France." *Dial* [Chicago] 48 (1 April 1910): 229–33. [reprint of his *Bernard Shaw in France*]
Dekobra, Maurice. "La Décadence du théâtre anglais." *La Revue des revues* (15 February 1910). [part 1 of 2]
———. "La Décadence du théâtre anglais." *La Revue des revues* (15 March 1910): 251–59. [part 2 of 2; Shaw discussed at 251–53]
Hamon, Augustin. *Bernard Shaw et ses traducteurs français*. Paris: A. Munier, 1910. [14 pp.][2]
———. "Le Capitalisme dans le théâtre de Bernard Shaw." *Le Mouvement socialiste* 218, 12th year, 3rd series (February 1910): 89–102.
———. "Le Théâtre de Bernard Shaw." *La Nouvelle Revue* (1 May 1910): 53–60.
———. "Les Idées morales et sociales dans le théâtre de Bernard Shaw." *La Revue du mois* 53 (10 May 1910): 564–96.
———. "Le Militarisme, la justice et la religion dans le théâtre de Bernard Shaw." *La Vie intellectuelle* [Brussels] (15 May 1910): 275–94.
———. "Le Théâtre de Bernard Shaw, son comique, ses caractères, sa philosophie, ses rapports avec les travaux des Francs-Maçons." *L'Acacia* (Revue Mensuelle d'Études Maçoniques) 15.5–6 (May–June 1910): 341–54.
———. "Conférences en Sorbonne (Faculté de Lettres) sur Diverses Comédies de Bernard Shaw." 1910–12. [238 pp., unpublished; Hamon Collection, University of Guelph, Guelph, Ontario, Canada]
Shaw, Bernard. "De Molière à Brieux." Translated by Augustin and Henriette Hamon. *L'Illustration* 68 (7 May 1910): 412–14. [excerpt from preface to *Three Plays by Brieux*]
———. "Correspondance: Lettre de M. Bernard Shaw sur le chat à neuf queues." *Le Temps* (24 September 1910): 2:6. [brief extracts quoted in translation as "May Use Lash on Apaches" in *New York Times* (25 September 1910)]
———. *Le Disciple du diable*. Translated by Augustin and Henriette Hamon. Paris: Calmann-Lévy, 1910.
———. *Le Disciple du diable*. Translated by Augustin and Henriette Hamon. Paris: G. Lévy, 1910.
———. *Trois Pièces pour puritains par Bernard Shaw, fragments caractéristiques de César et Cléopatre, Le Disciple du diable et La Conversion du capitaine Brassbound*. Translated by Augustin and Henriette Hamon. Paris: G. Lévy,

1910. [one act of each play, for copyright protection; complete publication as *Trois Pièces pour puritains*, 1935]

Waleffe, Maurice de. No title. *L'Action française* (13 May 1910). [on Shaw and Eugène Brieux]

———. No title. *La Dernière Heure* (14 May 1910). [on Shaw and Eugène Brieux]

1911

Hamon, Augustin. "Le Théâtre de Bernard Shaw." *L'Effort* 14 (January 1911): 53.

———. "La Métaphysique et la philosophie dans le théâtre de Bernard Shaw." *La Revue socialiste* (15 January 1911): 21–29.

———. "Molière et Bernard Shaw." *La Revue d'Europe et d'Amérique* (15 November 1911): 919–45.

———. "Le Théâtre de Bernard Shaw." *Les Annales de la jeunesse laïque* 15 (December 1911): 216–19.

———. "La Critique et le théâtre de Bernard Shaw." *Pan* (December 1911–January 1912): 33–42.

Henderson, Archibald. "Bernard Shaw intime." *Le Mercure de France* 91 (1 June 1911): 449–65.

Muret, Maurice. "Le Paradoxe au Théâtre—M. George Bernard Shaw." *Le Journal des débats* (5 August 1911): 1.[3]

Pfeiffer, Edouard. *La Société fabienne et le mouvement socialiste anglais contemporain.* Paris: Giard et Brière, 1911.

Rosmer, Alfred. "George Bernard-Shaw: L'Homme, Le Socialiste." *La Bataille syndicaliste* (15 February 1911).

Roz, Firmin. "Les Métamorphoses de Don Juan." *La Revue hebdomadaire* (22 September 1911): 461–77. [on "Don Juan in Hell"]

Shaw, Bernard. "De l'humour." *La Revue* 93 (1 December 1911): 357.

———. "Brieux: A Preface." In *Three Plays by Brieux*, 9–53. London: A. C. Fifield; New York: Brentano, 1911. [reprinted in Bernard F. Dukore, ed., *Bernard Shaw: The Drama Observed*, vol. 3 (University Park: Penn State University Press, 1993), 1188–1222]

1912

Anonymous. "Stage in France." *Daily Telegraph* (17 February 1912). [on *La Profession de Madame Warren*]

Anonymous. "Bernard Shaw and the French Critics." *Morning Post* [London] (19 December 1912). [on Hamon, Cestre, and Faguet]

Bert, Charles. "Le Théâtre." *Le Gil Blas* (16 February 1912). [on *La Profession de Madame Warren*]

Bidou, Henry. "*La Profession de Mrs Warren*." *Le Journal des débats* (19 February 1912).

———. "Candida." *Le Journal des débats* (19 February 1912).

Blum, Léon. "Digression sur M. Bernard Shaw." *Excelsior* (24 October 1912).

Boissard, Maurice. "*La Profession de Mrs Warren*." *Le Mercure de France* (16 March 1912): 412–13.

Bordeaux, Henry. "*Mrs. Warren's Profession.*" *La Revue hebdomadaire* (February 1912). [reprinted in *La Vie au théâtre: Troisième Série: 1911–1913* (Paris: Plon-Nourrit, 1913), 142–44]
Brisson, Adolphe. "Chronique Théâtrale." *Le Temps* (4 March 1912). [on *La Profession de Madame Warren*]
Cestre, Charles. *Bernard Shaw et son oeuvre*. Paris: Mercure de France, 1912. [1909 lectures]
Ciolkowska, Muriel. "Le Théâtre de Bernard Shaw." *L'Opinion* (10 February 1912). [reprinted by R. de Bury in *Le Mercure de France* (1 March 1912): 169–70]
Davray, Henry-D. No title. *Le Courrier européen* (10 March 1912): 186–88. [on *La Profession de Madame Warren*; same as *L'Action nationale* (10 April 1912)]
———. No title. *L'Action nationale* (10 April 1912): 211–13. [on *La Profession de Madame Warren*; same as *Le Courrier européen* (10 March 1912)]
d'Humières, Robert. "Une Lettre de M. Robert d'Humières." *Comoedia* (20 February 1912).
———. "Le Cas Bernard Shaw." *Le Mercure de France* (1 April 1912): 449–55.
E. H.-K. "Tolstoï et Shaw d'après leur échange de lettres." *La Grande Revue* 72 (10 March 1912): 122–28. [hitherto unpublished 14 February 1910 Shaw letter to Tolstoy, in full, in French, at 125–27; reported—with extracts—in *New York Times*, "Tolstoy Rebuked Shaw for Levity" (7 April 1912)]
Ernest-Charles, J. *L'Opinion* (24 February 1912): 245–47. [on *La Profession de Madame Warren*]
Faguet, Émile. "Un Livre sur Bernard Shaw." *La Revue* (1 October 1912): 316–25. [on Cestre's *Bernard Shaw et son oeuvre*]
Filon, Augustin. No title. *Le Journal des débats* (26 March 1912).
Flers, Robert de. "*La Profession de Mrs Warren.*" *Le Figaro* (17 February 1912).
Gignoux, Régis. No title. *Paris-Journal* (1912). [on *La Profession de Madame Warren*]
Grosfils, Paul. "George Bernard Shaw." *Bulletin de l'Oeuvre* (March 1912): 44–48.
Hamon, Augustin. *The Technique of Bernard Shaw's Plays*. Translated by Frank Maurice. London: C. W. Daniel, 1912. [reprinted by Folcroft Library Editions, 1972; third of nine Sorbonne lectures (1911); reprinted in Hamon 1913]
———. "L'Art dramatique et la comédie de Bernard Shaw." *La Société nouvelle* 7 (January 1912): 52–66.
———. "Bernard Shaw en Sorbonne." *Revue indépendante* 9 (February 1912): 134–41.
———. "Bernard Shaw romancier." *Paris Journal* (4 September 1912).
———. "A propos de Bernard Shaw." *Pan* 8–10 (September–October 1912): 586–93. [letter to Faguet about his 1 October 1912 article on Cestre in *La Revue*]
———. "The Technique of Bernard Shaw's Plays: Construction—Comicality—Characters—Ideas—Philosophy." *Open Road* 6.9 (December 1911): 328–36;

1.10 (January 1912): 42–48); 2.11 (February 1912): 121–28; 3.10 (March 1912): 185–92. [translated from *L'Acacia*, 1910]

Hamon, Augustin, and Henriette Hamon. "Bernard Shaw." *La Vie* (24 February 1912): 26–27.

———. "La Critique et 'La Profession de Madame Warren.'" *La Grande Revue* (10 April 1912): 567–76.

———. "'La Fenêtre' ouverte sur les grands écrivains. A propos de la Profession de Madame Warren." May 1912. [reprints in part their 10 April article in *La Grande Revue*, with additional material]

Kind, Paul. "Les Idées de Bernard Shaw." *Les Pages modernes* 51 (February 1912): 145–52. [part 1]

Laillet, H. "Bernard Shaw et son théâtre." *La Revue de Belgique* (1912): 718–27. [on *La Profession de Madame Warren*]

Lanson, Gustave. No title. *La Grande Revue* (25 February 1912): 850–53. [on *La Profession de Madame Warren*]

Locria, G. "L'Attitude et les idées de M. George-Bernard Shaw." *Les Idées contemporaines* (7 April 1912): 63–69.

Marx, Claude-Roger. "Bernard Shaw et 'la Profession de Mme Warren.'" *Comoedia illustré* (1 March 1912): 389–93.

Miomandre, Francis de. "*La Profession de Madame Warren*." *Le Théâtre* 319 (1 April 1912): 14–17.

Muret, Maurice. "La 'Consécration' de M. Bernard Shaw." *Le Journal des débats* (17 February 1912). [on *La Profession de Madame Warren*]

———. *Les Contemporains étrangers*. Paris: n.p., 1912.

Nayral, Jacques. "Le Théâtre." *Revue indépendante* (March 1912): 29–37. [on *La Profession de Madame Warren*]

Pawlowski, Gaston de. "*La Profession de Madame Warren*." *Comoedia* (17 February 1912): 1–2.

P. G. "Bernard Shaw en France." *Bulletin de l'Oeuvre* (January–February 1912). [translation of 2 May 1907 letter by Shaw to Aurélien-Marie Lugné-Poë]

Pratz, Claire de. "Paris Approves of Bernard Shaw." *Morning Leader* (19 February 1912): 6.

Rhys, Ernest. "Molière and Mr. Shaw." *Everyman* (19 November 1912).

Sabatier, G. "Theatre des Arts—La Profession de Madame Warren." *Petite République* (17 February 1912).

Schlumberger, Jean. "La Profession de Madame Warren (Théâtre des Arts). *La Nouvelle Revue française* (1 April 1912): 696–701.

Shaw, Bernard. "La Guerre" [reply to "Enquête internationale sur la guerre"]. *Le Monde illustré* 2862 (3 February 1912): 74–75. [retranslation, "How I Would Make War," in *New York American* (3 March 1912), magazine section; reprinted in *New York American* (30 August 1914) as "End War by Killing All Possible Mothers"]

———. "Préface aux *Pièces déplaisantes* de Bernard Shaw." Translated by

Augustin and Henriette Hamon. *Revue d'Europe et d'Amérique* (1 March 1912): 365–82.
———. *Don Juan aux enfers.* Translated by Augustin and Henriette Hamon. Paris: Eugène Figuière, 1912. [third act of *L'Homme et le surhomme*]
———. *L'Homme et le surhomme.* Translated by Augustin and Henriette Hamon. Paris: Eugène Figuière, 1912. [abridged acting version without act 3 "Don Juan in Hell" sequence]
———. "Rodin." *Nation* (9 November 1912). [reprinted in Stanley Weintraub, ed., *Bernard Shaw on the London Art Scene, 1885–1950* (University Park and London: Pennsylvania State University Press, 1989), 407–12]
———. "Rodin." Translated by Augustin and Henriette Hamon. *Le Gil Blas* (24 November 1912). [translation of "Rodin," *Nation* (9 November 1912)]
Sée, Edmond. No title. *Le Gil Blas* (1912). [on *La Profession de Madame Warren*]
Snell, Victor. No title. *L'Humanité* (1912). [on *La Profession de Madame Warren*]
Toulet, Paul Jean. "Notes de Théâtre." *Les Marges* (June 1912). [on *La Profession de Madame Warren*]

1913

Anonymous. "G.B.S. in Paris: The French Critics and 'You Never Can Tell.'" *Star* [London] (20 January 1913).
Anonymous. "Stage in France. Bernard Shaw's Play in Paris." *Daily Telegraph* [London] (30 January 1913).
Bidou, Henry. "Le Cas de Bernard Shaw." *Le Journal des débats* (10 March 1913).
Biguet, André. "Monsieur Bernard Shaw." *Montjoi* (29 May 1913).
Bithell, Jethro. "George Bernard Shaw pour nous autres Anglais." *Les Marges* (1913): 56–62.
Blavinhac, Albert. "Les Théâtres." *République française* (29 January 1913). [on *On ne peut jamais dire*]
Boissard, Maurice "Revue de la Quinzaine" [excerpt]. *Le Mercure de France* (1 April 1913): 627–28.
Boyd, E.-A. "Bernard Shaw and the French Critics." *Forum* 50.2 (13 August 1913): 205–16.
Catteau, Robert. "Les Répétitions générales." *Paris midi* (28 January 1913). [on *On ne peut jamais dire*]
Czolkowska, Muriel. *Revue critique des idées et des livres* (January 1913).
d'Arti, Léo. "Le Théâtre." *Évènement* (29 January 1913). [on *On ne peut jamais dire*]
de Saint-Albin. "M. G.-B. Shaw et la Médecine." *Bulletin du "Médecin de Paris"* (20 March 1913): 16–17. [on *Le Dilemme du docteur*]
Drault, Jean. "Les Premières." *Libre parole* (29 January 1913). [on *On ne peut jamais dire*]
Flers, Robert de. "Les Théâtres." *Le Figaro* (29 January 1913). [on *On ne peut jamais dire*]

Gaffié, L. "Bernard Shaw et son oeuvre théâtrale." *Théâtra* [Marseilles] (7 March 1913).

Gignoux, Régis. "Avant le Rideau." *Le Figaro* (27 January 1913). [on *On ne peut jamais dire*]

Gourmont, Remy de. "Bernard Shaw" in "Les Idées du jour." *La France* (27 February 1913). [reprinted in *Le Vase Magique* (1923): 79–80]

Gregh, Fernand. "Théâtres." *Liberté* (29 January 1913). [on *On ne peut jamais dire*]

Guet, C. "Les Premières." *Autorité* (29 January 1913). [on *On ne peut jamais dire*]

Guyot, Edouard. *Le Socialisme et l'évolution de l'Angleterre contemporaine (1880–1911)*. Paris: Félix Alcan, 1913. [Shaw discussed at 425–62]

Hamon, Augustin. *Le Molière du XXe siècle: Bernard Shaw*. Paris: Eugène Figuière, 1913.

Hamon, Augustin, and Henriette Hamon. *Considérations sur l'art dramatique à propos de la comédie de Bernard Shaw*. Paris: Eugène Figuière, 1913. [48 pp.]

———. "Considérations sur l'art dramatique" (À propos des *Pièces plaisantes* de Bernard Shaw). *Bibliothèque universelle* [Lausanne] 213 (September 1913): 520–51.

———. "Bernard Shaw en France et dans les pays de langue Française." *La Pensée Bretonne* (1 June 1913).

Hermant, Abel. "Les Théâtres." *Journal* (29 January 1913). [on *On ne peut jamais dire*]

J.G. "*On ne peut jamais dire*." *Comoedia* (28 January 1913).

Kostaki, N. L. "Le Mouvement dramatique à Paris." *La Politique* (22 March 1913). [on *On ne peut jamais dire*]

Le Breton, E. "Bernard Shaw." *Indépendance Bretonne* (1 February 1913).

Le Goffic, Charles. "Deux Celtes au théâtre." *Breton de Paris* (20 January 1913). [probably same as below]

———. No title. *La République française* (January 1913). [probably same as above]

L'Honeux, J. No title. *Revue de l'Université de Bruxelles* (January 1913).

Métives, Guy. "On ne peut jamais dire. . . ." *Excelsior* (28 January 1913). [on *On ne peut jamais dire*]

Montfort. No title. *Les Marges* (March 1913).

Nion, François de. "Les Répétitions générales." *L'Écho de Paris* (29 January 1913). [on *On ne peut jamais dire*]

Odier, Henri. "Georges-Bernard Shaw, un socialiste irlandais, auteur dramatique." In *Études de littérature anglaise contemporaine*, 57–94. Geneva: n.p., 1913. [probably four 1909 lectures at l'Athénée, Geneva]

Pawlowski, Gaston de. "*On ne peut jamais dire*." *Comoedia* (29 January 1913): 1–2.

Schlumberger, Jean. "*On ne peut jamais dire*, de Bernard Shaw." *La Nouvelle Revue française* (1 March 1913): 497–502.

Sée, Edmond. "Répétitions générales." *Le Gil Blas* (28 January 1913). [on *On ne peut jamais dire*]

Shaw, Bernard. "Considérations sur le théâtre contemporain." Translated by Augustin and Henriette Hamon. *Le Temps* (24 January 1913: 3:1–6; 26 January 1913: 3:6). [revised preface to *Pièces plaisantes*]

———. "Ce que je ne peux pas taire" [What I cannot silence]. *Fantasio* (1 March 1913).

———. "Haendel et l'Angleterre." Translated by Augustin and Henriette Hamon. *Revue musicale S. I. M.*4 (15 April 1913).

———. "Rodin's Bourgeois." *New Statesman* (31 May 1913). [reprinted in Stanley Weintraub, ed., *Bernard Shaw on the London Art Scene, 1885–1950* (University Park and London: Pennsylvania State University Press, 1989), 425–26]

———. "The Play and Its Author." Souvenir program of *Woman on Her Own* (8 December 1913). [on Eugène Brieux's *La Femme seule*; reprinted in Stanley Weintraub, ed., *SHAW, the Annual of Bernard Shaw Studies*, vol. 8 (University Park: Pennsylvania State University Press, 1988), 105–9) and in Bernard F. Dukore, ed., *Bernard Shaw: The Drama Observed*, vol. 4 (University Park: Pennsylvania State University Press, 1993), 1309–12)]

———. *Le Héros et le soldat.* Translated by Augustin and Henriette Hamon. *Les Cahiers d'aujourd'hui* 6 (August 1913). [act 1 only]

———. *L'Homme aimé des femmes.* Translated by Augustin and Henriette Hamon. Paris: Eugène Figuière, 1913.

———. *L'Homme du destin.* Translated by Augustin and Henriette Hamon. *Les Saisons* 3 (21 June 1913).

———. *L'Homme du destin.* Translated by Augustin and Henriette Hamon. Paris: Eugène Figuière, 1913.

———. *Non olet.* Translated by Augustin and Henriette Hamon. Paris: Eugène Figuière, 1913.

———. *On ne peut jamais dire.* Translated by Augustin and Henriette Hamon. Paris: Eugène Figuière, 1913.

———. *Pièces plaisantes et déplaisantes.* Translated by Augustin and Henriette Hamon. Paris: Eugène Figuière, 1913. [the seven plays published individually by Munier in 1908]

———. *La Profession de Madame Warren.* Translated by Augustin and Henriette Hamon. Paris: Eugène Figuière, 1913.

———. *La Profession de Mme Warren.* Translated by Augustin and Henriette Hamon. Paris: Aubier, 1913.

Simond, S., and A. Launie. "La Vie anglaise: Le Théâtre des fronts hauts." *La Revue* (1 January 1913).

Souday, Paul. "Les Premières." *Éclair* (29 January 1913). [on *On ne peut jamais dire*]

Uzanne, Octave. "L'Esprit d'origine étrangère: Bernard Shaw." *La Dépêche* [Toulouse] (26 February 1913).

1914

Bachelin, Henri. "Le 'Misanthrope' du XXe siècle: Bernard Schaw." *Comoedia* (14 January 1914). [part 1]

———. "Bernard Shaw." *Comoedia* (27 May 1914). [review of *Quatre Pièces plaisantes*]

Barbeau, A. No title. *Polybiblion* (March 1914): 241–42. [review of *Le Molière du XXème siècle: Bernard Shaw*]

Shaw, Bernard. *Le Disciple du diable*. Translated by Augustin and Henriette Hamon. Insert to *Comoedia* (8 June 1914): 1–6. [complete, but with abridged stage directions]

———. *Le Héros et le soldat*. Translated by Augustin and Henriette Hamon. Paris: Eugène Figuière, 1914.

1915

C. C. "G.B.S. and M. Hamon." *New Witness* (27 May 1915): 88–90. [review of *The Twentieth Century Molière: Bernard Shaw*]

Hamon, Augustin. *The Twentieth Century Molière: Bernard Shaw*. Translated by Eden and Cedar Paul. London: Allen and Unwin, 1915.

Lloyd, J. A. T. "Shaw—and Sense." *Daily Chronicle* (9 June 1915). [review of *The Twentieth Century Molière: Bernard Shaw*]

1916

Hamon, Augustin. "Dix Leçons faites à l'Université de Londres, Birkbeck College, 6 mai 1916 au 8 July 1916." Unpublished. [Shaw Papers, British Library, London]

1917

Dolléans, Edouard. "L'Épreuve de Bernard Shaw." *Revue politique et littéraire* 23 (24 November–1 December 1917): 728–31.

Shaw, Bernard. "Un Tour 'à l'oeil' au Front." Translated by Augustin and Henriette Hamon. *La Grande Revue* (April 1917): 193–206.

———. "English Socialist Societies." *Les Nations* (3 August 1917). [reprinted in *Independent Shavian* 34.1–2 (1996): 18–20]

1918

Michaud, Régis. "Bernard Shaw et le théâtre de la sincérité." In *Mystiques et réalistes anglo-saxons, d'Emerson à Bernard Shaw*, 255–94. Paris: Armand Colin, 1918.

1919

F. R. "À propos du nouveau receuil de pièces de M. Bernard Shaw." *La Revue hebdomadaire* (8 November 1919): 267–71.

Gillet, Louis. "Six Comédies de Bernard Shaw." *La Revue des deux mondes* (1 February 1919): 675–86.

Shaw, Bernard. *Cashel Byron, gentleman et boxeur*. Adapted by Louis Beaudoir. Paris: L'Édition française illustrée (puis G. Crès), 1919.

1920
Ruyssen, Henri. "Revue du théâtre anglais." *La Revue germanique* (1920): 284–319.
1921
Andréadès, André. "La Dernière Pièce de Bernard Shaw." *Le Figaro* (12 December 1921).
Claretie, Léo. "*Le Héros et le soldat.*" *La Revue mondiale* 142 (1 May 1921): 91.
Cru, Robert-L. "Moeurs anglaises." *Bonsoir* (31 December 1921). [on *Heartbreak House*]
Delattre, Floris. No title. *La Revue germanique* (1921). [on *The Quintessence of Bernard Shaw* by H. C. Duffin; previously published in *L'Opinion*]
Dubech, Lucien. "Chronique dramatique." *L'Action française* (3 April 1921). [on *Arms and the Man*]
Hamon, Augustin. "Comment j'ai connu Bernard Shaw." *Le Peuple* (22 and 23 April 1921).
Rageot, Gaston. "De Shakespeare à M. Bernard Shaw." *Revue politique et littéraire* 59 (4 June 1921): 366–68.
Schneider, Louis. "Les Premières à Paris: *Le Héros et le soldat.*" *La Suisse* (7 April 1921).
Shaw, Bernard. *Le Héros et le soldat.* Translated by Augustin and Henriette Hamon. *Les Annales* (11, 18, 25 September 1921). [excerpts]
———. *Le Dilemme du docteur.* Translated by Augustin and Henriette Hamon. *La Revue de Paris* 28 (15 October 1921): 673–705; (1 November 1921): 59–97; (15 November 1921): 316–38. [complete]
———. *Pièces déplaisantes.* Translated by Augustin and Henriette Hamon. Paris: Éditions Montaigne, 1921.
———. *La Profession de Madame Warren.* Translated by Augustin and Henriette Hamon. Paris: Éditions Montaigne, 1921.
Vautel, Clément. No title. *Chronique du mois* (April 1921). [on *Arms and the Man*]
1922
Claretie, Léo. No title. *La Revue mondiale* 148 (1 June 1922). [on *Arms and the Man*]
———. No title. *La Revue mondiale* 148 (1 June 1922). [on *Le Dilemme du docteur*]
———. "*La Profession de Mrs Warren.*" *La Revue mondiale* 148 (1 June 1922).
———. "*Candida.*" *La Revue mondiale* (15 December 1922).
Dubech, Lucien. "Chronique dramatique." *L'Action Française* (15 May 1922): 1. [on *La Profession de Madame Warren* and *Le Dilemme du docteur*]
———. "L'Anarchie de M. Bernard Shaw." *La Revue universelle* (1 June 1922): 667–72.
Ruyssen, Henri. "Le Théâtre anglais." *La Revue germanique* (1922): 287–302.
Shaw, Bernard. "The Genius of Molière." *Morning Post* (19 January 1922).

1923

Claretie, Léo. "*Pygmalion.*" *La Revue mondiale* 156 (1 November 1923): 95–96.
Gillet, Louis. "En écoutant *Vive Mathusalem.*" *La Revue des deux mondes* 18 (1 December 1923): 674–85.
Gourmont, Remy de. "Bernard Shaw." In *Le Vase magique,* 79–80. Paris: Le Divan, 1923. [reprint of *La France* (27 February 1913): 1]
Hamon, Augustin. "A propos de 'Pygmalion.'" *Comoedia* (7 October 1923).
Marcel, Gabriel. "*Pygmalion* de Bernard Shaw." *La Nouvelle Revue française* 21 (1 November 1923): 618–19.
Schneider, Louis. "Les Premières à Paris: *Pygmalion.*" *La Suisse* (4 October 1923).
Shaw, Bernard. *Comment il mentit au mari.* Translated by Augustin and Henriette Hamon. *La Grande Revue* 27 (August 1923): 177–97.
———. *On ne peut jamais dire.* Translated by Augustin and Henriette Hamon. Paris: Éditions Montaigne, 1923. [reprinted 1931]
———. *Pièces plaisantes.* Translated by Augustin and Henriette Hamon. Paris: Éditions Montaigne, 1923.
Veber, Pierre. "Première Représentation." *Le Petit Journal* (29 September 1923). [on *Pygmalion*]

1924

Andréadès, André. "La *Sainte Jeanne* de Bernard Shaw." *Revue politique et littéraire* 62 (20 December 1924): 854–57.
Antoine, André. "Le Manifeste de Bernard Shaw." *Comoedia* (18 March 1924).
Borgex, Louis. "'Sainte Jeanne' de Bernard Shaw au New Theatre de Londres." *Comoedia* (27 March 1924): 3.
Geistdoerfer, Michel. "Bernard Shaw et ses traducteurs Augustin et Henriette Hamon." *La Bretagne touristique* 26 (15 May 1924): 121–22.
Gémier, Firmin. "Bernard Shaw à l'Odéon." *Paris-Soir* (23 January 1924).
Gillet, Louis. "Une Nouvelle *Jeanne d'Arc* anglaise." *La Revue des deux mondes* 22 (1 August 1924): 687–97.
Graham, James. "Shaw on 'Saint Joan.'" *Sunday New York Times* (13 April 1924). [retranslation of Shaw's translated "La 'Jeanne d'Arc' de Bernard Shaw," *Comoedia* (16 March 1924); reprinted in Weintraub 1973]
Murry, John Middleton. "The Two Joans." *Adelphi* 1.12 (May 1924): 1043–1050.
Shaw, Bernard. *César et Cléopâtre.* Translated by Augustin and Henriette Hamon. *La Revue de Paris* 31, vol. 1 (1 February 1924): 542–60, (15 February 1924): 883–913; vol. 2 (1 March 1924): 62–100. [complete; incorporates new material on 891–92: see Dan H. Laurence, ed., *Bernard Shaw: A Bibliography,* 2 vols. (Oxford: Clarendon, 198)] item A46a]
———. *Pygmalion.* Translated by Augustin and Henriette Hamon. *Les Cahiers dramatiques.* Supplement to no. 30 of *Théâtre* and *Comoedia Illustré* 14 (15 March 1924): 1–37. [complete]
———. *Pygmalion.* Translated by Augustin and Henriette Hamon. Paris: J. Hébertot, 1924.
———. "La 'Jeanne d'Arc' de Bernard Shaw. Une lettre originale du dramaturge

irlandais." *Comoedia* (16 March 1924). [translation of 7 March 1924 letter in *Chicago Tribune* (24 March 1924); see next entry]

———. "Shaw Replies to French Critics." *Chicago Tribune* (24 March 1924). [reply to questions by Louis Borgex, London correspondent of *Comoedia*; letter of 7 March 1924]

———. No title. *Odéon-Magazine* 44 (April 1924): 7–9. Translated by Augustin and Henriette Hamon of "Shaw Replies to French Critics." *Chicago Tribune* (24 March 1924).

Smet, Robert de. "Les 'Adaptateurs' défigurent-ils leurs auteurs étrangers?" *Comoedia* (4 March 1924). [on the Hamons' translations of Shaw]

Thomas, Louis. "Une Clownerie déplacée: La 'Saint Joan' de Bernard Shaw au Théâtre Guild de New-York." *Comoedia* (13 January 1924).

———. "A propos de la 'Jeanne d'Arc' de Bernard Shaw. M. Louis Thomas répond à M. Hamon." *Comoedia* (22 February 1924).

Tittle, Walter. "Mr. Bernard Shaw Talks About St. Joan." *Outlook* 137 (25 June 1924): 311–13. [reprinted in Weintraub 1973]

1925

Achard, Paul. No title. *Paris-Midi* (29 April 1925). [on *Sainte Jeanne*]

Anonymous. "Mr. Shaw's Plays in Paris." *Times* (12 January 1925): 15.

Anonymous. "*Pygmalion*, de Bernard Shaw, aux Célestins." *Le Progrès* (Lyon) (17 November 1925).

Antoine, André. No title. *L'Information* (4 May 1925). [on *Sainte Jeanne*]

Aulard, François-Alphonse. "Bernard Shaw est de mauvaise humeur mais sa 'Sainte Jehanne' est un chef-d'oeuvre." *Le Quotidien* (20 September 1925).

Beaunier, André. No title. *L'Écho de Paris* (29 April 1925): 4.

Beauplan, Robert de. "*Sainte Jeanne*." *Comoedia* (1 June 1925).

Bernstein, Henry. "G.B.S. et Paris." *Le Temps* (7 September 1925). [part 1 of 2]

———. "G.B.S. et Paris." *Le Temps* (14 September 1925). [part 2 of 2]

———. "M. Henry Bernstein répond à M. Aulard." *Le Quotidien* (21 September 1925).

Berton, Claude. "*Sainte Jeanne*: Les Visages de la comédie parodique." *Les Nouvelles littéraires* (16 May 1925): 7.

Bidou, Henry. "*Sainte Jeanne*." *Le Journal des débats* (4 May 1925): 3.

Billy, André. "*Sainte Jeanne*." *Les Annales politiques et littéraires* 84 (10 May 1925).

———. "*Sainte Jeanne*." *Le Mercure de France* 180 (1 June 1925): 485–89.

Brisson, Pierre. "Le Théâtre." *Les Annales politiques et littéraires* 84 (10 May 1925).

Chenoy, Léon. "La Préface de Bernard Shaw pour 'Sainte Jeanne'." *Le Thyrse* 26 (8 November 1925): 397–99.

Dubech, Lucien. "*Sainte Jeanne*." *L'Action française* (3 May 1925): 2.

———. "Le Théâtre: *Tripe d'or.—Sainte Jeanne*." *La Revue universelle* (1 June 1925): 653–56.

F.A.G. "Shaw Doffs His Helmet Pariswards." *Boston Evening Transcript* (24 October 1925): III, 5:1–2. [translation of "Chronique théatrale: Réflexions . . . ." *Le Temps* (10 August 1925): 3:1–6]

Flers, Robert de. "*Sainte Jeanne.*" *Le Figaro* (11 May 1925). [English translation in T. F. Evans, ed., *Shaw, the Critical Heritage* (London: Routledge and Kegan Paul, 1976), 295–96]

Fréjaville, Gustave. "*Sainte Jeanne.*" *Le Journal des débats* (30 April 1925): 5.

Gignoux, Régis. "*Sainte Jeanne.*" *Comoedia* (29 April 1925).

Hamon, Augustin, and Henriette Hamon. "Chronique dramatique." *Le Journal des débats* 32 (18 May 1925): 792–93.

———. "Bernard Shaw et Sainte Jeanne." *La Griffe* (15 October 1925).

Harris, Frank. "George Bernard Shaw." *La Nouvelle Revue française* 142 (1 July 1925): 36–73. [translation by August Bréal of an essay in Harris's *Contemporary Portraits*, with some cuts]

Heugel, Jacques. "*Sainte Jeanne.*" *Le Menestrel* (8 May 1925).

Jung, Werner. *La "Jeanne d'Arc" de Bernard Shaw*. Brussels: La Renaissance de l'Occident, 1925.

Lièvre, Pierre. "G. B. Shaw et sa Jeanne d'Arc." *Les Marges* (15 July 1925): 231–37.

Lugné-Poë, Aurélien-Marie. No title. *L'Éclair* (29 April 1925). [on *Sainte Jeanne*]

Marcel, Gabriel. "*Sainte Jeanne.*" *L'Europe nouvelle* (9 May 1925): 620.

Mauriac, François. "*Sainte Jeanne* par Bernard Shaw au Théâtre des Arts." *La Nouvelle Revue française* 24 (1 June 1925): 1048–51.

Palmer, John. "The Productions of George Pitoëff." *Fortnightly Review* 118 n.s. (1 July 1925): 202–16. [on *Sainte Jeanne*]

Piéchaud, Martial. "*Sainte Jeanne.*" *La Revue hebdomadaire* (13 June 1925): 226.

Rageot, Gaston. "*Sainte Jeanne.*" *Revue politique et littéraire* 63 (6 June 1925): 385–87.

Ravennes, Jean. "*Sainte Jeanne.*" *La Revue française* (5 June 1925): 639–40.

Rivoire, André. "*Sainte Jeanne.*" *Le Temps* (4 May 1925).

Salomé, René. "Chronique dramatique: Deux autres Jeanne d'Arc.—'Le comédien et la grâce.'" *Les Études* 185 (5 October 1925): 79–92.

Saurat, Denis. "George Bernard Shaw." *Les Marges* (15 August 1925): 243–48.

———. "G. B. Shaw." *La Revue mondiale* (1 December 1925).

Shaw, Bernard. "Comment écrire une pièce populaire." Translated by Augustin and Henriette Hamon. *Les Annales politiques et littéraires* 84 (3 May 1925): 469–70. ["How to Write a Popular Play," excerpt from preface to *Three Plays by Brieux*]

———. *Sainte Jeanne*. Translated by Augustin and Henriette Hamon. *La Revue de Paris* 32 (15 May 1925): 294–318; (1 June 1925): 551–76; (15 June 1925): 764–99. [complete]

———. "Chronique théatrale: Réflexions . . . ." *Le Temps* (10 August 1925): 3:1–6. [retranslated (by F.A.G.) as "Shaw Doffs His Helmet Pariswards," *Boston Evening Transcript* (24 October 1925)]

———. "Chronique théatrale: Suite et fin d'une polémique. Lettre ouverte à

Henry Bernstein." *Le Temps* (16 November 1925): 2: 1–4. [followed by Bernstein's "Lettre confidentielle à Bernard Shaw"]

———. "Mon pseudo-antisémitisme ou post-scriptum à la controverse Bernstein-Shaw." *La Volonté* (23 December 1925).

———. *Sainte Jeanne.* Translated by Augustin and Henriette Hamon. Paris: Calmann-Lévy, 1925.

Speth, William. "*Sainte Jeanne.*" *La Revue mondiale* 165 (15 May 1925): 197–98.

Thiac, Robert de. "M. Georges Pitoëff nous parle de la Sainte-Jehanne de Bernard Shaw." *Comoedia* (22 April 1925): 3.

Veber, Pierre. No title. *Le Petit Journal* (29 April 1925). [on *Sainte Jeanne*]

1926

Anonymous. "*Pygmalion.*" *L'Indépendent belge* (6 October 1926).

Bidou, Henry. "*Le Disciple du diable.*" *Le Journal des débats* (12 April 1926): 3.

———. "*Le Disciple du diable.*" *Le Journal des débats* (16 April 1926): 637–39.

———. "Bernard Shaw." *Le Journal des débats* (13 November 1926): 1.

———. "Bernard Shaw." *Le Journal des débats* (19 November 1926): 848.

Cammaerts, Émile. "Molière and Bernard Shaw." *Nineteenth Century* (September 1926): 413–22. [short excerpt reprinted in T. F. Evans, ed., *Shaw, the Critical Heritage* (London: Routledge and Kegan Paul, 1976): 307–9]

Groos, René. "Bernard Shaw." *Le Mercure de France* 192 (15 December 1926): 513–26. [reprinted in *Esquisses* (1928)]

Hamon, Augustin. "*Le Disciple du diable.*" *La Revue mondiale* (1 April 1926): 258–62.

Hamon, Augustin, and Henriette Hamon. "Au Lecteur. En guise de préface." In *Le Disciple du diable,* translated by Augustin and Henriette Hamon, I–XXXVI. Paris: Calmann-Lévy, 1926. [dated 25 January 1926]

Muret, Maurice. "La 'Fausse Gloire' de M. Bernard Shaw." *Le Journal des débats* 272 (1 October 1926): 3. [reprinted as "That Man Shaw: A Disgrace to the Theatre," *Living Age* 331 (1926): 434–37]

Shaw, Bernard. "Considérations sur le christianisme." Translated by Augustin and Henriette Hamon. *La Revue nouvelle* 17 (15 April 1926): 1–7 [from preface to *Androcles and the Lion*]

———. *César et Cléopâtre.* Translated by Augustin and Henriette Hamon. Paris: Calmann-Lévy, 1926.

———. *Le Disciple du diable.* Translated by Augustin and Henriette Hamon. Paris: Calmann-Lévy, 1926.

———. *L'Homme du destin. Le Héros et le soldat.* Translated by Augustin and Henriette Hamon. Paris: Calmann-Lévy, 1926.

———. *La Première Pièce de Fanny.* Translated by Augustin and Henriette Hamon. *La Grande Revue* 120 (June 1926): 529–46; 121 (July–October): 67–79, 247–59, 395–415, 620–40. [complete]

1927

Bauer, Gérard. "Le Théâtre: *La Grande Catherine* de M. Bernard Shaw." *Les Annales politiques et littéraires* 88 (20 March 1927): 295.

Brion, Marcel. "Bernard Shaw." *La Grande Revue* (November 1927): 42–59.
Brisson, Pierre. "*Sainte Jeanne.*" *Le Temps* (27 June 1927): 3.
Lalou, René. *Panorama de la littérature anglaise contemporaine*. Paris: Kra, 161–73.
Shaw, Bernard. *L'Homme et le surhomme*. Translated by Augustin and Henriette Hamon. *La Revue de Paris* (15 January–15 February 1927).
———. *La Villa de crève-coeur*. Translated by Augustin and Henriette Hamon. *La Grande Revue* 124 (September 1927): 353–96; 124 (October 1927): 531–78; 125 (November 1927): 20–41. [complete]
———. *Bréviaire du révolutionnaire*. Translated by Augustin and Henriette Hamon. Paris: Éditions des cahiers libres, 1927.

1928

Achard, Paul. "Bernard Shaw est-il un mauvais Anglais?" *Paris-Midi* (13 February 1928).
Anonymous. "Mr. Shaw and the French." *Times* [London] (21 February 1928).
———. "Les Tenues pittoresques de Bernard Shaw à l'heure du bain." *L'Illustration* 85.2 (1 September 1928): 231.
Antoine, André. No title. *L'Information* (23 January 1928). [on *La Maison des coeurs brisés*]
———. No title. *L'Information* (23 December 1928). [on *César et Cléopâtre*]
Beauplan, Robert de. "*Sainte Jeanne* au Théâtre des Arts." *La Petite Illustration* 392 (28 July 1928): 1–2.
Bidou, Henry. "*La Maison des coeurs brisés*." *Le Journal des débats* 35.1 (27 January 1928): 164–66.
Boissy, Gabriel. "Mlle Falconetti chante et Bernard Shaw s'égare." *Comoedia* (31 December 1928).
Groos, René. *Esquisses: Charles Maurras, poète; Marcel Proust; Bernard Shaw*. Paris: Maison du Livre Français, 1928.
Hamon, Augustin, and Henriette Hamon. "L'Auteur de *Sainte Jeanne*." *L'Illustration* 392 (28 July 1928): 1–41.
Kemp, Robert. No title. *La Liberté* (18 January 1928). [on *La Maison des coeurs brisés*]
Kessel, Joseph. No title. *Gringoire* (21 December 1928). [on *César et Cléopâtre*]
Lasserre, Jean. "*L'Inca de Perusalem*." *L'Ami du peuple du soir* (31 December 1928).
Rageot, Gaston. "Un Ennemi des Anglais." *Revue politique et littéraire* 66 (18 February 1928): 121–23. [reprinted as "*Heartbreak House* in Paris," *Living Age* 334 (1928): 733–35]
Reboux, Paul. "*L'Inca de Perusalem*." *Paris-Soir* (31 December 1928).
Rey, Étienne. "*La Maison des coeurs brisés*." *Comoedia* (18 January 1928): 1–2.
Shaw, Bernard. "Bernard Shaw prophète," "Comment Bernard Shaw veut tuer les guerres," and "Où Bernard Shaw condamne la fiction de la neutralité." Translated by Augustin and Henriette Hamon. *Cri des peuples* (30 May 1928): 9–10, (6 June 1928): 19–20, and (13 June 1928): 19–20. [a three-part essay on the

League of Nations, the sixth of seven articles published in January–February 1919 on the Peace Conference.]

———. *César et Cléopâtre*. Translated by Augustin and Henriette Hamon. Paris: Éditions Montaigne, 1928.

———. *La Maison des coeurs brisés*. Program of Pitoëff production, translated by Augustin Hamon, Théâtre des Mathurins, Paris, 17 January 1928. [contains translated "Notice" by Shaw, written in the third person but signed with his name, p. 15]

———. *La Maison des coeurs brisés*. Translated by Augustin and Henriette Hamon. *Les Oeuvres libres* 83 (May 1928): 53–184. [without Shaw's preface]

———. *La Profession de Mme Warren*. Translated by Augustin and Henriette Hamon. Paris: Éditions Montaigne, 1928.

———. *Sainte Jeanne*. Translated by Augustin and Henriette Hamon. *La Petite Illustration* 392, Théâtre no. 211 (28 July 1928): 3–41. [complete, with some revisions by Shaw]

Speth, William. "*La Maison des coeurs brisés.*" *La Revue mondiale* 181.4 (15 February 1928): 419–21.

1929

Anonymous. "Un Paradoxe de Bernard Shaw." *Le Journal des débats* 36.2 (1 November 1929): 718.

Belfoe, A. M. A. "Le Théâtre à Londres: *La Voiture de pommes*, par Bernard Shaw." *Le Figaro* (28 October 1929).

Bernard, Jean-Jacques. "*César et Cléopâtre.*" *L'Europe nouvelle* (5 January 1929): 10.

Mas, Émile. "'César et Cléopatre' au Théâtre des Arts: Une Méchante Plaisanterie qui dure trop longtemps." *Le Petit bleu* (19 October 1929).

Sée, Henri. "Le Socialisme et le capitalisme expliqués par Bernard Shaw." *La Grande Revue* 8 (August 1929): 295–305. [review of *Guide de la femme intelligente en présence du socialisme et du capitalisme* in Hamon's translation]

———. "Le Socialisme et le capitalisme expliqués par Bernard Shaw." *Pages libres* 285 (August 1929): 17–27.

Shaw, Bernard. *Guide de la femme intelligente en présence du socialisme et du capitalisme*. Translated by Augustin and Henriette Hamon. Paris: Aubier, 1929.

———. *Guide de la femme intelligente en présence du socialisme et du capitalisme*. Translated by Augustin and Henriette Hamon. Paris: Éditions Montaigne, 1929.

1930

Amunategui, Francisco. "Bernard Shaw—*La Charrette de pommes.*" *La Revue nouvelle* (December 1930): 97–102.

MacCarthy, Desmond. "*Sainte Jeanne.*" *New Statesman* (21 June 1930). [reprinted in *Shaw* (London: MacGibbon and Kee, 1951), 170–75]

Shaw, Bernard. *La Charrette de pommes*. Translated by Augustin and Henriette Hamon. Paris: Aubier, 1930.

———. *La Charrette de pommes*. Translated by Augustin and Henriette Hamon. Paris: Éditions Montaigne, 1930.

1931

Beauplan, Robert de. "*La Charrette de pommes*." *L'Illustration* (25 April 1931).

Bidou, Henry. "*La Charrette de pommes*." *Le Journal des débats* (11 May 1931): 3.

Brisson, Pierre. "*La Charrette de pommes*." *Le Temps* (20 April 1931): 2.

Carbon, Émile. "De notre correspondant particulier: *The Apple Cart*." *Comoedia* (12 March 1931).

d'Uhalde, Jean. "Création au gymnase: *La Charrette de pommes*, la dernière oeuvre de M. Bernard Shaw." *Massalia* [Marseilles] (7 and 14 March 1931).

Ellehauge, Martin. *The Position of Bernard Shaw in European Drama and Philosophy*. Copenhagen: Levin and Munksgaard, 1931.

Hamon, Augustin, and Henriette Hamon. "Postface des traducteurs. Notes pour l'histoire dramatique." *L'Homme et le surhomme*. Translated by Augustin and Henriette Hamon. Paris: Éditions Montaigne, 1931: 289–91. [postface dated February 1931; limited edition of 300 copies]

Lalou, René. "*La Charrette de pommes*." *Les Nouvelles littéraires* (25 April 1931).

Pawlowski, Gaston de. "*La Charrette de pommes* au Théâtre des Arts." *Le Journal* (16 April 1931).

Pierre, Émile. "La Politique au théâtre." *Le Soleil* (10 March 1931).

Shaw, Bernard. "The Author's Apology." Translated by Augustin and Henriette Hamon. In *Oeuvres*, vol. 1. Paris: Aubier, 1931. [first publication of preface to the 1902 Stage Society edition of *Mrs Warren's Profession*]

———. "Épître dédicatoire à A. Bingham Walkley." Translated by Augustin and Henriette Hamon. In *Oeuvres*, vol. 2. Paris: Aubier, 1931. [first publication of "Epistle Dedicatory" to *Man and Superman*]

———. *L'Homme et le surhomme*. Translated by Augustin and Henriette Hamon. Paris: Éditions Montaigne, 1931. [limited edition of 300 copies]

———. *On ne peut jamais dire*. Translated by Augustin and Henriette Hamon. Paris: Éditions Montaigne, 1931.

———. *Pièces déplaisantes*. Translated by Augustin and Henriette Hamon. Paris: Aubier, 1931.

Speth, William. "Le Théâtre: *La Charrette de pommes*." *La Revue mondiale* 203 (1 May 1931): 93–95.

Zucker, Irving. *Le "Court Theatre" (1904–1914) et l'évolution du théâtre anglais contemporain*. Paris: Presses Modernes, 1931.

1932

Anonymous. No title. *Les Nouvelles littéraires* (5 November 1932): 2. [on *Trop vrai pour être beau*]

Brisson, Pierre. "*Trop vrai pour être beau*." *Le Temps* (26 December 1932): 2.

Dubech, Lucien. "'Trop beau pour être vrai' au Théâtre des Arts." *Candide* (29 December 1932).

Kochnitzky, Léon. "Le Strapontin volant." *Les Nouvelles littéraires* (23 July 1932). [on the reception of Shaw's plays in Poland]

Lalou, René. "Le Théâtre." *Les Nouvelles littéraires* (31 December 1932): 8.

Laurent, M. "Bernard Shaw nous parle de Rodin." *Les Annales politiques et littéraires* 99 (2 December, 1932): 487–88.

Lugné-Poë, Aurélien-Marie. "Le Théâtre." *L'Avenir* (18–19 December 1932). [on *Trop vrai pour être beau*]

M.J. "*Trop vrai pour être beau*." *Le Journal des débats* (17 December 1932).

Shaw, Bernard. *Androclès et le lion*. Translated by Augustin and Henriette Hamon. *Les Oeuvres libres* 133 (July 1932): 5–62. [without preface]

———. "La 'Société bourgeoise': A-t-elle fait faillite?" *La Revue mondiale* 43 (December 1932): 7–8.

———. *Le Lien déraisonnable*. Translated by Augustin and Henriette Hamon. Paris: Aubier, 1932.

1933

Bernard, J. J. "Témoignages: Bernard Shaw et Paris." *Masques* (April 1933): 65 ff.

Cru, Robert-L. "Un Pamphlet politique de M. Bernard Shaw." *Le Temps* (30 August 1933). [on *The Future of Political Science in America*]

Dubech, Lucien. "La Chronique des Théâtres." *L'Action française* (7 January 1933). [on *Trop vrai pour être beau*]

Dunton-Green, L. "G. B. Shaw, critique musical." *Revue musicale* (May 1933): 334–39.

Moore, Mina. *Bernard Shaw et la France*. Paris: Librairie Ancienne Honoré Champion, 1933.

Nargaud, Jacques. "'Pièces Plaisantes' de Bernard Shaw." *Le Petit bleu* (10 May 1933).

Shaw, Bernard. "Les Financiers maîtres du monde par Bernard Shaw." Translated by Augustin and Henriette Hamon. *Forces* (13 October 1933): 15. [excerpt from *Asiles d'aliénés politiques: Amérique et Europe*]

———. "N'allez pas à l'Université par G.-Bernard Shaw." *Marianne* (20 October 1933). [translation of "Mr. Shaw vs. Universities," *New York Times* (26 March 1933); reprinted as "Universities and Education" in Dan H. Laurence, ed., *Platform and Pulpit* (London: Rupert Hart-Davis, 1962), 259–61]

———. *Asiles d'aliénés politiques en Amérique et plus près de chez nous*. Translated by Augustin and Henriette Hamon. Paris: Aubier, 1933.

———. *Asiles d'aliénés politiques en Amérique et plus près de chez nous*. Translated by Augustin and Henriette Hamon. Paris: Éditions Montaigne, 1933.

———. *Les Aventures d'une jeune négresse à la recherche de Dieu*. Translated by Augustin and Henriette Hamon. Paris: Aubier, 1933.

———. *Les Aventures d'une jeune négresse à la recherche de Dieu*. Translated by Augustin and Henriette Hamon. Paris: Éditions Montaigne, 1933.

———. *Le Parfait Wagnérien*. Translated by Augustin and Henriette Hamon. Paris: Aubier, 1933.

———. *Le Parfait Wagnérien.* Translated by Augustin and Henriette Hamon. Paris: Éditions Montaigne, 1933.

———. *Pièces plaisantes.* Translated by Augustin and Henriette Hamon. Paris: Aubier, 1933.

1934

Fitz-Herbert, Patrice. "Aux Mathurins: Reprise de *Sainte Jeanne* de Bernard Shaw." *Vu* 352 (12 October 1934): 1617.

Heydet, Xavier. "*Bernard Shaw et la France* par Mina Moore." *Elsaessisches Literatur-Blatt* (1 March 1934). [part 1 of 2]

———. "*Bernard Shaw et la France* par Mina Moore." *Elsaessisches Literatur-Blatt* (1 April 1934). [part 2 of 2]

1935

Closset, François. *G. Bernard Shaw: Son oeuvre.* Paris: Éditions de *La Nouvelle revue critique*, 1935.

d'Hennezel, Henri. "Bernard Schaw." *Salut public* [Lyon] (16 November 1935).

Maurois, André. "Bernard Shaw, le prophète sceptique." *La Revue hebdomadaire* (16 and 23 March 1935): 308–25, 443–55. [reprinted in *Magiciens et logiciens* (1935)]

———. "Bernard Shaw." In *Magiciens et logiciens,* 101–38. Paris: Bernard Grasset, 1935. [translated by Hamish Miles as *Prophets and Poets* (New York and London: Harper, 1935), 97–138; reprinted in *Points of View from Kipling to Graham Greene* (New York: Frederick Ungar, 1968)]

Shaw, Bernard. *Le Socialiste insociable.* Translated by Augustin and Henriette Hamon. Paris: Éditions Montaigne, 1935.

———. *Trois Pièces pour puritains.* Translated by Augustin and Henriette Hamon. Paris: Aubier, 1935.

———. *Trois Pièces pour puritains.* Translated by Augustin and Henriette Hamon. Paris: Éditions Montaigne, 1935. [reprinted 1951]

1936

Hamon, Augustin. "Le Théâtre et la Question Sociale." *L'Humanité* (5 January 1936).

Shaw, Bernard. *Le Socialiste insociable.* Translated by Augustin and Henriette Hamon. Paris: Aubier, 1936.

Sobra, Adrien. "Les Femmes dans le théâtre de G. Bernard Shaw." *Revue de l'enseignement des langues vivantes* 2 (February 1936): 49–57; 3 (March 1936): 109–15; 4 (April 1936): 164–74; and 5 (May 1936): 198–211.

1937

Cru, Robert-L. "Une Autobiographie de Bernard Shaw." *Le Temps* (10 October 1937).

Delpech, Jeanine. "A propos de *Candide:* Des Influences subies par Bernard Shaw." *Les Nouvelles littéraires* (10 July 1937).

Hamon, Augustin, and Henriette Hamon. "Bernard Shaw à la radio: *Pygmalion.*" *Radio liberté* (29 October 1937): 38–39.

Heydet, Xavier. "Richard Wagner et Bernard Shaw." *Revue de l'enseignement des langues vivantes* (June 1937): 245–58.

———. *Littérature Comparée*, vol. 1, *Richard Wagner et Bernard Shaw*, vol. 2, *Hermann Bahr et Bernard Shaw*. Paris: Didier, 1937.

Maurois, André. "*Candide* de Bernard Shaw au Théâtre des Champs-Élysées." *Le Théâtre* (23 June 1937).

1938

Crémieux, Benjamin. No title. *La Lumière* (23 September 1938). [on *La Charrette de pommes*]

Daudé-Bancel, A. "La Réforme foncière au théâtre." *Terre et liberté* (October–November 1938): 85–86. [on *L'Argent n'a pas d'odeur* at the Théâtre des Mathurins]

Hamon, Augustin, and Henriette Hamon. "Le Théâtre de Bernard Shaw." *Tourisme et loisirs populaires* 11 (October–November 1938): 6.

Harris, Frank. *Bernard Shaw par Frank Harris*. Translated by Madeleine Vernon and Henry-D. Davray. Paris: Gallimard, 1938. [translation of *Frank Harris on Bernard Shaw: An Unauthorised Biography Based on Firsthand Information, with a Postscript by Mr Shaw* (1931)]

Heydet, Xavier. *Shaw-Kompendium*. Paris: Didier, 1936, ["Relevé complet, avec extraits et analyses, des travaux publiés en Allemagne sur Bernard Shaw, sa vie et son oeuvre"]

Lombard, Paul. "Le Théâtre et l'argent." *L'Homme libre* (24 September 1938).

Shaw, Bernard. *Androclès et le lion. Défense d'entrer. Pygmalion.* Translated by Augustin and Henriette Hamon. Paris: Aubier, 1938. [first publication of preface to *Androclès et le Lion* and of *Défense d'entrer (Overruled)*]

———. *Androclès et le lion. Défense d'entrer. Pygmalion.* Translated by Augustin and Henriette Hamon. Paris: Éditions Montaigne, 1938.

———. *Pygmalion.* Translated by Augustin and Henriette Hamon. Paris: Aubier, 1938. [reprinted 1952]

———. *Soviétisme et fascisme, suite au Guide de la femme intelligente.* Translated by Augustin and Henriette Hamon. Paris: Aubier, 1938.

———. *Soviétisme et fascisme, suite au Guide de la femme intelligente.* Translated by Augustin and Henriette Hamon. Paris: Éditions Montaigne, 1938.

1939

Eyrignoux, Louis. "La Dette de Shaw envers Samuel Butler, deux documents." *Études anglaises* 4 (October–December 1939): 361–64.

Shaw, Bernard. *Les Aventures d'une jeune négresse à la recherche de Dieu.* Translated by Augustin and Henriette Hamon. Paris: Aubier, 1939.

1941

Shaw, Bernard. *Le Dilemme du docteur. Mariage. Le Vrai Blanco Posnet.* Translated by Augustin and Henriette Hamon. In *Oeuvres*, vol. 10. Paris: Aubier, 1941. [first publication of "Préface sur les docteurs"]

———. *Mariage.* Translated by Augustin and Henriette Hamon. Paris: Éditions Montaigne, 1941.

———. *Le Vrai Blanco Posnet*. Translated by Augustin and Henriette Hamon. Paris: Éditions Montaigne, 1941.

1943

Shaw, Bernard. *La Commandante Barbara. Comment il mentit au mari*. Translated by Augustin and Henriette Hamon. Paris: Aubier, 1943.

1944

Shaw, Bernard. *La Commandante Barbara. Comment il mentit au mari*. Translated by Augustin and Henriette Hamon. Paris: Éditions Montaigne, 1944.

———. "Quelle sera la France de demain?" *La France Libre* [London] 8 (16 October 1944): 393–95. [translation of "What Next in France?" in *Tricolor* [New York] 2 (November 1944): 45–50]

1945

Shaw, Bernard. *La Commandante Barbara. Comment il mentit au mari*. Translated by Augustin and Henriette Hamon. Paris: Aubier, 1943.

———. *Pièces déplaisantes. Pièces plaisantes*. Translated by Augustin and Henriette Hamon. Paris: Aubier, 1945.

———. *Sainte Jeanne*. Translated by Augustin and Henriette Hamon. Paris: Aubier, 1945.

———. *La Seconde île de John Bull*. Translated by Augustin and Henriette Hamon. Paris: Aubier, 1945.

———. *La Seconde île de John Bull*. Translated by Augustin and Henriette Hamon. Paris: Éditions Montaigne, 1945.

1946

Hamon, Augustin. "Bernard Shaw et la France." *Adam International Review* 14.161 (August 1946): 17–18. [excerpt of Hamon's *Bernard Shaw et ses traducteurs français* (1910)]

Shaw, Bernard. *Genève*. Translated by Augustin and Henriette Hamon. Paris: Aubier, 1946.

———. *Genève*. Translated by Augustin and Henriette Hamon. Paris: Éditions Montaigne, 1946.

1947

Ransan, André. "Bernard Shaw." In *En déjeunant avec...*, 59–72. Paris: Les Deux Sirènes; Brussels: L'Écran du Monde, 1947.

Shaw, Bernard. "Bernard Shaw ne veut pas jouer au prophète" [Bernard Shaw does not want to play prophet]. *Ce Matin* [Paris] (29 March 1947).

———. "Molière and Shaw." Third-person draft for Archibald Henderson in *George Bernard Shaw: Man of the Century* (New York: D. Appleton, 1956). [reprinted in Bernard F. Dukore, ed., *Bernard Shaw: The Drama Observed*, vol. 4 (University Park: Pennsylvania State University Press, 1993), 1514–15]

1948

Shaw, Bernard. "Bernard Shaw pense à éviter la guerre." *Les Lettres françaises* (19 August 1948): 1:1–3, 3:1–2.

———. "The Acquired Habits of Napoleon." *New Statesman and Nation* 36 (9 October 1948): 304.

1949

Shaw, Bernard. *Sainte Jeanne*. Translated by Augustin and Henriette Hamon. Paris: Aubier, 1949.

1950

Chassé, Charles. "G. Bernard Shaw, auteur social et satiriste puritain." *France-Illustration* 265 (11 November 1950): 520.

Chauviré, Robert. "Bernard Shaw." *La Revue des deux mondes* 23 (1 December 1950): 476–84.

Guyard, Marius-François. "Bernard Shaw." *Études* 267 (October 1950): 397–99.

Haloche, Maurice. "G. B. Shaw." *Le Thyrse* (December 1950): 447–51.

Maurois, André. "Bernard Shaw par Bernard Shaw." *La Revue de Paris* 57 (December 1950): 5–11.

Perruchot, Henri. "Bernard Shaw, ou un cynisme de l'authenticité." *Synthèses* [Brussels] (December 1950): 50–61. [reprinted in Perruchot 1955]

Shaw, Bernard. *Le Héros et le soldat*. Translated by Augustin and Henriette Hamon. *Le Monde illustré, supplément théâtral et littéraire* 64 (12 August 1950). [published in Paris by France-Illustration]

———. *Mésalliance*. Translated by Augustin and Henriette Hamon. Paris: Aubier, 1950.

———. *Mésalliance*. Translated by Augustin and Henriette Hamon. Lille: Imprimerie Taffin-Lefort, 1950.

———. *Mon Portrait en seize esquisses*. Translated by Augustin and Henriette Hamon. Paris: Aubier, 1950.

———. *Pièces plaisantes*. Translated by Augustin and Henriette Hamon. Paris: Aubier, 1950.

1951

Ambrière, Francis. "Les Grandes Premières: *Sainte Jeanne* de Bernard Shaw." *Les Annales (conférencia)* (October 1951).

Baiwir, Albert. "The Legacy of George Bernard Shaw." *Revue des langues vivantes* [Brussels] 17 (1951): 2–10.

———. "Nouvelle lumière sur G. B. Shaw." *Revue des langues vivantes* [Brussels] 17 (1951): 176–80.

Dutt, Rajani Palme. "G. B. Shaw." *La Pensée* 34 (January 1951): 62–68.

Henderson, Archibald. "Bernard Shaw and France: Gaelic Triumph or Gallic Repulse?" *Carolina Quarterly* 3 (March 1951): 42–56.

Lalou, René. "George Bernard Shaw." *Revue de la société d'histoire du théâtre* 1 (1951).

Mann, Thomas. "G. B. Shaw prophète gouailleur d'une humanité émancipée des ténèbres." *Le Figaro* (1951). [reprinted in *Cahiers des saisons*, 1964]

Pearson, Hesketh. "Bernard Shaw et les femmes." *Nouvelles littéraires* 30.1953 (1951): 8.

Seresia, Cécile. "G. B. Shaw." *La Revue nouvelle* 4 [Brussels] (15 April 1951): 356–65.

Shaw, Bernard. *César et Cléopâtre*. Translated by Augustin and Henriette Hamon. Paris: Aubier, 1951.

———. *La Première Pièce de Fanny. La Dame brune des sonnets*. Translated by Augustin and Henriette Hamon. Paris: Aubier, 1951.

———. *Trois Pièces pour puritains*. Translated by Augustin and Henriette Hamon. Paris: Éditions Montaigne, 1951.

1952

Shaw, Bernard. *Androclès et le Lion. Défense d'entrer*. Translated by Augustin and Henriette Hamon. Paris: Aubier, 1952. [reprinted 1957]

———. *La Dame brune des sonnets. La Première Pièce de Fanny*. Translated by Augustin and Henriette Hamon. Paris: Éditions Montaigne, 1952.

———. *La Grande Catherine*. Translated by Augustin and Henriette Hamon. Paris: Aubier, 1952. [reprinted 1953]

———. *La Grande Catherine*. Translated by Augustin and Henriette Hamon. Paris: Éditions Montaigne, 1952.

———. *Pygmalion*. Translated by Augustin and Henriette Hamon. Paris: Aubier, 1952.

———. *Sainte Jeanne*. Translated by Augustin and Henriette Hamon. Paris: Aubier, 1952.

———. *Trop vrai pour être beau*. Translated by Augustin and Henriette Hamon. Paris: Aubier, 1952.

———. *Trop vrai pour être beau*. Translated by Augustin and Henriette Hamon. Paris: Éditions Montaigne, 1952.

1953

Eyrignoux, Louis. "Études critiques: Bernard Shaw et Mrs. Patrick Campbell." *Études anglaises* 6 (November 1953): 350–53.

Saint-Auclaire, Le comte de. "De Viviani à la *Jeanne d'Arc* de Bernard Shaw." *Les Oeuvres libres* (April 1953): 107–38.

Shaw, Bernard. *La Grande Catherine*. Translated by Augustin and Henriette Hamon. Paris: Aubier, 1952.

———. *La Maison des coeurs brisés*. Translated by Augustin and Henriette Hamon. Paris: Aubier, 1953.

———. *La Milliardaire*. Translated by Augustin and Henriette Hamon. Paris: Aubier, 1953.

1954

Shaw, Bernard. *Androclès et le lion. Défense d'entrer*. Translated by Augustin and Henriette Hamon. Paris: Aubier, 1954.

———. *Pygmalion*. Translated by Augustin and Henriette Hamon. Paris: Aubier, 1954.

1955

Anonymous. "Shaw Play Shocked Paris After 61 Years." Grimsby *Evening Telegraph* (5 April 1955). [on *La Profession de Madame Warren*]

Barzun, Jacques. "Shaw and Rousseau: No Paradox." *Shaw Bulletin* 1.8 (May 1955): 1–6.

Marcel, Gabriel. No title. *Les Nouvelles littéraires* (3 February 1955). [on *Pygmalion*]

Perruchot, Henri. *La Haine des masques: Montherlant, Camus, Shaw*. Paris: La Table Ronde, 1955, 157–206. [see Perruchot 1950]

Ravon, Georges. No title. *Semaine du monde* (20 January–3 February 1955). [on *Pygmalion*]

Shaw, Bernard. *La Maison des coeurs brisés*. Translated by Augustin and Henriette Hamon. Paris: Aubier, 1955.

———. *Pièces plaisantes: On ne peut jamais dire. L'Homme du destin*. Paris: Aubier, 1955.

———. *La Profession de Madame Warren*. Translated by Augustin and Henriette Hamon. Paris: Éditions Montaigne, 1955.

———. *Pygmalion*. New version by Claude-André Puget. Paris: A. Fayard, 1955.

———. *Pygmalion*. New version by Claude-André Puget. Paris: France-Illustration, 1955. [Theatrical supplement no. 184 to *Le Monde illustré*]

———. *Pygmalion*. New version by Claude-André Puget. Paris: Les Oeuvres Libres, 1955. [n.s., no. 112, September 1955]

———. *Le Soldat O'Flaherty, croix de Victoria 1915*. Translated by Augustin and Henriette Hamon. Paris: Aubier, 1955.

1956

Grindea, Miron. "G. B. S. and France." *Adam International Review* 255–256 (1956): 1–14.

LeCorre, Pierrette. "Les Cent Ans de George Bernard Shaw." *La Pensée* 70 (1956): 32–42.

Shaw, Bernard. "Shaw Writing to the Pitoëffs: Three Hitherto Unpublished Letters." *Adam International Review* 255–56 (1956): 14–15 [letters from 1928, in French]

———. *Le Disciple du diable*. Translated by Augustin and Henriette Hamon. Paris: Aubier, 1956.

———. *Pygmalion*. New version by Claude-André Puget. *Lisez-moi* 44 (June 1956). [published in Paris by Tallandier]

Sion, Georges. "Bernard Shaw, le baladin du monde occidental" [Bernard Shaw, the mountebank of the Occidental world]. *Revue générale belge* (August 1956): 1698–711.

1957

Eyrignoux, Louis. "Le Centenaire de la naissance de Bernard Shaw." *Études anglaises* 10 (1957): 123–27.

Maurois, André. "Le Théâtre de Bernard Shaw." *Les Annales (conférencia)* (January 1957).

Shaw, Bernard. *Androclès et le Lion. Défense d'entrer.* Translated by Augustin and Henriette Hamon. Paris: Aubier, 1957.

———. *Aux jours heureux du bon roi Charles.* Translated by Augustin and Henriette Hamon. Paris: Aubier, 1957.

———. *César et Cléopâtre.* Translated by Augustin and Henriette Hamon. Paris: Édition Montaigne, 1957.

Starr, William T. "Romain Rolland and George Bernard Shaw." *Shaw Bulletin* 2.3 (September 1957): 1–6.

1958

Kaye, Julian B. *Bernard Shaw and the Nineteenth-Century Tradition.* Norman: University of Oklahoma Press, 1958. [Shaw and Auguste Comte discussed at 40–48]

Rouché, Jacques. "Portraits: George Bernard Shaw." *Revue d'histoire du théâtre* 10 (1958): 300–303.

1959

Rostand, Jean. "Étude sur G.-B. Shaw et sa métabiologie." Preface to *Retour à Mathusalem: Pentateuque métabiologique.* Translated by Augustin and Henriette Hamon. Paris: Aubier, 1959: 7–15.

Shaw, Bernard. *Le Disciple du diable.* Translated by Augustin et Henriette Hamon. Paris: Éditions Montaigne, 1959.

———. *Retour à Mathusalem: Pentateuque métabiologique.* Translated by Augustin and Henriette Hamon. Paris: Aubier, 1959.

———. *Retour à Mathusalem: Pentateuque métabiologique.* Translated by Augustin and Henriette Hamon. Paris: Éditions Montaigne, 1959.

Serge, Jean. "Jean Serge raconte: *Le cas Dobedatt* ou le dilemme du docteur." *L'Avant-scène* 208 (15 November 1959): 42–43. [summary of adaptation by Jacques Deval of the Hamon translation of *Le Dilemme du docteur*]

1960

Wilson, Colin. "Shaw's Existentialism." *Shavian* 2.1 (February 1960): 4–6.

1961

Béra, M.-A. "G.B.S. ou Bernard Shaw?" *Les Langues modernes* 45.2 (March–April 1961): 107–19.

Cocteau, Jean. Préface. Bernard Shaw/Mrs. Patrick Campbell: Correspondance. Trans. Jean Bloch-Michel. Paris: Calmann-Lévy, 1961.

Shaw, Bernard. *Cher menteur.* Adapted and translated by Jean Cocteau. *L'Avant-scène* 242 (1 May 1961). [translation of *Dear Liar* (1960) by Jerome Kilty, based on correspondence of Shaw and Mrs. Patrick Campbell]

Stanton, Stephen S. "Shaw's Debt to Scribe." *PMLA* 76.5 (December 1961): 575–85.

1962

Bullough, Geoffrey. "Literary Relations of Shaw's Mrs Warren." *Philological*

Quarterly 41.1 (January 1962): 339–58. [Guy de Maupassant's "Yvette" and *Mrs Warren's Profession*]
Calvin, Judith S. "The GBSsence of Giraudoux." *Shaw Review* 5.1 (January 1962): 21–35.
Klein, John W. "Shaw and Brieux—an Enigma." *Drama* 67 (winter 1962): 33–35.
Shaw, Bernard. Bibliography to *Sainte Jeanne. Pygmalion*. Paris: Éditions Rombaldi, 1962. [chronological bibliography of works by Shaw in French translation at 405–16]

1963
Amalric, Jean-Claude. "Un Nouvel Alphabet pour l'anglais: The Shaw Alphabet." *Études anglaises* 16.1 (1963): 107–8.
Epstein, Rima. "Armin's Life and Work, Jean Anouilh: A French G.B.S., Hawthorne's Religious Beliefs." Master's thesis, Pennsylvania State University, 1963.

1964
Gerould, Daniel C. "*Saint Joan* in Paris." *Shaw Review* 7.1 (January 1964): 11–23. [reprinted in Weintraub 1973]
Mann, Thomas. "L'Impertinence libératrice." Translated by Louise Servicen. *Cahier des saisons* 37 (spring 1964): 167–72. [reprint of *Le Figaro*, 1951]
Maulnier, Thierry. "De Bernard Shaw à Jean Schlumberger." *La Revue de Paris* 71 (May 1964): 132–35.
Talley, Jerry B. "Religious Themes in the Dramatic Works of George Bernard Shaw, T. S. Eliot and Paul Claudel." Ph.D. diss., University of Denver, 1964.

1965
Dalmasso, Osvaldo de. "Molière, George Bernard Shaw y los médicos." *Lyra* 2 (September–December 1965): n.p.
Ducann, C. G. L. *Bernard Shaw et les femmes*. Paris: La Palatine, 1965.
Shaw, Bernard. *Don Juan aux Enfers*. Adaptation d'André Maurois. Paris: Aubier, 1965.

1966
Amalric, Jean-Claude. "Satire et comique plaisants et déplaisants: 'Mrs. Warren's Profession' et 'Arms and the Man' de Bernard Shaw." In *Études anglaises*, suppl. vol. 25, *Aspects du comique dans la littérature anglaise*, March 1965, 28–47. Paris: Didier, 1966.
Leary, Daniel J. "The Evolutionary Dialectic of Shaw and Teilhard. A Perennial Philosophy." *Shaw Review* 9.1 (1966): 15–34.

1967
Amalric, Jean-Claude. "Reliefs du festin shavien: Recueils et lettres publiés depuis la mort de Bernard Shaw." *Études anglaises* 20.2 (April 1967): 165–68.
Blanch, Robert J. "The Myth of Don Juan in *Man and Superman*." *Revue des langues vivantes* 33.2 (1967): 158–64.
Saint-Paulien [pseud. of Maurice I. Sicard]. "Le Séducteur de Kierkegaard, et le Don Juan misogyne et socialisé de George Bernard Shaw." In *Don Juan: Mythe et réalité*, 241–52. Paris: Plon, 1967.

Shaw, Bernard. *Pygmalion*. Translated by Augustin and Henriette Hamon. New revised and emended edition. Paris: Aubier-Montaigne, 1967.

1968

Searle, William. "The Saint and the Skeptics: Joan of Arc in the Works of Mark Twain, Anatole France, and Bernard Shaw." Ph.D. diss., University of California, Berkeley, 1968.

1971

McIlwaine, Robert Schields. "The Intellectual Farce of Bernard Shaw." Ph.D. diss., Duke University, 1971. [Beckett, Ionesco]

Mundell, Richard Frederick. "Shaw and Brieux: A Literary Relationship." 2 vols. Ph.D. diss., University of Michigan, 1971.

1972

Amalric, Jean-Claude. "Bernard Shaw." In *Encyclopaedia universalis*, vol. 14, 942–43. Paris: Encyclopaedia Universalis France, 1972.

1973

Valency, Maurice. *The Cart and the Trumpet: The Plays of George Bernard Shaw.* New York: Oxford University Press, 1973.

Weintraub, Stanley, ed. *"Saint Joan" Fifty Years After, 1923/24–1973/74.* Baton Rouge: Louisiana State University Press, 1973. [reprints Graham (1924), Tittle (1924) and Gerould (1964)]

1974

Appia, Henri. "A propos de *Pygmalion*, G. B. Shaw phonéticien." *Études anglaises* 27.1 (January–March 1974): 45–63.

Mouton, Janice Malmsten. "Joan of Arc on the Twentieth-Century Stage: Dramatic Treatments of the Joan of Arc Story by Bertolt Brecht, George Bernard Shaw, Jean Anouilh, Georg Kaiser, Paul Claudel, and Maxwell Anderson." Ph.D. diss., Northwestern University, 1974.

Shaw, Bernard. *Pièces déplaisantes*. Translated by Robert Soulat. Paris: L'Arche, 1974.

———. *Pièces plaisantes*. Translated by Lucette Andrieu, Marie Dubost, and Anne Villelaur. Paris: L'Arche, 1974.

1975

Fyfe, H. Hamilton. "Brieux and Bernard Shaw." *Independent Shavian* 13 (winter 1975): 24–25. [reprint of Fyfe 1906]

Senart, Philippe. "La Revue théâtrale: *Androclès et le lion*." *Nouvelle revue des deux mondes* (September 1975): 700–701.

1976

Amalric, Jean-Claude. "George Bernard Shaw, du réformateur victorien au prophète édouardien. Formation et évolution de ses idées (1856–1910)." Thesis for Doctorat d'État. Université de Paris-Sorbonne, 1976. [published as *Bernard Shaw: Du réformateur victorien au prophète édouardien* (1977)]

———. "Shaw critique musical." Conférence donnée au Centre Victorien de l'Université de Lyon II, 1976.

Cammaerts, Émile. "Émile Cammaerts on Molière and Shaw." In *Shaw, the Criti-*

cal Heritage, edited by T. F. Evans, 307–9. London: Routledge and Kegan Paul, 1976. [reprints short excerpt of "Molière and Bernard Shaw," *Nineteenth Century* (September 1926): 413–22]

Flers, Robert de. "Robert de Flers, notice, Le Figaro." In *Shaw, the Critical Heritage*, edited by T. F. Evans, 295–96. London: Routledge and Kegan Paul, 1976. [English translation of "Sainte Jeanne," *Le Figaro* (11 May 1925)]

Odin, Roger. "A propos d'une source trop négligée de la Jeanne d'Arc de George Bernard Shaw." *Revue d'histoire du théâtre* 28 (July–September 1976): 242–65.

Searle, William. *The Saint and the Skeptics: Joan of Arc in the Work of Mark Twain, Anatole France and Bernard Shaw.* Detroit: Wayne State University Press, 1976.

1977

Amalric, Jean-Claude. "Shaw in France in Recent Years." *Shaw Review* 20.1 (January 1977): 43–46. [reprinted in Amalric 1992]

———. *Bernard Shaw: Du réformateur victorien au prophète édouardien.* Paris: Didier, 1977.

Cohen, M. A. "The 'Shavianisation' of Cauchon." *Shaw Review* 20.2 (May 1977): 63–70. [reprinted in A. M. Gibbs, ed., *Bernard Shaw: 'Man and Superman' and 'Saint Joan,' a Casebook* (London: Macmillan, 1992), 203–13]

Senart, Philippe. "La Revue théâtrale: Pygmalion." *Nouvelle revue des deux mondes* (December 1977): 685–87.

1978

Ganz, Margaret. "Humor's Devaluations in a Modern Idiom: The Don Juan Plays of Shaw, Frisch, and Montherlant." In Maurice Charney, ed., *Comedy: New Perspectives* 1 (spring 1978): 117–36.

1979

Amalric, Jean-Claude. "Modèle actantiel et investissement thématique: Quelques Remarques sur *Arms and the Man.*" *Cahiers victoriens et édouardiens* 9–10 (October 1979): 87–94. [English translation in Amalric 1992]

Jomaron, Jacqueline. "Shaw." In *George Pitoëff, metteur en scène,* 158–82. Lausanne: L'Age d'Homme, 1979.

Shaw, Bernard. "Extraits de Lettres de Shaw à Pitoëff." In *George Pitoëff, metteur en scène,* by Jacqueline Jomaron, 179–82. Lausanne: L'Age d'Homme, 1979. [letters of 18 October 1927 and 13 September 1928 (in French); 13 January 1929, 23 January and 16 April 1930, 28 April 1931 (in English)]

1980

Amalric, Jean-Claude. "Shaw et la morale victorienne; le devoir d'immoralisme." Paper read at the second symposium of the Société Française d'Études Victoriennes et Édouardiennes. In *Actes du colloque, Confluents,* vol. 1 (1980), Lyon, 81–89. [English translation in Amalric 1992)]

1982

Poitou, Marc. "Du pèlerin de Bunyan au surhomme de Nietzsche: La Curieuse Généalogie du héros shavien." In *Vivante Tradition: Sources et racines,* 97–106. Paris: Centre d'Histoire des Idées dans les Iles Britanniques, 1982.

Taub, Michael. "The Martyr as Tragic Heroine: The Joan of Arc Theme in the Theatre of Schiller, Shaw, Anouilh and Brecht." Diss., University of North Carolina, 1982.

1983

Vitoux, M. P. "Le César de Mommsen et le César de George-Bernard Shaw." In *Présence de César: Actes du Colloque des 9–11 décembre 1983*, edited by R. Chevalier, 347–54. Paris: Belles Lettres, 1985.

1984

Amalric, Jean-Claude. "Shaw, Hamon, and Rémy de Gourmont." In *SHAW, the Annual of Bernard Shaw Studies*, edited by Stanley Weintraub, vol. 4, 129–37. University Park: Pennsylvania State University Press, 1984. [reprinted in Amalric 1992]

———. "Lecture sémiotique de *Man and Superman* de Bernard Shaw." *Études anglaises* 37.4 (October–December 1984): 412–23. [English translation in Amalric 1992]

Barzun, Jacques. "Shaw Versus Stendhal." *Partisan Review* 51 (1984): 613–19.

1985

Amalric, Jean-Claude. "A Playwright's Supertrips: Shaw's Visits to France." In *SHAW, the Annual of Bernard Shaw Studies*, vol. 5, *Shaw Abroad*, edited by Rodelle Weintraub, 67–80. University Park: Pennsylvania State University Press, 1985. [reprinted in Amalric 1992]

Hernadi, Paul. "Re-Presenting the Past: *Saint Joan* and *L'Alouette*." In *Interpreting Events: Tragicomedies of History on the Modern Stage*, 17–37. Ithaca, N.Y.: Cornell University Press, 1985. [reprinted in Harold Bloom, ed., *Major Literary Characters: Joan of Arc* (New York and Philadelphia: Chelsea House, 1992), 153–67]

1986

Amalric, Jean-Claude. "Du réaliste au surhomme: Les Métamorphoses du héros shavien." *Cahiers victoriens et édouardiens* 23 (April 1986): 59–69. [English translation in Amalric 1992]

———. "Bernard Shaw: *Man and Superman*, bibliographie sélective." *Cahiers victoriens et édouardiens* 24 (October 1986): 153–60.

1988

Kasimow, Harold. "The Conflict Between the Mystic and the Church as Reflected in Bernard Shaw's *Saint Joan* and Jean Anouilh's *The Lark*." *Mystics Quarterly* 14.2 (June 1988): 94–100.

Pharand, Michel W. "Eugène Brieux and Bernard Shaw: Iconoclasts of Social Reform." In *SHAW, the Annual of Bernard Shaw Studies*, vol. 8, edited by Stanley Weintraub, 97–104. University Park: Pennsylvania State University Press, 1988.

1991

Amalric, Jean-Claude. "Shaw's *Man and Superman* and the Myth of Don Juan: Intertextuality and Irony." *Cahiers victoriens et édouardiens* 33 (April 1991): 103–14. [reprinted in Amalric 1992]

———. "The Production of Shaw's Plays in France." In *Bernard Shaw: On Stage,*

Papers from the 1989 International Shaw Conference, editd by L. W. Connoly and Ellen M. Pearson, 81–87. Guelph: University of Guelph, 1991. [reprinted in Amalric 1992]

Pharand, Michel W. "Bernard Shaw, Romain Rolland, and the Politics of Pacifism: Above the Battle?" In *SHAW, the Annual of Bernard Shaw Studies,* vol. 11, *Shaw and Politics,* edited by T. F. Evans, 169–83. University Park: Pennsylvania State University Press, 1991.

———. "Shaw's Life Force and Bergson's *élan vital:* A Question of Influence." *Cahiers victoriens et édouardiens* 3 (April 1991): 87–101.

1992

Amalric, Jean-Claude. *Studies in Bernard Shaw.* Montpellier: Université Paul-Valéry, 1992.

Pharand, Michel W. "From Shavian Warrior to Gallic Waif: Bernard Shaw's *Saint Joan* on the French Stage." In *Text and Presentation: Journal of the Comparative Drama Conference,* vol. 12, edited by Karelisa Hartigan, 75–81. Gainesville, Fla.: Maupin House, 1992.

Russell, Phillips. "Yvette Guilbert *chez* Shaw." *Independent Shavian* 30.3 (1992): 61–62.

Shaw, Bernard. *Sainte Jeanne.* Translated by Anika Scherrer. Paris: L'Arche, 1992.

———. "Lettre au Times." In *Notre Amie la femme,* translated by Elisabeth Gille, 95–98. Lausanne: L'Age d'Homme, 1992. ["Sumptuary Regulations at the Opera," letter of 3 July 1905 to the *Times*]

1993

Steel, David. "George Bernard Shaw lecteur de *Retour de l'URSS.*" *Bulletin des Amis d'André Gide* 21 (April 1993): 189–93.

1994

Liébert, Georges. "Avant-propos." In *Bernard Shaw: Écrits sur la musique, 1876–1950,* translated by Georges Liébert, Béatrice Vierne, and Anne Chattaway, vii–xxxi. Paris: Robert Laffont, 1994. [see next item]

Shaw, Bernard. *Bernard Shaw: Écrits sur la musique, 1876–1950.* Translated by Georges Liébert, Béatrice Vierne, and Anne Chattaway. Paris: Robert Laffont, 1994. [selections from Dan H. Laurence, ed., *Shaw's Music: The Complete Musical Criticism,* 3 vols. (New York: Dodd, Mead, 1981)]

1995

Hare, Marion J. "Rodin, Shaw and the Six of Calais." In *The Six of Calais: Shaw Festival 1995.* Shaw Festival production program, 1995.

Pharand, Michel W. "Liaisons ténébreuses: Bernard Shaw and French Theatre." *Journal of Inquiry and Research* 61 [Osaka] (January 1995): 81–104.

Tehan, Arline Boucher. "The Sultan of Meudon and the Bishop of Everywhere." In "The Gates of Hell: The Story of Rodin." Unpublished. 1995. [on Shaw and Rodin]

Wellens, Oskar. "*Candida* in French (1907)." *Shavian* 7.7 (spring 1995): 6–11.

1996

Barzun, Jacques. "Berlioz and Shaw: An Affinity." In *SHAW, the Annual of Ber-*

nard *Shaw Studies,* vol. 16, *Unpublished Shaw,* edited by Dan H. Laurence and Margot Peters, 67–71. University Park: Pennsylvania State University Press, 1996.

Pharand, Michel W. "The River-God and the Thinker: Auguste Rodin Reinvents Bernard Shaw." *Journal of Inquiry and Research* [Osaka] 63 (February 1996): 137–52.

———. "Bernard Shaw, Proto-Existentialist: 'Don Juan in Hell' and Jean-Paul Sartre's *Huis clos.*" *Journal of Inquiry and Research* [Osaka] 64 (August 1996): 59–70.

Puelle, Leah. "A Begrudged Debt." *Pearl* (September 1995–May 1996): 2. [on Scribe]

1998

Galliou, Patrick. "George Bernard Shaw et Augustin Hamon: Les Premiers Temps d'une correspondance (1893–1913)." 4 vols. Ph.D. diss. Centre de Recherche Breton et Celtique, Université Bretagne Occidentale, Brest, 1998. [edition of Shaw-Hamon letters]

Pharand, Michel W. "Bernard Shaw's Bonaparte: Life Force or Death Wish?" In *Shaw and Other Matters: A Festschrift for Stanley Weintraub on the Occasion of His Forty-Second Anniversary at the Pennsylvania State University,* edited by Susan Rusinko, 41–52. London: Associated University Presses, 1998.

———. "The Siren on the Rock: Bernard Shaw vs. Sarah Bernhardt." In *SHAW, the Annual of Bernard Shaw Studies,* vol. 18, edited by Fred D. Crawford, 33–44. University Park: Pennsylvania State University Press, 1998.

2000

Crawford, Fred D. "Shaw in Translation." In *SHAW, the Annual of Bernard Shaw Studies,* vol. 20, edited by Dan H. Laurence and Fred D. Crawford, assisted by Mary Ann K. Crawford, 200–203. University Park: Pennsylvania State University Press, 2000. [chronological list of Shaw plays in French translation]

Notes

Abbreviations used in the notes:
Letters 1: Dan H. Laurence, ed., *Bernard Shaw: Collected Letters 1874–1897*
Letters 2: Dan H. Laurence, ed., *Bernard Shaw: Collected Letters 1898–1910*
Letters 3: Dan H. Laurence, ed., *Bernard Shaw: Collected Letters 1911–1925*
Letters 4: Dan H. Laurence, ed., *Bernard Shaw: Collected Letters 1926–1950*
Plays 1–7: Dan H. Laurence, ed., *The Bodley Head Bernard Shaw: Collected Plays with Their Prefaces*, 7 volumes

* * *

Preface

1. Already published by L'Arche are: *Androclès et le lion, Un Bourreau des coeurs, Candida, L'Homme et les Armes, L'Homme du destin, La Maison des coeurs brisés, Les Maisons des veufs, La Milliardaire, On ne peut jamais dire, La Profession de Madame Warren, Pygmalion,* and *Sainte Jeanne.* L'Arche's *Catalogue des pièces de théâtre 1999–2000* lists the following Shaw works as being "sous forme de manuscrit à L'Arche": *César et Cléopâtre, Comment il mentit au mari, Conversion du capitaine Brassbound, Disciple du diable, Fables tirées par les cheveux, La Grande Catherine, Idylle villageoise, Mariage,* and *Passion, poison et pétrification.*

Introduction: Shaw as Francophobe and Francophile

1. Saurat, "A G.B.S. Symposium," 8.
2. Shaw and Jean-Jacques Rousseau (1712–78) had ineffectual fathers, were music critics and amateur musicians, dressed unconventionally (Shaw in Jaeger suits and Rousseau in "Armenian" clothes), and believed in natural development over discipline in child rearing. See Barzun, "Shaw and Rousseau." In 1950, Shaw wrote that "Rousseau told the world two thundering lies, both of which the Churches swallowed with shut eyes and open mouth. Number one: men are born free. Number two: Get rid of your miracles and the whole world will fall at the feet of Jesus" ("A Tribute to a Great Churchman," 13 January 1950, in Tyson, *Shaw's Book Reviews* [1996], 539). For more on Rousseau and miracles, see the preface to *Androcles and the Lion,* in *Plays* 4, 485.
3. Shaw, unpublished letter to Mina Moore, quoted in her *Bernard Shaw et la France,* 71.
4. On 22 April 1886, in Weintraub, *Diaries,* 163. Shaw saw the English stage

version (by George Moore and translator Alexander Teixeira de Mattos) on 9 October 1891 (*Diaries,* 758).

5. Quoted in Wisenthal, *Shaw's Sense of History,* 15. Dumas's output was prodigious: plays, historical romances, journalism, and ten volumes of *Mes Mémoires.*

6. Shaw, letter to John Maynard Keynes, 30 November 1934, in *Letters* 4, 390. *Das Kapital* appeared in three volumes: 1867, 1885, 1894.

7. Weintraub's edition of Shaw's *Diaries* is indispensable for Shaw's early French readings.

8. Shaw, undated letter to H. G. Wells, c. 4–5 November 1934, in Smith, *Selected Correspondence,* 174. See Shaw's comments on Rousseau's "very ridiculous confession" (about flogging) in the preface to *Getting Married* (in *Plays* 3, 471).

9. Shaw, unpublished letter to Diana Watts, 22 July 1948, Charles Oringer Collection.

10. Laurence and Peters, *Unpublished Shaw,* 118.

11. Shaw, letter to the *Star,* 2 November 1888, in Laurence and Rambeau, *Agitations,* 12.

12. Laurence and Peters, *Unpublished Shaw,* 31, 32.

13. Shaw, "The Problem Play: A Symposium," *Humanitarian,* May 1895. Shaw's early theater reviews and other writings on drama are reprinted in Dukore, *Drama Observed.*

14. Shaw, "Preface to Three Plays by Brieux," 1909, in Dukore, *Drama Observed,* 1190–92.

15. Shaw, letter to William Archer, 24 January 1900, in *Letters* 2, 138.

16. Shaw, "The Revolutionist's Handbook," in *Plays* 2, 756.

17. Shaw, "Preface to Three Plays by Brieux," 1220. The reference is not to the novel but to *The Liquor Store* (1879), a stage adaptation by Zola and William B. Busnach.

18. Shaw, letter to Augustin Hamon, 21 March 1910, in *Letters* 2, 914.

19. Shaw, "Preface to Three Plays by Brieux," 1190.

20. Shaw, "Mr. George Moore's New Novel," 19 July 1887, in Tyson, *Shaw's Book Reviews* (1991), 303.

21. Shaw, letter to Erica Cotterill, 28 September 1905, in *Letters* 2, 563.

22. Shaw, "Preface to Three Plays by Brieux," 1188. It has been pointed out that when Shaw wrote in 1895, "But if I thought that people were picking up the French trick of reading dramatic works, I should be strongly tempted to publish my plays instead of bothering to get them performed," he "seems to be referring to a large-scale purchase of published playtexts," for which there appears to be no evidence. (Shaw, letter to T. Fisher Unwin, 9 September 1895, in *Letters* 1, 557; Kelly, "Imprinting the Stage," 52, n. 7.)

23. See Shaw's 1886 commentary on Proudhon's *Qu'est-ce que la Propriété?* (1840), in Laurence and Peters, *Unpublished Shaw,* 133–37.

24. Shaw, "Ideal London," 5 October 1886, in Tyson, *Shaw's Book Reviews* (1991), 205; see explanatory note in Tyson, *Shaw's Book Reviews* (1996), 365.

25. See Gibbs, *The Art and Mind of Shaw*, 150. See Kaye, *Bernard Shaw*, 40–48, for Shaw's treatment of "the ideal Comtian capitalist, Andrew Undershaft . . . [as] partially a critique of Comtianism" (45).

26. Weintraub, *Diaries*, 1175.

27. Shaw, "Idolatry of the Glory Merchant Is Sheer Illusion," 19 May 1946, in Tyson, *Shaw's Book Reviews* (1996), 529.

28. Shaw, "One of the Worst," *Saturday Review*, 28 December 1895. In 1894, Jewish officer Alfred Dreyfus (1859–1935) was accused of treason and sentenced to life on Devil's Island. On 13 January 1898, Zola published "J'accuse," an open letter denouncing the civil and military cover-up; the next year a retrial was ordered. Zola was sentenced to one year in prison for libel but escaped to England and spent a year in exile. He died in 1902; Dreyfus was acquitted in 1906. In 1909, Shaw praised Zola's smashing the conspiracy of "the officers and gentlemen who represented the old nobility and the old religion of France" ("Bernard Shaw on Shams of Rule and of Religion," 21 November 1909, in Tyson, *Shaw's Book Reviews* [1996], 230).

29. Quoted in Moore, *Bernard Shaw et la France*, 52.

30. Shaw, "Delsartism," *Our Corner*, September 1886. Deck had studied under François Delsarte and (according to Shaw) "had recognized in him a . . . faultless teacher of elocution, deportment, and gesture."

31. *Un Petit Drame* (in *Plays* 7, 528–32) first appeared in *Esquire* magazine (December 1959, 172–74), with translation by Norman Denny and introduction by Stanley Weintraub. Denny misreads the misprint *Ambeth* as *Macbeth*. Shaw's French text in *Esquire* is corrupt throughout.

32. Shaw's playlet may have been a reaction to his father's "chronic intoxication and subsequent surliness and abusiveness" (*Esquire*, 173). Like Arri, George Carr Shaw was left behind by his wife and daughter—and by Bernard—in 1876. Arri is most likely a parody of Mrs. Shaw's brother, Dr. Walter Gurly. For autobiographical references, see Weintraub's introduction in *Esquire*, 173.

33. See, for example, Shaw's heavily self-corrected manuscript draft of his letter to B. Guinandeau, 12 August 1892, in *Letters* 1, 354, about his reply to twenty-eight questions on British socialism for Georges Clemenceau's newspaper, *La Justice*.

34. Shaw, preface to *Misalliance*, in *Plays* 4, 39.

35. Quoted in "Shaw on *Saint Joan*," in Weintraub, *"Saint Joan" Fifty Years After*, 20.

36. See illustration in Hart-Davis, *A Catalogue*, 136.

37. Closset, *G. Bernard Shaw*, back cover.

38. Quoted in Rolland, *Deux Hommes*, 200–201.

39. Shaw, "Preface to Three Plays by Brieux," 1203; letter quoted in Grindea, "G.B.S. and France," 6.

40. Grindea, "G.B.S. and France," 1.

41. "Mr. Shaw and the French," *Times* [London], 21 February 1928, 14.

42. See Chase 1910, Boyd 1913, Ellehauge 1931, Henderson 1951, Grindea 1956, Amalric 1977, and Jomaron 1979 in appendix C.

43. Liébert, *Bernard Shaw: Écrits sur la musique,* back cover.

1. Shaw in the Picture-Galleries: "I am no critic of Art"

1. Shaw, "No Rules," *World,* 28 February 1894. Shaw's miscellaneous notes, reviews, and other writings on music are reprinted in Dan H. Laurence, ed., *Shaw's Music: The Complete Musical Criticism,* 3 vols.

2. Weintraub, *London Art Scene,* 42. Of the 181 pieces in *London Art Scene,* 170 had never been reprinted since their first publication.

3. Ibid., 242.

4. Ibid., 117–18.

5. Ibid., 152.

6. Ibid., 75, 127, 147, 222.

7. Ibid., 56, 78, 128, 270.

8. Ibid., 308, 409; Shaw, preface to *Saint Joan,* in Plays 6, 35.

9. Weintraub, *London Art Scene,* 405.

10. Shaw, "A Pride of Fausts," unsigned notes in *Dramatic Review,* 19 December 1885.

11. Weintraub, *London Art Scene,* 334–35.

12. Shaw, "The Effects of Electioneering," *World,* 6 July 1892.

13. Weintraub, *London Art Scene,* 194.

14. Shaw, "That Realism Is the Goal of Fiction," 117.

15. Weintraub, *London Art Scene,* 367, 368. Shaw's essay was reissued in 1908 as a small book, *The Sanity of Art.*

16. Weintraub, *London Art Scene,* 274–75, Shaw's emphasis.

17. Ibid., 121.

18. Shaw, speech of 11 March 1910, quoted in Weintraub, *London Art Scene,* 4.

19. Weintraub, *London Art Scene,* 121.

20. Ibid., 419.

21. Shaw, "Chestertonism and the War," 23 January 1915, quoted in Weintraub, *London Art Scene,* 36–37.

22. Weintraub, *London Art Scene,* 86, 144, 23.

23. The Gérôme is reproduced in Weintraub, *Unexpected Shaw,* 72.

24. See Whiting, "The Cleopatra Rug Scene," 15–17.

25. Meisel, "Cleopatra and 'The Flight into Egypt,'" 62.

26. Quoted in Pearson, *Bernard Shaw,* 221. Meisel writes that Shaw has predated the encounter by at least a dozen years ("Cleopatra and 'The Flight into Egypt,'" 62). The Merson is reproduced in Holroyd, *The Genius of Shaw,* 51.

27. Meisel, "Cleopatra and 'The Flight into Egypt,'" 63.

28. Hamon, letter to Georges Pitoëff, 23 January 1929, Hamon Collection, Special Collections of the McLaughlin Library, University of Guelph, Guelph, Canada. Referred to henceforth as Hamon Collection.

29. Weintraub, *London Art Scene,* 34–35.

30. Shaw, *Saint Joan*, in *Plays* 6, 99.
31. Weintraub, *London Art Scene*, 34.
32. Shaw, *Saint Joan*, 190. Fouquet (c. 1420–80); *Portrait de Charles VII* (c. 1446); *Boccace* (c. 1458).
33. Shaw, *Man and Superman*, in *Plays* 2, 534.
34. Weintraub, *London Art Scene*, 26. The *Hémicycle* is reproduced in Weintraub, *Unexpected Shaw*, 78.
35. Shaw, letter to J. Stanley Little, 26 August 1889, in *Letters* 1, 220.

2. Shaw in the Concert Halls: "I purposely vulgarized musical criticism"

1. Shaw, "No Rules," *World*, 28 February 1894.
2. Shaw, "The Religion of the Pianoforte," *Fortnightly Review*, February 1894.
3. Shaw, "Preface" (2 June 1935) to *London Music in 1888–89 as Heard by Corno di Bassetto*, in Laurence, *Shaw's Music*, vol. 1, 45.
4. Ibid., 55–56.
5. Weintraub, *Diaries*, 109.
6. Shaw, "Something Like a History of Music," 11 January 1887, in Tyson, *Shaw's Book Reviews* (1991), 236.
7. Shaw, "Wagner's Theories," *World*, 17 January 1894.
8. Shaw, "Preface," in Laurence, *Shaw's Music*, vol. 1, 58.
9. See Laurence, "Introduction," in Laurence, *Shaw's Music*, vol. 1, 20–21.
10. See Liébert, "Avant-propos," xxix–xxx.
11. Shaw, "Philémon et Baucis," *World*, 25 November 1891.
12. Lee, "The Skilled Voluptuary," 149.
13. Shaw, "Music of the Revolution," *Star*, 13 May 1889; "Samson et Dalila," *World*, 4 October 1893; "Garrick to the Life," *World*, 27 May 1891.
14. Shaw, letter to Ernest Newman, 25 October 1917, in *Letters* 3, 512.
15. Shaw, "Paris: A Pedant-Ridden Failure," *Star*, 11 April 1890; "A Backward Glance at the Opera Season," *World*, 6 August 1890; "Italian Opera and the French Dickens," *World*, 20 August 1890; "Concerts and Recitals," *World*, 17 May 1893; "Samson et Dalila"; "Yvette Guilbert," *World*, 16 May 1894; "Paris: A Pedant- Ridden Failure."
16. Shaw, "Spoof Opera, by a Ghost from the 'Eighties," *Nation* [London], 7 July 1917.
17. See Shaw, "Hamlet: A Foolish Opera," *World*, 30 July 1890; "Concerts," *Star*, 3 March 1890.
18. Shaw, "English Music," *World*, 14 March 1894, Shaw's emphases.
19. Shaw, "Aïda Gallicized," unsigned notes in *Dramatic Review*, 13 June 1885, Shaw's emphasis.
20. Shaw, "Bizet Italianized," *Star*, 20 May 1889.
21. See Shaw, "Philémon et Baucis."
22. Shaw, "The Music Season in London," *Bradford Observer*, 30 November 1891, unsigned.

23. Shaw, "No Rules"; see Shaw on Bruneau's love of Wagner's "good sense and logic" in *Die Walküre*, which Shaw thought absurd.

24. Shaw, "All About the Brigands," *Star*, 20 September 1889.

25. Shaw, "Causerie on Handel in England," *Ainslee's Magazine*, May 1913; no title, *Nation*, 1 August 1914; "Old Men and New Music," undated essay (c. 1930?), in Laurence, *Shaw's Music*, vol. 3, 751–52.

26. See Shaw, "Saint-Saëns and Raff," unsigned notes in *Dramatic Review*, 12 December 1885.

27. Shaw, "Paris: A Pedant-Ridden Failure"; "A Caged Critic," *World*, 14 June 1893.

28. Shaw, "What Impression Do I Produce?" *World*, 4 May 1892.

29. Shaw, "A Concert of Nearly Reasonable Length," *World*, 7 June 1893.

30. Shaw, "A Bodiless Spook," *World*, 18 October 1893. In July, Shaw recalled hearing Saint-Saëns play that Bach fugue "more than a dozen years ago" and found him "an excellent organist" ("Impervious to Counterpoint," *World*, 5 July 1893).

31. Shaw, "Half a Century Behind," *World*, 25 October 1893.

32. Shaw, "On Musical Criticism," *World*, 13 June 1894.

33. Shaw, "Model Testimony of Witnesses on Censorship," July 1909, in Dukore, *Drama Observed*, 1170.

34. Shaw, "Samson et Dalila."

35. Shaw, "No Rules."

36. Ibid.; Shaw, "Samson et Dalila."

37. Shaw, "A Ducal Opera," unsigned review in *Hornet*, 4 July 1877; "Hullah and Music," unsigned review in *Pall Mall Gazette*, 3 March 1886; "Signor Gayarré's Self-Complacency," unsigned review in *Hornet*, 25 April 1877.

38. Shaw, "Preface," Laurence, *Shaw's Music*, vol. 1, 57.

39. Shaw, "Going Fantee," *World*, 10 May 1893.

40. Shaw, "Ruskin on Music," *World*, 2 May 1894.

41. Shaw, "Composers and Professors in the Coming Century," *Musician*, 19 May 1897.

42. Shaw, "Municipal Bands and Opera Tricks," *World*, 2 July 1890.

43. Shaw, "The Basoche," *World*, 11 November 1891; Shaw, "Samson et Dalila."

44. Shaw, "The Merits of Meyerbeer," unsigned review in *Hornet*, 1 August 1877.

45. Shaw, "Garrick to the Life."

46. Weintraub, *Diaries*, 43, 44, 621.

47. See Shaw, "Staleness of the Opera Season," *World*, 6 June 1894.

48. Shaw, "The Religion of the Pianoforte."

49. Shaw, *The Perfect Wagnerite*, in Laurence, *Shaw's Music*, vol. 3, 530–31.

50. Shaw, "Italian Opera and the French Dickens," *World*, 20 August 1890; "Concerts Beyond Count," *World*, 9 July 1890.

51. Shaw, "Manon," *Dramatic Review*, 16 May 1885.

52. Shaw, "Art Corner," *Our Corner,* July 1885.
53. See Shaw, "Miss Eames Self-Possessed," *World,* 20 June 1894.
54. Shaw, "La Navarraise," *World,* 27 June 1894.
55. Shaw, "L'Amico Fritz," *World,* 1 June 1892.
56. Shaw, "Twenty Years Too Late," *World,* 30 May 1894.
57. Shaw, "German Opera at Drury Lane," *World,* 18 July 1894.
58. Shaw, "The New Magdalen and the Old," *Saturday Review,* 2 November 1895.
59. Shaw, "Miss Nethersole and Mrs Kendal," *Saturday Review,* 13 June 1896. Shaw called Mérimée's *Carmen* (1845) an "admirably told story" ("Romantic Music," 9 May 1885, unsigned notes in *Dramatic Review*).
60. Shaw, "Gluck's Orfeo," *World,* 15 April 1891.
61. Liébert, "Avant-propos," xxix–xxx. For parallels between *Carmen* and act 3 of *Man and Superman,* see Corballis, "Why the Devil," 170–74.
62. Shaw, "Mozart's Finality," *World,* 9 December 1891.
63. Corballis, "Why the Devil," 169, examples listed.
64. Shaw, "The Don Giovanni Centenary," *Pall Mall Gazette,* 31 October 1887, signed "By our Special Wagnerite."
65. In Shaw, *Man and Superman,* in *Plays* 2, 643, 645, Shaw's emphases.
66. Corballis, "Why the Devil," 169, 179, n. 9.
67. Shaw, "Men and Women of the Day: Madame Christine Nilsson and M. Faure," unsigned review in *Hornet,* 6 June 1877.
68. Shaw, "The Search for Another Messiah," unsigned notes in *Dramatic Review,* 29 August 1885.
69. Shaw, "A Pride of Fausts," unsigned notes in *Dramatic Review,* 19 December 1885.
70. Shaw, "Faust and Ancient Instruments," *World,* 28 May 1890.
71. Shaw, "Gounod's Music," *World,* 22 February 1893. See Shaw's amusing comments in "Philémon et Baucis."
72. Shaw, "Faust and Ancient Instruments," *World,* 28 May 1890.
73. Shaw, "Gluck's Orfeo."
74. Shaw, "Wagner's Birthday," *World,* 3 June 1891.
75. Shaw, "The Proms," unsigned review in *Hornet,* 22 August 1877.
76. Shaw, "Jean de Reszke's Romeo," *Star,* 17 June 1889; "The Opera Season," *Scottish Art Review,* September 1889. See Shaw's synopsis in "All About Romeo and Juliet," *Star,* 14 June 1889, with act 4's "most wonderful and passionate love duet."
77. Shaw, "Canterbury Kinfreederl and a Lighthouse," *Star,* 3 January 1890; Shaw, "Philémon et Baucis."
78. Weintraub, *Diaries,* 107, 308.
79. Shaw, "The Search for Another Messiah."
80. Shaw, "Mors et Vita," unsigned notes in *Dramatic Review,* 7 November 1885.
81. Shaw, "Art Corner," *Our Corner,* December 1885.

82. Shaw, "The Redemption at the Crystal Palace," *Dramatic Review*, 8 May 1886.

83. Shaw, "Gounod's Music."

84. Shaw, "Oh, Aint It Awful!" *World*, 1 April 1891.

85. Shaw, "Constructing an Oratorio," *World*, 18 April 1894; Shaw, "A Crowd of Concerts," *World*, 25 July 1894.

86. Shaw, "Half a Century Behind"; Shaw, "A Sulphurous Sublimity," *World*, 8 November 1893. Shaw had briefly reviewed a mediocre French *Mireille* (1864) in "Mireille," *World*, 17 June 1891.

87. Shaw, "Preface to Three Plays by Brieux," 1909, in Dukore, *Drama Observed*, 1198.

88. Shaw, "Modern Men: Sir Arthur Sullivan," unsigned article in *Scots Observer*, 6 September 1890.

89. Shaw, "Madame Angot Returns," *World*, 26 July 1893.

90. Shaw, "Irish Patriotism and Italian Opera," *World*, 15 November 1893.

91. Shaw, "Some Other Critics," *Saturday Review*, 20 June 1896. Meisel writes that the combination of political satire with the domestic and amorous interests of the ruler of a mythical kingdom in *La Grande Duchesse* is found in *The Apple Cart* (Meisel, *Shaw*, 391).

92. Shaw, "The Basoche."

93. Weintraub, *Diaries*, 768.

94. Shaw, "The Music Season in London."

95. See Shaw, "Three New Operas," *World*, 11 July 1894.

96. Weintraub, *Diaries*, 43. *Voyage* is untranslated, and the *Autobiography of Hector Berlioz* (1884) appeared four years after Shaw's readings.

97. Shaw, "Will Gluck Conquer London?" *World*, 12 November 1890.

98. Barzun, "Berlioz and Shaw," 69.

99. Shaw, "Cavalleria Rusticana," *World*, 28 October 1891.

100. Shaw, "Art Corner."

101. Shaw, "A Sulphurous Sublimity."

102. Shaw, "Berlioz's Episode," unsigned notes in *Dramatic Review*, 5 December 1885, Shaw's emphases.

103. Shaw, "The Fourth Brinsmead Concert," unsigned notes in *Dramatic Review*, 26 December 1885. Shaw noted a "magnificent performance" of the *Symphonie Fantastique* by the Hallé Orchestra in "Jack-Acting," *World*, 17 December 1890.

104. See Barzun, "Berlioz and Shaw," 69–70.

105. Barzun notes that Shaw recorded six sessions of Berlioz research in the British Museum between 26 February and 7 July 1880, "which suggests that the manuscript date of 29 February could be wrong" (ibid.," 71). See Weintraub, *Diaries*, 37–51.

106. Barzun, "Berlioz and Shaw," 68; for a summary of where Shaw departs from or distorts the facts of Berlioz's life, see 68–69.

107. Ibid., 71, 86, 79, 84.

108. Valency, *Cart,* 419.

109. Shaw, "Wagner's Theories."

110. Knapp and Chipman, *That Was Yvette,* 117–18. Arthur Symons, who saw Guilbert perform in Paris two months before Shaw did in London, praised her "tragic realism, touched with a sort of grotesque irony, which is a new thing on any stage," in a December 1915 *Vanity Fair* essay. See his *Plays, Acting, and Music,* 50.

111. Shaw, "Yvette Guilbert." *World,* Compare Symons's "Yvette Guilbert Last Night," *Star,* 4 December 1894: 2.

112. Shaw, "Yvette Guilbert."

113. Ibid.

114. Letter of Guilbert to Shaw, 19 March 1907, Bernard Shaw Papers, British Library, 50515, folio 14, Guilbert's emphases.

115. Hamon, *Le Molière,* 6.

116. Shaw, letter to Augustin Hamon, 2 July 1908, in *Letters* 2, 797.

117. Shaw, "Yvette Guilbert."

118. Guilbert, *The Song,* 316–17. This 1929 translation of Guilbert's 1927 memoirs contains ten new chapters (mostly about her visits to London and New York) and two additional "Portraits," one of Symons and one of Shaw, the latter a diary entry.

119. Quoted in Russell, "Yvette Guilbert *chez* Shaw," 62. Saint-Saëns, Twain, and Kipling were also honored at the 26 June 1907 Oxford ceremony. See Grunfeld, *Rodin,* 543–44.

3. The Old Grooves: Shaw and the French Theater

1. Quoted in John, "Actor as Puppet," 245. In his violent polemic "Le Comédien," Mirbeau called the actor "ce prostituteur de la beauté" (8). See Constant Coquelin's rejoinder, "Les Comédiens," in *Le Temps* (1 November 1882). Both essays appeared as a pamphlet (Paris: Brunox, 1883).

2. Shaw, "Delsartism," *Our Corner,* September 1886.

3. Quoted in Cole and Chinoy, *Actors on Acting,* 187–88, Delsarte's emphases. See his *System of Oratory* translated by Abby L. Alger (New York: Edgar S. Werner, 1893).

4. Shaw, "Delsartism."

5. Stokes et al., *Bernhardt, Terry, Duse,* 5. Popular handbooks included Bernier de Maligny's *Théorie de l'art du comédien* (1826, revised 1854) and Charles de Bussy's *Dictionnaire de l'art dramatique* (1866). See also Francïsque Sarcey's *Essai d'esthétique de théâtre* (1876).

6. Weintraub, *Diaries,* 408.

7. Shaw, "Royalty Theatre . . . French v. English Histrionics," *Star,* 1 February 1889, signed Julius Floemmochser.

8. Lemaître, *Souvenirs,* 319–20.

9. Hemmings, *Theatre Industry,* 177, 285, n.6.

10. Shaw, "The Stage as a Profession," *Morning Post,* 29 November 1897.

11. Shaw, preface to *Overruled,* in *Plays* 4, 838, 839. "Our school is one of

chronic sentimentality and solemn feebleness," Shaw wrote about English acting in "Ten Minutes With Mr Bernard Shaw," *Today,* 28 April 1894.

12. See Hemmings, *Theatre Industry,* 212–17. Talma (1763–1826), who opted for realistic (but often violently emotional) portrayals, could vary the same lines to suit the performance or the inspiration of the moment (218). Sarcey (1827–1899) was "an informed, often subtle and perceptive" critic whose preference for well-made plays "earned him the quite unmerited reputation of being a narrow traditionalist." See Carlson, *Theories of the Theatre,* 282.

13. Shaw, "L'Oeuvre," *Saturday Review,* 30 March 1895; Shaw, letter to William Archer, 18 April 1889, in *Letters* 1, 208. Sacha Guitry said that when Mounet spoke to you, he sounded as though he were shouting across a river (Gold and Fizdale, *Divine Sarah,* 99).

14. Shaw, letter to Ellen Terry, 12 October 1899, in *Letters* 2, 109.

15. Shaw, "Two Plays," *Saturday Review,* 8 June 1895.

16. Bernhardt, *L'Art du théâtre,* 48.

17. Shaw, "Royalty Theatre . . . French v. English Histrionics"; Shaw, "Mr John Hare," *Saturday Review,* 21 December 1895; Shaw, "Acting, by One Who Does Not Believe in It," 5 February 1889, paper read at the Church and Stage Guild, in Dukore, *Drama Observed,* 96, 97.

18. Shaw, "Acting, by One Who Does Not Believe in It," 97, Shaw's emphasis.

19. Shaw, "Mr John Hare."

20. Shaw, letter to Augustin Hamon, 3 July 1908, in *Letters* 2, 798.

21. Shaw, "Preface to Ellen Terry and Bernard Shaw: A Correspondence," 26 June 1929, in Dukore, *Drama Observed,* 1433; Shaw, "The Stage as a Profession."

22. For "The Dual Personality of the Actor," see Cole and Chinoy, *Actors on Acting,* 192–202.

23. Quoted ibid., 194.

24. See Carlson, *Theories of the Theatre,* 235–36. Alluding to *Masks or Faces?* on 5 February 1889, Shaw mentioned that Archer's research included a request to critic and dramatist Jules Lemaître (1853–1914) for information on French actors (see Dukore, *Drama Observed,* 94). See *Nineteenth Century* 21 (June 1887): 800–803, and *Harper's Weekly,* 12 November 1887.

25. Shaw, "Poor Shakespear!" *Saturday Review,* 6 July 1895; Shaw, "The Shooting Star Season," *Saturday Review,* 10 July 1897.

26. Valency, *The End,* 6.

27. Valency, *Cart,* 79.

28. Shaw, "On the Principles that Govern the Dramatist," *New York Times,* 2 June 1912.

29. Shaw, "The Author's Apology," preface to *Dramatic Opinions and Essays,* October 1906, in Dukore, *Drama Observed,* 1132–34.

30. Valency, *Cart,* 49.

31. See the following articles by Shaw: "Antoinette Rigaud," *Our Corner,* April 1886; "La Princesse Lointaine," *Saturday Review,* 22 June 1895; "The Chili Widow," *Saturday Review,* 12 October 1895; "The Return of Mrs Pat," *Saturday*

Review, 7 March 1896; "The Shooting Star Season"; "On Deadheads and Other Matters," *Saturday Review,* 31 October 1896; "Lorenzaccio," *Saturday Review,* 26 June 1897; and "Miss Nethersole and Mrs Kendal."

32. Shaw, "Two Plays"; Shaw, "Poor Shakespear!"; Shaw, "L'Oeuvre."
33. Shaw, "Quickwit on Blockhead," *Saturday Review,* 5 June 1897.
34. Shaw, "On the Principles that Govern the Dramatist."
35. Driver, *Romantic Quest,* 46.
36. Ibid., 47.
37. Stanton, "Introduction," xi.
38. Valency, *Flower,* 63.
39. Taylor, *The Rise and Fall,* 12.
40. Valency, *Flower,* 64.
41. See Driver, *Romantic Quest,* 47–48, and Stanton, "Introduction," xii–xv.
42. Valency, *Flower,* 67.
43. Ibid., 64–65, Valency's emphasis. For a fine scene-by-scene analysis of *Le Verre d'eau,* see Stanton, "Introduction," xvi–xix. Driver, *Romantic Quest* (49–52), adds four thematic characteristics: (1) Topicality: "Scribe's topicality was tailor-made to fit the taste of a middle class newly educated by the national system of schools and universities Napoleon had set up." (2) Avoidance of all metaphysical concerns and radical evil: "Metaphysics (in the realm of knowledge) and evil (in the realm of social morals) . . . cannot be reduced to logic." (3) Religion: "As long as religious opinions and sentiments do not raise fundamental questions about the given order of things." (4) Difficulties between the sexes: "Social incompatibility between married or engaged persons, money, differing moral standards, the presence of a 'third party' or a 'fallen woman,' and so on."
44. Quoted in Henderson, *Shaw, Playboy and Prophet,* 595.
45. Valency, *Flower,* 66.
46. Stanton, "Shaw's Debt to Scribe," 576, n. 8.
47. Bentley, "Foreword," ix.
48. Shaw, *The Quintessence of Ibsenism,* September 1891, 153; *The Quintessence of Ibsenism,* August 1913, 1293; both in Dukore, *Drama Observed.*
49. Bentley, "Foreword," xvi, xv, xviii.
50. Valency, *Cart,* 106.
51. Bentley, "Foreword," ix, xiv.
52. Stanton, "Introduction," xxxviii. For a synopsis of *La Bataille des dames,* see Stanton, "Shaw's Debt to Scribe," 579. "I am now preparing a study of Shaw's use of *La Bataille des Dames* in *Arms and the Man*" (578, n. 14). I was unable to trace this work.
53. Stanton, "Shaw's Debt to Scribe," 580–81. Valency believes *The Man of Destiny* was written in the style of *La Bataille des dames,* and that its plot resembles that of Sardou's *Dora* (1877) (see *Cart,* 145), which Shaw had seen as *Diplomacy* (1878), an adaptation by B. C. Stephenson and Clement Scott.
54. Holroyd, *Bernard Shaw,* 274–75.
55. Quoted in Gibbs, *Shaw: Interviews,* 120–21.

56. Bentley, "Foreword," xi.
57. Ibid., xii–xiii, x; Valency, *Cart*, 80. For a comparison of *Widowers' Houses* to Paul Hervieu's novel *L'Armature* (1895), see E.L.B. in *Le Réveil* (21 February 1908).
58. Shaw, "Robertson Redivivus," *Saturday Review*, 19 June 1897.
59. Stanton, "Introduction," xxxiii; Shaw, "Robertson Redivivus," *Saturday Review*, 19 June 1897.
60. Driver, *Romantic Quest*, 54.
61. Valency, *Flower*, 90.
62. Stanton, "Introduction," xxiii.
63. See the following articles by Shaw: "Acting, by One Who Does Not Believe in It," 103; "Two Bad Plays," *Saturday Review*, 20 April 1895; "Sardoodledom," *Saturday Review*, 1 June 1895; "Toujours Daly," *Saturday Review*, 13 July 1895; "Madame Sans-Gêne," *Saturday Review*, 17 April 1897; "The New Magda and the New Cyprienne," *Saturday Review*, 6 June 1896; and (on *La Tosca*) "Orchestral Concerts," *Star*, 31 January 1890.
64. Shaw, "The New Magda and the New Cyprienne."
65. Meisel, *Shaw*, 229.
66. Ibid., 266. For a plot synopsis of *Divorçons*, see 265–66. For a detailed summary, see Hart, *Sardou and the Sardou Plays*, 190–95.
67. Holroyd, *Bernard Shaw*, 198–99.
68. Shaw, "Toujours Daly."
69. Shaw, preface to *The Shewing-up of Blanco Posnet*, in Laurence, *Plays 3*, 716. Shaw saw *Mayfair* (1885), an adaptation of Sardou's *La Maison neuve* (1866), and refers often to *A Scrap of Paper*, or *Les Pattes de mouche* (1860). For a plot summary of the latter, see Stanton, "Introduction," xxiv–xxv.
70. Ervine, "Sardou," 13.
71. Shaw, "Alexander the Great," *Saturday Review*, 12 June 1897. "Nobody ever could, or did, or will improve on Dumas's romances and plays. . . . you get nothing above Dumas on his own mountain: he is the summit," Shaw wrote in July about Grundy's adaptation of *Mademoiselle de Belleisle* (1839), a play "expounded by its author with a dramatic perspicacity far beyond our most laborious efforts at play construction." But Grundy botched it with "pruderies," "wanton adulterations," and "blunders in stagecraft" ("Mr Grundy's Improvements on Dumas," *Saturday Review*, 17 July 1897).
72. Preface (1868) to *Un Père prodigue* (1859), quoted in Valency, *Cart*, 61.
73. Valency, *Flower*, 78, 79.
74. Shaw, "Slaves of the Ring," *Saturday Review*, 5 January 1895.
75. Quoted in Moore, *Bernard Shaw et la France*, 74–75, Dumas's emphases.
76. Shaw, "Two Plays"; Shaw, "Duse and Bernhardt," *Saturday Review*, 15 June 1895; Shaw, "Trilby and L'Ami des Femmes," *Saturday Review*, 9 November 1895.
77. Valency, *Cart*, 53. See also Moore, *Bernard Shaw et la France*, 74.
78. Carlson, *Theories of the Theatre*, 273–74. See Valency, *Cart*, 171.

79. Ellehauge, *The Position*, 359.
80. Quoted ibid., 112.
81. Meisel, *Shaw*, 143.
82. Shaw, "Two Plays." On the similarities of *La Dame aux camélias* to Scribe's *Adrienne Lecouvreur* (1849), see Stanton, "Introduction," xxvi–xxxii. In "Two Plays," Shaw refers in passing to Janet Achurch's 1893 performance as Adrienne, and in 1906 mentions "the old conventional mortuary ending of Adrienne Lecouvreur" ("Ibsen," *Clarion*, 1 June 1906). For a synopsis of the play, see Taylor, *The Rise and Fall*, 12–14.
83. Weintraub, *Diaries*, 176.
84. Shaw, letter to Elizabeth Robins, 19 October 1891, in *Letters* 1, 314.
85. For Coquelin on his role as Thouvenin, see Cole and Chinoy, *Actors on Acting*, 196.
86. Shaw, "The Stage as a Profession"; Shaw, "Bernard Shaw Talks About Actors and Acting," speech at the Royal Academy of Dramatic Art, London, 7 December 1928, published in *New York Times*, 6 January 1929; Shaw, "Preface to Ellen Terry and Bernard Shaw: A Correspondence," 1427; Shaw, "The Independent Theatre," *Saturday Review*, 26 January 1895.
87. Shaw, "*Vendetta!*" 11 September 1886, in Tyson, *Shaw's Book Reviews* (1991), 189.
88. Shaw, "Two Unimpressive Pamphlets," 23 July 1888, in Tyson, *Shaw's Book Reviews* (1991), 425.
89. Shaw, "*Vendetta!*" 11 September 1886, in Tyson, *Shaw's Book Reviews* (1991), 191. For Tyson's translation of those clauses, see 191–92.
90. Dumas *fils*, "Préface," 45. Valency quotes the lines in *Cart* (233), translating *disponible* as "expendable."
91. Shaw, "The Farcical Comedy Outbreak," *Saturday Review*, 9 May 1896; Shaw, "On Deadheads and Other Matters." Shaw also found many English "pieces of farcical clockwork," such as Wilde's *The Importance of Being Earnest*: "The humor is adulterated by stock mechanical fun" ("An Old New Play and a New Old One," *Saturday Review*, 23 February 1895).
92. Achard, "Georges Feydeau," 357, 363. "There is not a single detail, not one, which is not necessary to the action as a whole; there is not a single word which, at a given moment, does not have its repercussion in the comedy—and this one word, I have no idea why, buries itself in our subconscious, only to issue forth at the precise moment when it must illumine an incident we were not anticipating, but which we find entirely natural, and which delights us because it sounds improvised—and because we realize that we should have foreseen it" (357–58).
93. Baker, *Georges Feydeau*, 113, 149, n. 25.
94. Quoted in Carlson, *Theories of the Theatre*, 270.
95. Valency, *Cart*, 78. "I should be satisfied with the Théâtre Français," wrote Shaw, "if I were allowed to make a clean sweep of the mass of superstitions which M. Antoine quite rightly protests against" ("Ten Minutes with Mr Bernard

Shaw"). See excerpts from *Le Théâtre Libre* in Cole and Chinoy, *Actors on Acting*, 211–16.

96. Stanton, "Introduction," x.

97. Valency, *Cart,* 93, 152, 380.

98. Meisel, *Shaw,* 317. There were two adaptations: *The Romance of a Poor Young Man* by Edwards and Wallack, and *A Hero of Romance* by Westland Marston.

99. Quoted in Meisel, *Shaw,* 216.

100. Shaw, "Mr Irving Takes Paregoric," *Saturday Review,* 11 May 1895; Shaw, "Two Plays."

101. Meisel, *Shaw,* 218.

102. Quoted ibid., 218, 219.

103. See Stanton, "Introduction," xxxvii–xxxviii.

104. Shaw, "Preface to Three Plays by Brieux," 1909, in Dukore, *Drama Observed,* 1198, 1200.

105. Shaw, "The Drama, The Theatre, and the Films," *Fortnightly Review,* 1 September 1924, Shaw's emphasis.

106. Shaw, letter to Augustin Hamon, 26 November 1938, in *Letters* 4, 519.

107. Shaw, "Sullivan, Shakespeare, and Shaw," *Strand,* October 1947.

4. The Siren on the Rock: An Exasperation with Sarah Bernhardt

1. Gold and Fizdale, *Divine Sarah,* 3.

2. Stokes, "Sarah Bernhardt," 35.

3. Boulton, *Letters of D. H. Lawrence,* 58. Lawrence was so affected by the climactic scene of *La Dame aux camélias* that "he rushed from his seat and battered on the door of the theatre until an attendant let him out" (Stokes, "Sarah Bernhardt," 55).

4. Shaw, "Acting, by One Who Does Not Believe in It," 5 February 1889, in Dukore, *Drama Observed,* 103. On the Sardou-Bernhardt collaboration, see Aston, *Sarah Bernhardt,* 57–73. This excellent study details all of Bernhardt's London productions.

5. Stokes, "Sarah Bernhardt," 36.

6. Horville, "The Stage Techniques of Sarah Bernhardt," 37, 40. This fine essay uses contemporary reviews of Bernhardt's performances.

7. Quoted ibid., 58.

8. Shaw, "Acting, by One Who Does Not Believe in It," 103.

9. Stokes, "Sarah Bernhardt," 42.

10. Valency, *Cart,* 84.

11. Quoted in Trewin, "Bernhardt on the London Stage," 116.

12. Quoted ibid., 117.

13. See Shaw, "Royalty Theatre . . . French v. English Histrionics," *Star,* 1 February 1889.

14. Stokes, "Sarah Bernhardt," 32.

15. Lemaître, "Mme Sarah Bernhardt," 205.

16. Quoted in Horville, "The Stage Techniques," 43.
17. Stokes, "Sarah Bernhardt," 57.
18. Ibid.," 35.
19. Shaw, "On the Living and the Dead," *Saturday Review*, 25 December 1897.
20. Shaw, "Le Maître de Forges and The Money Spinner," *Our Corner*, August 1885.
21. Weintraub, *London Art Scene*, 123. See portrait by Jules Bastien-Lepage (1848–84) in Richardson, *Sarah Bernhardt*, 52.
22. Weintraub, *Diaries*, 295.
23. Shaw (unsigned), "From Our London Correspondent," *Manchester Guardian*, 19 July 1887. I am grateful to Bernard F. Dukore for providing a copy of this review.
24. Stokes, "Sarah Bernhardt," 43.
25. Quoted ibid., 44.
26. Quoted in Horville, "The Stage Techniques," 47.
27. Terry, *Ellen Terry's Memoirs*, 168.
28. Quoted in Horville, "The Stage Techniques," 45, 47, 57. See Stokes, "Sarah Bernhardt," for a detailed account and description of *Théodora* (37–44) and *Phèdre* (48–52). For a Nadar photograph of Bernhardt as Théodora (1884), see 14. For Bernhardt as Phèdre in hieratic postures (1895), see 49–50; for Bernhardt as Doña Sol (c. 1877), 33.
29. Stokes et al., "Introduction," *Bernhardt, Terry, Duse*, 8.
30. Weintraub, *Diaries*, 834.
31. Shaw, "The Musical Revolution," *Musical Courier*, September 1894. In his diary on 21 June 1894, Shaw noted that he planned to attend (but did not) "Bernhardt's lecture on 'Vocal Methods'" at the Brinsmead Galleries that day. See Weintraub, *Diaries*, 1035.
32. Quoted in Horville, "The Stage Techniques," 63.
33. Ibid., 31.
34. Lemaître, "Mme Sarah Bernhardt," 209.
35. Shaw, "L'Oeuvre," *Saturday Review*, 30 March 1895.
36. Shaw, letters to Janet Achurch, 23 April 1895 and 20 May 1897, and to Ellen Terry, 4 July 1897, in *Letters* 1, 529, 765–66, 780.
37. Horville, "The Stage Techniques," 60, 62.
38. For Guilbert's skit on Bernhardt's death scene in *Cléopâtre* and its hilarious song, "Le Petit Serpent de Sarah," see Guilbert, *La Chanson*, 211–12. The song "amusa beaucoup Sardou quand il l'entendit, mais agaça [irritated] Sarah" (211).
39. Horville, "The Stage Techniques," 61.
40. Quoted in Gold and Fizdale, *Divine Sarah*, 4.
41. Shaw, "Two Anonymous Communications," *Star*, 22 November 1889; Shaw, "Paris: A Pedant-Ridden Failure," *Star*, 11 April 1890.
42. Quoted in Horville, "The Stage Techniques," 60, 61.
43. Horville, "The Stage Techniques," 61–62.
44. Shaw, "Sardoodledom," *Saturday Review*, 1 June 1895.

45. Shaw, letter to Florence Farr, 6 June 1902, in *Letters* 2, 274.
46. Shaw, "At Several Theatres," *Saturday Review*, 9 October 1897.
47. Shaw, letter to Ellen Terry, 17 January 1915, in *Letters* 3, 283.
48. Dukore, "Introduction," *Drama Observed*, xxxii.
49. Shaw, "Duse and Bernhardt," *Saturday Review*, 15 June 1895.
50. Quoted in Horville, "The Stage Techniques," 42.
51. Ibid., 44.
52. Quoted ibid., 41.
53. Shaw, "The Theatre in England," *Argus* [Melbourne], 28 March 1896.
54. Gold and Fizdale, *Divine Sarah*, 255–56.
55. Shaw, "La Princesse lointaine," *Saturday Review*, 22 June 1895.
56. Quoted in Horville, "The Stage Techniques," 62.
57. Shaw, "Lorenzaccio," *Saturday Review*, 26 June 1897.
58. Quoted in Horville, "The Stage Techniques," 56.
59. Quoted in Gold and Fizdale, *Divine Sarah*, 261.
60. Shaw, letter to Augustin Hamon, 4 December 1906, in *Letters* 2, 664.
61. Shaw, letter to Ellen Terry, 15 May 1903, in *Letters* 2, 325.
62. Shaw, letter to Gertrude Kingston, 6 July 1917, in Laurence, *Selected Correspondence*, 139.
63. Shaw, "Lorenzaccio."
64. Shaw, "Handicaps of a Queen of Tragedy," *Sunday Chronicle* [Manchester], 1 April 1923. For a superb, detailed account of Bernhardt's voice, see Taranow, *Sarah Bernhardt*, 3–82.
65. Stokes, "Sarah Bernhardt," 58.
66. Shaw, "Handicaps of a Queen of Tragedy."
67. Stokes, "Sarah Bernhardt," 59.
68. Ibid., 58. See Symons on Bernhardt, Coquelin, and Réjane in his *Plays, Acting, and Music*.
69. Hemmings, *Theatre Industry*, 172.
70. Meisel, *Shaw*, 366, n. 21.
71. Laurence and Grene, *Shaw, Lady Gregory and the Abbey*, 167.
72. Bernhardt, *L'Art du théâtre*, 124.
73. Emboden, *Sarah Bernhardt*, 91.
74. Hart, "Illustrated Interviews," 535.
75. Quoted in Horville, "The Stage Techniques," 57.
76. Rolland, *Le Théâtre du peuple*, 31.
77. Bernhardt, *L'Art du théâtre*, 96–98.
78. Ibid., 177, 181, 183.
79. Shaw, "The Author's Apology," October 1906, in Dukore, *Drama Observed*, 1134.
80. See Shaw, "Preface to Three Plays by Brieux" (written 1909, published 1911), in Dukore, *Drama Observed*, 1188–222.
81. Bernhardt, *L'Art du théâtre*, 184.

82. Findlater, "Bernhardt and the British Player Queens," 94, Findlater's emphasis.

83. Trewin, "Bernhardt on the London Stage," 126.

84. Quoted ibid., 125, 119, 128, 120; Stokes, "Sarah Bernhardt," 58, 57. Stokes writes that Agate's adulation of French theater and tradition is symptomatic of his "philistinism and blindness to many kinds of innovation" (59).

85. Arnold, "The French Play in London," 85, 67. Arnold also faults the French rhymed alexandrine, "a form inadequate for true tragic poetry," for its lack of a "distinctive spirit of high poetry" and for "its incurable artificiality, its want of fluidity" (76, 70, 71).

86. For Bernhardt as theater manager, see Stokes, "Sarah Bernhardt," 16–30. She made a fortune yet often faced lawsuits for nonpayment of rent.

87. Quoted in Emboden, *Sarah Bernhardt*, 9.

88. Gold and Fizdale, *Divine Sarah*, 258.

89. Shaw was impervious to Bernhardt's charms for personal reasons. According to Dan H. Laurence, who spoke with Shaw's cousin and first full-time secretary, "Judy" Musters, at Folkestone on 23 June 1963, Musters recalled Shaw's remark that one of the reasons he probably did not like Bernhardt was that she resembled his aunt Georgina Shaw, whom he detested. Georgina separated from her husband (Shaw's youngest uncle Richard Frederick Shaw) and moved to London, where she often visited Shaw's mother. I am grateful to Mr. Laurence for this information and for alerting me to the following comment by Hesketh Pearson: "It is perhaps only fair to mention that Shaw confessed that his criticisms of the divine Sarah were worthless. 'I could never do her justice or believe in her impersonations because she was so like my aunt Georgina.' As with several of his funniest sallies, this was a simple statement of fact" (Pearson, *G.B.S.*, 149).

5. The Ruthless Revealer: An Encomium to Eugène Brieux

1. Brieux's epitaph is quoted in *Les Nouvelles Littéraires*, 16 December 1932.

2. See Mundell, "A Checklist of Brieux's Plays," in his "Shaw and Brieux," 522–29, for dates of French and English productions and translations into English. For the history of productions of early Brieux plays in London, see 23–25.

3. Brieux, *Damaged Goods. A Play by Brieux*, v. For Charlotte Shaw's role in popularizing Brieux abroad, see Dunbar, *Mrs. G.B.S.*, 185–86.

4. Fyfe, "Brieux and Bernard Shaw," 24.

5. Brieux, *Damaged Goods. A Play by Brieux*, vii.

6. For a discussion of governmental and medical efforts to combat venereal disease in England, see Brieux, foreword to *Damaged Goods. A Play by Brieux*, viii. For an early stage history of and reactions to *Damaged Goods*, see xii–xiii. For a discussion of American (1915) and British (1919) film versions of the play, see Kuhn, *Cinema*, 49–74.

7. Shaw, "Preface to Three Plays by Brieux," 1909, in Dukore, *Drama Observed*, 1197, 1203, 1204. Originally the preface to *Three Plays by Brieux* (New York: Brentano, 1911).

8. Shaw, "On the Nature of Drama," 28 February 1914, quoted by Charlotte Shaw in her (March 1914) foreword to *Damaged Goods. A Play by Brieux*, xiii.
9. Shaw, letter to Augustin Hamon, 24 January 1910, in *Letters* 2, 893.
10. Shaw, letter to Augustin Hamon, 21 March 1910, in *Letters* 2, 914.
11. Bernard Shaw Papers, British Library, 50515, folio 358.
12. Shaw, letter to Siegfried Trebitsch, 10 June 1911, in Weiss, *Letters to Trebitsch*, 153.
13. Bidou, *Le Journal des débats*, 13 May 1910; anonymous, *L'Action française*, 13 May 1910; de Waleffe, *La Dernière Heure*, 14 May 1910; all in Hamon Collection. For more complete bibliographical data of articles in French journals and newspapers, see appendix C.
14. Menken, preface to *Two Plays by Brieux*, vii.
15. Smith, *Main Currents*, 225.
16. Bennett, "Brieux, 17 Feb. '10," *Books and Persons*, 195, 197, 196, 200.
17. Shaw, "Preface to Three Plays by Brieux," 1196, 1201.
18. Published (in the Hamon translation) as "Comment écrire une pièce populaire" in *Les Annales politiques et littéraires*, 3 May 1925.
19. Brieux, "Préface," vi.
20. Shaw, "Preface to Three Plays by Brieux," 1218, 1219, 1218.
21. See Laurence and Leary, *Complete Prefaces*, vol. 3, 220. Shaw concludes, "But as far as the law is concerned the situation is unchanged."
22. Quoted in foreword to Brieux, *Damaged Goods. A Play by Brieux*, xiv, xv.
23. Brieux, *Damaged Goods (Les avariés)*, 9–10. Pollock thought the play "surpasses, in breadth of conception and in tragic force, any single play by the great Norwegian dramatist [Ibsen]" (12).
24. Brieux, *Les Trois Filles de M. Dupont*, 178, ellipses in text.
25. Brieux, *Maternité*, 357.
26. Shaw, preface to *Misalliance*, in *Plays* 4, 20.
27. Brieux, *Maternité*, 317.
28. Shaw, *Major Barbara*, in *Plays* 3, 173.
29. Quoted in Mundell, *Shaw and Brieux*, 153.
30. Klein, "Shaw and Brieux," 34. See also Moore, *Bernard Shaw et la France*, 79–80.
31. Brieux, *La Foi*, 118, 116; Shaw, *Saint Joan*, in *Plays* 6, 105–06.
32. Mauriac, *Discours de réception*, 16. Mauriac spoke on 16 November 1933 when assuming at the Académie Française the place left vacant by Brieux's death.
33. Bertrand, *Eugène Brieux*, 38, quoting the Paris edition of the *Daily Mail*, 24 August 1909. Brieux (51) recalled a group of laborers going to work at dawn: "Et je comparais mentalement cette foule à une procession sacrée. Je pensais alors à l'oeuvre encore inachevée, à l'universel progrès; et là, plus que jamais, j'ai senti que la religion de l'avenir sera l'amour de son prochain!" [And mentally I compared this crowd to a sacred procession. Then I was thinking of the still uncompleted work, of the universal progress; and then, more than ever, I felt that the religion of the future will be the love of one's neighbor!]

34. Ellehauge, *The Position,* 356.
35. Valency, *Cart,* 313–14.
36. Shaw, "The Play and Its Author," 8 December 1913, in *SHAW,* vol. 8, 106, 107, 109.
37. Ibid., 107–8.
38. Bennett, *The Journal of Arnold Bennett,* 342.
39. Lalou, *Histoire,* 154.
40. Quoted in Doisy, *Le Théâtre français contemporain,* 180. Copeau was twenty-eight when he became drama critic of *La Grande Revue* in 1907. American critic Waldo Frank compared "these papers which Copeau flung against the contemporary Parisian theater" with Shaw's "early fulminations" and found Shaw wanting. See Frank, "The Art of the Vieux Colombier," 127–29.
41. Mundell, "Shaw and Brieux," 14.
42. Bennett, *Books and Persons,* 200.
43. Shaw, letter to Siegfried Trebitsch, 18 April 1908, in Weiss, *Letters to Trebitsch,* 135.
44. See *Times,* 14 April 1908; reported by Weiss ibid., 136. Shaw wrote to Hamon that the discovery of a new version of *Maternité* "was a fearful blow to my wife, as her version is already set up and stereotyped" (21 March 1910, in *Letters 2,* 914).
45. Klein, "Shaw and Brieux," 35.
46. Shaw, letter to Augustin Hamon, 21 March 1910, in *Letters 2,* 914, 915.
47. Shaw, "Preface to Three Plays by Brieux," 1202.

6. Shaw Frenchified: Augustin and Henriette Hamon Rewrite Shaw

1. Lubek, "Politics and Psychology," 6–7. Five years later, many eminent men answered Hamon's questionnaire on war, peace, and militarism: Émile Durkheim, Remy de Gourmont, C. E. Maurice, Walter Crane, Havelock Ellis, and Leo Tolstoy. See Cooper's introduction (5–12) to Hamon, *Une Enquête.*
2. Shaw, letter to Augustin Hamon, 31 July 1893, in *Letters 1,* 400. Patrick Galliou, whose four-volume thesis prints 803 letters by Shaw and Hamon, estimates the entire corpus at around 1,700 letters (Galliou, "George Bernard Shaw et Augustin Hamon," vol. 1, 5). The four volumes of Shaw's *Collected Letters* print forty-one letters by Shaw, none by Hamon.
3. Weintraub, *Diaries,* 989.
4. Henderson, *Shaw: His Life and Works,* 306–7.
5. Lubek and Apfelbaum, "Early Social Psychological Writings of the 'Anarchist' Augustin Hamon," 20. *La Psychologie de l'anarchiste-socialiste* concludes that those attracted to the anarchist movement exhibit "the spirit of revolt, love of freedom, individualism, altruism, sense of justice, sense of logic, curiosity for knowledge, and proselytizing tendency" (6). Shaw's personality and inclinations certainly fit this description. See also Lubek and Apfelbaum, "Augustin Hamon aux origines de la psychologie sociale française," 35–48.
6. Lubek, "Politics and Psychology," 9. See Hamon's "Notes de Voyage en

Angleterre" (20 December 1894) in *L'Aube* (1896), and *Le Socialisme et le Congrès de Londres* (1897). Hamon claimed that he was put in touch with Shaw in 1890 by Peter Kropotkin (Hamon, Augustin and Henriette, "Au Lecteur," XI). Russian émigré Pëtr Aleksevich Kropotkin (1842–1921), geographer and Nihilist, led the anarchist movement in London from 1886 to 1914.

7. Shaw, letter to Augustin Hamon, 11 September 1897, in *Letters* 1, 808, 806.

8. Magny's articles appeared in October 1890, February, May, October 1891. The Harry Ransom Humanities Research Center of the University of Texas at Austin (henceforth the HRHRC) has two autographed letters signed (henceforth ALS) from Shaw to Magny (4 June 1889, 10 pp., and 12 June 1889, 5 pp.) with numerous corrections to Magny's translations. In 1895, Magny was translating "The Economic Basis of Socialism," the first essay in *Fabian Essays in Socialism* (see headnote of letter to Magny, 25 February 1895, in *Letters* 1, 487). For an unusual Freudian reading of Shaw's letters to Magny, see Peters, *Bernard Shaw*, 222–23.

9. Shaw, letter to Augustin Hamon, 25 January 1904, Hamon Collection.

10. Henderson, *Shaw, Playboy and Prophet*, 824.

11. Shaw, letter to Augustin Hamon, 25 January 1904.

12. See Hamon, *Le Molière*, 2.

13. Quoted in Grindea, "G.B.S. and France," 3.

14. Hamon, *Le Molière*, 3.

15. Holroyd, *Bernard Shaw*, 55.

16. Hamon, letter to Shaw, 16 November 1905, Galliou, "George Bernard Shaw et Augustin Hamon," vol. 1, 231, Hamon's emphases.

17. Shaw, letter to Augustin Hamon, 26 December 1905.

18. Shaw, letter to Siegfried Trebitsch, 10 December 1902, in *Letters* 2, 292.

19. Shaw, letters to Augustin Hamon, 13 June and 26 July 1922, in *Letters* 3, 773, 781. The revised 1967 Aubier-Montaigne edition has "Higgins," not "Hamon."

20. Quoted in Hamon, *Twentieth Century Molière*, 24. For evidence of Henriette Hamon's fluency in English, see her autographed postcard to Shaw, 6 July 1946, HRHRC, box 50, file 2.

21. Shaw, letter to Henry Arthur Jones, 25 July 1908, quoted in Holroyd, *Bernard Shaw*, 54. When actor Lewis Waller requested that Shaw translate Rostand's *Cyrano de Bergerac* (1897), Shaw wrote to Gilbert Murray, translator of the Greek dramatists: "There is a genuine vein of phantasy and grace of expression to be preserved—and more poetry, after all, than there is in Aristophanes" (letter of 3 December 1909, quoted in Bachelder, *Catalogue 104*, item 15).

22. ALS to Shaw from Comte Auguste Gilbert de Voisins, 6 October 1898, HRHRC, box 49, file 8. See also Laurence, *Shaw: An Exhibit*, item 640.

23. ALS to Shaw from Rémy Salvator, 1902, HRHRC, box 53, file 5.

24. ALS to Shaw from Georges Saint-Clair, 14 February 1903, HRHRC, box 53, file 5.

25. Shaw, letter to Augustin Hamon, 17 February 1905, in *Letters* 2, 513.

26. Shaw, letter to Stéphane Epstein-Etienne, 24 February 1905, in *Letters* 2, 518, 517.

27. Henri de Gérardel, "*César rencontre Cléopâtre*, d'après G. B. Shaw," typed manuscript signed (henceforth TMS), 21 pp, n.d., HRHRC, box 57, file 8, p. 1.

28. Shaw, letter to Arnold Bennett, 16 July 1910, in *Letters* 2, 933.

29. Zuber, "Problems of Propriety," 92.

30. Dell, letter to Shaw, 11 January 1912, Dan H. Laurence Collection, Special Collections, University of Guelph Library, Dell's emphasis.

31. De Gourmont, letter to Augustin Hamon, 20 February 1913, Amalric, *Studies,* 166.

32. Shaw, letter to Max Schiller, 25 August 1950, in *Letters* 4, 874. Romanian-born Schiller (1860–1952) had married Guilbert in 1897.

33. Quoted in Wisenthal, *Shaw's Sense of History,* 160.

34. Shaw, letter to Augustin Hamon, 26 December 1905.

35. See Moore, *Bernard Shaw et la France,* 191–95, who cites numerous mistranslations.

36. Hamon, letter to Shaw, 29 January 1904, Galliou, "George Bernard Shaw et Augustin Hamon," vol. 1, 184, Hamon's emphasis.

37. Hamon, letter to Shaw, 12 July 1906, ibid., 291, Hamon's emphasis.

38. Laurence, *Shaw: An Exhibit,* item 641.

39. Moore, *Bernard Shaw et la France,* 191.

40. D'Humières, "Le Cas Bernard Shaw," *Le Mercure de France,* 1 April 1912, 455.

41. Shaw, letter to Augustin Hamon, 1 May 1908, in *Letters* 2, 776–77.

42. Shaw, letter to Augustin Hamon, 15 May 1908, in *Letters* 2, 782–84, Shaw's emphasis.

43. Augustin and Henriette Hamon, "Au Lecteur," xiv.

44. Shaw, letter to Arnold Bennett, 16 July 1910.

45. Quoted in Grindea, "G. B. S. and France," 4. Shaw related the incident to Yvette Guilbert's husband in a letter of 25 August 1950. See *Letters* 4, 874.

46. Hamon, *Le Molière,* 7. This passage was cited by the *New Witness* (27 May 1915, 88–89) to ridicule Hamon's "qualifications" as translator.

47. See Wellens, "*Candida* in French (1907)," 7–8.

48. Quoted ibid., 10. For a summary of Belgian reviews, see 8–10.

49. Hamon, *Le Molière,* 2.

50. Shaw, letters to Augustin Hamon, 25 March 1905, 18 January 1906; Hamon, letter to Shaw, 6 April 1905, Galliou, "George Bernard Shaw et Augustin Hamon," vol. 1, 214; Shaw, letter to Hamon, 22 January 1906, in *Letters* 2, 602. Shaw's comments on *You Never Can Tell* in his letter of 27 August 1906 show an awareness of the delicate relationship between language and class in France. He questioned Hamon's frequent use of "Bien sûr—pour sûr—sûrement—&c &c. . . . this locution, in all french [sic] plays I have read, is never used by anyone of

higher rank than a concierge. The upper classes in these plays say Parfaitement, & other expressions of the kind, but not sûr." Hamon Collection.

51. Schlumberger, *La Nouvelle Revue française,* 1 April 1912, 699, Hamon Collection.

52. Hamon, *Trop vrai pour être beau,* TMS, n.d., 31, 67, 83, 44, Hamon Collection; Shaw, *Too True to be Good,* in *Plays* 6, 457.

53. Hamon, *César et Cléopâtre,* act 3, page proofs, n.d., p. 93, HRHRC, box 57, file 9.

54. "Maximes pour révolutionaires," n.d., 17, typed manuscript (henceforth TM), Hamon Collection. Hamon's awkward version was published as is. Shaw claimed his own aphorisms "eclipse Larochefoucauld's [sic]" (Shaw, letter to Siegfried Trebitsch, 10 December 1902). Shaw often quoted the maxim that very few people would fall in love if they had never read about it (see *Plays* 3, 15; *Plays* 4, 832; *Plays* 5, 22). See La Rochefoucauld's *Réflexions ou Sentences et Maximes morales* (1665).

55. "Maximes pour révolutionaires," n.d., 13, TM, Hamon Collection; Shaw, *Man and Superman,* in *Plays* 2, 793. The much-improved published version is: "Il y a abus du droit de vivre quand on ne le justifie pas constamment" (Augustin and Henriette Hamon, *L'Homme et le surhomme,* 283).

56. Shaw, MS notes, Hamon Collection. See "The Revolutionist's Handbook," *Plays* 2, 765.

57. Hamon, *Candida,* TMS, 86 pp., c. 1908, HRHRC, box 58, file 4, p. 21 (verso).

58. Hamon, *Le Disciple du diable,* page proofs for a limited edition, 138 pp., 1910, HRHRC, box 58, file 8, p. 85. See Aubier edition, 1956, p. 63.

59. Shaw, *Saint Joan,* in *Plays* 6, 207; Hamon, *Sainte Jeanne,* TMS (carbon), 139 pp., "Texte français revu et corrigé par Bernard Shaw en mars 1925," HRHRC, box 60, file 7, p. 136; Shaw, *Sainte Jeanne,* 41.

60. Hamon, *La Profession de Madame Warren,* page proofs, pp. 9–131 (60 pp.), 1908 (100 copies), HRHRC, box 59, file 10, pp. 68–70; Shaw, *Mrs Warren's Profession,* in *Plays* 1, 313–14.

61. Lubek and Apfelbaum, "Early Social Psychological Writings of the 'Anarchist' Augustin Hamon," 20, 21.

62. Quoted in Grindea, "G. B. S. and France," 5; emphasis (possibly Shaw's) in text.

63. Shaw, "Mr. Bernard Shaw in French," *Athenaeum* 4197 (4 April 1908): 418; C. G., "Mr. Bernard Shaw in French," *Athenaeum* 4198 (11 April 1908).

64. Shaw, letter to Dr. Ch. Barbaud, 5 June 1908, Smith, *RWA Auction Catalog,* 316.

65. Quoted in Graham, "Shaw on *Saint Joan,*" in Weintraub, "*Saint Joan,*" 20, 21. This is a retranslation of "La 'Jeanne d'Arc' de Bernard Shaw. Une lettre originale du dramaturge irlandais," *Comoedia,* 16 March 1924.

66. For Hamon's translations of Shaw in order of publication, see Horn-Monval, *Répertoire,* 173–80. For Shaw's plays produced in France from 1908 to

1955 (sixteen plays and twenty-seven productions, all in Paris except two, eleven at the Théâtre des Arts), see Henderson, *Shaw: Man of the Century*, 921. For an account of the Pitoëff productions, see Jomaron, *Georges Pitoëff*, 158–81; for a list of those productions, see appendix A.

67. Shaw, letter to Augustin Hamon, 9 January 1907, in *Letters* 2, 669.
68. Hamon, *The Technique of Bernard Shaw's Plays*, 63–64.
69. Grindea, "G.B.S. and France," 3, n. 4.
70. Shaw, letter to Augustin Hamon, 9 May 1913, in *Letters* 3, 170.
71. Hamon, *La Comédie*, 85 pp., Bernard Shaw Papers, British Library, 50575.
72. Shaw, "The Play and Its Author," 8 December 1913, in *SHAW*, vol. 8, 106.
73. Henderson, *Shaw, Playboy and Prophet*, 824.
74. Henderson, *Shaw: Man of the Century*, 737.
75. Hamon, *Twentieth Century Molière*, 310–16. Hamon notes that the idea for a Molière-Shaw connection came from a passing reference in the essay on Shaw by Augustin Filon in *La Revue des deux mondes* (1905); Hamon believed that "une forte parenté" [a strong kinship] united Shavian and Molièresque comic theater (8).
76. Moore, *Bernard Shaw et la France*, 55, 56.
77. See Barbeau, *Polybiblion*, March 1914; Blum, *Excelsior*, 24 October 1912; *Dundee Advertiser*, 9 November 1912; *New Witness*, 27 May 1915; all in Hamon Collection.
78. Rhys, *Everyman*, 19 November 1912; *Pall Mall Gazette*, 2 June 1915; Boissard, *Le Mercure de France*, 1 April 1913; Bithell, *Les Marges*, 1913; all in Hamon Collection; Maurois, *Magiciens et logiciens*, 137.
79. Bidou, *Le Journal des débats*, 10 March 1913, Hamon Collection.
80. Augustin and Henriette Hamon, "'La Fenêtre' ouverte sur les grands écrivains. A propos de la Profession de Madame Warren" (May 1912), an addition to their essay in *La Grande Revue*, 10 April 1912, 567–76.
81. Hamon, "Épitre dédicatoire," *Le Molière*, proof sheets, pp. 1–13, n.d., HRHRC, box 70, file 6, pp. 9–10.
82. Cammaerts, "Molière and Bernard Shaw" (1926) in Evans, *Shaw, The Critical Heritage*, 308. Cammaerts asks whether "the idea of having his *Fanny's First Play* criticised on the stage by the critics of the day was derived from *La Critique de l'École des Femmes*" (308).
83. Abbott, *The Vital Lie*, 47.
84. Barzun, "Eros, Priapos, and Shaw," 83. John A. Bertolini parallels Don Juan's escape to heaven with Alceste's wish to escape "from the vices and injustices of humanity to a desert where he can have honor" (*Playwriting Self*, 180, n. 18).
85. Shaw, letter to Augustin Hamon, 9 April 1927, in *Letters* 4, 51. In 1909, Shaw had written that *Le Misanthrope* seemed "Molière's dullest and worst play," and *Le Festin de Pierre*, his "best philosophic play, is as brilliant and arresting as Le Misanthrope is neither the one nor the other" ("Preface to Three Plays by Brieux," 1909, in Dukore, *Drama Observed*, 1195–96; see 1195 for Shaw's summary of Molière's achievements).

86. Shaw, letter to Thomas Demetrius O'Bolger, February 1916, in *Letters* 3, 374.

87. Henderson, *Shaw: Man of the Century*, 55. Henderson refers to the *Times* (London) of 19 January 1922.

88. Shaw, letter to Augustin Hamon, 10 March 1922, in *Letters* 3, 764, 765. Paul Bourget's essay was "Molière et le génie Français" in *L'Illustration*, 14 January 1922. Shaw commented at length to Hamon on Aristide Briand on 24 October 1910 (see *Letters* 2, 946–47).

89. Henderson, *Shaw: Man of the Century*, 738, 739.

90. Henderson, "Bernard Shaw and France," 50–51; reprinted in Dukore, *Drama Observed*, 1514–15.

91. Hamon, "A propos de Bernard Shaw," *Pan* 8–10 (September–October 1912), 589, 590, Hamon Collection.

92. Hamon, letters to Jules Delacre, 26 March 1924, 2 June 1924, 12 July 1924; Delacre, letter to Augustin Hamon, 7 July 1924; all in Hamon Collection, Hamon's and Delacre's emphases.

93. Hamon, letter to Georges Pitoëff, 23 January 1929, Hamon Collection, Hamon's emphasis.

94. Roux, letter to Augustin Hamon, 4 January 1931; Hamon, letter to J. R. Roux, 19 February 1931; both in Hamon Collection.

95. Hamon, letter to François Closset, 18 December 1931, Hamon Collection.

96. Moore, letter to Augustin Hamon, 23 January 1931; Hamon, letter to Mina Moore, 10 February 1931; both in Hamon Collection, Hamon's emphases.

97. Sobra, letters to Augustin Hamon, 8 April and 18 May 1933, Hamon Collection.

98. Hamon, *Le Molière*, 6.

99. Typed letter signed to Shaw from Jean-Marie Rojé, 8 September 1946, HRHRC, box 53, file 3.

100. ALS to Shaw from Pierre Montillier, 24 June 1948, HRHRC, box 52, file 1.

101. ALS to Shaw from Maurice Grinberg, 15 January 1949, HRHRC, box 50, file 1.

102. Peters, "Intersections," 260. Compare Shaw's equally troublesome relationship with his German translator Trebitsch in Weintraub, "Indulging the Insufferable."

7. Outrageous: Shaw and the French Press

1. Filon, *The English Stage*, 283.

2. ALS of Jacques-Émile Blanche to Shaw, 2 March 1911, British Library, 50516. Henry James had taken Blanche to see *Candida* in Paris, and both found "the translation & acting (without mentioning the staging) preposterous."

3. See Henderson, *Shaw: Man of the Century*, 498. Henderson quotes from a letter by Filon of 2 December 1904 but does not mention when he wrote his own letters.

4. Filon, "M. Bernard Shaw et son théâtre" (*La Revue des deux mondes* 30, 15 November 1905, 431, 410–11, 433).

5. For Gourmont's ideas that Shaw may have shared, see Amalric, "Shaw, Hamon and Rémy de Gourmont," in his *Studies,* 163–64. He concludes that despite some similarities and Shaw's possible familiarity with Gourmont via Hamon, "internal evidence is not sufficient to show anything more than convergent trends of thought" (164). Ellehauge finds Gourmont's influence in such ideas as "the dissociation of love from sexual passion" and "racial improvement by the mating of men and women on scientific principles," the latter forming "a striking parallel" between Gourmont's "La Morale de l'amour" and "The Revolutionist's Handbook" (Ellehauge, *The Position,* 363). See also Moore, *Bernard Shaw et la France,* 89.

6. Grosfils, *Bulletin de l'oeuvre,* March 1912, 46; Brion, *La Grande Revue,* November 1927, 42, 45; both in Hamon Collection.

7. Cestre, *Bernard Shaw,* 95. See also 93–96.

8. Hermeline, *L'Univers,* 20 November 1908; Dekobra, *La Revue des revues,* 15 March 1910; Faguet, *La Revue,* 1 October 1912; Muret, *Le Journal des débats,* 17 February 1912; Dubech, *L'Action française,* 15 May 1922; Dubech, *Candide,* 29 December 1932; Dubech, *L'Action française,* 7 January 1933; all in Hamon Collection.

9. Saurat, *Les Marges,* 15 August 1925; Locria, *Les Idées contemporaines,* 7 April 1912; Nayral, *Revue indépendante,* March 1912; Hermant, *Journal,* 29 January 1913; Faguet, *La Revue,* 1 October 1912; Boissard, *Le Mercure de France,* 1 April 1913; Gaffié, *Théâtra,* 7 March 1913; Uzanne, *La Dépêche,* 26 February 1913; Gillet, *La Revue des deux mondes,* 1 February 1919; all in Hamon Collection.

10. These letters were reprinted in *Der Jude* 9 (January 1926) with Shaw's "Nachwort zur Bernstein-Shaw-Kontroverse." The postscript appeared retranslated as "Mr. Bernard Shaw on the Jews: Repudiation of Anti-Semitism" in *Jewish Guardian* 7 (1 January 1926). Both "Lettre ouverte" (16 November) and "Postscriptum" (23 December) were published as "Bernard Shaw on the Jews. The 'Persecution Complex'" in *Jewish Chronicle* 2967 (12 February 1926).

11. Shaw made identical comments to Hamon two weeks earlier: "The truth is that there is no anti-semitism in England, although there is a literary clique headed by Chesterton and Belloc who profess it as a sort of Catholic literary affectation. But England is politically and officially Zionist." Letter to Augustin Hamon, 3 December 1925, in *Letters* 3, 923.

12. Shaw, letter to Augustin Hamon, 9 April 1927, in *Letters* 4, 57. One week after Bernstein's articles in *Le Temps* (7 and 14 September 1925), historian François Aulard, in *Le Quotidien* (20 September 1925), published "Bernard Shaw est de mauvaise humeur mais sa 'Sainte Jehanne' est un chef-d'oeuvre," [Bernard Shaw is in a bad mood but his 'Sainte Jehanne' is a masterpiece], defending Shaw against Bernstein. "M. Henry Bernstein Répond à M. Aulard" appeared the next

day in the same newspaper. See "Newspaper cuttings belonging to Shaw," Bernard Shaw Papers, British Library, 50740.

13. Shaw, letter to Augustin Hamon, 14 April 1921, in *Letters* 3, 715.

14. Shaw, letters to Augustin Hamon, 13 June 1922 and 26 November 1924, in *Letters* 3, 773, 891.

15. Shaw, letter to A.-M. Lugné-Poë, 17 February 1906, in *Letters* 2, 605, 606. "You could play the part of Crofts well. Madame Lugné Poë might make a hit as Mrs Warren. . . . My works might make L'Oeuvre a reality instead of a name," Shaw wrote to him c. November 1907 (*Letters* 2, 730). In 1908 Shaw went to see Després in Bernstein's *La Rafale* to judge if she would be able to play in *Mrs Warren* to a Parisian audience; she did, but only in a revival from 9 May to 8 June 1922. See headnotes to letters to Augustin Hamon, 22 January 1906 and 26 July 1922, in *Letters* 2, 601, 779.

16. Shaw, letter to Georges Pitoëff, 16 November 1927, in *Letters* 4, 77.

17. Shaw, letter to Georges and Ludmilla Pitoëff, 13 January 1929, in *Letters* 4, 123–25.

18. Shaw, letter to Augustin Hamon, 17 January 1929, in *Letters* 4, 126.

19. Shaw, letter to Georges Pitoëff, 23 January 1930, in *Letters* 4, 173. According to Whitton (*Stage Directors*, 98), Georges "could be extremely monotonous. But contemporary accounts make it abundantly clear that he had an unsettling presence which made a deep impression on spectators."

20. Kessel, *Gringoire*, 21 December 1928, quoted in Jomaron, *Georges Pitoëff*, 176.

21. Shaw, letter to Georges Pitoëff, 23 January 1930, 173–74. Shaw had been more gracious (prior to the *César et Cléopâtre* fiasco) before the Pitoëffs came to England, asking (on 2 June 1928) how he could make their visit interesting aside from "mes efforts funestes de m'exprimer en français" [my baleful efforts to express myself in French]. On 10 October he urged Georges to produce *Heartbreak House* and play Shotover, who must be "un homme imaginative et un slav. Aucun Français ne pouvait le toucher. Elie est un très beau rôle: le seul dans mes pièces assez exquise pour Madame Pitoëff" [an imaginative man and a Slav. No Frenchman could touch him. Elie is a very lovely role: the only one in my plays exquisite enough for Madame Pitoëff] (Shaw, "Shaw Writing to the Pitoëffs," 15, 14).

22. Shaw, letter to Siegfried Trebitsch, 28 April 1931, in *Letters* 4, 236.

23. *Daily Telegraph*, 9 May 1908; Nozière, *Le Gil Blas*, 10 May 1908; Blum, *La Grande Revue*, 10 June 1908; Ernest-Charles, *L'Opinion*, 16 May 1908; d'Humières, *Comoedia*, 10 May 1908; Leblanc-Maeterlinck, *Le Figaro*, 30 May 1908; all in Hamon Collection.

24. For an interesting comparison of *Mrs Warren's Profession* and *Yvette*, see Bullough, "Literary Relations," 339–49.

25. Davray, *Le Courrier européen*, 10 March 1912; Davray, *L'Action nationale*, 10 April 1912; Nayral, *Revue indépendante*, March 1912; Dubech, *L'Action française*, 15 May 1922; Lanson, *La Grande Revue*, 25 February 1912; all in Hamon Collection.

26. Blavinhac, *République française,* 29 January 1913; Souday, *Éclair,* 29 January 1913; Sée, *Le Gil Blas,* 28 January 1913; Métives, *Excelsior,* 28 January 1913; de Flers, *Le Figaro,* 29 January 1913; Hermant, *Journal,* 29 January 1913; all in Hamon Collection.

27. Veber, *Le Petit Journal,* 29 September 1923; Shaw, letter to Augustin Hamon, 7 December 1923, in *Letters* 3, 857. The 1916 printed version's "What Happened Afterwards" makes it clear that Eliza is to marry Freddy.

28. Marcel, *Les Nouvelles littéraires,* 3 February 1955; Ravon, *Semaine du monde,* 20 January–3 February 1955; Marcabru, *Arts,* 26 January 1955; Lebesque, *Carrefour,* 26 January 1955; Volmane, *Aux écoutes de la finance,* 27 January 1955; J. L., *Le Figaro littéraire,* 22 January 1955; all in Hamon Collection.

29. Dussane, *J'étais dans la salle,* 93–94.

30. Shaw, letter to Augustin Hamon, 13 June 1922, 772.

31. Robert, "The Language of Theater," 115.

32. Ibid., 117, 118.

33. Amalric, "Shaw in France in Recent Years," 43–44.

34. Henderson, *Shaw: Man of the Century,* 503.

35. Rostand, "Étude sur G.-B. Shaw," 7, 13–14, 15. See also Bowler, "Anti-Darwinism in France," in *The Eclipse of Darwinism,* 107–17. Rostand praised the translation, in which "la scrupuleuse fidélité au texte se concilie avec une rare élégance de style" (7). Rostand (1894–1977), author of *La Biologie et l'avenir humain* (1950), was known for his work on parthenogenesis.

36. Cocteau, *Cher menteur,* 26.

37. Ibid., 5.

38. See Amalric, "Shaw in France in Recent Years," 43.

39. Shaw, letter to Max Schiller, 25 August 1950, in *Letters* 4, 874, Shaw's emphasis.

8. The Trials of Jeanne d'Arc: From Peasant-Warrior to Piteous Waif

1. See Taub, "The Martyr as Tragic Heroine," 13–24.

2. Valency, *Cart,* 377.

3. Crompton, *Shaw the Dramatist,* 196.

4. See Terry, *Jeanne d'Arc,* 60–62, 72–73. Post-Shavian French Joan plays include Joseph Delteil's *Jeanne d'Arc* (1925), Robert Brasillach's *Procès de Jeanne d'Arc* (1932), Paul Claudel's *Jeanne d'Arc au bûcher* (1933), Maurice Maeterlinck's *Jeanne d'Arc* (1948), Thierry Maulnier's *Jeanne et ses juges* (1949), Jacques Audiberti's *Pucelle* (1950), and Jean Anouilh's *L'Alouette* (1953). For a brief survey, see Hunt, "Saint Joan of Arc," 302–33.

Shaw had the last word on Joan in England, aside from Christopher Fry's *The Lark* (1955), adapted from Anouilh. The United States was slower to bring her to the stage: Maxwell Anderson's *Joan of Lorraine* (1946); Lillian Hellman's *The Lark* (1955), also adapted from Anouilh; Robert Hogan's spoof *Saint Jane* (1966); the rock opera *The Survival of Saint Joan* (1971), in which Joan is burned by mistake; Al Carmines's pop opera *Joan* (1972), with a lesbian Joan in nun's habit;

Lawrence Grossman's musical comedy *Goodtime Charlie* (1974); and Jules Feiffer's farce *Knock Knock* (1976). See Weintraub, *Unexpected Shaw,* 181–82. For Peter Barnes's response to *Saint Joan, Red Noses* (1985), see *Modern Drama* 30.3 (September 1987): 340–51. See also Newman, "Joan of Arc in English Literature," 431–39, and Daemmrich, *Themes and Motifs,* 152–54.

Studies of Saint Joan in drama abound: Jean Bastaire, "De Christine de Pisan à Jean Anouilh. Jeanne d'Arc à travers la littérature," *La Revue des lettres modernes* 71–73 (1962): 11–31; Werner Brettschneider, *Die Jungfrau von Orleans im Wandel der Literatur* (Hollfeld: Bange, 1970); Ulrich Fischer, *Der Fortschritt im Jeanne-d'Arc-Drama des 20. Jahrhunderts* (Frankfurt: Lang, 1982); Janice Malsten Mouton, "Joan of Arc on the Twentieth-Century Stage" [Brecht, Shaw, Anouilh, Kaiser, Claudel, Anderson] (Ph.D. diss., Northwestern University, 1974); Barry Munitz, "Joan of Arc and Modern Drama" (Ph.D. diss., Princeton University, 1968); H. M. O'Connor, "Jeanne d'Arc dans le théâtre contemporain français, anglais, et américain" (Ph.D. diss., Université Laval, 1956); Joachim Schondorff, *Die Heilige Johanna: Schiller, Shaw, Brecht, Claudel, Mell, Anouilh* (München: Langen, 1965); and Taub, cited earlier.

5. Meisel, *Shaw,* 366, n. 21.

6. Shaw, letter to Mrs. Patrick Campbell, 8 September 1913, in *Letters* 3, 201–02.

7. Thomas, "Une Clownerie déplacée," *Comoedia,* 13 January 1924.

8. Thomas, "A propos de la 'Jeanne d'Arc' de Bernard Shaw," *Comoedia,* 22 February 1924.

9. Shaw, letter to René Viviani, 13 March 1924, in *Letters* 3, 869–70.

10. Huizinga, "Bernard Shaw's Saint," 54, 57.

11. Quoted in Graham, "Shaw on *Saint Joan,*" 16. This is a retranslation of "La 'Jeanne d'Arc' de Bernard Shaw. Une lettre originale du dramaturge irlandais," *Comoedia,* 16 March 1924); the corrected TM of Shaw's original letter of 7 March 1924 is in the Boston Public Library. Shaw's broadside was directed to A.-Louis Thomas's second article, "A propos de la 'Jeanne d'Arc' de Bernard Shaw, M. Louis Thomas répond à M. Hamon," *Comoedia,* 22 February 1924, which was a response to Hamon's objections to an earlier critique by Thomas, "La 'Saint Joan' de Bernard Shaw au Théâtre Guild de New-York," *Comoedia* 13 January 1923. Graham reprints Shaw's twice-translated letter as it appeared in the *Sunday New York Times,* 13 April 1924.

12. Grindea, "G. B. S. and France," 9.

13. Quoted in Graham, "Shaw on *Saint Joan,*" 17–19.

14. Mauriac, "*Sainte Jeanne* par Bernard Shaw au Théâtre des Arts," *La Nouvelle Revue française* 24 (1 June 1925): 1048, 1050, Hamon Collection.

15. Shaw, "Preface for Politicians," *John Bull's Other Island,* in *Plays* 2, 811.

16. Quoted in Graham, "Shaw on *Saint Joan,*" 17.

17. Huizinga, "Bernard Shaw's Saint," 106. Moore's *Bernard Shaw et la France* quotes Quicherat: "Johanna erat simplex puella, bona et catholica" (111, n. 3).

18. Shaw, preface to *Saint Joan*, in *Plays* 6, 49; Shaw, "Saint Joan: A Radio Talk," in *Plays* 6, 221.

19. Shaw, letter to Bertha Newcombe, 5 January 1924, in *Letters* 3, 858, Shaw's emphasis. See the photograph of the head in Weintraub, *Unexpected Shaw*, 87.

20. Quoted in Tyson, *The Story*, 20.

21. Shaw, letter to Ben Turner, 27 June 1923, in *Letters* 3, 842; Shaw, letter to Thea Holme, 2 February 1939, in *Letters* 4, 526.

22. Walkley, unsigned notice in the *Times*, 27 March 1924.

23. Agate, notice in the *Sunday Times*, 30 March 1924.

24. Moore, *Bernard Shaw et la France*, 104–5.

25. Shaw, letter to Thea Holme, 2 February 1939, 526.

26. Quoted in Valency, *Cart*, 375.

27. For ambiguities concerning Shaw's knowledge of Murray's book through Father Joseph Leonard, Charlotte Shaw, and Sydney Cockerell, see Tyson, *The Story*, 4–6. For Shaw's insistence on adhering to history, see Wisenthal, *Shaw's Sense of History*, 44–5. Shaw does not mention Quicherat's critical study, *Aperçus nouveaux sur l'histoire de Jeanne d'Arc* (Paris, 1850).

28. Shaw, letter to John Middleton Murry, 1 May 1924, in *Letters* 3, 875. See Mark Twain's *Personal Recollections of Joan of Arc* (1896), Anatole France's *Vie de Jeanne d'Arc* (1908), and Andrew Lang's *The Maid of France, Being the Study of the Life and Death of Jeanne d'Arc* (1908) and *La Jeanne d'Arc de M. Anatole France* (1909). For contemporary reviews on France and Lang, see Terry, *Jeanne d'Arc*, 90–93, 97–98. See the fine essay by Salomon, "Escape From History," on Twain's "lifelong dislike of the French nation" (109), "deep-seated dislike of Catholicism" (110), and "abysmal ignorance of the historical forces at work in the Middle Ages" (111). Shaw claimed to have read "all the chief sources," including Michelet's *Histoire de France* (1834; Joan's story printed separately as *Jeanne d'Arc*, 1853), Henri Martin's *Jeanne d'Arc* (1857), and Henri Wallon's *Jeanne d'Arc* (1860). See Tyson, *The Story*, 19, 120.

29. Henderson, *Table-Talk of G.B.S.*, 34–36.

30. Tyson, *The Story*, 21, 57, 58, 59, 22, 22–23.

31. Ibid., 57. To see where Shaw diverges from and adheres to Murray, see Tyson's detailed study; also compare Shaw's text to the "Extracts from the Trial and Rehabilitation Transcripts" (Murray's version) in Weintraub, *Saint Joan*, 203–28.

32. Huizinga, "Bernard Shaw's Saint," 104. For an interesting discussion of "the redemptive power of the imagination," which is "the key to the dramatic statement of the entire play," see Tyson, *The Story*, 76–81. See Sullivan's fascinating essay on how Jeanne's identification of her voices with Saints Michael, Catherine, and Margaret "is not so much represented in as constituted by" the trial transcripts (90), where the clerics' questions "dictate that she express her experience in terms of" certain assumptions (101). Other recent revaluations of

the trial include Monica Furlong, ed., *The Trial of Joan of Arc* (Evesham, Worcestershire: Arthur James, 1996), where Jeanne's insistence on cross-dressing is seen as a prime cause of her sentence, and Karen Sullivan, *The Interrogation of Joan of Arc* (Minneapolis: University of Minnesota Press, 1999).

33. Shaw, "Beethoven's *Unsterbliche Geliebte*," *World,* 1 November 1893.

34. Shaw, "Ten Minutes with Mr Bernard Shaw," questionnaire in *To-day,* 28 April 1894, in *Plays* 1, 480–81.

35. Valency, *Cart,* 391.

36. Cohen, "The 'Shavianization' of Cauchon," 63, Cohen's emphasis.

37. Shaw, letter to the Reverend Joseph Leonard, 11 December 1922, in *Letters* 3, 795; Shaw, "Saint Joan: A Radio Talk," in *Plays* 6, 222, 223; Shaw, "Saint Joan Banned: Film Censorship in the United States," in *Plays* 6, 237. Leonard disagreed: "I would describe it [the trial] as illegal and unjust. Cauchon was clearly out for her death" (quoted in headnote to Shaw's letter to Leonard, 15 December 1922, in *Letters* 3, 797). Raknem sides with Vita Sackville-West in her assessment of the trial as (in her words) "a preordained and tragic farce." See his *Joan of Arc,* 201–2.

38. Huizinga, "Bernard Shaw's Saint," 103.

39. Shaw, preface to *Saint Joan,* in *Plays* 6, 19.

40. Cohen, "The 'Shavianization' of Cauchon," 70. Although I limit my discussion to Shaw's handling of the character of Jeanne, much has been written about his portrayal of Pierre Cauchon. See Huizinga, "Bernard Shaw's Saint," 103–4, and especially Cohen, who believes that Shaw's portrait of Cauchon is largely false from a historical standpoint. Cauchon "arranged for her [Joan] to be burnt summarily, unlike Shaw's protagonist, who is angered by the way in which the English speed the victim to the bonfire" (65). "The rabid nationalism of Stogumber, partly a personification of World War One jingoism, or the cynical power politics of Warwick, partly representative of the Perfidious Albion under whom Ireland had suffered for centuries, could not have been brought home anything like so sharply had Cauchon not been Shavianized into a non-villain and been portrayed as the tool of English policy which he actually was" (67). "Thus the work ends with the lonely saint ranged against virtually everybody, . . . an essentially Shavian point which could not have been made had Cauchon appeared as the accomplice of the English and the trial been exposed for what it was: a device to deprive French nationalism of its most effective leader" (69). For Shaw's views on Cauchon (based on Murray), see his letter to Father Leonard, 15 December 1922, 798–800.

41. Gerould, "*Saint Joan* in Paris," 12. This invaluable essay paraphrases numerous French reviews of *Sainte Jeanne* and elaborates on issues treated only briefly here.

42. Quoted in Frank, *Georges Pitoëff,* 102. Most Parisians agreed. André Antoine noted on 27 June 1927 one critic's remark that Thorndike, "question de race probablement" [probably due to her race], lacked Ludmilla's "fièvre intérieure dévorant l'héroïne" [inner fever devouring the heroine] (Quoted in Antoine, *Le Théâtre,* 400).

43. Palmer, "The Productions of George Pitoëff," 205. For Pitoëff's theatrical background and dramatic outlook, see 202–10. For a detailed chronology of the Pitoëffs' Paris productions from 1919 to 1939, see Pitoëff, *Notre Théâtre*, 102–8.

44. In Paris, the Pitoëffs went from one base to another: Comédie des Champs-Élysées (1922–24), Théâtre des Arts (1925–27, 1928–31), Théâtre des Mathurins (1927–28), Théâtre de l'Avenue (1932), Théâtre du Vieux-Colombier (1933–34), and back to the Mathurins, where Georges spent his last five years plagued by ill health. A large family prevented the Pitoëffs from ever becoming financially comfortable. Shaw wrote to Hamon: "Either Ludmilla must learn birth control or Pitoeff selfcontrol" (2 February 1927, in *Letters* 4, 39).

45. Shaw, letter to Lugné-Poë, c. November 1907, in *Letters* 2, 729–30. The letter appeared in French in *Bulletin de l'Oeuvre*, January–February 1912, dated 2 May 1907.

46. Quoted in Gerould, "*Saint Joan* in Paris," 17.

47. Quoted in Hort, *La Vie héroique des Pitoëff*, 224.

48. Pitoëff, *Notre Théâtre*, 19, 90. See illustrations at 25–26.

49. Whitton, *Stage Directors*, 103.

50. Tyson, *The Story*, 130, n. 80.

51. Hort, *La Vie héroique des Pitoëff*, 317–18. See Jomaron, *Georges Pitoëff*, for descriptions of the triptych (166) and the six tableaux (166–68). Like Shaw, Pitoëff claimed to have "fouillé minutieusement" [scrupulously searched] fifteenth-century documentation (Pitoëff in *Comoedia*, 22 April 1925, quoted in Jomaron, 167).

52. Shaw, letter to Augustin Hamon, 3 December 1925, in *Letters* 3, 922, Shaw's emphasis.

53. Gerould, "*Saint Joan* in Paris," 16. For Van Dongen's poster, see Conolly and Pearson, *Bernard Shaw: On Stage*, 88, and Henderson, *Shaw, Playboy and Prophet*, between 544 and 545.

54. Lenormand, *Les Pitoëff, souvenirs*, 120–21, 124.

55. Hort, *La Vie héroique des Pitoëff*, 317.

56. Gerould, "*Saint Joan* in Paris," 16. On Ludmilla's religious crisis, see Pitoëff, *Ludmilla, ma mère*, 140–41.

57. Lenormand, *Les Pitoëff, souvenirs*, 122, 125.

58. Quoted in Pitoëff, *Ludmilla, ma mère*, 141.

59. Lenormand, *Les Pitoëff, souvenirs*, 124.

60. Gerould, "*Saint Joan* in Paris," 17.

61. Ibid., 13.

62. Hort, *La Vie héroique des Pitoeff*, 233; Tyson, *The Story*, 98–99.

63. Gerould, "*Saint Joan* in Paris," 12.

64. Quoted in Pitoëff, *Ludmilla, ma mère*, 137–38.

65. Quoted in headnote to Shaw's letter to Augustin Hamon, 8 May 1925, in *Letters* 3, 911.

66. Blanchart, "Jeanne d'Arc vue par Bernard Shaw," *La Nouvelle Revue critique*, n.d., 379–87, Hamon Collection.

67. Quoted in Frank, *Georges Pitoëff*, 101, du Gard's emphasis.
68. Gerould, "*Saint Joan* in Paris," 15.
69. Quoted in Graham, "Shaw on *Saint Joan*," 17.
70. Gerould, "*Saint Joan* in Paris," 18, 19.
71. Ibid., 17, 19. Robert de Flers was entranced: "This play brings tears to the eyes of the audience each evening." See his (translated) *Le Figaro* review of 11 May 1925 in Evans, *Shaw, the Critical Heritage*, 295–96.
72. Gerould, "*Saint Joan* in Paris," 20. Gerould cites André Billy in *Le Mercure de France*, 1 June 1925. René Salomé in *Les Études*, 5 October 1925, in Hamon Collection, called the château de Chinon "un magazin de pantins grotesques ou de déplaisants automates" [a shop of grotesque puppets or of unpleasant automatons], and Charles VII "d'une bouffonnerie énorme et d'une écoeurante bassesse" [a tremendous buffoon and disgustingly base] in the midst of which Joan was denied all grace. Of the Protestant Joan, Paul Claudel exclaimed: "What a monstrosity" (quoted in Gerould, "*Saint Joan* in Paris," 21).
73. Palmer, "The Productions of George Pitoëff," 216.
74. Gerould, "*Saint Joan* in Paris," 20.
75. Ibid., 21, Gerould's emphasis.
76. MacCarthy, *New Statesman*, 21 June 1930, in his *Shaw*, 171, 172–73, 171, 173.
77. Quoted in Hort, *La Vie héroique des Pitoëff*, 314–15.
78. *Daily Herald*, 11 June 1930, Hamon Collection.
79. Quoted in Hort, *La Vie héroique des Pitoëff*, 315, 316.
80. Pitoëff, *Ludmilla, ma mère*, 138. See also 138–40.
81. Quoted in Huizinga, "Bernard Shaw's Saint," 93.
82. Quoted in Hill, *Playing Joan*, 38–9.
83. Hort, *La Vie héroique des Pitoëff*, 318.
84. Shaw, letter to Augustin Hamon, 8 December 1937, in *Letters* 4, 485.
85. Quoted in Tyson, *The Story*, 99.
86. Ibid., 95–96.
87. Huizinga, "Bernard Shaw's Saint," 91.
88. Quoted in Grindea, "G.B.S. and France," 8.
89. Quoted in Laurence and Grene, *Shaw, Lady Gregory and the Abbey*, 167.
90. Palmer, "The Productions of George Pitoëff," 211–13.
91. Ibid., 213.
92. Gerould, "*Saint Joan* in Paris," 22. See also 22, n. 66. In 1931, Brisson was very entertained by *La Charrette de pommes* but dismissed the preface as a "pamphlet embrouillé qui se perd dans l'idéologie" [muddled lampoon that loses itself in ideology] (*Le Temps*, 20 April 1931).
93. Quoted in Graham, "Shaw on *Saint Joan*," 17.
94. Shaw, letter to Max Schiller, 25 August 1950, in *Letters* 4, 874.
95. Huizinga, "Bernard Shaw's Saint," 88, 92.
96. Shaw, letter to Augustin Hamon, 25 May 1928, in *Letters* 4, 98–99.

97. Patrice Fitz-Herbert, "Aux Mathurins: Reprise de *Sainte Jeanne* de Bernard Shaw," *Vu* 352 (12 October 1934): 1617, Hamon Collection.

98. In *La Lumière,* 23 September 1938), quoted in Jomaron, *Georges Pitoëff,* 178.

99. Shaw, letter to Augustin Hamon, 8 December 1937, in *Letters* 4, 485.

100. Dubech, *La Revue universelle,* 1 June 1925, 653–56; see Gerould, "*Saint Joan* in Paris," 21, n. 58. Dubech's *vaudeville philosophique* may echo *vaudeville idéologique,* a term applied to the plays of Alfred Savoir (1883–1934)—author of *La Petite Catherine* (1930)—dubbed "the Bernard Shaw of the Boulevard." See Knapp, *French Theatre,* 281–83.

101. Gerould, "*Saint Joan* in Paris," 23.

102. Jacobs, "The Role of Joan of Arc," 108.

103. Quoted in Marsh, "Le Théâtre à Paris," 288, 290.

104. Dussane, *Notes de théâtre,* 121.

105. Ibid., 121–22. For the ambiguities surrounding Vermorel's *Jeanne avec nous,* see Jacobs, "The Role of Joan of Arc," 114–19, who maintains that nothing "could lead one to conclude that it was taken by audiences to be anti-Nazi or anti-Vichy" (114), and that this misconception rests on its December 1945 production, which "prompted reviewers to deal almost exclusively with the impact and meaning it had had for occupied audiences, and moreover to brand it the first Resistance play to be performed in Paris" (115). "The 1942 critics generally ignored aspects of the play which were manifestly an incitement to revolt against imposed order" (117), and the play ran almost continuously for nearly eight months without being banned by the Propaganda-staffel or its French theatrical equivalent, the Comité d'Organization des Entreprises de Spectacle (118). Compare Marsh, "Le Théâtre à Paris," 292–94, for excerpts of *Jeanne avec nous,* which he calls the only "résistance play" put on during the war whose message the public really understood (292).

106. Jacobs, "The Role of Joan of Arc," 109, 110.

107. Ibid., 110, 111.

108. Hobson, *The French Theatre of To-day,* 36.

109. Ibid., 39.

110. Jacobs, "The Role of Joan of Arc," 109–10.

111. Ibid., 110.

112. See *Comoedia,* 2 May 1942.

113. Gide, *Journal,* 135.

9. Jeanne After Joan: Shaw's Joan and Two French Incarnations

1. Quoted in Calvin, "The GBSsence," 22.

2. Giraudoux, "Discours sur le théâtre," 19 November 1931, in *Oeuvres,* 574.

3. Quoted in Calvin, "The GBSsence," 22.

4. See Cohen, *Giraudoux,* 144–46.

5. Quoted in Giraudoux, *Four Plays,* vol. 1, ix. Although Valency defends his

adaptations—"At the least, they are an approximation; at the best, an equivalent" (xxi)—Cohen shows where Valency severely emasculates the text (see *Giraudoux*, notes at 66, 73, 81, 122).

6. Giraudoux, *Oeuvres*, 577.
7. Quoted in Hobson, *French Theatre Since 1830*, 39.
8. Quoted in Wisenthal, *Shaw and Ibsen*, 220.
9. "Trissontin's Revenge," *Times Literary Supplement*, 18 July 1958, 402, quoted in Calvin, "The GBSsence," 25.
10. Mankin, *Precious Irony*, 107; see also Inskip, *Jean Giraudoux*, 101.
11. Giraudoux, *Ondine*, *Théâtre*, vol. 3, 329.
12. Shaw, *Saint Joan*, in *Plays* 6, 183.
13. Ibid., 202.
14. Ibid., 206.
15. Giraudoux, *Théâtre*, vol. 3, 344.
16. Cohen, *Giraudoux*, 81.
17. Valency, *The End*, 433.
18. Shaw, *Pygmalion*, in *Plays* 4, 782.
19. Calvin, "The GBSsence," 35, 32. Calvin's Joan/Ondine analogy is more convincing than *John Bull's Other Island*'s Father Keegan and *La Folle de Chaillot*'s comtesse Aurélia as "hyper-sane lunatics" (see 27–29).
20. Frank, *Georges Pitoëff*, 21.
21. Poirot-Delpech, *Manchester Guardian Weekly*, 11 October 1987, 11. See also Anouilh, *Drôle de Père*, 20.
22. Howarth, "History in the Theatre," 155.
23. Comparing *La Foire d'empoigne* to *The Man of Destiny*, Howarth sees "something reminiscent of the Shavian manner" in Anouilh's play: "If Shaw's purpose was to debunk the heroic by bringing it down to human proportions, Anouilh's was to challenge all our assumptions about what constitutes 'history.' For the serious, dignified cause and effect of the professional historians he substitutes a crude and vulgar rat-race (the *foire d'empoigne* of his title)" ("Bonaparte on Stage," 157, 159). Exclaims Napoleon: "Quelle foire d'empoigne, l'histoire de France!" [What a free-for-all is the history of France!] (Anouilh, *La Foire d'empoigne* in *Pièces costumées*, 320). Whereas in *The Man of Destiny* Shaw manipulates the facts to suit his fiction, Anouilh disregards historical verisimilitude; his Napoleon indulges in self-conscious posturing and role-playing exceeding Shaw's. Fouché refers to Napoleon as "un acteur pareil" who, like Shaw's general, had taken diction lessons from Talma. Like his Jeanne d'Arc, Anouilh's Napoleon is always aware of life-as-theater: "Mon petit ami, nous ne sommes pas au théâtre. Ou plutôt, si, nous y sommes . . . mais pas dans la tragédie, dans le mélo. . . . Moi, je suis un acteur de drame historique" [We are not in the theater. Or rather, yes, we are . . . but not in tragedy, in melo[drama]. . . . Myself, I am an actor of historical drama] (*Pièces costumées*, 323).
24. Quoted by Gross, *New York Times*, 5 October 1987.
25. Valency, *Cart*, 308.

26. Anouilh, *La Vicomtesse d'Eristal*, 37, 38–39.
27. Jolivet, *Le Théâtre de Jean Anouilh*, 126.
28. Paul Gordeaux, quoted in Quéant, "*L'Alouette* de Jean Anouilh," 83; quoted in de Comminges, *Anouilh*, 53.
29. Quoted in de Comminges, *Anouilh*, 19.
30. Jolivet, *Le Théâtre de Jean Anouilh*, 126.
31. De Comminges, *Anouilh*, 23–24, 39–40.
32. Quoted in Quéant, "*L'Alouette* de Jean Anouilh," 84.
33. Eliot, "A Commentary," 4, and "Shaw, Robertson and 'The Maid,'" 390.
34. Taub, "The Martyr as Tragic Heroine," 124.
35. Quoted in Falb, *Jean Anouilh*, 113.
36. Taub, "The Martyr as Tragic Heroine," 125.
37. Harvey, *Anouilh, a Study in Theatrics*, 95, 98.
38. Anouilh, *Pièces costumées*, 11, 30.
39. Quoted in de Comminges, *Anouilh*, 20.
40. Bentley, "The Road from Rouen," 256–57, Bentley's emphasis.
41. Howarth, "History in the Theatre," 157.
42. Kasimov, "The Conflict," 96.
43. Howarth, "History in the Theatre," 154, 155.
44. Hernadi, "Re-Presenting the Past," 157, Hernadi's emphasis.
45. Bentley, in Turco, Jr., "Shaw 40 Years Later," 16, Bentley's emphasis.
46. Bastaire, *Pour Jeanne d'Arc*, 147.
47. Anouilh, *Pièces costumées*, 21, 23.
48. For other cross-cultural and multilingual transformations, see two 1955 plays based on *L'Alouette*: the British translation by Christopher Fry and the American adaptation by Lillian Hellman. See Knepler, "The Lark," 15–28, especially on how the versions reflect national differences with respect to sexuality (22–23) and religion (24–25). Knepler demonstrates the superiority of Hellman's adaptation over Fry's translation.
49. Pernoud, *Jeanne d'Arc*, 124. See Dukore, "'Responsibility to Another'?" which argues that Greene altered lines to dilute Shaw's Protestantism or insert a Catholic viewpoint. Jacques Rivette's 1994 six-hour film *Jeanne La Pucelle* owes a silent debt to Shaw, "who contributed a few episodes and characters, possibly via Preminger's film" (Goy-Blanquet, "French Maid of All Work," 18). For Anouilh's *The Rehearsal* as a parallel to *Heartbreak House*, see Epstein, "Armin's Life and Work," 48–51.

10. The Disabled Skeptic: A Limited Esteem for Anatole France

1. Quoted in Grindea, "G.B.S. and France," 10.
2. Pearson, *Bernard Shaw*, 322. Robert d'Humières's version: "'Toute courtisane ne peut pas se dire marchande d'amour.' L'héroïque modestie de son sourire impliquerait sans doute, comme le sied entre gens courtois, qu'il s'humiliait ainsi lui-même" ["Every courtesan cannot claim to be a love-merchant." The heroic modesty of his smile doubtless would imply that he was in this way humiliating

himself, as befits courteous people] (d'Humières, "Le Cas Bernard Shaw," *Le Mercure de France,* 1 April 1912, 450. Shaw later told Hamon that d'Humières "misquoted France, who said 'Quand on est courtisane, on a le droit de se dire marchande de plaisir,' in goodhumored depreciation of my calling him a man of genius, and not at all in ridicule of my calling myself one." Letter to Augustin Hamon, 30 April 1912; transcription courtesy of Dan H. Laurence from his personal (not Guelph) archive. For a third version of the interchange, see Henderson, *Shaw: His Life and Works,* 494–95, who places it at a Paris supper.

3. See especially France's *Les Opinions de M. Jérôme Coignard* (1893).

4. See Virtanen, *Anatole France,* 164–65.

5. See France's *Monsieur Bergeret à Paris* (1901), about the participation in the Dreyfus Affair of a man formerly aloof from political strife—France's own case.

6. Axelrad, *Anatole France,* 390–91.

7. Shaw, "Lord Sandhurst and Blanco Posnet," in *Plays* 3, 810.

8. Shaw, "How My Enemies Made Me Famous and Wealthy," Shaw's emphasis.

9. Shaw, letter to John Lane, 2 June 1908, in *Letters* 2, 788, 789.

10. Tylden-Wright, *Anatole France,* 204–5. The preface appeared in *L'Aurore* at the end of December 1903, in Combes, *Une Campagne laïque,* on 5 January 1904, and reprinted as *Le Parti Noir* in March 1904. It was expanded to twice its length and reissued as *L'Église et la République* on 1 January 1905.

11. France, preface to Combes, *Une Campagne laïque,* XI. France praises Combes for upholding the controversial 1 July 1901 Law of the Congregations that forced all religious orders to apply for authorization to teach. Combes closed more than 2,500 clerically operated schools in an effort to achieve complete state control of public instruction (Jefferson, *Anatole France,* 124). France condemns the monks for teaching that one can escape eternal damnation only by observing "des règles de vie minutieuses et compliquées" [minute and complicated regulations of life] (XXVIII) and finds odious the iconography of furnaces and horned devils armed with pitchforks. For the background to Combes's fanatical anticlericalism, see Tylden-Wright, *Anatole France,* 196–98; for the downfall of his Ministry, 205–7. For a lucid account of France's participation in the Dreyfus Affair, see Jefferson, *Anatole France,* 94–111; for the Combes controversy, 122–35.

12. Tylden-Wright, *Anatole France,* 285.

13. Anonymous, "Anatole France," 9.

14. Quoted in May, *Anatole France,* 102.

15. Pearson, *Bernard Shaw,* 322.

16. Axelrad, *Anatole France,* 390.

17. Shaw, letter to Gilbert Murray, 5 November 1914, in *Letters* 3, 261. The open letter appeared in the *Manchester Guardian* on 23 December 1914.

18. Smith, *Shaw on Religion,* 137; reprinted in Laurence and Leary, *Complete Prefaces,* 574.

19. Smith, *Shaw on Religion,* 136, 137. Three years later France asked Shaw to

contribute to his journal *Les Nations*. "English Socialist Societies" appeared (in English) on 3 August 1917 and is reprinted in the *Independent Shavian* 34.1–2 (1996): 18–20.

20. Shaw, "Tolstoy: Tragedian or Comedian?" May 1921, in Dukore, *Drama Observed*, 1376–77, Shaw's emphasis. Simon de Nantua is a moralizing traveling salesman. "Il avait toujours raison... J'y acquis pourtant la connaissance d'une grande vérité: c'est qu'il ne faut pas avoir toujours raison" [He was always right. ... Yet from this I learned a great truth: one must not always be right] (France, *Le Petit Pierre*, 169).

21. See Virtanen, *Anatole France*, 44–45.

22. Shaw, letter to Siegfried Treibitsch, 19 August 1913, in Weiss, *Letters to Trebitsch*, 166; for the *Neue Rundschau* comment, see 166, n. 1 to Shaw's letter.

23. Sackville-West, *Saint Joan of Arc*, 382.

24. Shaw, letter to *The Catholic Herald*, 9 January 1948, in *Plays* 6, 243.

25. Sackville-West, *Saint Joan of Arc*, 13–14.

26. Shaw, letter to John Middleton Murry, 1 May 1924, in *Letters* 3, 876.

27. Shaw, preface to *Saint Joan*, in *Plays* 6, 42. Shaw's earlier comments about "an Anti-Feminist" historian and the "nineteenth century prejudices and biases" of Joan's "ideal biographer" seem aimed at France; see 20.

28. "Chronique théatrale: Réflexions...," *Le Temps*, 10 August 1925; retranslated as "Shaw Doffs His Helmet Pariswards," *Boston Evening Transcript*, 24 October 1925, III, 5:1–2.

29. Searle, *The Saint and the Skeptics*, 59, 86, 64.

30. France, *Vie de Jeanne d'Arc*, vol. 2, 461. Ironically, parts of the letter undermine France's thesis. Dr. Georges Dumas admits that contemporary neurologists attach less importance than did Charcot to unilateral visual hallucinations in diagnosing hysteria, and that Jeanne's occasional resistance to her voices and her ability to summon her saints "n'est plus dans la manière classique des hystériques, en général assez passives" [is no longer in the classical manner of hysterics, who are generally rather passive] (461, 464).

31. Shaw, preface to *Saint Joan*, in *Plays* 6, 33. Shaw commented on an essay by Sir Francis Galton (1822–1911), "Eugenics: Its Definition, Scope and Aims," in *Sociological Papers*, vol. 1, 74–75 (London: Macmillan, 1905).

32. Searle, *The Saint and the Skeptics*, 72, 73. For France on miracles, see 64–66.

33. France, *Vie de Jeanne d'Arc*, "Préface," xlvii; see xlvii–xlix.

34. Huizinga, "Bernard Shaw's Saint," 94.

35. France, *Vie de Jeanne d'Arc*, "Préface," lxiv, lxv, lxviii.

36. Shaw, preface to *Saint Joan*, in *Plays* 6, 47.

37. France, *Vie de Jeanne d'Arc*, "Préface," lv.

38. Shaw, preface to *Saint Joan*, in *Plays* 6, 26, 51, 19.

39. Shaw, letter to the *New York Times*, 14 September 1936, *London Mercury*, October 1936, reprinted as "Saint Joan Banned: Film Censorship in the United States," in *Plays* 6, 233, 237.

40. Shaw, letter to Cecil Gray, 31 January 1946, in Laurence, *Selected Correspondence*, 222.

41. Shaw, letter to Diana Watts, 22 July 1948, collection of Charles Oringer.

42. Murry, "The Two Joans," 1044–45, 1046, 1047, 1049.

43. Quoted in Salemson, "Anatole France: A Post-Mortem," 26, 30, 30, 32, 35, 31. The satirical *Le Canard enchaîné* reported the poll on 11 December 1929 under the heading "Anatole France jugé par ses inférieurs."

44. Hamon, "Bernard Shaw romancier," *Paris Journal*, 4 September 1912, Hamon Collection.

45. *English Mail* [Frankfurt-am-Main], 14 May 1908, Hamon Collection.

46. Ernest-Charles, "Bernard Shaw et *Candida* (au Théâtre des Arts)," *L'Opinion*, 16 May 1908, Hamon Collection.

47. Anonymous, *Le Progrès* [Lyon], 17 November 1925; d'Hennezel, *Salut public* [Lyon], 16 November 1935; Roz, *Revue bleue*, 16 June 1908; Gregh, *Liberté*, 29 January 1913; all in Hamon Collection.

48. Quoted from Pharand, "'Almost Wholly Cerebral,'" 97.

49. Unpublished letter of 14 April 1928, quoted from Jay Parini, *John Steinbeck: A Biography* (New York: Holt, 1995), in Pfeiffer, "A Continuing Checklist of Shaviana," 239.

50. Detractors and the flaws they found in France include André Breton (servility), Louis Aragon (complacency), Charles-Louis Philippe (dilettantism), François Mauriac (garrulousness), Blaise Cendrars (ennui), Paul Valéry (lack of originality), André Gide (lack of penumbra). Georges Bernanos caricatured France in 1926 as an odious old skeptic in *Sous le soleil de Satan*. See Virtanen, *Anatole France*, 157–66.

51. Patch, *Thirty Years with G.B.S.*, 186.

52. For a photograph of the window, see Shenfield, *Shaw: A Pictorial Biography*, 118. For photographs of Thorndike as Saint Joan, see Holroyd, *The Genius of Shaw*, 87.

53. I am much indebted in this chapter to the insights and suggestions of Dan H. Laurence.

11. Shaw's Man of Destiny: The Decline and Fall of Napoleon Bonaparte

1. Howarth, "Bonaparte on Stage," 139.

2. *The Man of Destiny* was written in 1895, performed in 1897, published in 1898.

3. Quoted in Berst, "The Man of Destiny," 93, 86, 88.

4. Quoted in headnote to Shaw's letter to Ellen Terry, 5 August 1897, in *Letters* 1, 791.

5. Maurice Muret, "La 'Consécration' de M. Bernard Shaw," *Le Journal des débats*, 17 February, 1912), Hamon Collection. When Henderson asked Yvette Guilbert if she thought *The Man of Destiny* would succeed in Paris, she replied: "I rather fear not. Shaw's portrait is too true to the original to suit the French!" (Quoted in Henderson, *Shaw: His Life and Works*, 341.) Yet compare Grosfils:

"M. Shaw nous procure une vision extraordinairement exacte du général Bonaparte, *l'homme du destin,* et le décor qui l'entoure réduit à de justes proportions le romantisme exagéré qui, tant de fois, dénature [distorts] l'esprit du personnage" (*Bulletin de l'Oeuvre,* March 1912, 47, Grosfils's emphasis).

6. Berst, "The Man of Destiny," 85.
7. Moore, *Bernard Shaw et la France,* 122.
8. Shaw, letter to T. Fisher Unwin, 27 August 1895, in *Letters* 1, 552.
9. Weintraub, *Diaries,* 1102–3.
10. Berst, "The Man of Destiny," 110. See also 112–14.
11. Shaw, *The Man of Destiny,* in *Plays* 1, 618.
12. Weintraub, *Unexpected Shaw,* 68.
13. Weintraub, *Diaries,* 1023.
14. Weintraub, *Unexpected Shaw,* 70.
15. Shaw, *The Man of Destiny,* 638.
16. Dukore, *1992: Shaw and the Last Hundred Years,* 60.
17. Shaw, *The Man of Destiny,* 642, 612.
18. Dukore, *1992: Shaw and the Last Hundred Years,* 59.
19. Berst, "The Man of Destiny," 87, 94. "Shaw's satire is directed against those qualities which he regards as irrelevant to true greatness, and true greatness is represented as having a sure instinct for the creation of an image which will please the common man" (Horsley, *Fictions,* 55; see 54–60).
20. Shaw, *The Man of Destiny,* 630, 631, 632, 633.
21. Meisel, *Shaw,* 358.
22. Shaw, *The Man of Destiny,* 661.
23. Valency, *Cart,* 144.
24. Shaw, *The Man of Destiny,* 657, 659.
25. Shaw, *The Perfect Wagnerite,* in Laurence, *Shaw's Music,* vol. 3, 466–67.
26. Shaw, *The Man of Destiny,* 607–8.
27. "The Revolutionist's Handbook," in *Plays* 2, 751.
28. Shaw, letter to Gilbert Murray, 14 July 1915, in *Letters* 3, 301, Shaw's emphasis.
29. Berst, "The Man of Destiny," 92–93. For a comparison of *Madame Sans-Gêne* and *The Man of Destiny,* see Harris, "Victorien Sardou," 147–73.
30. Shaw, "Toujours Daly," *Saturday Review,* 13 July 1895.
31. Shaw, "Madame Sans-Gêne," *Saturday Review,* 17 April 1897.
32. Shaw, letter to Ellen Terry, 1 November 1895, in *Letters* 1, 565.
33. Sardou, *Madame Sans-Gêne*. Catherine's lines are from the end of act 1, scene 14.
34. Ganz, *G. B. Shaw,* 74.
35. Howarth, "Bonaparte on Stage," 139.
36. Valency, *Cart,* 146.
37. Wisenthal, *Shaw's Sense of History,* 62–63.
38. Shaw, *Back to Methuselah,* in *Plays* 5, 531.
39. Ibid., 532.

40. Quoted in Moore, *Shaw et la France*, 126–27.
41. Shaw, *Back to Methuselah*, 534–35.
42. Ibid., 535, 538, 535–36, 539.
43. Shaw, "Common Sense About the War," *Collected Works*, vol. 21, 107–8.
44. Shaw, unsent letter to H. G. Wells, 1 July 1921, in *Letters* 3, 724–25. In *The Outline of History* (1920), Wells had called Napoleon "hard, compact, capable, unscrupulous, imitative, and neatly vulgar" (quoted in Laurence and Leary, *Complete Prefaces*, vol. 3, 249, n. 5).
45. Shaw, "Toast to Albert Einstein," 233.
46. Shaw, "Preface on Bosses," in *Plays* 6, 856–58, 876.
47. Shaw, letter to Friedrich Adler, 2 October 1927, in *Letters* 4, 69.
48. Shaw, *Everybody's Political What's What?* 34, 338, 131, 134. For other remarks, see 32, 123.
49. Shaw, "Idolatry of the Glory Merchant Is Sheer Illusion," 19 May 1946, in Tyson, *Shaw's Book Reviews* (1996), 528, 529.
50. Shaw, *Everybody's Political What's What?* 339.
51. Shaw, "The Acquired Habits of Napoleon," *New Statesman and Nation* 36 (9 October 1948): 304. Shaw's letter is probably a critique of Taylor's 25 September review (at 263) of *Napoleon's Memoirs*, edited by Somerset de Chair. Taylor replied to Shaw in the 16 October issue (at 326), writing that "Napoleon started France on her way downhill. For my part, I find the historic truth in the Emperor of Turania rather than in the Man of Destiny."

12. The Politics of Pacifism: At War with Romain Rolland

1. See Fisher, *Romain Rolland*, 355–58.
2. Quoted in Starr, "Romain Rolland," 1.
3. Rolland, *Deux Hommes*, 211–12.
4. Rolland, *Journal*, 875.
5. Ibid., 859.
6. Quoted in Francis, "Romain Rolland," 197.
7. For Rolland's pacifist ideology, see Fisher, *Romain Rolland*, 38–48.
8. Shaw, *What I Really Wrote About the War* (1930), in *Collected Works*, vol. 21, 1.
9. Rolland, "Pro Aris," *Au-dessus de la mêlée*, 10.
10. Fisher, *Romain Rolland*, 43.
11. See Grunfeld, *Rodin*, 624–25.
12. Rolland, *Journal*, 160 and 125. For a partial list of signatories, see 1842–43.
13. Quoted in Rolland, *Journal*, 126.
14. Ibid., 126.
15. Quoted ibid., 1007.
16. See Rolland, "Pour l'Internationale de l'esprit," first published in *Revue politique internationale* [Lausanne], March–April 1918. For Rolland's approba-

tion of the Russian Revolution and his reservations about Marxist-Leninist ideology, see Fisher, *Romain Rolland*, 53–58.

17. Of the 952 signatures, Spain had 100, France 58, Germany 21, the United States 14, Italy 10, Belgium 10, Switzerland 6, England 5, Sweden 4, Russia 4. For a partial list, see Fisher, *Romain Rolland*, 314–15; for dissenting opinions on the declaration, see 68–76. For the full text of the Declaration, see Rolland, *Journal*, 1769–71, or *Quinze Ans de combat*, 1–3. The latter prints Rolland's introduction (7–10) "sur le malentendu mortel qui risque de séparer les intellectuels et le peuple ouvrier" [on the deadly misunderstanding that risks separating intellectuals and working class], appended to the English translation of the declaration in E. D. Morel's *Foreign Affairs*, August 1919. Rolland concludes that intellectuals must illuminate the road that workers must build.

18. Rolland, *Journal*, 1819.
19. Rolland, *Quinze Ans de combat*, lxiv.
20. Rolland, *Journal*, 1791, 1818, 1814, 1819.
21. Ibid., 1796.
22. Ibid., 1815.
23. Ibid., 1770.
24. Rolland, *Quinze Ans de combat*, 9
25. Rolland, *Au-dessus de la mêlée*, 30.
26. Rolland, *Journal*, 1917.
27. Quoted in Rolland, *Par la révolution, la paix*, 13–14.
28. Ibid., 14.
29. Ibid., 14.
30. Ibid., 15, Rolland's emphasis.
31. Quoted in Starr, "Romain Rolland," 5.
32. Rolland, *Liluli*, 125.
33. Ibid., 115–16, 186, 214.
34. Rolland, *Le Théâtre du peuple*, 116–17. The work appeared between 1900 and 1903 in *La Revue d'art dramatique* and as a book in 1903. Rolland appends a manifesto for an International Congress on Popular Theatre propounding the breakdown of religious, political, moral, and social barriers, with Art as the savior of humanity. See 209–11.
35. Rolland, *Péguy*, 250.
36. Ibid., 251.
37. See Fisher, *Romain Rolland*, 313, n. 40.
38. Ibid., 76
39. Shaw, letter to E. D. Morel, 30 March 1919, quoted in Rolland, *Quinze Ans de combat*, xiv.
40. See Fisher, *Romain Rolland*, 160. After World War II, the scope and purpose of the CIC were encompassed by the program projected at the United Nations for UNESCO. See headnote to Shaw's letter to Henri Barbusse, 4 May 1932, in *Letters* 4, 291.

41. Shaw, letters to Barbusse, 4 May 1932; Murray, 8 July 1938; and Hamon, 6 May 1932; all in *Letters* 4, 292, 505, 295.

42. Shaw, "Author's Note" (*Malvern Festival Book*, 1938) to *Geneva*, in *Plays* 7, 166.

43. Shaw, letter to Gilbert Murray, 23 October 1940, in *Letters* 4, 585.

44. Quoted in Starr, "Romain Rolland," 6. Rolland became professor of the history of music at the Sorbonne in 1910 and that year published *Beethoven*, one of his many studies on the composer.

45. Shaw, letter to C. H. Norman, 18 September 1940, in *Letters* 4, 578, Shaw's emphases.

13. The River-God and the Thinker: At Meudon with Auguste Rodin

1. With Anatole France and Joan of Arc in the Ethical Church; in the "Fabian" window with Sidney Webb, William Morris, and H. G. Wells in Beatrice Webb House, Surrey. For an excellent color photograph of the "Fabian" window, see Holroyd, *The Genius of Shaw*, 129.

2. Quoted in Pearson, *Bernard Shaw*, 317.

3. Quoted in Grunfeld, *Rodin*, 506.

4. Quoted in Pearson, *Bernard Shaw*, 317.

5. Letter to Siegfried Trebitsch, 1 March 1906, in Weiss, *Letters to Trebitsch*, 95.

6. Quoted in Holroyd, *Bernard Shaw*, 181.

7. Quoted in Pearson, *Bernard Shaw*, 317.

8. Holroyd, *Bernard Shaw*, 183.

9. Quoted in Grunfeld, *Rodin*, 507–8. Rilke based his article on a 19 April 1906 letter to his wife, Clara, written the day after Shaw's third sitting. For a slightly different translation, see Hull, *Selected Letters of Rainer Maria Rilke*, 86–88, with close-up of the bust in profile facing 88.

10. Shaw, *Collected Works*, vol. 29, 240–41. "Rodin" appeared in the *Nation*, 9 November 1912. Reprinted as "G.B.S. on Rodin" in the *New York Review of Books*, 1 December 1912; as "A Memory of Rodin" in the *Nation*, 24 November 1917; under that title in the *Lantern* (San Francisco) in January 1918; as "Rodin" in *Pen Portraits and Reviews* (1931); as "Rodin" in Weintraub, *London Art Scene*, 407–11. The Hamon translation appeared in *Le Gil Blas*, 24 November 1912, which Shaw instructed him to send to Rodin: "Voulez vous me pardonner cette exploitation de nos séances de 1906?" (Shaw to Rodin, 5 December 1912, in *Letters* 3, 131). "Rodin" was to be a review-article of *Art: Conversations with Paul Gsell* (Hodder and Stoughton, 1912)—a translation of *L'Art: Entretiens réunis par Paul Gsell* (Grasset, 1911), interviews with Rodin—but Shaw never mentions the popular book, of which excerpts had appeared in French newspapers and periodicals (see Rodin, *Art*, 115, n. 4).

11. Quoted in Laurent, "Bernard Shaw nous parle de Rodin," 487–88.

12. Shaw, *Collected Works*, vol. 29, 243.

13. Shaw, letter to Sydney Cockerell, 20 April 1906, in *Letters* 2, 618.

14. Shaw, *Collected Works*, vol. 29, 241.
15. Gernsheim and Gernsheim, *Alvin Langdon Coburn*, 40.
16. Quoted in Grunfeld, *Rodin*, 506.
17. Laurent, "Bernard Shaw nous parle de Rodin," 488.
18. Quoted in Grunfeld, *Rodin*, 511.
19. Shaw, letter to Lillah McCarthy, 30 May 1906, in *Letters* 2, 625.
20. Shaw, *Collected Works*, vol. 29, 239.
21. Holroyd, *Bernard Shaw*, 184.
22. Shaw, letter to Harris, 24 May 1919, in Weintraub, *Playwright*, 140.
23. The caricature is in Weiss, *Letters to Trebitsch*, 99. See also Shaw's long, amusing letter (in French) to Rodin, in *Letters* 2, 754–55, with Shaw's sketches at 755.
24. Ludovici, *Personal Reminiscences*, 121.
25. Quoted in Pearson, *Bernard Shaw*, 319.
26. Quoted in Shaw's letter to Thomas Demetrius O'Bolger, February 1916, in *Letters* 3, 371.
27. Holroyd, *Bernard Shaw*, 184.
28. Quoted in Van Vorst, "Rodin and Bernard Shaw," 534.
29. Quoted in Pearson, *Bernard Shaw*, 318.
30. Quoted in Laurent, "Bernard Shaw nous parle de Rodin," 488.
31. Shaw, *Collected Works*, vol. 29, 242.
32. Shaw, letter to Rodin, 5 December 1912, in *Letters* 3, 131.
33. Weintraub, *Playwright*, 141. Shaw told Epstein that "Rodin with his callipers was extremely conscientious in getting the visible physical facts right, whereas you disregard them to the point of flat mendacity. . . . You strip from me the mask of my civilisation, . . . I became a Brooklyn navvy in your hands. My skin thickened, my hair coarsened, I put on five stone in weight, . . . and without the peculiar critical lift at the outer ends of my eyebrows I am only a barbarous joker and not a high comedian" (quoted in Pearson, *Bernard Shaw*, 318, 320–21). The bust was done in June and July 1934; the following year Shaw called it a "Neanderthal Shaw" (quoted in Weintraub, *Unexpected Shaw*, 96). For a photograph, see *Letters* 4, facing 500. For illustrations of works by Beerbohm, Collier, Davidson, Epstein, John, Karsh, Lady Kennett, Low, Strobl, Topolski, and Troubetskoy, see Loewenstein, *Bernard Shaw Through the Camera*, 60–78.
34. Quoted in Weintraub, *London Art Scene*, 411.
35. Weintraub, *Playwright*, 140; Shaw, *Collected Works*, vol. 29, 238.
36. Shaw, undated letter (c. 23 February 1912), in *Letters* 3, 79.
37. Quoted in Weintraub, *London Art Scene*, 411. With unusual modesty, Shaw wrote to Rodin on 22 April 1914: "Vous êtes le seul homme auprès de qui je me sens vraiment humble" [You are the only man beside whom I feel truly humble] (*Letters* 3, 231). In 1996, between ten and fifteen thousand plaster body parts were discovered in the basement of Rodin's Meudon villa; a photograph shows four, possibly six, busts of Shaw (see MacIntyre, "Vaults," 14).
38. Holroyd, *Bernard Shaw*, 183.

39. Quoted in Gernsheim and Gernsheim, *Alvin Langdon Coburn,* 40.
40. Quoted in Grunfeld, *Rodin,* 191.
41. *Le Penseur (Bernard Shaw)* is reproduced in Butler, *Rodin,* 392, and Weintraub, *Unexpected Shaw,* 95. For Rodin's *Le Penseur* in front of the Panthéon, see Butler, *Rodin,* 428. Two days after Shaw left, Rodin fired Rilke. Butler claims Rodin "resented his protégé's losing his heart to a new hero. Rodin must have been not only jealous but angry, for Shaw had engaged—wittily, slyly, yet mercilessly—in a competition, in the week of all weeks when Rodin alone should have been the focus of everyone's attention.... It was Rilke who paid the price for the mischievous Englishman's visit" (391).
42. Quoted in Grunfeld, *Rodin,* 224–25.
43. For a discussion of doubts as to the incident's veracity, see McNamara and Elsen, *Rodin's "Burghers,"* 9. For background to the revival of French nationalism, see 10–12.
44. Quoted in McNamara and Elsen, *Rodin's "Burghers,"* 72.
45. Quoted Grunfeld, *Rodin,* 251.
46. Quoted in McNamara and Elsen, *Rodin's "Burghers,"* 71.
47. Quoted ibid., 79, 66, and in Grunfeld, *Rodin,* 352.
48. Quoted in Grunfeld, *Rodin,* 284, and in McNamara and Elsen, *Rodin's "Burghers,"* 74.
49. Shaw, letter to Rodin, 24 May 1913, in *Letters* 3, 180–81.
50. Quoted in Weintraub, *London Art Scene,* 426.
51. Quoted in Weintraub, *Unexpected Shaw,* 89.
52. McNamara and Elsen, *Rodin's "Burghers,"* 63.
53. From Shaw's "Prefatory Note" of 28 May 1935, in *Plays* 6, 973–75. *The Six of Calais* is at 976–91. Shaw's shorthand MS dated "In the Atlantic 13 / 5 / 34" is titled (in longhand) "Les Bourgeois de Calais," and the introduction of *The Six of Calais* is titled "The Burgesses of Calais." HRHRC, box 29, file 2.
54. Shaw, "Prefatory Note," 973.
55. Rodin inspired the feistiest burgher: "Auguste Rodin contributed the character of Peter Hardmouth; but his manner of creation was that of a sculptor and not that of a playwright. Nothing remained for me to do but to correct Froissart's follies and translate Rodin into words" ("Author's Note" in the program of the play's first performance, in *Plays* 6, following 991).
56. Shaw "Prefatory Note," 973–74.

14. Creative Evolution: The Rise of the Life Force

1. Shaw, letter to Frederick H. Evans, 27 August 1895, in *Letters* 1, 551.
2. Berst, "In the Beginning," 39.
3. Shaw, *Passion Play,* in *Plays* 7, 506, 508.
4. Shaw, preface to *Androcles and the Lion* (1915), in *Plays* 4, 563–64.
5. Shaw, preface to *Back to Methuselah* (1921), in *Plays* 5, 282.
6. Shaw, "What Is My Religious Faith?" 78. The essay first appeared in 1945

in the *Rationalist Annual*. For a detailed list of writings by and about Shaw on his religious and philosophical ideas, see Carpenter, "Shaw and Religion/Philosophy."

7. Ellehauge, *The Position*, 272.

8. Shaw, postscript to *Back to Methuselah* (1944), in *Plays* 5, 692.

9. See Smith, *Religious Speeches*, 33–34, 49, 77–78.

10. Rose, *Edwardian Temperament*, 74.

11. See Butler's *Luck or Cunning* (1886), Galton's *Natural Inheritance* (1889), and Ward's "gynaecocentric theory"—female dominance and man's eventual subjugation of her—in Mills, "Shaw's Debt to Lester Ward."

12. Shaw, letter to E. C. Chapman, 29 July 1891, in *Letters* 1, 301.

13. Shaw, preface to *Back to Methuselah* (1921), 271. Referring to the "psychoLamarckism" of that preface, one critic finds it curious that "Shaw seems to have felt that he was part of a new wave of support for Lamarckism, but in fact his claim that it represented the spiritual salvation of the evolution movement was no longer fashionable, even outside science" (Bowler, *The Eclipse of Darwinism*, 105).

14. Quoted in Ellehauge, *The Position*, 240.

15. Shaw, letter to H. G. Wells, 12 December 1901, in Smith, *Selected Correspondence*, 8.

16. Shaw, preface to *Back to Methuselah* (1921), 294.

17. Shaw, preface to *Misalliance*, in *Plays* 4, 127.

18. Gibbs, "Shaw and Creative Evolution," 77–78.

19. Shaw, preface to *Back to Methuselah* (1921), 273–74.

20. Shaw, letter to Julie Moore, 15 October 1909, in *Letters* 2, 873.

21. Gibbs, "Shaw and Creative Evolution," 80.

22. Quoted in Rose, *Edwardian Temperament*, 79.

23. Wells et al., *The Science of Life*, 638.

24. Shippey, "Skeptical Speculations," 202, 203.

25. Shaw, preface to *Back to Methuselah* (1921), 323.

26. Bergson, *L'Évolution créatrice*, in *Oeuvres*, 560–61.

27. Bergson, *Mélanges*, 1524.

28. Bergson, *L'Évolution créatrice*, in *Oeuvres*, 569.

29. Monk, *Bertrand Russell*, 232.

30. Bergson's British lectures include: "La Perception du changement," Oxford University, 26 and 27 May 1911; "Life and Consciousness," Birmingham University, 29 May 1911, in *Hibbert Journal*, October 1911, and *Huxley Memorial Lectures* (1914); "The Nature of the Soul," University College, London, October 1911; four 1911 lectures at Leeds University, 20, 21, 27, 28 October; "'Phantasms of the Living' and 'Psychical Research'," presidential address to the British Society for Psychical Research—Shaw had attended meetings between 1885 and 18879–London, 28 May 1913, in *Proceedings*, vol. 26, 1913; "The Problem of Personality" (The Gifford Lectures), University of Edinburgh, April–May 1914; "Le Possible et le réel," Oxford, 24 September 1920, revised and published in November 1930 in Swedish in *Nordisk Tidskrift* as Bergson's Nobel Prize acceptance speech.

31. Hamon, *Le Molière*, 91. See also 85–92.

32. Berst, *Bernard Shaw*, 309–10.

33. Between 1890 and 1911, 115 items on Bergson appeared in some forty periodicals: *Athenaeum, Contemporary Review, Current Literature, Dial, Dublin Review, Fortnightly Review, Forum, Hibbert Journal, Living Age, Mind, New Age, Outlook, Spectator, Westminster Review*, and journals of psychology, philosophy, theology, science, and medicine. See Gunter, *Henri Bergson*, 86–115. See, in particular, T. E. Hulme's articles in *New Age* (three in 1909 and ten in 1911), whose new publisher-editor, socialist A. R. Orage, Shaw had financed with a gift of £500 in May 1907 (see *Letters* 2, 809).

34. See Amalric, "A Playwright's Supertrips," and appendix B.

35. Shaw, letter to H. G. Wells, 7 July 1921, in Smith, *Selected Correspondence*, 105.

36. Shaw, letter to William Archer, 19 April 1919, in *Letters* 3, 601.

37. Shaw, "Causerie on Handel in England," *Ainslee's Magazine*, May 1913.

38. Bergson, *L'Évolution créatrice*, 114.

39. Wilson, *Bernard Shaw*, 170–71.

40. Quoted in Ellehauge, *The Position*, 250.

41. Bergson, *L'Évolution créatrice*, in *Oeuvres*, 38, Bergson's emphasis.

42. Kolakowski, *Bergson*, 85, 61.

43. Shaw, letter to Augustin Hamon, 10 December 1912, in *Letters* 3, 137. Shaw substituted four mentions of *La Force de vie* with *L'Élan vitale* [sic]. See Hamon, *L'Homme et le surhomme*, page proofs, n.d., 169–70, Hamon Collection.

44. Shaw, letter to Josephine Preston Peabody, 29 December 1904, in *Letters* 2, 475.

45. Shaw, letter to editor of *Le Monde illustré*, undated (c. January 1912), in *Letters* 3, 69; preface to *Back to Methuselah* (1921), 290.

46. Shaw, letter to Charles Trevelyan, 14 March 1918, in *Letters* 3, 542.

47. Russell, *Portraits*, 78. Bergson's biographers interpret the event differently: "Fort impoliment Shaw aurait répliqué à Bergson qu'il comprenait mieux sa philosophie que Bergson ne la comprenait!" [Very impolitely Shaw would have retorted to Bergson that he better understood his philosophy than Bergson did!] (Soulez and Worms, *Bergson*, 132).

48. Russell, *A History*, 791. This remark might be somewhat derogatory, given Russell's anti-Bergsonian stance. See his famous criticism in *Monist* 22.3 (July 1912): 321–47. "I think his [Bergson's] philosophy is the outcome of some mystic illumination which I don't quite understand," he wrote to Ottoline Morrell (quoted in Monk, *Bertrand Russell*, 247).

49. Moore, *Bernard Shaw et la France*, 91.

50. Laurence, *The Fifth Gospel of Bernard Shaw*, 16.

51. Chevalier, *Entretiens*, 13. The ex-pupil kept detailed notes of his conversations at Bergson's Paris home, at (note the name) 32 rue Vital.

52. Kolakowski, *Bergson*, vii.

53. Chevalier, *Entretiens*, 12.

54. Quoted ibid.

55. Smith, *The London Heretics*, 215. For an account of the New Theology controversy, see 215–23.

56. Shaw, letter to C. H. Norman, 24 September 1908, in *Letters* 2, 810.

57. Smith, *Religious Speeches*, 18–19.

58. Mossé-Bastide, *Henri Bergson*, vol. 2, 239.

59. Quoted in Weintraub, "Saint Joan," 21.

15. Optimistic Vitalism: Converging Toward Gods

1. Barzun, "Shaw and Rousseau," 5. Barzun writes that although Voltaire sharply criticized the established order, he was on the whole pleased with his age. "Had the government under which he lived been more business-like, less church-ridden, better able to maintain prosperity, he would have been content to perpetuate all distinctions of class and income for the benefit of the enlightened minority which he deemed alone capable of civilization" (2). Compare *Black Girl* and Voltaire's *L'ingénu* (1767), the parable of a Huron Indian who returns to France with some explorers, is given a New Testament, and proceeds to test the book's precepts.

2. Maurois, *Magiciens et logiciens*, 137–38.

3. Quoted in Laurence, "Approaching the Challenge," 31.

4. Shaw, letter to Hesketh Pearson, 13 April 1924, in *Letters* 4, 875.

5. Shaw, preface to *John Bull's Other Island*, in *Plays* 2, 837. Shaw repeated the observation in the preface to *Three Plays by Brieux* (1909) in "Brieux and Voltaire," writing that Voltaire's "religious opinions were almost exactly those of most English Nonconformists today" (Dukore, *Drama Observed*, 1220).

6. Shaw, preface to *John Bull's Other Island*, in *Plays* 2, 837, 837–38.

7. Shaw characterized Mabel Shaw as a woman "who broke off her engagement with a clergyman . . . to bury herself in the wilds of Africa and lead negro children to Christ." Letter to Nancy Astor, 12 May 1930, in *Letters* 4, 187.

8. Shaw, letter to Mabel Shaw, 39 January 1928, in *Letters* 4, 89.

9. Shaw, letter to Joseph Fels, 23 March 1909, in *Letters* 2, 839. For similar comments by Shaw in the *Daily Chronicle*, see "Nationalisation, Restoration, Taxation," 4 April 1893, in Tyson, *Shaw's Book Reviews* (1996), 176, and explanatory note at 179–80.

10. Rolland, *Liluli*, 50, 157, Rolland's emphases.

11. Shaw, *The Adventures of the Black Girl*, in Weintraub, *Portable Shaw*, 639. For five early responses (four rebuttals) to Shaw's fable, see Hugo, "The Black Girl," 161–84.

12. Weintraub, *Portable Shaw*, 671.

13. Ibid., 673.

14. Ibid., 672.

15. Ibid., 672–73.

16. Ibid., 674, 675. The Irish socialist of *Black Girl* is obviously autobiographi-

cal, and this is the only instance where Shaw, a partner in a celibate marriage, imagines a sexual union for himself (with children as an outcome).

17. Shaw, letter to Laurentia McLachlan, 14 April 1932, in *Letters* 4, 281–82.
18. Weintraub, *Portable Shaw*, 672.
19. Shaw, letter to Otto Kyllmann, 9 April 1932, quoted in *Letters* 4, 288; Shaw, letter to Clara M. Kennedy, 24 July 1944, in *Letters* 4, 719.
20. Bertolini, *Playwrighting Self*, 153–54.
21. Shaw, letter to Sydney Cockerell, 29 September 1944, in *Letters* 4, 724. Shaw's own suggestion and Farleigh's illustration are reproduced in Holroyd, *The Genius of Shaw*, 84–85.
22. Abbott, *The Vital Lie*, 52.
23. Leary, "The Heralds," 11–12.
24. Leary, "The Heralds," 6.
25. Ibid., 21; quoted in Smith, *Bishop of Everywhere*, 92, Teilhard's emphasis. For an overview of Teilhard's ideas in relation to Julian Huxley's "Evolutionary Humanism" and Shaw's creative evolution, see 85–121 passim. C. E. M. Joad provided a coherent account of the Life Force in his 1946 essay, "Shaw's Philosophy": Life (consciousness) must transcend matter (body) into immortal pure thought (mind), eventually producing an organ (brain) for that purpose. Cosmic purpose—effort in improving the race (salvation)—struggles against individual pleasure—hedonism and egotism (damnation). Femaleness (primitive) seduces Maleness (civilized) with the Life Force (sex). Domesticity (beauty, security, family, continuity) can tame the Visionary (intellect, adventure, creativity, individuality) but not the Genius (artist), who drives Life to higher levels by refining society's awareness with new insights into truth, morality, and beauty (art). Art should transcend sex (higher consciousness), not glorify it (romanticism). The artist captures an evanescent glimpse of intenser awareness by bringing the Life Force into being. The object of pure thought is contemplation; this is the goal of evolution. See Joad, "Shaw's Philosophy," 184–205.
26. Shaw, *Man and Superman*, in *Plays* 2, 680.
27. Leary, "The Heralds," 19.
28. Rose, *Edwardian Temperament*, 81.
29. Shaw, *Postscript: After Twentyfive Years* (1944), in *Plays* 5, 703.
30. Quoted in Leary, "The Heralds," 29.
31. Quoted in Smith, *Bishop of Everywhere*, 120.
32. Shaw, *Back to Methuselah* (1921), in *Plays* 5, 433.
33. Leary, "The Heralds," 25.

16. Shaw's Protoexistentialism: In Hell with Jean-Paul Sartre

1. "No exit" is *pas de sortie, aucune sortie,* or *sortie interdite* [exit forbidden]. *Huis clos* is proper to jurisprudence: *huis* is "door" and *huis clos* means "behind closed doors." *Prononcer un huis clos* means "to clear the court." Echoes of judgment and criminality fitting to Sartre's world of recriminations are absent from the expression "no exit."

2. Shaw, *Man and Superman,* in *Plays* 2, 632. Valency thinks that "Shaw did not have this figure in mind. His Don Juan . . . plainly shows the influence of Molière" (*Cart,* 220).
3. Shaw, *Man and Superman,* 689.
4. Sartre, *Théâtre,* vol. 1, 168.
5. Shaw, "Maxims for Revolutionists," in *Plays* 2, 783.
6. Dietrich, "Shaw and Yeats," 70.
7. Valency, *Cart,* 192.
8. Nathan, "The *House,*" 35, 37.
9. Wilson, *Religion and the Rebel,* 241, 287. See 285–87.
10. Coakley, "Review," 298.
11. Dukore, *Bernard Shaw, Playwright,* 218, 242, 223.
12. Shaw, "Epistle Dedicatory" to *Man and Superman,* in *Plays* 2, 503.
13. Shaw, "Shaw Unperturbed by Immortality," in *Plays* 6, 230.
14. Contat and Rybalka, *Les Écrits de Sartre,* 100. See also: "On trouve sous-jacent dans la philosophie sartrienne le schéma temporel exploité dramatiquement dans *Huis clos:* a) notre image se forme dans l'esprit d'autrui à travers nos actes (PRÉSENT); b) en fixant cette image, autrui nie notre liberté de devenir (NÉGATION DU FUTUR); c) cette image ne peut être modifiée par la justification des motifs qui ont présidé à l'acte créateur (NÉGATION DU PASSÉ)" [Underlying Sartrean philosophy is the temporal schema exploited dramatically in *Huis clos:* a) our image is formed in the other's mind through our actions (PRESENT); b) in fixing this image, the other denies our freedom of becoming (NEGATION OF THE FUTURE); c) this image can not be modified by the justification of the motives which have governed the creative act (NEGATION OF THE PAST)] (Lorris, *Sartre dramaturge,* 84).
15. See "The New Theology," in Weintraub, *Portable Shaw,* 309–10.
16. Sartre, *L'Existentialisme,* 64.
17. Shaw, *Man and Superman,* 667.
18. Dukore, *Bernard Shaw, Playwright,* 220.
19. McDowell, "Heaven," 258.
20. Weintraub, *Portable Shaw,* 310.
21. Sartre, *L'Existentialisme,* 67.
22. Weintraub, *Portable Shaw,* 314.
23. Shaw, *Man and Superman,* 654, 656, 636.
24. Shaw, "Don Juan in Hell," 4 June 1907, in *Plays* 2, 801.
25. Shaw, *Man and Superman,* 650, 651.
26. Sartre, *L'Existentialisme,* 37, 80–81.
27. Shaw, *Man and Superman,* 658.
28. The cousin's death—a plausible suicide—is ambiguous. The point is Inès's feeling of responsibility and her implication of her cousin's wife, Florence: "Alors il y a eu ce tramway. Je lui disais tous les jours: eh bien, ma petite! Nous l'avons tué" [Then there was this tramway. I used to tell her every day: well, my little one! We've killed him] (Sartre, *Théâtre,* vol. 1, 144).

29. Shaw, *Man and Superman*, 675.
30. Ibid., 670, 675, 677, 678.
31. Shaw, "Don Juan in Hell," 801.
32. Sartre, *L'Existentialisme*, 55.
33. Sartre, *Théâtre*, vol. 1, 165.
34. Sartre, *L'Existentialisme*, 82.
35. Shaw, *Man and Superman*, 656, 547.
36. Ibid., 545.
37. Sartre, *Théâtre*, vol. 1, 154. Compare Mangan: "Let's all strip stark naked. We may as well do the thing thoroughly when we're about it. We've stripped ourselves morally naked: well, let us strip ourselves physically naked as well, and see how we like it" (Shaw, *Heartbreak House*, in *Plays* 5, 166).
38. Sartre, *Théâtre*, vol. 1, 154, 167. That Sartre first published his play in *L'Arbalète* (no. 8, April 1944, 37–80) as *Les Autres* [The others] underlines the importance of Garcin's maxim. In "Sartre donne les clefs de *L'enfer, c'est les Autres*," in *Le Figaro littéraire*, 7–13 January 1965, he clarified the aphorism: "'L'enfer, c'est les autres' a été toujours mal compris. On a cru que je voulais dire par là que nos rapports avec les autres étaient toujours empoisonnés, que c'étaient toujours des rapports interdits. Or, c'est tout autre chose que je veux dire. Je veux dire que si les rapports avec autrui sont tordus, viciés, alors l'autre ne peut être que l'enfer. . . . Les autres sont, au fond, ce qu'il y a de plus important en nous-mêmes, pour notre propre connaissance de nous-même" ['Hell is other people' has always been misunderstood. By that it was believed that I meant that our relations with others were always poisoned, that they were always forbidden relations. However, what I mean is something else altogether. I mean that if relations with others are twisted, vitiated, then the other can be nothing but hell. . . . Others are, in the end, what is most important in ourselves, for our own self-awareness] (quoted in Contat and Rybalka, *Les Écrits de Sartre*, 101).
39. Sartre, *Théâtre*, vol. 1, 147.
40. Ibid., 149.
41. Shaw, "Don Juan in Hell," 4 June 1907, in *Plays* 2, 800.
42. Quoted in Contat and Rybalka, *Les Écrits de Sartre*, 141.
43. Shaw, *Man and Superman*, 687.
44. Cohn, "Hell on the Twentieth-Century Stage," 53.
45. Shaw, *Man and Superman*, 681.
46. Sartre, *Théâtre*, vol. 1, 177.
47. Shaw, *Man and Superman*, 685. Compare Shotover's warning to avoid being "a drifting skipper": "Navigation. Learn it and live; or leave it and be damned" (*Heartbreak House*, 177). Nathan argues that the characters in *No Exit* and *Heartbreak House* "hold the mirror up to each other and reveal their cowardice, concupiscence and improvidence" and have failed to make a commitment to life because of their inauthenticity ("The *House*," 36). Like Sartre's people, Shaw's "are caught in the grip of delusion and dependency upon others' responses to their machinations" (38). Nathan discusses *Heartbreak House* in relation to the theater

of the absurd (39–42), while another critic dubs Shaw "the god father . . . to the theatre of the absurd" (Kaufmann, *G. B. Shaw*, 11). Grosfils compares the London premiere (1893) of *Widowers' Houses* to the notorious Paris premiere (1896) of Alfred Jarry's landmark *Ubu Roi:* "elle fut épique" (*Bulletin de l'Oeuvre*, March 1912, 45).

48. Shaw, "Epistle Dedicatory," 523.
49. Weintraub, *Portable Shaw*, 313.
50. Shaw, *Man and Superman*, 679–80.
51. Sartre, *L'Existentialisme*, 62. See also: "Nous ne définissons l'homme que par rapport à un engagement" [We define man only in relation to a commitment] (Sartre, *L'Existentialisme*, 78); "Tel est l'homme que nous concevons: homme total. Totalement engagé et totalement libre" [Such is the man we imagine: a whole man. Wholly committed and wholly free] (Sartre, *Qu'est-ce que la littérature?*, 28). Wilson believes that Undershaft "anticipated Sartre's doctrine of 'commitment'" (*Religion and the Rebel*, 265), that "there is more than a hint of Undershaft about Romain Gary, Jean-Paul Sartre, and Albert Camus" ("Shaw's Existentialism," 6), and that Shaw "comes closer to the ideal of the existentialist than Sartre, or Camus, or Marcel" ("Beyond the Outsider," 58).
52. Sartre, *L'Existentialisme*, 21.
53. Wilson, *The Strength to Dream*, 68, Wilson's emphasis.
54. Sartre, *L'Être et le néant*, 174, 172, Sartre's emphases.
55. Shaw, *Man and Superman*, 662.
56. Weintraub, *Portable Shaw*, 314. See Shaw to Lady Augusta Gregory (19 August 1909): "To me the sole hope of human salvation lies in teaching Man to regard himself as an experiment in the realization of God" (*Letters* 2, 858); and to Leo Tolstoy (14 February 1910): "To me God does not yet exist; but there is a creative force constantly struggling to evolve an executive organ of godlike knowledge and power: that is, to achieve omnipotence and omniscience; and every man and woman born is a fresh attempt to achieve this object. . . . God has made many mistakes in His attempts to make a perfect being. . . . we are here to help God, to do His work, to remedy His old errors, to strive towards Godhead ourselves" (*Letters* 2, 901–2).
57. Sartre, *L'Être et le néant*, 653; Weintraub, *Portable Shaw*, 314.
58. Sartre, *L'Être et le néant*, 653, 664.
59. Smith, *Religious Speeches*, 35.
60. Valency, *Cart*, 291.
61. Wilson, *Religion and the Rebel*, 298.
62. Shaw, *Man and Superman*, 664.
63. Weintraub, *Portable Shaw*, 314.
64. Sartre, *L'Existentialisme*, 95.
65. Wisenthal, *The Marriage of Contraries*, 48.
66. Shaw, *Man and Superman*, 689.
67. Shaw, "Don Juan in Hell," 803.
68. Wisenthal, *The Marriage of Contraries*, 45.

69. McDowell, "Heaven," 259.
70. Amalric, "*Man and Superman:* A Semiotic Reading," in his *Studies,* 96.
71. Wallmann, "See No Evil," 125–26.
72. Dukore, *Bernard Shaw, Playwright,* 222, 246, 251, 230.
73. Gilbert, "Revolutionary Revival," 24.

Conclusion. Irreconcilable Differences

1. Bentley, "The Road from Rouen," 255.
2. Shaw, "Bassetto's Destructive Force," *Star,* 7 March 1890.
3. Starkie, *From Gautier to Eliot,* 214.
4. Shaw, letter to Tighe Hopkins, 31 August 1889, in *Letters* 1, 222.
5. Kolakowski, *Bergson,* 11.
6. Henderson, "Bernard Shaw and France," 48.
7. Palmer, "The Productions of George Pitoëff," 208.
8. Blum, "Digression sur M. Bernard Shaw," *Excelsior,* 24 October 1912, Hamon Collection. Ellehauge reads Blum's "Du Mariage" and the preface to *Getting Married* as attacks on the property-principle of marriage and on the ideal of virginity (Ellehauge, *The Position,* 363).
9. Ervine, *Bernard Shaw,* 378.
10. Barbeau in *Polybiblion,* March 1914, 241, Hamon Collection.
11. Heydet, review of *Bernard Shaw et la France, Elsaessisches Literatur-Blatt,* 1 March and 1 April 1934.
12. Maurois, *Magiciens et logiciens,* 101.
13. Hamon, "Épitre dédicatoire," *Le Molière,* proof sheets, pp. 1–13, n.d., HRHRC, box 70, file 6, p. 13.
14. Amalric, "The Production of Shaw's Plays in France," in his *Studies,* 198, Amalric's emphasis. Berst notes that Shaw's eclectic proclivities — spiritual (morality play), intellectual (dialectic), dramatic (contention), aesthetic (ambiguity) — "lead him unabashed into numerous paradoxes which have caused some critics to be confused by an ostensible conflict of his genres" (Berst, *Bernard Shaw,* 299).
15. Cazamian, *History of English Literature,* 1310, 1313, 1319.
16. Liébert, "Avant-propos," xxv.
17. Eric Bentley claims that for all the sex in Shaw's plays, the element that people miss in them is "the torridity of sexual romance": "If the characteristic act of the French drama of the period was the plunge into bed, that of the Shavian drama is the precipitate retreat from the bedroom door" ("Foreword," xxi).
18. Henderson, *Shaw: Man of the Century,* 504–05.
19. Henderson quoted in Elliot, *Dear Mr Shaw,* 19. My version. Synonyms for *saltimbanque* include "mountebank," "charlatan," and "humbug."
20. Quoted in Rattray, *Bernard Shaw: A Chronicle,* 334.
21. D'Humières, "Le Cas Bernard Shaw" (*Le Mercure de France,* 1 April 1912, 453).
22. Shaw, "The Play of Ideas," 6 May 1950, in West, *Shaw on Theatre,* 290.

This line, last of the third paragraph in West (1958), is in the first publication—*New Statesman and Nation* 39 (6 May 1950): 5109–but missing in Dukore, *Drama Observed* (1993), 1524.

Appendix A. Shaw on Stage: The Pitoëff Productions

1. See Hort, *La Vie héroique des Pitoëff*, 533–45, and Pitoëff, *Notre Théâtre*, 100–8. See Hort for particulars about staging, sets, costumes, and stage roles played by Georges. See Henderson, *Shaw: Man of the Century*, 920–21, for performances in Belgium (Brussels, Antwerp, Louvain, Ostend) and France (Paris, Nice, Lyon). See Jomaron, *Georges Pitoëff*, 158–81, for an account of the Pitoëff productions of *Androclès et le Lion, Sainte Jeanne, La Maison des Coeurs Brisés, César et Cléopâtre*, and *La Charrette de pommes*.

Appendix B. Shaw in France: Travels Across the Channel

1. Shaw, "Paris: A Pedant-Ridden Failure," *Star*, 11 April 1890.
2. Amalric, "A Playwright's Supertrips," 173. I am indebted to this well-documented essay for details of the Shaws' travel itineraries.
3. Ibid., 181. Shaw's visual record was destroyed: writing to Harley Granville Barker from Paris on 7 May 1906, he remarked, "All my photographs (9 dozen) are ruined by a defect in the shutter of my most expensive camera" (*Letters* 2, 622).
4. Quoted in headnote to Shaw's letter to Harley Granville Barker, 7 May 1906, in *Letters* 2, 620. The *Labour Leader* published Shaw's letter on 11 May.
5. Shaw, letter to Harley Granville Barker, 621.
6. Shaw, "Joy Riding at the Front," *What I Really Wrote About the War*, in *Collected Works*, vol. 21, 256, 257, 257–58, 260, 261, 262.
7. Amalric, "A Playwright's Supertrips," 183.
8. Weintraub, *Playwright*, 213–14.
9. Quoted in Amalric, "A Playwright's Supertrips," 185. Amalric translates from *Les Nouvelles littéraires*, 2 May 1931, 10.
10. The following year, the Shaws traveled through France for the last time, from Calais to Paris and Monte-Carlo on 15 and 16 December, to join the *Empress of Britain* at Monaco and embark on a world tour.

Appendix C. Shaw in Print: A Chronological Bibliography of Works by and about Bernard Shaw in French and on Shaw and French Culture and Literature

1. Entries with incomplete data were excluded, such as the following from the Hamon Collection: Paul Blanchart, "Jeanne d'Arc vue par Bernard Shaw," *La Nouvelle Revue critique*, 379–87; George Crofts, "Georges-Bernard SHAW," *Les Hommes du jour*, 2; Gérard d'Houville, "Propos de Théâtre," *La Revue de Paris*, 904–8 (on *Sainte Jeanne*). In *Shaw: Man of the Century*, Henderson cites many critics and periodicals not found in the Davis bibliography: Claude Bralt, J. Ernest-

Charles, Émile Faguet, J. Van Kan, Valérie Larbaud, Felicien Pascal, Raymond Recouly, Henri de Régnier, Firmin Roz; *Le Divan, L'Éventail, Pages libres, La Rampe, L'Opinion, L'Art moderne, La Revue socialiste, Gazette de France, Le Mouvement socialiste, La Revue du mois, L'Acacia, L'Effort, La Revue des revues.*

2. In *Shaw: Man of the Century,* Henderson inexplicably errs when writing that "an anonymous pamphlet, *Bernard Shaw et ses traducteurs français* (Meunier [sic], Paris, 1910) appeared containing a caustic and violent assault upon the Hamon pair as incompetent, constituting permanent bars to the acceptance of Shaw's plays by the French public" (496). In *Bernard Shaw et la France* (206), Moore had listed it as a work by Augustin Hamon, which the Harry Ransom Humanities Research Center's TMS confirms. In it Hamon instructs that the pamphlet should be printed in five hundred copies, "sur beau papier, format ou petit quarto ou in octavo, de façon que ce soit très élégant," which describes the HRHRC's published copy. Shaw made numerous changes to Hamon's TMS, including an addition about Rodin's bust: "De ce chef d'oeuvre Shaw lui même dit que c'est la vérité, tous les autres n'étant que le Bernard Shaw legendaire inventé par les journalistes." See HRHRC, box 70, file 6.

3. Moore, in *Bernard Shaw et la France,* 210, lists an undated piece by Muret titled "L'Enfant terrible du théâtre anglais," *Bibliothèque universelle* (Lausanne), 116th year, vol. 64.

Works Cited

Abbott, Anthony S. *The Vital Lie: Reality and Illusion in Modern Drama.* Tuscaloosa: University of Alabama Press, 1989.

Achard, Marcel. "Georges Feydeau." 1948. Translated by Mary Douglas Dirks. Appendix to *Let's Get a Divorce! and Other Plays,* edited by Eric Bentley, 350–64. New York: Hill and Wang, 1958.

Agate, James. Notice [on *Saint Joan*]. *Sunday Times* (30 March 1924).

Amalric, Jean-Claude. *Bernard Shaw: Du réformateur victorien au prophète édouardien* [Bernard Shaw: from Victorian reformer to Edwardian prophet]. Paris: Didier, 1977.

———. "Shaw in France in Recent Years." *Shaw Review* 20.1 (January 1977): 43–46.

———. "A Playwright's Supertrips: Shaw's Visits to France." In *Studies in Bernard Shaw,* 169–89. Montpellier: Université Paul-Valéry, 1992.

Anonymous. "Anatole France. Homage to the English Genius." *Times* [London] (11 December 1913): 9–10.

———. "Mr. Shaw and the French." *Times* [London] (21 February 1928): 14.

———. "Bernard Shaw et la France." *Adam International Review* 14.161 (August 1946): 17–18.

Anouilh, Caroline. *Drôle de Père.* Paris: Michel Lafon, 1990.

Anouilh, Jean. *Pièces costumées.* Paris: La Table Ronde, 1960.

———. *La Vicomtesse d'Eristal n'a pas reçu son balai mécanique: Souvenirs d'un jeunne homme* [The viscountess of Eristal has not received her mechanical broom: recollections of a young man]. Paris: La Table Ronde, 1987.

Antoine, André. *Le Théâtre.* Vol. 2. Paris: Les Éditions de France, 1932.

Arnold, Matthew. "The French Play in London." *Nineteenth Century* (August 1879). Reprinted in *The Complete Prose Works of Matthew Arnold,* vol. 9, *English Literature and Irish Politics,* edited by R. H. Super, 64–85. Ann Arbor: University of Michigan Press, 1973.

Aston, Elaine. *Sarah Bernhardt: A French Actress on the English Stage.* Oxford, New York, Munich: Berg, 1989.

Axelrad, Jacob. *Anatole France: A Life Without Illusions 1844–1924.* New York and London: Harper, 1944.

Bachelder, Robert. *Catalogue 104.* N.p.: 1966.

Baker, Stuart E. *Georges Feydeau and the Aesthetics of Farce.* Ann Arbor: UMI Research Press, 1981.

Barzun, Jacques. "Shaw and Rousseau: No Paradox." *Shaw Bulletin* 1.8 (May 1955): 1–6.

———. "Eros, Priapos, and Shaw." In *The Play and Its Critics: Essays for Eric Bentley,* edited by Michael Bertin, 67–88. New York and London: University Presses of America, 1986.

———. "Berlioz and Shaw: An Affinity." In *SHAW, the Annual of Bernard Shaw Studies,* vol. 16, *Unpublished Shaw,* edited by Dan H. Laurence and Margot Peters, 67–87. University Park: Pennsylvania State University Press, 1996.

Bastaire, Jean. *Pour Jeanne d'Arc: Petit traité d'incarnation.* Paris: Du Cerf, 1979.

Bennett, Arnold. "Brieux, 17 Feb. '10." In *Books and Persons, Being Comments on a Past Epoch, 1908–1911,* 195–200. New York: Doran, 1917.

———. *The Journal of Arnold Bennett.* New York: Literary Guild, 1933.

Bentley, Eric. "Foreword." *Plays by George Bernard Shaw.* New York: New American Library, 1960.

———. "The Road from Rouen to New York." In *What Is Theatre?* 254–57. 1956. Reprint, New York: Atheneum, 1968.

Bergson, Henri. *L'Évolution créatrice* [Creative evolution]. Paris: Alcan, 1910.

———. *Oeuvres.* Annotated by André Robinet. Paris: Presses Universitaires de France, 1959.

———. *Mélanges.* Edited by André Robinet. Paris: Presses Universitaires de France, 1972.

Bernhardt, Sarah. *L'Art du théâtre: La Voix, le geste, la prononciation* [The art of the theater: voice, gesture, pronunciation]. Paris: Nilsson, 1923.

Berst, Charles A. *Bernard Shaw and the Art of Drama.* Urbana: University of Illinois Press, 1973.

———. "In the Beginning: The Poetic Genesis of Shaw's God." In *SHAW, the Annual of Bernard Shaw Studies,* vol. 1, *Shaw and Religion,* edited by Charles A. Berst, 5–41. University Park: Pennsylvania State University Press, 1981.

———. "The Man of Destiny: Shaw, Napoleon, and the Theatre of Life." In *SHAW, the Annual of Bernard Shaw Studies,* vol. 7, *The Neglected Plays,* edited by Alfred Turco, Jr., 85–118. University Park: Pennsylvania State University Press, 1987.

Bertolini, John A. *The Playwrighting Self of Bernard Shaw.* Carbondale and Edwardsville: Southern Illinois University Press, 1991.

Bertrand, Adrien. *Eugène Brieux.* Paris: Sansot, 1910.

Boulton, James T., ed. *The Letters of D. H. Lawrence.* Vol. 1, 1901–13. Cambridge: Cambridge University Press, 1979.

Bowler, Peter J. *The Eclipse of Darwinism: Anti-Darwinian Evolution Theories in the Decades Around 1900.* Baltimore and London: Johns Hopkins University Press, 1983.

Brieux, Eugène. *Three Plays by Brieux.* With a preface by Bernard Shaw. New York: Brentano, 1911.

———. *Two Plays by Brieux.* With a preface by H. L. Mencken. Boston: John W. Luce, 1913.

———. *"Woman on Her Own," "False Gods" and "The Red Robe": Three Plays by*

Brieux. The English versions by Mrs. Bernard Shaw, J. F. Fagan, and A. Bernard Miall. With an introduction by Brieux. New York: Brentano's, 1916.

———. *Damaged Goods. A Play by Brieux*. With a foreword by Mrs. Bernard Shaw. London: Fifield, 1917.

———. "Préface." *Théâtre complet de Brieux*. Vol. 1. Paris: Stock, 1921.

———. *Les Trois filles de M. Dupont. Théâtre complet de Brieux*. Vol. 3. Paris: Stock, 1922.

———. *Maternité. Théâtre complet de Brieux*. Vol. 4. Paris: Stock, 1922.

———. *La Foi. Théâtre complet de Brieux*. Vol. 8. Paris: Stock, 1928.

———. *Damaged Goods* [Les avariés]. New English version by Sir John Pollock. London: Jonathan Cape, 1943.

Bullough, Geoffrey. "Literary Relations of Shaw's Mrs Warren." *Philological Quarterly* 41.1 (January 1962): 339–58.

Butler, Ruth. *Rodin: The Shape of Genius*. New Haven and London: Yale University Press, 1993.

Calvin, Judith S. "The GBSsence of Giraudoux." *Shaw Review* 5.1 (January 1962): 21–35.

Carlson, Marvin. *Theories of the Theatre: A Historical and Critical Survey, from the Greeks to the Present*. Ithaca and London: Cornell University Press, 1984.

Carpenter, Charles A. "Shaw and Religion/Philosophy: A Working Bibliography." In *SHAW, the Annual of Bernard Shaw Studies*, vol. 1, *Shaw and Religion*, edited by Charles A. Berst, 225–46. University Park: Pennsylvania State University Press, 1981.

Cazamian, Louis. 1927. "Modern Times (1660–1967)." In *A History of English Literature*, by Émile Legouis and Louis Cazamian. Revised edition. London: Dent, 1967.

Cestre, Charles. *Bernard Shaw et son oeuvre*. Paris: Mercure de France, 1912.

Chevalier, Jacques. *Entretiens avec Bergson*. Paris: Plon, 1959.

Closset, François. *G. Bernard Shaw: Son Oeuvre*. Paris: Nouvelle Revue Critique, 1935.

Coakley, James. Review of *Shaw's People: Victoria to Churchill* by Stanley Weintraub, *Bernard Shaw: The Ascent of the Superman* by Sally Peters, and *George Bernard Shaw and the Socialist Theatre* by Tracy C. Davis. *Comparative Drama* (summer 1998): 297–302.

Cocteau, Jean. *Cher menteur* [Dear liar]. *L'Avant-scène* 242 (1 May 1961): 3–26.

Cohen, M. A. "The 'Shavianization' of Cauchon." *Shaw Review* 20.2 (May 1977): 63–70.

Cohen, Robert. *Giraudoux, the Three Faces of Destiny*. Chicago: University of Chicago Press, 1968.

Cohn, Ruby. "Hell on the Twentieth-Century Stage." *Wisconsin Studies in Contemporary Literature* 5 (winter–spring 1964): 48–53.

Cole, Toby, and Helen Krich Chinoy, eds. *Actors on Acting*. 1949. Reprint, New York: Crown, 1970.

Combes, Émile. *Une Campagne laïque (1902–1903)* [A secular campaign]. Paris: H. Simonis Empis, 1904.
Conolly, L. W., and Ellen M. Pearson, eds. *Bernard Shaw: On Stage, Papers from the 1989 International Shaw Conference.* Guelph: University of Guelph, 1991.
Contat, Michel, and Michel Rybalka, eds. *Les Écrits de Sartre: Chronologie, bibliographie commentée* [The writings of Sartre: chronology, annotated bibliography]. Paris: Gallimard, 1964.
Corballis, Richard. "Why the Devil Gets all the Good Tunes: Shaw, Wagner, Mozart, Gounod, Bizet, Boito, and Stanford." In *SHAW, the Annual of Bernard Shaw Studies,* vol. 12, edited by Fred D. Crawford, 165–80. University Park: Pennsylvania State University Press, 1997.
Crompton, Louis. *Shaw the Dramatist.* Lincoln: University of Nebraska Press, 1969.
Daemmrich, Horst S., and Ingrid Daemmrich. *Themes and Motifs in Western Literature: A Handbook.* Tübingen: Francke, 1987.
Davis, W. Eugene, gen. ed. *George Bernard Shaw: An Annotated Bibliography of Writings about Him.* 3 vols. DeKalb: Northern Illinois University Press, 1986–87.
De Comminges, Elie. *Anouilh, littérature et politique.* Paris: Nizet, 1977.
Dietrich, R. F. "Shaw and Yeats: Two Irishmen Divided by a Common Language." In *SHAW, the Annual of Bernard Shaw Studies,* vol. 15, *Shaw: The Neglected Plays,* edited by Fred D. Crawford, 65–84. University Park: Pennsylvania State University Press, 1995.
Doisy, Marcel. *Le Théâtre français contemporain* [Contemporary French theater]. Brussels: La Boétie, 1947.
Driver, Tom F. *Romantic Quest and Modern Query: A History of the Modern Theatre.* New York: Delacorte, 1970.
Dukore, Bernard F. *Bernard Shaw, Playwright: Aspects of Shavian Drama.* Columbia: University of Missouri Press, 1973.
Dukore, Bernard F., ed. *Bernard Shaw: The Drama Observed.* 4 vols. University Park: Pennsylvania State University Press, 1993.
———, ed. *SHAW, the Annual of Bernard Shaw Studies,* vol. 14, *1992: Shaw and the Last Hundred Years,* edited by Fred D. Crawford. University Park: Pennsylvania State University Press, 1994.
———. "'Responsibility to Another'? Graham Greene's Screen Version of Bernard Shaw's *Saint Joan.*" *Theatre History Studies* 16 (June 1996): 3–13.
Dumas *fils,* Alexandre. "Préface" à *L'Ami des femmes. Théâtre complet avec préfaces inédites.* Vol. 4. Paris: Calmann Lévy, 1890.
Dunbar, Janet. *Mrs. G.B.S.: A Portrait.* New York: Harper, 1963.
Dussane, Béatrix. *Notes de Théâtre, 1940–1950* [Theater notes]. Paris: Lardanchet, 1951.
———. *J'étais dans la salle* [I was in the audience]. Paris: Mercure de France, 1963.

Eliot, T. S. "A Commentary." *Criterion* 3 (October 1924): 4.
———. "Shaw, Robertson and 'The Maid'." *Criterion* 4 (April 1926): 389–90.
Ellehauge, Martin. *The Position of Bernard Shaw in European Drama and Philosophy.* 1931. Reprint, New York: Haskell House, 1966.
Elliot, Vivian, ed. *Dear Mr Shaw: Selections from Bernard Shaw's Postbag.* London: Bloomsbury, 1987.
Emboden, William. *Sarah Bernhardt.* New York: Macmillan, 1975.
Epstein, Rima. "Armin's Life and Work, Jean Anouilh: A French G.B.S., Hawthorne's Religious Beliefs." Master's thesis, Pennsylvania State University, 1963.
Ervine, St. John. "Sardou." *Observer* (13 September 1931): 13.
———. *Bernard Shaw: His Life, Work and Friends.* New York: Morrow, 1956.
Evans, T. F., ed. *Shaw, the Critical Heritage.* London: Routledge and Kegan Paul, 1976.
Falb, Lewis W. *Jean Anouilh.* New York: Frederick Ungar, 1977.
Filon, Augustin. *The English Stage, Being an Account of the Victorian Drama by Augustin Filon.* Translated by Frederic Whyte. London: John Milne, 1897.
Findlater, Richard. "Bernhardt and the British Player Queens: A Venture into Comparative Theatrical Mythology." In *Bernhardt and the Theatre of Her Time,* edited by Eric Salmon, 91–109. Westport, Conn., and London: Greenwood, 1984.
Fisher, David James. *Romain Rolland and the Politics of Intellectual Engagement.* Berkeley: University of California Press, 1988.
France, Anatole. *Le Petit Pierre* [Little Peter]. 1918. Paris: Calmann-Lévy, 1924.
———. *Vie de Jeanne d'Arc* [Life of Joan of Arc]. 1908. 2 vols. Paris: Calmann-Lévy, 1927.
Francis, R. A. "Romain Rolland and Some British Intellectuals During the First World War." *Journal of European Studies* 10 (1980): 189–209.
Frank, André. *Georges Pitoëff.* Paris: L'Arche, 1958.
Frank, Waldo. "The Art of the Vieux Colombier." 1918. In *Salvos: An Informal Book About Books and Plays,* 119–67. Reprint, New York: Boni and Liveright, 1924.
Fyfe, H. Hamilton. "Brieux and Bernard Shaw." 1906. Reprinted in *Independent Shavian* 13 (winter 1975): 24–25.
Galliou, Patrick. "George Bernard Shaw et Augustin Hamon: Les Premiers Temps d'une correspondance (1893–1913)." 4 vols. Ph.D. diss. Centre de Recherche Breton et Celtique, Université Bretagne Occidentale, Brest, 1998.
Ganz, Arthur. *G. B. Shaw.* London: Macmillan, 1983.
Gernsheim, Helmut, and Alison Gernsheim, eds. *Alvin Langdon Coburn, Photographer: An Autobiography.* New York: Praeger, 1966.
Gerould, Daniel C. "*Saint Joan* in Paris." *Shaw Review* 7.1 (January 1964): 11–23.
Gibbs, A. M. *The Art and Mind of Shaw: Essays in Criticism.* New York: St. Martin's, 1983.

———. "Shaw and Creative Evolution." In *Irish Writers and Religion,* edited by Robert Welsh, 75–88. Gerrards Cross: Colin Smythe, 1992.

———, ed. *Shaw: Interviews and Recollections.* London: Macmillan, 1990.

———, ed. *Bernard Shaw: "Man and Superman" and "Saint Joan," A Casebook.* London: Macmillan, 1992.

Gide, André. *Journal, 1939–1949: Souvenirs.* Paris: Gallimard, 1972.

Gilbert, W. Stephen. "Revolutionary Revival." *Plays and Players* (September 1976): 24.

Giraudoux, Jean. *Oeuvres littéraires diverses* [Various literary works]. Paris: Grasset, 1958.

———. *Théâtre.* Vol. 3. Paris: Grasset, 1959.

———. *Four Plays, Adapted, and with an Introduction by Maurice Valency.* 1958. Vol. 1. Reprint, New York: Hill and Wang, 1966.

Gold, Arthur, and Robert Fizdale. *The Divine Sarah: A Life of Sarah Bernhardt.* New York: Knopf, 1991.

Goy-Blanquet, Dominique. "French Maid of All Work." *Times Literary Supplement* (18 March 1994): 18.

Graham, James. "Shaw on *Saint Joan.*" In *"Saint Joan" Fifty Years After, 1923/24–1973/74,* edited by Stanley Weintraub, 15–22. Baton Rouge: Louisiana State University Press, 1973.

Grindea, Miron. "G.B.S. and France." *Adam International Review* 255–56 (1956): 1–14.

Gross, Jane. No title. *New York Times* (5 October 1987).

Grunfeld, Frederic V. *Rodin: A Biography.* New York: Holt, 1987.

Guicharnaud, Jacques. *Modern French Theatre from Giraudoux to Genet.* 1960. Revised edition, New Haven: Yale University Press, 1967.

Guilbert, Yvette. *La Chanson de ma vie (Mes Mémoires)* [The song of my life (my memoirs)]. Paris: Grasset, 1927.

———. *The Song of My Life: My Memories.* Translated by Béatrice de Holthoir. London: Harrap, 1929.

Gunter, Pete A. Y. *Henri Bergson: A Bibliography.* Revised second edition. Bowling Green, Ohio: Philosophy Documentation Center, Bowling Green State University, 1986.

Hamon, Augustin. *Une Enquête sur la guerre et le militarisme* [An inquiry into war and militarism]. 1899. Introduction by Sandi E. Cooper. Reprint, New York and London: Garland, 1972.

———. *The Technique of Bernard Shaw's Plays.* Translated by Frank Maurice. London: C. W. Daniel, 1912. Reprint, Folcroft, Pa.: Folcroft Library Editions, 1972.

———. *Le Molière du XXe siècle: Bernard Shaw.* Paris: Eugène Figuière, 1913.

———. *The Twentieth Century Molière: Bernard Shaw.* Translated by Eden and Cedar Paul. London: Allen, 1915.

Hamon, Augustin, and Henriette Hamon. "Au Lecteur. En guise de préface" [To the reader. By way of preface]. In *Le Disciple du diable: Mélodrame en trois actes,* translated by Augustin and Henriette Hamon, 1–36. Paris: Calmann-Lévy, 1926.

Harris, Truett Wilson. "Victorien Sardou in the Modern Theater." Ph.D. diss., Brown University, 1956.

Hart, Edward John. "Illustrated Interviews No. XL—Sarah Bernhardt." *Strand Magazine* (May 1895): 526–36.

Hart, Jerome A. *Sardou and the Sardou Plays.* Philadelphia and London: Lippincott, 1913.

Hart-Davis, Rupert, comp. *A Catalogue of the Caricatures of Max Beerbohm.* Cambridge, Mass.: Harvard University Press, 1972.

Harvey, John. *Anouilh, a Study in Theatrics.* New Haven: Yale University Press, 1964.

Hemmings, F.W.J. *The Theatre Industry in Nineteenth-Century France.* Cambridge: Cambridge University Press, 1993.

Henderson, Archibald. *George Bernard Shaw: His Life and Works.* Cincinnati: Stewart, 1911.

———. *Table-Talk of G.B.S. Conversations on Things in General Between Bernard Shaw and His Biographer.* New York: Harper, 1925.

———. *Bernard Shaw, Playboy and Prophet.* New York: Appleton, 1932.

———. "Bernard Shaw and France: Gaelic Triumph or Gallic Repulse?" *Carolina Quarterly* 3 (March 1951): 42–56.

———. *George Bernard Shaw: Man of the Century.* New York: Appleton, 1956.

Hernadi, Paul. "Re-Presenting the Past: 'Saint Joan' and 'L'Alouette.'" 1985. In *Major Literary Characters: Joan of Arc,* edited by Harold Bloom, 153–67. Reprint, New York and Philadelphia: Chelsea House, 1992.

Hill, Holly. *Playing Joan: Actresses on the Challenge of Shaw's "Saint Joan."* New York: Theatre Communications Group, 1987.

Hobson, Harold. *The French Theatre of To-day: An English View.* 1953. Reprint, New York: Benjamin Blom, 1965.

———. *French Theatre Since 1830.* London: Calder, 1978.

Holroyd, Michael. *Bernard Shaw.* Vol. 2, *1898–1918, The Pursuit of Power.* London: Chatto and Windus, 1989.

———, ed. *The Genius of Shaw: A Symposium.* New York: Holt, Rinehart and Winston, 1979.

Horn-Monval, Madeleine. *Répertoire bibliographique des traductions et adaptations françaises du théâtre étranger du XVe siècle à nos jours* [Bibliographical repertory of French translations and adaptations of foreign plays from the fifteenth century to the present]. Vol. 5. Paris: Centre National de la Recherche Scientifique, 1963.

Horsley, Lee. *Fictions of Power in English Literature: 1900–1950.* London and New York: Longman, 1995.

Hort, Jean. *La Vie héroïque des Pitoëff* [The heroic life of the Pitoëffs]. Geneva: Pierre Cailler, 1966.
Horville, Robert. "The Stage Techniques of Sarah Bernhardt." Translated by Eric Salmon. In *Bernhardt and the Theatre of Her Time,* edited by Eric Salmon, 35–65. Westport, Conn., and London: Greenwood, 1984.
Howarth, W. D. "History in the Theatre: The French and English Traditions." *Trivium* 1 (1966): 151–68.
———. "Bonaparte on Stage: The Napoleonic Legend in Nineteenth-Century French Drama." In *Themes in Drama: Historical Drama,* edited by James Redmond, 139–61. Cambridge: Cambridge University Press, 1986.
Hugo, Leon H. "The Black Girl and Some Lesser Quests: 1932–1934." In *SHAW, the Annual of Bernard Shaw Studies,* vol. 9, *Shaw Offstage: The Nondramatic Writings,* edited by Fred D. Crawford, 161–84. University Park: Pennsylvania State University Press, 1989.
Huizinga, Johan. "Bernard Shaw's Saint." 1925. In *Major Literary Characters: Joan of Arc,* edited by Harold Bloom, 85–107. Reprint, New York and Philadelphia: Chelsea House, 1992.
Hull, R.F.C., trans. *Selected Letters of Rainer Maria Rilke, 1902–1926.* London: Macmillan, 1947.
Hunt, H. J. "Saint Joan of Arc in Some Recent French Dramas." *French Studies* 1 (1947): 302–33.
Inskip, Donald. *Jean Giraudoux: The Making of a Dramatist.* London: Oxford University Press, 1958.
Jacobs, Gabriel. "The Role of Joan of Arc on the Stage of Occupied Paris." In *Vichy France and the Resistance: Culture and Ideology,* edited by Roderick Kedward and Roger Austin, 106–22. Totowa, N.J.: Barnes and Noble, 1985.
Jefferson, Alfred Carter. *Anatole France: The Politics of Skepticism.* New Brunswick, N.J.: Rutgers University Press, 1965.
Joad, C.E.M. "Shaw's Philosophy." In *G.B.S.: A Critical Survey,* edited by Louis Kronenberger. New York: World, 1953.
John, S. Beynon. "Actor as Puppet: Variations on a Nineteenth-Century Theatrical Idea." In *Bernhardt and the Theatre of Her Time,* edited by Eric Salmon, 243–68. Westport, Conn., and London: Greenwood, 1984.
Jolivet, Philippe. *Le Théâtre de Jean Anouilh.* Paris: Michel Brient, 1963.
Jomaron, Jacqueline. *Georges Pitoëff, metteur en scène* [Georges Pitoëff, producer]. Lausanne: L'Age d'Homme, 1979.
Kasimow, Harold. "The Conflict Between the Mystic and the Church as Reflected in Bernard Shaw's *Saint Joan* and Jean Anouilh's *The Lark.*" *Mystics Quarterly* 14.2 (June 1988): 94–100.
Kaufmann, R. J., ed. *G. B. Shaw: A Collection of Critical Essays.* Englewood Cliffs, N.J.: Prentice-Hall, 1965.
Kaye, Julian B. *Bernard Shaw and the Nineteenth-Century Tradition.* Norman: University of Oklahoma Press, 1958.

Kelly, Katherine E. "Imprinting the Stage: Shaw and the Publishing Trade, 1883–1903." In *The Cambridge Companion to George Bernard Shaw*, edited by Christopher Innes, 25–54. Cambridge: Cambridge University Press, 1998.

Klein, John W. "Shaw and Brieux—an Enigma." *Drama* 67 (winter 1962): 33–35.

Knapp, Bettina L. *French Theatre 1918–1939.* New York: Barnes, 1968.

Knapp, Bettina L., and Myra Chipman. *That Was Yvette: The Biography of a Great Diseuse.* London: Frederick Muller, 1966.

Knepler, Henry W. "*The Lark*, Translation vs. Adaptation: A Case History." *Modern Drama* 1.1 (1958): 15–28.

Kolakowski, Leszek. *Bergson.* Oxford: Oxford University Press, 1985.

Kuhn, Annette. *Cinema, Censorship and Sexuality, 1909–1925.* London: Routledge, 1988.

Lalou, René. *Histoire de la littérature française contemporaine, 1870 à nos jours* [History of contemporary French literature, 1870 to the present]. Revised and enlarged edition. Paris: Crès, 1923.

Laurence, Dan H. *The Fifth Gospel of Bernard Shaw.* New Orleans: Graduate School of Tulane University, 1981.

———. *Bernard Shaw: A Bibliography.* 2 vols. Oxford: Clarendon Press, 1983.

———. "Approaching the Challenge." In *SHAW, the Annual of Bernard Shaw Studies*, vol. 16, *Unpublished Shaw*, edited by Dan H. Laurence and Margot Peters, 17–34. University Park: Pennsylvania State University Press, 1996.

———, ed. *Bernard Shaw: Collected Letters 1874–1897.* New York: Dodd, Mead, 1965.

———, ed. *Bernard Shaw: Collected Letters 1898–1910.* New York: Dodd, Mead, 1972.

———, ed. *The Bodley Head Bernard Shaw: Collected Plays with Their Prefaces.* 7 vols. London: Max Reinhardt, the Bodley Head, 1970–74.

———, ed. *Shaw: An Exhibit.* Austin: University of Texas at Austin, 1977.

———, ed. *Shaw's Music: The Complete Musical Criticism.* 3 vols. New York: Dodd, Mead, 1981.

———, ed. *Bernard Shaw: Collected Letters 1911–1925.* New York: Viking, 1985.

———, ed. *Bernard Shaw: Collected Letters 1926–1950.* New York: Viking, 1988.

———, ed. *Selected Correspondence of Bernard Shaw: Theatrics.* Toronto: University of Toronto Press, 1995.

Laurence, Dan H., and Nicholas Grene, eds. *Shaw, Lady Gregory and the Abbey: A Correspondence and a Record.* Gerrards Cross: Colin Smythe, 1993.

Laurence, Dan H., and Daniel J. Leary, eds. *Bernard Shaw: The Complete Prefaces.* 3 vols. London: Allen Lane, Penguin, 1993–97.

Laurence, Dan H., and James Rambeau. *Agitations: Letters to the Press 1875–1950.* New York: Frederick Ungar, 1985.

Laurent, M. "Bernard Shaw nous parle de Rodin" [Bernard Shaw speaks to us about Rodin]. *Les Annales politiques et littéraires* 99 (2 December 1932): 487–88.

Leary, Daniel J. "The Heralds of Convergence: Teilhard and Shaw." In *Voices of Convergence*, 1–32. Milwaukee: Bruce, 1969.

Lee, Josephine. "The Skilled Voluptuary: Shaw as Music Critic." In *SHAW, the Annual of Bernard Shaw Studies,* vol. 12, edited by Fred D. Crawford, 147–64. University Park: Pennsylvania State University Press, 1997.

Lemaître, Frédérick. *Souvenirs de Frédérick Lemaître publiés par son fils* [Recollections of Frédérick Lemaître published by his son]. Paris: Ollendorff, 1880.

Lemaître, Jules. "Mme Sarah Bernhardt." In *Les Contemporains. Études et portraits littéraires* [Contemporaries. Studies and literary portraits]. Second series. Paris: Boivin, 1903.

Lenormand, Henri-René. *Les Pitoëff, souvenirs* [The Pitoëffs, recollections]. Paris: Odette Lieutier, 1943.

Liébert, Georges. "Avant-propos." In *Bernard Shaw: Écrits sur la musique, 1876–1950* [Bernard Shaw: writings on music], translated by Georges Liébert, Béatrice Vierne, and Anne Chattaway, vii–xxxi. Paris: Robert Laffont, 1994.

Loewenstein, Fritz Erwin. *Bernard Shaw Through the Camera*. London: B. and H. White, 1948.

Lorris, Robert. *Sartre dramaturge*. Paris: Nizet, 1975.

Lubek, Ian. "Politics and Psychology: Anarchist Social Psychology in Fin-de-siècle France." Paper read at the annual convention of the American Psychological Association, 25 August 1984, Toronto, Canada.

Lubek, Ian, and Erika Apfelbaum. "Augustin Hamon aux origines de la psychologie sociale française" [Augustin Hamon at the origins of French social psychology]. *Recherches de psychologie sociale* 4, Université de Paris VIII (1982): 35–48.

———. "Early Social Psychological Writings of the 'Anarchist' Augustin Hamon." Unpublished manuscript. Guelph: University of Guelph, 1982.

Ludovici, Anthony M. *Personal Reminiscences of Auguste Rodin*. London: John Murray, 1926.

MacCarthy, Desmond. *Shaw*. London: MacGibbon and Kee, 1951.

MacIntyre, Ben. "Vaults Surrender Rodin Treasures." *Times* (London) (22 May 1996).

Mankin, Paula A. *Precious Irony: The Theatre of Jean Giraudoux*. The Hague and Paris: Mouton, 1971.

Marsh, Patrick. "Le Théâtre à Paris sous l'occupation allemande" [Theater in Paris under the German Occupation]. *Revue de la Société d'Histoire du Théâtre* (July–September 1981): 197–369.

Mauriac, François. *Discours de réception à l'Académie Française* [Acceptance speech at the French Academy]. Paris: Grasset, 1934.

Maurois, André. *Magiciens et logiciens* [Magicians and logicians]. Paris: Grasset, 1935.

May, James Lewis. *Anatole France: The Man and His Work. An Essay in Critical Biography*. 1924. Reprint, London: Kennikat, 1970.

McDowell, Frederick P. W. "Heaven, Hell, and Turn-of-the-Century London: Reflections upon Shaw's 'Man and Superman.'" *Drama Survey* 2.3 (February 1963): 245–68.

McNamara, Mary Jo, and Albert Elsen. *Rodin's "Burghers of Calais."* N.p.: Canton, Fitzgerald, 1977.

M.E. "Brilliant New St. Joan." *Daily Herald* (11 June 1930).

Meisel, Martin. "Cleopatra and 'The Flight into Egypt'." *Shaw Review* 7.2 (May 1964): 62–63.

———. *Shaw and the Nineteenth-Century Theater*. 1963. Reprint: Princeton, N.J.: Princeton University Press, 1984.

Mills, Carl Henry. "Shaw's Debt to Lester Ward in 'Man and Superman'." *Shaw Review* 14.1 (January 1971): 2–13.

Monk, Ray. *Bertrand Russell: The Spirit of Solitude, 1872–1921*. New York and London: Free Press, 1996.

Moore, Mina. *Bernard Shaw et la France*. Paris: Honoré Champion, 1933.

Mossé-Bastide, Rose-Marie, ed. *Henri Bergson: Écrits et paroles* [Henri Bergson: writings and words]. Vol. 2. Paris: Presses Universitaires de France, 1959.

Mundell, Richard Frederick. "Shaw and Brieux: A Literary Relationship." 2 vols. Ph.D. diss., University of Michigan, 1971.

Murry, John Middleton. "The Two Joans." *Adelphi* 1.12 (May 1924): 1043–50.

Nathan, Rhoda B. "The *House* with No Exit: The Existentialist Shaw." *Independent Shavian* 25.3 (1987): 35–42.

Newman, Carol Montgomery. "Joan of Arc in English Literature." *Sewanee Review* 34 (1926): 431–39.

Palmer, John. "The Productions of George Pitoëff." *Fortnightly Review*, n.s., 118 (1 July 1925): 202–16.

Patch, Blanche. *Thirty Years with G.B.S.* London: Victor Gollancz, 1951.

Pearson, Hesketh. *Bernard Shaw: His Life and Personality*. Montreal: Reprint Society of Canada, 1942.

———. *G.B.S.: A Full Length Portrait*. New York and London: Harper and Brothers, 1942.

Pernoud, Régine. *Jeanne d'Arc*. Paris: Éditions du Seuil, 1981.

Peters, Margot. "Intersections." In *SHAW, the Annual of Bernard Shaw Studies*, vol. 17, *Shaw and Science Fiction*, edited by Milton T. Wolf, 233–45. University Park: Pennsylvania State University Press, 1997.

Peters, Sally. *Bernard Shaw: The Ascent of the Superman*. New Haven and London: Yale University Press, 1996.

Pfeiffer, John R. "A Continuing Checklist of Shaviana." In *SHAW, the Annual of Bernard Shaw Studies*, vol. 16, *Unpublished Shaw*, edited by Dan H. Laurence and Margot Peters, 233–45. University Park: Pennsylvania State University Press, 1996.

Pharand, Michel W. "'Almost Wholly Cerebral': Richard Aldington on Bernard Shaw." In *SHAW, the Annual of Bernard Shaw Studies,* vol. 18, edited by Fred D. Crawford, 93–100. University Park: Pennsylvania State University Press, 1998.

Pitoëff, Aniouta. *Ludmilla, ma mère. Vie de Ludmilla et de Georges Pitoëff* [Ludmilla, my mother. Life of Ludmilla and Georges Pitoëff]. Paris: René Julliard, 1955.

Pitoëff, Georges. *Notre Théâtre, textes et documents* [Our theater, texts and documents]. Textes et documents réunis par Jean de Rigault. Paris: Messages, 1949.

Poirot-Delpech, Bertrand. *Manchester Guardian Weekly* (11 October 1987), 11.

Pollock, John. Introduction. In *Damaged Goods (Les Avariés),* by Eugène Brieux, 5–12. London: Jonathan Cape, 1943.

Quéant, Olivier, ed. "*L'Alouette* de Jean Anouilh au Théâtre Montparnasse, ou le triomphe d'un demi-chef-d'oeuvre" [*L'Alouette* of Jean Anouilh at the Théâtre Montparnasse, or the triumph of a half-masterpiece]. In *Théâtre de France,* vol. 4, 83. Paris: Publications de France, 1954.

———. "*L'Alouette* de Jean Anouilh au Théâtre Montparnasse, ou la virtuosité au service de la vulgarité" [*L'Alouette* of Jean Anouilh at the Théâtre Montparnasse, or virtuosity in the service of vulgarity]. In *Théâtre de France,* vol. 4, 84. Paris: Publications de France, 1954.

Raknem, Ingvald. *Joan of Arc in History, Legend and Literature.* Oslo: Universitetsforlaget, 1971.

Rattray, R. F. *Bernard Shaw: A Chronicle.* New York: Roy, 1951.

Richardson, Joanna. *Sarah Bernhardt and Her World.* New York: G. B. Putnam's Sons, 1977.

Robert, Lucie. "The Language of Theater." In *Essays on Modern Quebec Theater,* edited by Joseph I. Donohoe, Jr., and Jonathan M. Weiss, 109–29. East Lansing: Michigan State University Press, 1995.

Rodin, Auguste. *Art: Conversations with Paul Gsell.* Translated by Jacques de Caso and Patricia B. Sanders. Berkeley and Los Angeles: University of California Press, 1984.

Rolland, Romain. *Le Théâtre du peuple: Essai d'esthétique d'un théâtre nouveau* [The people's theater: an essay on designing a new theater]. 1903. Reprint, Paris: Hachette, 1913.

———. *Au-dessus de la mêlée* [Above the battle]. 58th edition. Paris: Ollendorff, 1915.

———. *Liluli.* Paris: Albin Michel, 1919.

———. *Par la révolution, la paix* [Peace through revolution]. Paris: Éditions Sociales Internationales, 1935.

———. *Quinze ans de combat (1919–1934)* [Fifteen years of struggle]. 9th edition. Paris: Rieder, 1935.

———. *Péguy.* 1944. 2 vols. Buenos Aires: Viau-Feugere, 1946.

———. *Journal des années de guerre, 1914–1919* [Diary of the war years]. Text prepared by Marie Romain Rolland. Paris: Albin Michel, 1952.

———. "Pour l'Internationale de l'esprit" [For the International of the spirit]. In *L'Esprit libre: Au-dessus de la mêlée, Les Précurseurs* [Free spirit: above the battle, the forerunners], 328–37. Paris: Albin Michel, 1953.

———. *Deux Hommes se rencontrent. Correspondance entre Jean-Richard Bloch et Romain Rolland (1910–1918)* [Two men meet: letters of Jean-Richard Bloch and Romain Rolland]. Paris: Albin Michel, 1964.

Rose, Jonathan. *The Edwardian Temperament, 1895–1919*. Athens, Ohio: Ohio University Press, 1986.

Rostand, Jean. "Étude sur G.-B. Shaw et sa métabiologie" [Study of G.-B. Shaw and his metabiology]. Preface to *Retour à Mathusalem: Pentateuque métabiologique,* translated by Augustin and Henriette Hamon, 7–15. Paris: Aubier, 1959.

Russell, Bertrand. *Portraits from Memory and Other Essays*. New York: Simon and Schuster, 1956.

———. *A History of Western Philosophy*. 1945. Reprint, New York: Simon and Schuster, 1972.

Russell, Phillips. "Yvette Guilbert *chez* Shaw." *Independent Shavian* 30.3 (1992): 61–62.

Sackville-West, Vita. *Saint Joan of Arc*. New York: Literary Guild, 1936.

Salemson, Harold J. "Anatole France: A Post-Mortem Five Years Later." *Le Tambour* 5 (November 1929): 25–37.

Salmon, Eric, ed. *Bernhardt and the Theatre of Her Time*. Westport, Conn., and London: Greenwood, 1984.

Salomon, Roger B. "Escape From History: Mark Twain's *Joan of Arc.*" 1961. In *Major Literary Characters: Joan of Arc,* edited by Harold Bloom, 108–18. Reprint, New York and Philadelphia: Chelsea House, 1992.

Sardou, Victorien. *Madame Sans-Gêne. L'Illustration théâtrale* 75 (21 December 1907): n.p.

Sartre, Jean-Paul. *L'Être et le néant: Essai d'ontologie phénoménologique* [Being and nothingness: an essay on phenomenological ontology]. Paris: Gallimard, 1943.

———. *L'Existentialisme est un humanisme* [Existentialism is a humanism]. Paris: Nagel, 1946.

———. *Qu'est-ce que la littérature?* [What is literature?]. Paris: Gallimard, 1946.

———. *Théâtre*. Vol. 1. Paris: Gallimard, 1947.

Saurat, Denis. no title. "A G.B.S. Symposium." *Adam International Review* 14.161 (August 1946): 8.

Scheifley, William H. *Brieux and Contemporary French Society*. New York: Putnam's, 1917.

Searle, William. *The Saint and the Skeptics: Joan of Arc in the Work of Mark Twain, Anatole France, and Bernard Shaw*. Detroit: Wayne State University Press, 1976.

Shaw, Bernard. "A Reminiscence of Hector Berlioz." 1880. In *SHAW, the Annual of Bernard Shaw Studies,* vol. 16, *Unpublished Shaw,* edited by Dan H.

Laurence and Margot Peters, 71–87. University Park: Pennsylvania State University Press, 1996.

———. "From Our London Correspondent." *Manchester Guardian* (19 July 1887).

———. "That Realism Is the Goal of Fiction." 1888. In *SHAW, the Annual of Bernard Shaw Studies*, vol. 16, *Unpublished Shaw*, edited by Dan H. Laurence and Margot Peters, 111–18. University Park: Pennsylvania State University Press, 1996.

———. *Selected Passages from the Works of Bernard Shaw*. Chosen by Charlotte F. Shaw. London: Constable, 1912.

———. "The Play and Its Author." Souvenir program of *Woman on Her Own* (8 December 1913). In *SHAW, the Annual of Bernard Shaw Studies*, vol. 8., edited by Stanley Weintraub, 105–9. University Park: Pennsylvania State University Press, 1988.

———. *Sainte Jeanne*. Translated by Augustin and Henriette Hamon. *La Petite Illustration* 392, Théâtre no. 211 (28 July 1928): 3–41.

———. "How My Enemies Made Me Famous and Wealthy." *Centenarian Magazine* (East Aurora, N.Y., 1930).

———. *The Collected Works of Bernard Shaw*. 30 vols. London: Constable, 1930–32.

———. *L'Homme et le surhomme*. Translated by Augustin and Henriette Hamon. Paris: Éditions Montaigne, 1931.

———. *Everybody's Political What's What?* New York: Dodd, Mead, 1944.

———. "What Is My Religious Faith?" In *Sixteen Self Sketches*, 73–79. London: Constable, 1949.

———. "Shaw Writing to the Pitoëffs: Three Hitherto Unpublished Letters." *Adam International Review* 255–56 (1956): 14–15.

———. "Un Petit Drame." *Esquire* (December 1959): 172–74.

———. "Toast to Albert Einstein." 1930. In *SHAW, the Annual of Bernard Shaw Studies*, vol. 15, edited by Fred. D. Crawford, 233. Reprint, University Park: Pennsylvania State University Press, 1995.

Shenfield, Margaret. *Bernard Shaw: A Pictorial Biography*. New York: Viking, 1962.

Shippey, Tom. "Skeptical Speculations and *Back to Methuselah*." In *SHAW, the Annual of Bernard Shaw Studies*, vol. 17, *Shaw and Science Fiction*, edited by Milton T. Wolf, 199–213. University Park: Pennsylvania State University Press, 1997.

Smith, Hugh Allison. *Main Currents of Modern French Drama*. New York: Holt, 1925.

Smith, Jim, and Pat Smith. *RWA Auction Catalog #45*. Wells, Maine: n.p., n.d.

Smith, J. Percy, ed. *Selected Correspondence of Bernard Shaw: Bernard Shaw and H. G. Wells*. Toronto: University of Toronto Press, 1995.

Smith, Warren Sylvester. *The London Heretics, 1870–1914*. London: Constable, 1967.

———. *Bishop of Everywhere: Bernard Shaw and the Life Force*. University Park: Pennsylvania State University Press, 1982.

———, ed. *The Religious Speeches of Bernard Shaw*. University Park: Pennsylvania State University Press, 1963.

———, ed. *Shaw on Religion*. New York: Dodd, Mead, 1967.

Soulez, Philippe, and Frédéric Worms. *Bergson*. Paris: Flammarion, 1997.

Stanton, Stephen S., ed. "Introduction." In *"Camille" and Other Plays*, vii–xxxix. New York: Hill and Wang, 1957.

———. "Shaw's Debt to Scribe." *PMLA* 76 (December 1961): 575–85.

Starkie, Enid. *From Gautier to Eliot: The Influence of France on English Literature 1851–1939*. 1960. Reprint, London: Hutchinson, 1962.

Starr, William T. "Romain Rolland and George Bernard Shaw." *Shaw Bulletin* 2.3 (September 1957): 1–6.

Stokes, John. "Sarah Bernhardt." In *Bernhardt, Terry, Duse: The Actress in Her Time*, by John Stokes, Michael R. Booth, and Susan Bassnett, 13–63. Cambridge: Cambridge University Press, 1988.

Stokes, John, Michael R. Booth, and Susan Bassnett. *Bernhardt, Terry, Duse: The Actress in Her Time*. Cambridge: Cambridge University Press, 1988.

Sullivan, Karen. "'I Do Not Name to You the Voice of St. Michael': The Identification of Joan of Arc's Voices." In *Fresh Verdicts on Joan of Arc*, edited by Bonnie Wheeler and Charles T. Wood, 85–111. New York and London: Garland, 1996.

Symons, Arthur. *Plays, Acting, and Music: A Book of Theory*. New York: Dutton, 1909.

Taranow, Gerda. *Sarah Bernhardt: The Art Within the Legend*. Princeton: Princeton University Press, 1972.

Taub, Michael. "The Martyr as Tragic Heroine: The Joan of Arc Theme in the Theatre of Schiller, Shaw, Anouilh and Brecht." Ph.D. diss., University of North Carolina, 1982.

Taylor, John Russell. *The Rise and Fall of the Well-Made Play*. New York: Hill and Wang, 1967.

Terry, Altha Elizabeth. *Jeanne d'Arc in Periodical Literature, 1894–1929, with special reference to Bernard Shaw's "Saint Joan."* New York: Institute of French Studies, 1930.

Terry, Ellen. *Ellen Terry's Memoirs*. Originally titled *The Story of My Life*. 1908. Reprint, New York: G. P. Putnam's Sons, 1932.

Thomas, A.-Louis. "Une Clownerie déplacée: La 'Saint Joan' de Bernard Shaw au Théâtre Guild de New-York" [A misplaced clowning about: Bernard Shaw's "Saint Joan" at the Theater Guild of New York]. *Comoedia* (13 January 1924).

———. "A propos de la 'Jeanne d'Arc' de Bernard Shaw, M. Louis Thomas répond à M. Hamon." *Comoedia* (22 February 1924).

Trewin, J. C. "Bernhardt on the London Stage." In *Bernhardt and the Theatre of*

Her Time, edited by Eric Salmon. Westport, Conn., and London: Greenwood, 1984.

Turco, Alfred, Jr. "Shaw 40 Years Later—Eric Bentley Speaks His Mind on Eleven Neglected Plays: *Getting Married, Overruled, On The Rocks,* and Others." In *SHAW, the Annual of Bernard Shaw Studies*, vol. 7, *Shaw: The Neglected Plays*, edited by Alfred Turco, Jr., 7–29. University Park: Pennsylvania State University Press, 1987.

Tylden-Wright, David. *Anatole France*. New York: Walker, 1967.

Tyson, Brian. *The Story of Shaw's "Saint Joan."* Kingston: McGill-Queen's University Press, 1982.

———, ed. *Bernard Shaw's Book Reviews, Originally Published in the "Pall Mall Gazette" from 1885–1888*. University Park: Pennsylvania State University Press, 1991.

———, ed. *Bernard Shaw's Book Reviews*. Vol. 2, *1884–1950*. University Park: Pennsylvania State University Press, 1996.

Valency, Maurice. *The Flower and the Castle: An Introduction to Modern Drama*. London and New York: Macmillan, 1963.

———. *The Cart and the Trumpet: The Plays of George Bernard Shaw*. 1973. Reprint, New York: Schocken, 1983.

———. *The End of the World: An Introduction to Contemporary Drama*. 1980. Reprint, New York: Schocken, 1983.

Van Vorst, Marie. "Rodin and Bernard Shaw." *Putnam's Monthly* (October 1907–March 1908): 534–35.

Virtanen, Reino. *Anatole France*. New York: Twayne, 1968.

Walkley, Arthur Bingham. Unsigned notice [on *Saint Joan*] in the *Times* (London) (27 March 1924).

Wallmann, Jeffrey M. "See No Evil, Hear No Evil, Speak No Evil: The Alienation Factors in Shaw's Dramas." In *SHAW, the Annual of Bernard Shaw Studies*, vol. 18, edited by Fred D. Crawford, 113–29. University Park: Pennsylvania State University Press, 1997.

Weintraub, Stanley. *The Unexpected Shaw: Biographical Approaches to G.B.S. and His Work*. New York: Frederick Ungar, 1982.

———. "Indulging the Insufferable: Shaw and Siegfried Trebitsch." In *Shaw's People: Victoria to Churchill*, 195–211. University Park: Pennsylvania State University Press, 1996.

———, ed. *Saint Joan*. Indianapolis and New York: Bobbs-Merrill, 1971.

———, ed. *"Saint Joan" Fifty Years After, 1923/24–1973/74*. Baton Rouge: Louisiana State University Press, 1973.

———, ed. *The Playwright and the Pirate, Bernard Shaw and Frank Harris: A Correspondence*. University Park and London: Pennsylvania State University Press, 1982.

———, ed. *The Portable Bernard Shaw*. 1977. Harmondsworth, England: Penguin, 1983.

———, ed. *Bernard Shaw: The Diaries 1885–1897*. 2 vols. University Park and London: Pennsylvania State University Press, 1986.

———, ed. *Bernard Shaw on the London Art Scene, 1885–1950*. University Park and London: Pennsylvania State University Press, 1989.

Weiss, Samuel A., ed. *Bernard Shaw's Letters to Siegfried Trebitsch*. Stanford, Calif.: Stanford University Press, 1986.

Wellens, Oskar. "*Candida* in French (1907)." *Shavian* 7.7 (spring 1995): 6–11.

Wells, H. G., Julian Huxley, and G. P. Wells. *The Science of Life*. New York: Literary Guild, 1934.

West, E. J., ed. *Shaw on Theatre*. New York: Hill and Wang, 1959.

Whiting, George W. "The Cleopatra Rug Scene: Another Source." *Shaw Review* 3.1 (January 1960): 15–17.

Whitton, David. *Stage Directors in Modern France*. Manchester: Manchester University Press, 1987.

Wilson, Colin. *Religion and the Rebel*. London: Victor Gollancz, 1957.

———. "Beyond the Outsider." In *Declaration*, edited by Tom Maschler, 31–59. London: MacGibbon, 1958.

———. "Shaw's Existentialism." *Shavian* 2.1 (February 1960): 4–6.

———. *The Strength to Dream: Literature and the Imagination*. London: Victor Gollancz, 1962.

———. *Bernard Shaw: A Reassessment*. London: Hutchinson, 1969.

Wisenthal, J. L. *The Marriage of Contraries, Bernard Shaw's Middle Plays*. Cambridge, Mass.: Harvard University Press, 1974.

———. *Shaw's Sense of History*. Oxford: Clarendon Press, 1988.

———, ed. *Shaw and Ibsen: Bernard Shaw's "The Quintessence of Ibsenism" and Related Writings*. Toronto: University of Toronto Press, 1979.

Zuber, Ortrun. "Problems of Propriety and Authenticity in Translating Modern Drama." In *The Languages of Theatre: Problems in the Translation and Transposition of Drama,* edited by 92–103. Ortrun Zuber, Oxford: Pergamon, 1980.

Index

Académie Française, 57, 61, 84, 85, 88
Achurch, Janet, 75, 337n.82
Agate, James, 82, 154, 341n.84
Alain (Émile-Auguste Chartier), 213
Albert Hall, 36, 39, 75
Aldington, Richard, 193
Alice in Wonderland, 253
Amalric, Jean-Claude, 144, 272, 278, 283, 286; *Bernard Shaw: Du réformateur victorien au prophète édouardien*, 10, 289; "Shaw, Hamon and Rémy de Gourmont," 349n.5; "Shaw in France in Recent Years," 289
Anderson, Maxwell, 351n.4
Anouilh, Jean, 9; *L'Alouette*, 175–81, 351n.4; *Antigone*, 176, 177; *La Foire d'empoigne*, 176, 358n.23; *Ornifle, ou le courant d'air*, 176; *The Rehearsal*, 359n.49
Antier, Benjamin: *L'Auberge des Adrets*, 68
Antoine, André, 87, 107, 162; *Le Théâtre*, 354n.42; *Le Théâtre Libre*, 67, 337n.95
Apfelbaum, Erika, 117
Aragon, Louis, 362n.50
Archer, William, 4, 42, 50, 60, 129, 197; *Masks or Faces?* 54, 334n.24
Aristophanes, 334n.21
Arnaud, René, 168
Arnold, Matthew, xv, 83, 341n.85
Astor, Lady Nancy, 164
Atkinson, Brooks, 178
Audiat, Pierre, 162
Audiberti, Jacques, 351n.4
Augier, Émile, 57, 67, 82, 137; *La Ceinture dorée*, 60–61; *Le Mariage d'Olympe*, 61, 69

Aulard, François, 349n.12
Axelrad, Jacob, 184

Bach, Johann Sebastian, 25, 28, 29, 330n.30
Balzac, Honoré de, 232; *La Peau de chagrin*, 2; *Vautrin*, 2
Banville, Théodore de, 74; *Gringoire*, 2
Barbaud, Ch., 117
Barbeau, A., 121, 276, 277
Barbier, Jules, 74, 76, 283
Barbusse, Henri, 213, 220, 221
Baring, Maurice, 82
Barker, Harley Granville, 186, 284, 377n.3
Barnes, Peter: *Red Noses*, 352n.4
Barrett, W. A., 39–40
Barrie, James, 131
Barzun, Jacques, 1, 39, 40, 41, 123, 253, 332n.105, 371n.1
Bastaire, Jean, 180, 352n.4
Bastien-Lepage, Jules, 339n.21
Bateson, William, 242
Baudot, Jules, 150
Bax, Belfort: *Men's Wrongs*, 62
Beatty, Edith, 6
Beatty, Packenham, 6
Beaumarchais (Pierre Augustin Caron), 1, 130; *Le Barbier de Séville*, 4; *Le Mariage de Figaro*, 4
Becque, Henry, 277
Bedford, Mary, 212
Beerbohm, Max, 8, 45, 225, 367n.33
Beethoven, Ludwig van, 28, 30, 37, 222
Belloc, Hilaire, 136, 349n.11
Benedict XV, Pope, 149
Bennett, Arnold, 89, 96, 97, 106, 111, 211
Bentley, Eric, 59, 60, 61, 177, 178, 274, 376n.17

Bergson, Henri, xv, 8, 9, 145, 240, 243–52, 259, 261, 275, 279, 370n.47; articles in British periodicals, 370n.33; *Creative Evolution,* 246; *Les Deux sources de la morale et de la religion,* 244; *Durée et simultanéité,* 244; *Essai sur les données immédiates de la conscience,* 244, 251; *L'Évolution créatrice,* 243, 244, 247, 249, 250, 251; *Laughter,* 246; lectures in Britain, 369n.30; *Matière et mémoire,* 244; *Matter and Memory,* 246; *Le Rire,* 244, 245; *Time and Free Will,* 246
Berlioz, Hector, 2, 17, 24, 25, 26, 52, 332nn.105, 106; *Autobiography of Hector Berlioz,* 332n.96; *La Damnation de Faust,* 39; *Mémoires,* 39, 41; *Symphonie Fantastique,* 39; *Symphonie Funèbre et Triomphale,* 39–40; *Te Deum,* 39; *Traité d'instrumentation et d'orchestration,* 59; *Voyage Musical en Allemagne et en Italie,* 39, 332n.96
Bernanos, Georges: *Sous le soleil de Satan,* 362n.50
Bernard, Tristan, 173
Bernhardt, Sarah Henriette Rosine, xv, 8, 41, 42, 45, 49, 52–53, 54, 70–83, 166, 275, 283, 338nn.4, 6, 339n.38, 340nn.64, 68, 341n.89; *L'Art du théâtre* 81; "Vocal Methods" (lecture), 339n.31
Bernini, Giovanni, 227
Bernstein, Henry, 133–36, 169, 349n.12; *La Rafale,* 350n.15
Berst, Charles A., 198–99, 200, 239, 246, 376n.14
Bertolini, John A., 259, 290, 347n.84
Besant, Annie, 15
Besnard, Paul Albert, 16
Bidou, Henry, 88, 121–22, 162
Billet, Pierre Célestin, 15
Binyon, Laurence, 17
Bisson, Alexandre, 55; *Monsieur le directeur* (Bisson et Carré), 56; *Les Surprises du divorce* (Bisson et Carré), 53
Bithell, Jethro, 121
Bizet, Georges, 24, 33–34; *Carmen,* 25, 33; *Les Pêcheurs de perles,* 27

Blake, William, 8
Blanchart, Paul, 163
Blanche, Jacques-Émile, 129, 348n.2
Blavinhac, Albert, 142
Bloch, Jean-Richard, 9, 208; *Destin du théâtre,* 169
Blum, Jean, 130
Blum, Léon, 120, 139, 276; "Du Mariage," 376n.8
Boisgobey, Fortuné Du, 2
Boissard, Maurice, 121, 133
Boissy, Gabriel, 77, 80, 152
Bonheur, Rosa, 17
Bossuet, Jacques Bénigne, 1
Boubée, Joseph, 150
Bouguereau, Adolphe William, 18, 20
Bouhélier, Saint-Georges de, 171
Boulestin, M., 137
Bourget, Paul, 124; "Molière et le génie Français," 348n.88
Bovet, Marie Anne de, 36
Brahms, Johannes, 25
Brandes, Georg, 8
Brantôme, Pierre de Bourdelles, Seigneur de: *Discours sur les duels,* 1
Brasillach, Robert, 351n.4
Brasseur, Pierre, 145
Brecht, Bertolt, 57
Breton, André, 362n.50
Breton, Émile Adelard, 15
Briand, Aristide, 124, 348n.88
Brieux, Eugène, xv, 3, 4, 8, 56, 67, 82, 84–97, 117, 186, 275, 342n.33; *L'Armature,* 91; *Les Avariés,* 85, 87, 89, 90, 91, 97; *Le Berceau,* 89, 91, 93; *Les Bienfaiteurs,* 91, 93, 284; *Blanchette,* 92, 95; *Le Bourgeois aux champs,* 87; *Damaged Goods,* 85, 90; *Damaged Goods. A Play by Brieux* (Charlotte Shaw), 85, 91, 341n.6, 342n.8; *La Déserteuse,* 91; *L'Engrenage,* 91; *La Femme seule,* 91, 95, 96; *La Femme seule (Woman on Her Own)* (Charlotte Shaw), 85; *La Foi,* 87, 91, 94; *La Française,* 95, 97; *Les Hannetons,* 85, 91; *Maternité,* 84–85, 91, 92, 93; *Ménage d'artistes,* 89, 91; *Les*

Remplaçantes, 91; *Résultat des courses,* 91; *La Robe rouge,* 91; *Simone,* 91, 97; *Suzette,* 89, 91, 93, 96; *Three Plays by Brieux,* 85; *Les Trois Filles de M. Dupont,* 85, 91, 92; *Woman on Her Own,* 95
Brighouse, Harold, 150
Brion, Marcel, 131
Brisson, Pierre, 134, 167, 356n.92
British Museum, 17, 30, 39, 40, 332n.105
Bruneau, Alfred, 330n.23; *Le Rêve,* 27
Bunyan, John, 8, 240
Burne-Jones, Edward, 18
Bussy, Charles de: *Dictionnaire de l'art dramatique,* 333n.5
Butler, Samuel, 8, 241, 279; *Luck or Cunning,* 369n.11
Byron, George Gordon, Lord, 208

Caesar, Julius, 201
Calvé, Emma, 25, 32, 33
Cammaerts, Émile, 123, 347n.82
Campbell, Mrs. Patrick, 145, 150, 285
Campbell, Reverend Reginald John: *The New Theology,* 250, 251
Camus, Albert, 263, 375n.51
Cane, Hall, 131
Canova, Antonio, 227
Carmen. See Bizet; Mérimée
Carmines, Al, 351n.4
Carnot, Sadi, 102
Carpenter, Edward, 102
Carré, Fabrice. See Bisson
Carton, R. C.: *The Squire of Dames,* 64
Casarès, Maria, 145
Casement, Sir Roger, 209
Caserio, Santo, 102
Cauchon, Pierre, 155, 163, 176, 178, 179, 354n.40
Cazamian, Louis, 278
Cazin, Jean Charles, 15
Cendrars, Blaisel, 362n.50
Censorship, 18, 63, 71, 85, 87, 144–45, 171, 259, 354n.37
Cestre, Charles, 131; *Bernard Shaw et son oeuvre,* 10, 119, 125
Cézanne, Paul, 20

Chadwick, Julia, 150
Chair, Somerset de: *Napoleon's Memoirs,* 364n.51
Chapelin, Jean, 149
Chapman, Frederick, 184
Charcot, Jean-Martin, 361n.30
Charlemagne, 206
Chateaubriand, François René de, 40
Chaucer, Geoffrey, 231
Chauchard, Paul, 145
Chesterton, Gilbert Keith, 136, 232, 349n.11
Claretie, Jules, 130
Claudel, Paul, 170, 171, 176, 351n.4, 356n.72
Clemenceau, Georges, 124, 327n.33
Closset, François, 9, 126; *G. Bernard Shaw: son oeuvre,* 10
Coburn, Alvin Langdon, 225; *Le Penseur (Bernard Shaw),* 232
Cockerell, Sydney, 227, 353n.27
Cocteau, Jean, 146, 158; *Cher menteur,* 145
Cohen, M. A., 156, 157, 358n.5
Cohn, Ruby, 268
Collier, John, 231, 367n.33
Combes, Émile: *Une Campagne de laïque (1902–3),* 183–84, 360nn.10–11
Comédie des Champs-Élysées, 355n.44
Comédie-Française, 49, 52, 56, 70, 71, 135, 146, 165, 275, 337
Comédie-Montaigne, 136
Comte, Auguste, xv, 5, 67, 134
Conrad, Joseph, xv, 110
Conservatoire de Paris, 50, 51
Constant, Joseph-Benjamin, 17
Copeau, Jacques, 96, 158, 343n.40
Coppée, François: *Pour la couronne,* 56
Coquelin, Benoît Constant, 53–54, 284, 337n.85, 340n.68; "L'art du comédien," 54; *L'Art et le comédien,* 54; "Les Comédiens," 333n.1; "A Reply to Mr. Henry Irving," 54
Corballis, Richard, 34
Corelli, Marie, 184; *Vendetta!,* 66
Corneille, Pierre, 1
Corot, Jean-Baptiste-Camille, 17

Courbet, Gustave, 17
Courteline, Georges, 277
Covent Garden, 26, 30, 31, 32, 35, 38
Crane, Walter, 184, 343n.1
Crawford, Fred D., 290
Crawford, MaryAnn K., 290
creative evolution, 145, 239–52, 259, 260, 274
Crémieux, Benjamin, 169
Croce, Benedetto, 84, 213
Cromwell, Oliver, 201
Crystal Palace, 36, 37, 39
Cuénot, Lucien, 145
Curie, Marie, 213

Dante Alighieri, 269; *Inferno*, 262, 267
Darwin, Charles: *The Origin of Species by Means of Natural Selection*, 241
Davidson, Jo, 367n.33
Davis, W. Eugene: *G. B. Shaw: An Annotated Bibliography of Writings About Him*, 289
Davray, Henry-D., 107, 141, 212
Debroka, Maurice, 131
Debussy, Claude, 27
Deck, Richard, 6, 327n.30
Dekobra, Maurice, 131
Delacre, Jules, 125–26
Delacroix, Eugène, 17
Delaroche, Paul: *Hémicycle*, 22, 329n.34; *Napoleon at Fontainebleau*, 199; *Napoleon at Saint Helena*, 199; *Napoleon Crossing the Alps*, 199
Délibes, Léo: *Lakmé*, 27
Dell, Robert, 107
Delorme, Danièle, 145
Delsarte, François, 49–50; *System of Oratory*, 333n.3
Delteil, Joseph, 351n.4
Desailly, Jean, 145
Descartes, René, 247, 264
Descave, Lucien, 162
Deslandes, Raimond: *Antoinette Rigaud*, 55
De Smet, Gustave, 231
de Smet, Robert, 103, 117, 125–26
Després, Suzanne, 137, 350n.15

Deville, Gabriel, 1
de Waleffe, Maurice, 88
d'Hennezel, Henri, 192
d'Humières, Robert, 109–11, 139–40, 279, 359n.2
Dickens, Charles, 186, 278
Diderot, Denis: *Paradoxe sur le comédien*, 50
Dongen, Kees Van, 160, 355n.53
Donnay, Maurice: *La Douloureuse*, 54, 56, 123
Dos Passos, John, 221
Doumic, René, 80
Doyle, Arthur Conan, 131
Dreiser, Theodore, 221
Dreyfus, Alfred, 5, 184, 188, 327n.28, 360nn.5, 11
Driver, Tom F., 58
Dubech, Lucien, 131, 141, 169, 357n.100
Dubost, Marie, 145
Dubufe, Louis Edouard, 15
du Gard, Roger Martin, 163
Duhamel, Georges, 162, 213, 220
Dukore, Bernard F., 77, 263, 264, 273, 326n.13
Dumas *fils*, Alexandre, 31, 57, 63–66, 67, 81, 82, 97, 134, 142; *L'Ami des femmes*, 64 (preface to, 66); *La Dame aux camélias*, 61, 70, 74, 337n.82, 338n.3 (preface to, 65); *Denise*, 65; *L'Étrangère*, 68, 70; *La Femme de Claude*, 56, 64; *Le Fils naturel*, preface to, 64; "L'Homme-Femme: réponse à M. Henri D'Ideville," 65–66
Dumas *père*, Alexandre, 1, 326n.5; *Mademoiselle de Belleisle*, 336n.71; *Le Mariage sous Louis XV*, 63; *Les Trois Mousquetaires*, 31, 36
Dupanloup, Félix, 149
Duran, Émile Auguste Carolus, 15
Durkheim, Émile, 343n.1
Duse, Eleonora, 56, 64, 65, 75, 77, 78
Dussane, Béatrix, 143, 170

Eastman, Max, 213
Edwards, Pierrepont: *The Romance of a*

Poor Young Man (Edwards and Wallack), 68, 338n.98
Einstein, Albert, 205, 213, 221
élan vital, 9, 240, 243, 246, 247, 248–49, 250, 252, 370n.43
Elgar, Edward, 26
Eliot, T. S., 84, 178
Elisabeth, Reine d'Angleterre (silent film), 77
Ellehauge, Martin, 65, 95, 349n.5, 376n.8
Ellis, Havelock, 102, 343n.1
Epstein, Jacob, 225, 228, 231, 367n.33
Epstein-Etienne, Stéphane, 106, 345n.26
Ernest-Charles, J., 139, 192
Ervine, St. John, 276; *Bernard Shaw*, 63
Evans, Frederick H., 239

Fabre, Joseph: *La Délivrance d'Orléans*, 150
Faguet, Émile, 125, 130, 131, 133
Farleigh, John, 259, 372n.21
Farr, Florence, 77, 79
Faure, Jean Baptiste, 34
Faust. See Berlioz; Goethe; Gounod
Feiffer, Jules, 352n.4
Feuillet, Octave: *Le Roman d'un jeune homme pauvre*, 68; *Le Sphinx*, 70
Feydeau, Georges, 57, 278; *Champignol malgré lui*, 66; *Hortense a dit: "Je m'en fous!,"* 67; *L'Hotel du Libre-Échange*, 66; *Hotel Paradiso*, 66; *Le Système Ribadier* (Feydeau et Hennequin), 56, 67
Filon, Augustin, 56–57, 347n.75, 348n.3; *The English Stage*, 56; *M. Bernard Shaw et son théâtre*, 130; *Le Théâtre anglais: Hier, aujourd'hui, demain*, 56, 129
Flameng, François, 20, 199
Flameng, Leopold, 31
Flaubert, Gustave, 191
Flers, Robert de, 142, 356n.71
Fouquet, Jean: *Boccaccio*, 22; *Portrait of Charles VII*, 329n.32
Fourier, Charles: *Le Nouveau Monde industriel et sociétaire*, 5
Fra Angelico, 36–37
France, Shaw's trips to. See 283–87
France, Anatole, xv, 1, 8, 150, 152, 155, 182–93, 208, 213, 360n.19, 361n.27, 366n.1; *La Comédie de celui qui épousa une femme muette (The Man Who Married a Dumb Wife)*, 186; *L'Ile des Pingouins*, 183, 191; *Jocaste et le chat maigre*, 186; *Monsieur Bergeret à Paris*, 360n.5; *Les Opinions de M. Jérôme Coignard*, 360n.3; *Vie de Jeanne d'Arc*, 187–90, 353n.28
Frank, André, 175
Frank, Waldo, 191, 343n.40
Frazer, James G., 184
French, Shaw on the, 4, 5, 7, 15, 104, 119, 135, 152, 187–88, 278, 279, 284, 286, 326n.22. See also Paris and Parisians.
French actors and acting, Shaw on, 49–54
French and Swiss theatres, the Pitoëff productions in, 281, 355n.43
French art and artists: influence on Shaw of, 20–22, 199, 235, 368n.55; Shaw on, 15–23, 226–32, 234–35, 367nn.33, 37, 378n.2
French drama and literature: influence on Shaw of, 58–61, 62, 65, 67, 68–69, 93–95, 202–3, 332n.91, 335n.53, 349n.5, 250n.24, 363n.29, 370n.43, 373n.2; Shaw's influence on, 169, 177, 179–81, 250–51, 357n.100, 358n.23, 359n.49
French drama and theatre: Shaw on, 54–69, 152, 274
French music and musicians: Shaw on, 24–45, 330n.30
French productions of Shaw's plays: Shaw on, 136–38, 164–66, 169, 287, 350n.21
French Revolution, 1, 5
French translation and translators: Shaw on, 64, 87, 102, 104, 108, 113, 114–16, 117–18, 134, 345n.50
French, translation of Shaw's works into, 103–18, 346n.66
French translators of Shaw's works (other than the Hamons), 103, 105–6, 117, 126, 128, 186
French views of the Hamon translations, 107, 108, 109–11, 113, 117, 151, 154, 161, 163, 164, 348n.2, 351n.35, 378n.2

French views of Shaw and his works, 9,
  10–11, 44–45, 88, 89, 130–33, 135,
  139–46, 151, 153, 159–64, 167, 170,
  171, 175–76, 177, 192–93, 197, 208–9,
  220, 254, 276–79, 354nn.41, 42,
  356nn.71, 72, 92, 362n.5
Freud, Sigmund, 76, 344n.8
Froissart, Jean, 233, 235, 368n.55
Fry, Christopher, 351n.4, 359n.48
Fyfe, H. Hamilton, 85

Gaffié, L., 85
Gallet, Louis, 27
Galliou, Patrick, 343n.2
Galsworthy, John, 184, 211
Galton, Sir Francis, 189, 241; "Eugenics:
  Its Definition, Scope and Aims,"
  361n.31; *Natural Inheritance*, 369n.11
Ganz, Arthur, 203
Garnett, Edward, 150
Garnier, Jules Arsène, 17–18
Gary, Romain, 375n.51
Gautier, Marguerite, 3, 65, 70
Gautier, Théophile: *Mademoiselle de
  Maupin*, 4, 40
"G.B.S. et la France," 275
Gémier, Firmin, 136, 158
Gérardel, Henri de, 106
Gérôme, Jean Léon, 328n.23; *Ave Caesar,
  Morituri Te Salutant*, 21; *The Christian
  Martyrs' Last Prayer*, 21; *Cléopâtre
  apportée à César dans un tapis*, 21; *The
  Gladiators*, 21; *Master of the Harem*, 21
Gérôme, Raymond, 146
Gerould, Daniel C., 162, 164; "*Saint Joan*
  in Paris," 289
Gevaert, François Auguste, 24–25; *Traité
  général d'instrumentation*, 25; *Histoire
  et théorie de la musique de l'antiquité*,
  25
Gibbs, A. M., 5, 242
Gide, André, 84, 171, 362n.50
Gielgud, Sir John, 83
Gignoux, Régis, 162
Gilbert, W. Stephen, 273
Gillet, Louis, 133
Ginisty, Paul, 162

Giraudoux, Jean, 9, 172–75; *Amphitryon
  38*, 175; *L'Apollon de Bellac*, 175; *La
  Folle de Chaillot*, 358n.19; *Intermezzo*,
  175; *Ondine*, 173, 175
Gluck, Christoph Willibald: *Orfeo ed
  Euridice*, 25
Goethe, Johann Wolfgang von, 34, 35,
  201, 260; *Faust*, 17, 36, 240
Gorky, Maxim, 213, 221
Gosse, Edmund, 183, 211
Got, Edmond, 72
Gounod, Charles, 6, 24, 27, 28, 29, 32,
  39, 76, 275, 283; "Ave Maria," 35; *Le
  Cinq Mars*, 35; *Faust*, 34–35, 228;
  Messe Solennelle, 35; *Mireille*, 26, 37;
  Mors et Vita, 35–37; *Philémon et
  Baucis*, 25, 35; *Rédemption*, 36–37;
  Roméo et Juliette, 35
Gourmont, Remy de, 107–8, 130–31,
  343n.1; "La Morale de l'amour,"
  349n.5
Grandmont, Éloi de, 144
Greene, Graham, 181, 359n.49
Gregh, Fernand, 193
Gregory, Lady Isabella Augusta, 80, 166,
  375n.56
Grinberg, Maurice, 128
Grindea, Miron, 152, 182
Grosfils, Paul, 131, 362n.5, 375n.47
Grossman, Lawrence, 352n.4
Grundy, Sydney, 63; *Mademoiselle de
  Belleisle*, 336n.71
Gsell, Paul: *Art: Conversations with Paul
  Gsell*, 366n.10; *L'Art: Entretiens réunis
  par Paul Gsell*, 366n.10
Guilbert, Yvette, xv, 41–45, 76, 146,
  333n.110, 339n.38, 345n.45, 362n.5
Guitry, Sacha, 334n.13
Gurly, Dr. Walter, 327n.32

Hahn, Reynaldo, 74
Haig, Sir Douglas, 285
Halévy, Ludovic, 74
Hamon, Augustin, xv, 1, 7–8, 11, 44, 69,
  78, 87, 97, 101–28, 130, 134, 135, 136,
  137, 138, 142, 143, 146, 151, 154, 161,
  168, 169, 170, 186, 191, 208, 212, 213,

221, 231, 246, 248, 249, 253, 275, 277, 284, 285, 290, 342n.18, 343nn.1, 2, 345nn.46, 50, 347n.75, 348n.88, 349n.11, 355n.44, 360n.2, 366n.10; *Bernard Shaw et ses traducteurs français,* 378n.2; "Bernard Shaw en France et dans les Pays de langue Française," 289; *La Comédie,* 119; *Déterminisme et responsabilité,* 101; *Une Enquête sur la guerre et le militarisme,* 101; *Étude sur les eaux potables et le plomb,* 101; *La France sociale et politique,* 101, 102; "Au Lecteur: En guise de préface," 289; *Le Molière du XXe siècle: Bernard Shaw,* 10, 119–22, 128, 245, 278; "Notes de Voyage en Angleterre," 343n.6; *La Psychologie de l'anarchiste-socialiste,* 101, 102, 343n.5; *La Psychologie du militaire professionnel,* 101, 102; *Le Socialisme et le Congrès de Londres,* 343n.6; *Survivances animiques et polythéiques en Bretagne,* 101; "The Technique of Bernard Shaw's plays," 118; "Le Théâtre de Bernard Shaw," 119; *The Twentieth Century Molière: Bernard Shaw,* 119

Hamon, Augustin, and Hamon, Henriette, translations by: *Androclès et le lion,* 377n.1; *Candida,* 110, 111–12, 115, 117, 192, 209, 348n.2; *La Charrette de pommes,* 138, 287, 356n.92, 377n.1; *César et Cléopâtre,* 21, 126, 137, 350n.21, 377n.1; "Comment écrire une pièce populaire," 342n.18; *Comment il mentit au mari,* 125; "De Molière à Brieux," 88; *Le Dilemme du docteur,* 136; *Le Disciple du diable,* 111, 116; *La Grande Catherine,* 146; *Le Héros et le soldat,* 136, 144, 209; *L'Homme aimé des femmes,* 209; *L'Homme du destin,* 209; *L'Homme et le surhomme,* 114–15, 248, 346n.55, 370n.43; *La Maison des Coeurs Brisés,* 377n.1; *Non Olet [L'Argent n'a pas d'odeur],* 209; *On ne peut jamais dire,* 108, 141–42, 193, 209; *Pièces déplaisantes,* 107; *Pièces plaisantes et déplaisantes,* 118, 119; *La Première Pièce de Fanny,* 125; *La Profession de Madame Warren,* 9, 113, 116, 141; *Pygmalion,* 142–44, 192; *Retour à Mathusalem,* 145; *Sainte Jeanne,* 9, 10, 108, 116, 117, 134, 136, 137, 143, 146, 157, 158, 159, 160, 161, 162, 163, 164, 166, 168, 169, 170, 171, 177, 209, 276, 279, 290, 354n.41, 377n.1

Hamon, Augustin, translations defended by, 125–27, 161. *See also* French views of the Hamon translations

Hamon, Henriette, xv, xvi, 8, 102, 105, 106, 109, 113, 117, 128, 136, 154, 161, 284, 285, 289, 290, 344n.20, 349n.5, 352n.11, 370n.43

Handel, George Frederick, 25, 36, 37
Hankin, St. John, 85
Haraucourt, Edmond: *La Passion,* 283
Harris, Frank, 134, 229; *Frank Harris on Bernard Shaw,* 193; *My Life and Loves,* 286
Hartmann, Édouard de, 145
Hearn, Lafcadio, 184
Heinemann, William, 210, 211
Hellman, Lillian, 351n.4, 359n.48
Hemmings, F. W. J., 52
Henderson, Archibald, 45, 69, 102, 103, 119, 123, 124, 129–30, 145, 275, 279, 362n.5; *George Bernard Shaw: Man of the Century,* 289, 347n.66, 378n.2; "La Carrière de Bernard Shaw," 130
Henley, William Ernest, 68
Hennequin, Maurice, 56
Hermann-Paul, 107
Hermant, Abel, 133, 142
Hermeline, Charles, 131
Hernadi, Paul, 180
Hérold, Ferdinand: *Zampa,* overture to, 27
Hervey, Arthur: *Masters of French Music,* 24, 29
Hervieu, Paul Ernest: *L'Armature,* 336n.57
Hesse, Hermann, 213
Heydet, Xavier, 277
Hitler, Adolph, 5, 206
Hobson, Harold, 171
Hofmannsthal, Hugo von, 106

Hogan, Robert, 351n.4
Holroyd, Michael, 60, 62, 104, 228
Holt, Jany, 170
Horn-Monval, Madeleine: *Répertoire bibliographique des traductions et adaptations françaises du théâtre étranger du XVe siècle à nos jours*, 289–90, 346n.66
Hort, Jean, 159, 161, 165
Horville, Robert, 71
Houdon, Jean-Antoine, 227, 259
Housman, Laurence, 218
Howarth, W. D., 179–80, 358n.23
Hugo, Victor, 1; *Hernani*, 70, 72, 74, 79; *Les Misérables*, 2; *Ruy Blas*, 51, 70, 76
Huizinga, Johan, 152, 153, 156, 157, 166, 189
Hulme, T. E., 370n.33; *L'Humanité nouvelle*, 102, 103, 130
Hunt, Holman, 18
Huss, John, 153
Hutchins, Will, 150
Huxley, Julian, 242, 372n.25

Ibsen, Henrik, 8, 56, 84, 101, 129, 158, 193, 240; *A Doll's House*, 59; *Ghosts*, 97; *The League of Youth*, 59; *Peer Gynt*, 284; *Rosmersholm*, 75; *The Wild Duck*, 75
Impressionism, 8, 16, 18–19
Irving, Henry, 56, 65, 79; "An Actor's Notes," 54

Jacobs, Gabriel, 170, 171
Jacobs, W. W., 184
James, Henry, xv, 348n.2
James, William, 250; *Principles of Psychology*, 251
Jarry, Alfred: *Ubu Roi*, 375n.47
Jerome, Jerome K., 184
Joad, C. E. M., 372n.25
Joan of Arc, plays about: *L'Alouette* (Anouilh), 351n.4; *Goodtime Charlie* (Grossman), 352n.4; *Jeanne avec nous* (Vermorel), 170, 171, 175, 357n.105; *Jeanne d'Arc* (Barbier), 74, 76, 283; *Jeanne d'Arc* (Baudot), 150; *Jeanne d'Arc* (Delteil), 351n.4; *Jeanne d'Arc* (Mackaye), 150; *Jeanne d'Arc* (Maeterlinck), 351n.4; *Jeanne d'Arc* (Péguy), 150, 168; *Jeanne d'Arc* (Wallon), 353n.28; *Jeanne d'Arc à Poitiers* (Boubée), 150; *Jeanne d'Arc at Vaucouleurs* (Hutchins), 150; *Jeanne d'Arc au bûcher* (Claudel), 170, 351n.4; *Jeanne d'Arc et ses juges* (Maulnier), 351n.4; *Jeanne d'Arc la pucelle de France* (Bouhélier), 171; *Jeanne d'Arc, Maid of Orleans* (Murray), 155; *Jeanne et Hauviette* (Péguy), 150; *Joan* (Carmines), 351n.4; *Joan of Arc* (Southey), 149; *Joan of Arc: Three Scenes from her Life* (Chadwick), 150; *Joan of Lorraine* (Anderson), 351n.4; *Knock Knock* (Feiffer), 352n.4; *The Lark* (Fry), 351n.4; *The Lark* (Hellman), 351n.4; *The Maid of France* (Brighouse), 150; *Le Mystère de la charité de Jeanne d'Arc* (Péguy), 150, 169; *Poëme héroïque: La Pucelle ou la France délivrée* (Chapelin), 149; *Procès de Jeanne d'Arc* (Brasillach), 351n.4; *Le Procès de Jeanne d'Arc* (Moreau), 150; *Pucelle* (Audiberti), 351n.4; *La Pucelle d'Orléans* (Voltaire), 149, 152, 254, 255; *Saint Jane* (Hogan), 351n.4; *Saint Joan* (Shaw) (See Shaw); *The Survival of Saint Joan*, 351n.4; *La Tapisserie de Sainte Geneviève et de Jeanne d'Arc* (Péguy), 150; *The Trial of Jeanne d'Arc* (Garnett), 150; *La Vierge au grand coeur* (Porché), 162, 171; *La Vocation de Jeanne d'Arc* (Baudot), 150; *Le Vray procès de Jehanne d'Arc* (Arnaud), 168
John, Augustus, 225, 231, 367n.33
Jomaron, Jacqueline: *Georges Pitoëff, metteur en scène*, 290, 355n.51
Jones, Henry Arthur, 105
Jouvet, Louis, 128
Joyce, James, xv; *Ulysses*, 84
Jullien, Jean Lucien Adolphe: *Hector Berlioz: Sa vie et ses oeuvres*, 2, 39; *Richard Wagner, sa vie et ses oeuvres*, 2, 25

Kant, Emmanuel, 240
Karsh, Yousuf, 225
Kasimov, Harold, 179
Kean, Edmund, 52
Kemble, Charles, 52
Kennet of the Dene, Lady, 231, 367n.33
Kerr, Alfred, 186
Kessel, Joseph, 138
Kilty, Jerome: *Dear Liar*, 145
Kingston, Gertrude, 79
Kipling, Rudyard, 110, 211, 333n.119
Klein, John W., 97
Knox, John, 255
Kropotkin, Peter, 102, 343n.6

Labiche, Eugène, 134, 142; *La Cagnotte*, 2
La Fontaine, Jean de, 17
Lalou, René, 96
Lamarck, Jean-Baptiste, 19, 240, 241–43, 251, 259, 261, 264; *Philosophie zoologique*, 241
Lamarckism, 145, 241, 242, 244, 252, 369n.13
Lamartine, Alphonse de, 76
La Motte-Fouqué, Friedrich de: *Undine*, 173
Lane, John, 183
Lang, Andrew, 155; *La Jeanne d'Arc de M. Anatole France*, 353n.28; *The Maid of France*, 150, 353n.28
Lanson, Gustave, 141
La Rochefoucauld, François de, 2; *Réflexions ou Sentences et Maximes morales*, 346n.54
Laurence, Dan H., 25, 105, 109, 328n.1, 341n.89, 360n.2, 362n.53; *Bernard Shaw: A Bibliography*, 290
Lawrence, D. H., 70, 72, 338n.3
Lawrence, T. E., 206
Lazerges, Jean-Baptiste-Paul, 16
Leary, Daniel J., 260, 261
Lebesque, Morvan, 143, 178
Leblanc-Maeterlinck, Georgette, 140
Lee, George John Vandeleur, 24
Leibniz, Gottfried Wilhelm, 247; *Théodicée*, 256
Leighton, Frederick, 18, 227

Lemaire, Madeleine Jeanne, 16
Lemaître, Frédérick, 50–51
Lemaître, Jules, 56, 72, 74, 75, 129, 334n.24
Lemarchand, Jacques, 178
Lenepveu, Jules Eugène: *Le Départ de Vaucouleurs*, 22
Lenormand, Henri-René, 160
Leonard, Reverend Joseph, 157, 353n.27, 354n.37
Leoncavallo, Ruggiero: *I Pagliacci*, 25
Lepage, Jules-Bastien, 74
Lévy, Arthur: *Napoléon intime*, 198; *The Private Life of Napoleon*, 198
Lewes, George Henry, 68
Liébert, Georges, 33, 278
Life Force, 8, 92, 95, 118, 154, 157, 175, 198, 200, 201, 204, 206, 207, 227, 228, 231, 232, 238, 239, 240, 241, 242, 243, 246, 247, 248, 249, 250, 252, 260, 261, 262, 264, 266, 269, 271, 273, 274, 372n.25
Lissagaray, Prosper Olivier: *Histoire de la Commune de 1817*, 2
Locria, G., 132
Lord Chamberlain, 28, 71, 183
Low, David, 225, 367n.33
Lubek, Ian, 117
Ludovici, Anthony, 230
Lugné-Poë, Aurélien-Marie, 56, 136, 137, 158, 284
Luther, Martin, 201, 255

Macaire, Robert, 68
MacCarthy, Desmond, 164
Mackaye, Percy, 150
Madame Tussaud, 62
Madelin, Louis: *La Révolution*, 5
Maeterlinck, Maurice, xv, 130, 140, 351n.4; *Pelléas et Mélisande*, 56, 74
Magny, Jules, 103, 344n.8
Maligny, Bernier de: *Théorie de l'art du comédien*, 333n.5
Manet, Édouard, 234
Mann, Heinrich, 213
Mann, Thomas, 84
Manon. *See* Massenet; Prévost; Puccini

Marais, Jean, 142–43, 145
Marcabru, Pierre, 143
Marcel, Gabriel, 142, 375n.51
Marchand, Jules Louis, 16
"La Marseillaise," 26
Marsh, Edward, 184
Marston, Westland: *A Hero of Romance*, 338n.98
Martin, Henri: *Jeanne d'Arc*, 353n.28
Marx, Karl, 97; *Das Kapital*, 1, 326n.6
Mascagni, Pietro: *Cavalleria Rusticana*, 25
Massenet, Jules, 25, 30; *Hérodiade*, prelude to, 31; *Manon*, 31–32; *La Navarraise*, 32; *Werther*, 32
Massingham, Henry William, 184, 218
Matisse, Henri, 20
Mattos, Alexander Teixeira de, 326n.4
Maulnier, Thierry, 351n.4
Maupassant, Guy de, xv, 1, 67; *Yvette*, 141, 350n.24
Maurel, Victor, 25, 35
Maurey, Max, 107
Mauriac, François, 95, 153, 342n.32, 362n.50
Maurice, C. E., 343n.1
Maurice, Saint, 153, 160, 353n.19
Maurois, André, 121, 146, 158, 253, 277–78
May, Lewis, 184
Meilhac, Henri, 142; *Frou Frou* (Meilhac et Halévy), 74, 75; *Ma Cousine*, 56
Meisel, Martin, 21, 62, 65, 68, 80, 150, 328n.26, 332n.91
Meissonier, Jean-Louis-Ernest, 16; *Campagne of France*, 199; *Napoleon in 1814*, 199
Mellot, Marthe, 75
Mencken, H. L., 191; *Two Plays by Brieux*, preface to, 89
Mendelssohn, Felix, 25
Mendès, Catulle, 134
Mercure, Jean, 145
Mérimée, Prosper: *Carmen*, 33, 56, 331nn.59, 61
Merivale, Herman: *The Queen's Proctor*, 62
Merson, Luc-Olivier, 328n.26; *Repos en Égypte*, 21

Messager, André: *La Basoche*, 38; *Fauvette*, 38; *Mirette*, 38
Métives, Guy, 142
Meyerbeer, Giacomo, 24, 25, 28, 32; *L'Africaine*, 29; *Dinorah*, 26; *Les Huguenots*, 26, 29, 31; *Le Prophète*, 29, 30
Michelangelo, 29, 31, 228
Michelet, Jules, 189; *Histoire de France*, 149, 353n.28; *Jeanne d'Arc*, 353n.28
Mill, John Stuart, 134
Millerand, Alexandre, 124
Millet, Jean François, 17
Mirbeau, Octave: "Cabotinisme," 49; "Le Comédien," 49, 333n.1
Molière (Jean-Baptiste Poquelin), 1, 10, 54, 57, 84, 88, 89, 117, 119–22, 142, 146, 184, 246, 253, 254, 277, 278, 280, 347n.75, 373n.14; *Le Bourgeois Gentilhomme*, 144, 283; *La Critique de l'École des Femmes*, 347n.82; *L'Étourdi*, 2, 53; *Le Festin de Pierre*, 347n.85; *Le Misanthrope*, 121, 123, 144, 347n.85; *Tartuffe*, 124
Molière du XXe siècle, Le Bernard Shaw. See Hamon, Augustin
Monet, Claude, 18–19, 20; *Impression: Soleil levant*, 18
Montgomery, Field Marshall Viscount, 206–7; *Military Leadership*, 206
Montillier, Pierre, 128
Monvel, Louis-Maurice Boutet de, 22
Moore, George, xv, 211, 326n.4; "Mummer Worship," 49
Moore, Mina, 5, 109, 154, 249; *Bernard Shaw et la France*, xv, 10, 120, 127, 290, 378n.2
Morand, Paul, 191
Moreau, Émile, 150
Moreau, Gustave, 17
Moreau, Jeanne, 142–43
Morel, E. D., 365n.17
Morrell, Ottoline, 370n.48
Morris, William, 231, 366n.1
Mounet, Jean Sully (Mounet-Sully), 52–53, 54, 334n.13
Mozart, Wolfgang Amadeus, 8, 25, 30, 31, 40; *Don Giovanni*, 34

Muraour, Ali Ben, 103, 105
Muret, Maurice, 131, 197; "De Nora à Candida," 112, 129
Murray, Gilbert, 79, 184, 201, 221, 344n.21
Murray, T. Douglas, 156, 157, 353n.27, 354n.37; "Extracts from the Trial and Rehabilitation Transcripts," 353n.31; *Jeanne d'Arc, Maid of Orleans, Deliverer of France*, 155
Murry, John Middleton, 190–91; "The Two Joans," 190
Musset, Alfred de: *Lorenzaccio*, 56, 74, 78, 79
Mussolini, Benito, 127, 206
Musters, "Judy," 341n.89

Nathan, Rhoda, 374n.47
Nayral, Jacques, 132, 141
Neveaux, Georges, 146
Nietzsche, Friedrich, 8, 193, 240, 279
Noally, Francisque, 16
Nordau, Max, 19; *Degeneration*, 18
Noufflard, Georges: *Richard Wagner d'après lui-même*, 25
Nozière, Fernand, 139

Offenbach, Jacques, 25; *Les Brigands*, 27; *La Grande Duchesse de Géroldstein*, 37–38, 332n.91
Orage, Alfred Richard, 370n.33

Palmer, John, 158, 164, 166, 167, 275
Paris and Parisians, Shaw on, 9–10, 26, 30, 36, 87, 134, 137, 139, 152, 163, 165, 187, 247, 283
Paris, L'Opéra de, 26, 32, 34, 38
Patch, Blanche, 193
Pawlowski, Gaston de, 162
Pax, Paulette, 142
Pearson, Hesketh, 21, 182, 341n.89
Péguy, Charles, 150, 153, 168, 169, 170, 171
Perret, Aimé, 16
Perros, Georges, 145
Pétain, Philippe, 176
Pfeiffer, John R.: "Shaw and Other Playwrights: A Bibliography of Secondary Writings," 290
Philippe, Charles-Louis, 362n.50
pièce à thèse (thesis play), 54, 63, 67, 68, 135
pièce bien faite (well-made play), 54, 57–63, 67, 69, 335n.43
Pinero, Arthur Wing, 131, 211; *The Second Mrs. Tanquery*, 69
Pirandello, Luigi, 57, 84, 158, 176
Pitoëff, Aniouta, 165, 355n.56
Pitoëff, Georges, xv, 8, 21, 108, 126, 137–38, 157–69, 177, 275, 287, 290, 350nn.19, 21, 355nn.44, 45, 51; *Notre Théâtre*, 355n.43
Pitoëff, Georges and Ludmilla, productions by, 281
Pitoëff, Ludmilla, xv, 8, 80, 137, 143, 157–69, 275, 350n.21, 354n.42, 355n.44, 56
Poincaré, Raymond, 124, 235
Pollock, John, 85, 91, 342n.23
Pollock, W. H., 50
Porché, François, 162, 171
Preminger, Otto, 181
Pre-Raphaelites, 18
Prévost, Abbé (Antoine-François Prévost d'Exiles): *Manon Lescaut*, 3
Proudhon, Pierre Joseph, xv, 67, 97; *Qu'est-ce que la Propriété?* 5, 326n.23
Puccini, Giacomo: *Manon Lescaut*, 25
Puget, Claude-André, 142–43
Puvis de Chavannes, Pierre, 17

Quicherat, Jules, 156, 352n.17; *Aperçus nouveaux sur l'histoire de Jeanne d'Arc*, 353n.27; *Procès de condamnation et de réhabilitation de Jeanne d'Arc*, 155, 187
Quixote, Don, 286

Rabelais, François, 2; *Gargantua*, 17; *Pantagruel*, 17
Racine, Jean, 82, 278; *Andromaque*, 70, 80; *Phèdre*, 70, 71, 339n.28
Ravon, Georges, 143
Reding, Victor, 44, 112
Regnard, Jean François, 142

Rehan, Ada, 77
Réjane, Gabrielle, 54, 56, 340n.68
Renan, Ernest, 191, 192, 193
Rétoré, Guy, 145
Rey, Étienne, 162
Rhys, Ernest, 121
Richelieu, Armand Jean Duplessis, Cardinal, Duc de, 1
Rilke, Rainer Maria, 225, 226, 366n.9, 368n.41
Rivette, Jacques: *Jeanne La Pucelle* (film), 359n.49
Rivoire, André, 163
Robins, Elizabeth, 65
Rodin, Auguste, xv, 8, 17, 44–45, 210, 225–38, 246, 247, 275, 284, 366n.10, 367n.37, 368n.55, 378n.2; *Les Bourgeois de Calais*, 20, 232–35; *Le Penseur*, 232, 368n.41
Rojé, Jean-Marie, 128
Rolland, Romain, xv, 8, 9, 81, 208–22, 256–57, 273, 365n.34; *Above the Battle*, 209; *Au-dessus de la mêlée*, 209–12; *Beethoven*, 366n.44; *Déclaration d'indépendance de l'esprit*, 212–17, 365n.17; *Liluli*, 218–20, 256; *Par la révolution, la paix*, 218; *Péguy*, 220; "Pro Aris," 210–12; *Le Théâtre du peuple*, 219
Rose, Jonathan, 240, 260
Rossetti, Dante Gabriel, 18
Rostand, Edmond, 1, 54, 81, 82, 145; *L'Aiglon*, 74; *Cyrano de Bergerac*, 344n.21; *La Princesse lointaine*, 52, 56, 74, 78
Rostand, Jean, 145; *La Biologie et l'avenir humain*, 351n.35
Rouché, Jacques, 107
Rouleau, Raymond, 170
Rousseau, Jean-Jacques, 1, 186, 253, 325n.2, 326n.8; *Les Confessions*, 2
Roux, J. R., 126
Roz, Firmin, 192
Roze, Marie, 31–32
Russell, Bertrand, 191, 213, 221, 249, 370n.48

Sackville-West, Vita, 354n.37; *Saint Joan of Arc*, 187
Saint-Clair, Georges, 106
Saint-Saëns, Camille, xv, 8, 25, 26, 28–29, 30, 37, 38, 330n.30, 333n.119; *Ascanio*, 28; *Le Rouet d'Omphale*, 28; *Samson et Dalila*, 28
Salou, Louis, 164
Salvator, Rémy, 105
Sand, George, 17
Sanger, Margaret, 91
Sarcey, Francïsque, 52, 55, 56, 72, 334n.12; *Essai d'esthétique de théâtre*, 333n.5
Sardou, Victorien, xv, 8, 55, 57, 59, 67, 69, 81, 82, 103, 146, 274, 338n.4, 339n.38; *Delia Harding*, 61; *Divorçons*, 62, 336n.66; *Dora*, 61, 335n.53; *Fédora*, 61, 63, 71, 74; *Gismonda*, 61, 74, 77; *Madame Sans-Gêne*, 61, 62, 202–3, 363n.29; *La Maison neuve*, 336n.69; *Mayfair*, 336n.69; *Les Pattes de mouche*, 336n.69; *A Scrap of Paper*, 336n.69; *Théodora*, 71, 72, 74, 76, 339n.28; *La Tosca*, 62, 71, 74
Sargent, John Singer, 20
Sartre, Jean-Paul, 9, 262–73; *Being and Nothingness*, 263; *L'Existentialime est un humanisme*, 375n.51; "L'Existentialime est un humanisme," 264; *Huis clos*, 262–68; *Les Mains sales*, 263; *No Exit*, 262, 263; *Qu'est-ce que la littérature?* 375n.51; "Sartre donne les clefs de L'enfer, c'est les Autres," 374n.38
Saurat, Denis, 1, 253
Savoir, Alfred: *La Petite Catherine*, 357n.100
Schiller, Friedrich von, 155; *Die Jungfrau von Orleans*, 149
Schiller, Dr. Max, 44, 146, 152, 345n.32
Schlumberger, Jean, 113
Schnitzer, Arthur, 106
Schopenhauer, Arthur, 193, 240, 279
Scott, Clement. *See* Stephenson, B. C.
Scribe, Augustin-Eugène, 8, 9, 29, 55, 57–

60, 67, 137, 142, 146, 274, 275; *Adrienne Lecouvreur*, 337n.82; *La Bataille des dames*, 59, 335nn.52, 53; *Une Chaîne*, 69, 335n.43; *Le Verre d'eau*, 58

Searle, William, 188, 189

Seberg, Jean, 181

Sée, Edmond, 142, 162

sex: Shaw on, 51–52, 90, 137; in Shaw's plays, 80, 92, 96, 133, 139, 166, 276, 371n.16, 376n.17

Shakespeare, William, 52, 193, 240, 259, 278; *Hamlet*, 79; *Henry VI, Part One*, 149, 151; *Macbeth*, 79

Shaw, Charlotte, 7, 24, 52, 82, 84, 85, 91, 95, 225, 226, 228, 230, 253, 283, 286, 341n.3, 342n.8, 353n.27

Shaw, George Bernard, dramatic works by: *Androcles and the Lion*, 21, 45, 158, 176, 186, 240, 325n.2; *The Apple Cart*, 127, 177, 332n.91; *Arms and the Man*, 59, 102, 105, 106, 118, 128, 129, 131, 134, 335n.52; *Back to Methuselah*, 203, 205, 242, 249, 260, 261, 263, 273; *Caesar and Cleopatra*, 21, 106, 118, 145; *Candida*, 44, 60, 62, 68, 87, 110, 111–12, 115, 117, 118, 124, 129, 133, 139–41, 142, 145, 158, 278; *Captain Brassbound's Conversion*, 60, 85; *The Devil's Disciple*, 59–60, 118, 129, 145; *The Doctor's Dilemma*, 97, 273; "Don Juan in Hell," 34, 146, 260, 262–73; *Fanny's First Play*, 95, 326n.8; *Geneva*, 221; *Getting Married*, 62, 67, 85, 92, 376n.8; *Great Catherine*, 255–56, 259; *Heartbreak House*, 68, 97, 137, 138, 145, 263, 273, 350n.21, 359n.49, 374nn.37, 47; *The Household of Joseph*, 60; *In Good King Charles's Golden Days*, 128; *Jitta's Atonement*, 104; *John Bull's Other Island*, 255, 273, 358n.19; *Major Barbara*, 93, 146, 273; *Man and Superman*, 4, 9, 22, 34, 44, 59, 60, 68, 103, 114–15, 118, 129, 244, 247, 249, 250, 258, 263, 264, 269, 271, 276, 331n.61; *The Man of Destiny*, 16, 20, 108, 118, 162, 197–208, 335n.53, 358n.23, 362n.5, 363n.29; *The Millionairess*, 206; *Misalliance*, 93; *Mrs Warren's Profession*, 65, 68, 96, 107, 113, 118, 121, 124, 129, 137, 139, 144, 158, 208, 209, 350nn.15, 24; *Overruled*, 51, 87; *Passion Play*, 239; *Un Petit Drame*, 6–7; *The Philanderer*, 92, 121; *Plays Pleasant*, 176; *Plays Unpleasant*, 176; *Pygmalion*, 10, 95, 105, 139, 145, 175; *Saint Joan*, 8, 9, 22, 56, 68, 80, 93, 128, 138, 145, 150, 151, 153, 154, 155, 156, 157, 158, 161, 163, 166, 167, 169, 171, 175, 176, 177, 178, 179, 180, 181, 187, 190, 193, 199, 220, 235, 247, 255, 263, 273, 274; *The Shewing-Up of Blanco Posnet*, 62–63, 68, 85; *The Six of Calais*, 20, 235–38, 368n.53; *Three Plays for Puritans*, 176; *Too True to Be Good*, 114, 206, 273; *Widowes' Houses*, 3, 60–61, 68, 106, 336n.57, 375n.47; *You Never Can Tell*, 68, 139, 345n.50. *See also* Hamon, Augustin, and Hamon, Henriette, translations by; women in Shaw's plays

Shaw, George Bernard, nondramatic works by: "The Acquired Habits of Napoleon," 207; "Acting, by One Who Does Not Believe in It," 71; *The Adventures of the Black Girl in Her Search for God*, 253–59, 371nn.1, 16; "Berlioz's Episode," 39; "Brieux: A Preface" (*See* "Preface to Three Plays by Brieux"); "Censorship as a Police Duty," 87; "Christianity and Equality," 251; "Common Sense About the War," 204, 212; "A Degenerate's View of Nordau," 19; "Dramatic Censorship," 85; *Dramatic Opinions and Essays*, preface to, 55; "Duse and Bernhardt," 77; "English Voltaireanism," 255; *Everybody's Political What's What?* 87, 206; "From Our London Correspondent," 72; "Handicaps of a Queen of Tragedy," 79; "How to Write a Popular Play," 90; "The Ideal of Citizenship," 251; "Idolatry of the

Shaw, nondramatic—*continued*
  Glory Merchant Is Sheer Illusion," 206; "The Illusions of Socialism," 102; *Immaturity*, 70; "Joy Riding at the Front," 285; "Maxims for Revolutionists," 114, 263; "The Merits of Meyerbeer," 30; "The New Theology," 251, 263–64, 271; "On the Nature of Drama," 91; *Our Theatres in the Nineties*, 55; "Paris: A Pedant-Ridden Failure," 283; *The Perfect Wagnerite*, 25, 31; "The Play and Its Author," 95; "Preface to Three Plays by Brieux," 69, 87, 371n.5; "The Problem Play: A Symposium," 3; "Quickwit on Blockhead," 56; *The Quintessence of Ibsenism*, 59, 247; "The Religion of the British Empire," 251; "The Religion of the Future," 270; "The Religion of the Pianoforte," 31; "A Reminiscence of Hector Berlioz," 40–41; "The Revolutionist's Handbook," 4, 201, 349n.5; *Rhinegold*, 60–61; "Rodin," 17, 231, 366n.10; "Royalty Theater . . . French v. English Histrionics," 50, 72; "Sardoodledom," 2, 61, 77, 202; "The Stage as a Profession," 51, 53; "That Realism Is the Goal of Fiction," 2, 18–19; "Tolstoy: Tragedian or Comedian?" 186; "The Transition to Social Democracy," 103; "Treatise on Parents and Children," 93; "What I Owe to German Culture," 85; *What I Really Wrote About the War*, 285–86
Shaw, George Carr, 327n.32
Shaw, Georgina, 341n.89
Shaw, Mabel, 255, 371n.7
Shaw, Richard Frederick, 341n.89
Shelley, Percy Bysshe, 8, 240
Shippey, Tom, 243
Simon, Michel, 142
Sinclair, Upton, 97, 213, 221
Sloane, William Milligan: *Life of Napoleon Bonaparte*, 198–99
Smith, Hugh Allison, 89
Smith, Warren Sylvester, 261
Smithson, Harriet, 52
Sobra, Adrien, 127
Socrates, 257
Sophocles, 82, 87, 91
Souday, Paul, 142
Southey, Robert, 149
Spencer, Herbert, 250
Stanton, Stephen S., 59, 60, 67, 68
Starkie, Enid, 275
Steinbeck, John, 193
Stendhal (Henri Beyle), 191
Stephenson, B. C.: *Diplomacy* (Stephenson and Scott), 63, 335n.53
Stevenson, Robert Louis: *Macaire; A Melodramatic Farce* (Stevenson and Henley), 68
Stieglitz, Alfred, 213
Stokes, John, 50, 79
Stopes, Marie, 91
Strauss, Richard, 26
Strindberg, August, 84
Strobl, Sigmund, 225, 259, 367n.33
Sudermann, Hermann: *Heimat*, 74, 77
Sutro, Alfred, 184
Svevo, Italo, 84
Symons, Arthur, 79, 333nn.110, 118, 340n.68

Taglione, Maria, 105
Tagore, Rabindranath, 213
Taine, Hippolyte, 67
Talma, François Joseph, 52, 334n.12, 358n.23
Taylor, A. J. P., 207, 364n.51
Teilhard de Chardin, Pierre, 9, 145, 259–61, 372n.25; *L'Apparition de l'homme*, 259; *L'Avenir de l'homme*, 259; *Le Milieu divin*, 259; *Le Phénomène humain*, 259, 260
Terry, Ellen, 52, 74, 75, 77, 79, 202
Théâtre des Arts, 139, 142, 162, 166, 169, 177, 347n.66, 355n.44
Théâtre de l'Avenue, 177, 355n.44
Théâtre-Français. *See* Comédie-Française
Théâtre Gramont, 144
Théâtre de l'Odéon, 52, 107, 158
Théâtre de l'Oeuvre, 136, 158, 350n.15
Théâtre du Marais, 125
Théâtre des Mathurins, 137, 355n.44

Théâtre Montparnasse Gaston Baty, 177
Théâtre National Populaire, 171
Théâtre du Nouveau Monde, 144
Théâtre du Parc, 44, 112
Théâtre de la Renaissance, 80, 162
Théâtre du Vieux-Colombier, 158, 355n.44
Thomas, Ambroise: *Hamlet*, 26
Thomas, A.-Louis, 151–52, 157; "Une Clownerie déplacée," 151, 352n.11; "À propos de la 'Jeanne d'Arc' de Bernard Shaw," 352n.11
Thorndike, Dame Sybil, 150, 158, 163, 164, 165, 166, 167, 193, 354n.42, 362n.52
Thorwaldsen, Bertel, 227
Tissot, Jacques-Joseph, 16
Tolstoy, Leo, 102, 158, 186, 343n.1, 375n.56
Topolski, Feliks, 225, 367n.33
Touchard, P. A., 146
Toulouse-Lautrec, Henri Marie de, 45
Trebitsch, Siegfried, 88, 97, 104, 105, 128, 138, 186, 225, 230, 346n.54, 348n.102
Troubetskoy, Paul, 227, 231, 367n.33
Twain, Mark, 155, 333n.119; *Personal Recollections of Joan of Arc*, 150, 353n.28
Tyson, Brian, 66, 155

Unwin, T. Fisher, 198
Uzanne, Octave, 133

Valency, Maurice, 41, 54, 57, 59, 61, 64, 67, 68, 149, 156, 176, 201, 203, 263, 271, 335n.53, 357n.5, 373n.14
Valéry, Paul, 84, 362n.50
Vandel, Albert, 145
Van Dongen, Kees, 160
Van Dyck, Ernest, 35
Vaneck, Pierre, 145
Veber, Pierre, 142, 162
Verdi, Giuseppe, 28; *Falstaff*, 25
Vermorel, Claude, 170, 357n.105
Vildrac, Roger, 162
Viviani, René, 151
Vizetelly, Henry Richard, 3, 4
Voisins, Auguste Gilbert de, 105

Volmane, Véra, 143
Voltaire (François Marie Arouet), xv, 1, 145, 151, 178, 180, 191, 193, 253–59, 275, 278, 371n.5; *Candide, ou l'Optimisme*, 253, 256; *L'Homme aux Quarante Écus*, 255, 256; *L'ingénu*, 371n.1; *Mahomet*, 255; *La Pucelle d'Orléans*, 149, 152, 154, 255; *Zaïre*, 70

Wagner, Richard, 2, 8, 25, 26, 27, 30, 84, 101, 240; *Die Walküre*, 330n.23
Walkley, Arthur Bingham, 72, 82, 129, 154, 183
Waller, Lewis, 344n.21
Wallon, Henri, 353n.28
war. *See* World War I; World War II
Ward, Lester, 241, 369n.11
Webb, Beatrice, 366n.1
Webb, Sydney, 131–32, 283, 366n.1
Weintraub, Stanley, 15, 20, 21, 22, 38, 327n.31; *Bernard Shaw on the London Art Scene 1885–1950*, 5
Wellens, Oskar, 112; "*Candida* in French (1907)," 290
Wells, G. P., 242
Wells, H. G., 184, 203, 208, 211, 221, 225, 241, 242, 247, 366n.1; *The Outline of History*, 205, 207, 364n.44
Whistler, James Abbott McNeill, 19
Whitman, Walt, xv
Wilde, Oscar, 70, 82; *The Importance of Being Earnest*, 337n.91; *Lady Windemere's Fan*, 69; *Salomé*, 71
Wilson, Colin, 247, 248, 263, 269, 271, 375n.51
Wilson, Edmund, 191
Wisenthal, J. L., 203, 271, 272, 353n.27
women in Shaw's plays, 92, 139–41, 142–44, 158–69, 173–75, 202–3, 236–37, 256–58, 259, 276
Woolf, Virginia, 84
World War I, 119, 154, 183, 185, 203, 204, 209–17, 220–21, 285–86, 354n.40
World War II, 169–71, 176–77, 206–7, 222, 357n.105, 365n.40
Wycliffe, John, 153

Yeats, William Butler, 82, 84, 211

Zangwill, Israel, 184, 213
Zola, Émile, xv, 18, 19, 27, 33, 97, 192, 208, 275; *L'Assommoir*, 4; *La Bête humaine*, 2, 3; *La Fécondité*, 4; "J'accuse!" 184, 327n.28; *The Liquor Store* (Zola and Busnach), 326n.17; *Nana*, 4; "Le Naturalisme au théâtre," 2, 67; *Le Rêve*, 2; *Le Roman expérimental*, 2, 67; *La Terre*, 3; *Thérèse Raquin*, 1, 2
Zuber, Jean Henri, 16
Zuber, Ortrun, 107
Zweig, Stefan, 213

Michel W. Pharand teaches in the English and Theater Departments of the University of Ottawa, Canada. He has published on Shaw, Robert Graves, Lawrence Durrell, Richard Aldington, Tennessee Williams, and Rohinton Mistry. His edition of Graves's *The Greek Myths* will appear in 2001.